Prose Models

Tenth Edition

Gerald Levin

Professor Emeritus
University of Akron

HARCOURT BRACE COLLEGE PUBLISHERS

Fort Worth Philadelphia San Diego New York Orlando Austin San Antonio
Toronto Montreal London Sydney Tokyo

PUBLISHER *Ted Buchholz*
EDITOR-IN-CHIEF *Christopher P. Klein*
ACQUISITION EDITORS *Stephen T. Jordan, John P. Meyers*
SENIOR PROJECT EDITOR *Cliff Crouch*
SENIOR PRODUCTION MANAGER *Serena Manning*
ART DIRECTOR *Peggy Young*

Library of Congress Catalogue Card Number

95-78216

International Standard Book Number: 0-15-502167-2

Address for editorial correspondence:
Harcourt Brace College Publishers 301 Commerce Street, Suite 3700 Fort Worth, Texas 76102

Address for orders:
Harcourt Brace, Inc. 6277 Sea Harbor Drive Orlando, Florida, 32887

Phone:
800/782-4479, or (in Florida only) 800/433-0001

Printed in the United States of America

5 6 7 8 9 0 1 2 3 4 016 8 7 6 5 4 3 2 1

Preface

This tenth edition of *Prose Models* offers 104 models for composition that are drawn from both contemporary and classic essayists. The book contains numerous and varied examples of the rhetorical modes of writing as well as detailed discussions of the paragraph, the sentence, and diction. A major part of the book is devoted to argument and persuasion, with particular attention given to inductive and deductive reasoning.

To quote James Sledd, "Nobody ever learned to write without reading." In his essay on composition, Mark Twain refers to the "model-chamber" or store of effective sentences gathered by the writer from many kinds of reading. These statements express the philosophy of this book. Student writers need to understand the methods of prose composition and to observe these methods in practice. Discussion of the writing process and exercises in invention enhance writing skills, but analysis and discussion of a wide selection of readings are just as essential.

ABOUT THE SELECTIONS

These readings, far more numerous than most other books on the market, have been carefully selected to elicit active classroom discussion and thoughtful student essays. The models are strong both in range of topics and as models for rhetorical purpose. Thirty-four new selections join the 70 readings that have proved especially effective in classrooms.

Writers new to *Prose Models* include Alan M. Dershowitz, Ian Frazier, Walker Gibson, Vicki Hearne, Perri Klass, Leonard Kriegel, N. Scott Momaday, William Raspberry, Esmerelda Santiago, Deborah Tannen, Paul Theroux, Susan Allen Toth, James Trefil, and Bailey White.

The readings connect in theme in various ways. For example, John Holt, Kenneth B. Clark, John Henry Newman, and William Zinsser discuss the purpose of education; and Peter H. Rossi, Leanne G. Rivlin, Hilary de Vries, and Anna Quindlen present different perspectives on homelessness in America. The thematic table of contents suggests other connections, as does the Instructor's Manual.

ORGANIZATION

Part 1 of the book addresses matters of organization in the paragraph and essay; Part 2 demonstrates essay and paragraph development (description, narration, and methods of exposition, including example, classification/division, definition, comparison/contrast, analogy, process, and cause/effect). Part 3 presents argument and persuasion; several documented essays illustrate uses of primary and secondary sources in the humanities and the social sciences. Contrasting essays deal with two controversial issues: women in combat and legalizing drugs. Part 4 explains usage, tone, imagery and other matters of diction; Part 5 illustrates sentences style; and Part 6 concludes the book with three essays on writing.

PEDAGOGY

Each of the readings is introduced by a headnote containing information about the author and the reading. Questions and suggestions for writing follow all selections except the supplementary essays on writing. Vocabulary studies following most of the readings invite the student to look up unfamiliar words and find the exact meaning of familiar ones.

INSTRUCTOR'S MANUAL

The Instructor's Manual to accompany *Prose Models*, Tenth Edition, suggests ways to teach the selections and provides answers to the exercises. To show how this reader can be combined with a handbook, a one-semester model syllabus links the sections of *Prose Models* with the corresponding sections of the *Harbrace College Handbook*, Twelfth Edition.

ACKNOWLEDGMENTS

I express my gratitude to the following teachers of writing who made suggestions for the tenth edition: Chris Baker, Lamar University; Noel Berky, Sauk Valley Community College; Mark Christensen, Bemidji State University; Anthony Gargano, Cypress College; Harold Knox, Sacramento City College; Peggy Richards, University of Akron; Beverly Ricks, University of Akron; Susan Tilka, Southwest Texas State University; and Anthony Zigler, University of Akron. I also owe a continuing debt to William Francis, Alan Hart, Bruce Holland, Robert Holland, Alice MacDonald, Sally K. Slocum, and Linda

Weiner, former colleagues at the University of Akron, who made suggestions for previous editions and gave me their advice and support over many years.

I thank my acquisitions editor at Harcourt Brace College Publishers, Stephen T. Jordan, and my freelance developmental editor, Sarah Helyar Smith, for their help and suggestions. I thank also senior project editor Clifford Crouch, art director Peggy Young, and production manager Serena Manning.

I owe a considerable debt to my wife, Lillian Levin, for her support and help over many editions. Christopher, Daniel, and Sarah Rubin and Matthew and Meredith Ziegler were always in mind.

Gerald Levin

To the Student: How to Use this Book

Part 1 of *Prose Models* discusses matters common to various kinds of writing. These include stating and highlighting your central idea or thesis, organizing your ideas and supporting details, and showing how these details connect. Part 2 deals with ways of developing ideas in expository essays—those whose purpose is to explain ideas and processes. Parts 1 and 2, in addition, illustrate how to organize and develop paragraphs—the basic units of the essay. Part 3 deals with various kinds of arguments and their use in persuasive writing; Parts 4 and 5, with choosing effective diction and building sentences in effective ways. Part 6 concludes the book with a series of essays on the art of composition.

In your reading, you probably have noticed that a particular writer often favors similar kinds of sentences and certain expressions and ways of phrasing ideas, or builds paragraphs and essays in similar ways. The word *style* describes these recurrent patterns in a writer. Though still connected for many people with what is "correct" or "proper" in writing (style for the eighteenth-century writer Jonathan Swift was "proper words in proper places"), style refers commonly to individual choices in diction and sentence construction as well as in organization. It is in this sense that people refer to a "Hemingway style" in fiction.

However, much of what we describe as style in speaking and writing is probably not a matter of choice at all. Your writing is governed strongly by habits that develop without your being aware of them. One writer may favor long, heavily coordinated sentences, as in the speech of a nonstop talker. Another person, used to speaking in clipped sentences, may write in very short sentences or very short paragraphs. Habits of speech strongly influence how you write, though written communication requires more attention to such matters as sentence structure, punctuation, the organization of the whole essay.

You do have control, then, over your writing. Though you will continue to speak and write in ways natural to you, you can make your writing more expressive and effective. The more writing you do, the more aware you will become of your own habitual choices. As your awareness increases, you will have the opportunity to experiment with new ways of writing—as college gives you the opportunity to think about new ideas in new ways. The discovery and mastery of your own style of writing and thinking is one important purpose of this book.

The readings in this book are examples of effective writing by mostly contemporary American and British authors. They show how various writers choose to organize and develop their impressions and ideas. The readings do not, however, represent every kind of effective writing, nor are they "models" in the sense of representing the best and only ways to write sentences, paragraphs, and essays. They illustrate, rather, some choices possible in writing; they are models in being effective solutions to problems you will face in the course of writing your own essays. The readings have also been selected to help you draw on your own experiences and observations in writing your own essays. You will discover that many of the selections connect in theme or point of view. The expository and argumentative essays—many dealing with important issues of our time—offer an opportunity for you to work out your own ideas and bring your experience to bear on the issue under discussion. Essays that interest or move you can serve as resources to which you will return for inspiration and help in planning and revising your own.

The readings constitute in this way a repertory of choices available in practicing and refining your writing skills. The study and discussion of paragraphs and essays is only one part of the process of writing, but it is an indispensable part. For you learn to write as you learn to speak—by reading and listening to the words of others. Thus, in planning, drafting, and revising your own essays, you will have many opportunities to return to your reading and perhaps discover new ways to build and develop your ideas.

You will discover that principles of organization and development in paragraphs and sentences occur also in the whole essay; thus the topic sentence of the paragraph bears a close relationship to the main clause that organizes a sentence and to the thesis that organizes the essay. You will have an opportunity, then, to consider topics of organization and development in the smaller and larger units of the essay. Though each reading illustrates a particular way of organizing ideas or developing them, each also employs other methods discussed in the book. The questions often call attention to these, and your instructor may use a reading to focus discussion on another topic.

A final word on the vocabulary list that follows many of the readings: These lists contain unfamiliar words as well as many you use every day. The familiar words are singled out because the author of the reading uses them in a special or unusual way. Often you will recognize the general meaning of a word, but you will need your dictionary to discover a subtle meaning that the author has in mind. In preparing for class discussion of these essays, you will gain the most if you keep a dictionary at hand and check the meanings of these words and others about whose meaning you are doubtful. A log of words and their definitions can be of immense help in your reading for composition and other courses.

Contents

*Complete section, chapter, or essay.

CONTENTS BY THEME

People and Places

Childhood and Adolescence

Education

Urban and Rural Life

Social and Personal Values

Ethnicity

Nature

Media

Social and Political Issues

Women and Society

Women and Combat

Hunger, Poverty, Homelessness

Drugs

Technology

War

Language

Reading and Writing

Part 1

ORGANIZING THE ESSAY

INTRODUCTION:
THE ESSAY AND THE PARAGRAPH

The Nature of the Essay. If asked what an essay is, many would say that it is a piece of writing that states one or more ideas or impressions, develops these fully, and has a clearly marked beginning, middle, and end. The essay may be addressed to a single reader—perhaps in the form of a letter—or to a general audience, the readers of a newspaper or magazine, or a special audience, the readers of a technical journal. Many essays today—those written by newspaper and magazine columnists, television commentators, scholars, students —meet this definition.

But many essays in newspapers, magazines, and journals do not work out ideas completely; the essayist may do no more than explore an idea or an impression of a person or place briefly. The etymology of the word indeed suggests that an essay was for many writers of the past a trying-out or weighing of an idea, a first attempt at expression that might be followed by a second or third attempt. The essayist might put words on paper and not revise them; or might rephrase ideas, introduce new ideas and details, or recast the whole essay or parts of it. One of the creators of the modern essay, the sixteenth-century French writer Michel de Montaigne, states that some of his late essays added to "other parts of my portrait." "I add, but I do not correct," he writes in the third book of his essays, though he did make corrections later. It would be better to restate ideas in new essays. Montaigne adds that he fears

> to lose by the change; my understanding does not always advance, it also goes backwards. I do not distrust my thoughts less because they are the second or third, than because they are the first, or my present less than my past thoughts. Besides, we often correct ourselves as foolishly as we correct others. ("Of Vanity," *Essays*)

For Montaigne and for the British essayist and novelist Virginia Woolf, the essay is first of all an expression of personal ideas:

> A very wide definition obviously must be that which will include all the varieties of thought which are suitably enshrined in essays. . . . Almost all essays begin with a capital I—"I think," "I feel"—and when you have said that, it is clear that you are not writing history or philosophy or biography or anything but an essay, which may be

brilliant or profound, which may deal with the immortality of the soul, or the rheumatism in your left shoulder, but is primarily an expression of personal opinion. ("The Decay of Essay-Writing")

Since Montaigne's day, the essay has broadened to include "all the varieties of thought," as Woolf states. The contemporary essay sometimes expresses personal opinion and feelings and as such sometimes seems extemporaneous and unfinished. But the contemporary essay may be entirely objective in tone and approach to the subject, omitting personal opinions and feelings.

Organizing and Developing the Essay. The contemporary essay may narrate experiences, describe persons and places, explain an idea or a process, give the history of an event, or argue a point and seek to persuade us to accept it. Essays indeed have been traditionally classified as narrative, descriptive, expository, and argumentative, depending on the chief method used to organize and develop the essay. We commonly refer to novels as narratives, word pictures as descriptions, sets of directions as expositions, and defenses of opinion as arguments. This traditional classification does not, however, tell us why the essayist chooses to narrate or describe, explain or argue. We need to know the purpose that the writer has in doing so.

Thus an autobiographical essay or memoir like Sally Carrighar's recollection of her father (p. 41) may use narrative and description to express the writer's sense of the past or help us to understand it. Narratives in the form of short stories and novels may entertain us, or, like John Steinbeck's *The Grapes of Wrath*, seek to move us or persuade us to take action. An explanatory essay helps us to understand a process or, as in Jearl Walker's essay on how to cook outdoors (p. 227), teaches us to perform it. Usually argument is used as a means of persuasion. Though essays may depend on a single method of development, most depend upon more than one method. Description usually gives support to narrative. And exposition often aids in expressing feelings and attitudes, and often joins with argument, as in an advertisement that explains how a product works and gives us reasons for buying it.

The Nature of the Paragraph. In this section and those following in Parts One and Two, we will see how individual paragraphs and complete essays illustrate a principle of organization and development of ideas. In looking at paragraphs, we need to remember that they form complete essays and do not stand alone, except where the essay consists of a single paragraph, as in E. B. White's "In an Elevator" (p. 55).

Some paragraphs develop a single impression or idea; some develop related impressions or ideas. The paragraphs that follow in this and later sections are of this type. Other paragraphs, it should be noted, are transitional, marking a turn to a new idea, and some are summary paragraphs—stating or reiterating the central idea or thesis, without developing it:

[*Transitional*] But mass transportation needn't necessarily wait for breakthroughs in energy technology. In fact, in the nineteenth century, cities developed their first systems based on the use of one of mankind's oldest suppliers of energy: the horse.

[*Summary*] The organization of mass transportation systems was an important step forward in urban social organization, but it hardly marked a major breakthrough in technology. Horses, after all, had been used to pull wagons from time immemorial. Aside from the rather mundane development that saw rails put in city streets, there was very little to distinguish the early-nineteenth-century transportation engineer from his Roman (or even Sumerian) counterpart. (James C. Trefil, *The Growth of Cities*)

The essays and paragraphs that follow by no means show all possible ways of organizing and developing ideas. But the methods illustrated are common ones that all writers draw upon.

1

Topic Sentence, Thesis, and Unity

Topic Sentence and Unity in the Paragraph

In reading an essay, we depend on the opening sentence of each paragraph to direct us from one idea to the next. As in the following paragraph from Eric Sevareid's essay describing his hometown in North Dakota (pp. 29–34), the opening sentence sometimes directs us through a topic sentence or statement of the central idea:

> *Sights have changed:* there is a new precision about street and home, a clearing away of chicken yards, cow barns, pigeon-crested cupolas, weed lots and coulees, the dim and secret adult-free rendezvous of boys. An intricate metal "jungle gym" is a common backyard sight, the sack swing uncommon. . . . ("Velva, North Dakota" [italics added])

Not all opening sentences state the central idea fully. Some state just the subject or topic of the paragraph—occasionally through a single word, as in another paragraph of Sevareid's:

> *Consolidation.* The nearby hamlets of Sawyer and Logan and Voltaire had their own separate banks and papers and schools in my days of dusty buggies and Model Ts marooned in the snowdrifts. Now these hamlets are dying. . . . [italics added]

The subject or topic may also be introduced through a question that Sevareid answers in the remainder of the paragraph:

> *But now I must ask myself:* Are they nearer to one another? And the answer is no; yet I am certain that this is good. The shrinking of time and distance has made contrast and relief available to their daily lives. They do not know one another quite so well because they are not so much obliged to. . . . [italics added]

In paragraphs that open with a statement of the subject or topic, the central or topic idea may follow immediately, as in the paragraph just cited, or details and explanatory statements may build to the central idea. Paragraphs of this kind sometimes generate suspense or a sense of climax, for the reader must wait for the central statement in order to gain the full impact. When the details alone make the point, the paragraph is said to have an *implied* topic sentence, the central idea or generalization remaining unstated.

The topic sentence helps in unifying the paragraph. A unified paragraph not only develops one idea at a time but also makes each idea and detail relevant to the topic idea. The reader sees the relation of ideas and details. A disunified paragraph, by contrast, seems disconnected, its ideas and details introduced without transition or apparent reason.

Mark Twain

Growing up in Hannibal, Missouri, on the Mississippi River, SAMUEL CLEMENS had one ambition in life—to become a steamboatman. "Boy after boy managed to get on the river," Twain tells us in Life on the Mississippi (1883). "The minister's son became an engineer. The doctor's and the postmaster's sons became 'mud clerks'. . . . " Twain left Hannibal in 1853 and worked as a printer in St. Louis and other cities. In 1857 he became a cub pilot on a Mississippi steamboat, secured his license two years later, and worked as a pilot until 1861. Later, working as a newspaper reporter, he adopted the pen name "Mark Twain," after the term leadsmen used on river boats for "two fathoms deep." In the excerpt reprinted below, Twain describes the trials of learning the shape of the Mississippi under a senior pilot, Horace Bixby. Bixby says "I'll learn a man," Twain says in a note, because "'teach' is not in the river vocabulary." In the excerpt in Part Five of this book (pp. 535), Twain describes his early ambition.

THE SHAPE OF THE RIVER

I went to work now to learn the shape of the river; and of all the ꞁ eluding and ungraspable objects that ever I tried to get mind or hands on, that was the chief. I would fasten my eyes upon a sharp, wooden point that projected far into the river some miles ahead of me, and go to laboriously photographing its shape upon my brain; and just as I was beginning to succeed to my satisfaction, we would draw up toward it and the exasperating thing would begin to melt away and fold back into the bank! If there had been a conspicuous dead tree standing upon the very point of the cape, I would find that tree inconspicuously merged into the general forest, and occupying the middle of a straight shore, when I got abreast of it! No prominent hill would stick to its shape long enough for me to make up my mind what its form really was, but it was as dissolving and changeful as if it had been a mountain of butter in the hottest corner of the tropics. Nothing ever had the same shape when I was coming down-stream that it had borne when I went up. I mentioned these little difficulties to Mr. Bixby. He said,

"That's the main virtue of the thing. If the shapes didn't change every three seconds they wouldn't be of any use. Take this place where we are now, for instance. As long as that hill over yonder is only one hill, I can boom right along the way I'm going; but the moment it splits at the top and forms a V, I know I've got to scratch to starboard in a hurry, or I'll bang this boat's brains out against a rock; and then the moment one of the prongs of the V swings behind the other, I've got to waltz to larboard again, or I'll have a misunderstanding with a snag that would snatch the keelson out of this steamboat as neatly as if it were a sliver in your hand. If that hill didn't change its shape on bad nights there would be an awful steamboat graveyard around here inside of a year."

It was plain that I had got to learn the shape of the river in all the different ways that could be thought of—upside down, wrong end first, inside out, fore-and-aft, and "thort-ships"—and then know what to do on gray nights when it hadn't any shape at all. So I set about it. In the course of time I began to get the best of this knotty lesson, and my self-complacency moved to the front once more. Mr. Bixby was all fixed, and ready to start it to the rear again. He opened on me after this fashion:

"How much water did we have in the middle crossing at Hole-in-the-Wall, trip before last?"

I considered this an outrage. I said:

3

"Every trip, down and up, the leadsmen are singing through that tangled place for three quarters of an hour on a stretch. How do you reckon I can remember such a mess as that?"

"My boy, you've got to remember it. You've got to remem-   4
ber the exact spot and the exact marks the boat lay in when we had the shoalest water, in every one of the five hundred shoal places between St. Louis and New Orleans; and you mustn't get the shoal soundings and marks of one trip mixed up with the shoal soundings and marks of another, either, for they're not often twice alike. You must keep them separate."

When I came to myself again, I said,   5

"When I get so that I can do that, I'll be able to raise the dead, and then I won't have to pilot a steamboat to make a living. I want to retire from this business. I want a slush-bucket and a brush; I'm only fit for a roustabout. I haven't got brains enough to be a pilot; and if I had I wouldn't have strength enough to carry them around, unless I went on crutches."

"Now drop that! When I say I'll learn a man the river I   6
mean it. And you can depend on it, I'll learn him or kill him."

VOCABULARY

paragraph 1: starboard, larboard, keelson
paragraph 4: leadsmen

QUESTIONS

1. Twain states the topic idea of paragraph 1 in his opening sentence. How does he illustrate this idea, and in what order does he present his examples?
2. What point is Bixby making in paragraph 2, and where does he state it? How does he develop it?
3. What is Twain showing about himself as a student and about Bixby as a teacher?

SUGGESTIONS FOR WRITING

1. In one or two well developed paragraphs, describe your own experience learning a difficult job. Like Twain, explain in detail what you had to learn.

2. Describe a similar episode that shows something about you as a student and something about the teacher. Open your paragraphs with topic sentences that state the subject of the paragraph or an idea illustrated by the details that follow.

James Stevenson

JAMES STEVENSON *has written articles and profiles for* The New Yorker, *and his cartoons often appear in that magazine. He is the author and illustrator of a number of children's books. His description of a steep road in Los Angeles—from one of his profiles—introduces the reader to a director of horror films, John Carpenter. Notice how Stevenson creates a feeling of suspense in his selection of details and building of the paragraph.*

LOMA VISTA DRIVE

Partway down the long, very steep slope of Loma Vista Drive, descending through Beverly Hills, with the city of Los Angeles spread out far below the houses of sparkling opulence on either side, there is a sign warning "Use Lowest Gear" and, shortly after that, a sign that says "Runaway Vehicle Escape Lane 600 Feet Ahead." Just before Loma Vista crosses Doheny Road, it expands on the right into a third lane, composed of a succession of low, uneven piles of loose gravel nestled against cement block set in an embankment. The operator of a runaway vehicle is apparently expected to steer his car into this soft and receptive lane and come to a halt like a baseball player sliding into third. It seems a perfectly reasonable solution; the unsettling aspect is the underlying assumption that automobiles will so frequently go berserk hereabouts that some accommodation must be made for them. Similarly, along the heavily populated canyon roads of Beverly Hills there are signs forbidding cigarettes and matches: these dry hills may burst into flame at any time. The houses above Sunset Boulevard are stuck in the nearly vertical slopes like cloves in a ham; how they stay there is mysterious. It seems likely that, if they do not catch fire first, a good rain will send them tumbling down the mountain; already, earth has slid out from under retaining walls, terraces, swimming pools, driveways, even roads. In some places, tons of concrete have been poured like icing over a section of hillside to hold it back— and the concrete has even been painted green—but the earth has begun to slip away beneath that, too, leaving edges of concrete sticking out against the sky. In addition, of course, the entire area sits close to the quiescent but menacing San Andreas Fault. Gazing up the perilous roads at the plucky, high-risk homes perched in the tinderlike hills near the great rift, a visitor feels that this may be a community where desire and imagination automatically take precedence over danger, and even over reality.

VOCABULARY

opulence, assumption, berserk, quiescent, rift, precedence

QUESTIONS

1. Stevenson builds up to his central idea instead of starting the paragraph with it. How does the opening sentence introduce the topic or subject of the paragraph and prepare the reader for the details that follow?
2. How do the details develop the central idea stated in the final sentence?
3. Did Stevenson need to state the central idea, or could he have depended on the details to state it implicitly?
4. How is the paragraph appropriate as an introduction to a man who makes horror films?

SUGGESTIONS FOR WRITING

1. In a paragraph of your own, give an account of a drive down an unusual street. Describe the street for someone who has not seen it—building through a series of details to a central idea as Stevenson does.

2. Write a second paragraph describing the street from the point of view of a person seeing it for the first time. Let your details develop an idea; do not state it explicitly. Your details should be vivid enough and well enough organized to make the idea clear to your reader.

Thesis and Unity in the Essay

The thesis of an essay is its central or controlling idea, the proposition or chief argument—the point of the essay. The topic sentence of a paragraph may be either a full or a partial statement of the controlling idea. The thesis is always a full statement of it.

Where the thesis appears depends largely on the audience. If we believe that our readers require no introduction to it (no background or explanation of the issue or important terms) we may state it in the opening paragraph. Many newspaper editorials begin this way—a practice consistent with that of putting the essential information in the opening sentences of a news story. Many essayists, by contrast, prefer to build to a full statement of the thesis—introducing it in the opening paragraphs, perhaps with an explanation of important terms and the issues to be discussed. William Zinsser does this in the opening paragraphs of the essay on writing that concludes this book:

> Clutter is the disease of American writing. We are a society strangling in unnecessary words, circular constructions, pompous frills and meaningless jargon. ("Simplicity")

Zinsser illustrates this opening statement in the succeeding paragraph, then states his thesis in the opening sentence of a paragraph that follows shortly:

> But the secret of good writing is to strip every sentence to its cleanest components.

The remainder of the essay shows how to do so, the conclusion restating the thesis in light of what Zinsser has demonstrated:

> Writing is hard work. A clear sentence is no accident. Very few sentences come out right the first time, or even the third time. . . .

If the thesis needs extensive background and discussion to be understood or perhaps is highly controversial, we may decide to build up to it instead of stating it toward the beginning of the essay. In some essays we may not state the thesis at all, letting the reader draw conclusions from the details or facts provided. In such essays the thesis is said to be *implied*.

George Orwell

> GEORGE ORWELL (1903–1950) *was the pseudonym of the English novelist and essayist Eric Hugh Blair. Orwell was born in India, where his father was a customs official in the British civil government. After attending school in England, Orwell took a job with the Imperial Police in Burma, serving from 1922 to 1927. On leaving the police service, he returned to Europe, where he began his career as journalist and novelist. The rise of totalitarianism in Europe is the subject of numerous essays and books, particularly in his fable* Animal Farm *(1945) and the novel* Nineteen Eighty-four *(1949). In "Shooting an Elephant," Orwell skillfully combines description of a small Burmese town and British colonial officials with a narrative of what happened to him when summoned to deal with a crazed elephant. In narrating the incident, Orwell is arguing a thesis in a special way—through an episode typical of a situation faced by colonial powers. Orwell also has something important to say about human nature. Although Great Britain no longer governs India or Burma, Orwell's ideas remain pertinent to today's political issues.*

SHOOTING AN ELEPHANT

In Moulmein, in lower Burma, I was hated by large numbers of people—the only time in my life that I have been important enough for this to happen to me. I was subdivisional police officer of the town, and in an aimless, petty kind of way anti-European feeling was very bitter. No one had the guts to raise a riot, but if a European woman went through the bazaars alone somebody would probably spit betel juice over her dress. As a police officer, I was an obvious target and was baited whenever it seemed safe to do so. When a nimble Burman tripped me up on the football field and the referee (another Burman) looked the other way, the crowd yelled with hideous laughter. This happened more than once. In the end the sneering yellow faces of young men that met me everywhere, the insults hooted after me when I was at a safe distance, got badly on my nerves. The young Buddhist priests were the worst of all. There were several thousands of them in the town and none of them seemed to have anything to do except stand on street corners and jeer at Europeans.

All this was perplexing and upsetting. For at that time I had already made up my mind that imperialism was an evil thing and the sooner I chucked up my job and got out of it the better. Theoretically—and secretly, of course—I was all for the Burmese and all against their oppressors, the British. As for the job I was doing, I hated it more bitterly than I can perhaps make clear. In a job like that you see the dirty work of Empire at close quarters. The wretched prisoners huddling in the stinking cages of the lock-ups, the gray, cowed faces of the long-term convicts, the scarred buttocks of the men who had been flogged with bamboos—all these oppressed me with an intolerable sense of guilt. But I could get nothing into perspective. I was young and ill educated and I had had to think out my problems in the utter silence that is imposed on every Englishman in the East. I did not even know that the British Empire is dying, still less did I know that it is a great deal better than the younger empires that are going to supplant it. All I knew was that I was stuck between my hatred of the empire I served and my rage against the evil-spirited little beasts who tried to make my job impossible. With one part of my mind I thought of the British Raj as an unbreakable tyranny, as something clamped down, in *saecula saeculorum*,

2

upon the will of prostrate peoples; with another part I thought that the greatest joy in the world would be to drive a bayonet into a Buddhist priest's guts. Feelings like these are the normal by-products of imperialism; ask any Anglo-Indian official, if you can catch him off duty.

One day something happened which in a roundabout way was enlightening. It was a tiny incident in itself, but it gave me a better glimpse than I had had before of the real nature of imperialism—the real motives for which despotic governments act. Early one morning the sub-inspector at a police station the other end of the town rang me up on the 'phone and said that an elephant was ravaging the bazaar. Would I please come and do something about it? I did not know what I could do, but I wanted to see what was happening and I got on to a pony and started out. I took my rifle, an old .44 Winchester and much too small to kill an elephant, but I thought the noise might be useful in *terrorem*. Various Burmans stopped me on the way and told me about the elephant's doings. It was not, of course, a wild elephant, but a tame one which had gone "must."* It had been chained up, as tame elephants always are when their attack of "must" is due, but on the previous night it had broken its chain and escaped. Its mahout,* the only person who could manage it when it was in that state, had set out in pursuit, but had taken the wrong direction and was now twelve hours' journey away, and in the morning the elephant had suddenly reappeared in the town. The Burmese population had no weapons and were quite helpless against it. It had already destroyed somebody's bamboo hut, killed a cow and raided some fruit-stalls and devoured the stock; also it had met the municipal rubbish van and, when the driver jumped out and took to his heels, had turned the van over and inflicted violences upon it.

The Burmese sub-inspector and some Indian constables were waiting for me in the quarter where the elephant had

3

4

---

* *must*: state of sexual heat in male elephant. [All notes are the editor's.]
* *mahout*: the elephant driver and sometimes owner.

been seen. It was a very poor quarter, a labyrinth of squalid bamboo huts, thatched with palm-leaf winding all over a steep hillside. I remember that it was a cloudy, stuffy morning at the beginning of the rains. We began questioning the people as to where the elephant had gone and, as usual, failed to get any definite information. That is invariably the case in the East; a story always sounds clear enough at a distance, but the nearer you get to the scene of events the vaguer it becomes. Some of the people said that the elephant had gone in one direction, some said that he had gone in another, some professed not even to have heard of any elephant. I had almost made up my mind that the whole story was a pack of lies, when we heard yells a little distance away. There was a loud, scandalized cry of "Go away, child! Go away this instant!" and an old woman with a switch in her hand came round the corner of a hut, violently shooing away a crowd of naked children. Some more women followed, clicking their tongues and exclaiming; evidently there was something that the children ought not to have seen. I rounded the hut and saw a man's dead body sprawling in the mud. He was an Indian, a black Dravidian coolie, almost naked, and he could not have been dead many minutes. The people said that the elephant had come suddenly upon him round the corner of the hut, caught him with its trunk, put its foot on his back and ground him into the earth. This was the rainy season and the ground was soft, and his face had scored a trench a foot deep and a couple of yards long. He was lying on his belly with arms crucified and head sharply twisted to one side. His face was coated with mud, the eyes wide open, the teeth bared and grinning with an expression of unendurable agony. (Never tell me, by the way, that the dead look peaceful. Most of the corpses I have seen looked devilish.) The friction of the great beast's foot had stripped the skin from his back as neatly as one skins a rabbit. As soon as I saw the dead man I sent an orderly to a friend's house nearby to borrow an elephant rifle. I had already sent back the pony, not wanting it to go mad with fright and throw me if it smelt the elephant.

The orderly came back in a few minutes with a rifle and five ₅ cartridges, and meanwhile some Burmans had arrived and told us that the elephant was in the paddy fields below, only a few hundred yards away. As I started forward practically the whole population of the quarter flocked out of the houses and followed me. They had seen the rifle and were all shouting excitedly that I was going to shoot the elephant. They had not shown much interest in the elephant when he was merely ravaging their homes, but it was different now that he was going to be shot. It was a bit of fun to them, as it would be to an English crowd; besides they wanted the meat. It made me vaguely uneasy. I had no intention of shooting the elephant—I had merely sent for the rifle to defend myself if necessary—and it is always unnerving to have a crowd following you. I marched down the hill, looking and feeling a fool, with the rifle over my shoulder and an ever-growing army of people jostling at my heels. At the bottom, when you got away from the huts, there was a metalled road and beyond that a miry waste of paddy fields a thousand yards across, not yet ploughed but soggy from the first rains and dotted with coarse grass. The elephant was standing eight yards from the road, his left side toward us. He took not the slightest notice of the crowd's approach. He was tearing up bunches of grass, beating them against his knees to clean them, and stuffing them into his mouth.

I had halted on the road. As soon as I saw the elephant I ₆ knew with perfect certainty that I ought not to shoot him. It is a serious matter to shoot a working elephant—it is comparable to destroying a huge and costly piece of machinery—and obviously one ought not to do it if it can possibly be avoided. And at that distance, peacefully eating, the elephant looked no more dangerous than a cow. I thought then and I think now that his attack of "must" was already passing off; in which case he would merely wander harmlessly about until the mahout came back and caught him. Moreover, I did not in the least want to shoot him. I decided that I would watch him for a little while to make sure that he did not turn savage again, and then go home.

But at that moment I glanced round at the crowd that had ⁷ followed me. It was an immense crowd, two thousand at the least and growing every minute. It blocked the road for a long distance on either side. I looked at the sea of yellow faces above the garish clothes—faces all happy and excited over this bit of fun, all certain that the elephant was going to be shot. They were watching me as they would watch a conjurer about to perform a trick. They did not like me, but with the magical rifle in my hands I was momentarily worth watching. And suddenly I realized that I should have to shoot the elephant after all. The people expected it of me and I had got to do it; I could feel their two thousand wills pressing me forward, irresistibly. And it was at this moment, as I stood there with the rifle in my hands, that I first grasped the hollowness, the futility of the white man's dominion in the East. Here was I, the white man with his gun, standing in front of the unarmed native crowd—seemingly the leading actor of the piece; but in reality I was only an absurd puppet pushed to and fro by the will of those yellow faces behind. I perceived in this moment that when the white man turns tyrant it is his own freedom that he destroys. He becomes a sort of hollow, posing dummy, the conventionalized figure of a sahib. For it is the condition of his rule that he shall spend his life in trying to impress the "natives," and so in every crisis he has got to do what the "natives" expect of him. He wears a mask, and his face grows to fit it. I had got to shoot the elephant. I had committed myself to doing it when I sent for the rifle. A sahib has got to act like a sahib; he has got to appear resolute, to know his own mind and do definite things. To come all that way, rifle in hand, with two thousand people marching at my heels, and then to trail feebly away, having done nothing— no, that was impossible. The crowd would laugh at me. And my whole life, every white man's life in the East, was one long struggle not to be laughed at.

But I did not want to shoot the elephant. I watched him   8
beating his bunch of grass against his knees with that preoc-
cupied grandmotherly air that elephants have. It seemed to
me that it would be murder to shoot him. At that age I was
not squeamish about killing animals, but I had never shot an
elephant and never wanted to. (Somehow it always seems
worse to kill a *large* animal.) Besides, there was the beast's
owner to be considered. Alive, the elephant was worth at
least a hundred pounds; dead, he would only be worth the
value of his tusks, five pounds, possibly. But I had got to act
quickly. I turned to some experienced-looking Burmans who
had been there when we arrived, and asked them how the elephant had been behaving. They all said the same thing: he
took no notice of you if you left him alone, but he might
charge if you went too close to him.

It was perfectly clear to me what I ought to do. I ought to   9
walk up to within, say, twenty-five yards of the elephant and
test his behavior. If he charged, I could shoot; if he took no
notice of me, it would be safe to leave him until the mahout
came back. But also I knew I was going to do no such thing. I
was a poor shot with a rifle and the ground was soft mud into
which one would sink at every step. If the elephant charged
and I missed him, I should have about as much chance as a
toad under a steam-roller. But even then I was not thinking
particularly of my own skin, only of the watchful yellow faces
behind. For at that moment, with the crowd watching me, I
was not afraid in the ordinary sense, as I would have been if
I had been alone. A white man mustn't be frightened in front
of "natives"; and so, in general, he isn't frightened. The sole
thought in my mind was that if anything went wrong those
two thousand Burmans would see me pursued, caught, tram-
pled on, and reduced to a grinning corpse like that Indian up
the hill. And if that happened it was quite probable that some
of them would laugh. That would never do. There was only
one alternative. I shoved the cartridges into the magazine
and lay down on the road to get a better aim.

The crowd grew very still, and a deep, low, happy sigh, as 10
of people who see the theater curtain go up at last, breathed
from innumerable throats. They were going to have their bit
of fun after all. The rifle was a beautiful German thing with
crosshair sights. I did not then know that in shooting an elephant one would shoot to cut an imaginary bar running from
ear-hole to ear-hole. I ought, therefore, as the elephant was
sideways on, to have aimed straight at his ear-hole; actually I
aimed several inches in front of this, thinking the brain would
be further forward.

When I pulled the trigger I did not hear the bang or feel the 11
kick—one never does when a shot goes home—but I heard the
devilish roar of glee that went up from the crowd. In that
instant, in too short a time, one would have thought, even for
the bullet to get there, a mysterious, terrible change had come
over the elephant. He neither stirred nor fell, but every line of
his body had altered. He looked suddenly stricken, shrunken,
immensely old, as though the frightful impact of the bullet had
paralyzed him without knocking him down. At last, after what
seemed a long time—it might have been five seconds, I dare
say—he sagged flabbily to his knees. His mouth slobbered. An
enormous senility seemed to have settled upon him. One
could have imagined him thousands of years old. I fired again
into the same spot. At the second shot he did not collapse but
climbed with desperate slowness to his feet and stood weakly
upright, with legs sagging and head drooping. I fired a third
time. That was the shot that did for him. You could see the
agony of it jolt his whole body and knock the last remnant of
strength from his legs. But in falling he seemed for a moment
to rise, for as his hind legs collapsed beneath him he seemed
to tower upward like a huge rock toppling, his trunk reaching
skyward like a tree. He trumpeted, for the first and only time.
And then down he came, his belly toward me, with a crash that
seemed to shake the ground even where I lay.

I got up. The Burmans were already racing past me across 12
the mud. It was obvious that the elephant would never rise

again, but he was not dead. He was breathing very rhythmically with long rattling gasps, his great mound of a side painfully rising and falling. His mouth was wide open—I could see far down into caverns of pale pink throat. I waited a long time for him to die, but his breathing did not weaken. Finally I fired my two remaining shots into the spot where I thought his heart must be. The thick blood welled out of him like red velvet, but still he did not die. His body did not even jerk when the shots hit him, the tortured breathing continued without a pause. He was dying, very slowly and in great agony, but in some world remote from me where not even a bullet could damage him further. I felt that I had got to put an end to that dreadful noise. It seemed dreadful to see the great beast lying there, powerless to move and yet powerless to die, and not even to be able to finish him. I sent back for my small rifle and poured shot after shot into his heart and down his throat. They seemed to make no impression. The tortured gasps continued as steadily as the ticking of a clock.

In the end I could not stand it any longer and went away.   13 I heard later that it took him half an hour to die. Burmans were bringing dahs* and baskets even before I left, and I was told they had stripped his body almost to the bones by the afternoon.

Afterward, of course, there were endless discussions about   14 the shooting of the elephant. The owner was furious, but he was only an Indian and could do nothing. Besides, legally I had done the right thing, for a mad elephant has to be killed, like a mad dog, if its owner fails to control it. Among the Europeans opinion was divided. The older men said I was right, the younger men said it was a damn shame to shoot an elephant for killing a coolie, because an elephant was worth more than any damn Coringhee coolie. And afterward I was very glad that the coolie had been killed; it put me legally in the right and it gave me a sufficient pretext for shooting the elephant. I often wondered whether any of the others grasped that I had done it solely to avoid looking a fool.

* *dahs*: knives for butchering animals.

VOCABULARY

paragraph 2: imperialism, supplant, prostrate
paragraph 4: Dravidian
paragraph 7: dominion, sahib
paragraph 8: squeamish
paragraph 11: glee, sagged, slobbered, senility
paragraph 14: pretext

QUESTIONS

1. Orwell states in paragraph 3: "One day something happened which in a roundabout way was enlightening. It was a tiny incident in itself, but it gave me a better glimpse than I had had before of the real nature of imperialism—the real motives for which despotic governments act." The incident, in its details, reveals the psychology of the imperialist ruler. What effects do the stuffy, cloudy weather and the behavior of the Burmese and their attitude toward the elephant have on his psychology? Why is the dead coolie described in detail in paragraph 4? Why is the shooting of the elephant described in detail in paragraph 11? In general, how does the incident reveal the motives Orwell mentions?

2. The incident reveals more than just the motives of the imperialist ruler: What does it reveal about mob and crisis psychology and the policeman in the middle?

3. Where in the essay is the thesis stated, and how do you account for its placement? Does Orwell restate it?

4. The exact diction contributes greatly to the development of the thesis, for Orwell does not merely *tell us*, he makes us see. In paragraph 11, for example, he states: ". . . I heard the devilish roar of *glee* that went up from the crowd." He might have chosen *laughter*, *hilarity*, or *mirth* to describe the behavior of the crowd, but *glee* is the exact word because it connotes something that the other three words do not—malice. And the elephant "*sagged* flabbily to his knees," not *dropped* or *sank*, because *sagged* denotes weight and, in the context of the passage, age. What does Orwell mean in the same paragraph by "His mouth *slobbered*" and "An enormous *senility* seemed to have settled upon him"? In paragraph 12 why "*caverns* of pale pink throat" rather than *depths*? In paragraph 4 why is

the corpse *grinning* rather than *smiling*? (Consult the synonym listings in your dictionary, or compare definitions.)

SUGGESTIONS FOR WRITING

1. Illustrate the last sentence of the essay from your own experience. Build the essay to the moment when you acted to avoid looking like a fool. Make your reader see and feel what you saw and felt.

2. Orwell states: "And my whole life, every white man's life in the East, was one long struggle not to be laughed at." Drawing on your experience and observation, discuss what you see as the feelings and motives of people charged with enforcing rules of some sort—perhaps hall monitors in high school, or lifeguards at a swimming pool, or supervisors at a playground, or babysitters. Use your discussion to draw a conclusion, as Orwell does.

Peggy and Pierre Streit

PEGGY *and* PIERRE STREIT *collaborated on numerous articles on life in the Middle East and Asia. Pierre Streit also produced documentaries for television and business corporations. In a recent article,* Barbara Crossette *writes that the thousands of subcastes in the Hindu caste system fall into major divisions or* varnas *in a descending hierarchy—the learned and warrior castes, followed by the merchant, laboring, servant, and other castes:* "Under them all are the outcastes, people considered impure and therefore untouchable, who do the lowliest jobs" *(New York Times Magazine, May 19, 1991). Through the influence of the great Hindu political leader Mahatma Gandhi, the untouchable caste is now called* Harijan—*meaning "Child of God." In 1949 the Indian government outlawed discrimination against Harijans but, as the Streits show in the 1959 article, traditional attitudes remain powerful.*

A WELL IN INDIA

The hot dry season in India. . . . A corrosive wind drives   ₁
rivulets of sand across the land; torpid animals stand at the

edge of dried-up water holes. The earth is cracked and in the rivers the sluggish, falling waters have exposed the sludge of the mud flats. Throughout the land the thoughts of men turn to water. And in the village of Rampura these thoughts are focused on the village well.

It is a simple concrete affair, built upon the hard earth worn by the feet of five hundred villagers. It is surmounted by a wooden structure over which ropes, tied to buckets, are lowered to the black, placid depths twenty feet below. Fanning out from the well are the huts of the villagers—their walls white from sun, their thatched roofs thick with dust blown from the fields.

At the edge of the well is a semi-circle of earthen pots and, crouched at some distance behind them, a woman. She is an untouchable—a sweeper in Indian parlance—a scavenger of the village. She cleans latrines, disposes of dead animals and washes drains. She also delivers village babies, for this—like all her work—is considered unclean by most of village India.

Her work—indeed, her very presence—is considered polluting, and since there is no well for untouchables in Rampura, her water jars must be filled by upper-caste villagers.

There are dark shadows under her eyes and the flesh has fallen away from her neck, for she, like her fellow outcastes, is at the end of a bitter struggle. And if, in her narrow world, shackled by tradition and hemmed in by poverty, she had been unaware of the power of the water of the well at whose edge she waits—she knows it now.

Shanti, 30 years old, has been deserted by her husband, and supports her three children. Like her ancestors almost as far back as history records, she has cleaned the refuse from village huts and lanes. Hers is a life of inherited duties as well as inherited rights. She serves, and her work calls for payment of one chapatty—a thin wafer of unleavened bread—a day from each of the thirty families she cares for.

But this is the hiatus between harvests; the oppressive lull before the burst of monsoon rains; the season of flies and dust, heat and disease, querulous voices and frayed tempers—and the season of want. There is little food in Rampura for anyone, and though Shanti's chores have continued as before, she has received only six chapatties a day for her family—starvation wages.

Ten days ago she revolted. Driven by desperation, she defied an elemental law of village India. She refused to make her sweeper's rounds—refused to do the work tradition and religion had assigned her. Shocked at her audacity, but united in desperation, the village's six other sweeper families joined in her protest. 8

Word of her action spread quickly across the invisible line that separates the untouchables' huts from the rest of the village. As the day wore on and the men returned from the fields, they gathered at the well—the heart of the village—and their voices rose, shrill with outrage: a *sweeper* defying them all! Shanti, a sweeper *and* a woman challenging a system that had prevailed unquestioned for centuries! Their indignation spilled over. It was true, perhaps, that the sweepers had not had their due. But that was no fault of the upper caste. No fault of theirs that sun and earth and water had failed to produce the food by which they could fulfill their obligations. So, to bring the insurgents to heel, they employed their ultimate weapon; the earthen water jars of the village untouchables would remain empty until they returned to work. For the sweepers of Rampura the well had run dry. 9

No water; thirst, in the heat, went unslaked. The embers of the hearth were dead, for there was no water for cooking. The crumbling walls of outcaste huts went untended, for there was no water for repairs. There was no fuel, for the fires of the village were fed with dung mixed with water and dried. The dust and the sweat and the filth of their lives congealed on their skins and there it stayed, while life in the rest of the village—within sight of the sweepers—flowed on. 10

The day began and ended at the well. The men, their dhotis wrapped about their loins, congregated at the water's edge in the hushed post-dawn, their small brass water jugs in 11 hand, their voices mingling in quiet conversation as they rinsed their bodies and brushed their teeth. The buffaloes were watered, their soft muzzles lingering in the buckets before they were driven off to the fields. Then came the women, their brass pots atop their heads, to begin the ritual of water drawing: the careful lowering of the bucket in the well, lest it come loose from the rope; the gratifying splash as it touched the water; the maneuvering to make it sink; the squeal of rope against wooden pulley as it ascended. The sun rose higher. Clothes were beaten clean on the rocks surrounding the well as the women gossiped. A traveler from a near-by road quenched his thirst from a villager's urn. Two little boys, hot and bored, dropped pebbles into the water and waited for their hollow splash, far below.

As the afternoon wore on and the sun turned orange   12
through the dust, the men came back from the fields. They doused the parched, cracked hides of their water buffaloes and murmured contentedly, themselves, as the water coursed over their own shoulders and arms. And finally, as twilight closed in, came the evening procession of women, stately, graceful, their bare feet moving smoothly over the earth, their full skirts swinging about their ankles, the heavy brass pots once again balanced on their heads.

The day was ended and life was as it always was—almost.   13
Only the fetid odor of accumulated refuse and the assertive buzz of flies attested to strife in the village. For, while tradition and religion decreed that sweepers must clean, it also ordained that the socially blessed must not. Refuse lay where it fell and rotted.

The strain of the water boycott was beginning to tell on the   14
untouchables. For days they had held their own. But on the third their thin reserve of flesh had fallen away. Movements were slower; voices softer; minds dull. More and more the desultory conversation turned to the ordinary: the delicious memory of sliding from the back of a wallowing buffalo into a pond; the feel of bare feet in wet mud; the touch of fresh water on parched lips; the anticipation of monsoon rains.

One by one the few tools they owned were sold for food. 15
A week passed, and on the ninth day two sweeper children
were down with fever. On the tenth day Shanti crossed the
path that separated outcaste from upper caste and walked
through familiar, winding alleyways to one of the huts she
served.

"Your time is near," she told the young, expectant mother. 16
"Tell your man to leave his sickle home when he goes to the
fields. I've had to sell mine." (It is the field sickle that cuts the
cord of newborn babies in much of village India.) Shanti, the
instigator of the insurrection, had resumed her ancestral
duties; the strike was broken. Next morning, as ever, she
waited at the well. Silently, the procession of upper-caste
women approached. They filled their jars to the brim and
without a word they filled hers.

She lifted the urns to her head, steadied them, and started 17
back to her quarters—back to a life ruled by the powers that
still rule most of the world: not the power of atoms or electricity, nor the power of alliances or power blocs, but the elemental powers of hunger, of disease, of tradition—and of
water.

VOCABULARY

paragraph 1: corrosive, rivulets
paragraph 3: untouchable, parlance
paragraph 4: upper-caste
paragraph 7: hiatus, monsoon
paragraph 9: insurgents
paragraph 10: unslaked, congealed
paragraph 13: fetid

QUESTIONS

1. The Streits build to a statement of their thesis at the end of paragraph 5. Why is it necessary to portray the world of the untouchable before stating the thesis?

2. Where in the essay is the thesis restated? Is the restatement
   more informative or detailed than the original statement of it?

3. What is the attitude of the authors toward the world they portray and the fate of Shanti? Do they seem to be taking sides?

4. Is it important to the thesis that Shanti is a woman? Are the authors concerned with her as a woman, in addition to their concern for her as an untouchable?

5. Is the concern of the essay equally with the power of water and the power of tradition? Or are these considerations subordinate to the portrayal of the untouchable and the courage shown?

6. Are we given a motive directly for what Shanti does—or is the motive implied?

SUGGESTIONS FOR WRITING

1. Develop an idea relating to the power of tradition and illustrate it from personal experience and observation. Provide enough background so that your reader understands why the tradition is important to the people who observe it.

2. Describe a conflict between you and your parents or school officials or between a person and a group of some sort. Explain how the conflict arose from a basic difference in attitude, ideas, or feelings—a difference that reveals something important about you and the other people involved.

Eric Sevareid

Born in 1912 in Velva, North Dakota, ERIC SEVAREID graduated from the University of Minnesota in 1935 and immediately began his career as a journalist with the Minneapolis Journal. He later reported for the Paris edition of The New York Herald Tribune. In 1939 Sevareid began his long association with the Columbia Broadcasting Company as a war correspondent in Europe. From 1964 to 1977 he delivered his commentary on the CBS Evening News. His books include Small Sounds in the Night (1956) and an autobiography, Not So Wild a Dream (1976). Like Orwell in "Shooting an Elephant," Sevareid builds through a careful presentation of detail to increasingly broad truths about the world of his youth and human nature generally.

VELVA, NORTH DAKOTA

My home town has changed in these thirty years of the American story. It is changing now, will go on changing as America changes. Its biography, I suspect, would read much the same as that of all other home towns. Depression and war and prosperity have all left their marks; modern science, modern tastes, manners, philosophies, fears and ambitions have touched my town as indelibly as they have touched New York or Panama City.

Sights have changed: there is a new precision about street and home, a clearing away of chicken yards, cow barns, pigeon-crested cupolas, weed lots and coulees, the dim and secret adult-free rendezvous of boys. An intricate metal "jungle gym" is a common backyard sight, the sack swing uncommon. There are wide expanses of clear windows designed to let in the parlor light, fewer ornamental windows of colored glass designed to keep it out. Attic and screen porch are slowly vanishing and lovely shades of pastel are painted upon new houses, tints that once would have embarrassed farmer and merchant alike.

Sounds have changed; I heard not once the clopping of a horse's hoofs, nor the mourn of a coyote. I heard instead the shriek of brakes, the heavy throbbing of the once-a-day Braniff airliner into Minot, the shattering sirens born of war, the honk of a diesel locomotive which surely cannot call to faraway places the heart of a wakeful boy like the old steam whistle in the night. You can walk down the streets of my town now and hear from open windows the intimate voices of the Washington commentators in casual converse on the great affairs of state; but you cannot hear on Sunday morning the singing in Norwegian of the Lutheran hymns; the old country seems now part of a world left long behind and the old-country accents grow fainter in the speech of my Velva neighbors.

The people have not changed, but the *kinds of* people have changed; there is no longer an official, certified town drunk, no longer a "Crazy John," spitting his worst epithet, "rotten chicken legs," as you hurriedly passed him by. People so sick are now sent to places of proper care. No longer is there an official town joker, like the druggist MacKnight, who would spot a customer in the front of the store, have him called to the phone, then slip to the phone behind the prescription case, and imitate the man's wife to perfection with orders to bring home more bread and sausage and Cream of Wheat. No longer anyone like the early attorney, J. L. Lee, who sent fabulous dispatches to that fabulous tabloid, the *Chicago Blade*, such as his story of the wild man captured on the prairie and chained to the wall in the drugstore basement. (This, surely, was Velva's first notoriety; inquiries came from anthropologists all over the world.)

No, the "characters" are vanishing in Velva, just as they are 5 vanishing in our cities, in business, in politics. The "well-rounded, socially integrated" personality that the progressive schoolteachers are so obsessed with is increasing rapidly, and I am not at all sure that this is good. Maybe we need more personalities with knobs and handles and rugged lumps of individuality. They may not make life more smooth; more interesting they surely make it.

They eat differently in Velva now; there are frozen fruits and 6 sea food and exotic delicacies we only read about in novels in those meat-and-potato days. They dress differently. The hard white collars of the businessmen are gone with the shiny alpaca coats. There are comfortable tweeds now, and casual blazers with a touch in their colors of California, which seems so close in time and distance.

It is distance and time that have changed the most and 7 worked the deepest changes in Velva's life. The telephone, the car, the smooth highway, radio and television are consolidating the entities of our country. The county seat of Towner now seems no closer than the state capital of Bismarck; the voices and concerns of Presidents, French premiers and Moroccan pashas are no farther away than the portable radio on Aunt Jessey's kitchen table. The national news magazines are stacked each week in Harold Anderson's drugstore beside the new soda fountain, and the excellent Minot Daily News smells hot from the press each afternoon.

Consolidation. The nearby hamlets of Sawyer and Logan   8
and Voltaire had their own separate banks and papers and schools in my days of dusty buggies and Model T's marooned in the snowdrifts. Now these hamlets are dying. A bright yellow bus takes the Voltaire kids to Velva each day for high school. Velva has grown—from 800 to 1,300—because the miners from the Truax coal mine can commute to their labors each morning and the nearby farmers can live in town if they choose. Minot has tripled in size to 30,000. Once the "Magic City" was a distant and splendid Baghdad, visited on special occasions long prepared for. Now it is a twenty-five minute commuter's jump away. So P. W. Miller and Jay Louis Monicken run their businesses in Minot but live on in their old family homes in Velva. So Ray Michelson's two girls on his farm to the west drive up each morning to their jobs as maids in Minot homes. Aunt Jessey said, "Why, Saturday night I counted sixty-five cars just between here and Sawyer, all going up to the show in Minot."

The hills are prison battlements no longer; the prairies no   9
heart-sinking barrier, but a passageway free as the swelling ocean, inviting you to sail home and away at your whim and your leisure. (John and Helen made an easy little jaunt of 700 miles that week-end to see their eldest daughter in Wyoming.)

Consolidation. Art Kumm's bank serves a big region now;   10
its assets are $2,000,000 to $3,000,000 instead of the $200,000 or $300,000 in my father's day. Eighteen farms near Velva are under three ownerships now. They calculate in sections; "acres" is an almost forgotten term. Aunt Jessey owns a couple of farms, and she knows they are much better run. "It's no longer all take out and no put in," she said. "Folks strip farm now; they know all about fertilizers. They care for it and they'll hand on the land in good shape." The farmers gripe about their cash income, and not without reason at the moment, but they will admit that life is good compared with those days of drought and foreclosure, manure banked

against the house for warmth, the hand pump frozen at 30 below and the fitful kerosene lamp on the kitchen table. Electrification has done much of this, eased back-breaking chores that made their wives old as parchment at forty, brought life and music and the sound of human voices into their parlors at night.

And light upon the prairie. "From the hilltop," said Aunt 11 Jessey, "the farms look like stars at night."

Many politicians deplore the passing of the old family-size 12 farm, but I am not so sure. I saw around Velva a release from what was like slavery to the tyrannical soil, release from the ignorance that darkens the soul and from the loneliness that corrodes it. In this generation my Velva friends have rejoined the general American society that their pioneering fathers left behind when they first made the barren trek in the days of the wheat rush. As I sit here in Washington writing this, I can feel their nearness. I never felt it before save in my dreams.

But now I must ask myself: Are they nearer to one another? 13 And the answer is no; yet I am certain that this is good. The shrinking of time and distance has made contrast and relief available to their daily lives. They do not know one another quite so well because they are not so much obliged to. I know that democracy rests upon social discipline, which in turn rests upon personal discipline; passions checked, hard words withheld, civic tasks accepted, work well done, accountings honestly rendered. The old-fashioned small town was this discipline in its starkest, most primitive form; without this discipline the small town would have blown itself apart.

For personal and social neuroses festered under this hard 14 scab of conformity. There was no place to go, no place to let off steam; few dared to voice unorthodox ideas, read strange books, admire esoteric art or publicly write or speak of their dreams and their soul's longings. The world was not "too much with us," the world was too little with us and we were too much with one another.

The door to the world stands open now, inviting them to 15 leave anytime they wish. It is the simple fact of the open door that makes all the difference; with its opening the stale air rushed out. So, of course, the people themselves do not have to leave, because, as the stale air went out, the fresh air came in.

Human nature is everywhere the same. He who is not   16 forced to help his neighbor for his own existence will not only give him help, but his true good will as well. Minot and its hospital are now close at hand, but the people of Velva put their purses together, built their own clinic and homes for the two young doctors they persuaded to come and live among them. Velva has no organized charity, but when a farmer falls ill, his neighbors get in his crop; if a townsman has a financial catastrophe his personal friends raise a fund to help him out. When Bill's wife, Ethel, lay dying so long in the Minot hospital and nurses were not available, Helen and others took their turns driving up there just to sit with her so she would know in her gathering dark that friends were at hand.

It is personal freedom that makes us better persons, and   17 they are freer in Velva now. There is no real freedom without privacy, and a resident of my home town can be a private person much more than he could before. People are able to draw at least a little apart from one another. In drawing apart, they gave their best human instincts room for expansion.

VOCABULARY

paragraph 1: indelibly
paragraph 4: certified, epithet, tabloid, notoriety, anthropologists
paragraph 5: progressive
paragraph 6: alpaca, blazers
paragraph 7: pashas
paragraph 8: consolidation, commute
paragraph 9: battlements, whim, jaunt
paragraph 10: foreclosure
paragraph 12: deplore, corrodes, trek
paragraph 13: starkest
paragraph 14: neuroses, scab, unorthodox, esoteric

QUESTIONS

1. Where does Sevareid indicate his attitude toward his hometown? What is his thesis?

2. What details in the whole essay support the dominant impression Sevareid creates of the town in his opening paragraph? Is any of this detail unrelated to this impression?

3. What are the causes of the change in life in Velva? Does Sevareid indicate a main cause?

4. What does Sevareid mean by *discipline* in the statement in paragraph 13, "without this discipline the small town would have blown itself apart"?

5. Sevareid points up a series of paradoxes toward the end. What are these, and what do they contribute to the tone of the conclusion?

SUGGESTIONS FOR WRITING

1. Describe important changes that have occurred in the town or the neighborhood in which you grew up, and discuss the reasons. Use these changes to develop a thesis of your own.

2. Sevareid writes that much was lost; the changes that occurred in farming and the general life of Velva were perhaps for the better. Develop your essay further by explaining why you would—or would not—say the same thing about the changes that occurred in your town or neighborhood.

2

Main and Subordinate Ideas

The Paragraph

An author may develop the main or central idea of a paragraph through a series of subordinate ideas. Consider the opening sentences of the following paragraph on country superstitions.

> In the folklore of the country, numerous superstitions relate to winter weather. Back-country farmers examine their corn husks—the thicker the husk, the colder the winter. They watch the acorn crop—the more acorns, the more severe the season. They observe where white-faced hornets place their paper nests—the higher they are, the deeper will be the snow. They examine the size and shape and color of the spleens of butchered hogs for clues to the severity of the season. They keep track of the blooming of dogwood in the spring—the more abundant the blooms, the more bitter the cold in January. When chipmunks carry their tails high and squirrels have heavier fur and mice come into country houses early in the fall, the superstitious gird themselves for a long, hard winter. Without any scientific basis, a wider-than-usual black band on a woolly-bear caterpillar is accepted as a sign that winter will arrive early and stay late. Even the way a cat sits beside the stove carries its message to the credulous. According to a belief once widely held in the Ozarks, a cat sitting with its tail to the fire indicates very cold weather is on the way. (Edwin Way Teale, *Wandering Through Winter*)

The first sentence is the main idea; the second sentence, a subordinate idea that develops it through illustration:

> In the folklore of the country, numerous superstitions relate to winter weather.
> Back-country farmers examine their corn husks—
> the thicker the husk, the colder the winter.

We have indented to show the levels of subordination in these sentences. Notice that the third sentence has the same importance as the second in developing the main idea:

> They watch the acorn crop—
>> the more acorns, the more severe the season.

Of course, in writing paragraphs you do not indent in this way to show the relative importance of your ideas. But you do in writing essays: the break for a new paragraph—through an indentation—tells the reader that you are introducing a new or related idea or topic. Within the paragraph you need ways of substituting for the indentations shown above. One of these ways is the use of parallel phrasing to show that ideas have the same importance:

They watch the acorn crop . . .
They observe . . .
They examine . . .

In longer paragraphs, you can distinguish the main idea by repeating or restating it at the end. We will see later in the book that the beginning and ending are usually the most emphatic parts of sentences because of their prominence. The same is true of paragraphs and essays.

Lytton Strachey

LYTTON STRACHEY (1890–1932), *one of England's great biographers, was particularly interested in revered figures of the nineteenth century, and earlier English history, whose human qualities he wanted to discover. In his biographies, Strachey looks at the strengths and failings of his subjects, joining fact with the imagined creation of their inner life. We see this method in his portrait of Queen Victoria. Born in 1819, Victoria became queen in 1837 at the age of eighteen, and in 1840 married a first cousin her own age, the German prince Albert of Saxe-Coburg. When Albert died of a sudden illness in 1861, at the age of 42, she entered a long period of private mourning—for the remainder of her life preserving her physical surroundings as they had existed in his lifetime. Strachey shows how little the author needs to say when the right details are chosen and organized carefully.*

QUEEN VICTORIA
AT THE END OF HER LIFE

[1]She gave orders that nothing should be thrown away—and nothing was. [2]There, in drawer after drawer, in wardrobe after wardrobe, reposed the dresses of seventy years. [3]But not only the dresses—the furs and the mantles and subsidiary frills and the muffs and the parasols and the bonnets—all were ranged in chronological order, dated and complete. [4]A great cupboard was devoted to the dolls; in the china room at Windsor a special table held the mugs of her childhood, and her children's mugs as well. [5]Mementoes of the past surrounded her in serried accumulations. [6]In every room the tables were powdered thick with the photographs of relatives; their portraits, revealing them at all ages, covered the walls; their figures, in solid marble, rose up from pedestals, or gleamed from brackets in the form of gold and silver statuettes. [7]The dead, in every shape—in miniatures, in porcelain, in enormous life-size oil-paintings—were perpetually about her. [8]John Brown stood upon her writing table in solid gold.* [9]Her favorite horses and dogs, endowed with a new durability, crowded round her footsteps. [10]Sharp, in silver gilt, dominated the dinner table; Boy and Boz lay together among unfading flowers in bronze. [11]And it was not enough that each particle of the past should be given the stability of metal or of marble: the whole collection, in its arrangement, no less than its entity, should be immutably fixed. [12]There might be additions, but there might never be alterations. [13]No chintz might change, no carpet, no curtain, be replaced by another; or, if long use at last made it necessary, the stuffs and the patterns must be so identically reproduced that the keenest eye might not detect the

---

* John Brown (1826–1883) was the Scottish attendant to Victoria's husband, Prince Albert, and after the death of the Prince in 1861, to the Queen herself.—Ed.

difference. [14]No new picture could be hung upon the walls at Windsor, for those already there had been put in their places by Albert, whose decisions were eternal. [15]So, indeed, were Victoria's. [16]To ensure that they should be the aid of the camera was called in. [17]Every single article in the Queen's possession was photographed from several points of view. [18]These photographs were submitted to Her Majesty, and when, after careful inspection, she had approved of them, they were placed in a series of albums, richly bound. [19]Then, opposite each photograph, an entry was made, indicating the number of the article, the number of the room in which it was kept, its exact position in the room and all its principal characteristics. [20]The fate of every object which had undergone this process was henceforth irrevocably sealed. [21]The whole multitude, once and for all, took up its steadfast station. [22]And Victoria, with a gigantic volume or two of the endless catalogue always beside her, to look through, to ponder upon, to expatiate over, could feel, with a double contentment, that the transitoriness of this world had been arrested by the amplitude of her might.

VOCABULARY

sentence 3: subsidiary, frills, parasols
sentence 5: mementoes, serried
sentence 11: immutably
sentence 13: chintz
sentence 20: irrevocably
sentence 22: expatiate, transitoriness, amplitude

QUESTIONS

1. In his portrait of Victoria in her old age, Strachey develops and illustrates several major ideas that build to his central or topic idea. What are these ideas?

2. Strachey states in sentence 2 that Victoria saved the dresses of seventy years; in sentence 3, that she saved her furs and bonnets, as well as other articles of clothing—and arranged and dated them chronologically. How does Strachey show that he is moving from one surprising, even astonishing, fact to an even more surprising one?

3. Compare sentences 11 and 12 with those that follow. How does Strachey indicate that he is building the paragraph to even more surprising details?

4. What contributes to the climactic effect of the final sentence of the paragraph?

5. Has Strachey made Queen Victoria human to you? Or is she merely an eccentric?

SUGGESTIONS FOR WRITING

1. Write a character sketch of an unusual friend or teacher, centering on a dominant trait and presenting related traits as Strachey does. Present these related traits in the order of rising importance—as illustrations of the dominant trait.

2. Rewrite Strachey's paragraph, beginning with his concluding sentence and achieving a sense of climax in your reordering of ideas and details.

The Essay

The thesis is the most important idea in an essay. When an essay builds to its thesis through a series of subordinate ideas and details, we may sense a rising importance of ideas in it, even perhaps a sense of climax. As in the paragraph, it is important that we sense the relative importance of these ideas and details. An essay in which all seem to have the same importance would be extremely hard to read.

We can sense this relative importance of ideas even in the topic sentences, as in these sentences that open the first seven paragraphs of Sevareid's essay on Velva, North Dakota. The different indentations show the relative weight of each idea:

My home town has changed in these thirty years. . . .
    Sights have changed. . . .
    Sounds have changed. . . .
    The people have not changed, but the *kinds of* people have changed.
        No, the "characters" are vanishing in Velva. . . .
    They eat differently in Velva now. . . .
It is distance and time that have changed the most and worked the deepest changes in Velva's life.

Sevareid builds to his thesis through a series of increasingly broad generalizations. Here are the opening sentences of the last six paragraphs:

> Many politicians deplore the passing of the old family-size farm, but I am not so sure.
> But now I must ask myself: Are they nearer to one another?
> For personal and social neuroses festered under this hard scab of conformity.
> The door to the world stands open now. . . .
> Human nature is everywhere the same.
> It is personal freedom that makes us better persons, and they are freer in Velva now [*thesis*].

Sevareid's sentences show that we do not always need formal transitions to tell us which ideas are main and which are subordinate. The clear, logical relationship of Sevareid's ideas shows their relative importance. But, as in the paragraph, formal transitions are sometimes needed (pp. 79–100). Having a sense of the relative importance of our ideas and details is important as we write.

Sally Carrighar

The writer and naturalist SALLY CARRIGHAR *was born in Cleveland, Ohio, the scene of the introduction to her autobiography,* Home to the Wilderness (1973), *reprinted here. After graduation from Wellesley College, Carrighar discovered an interest in birds and animals, and she decided to become a nature writer: "There could be no finer subject than woods and fields, streams, lakes, and mountainsides and the creatures who live in that world. It would be a subject of inexhaustible interest, a supreme joy to be learning to tell it all straight and truthfully." For nine years Carrighar lived in an isolated Alaskan village, studying Eskimo life and the animals of the Arctic region. She has written about this experience and about wildlife generally in* Icebound Summer (1953), Wild Voice of the North (1959), Wild Heritage (1965), *and other books. In the passage that follows, she describes experiences and people that awakened her imagination and curiosity about life.*

THE BLAST FURNACE

We were a father and his first-born, a four-year-old girl, setting out every Sunday afternoon to see the industrial marvels of Cleveland, Ohio. The young man had grown up in a smaller Canadian town and he was delighted with Cleveland, which hummed and clanged with the vast new developments steel had made possible. In temperament he was anything but an engineer; here however he was excited to feel that he had jumped into the very heart of the torrent of progress.

Most often we walked on the banks of the Cuyahoga River to see the drawbridge come apart and rise up, like giant black jaws taking a bite of the sky, so that boats could go through: the long freighters that brought iron ore from Lake Superior, other large and small freighters, fishing boats, passenger steamers. My father's eyes never tired of watching them make their smooth way up and down the river. His father, born in Amsterdam of a seagoing family, had been a skipper on the Great Lakes. Perhaps my father too should have been a sailor, but he was something nearly as satisfying—he worked for a railroad.

And so we went to the roundhouse where the steam engines stood when they were not pulling trains. They had all entered through the same door but inside their tracks spread apart, as gracefully as the ribs of a lady's fan. My father knew a great deal about engines, he knew the names of some of these and he walked among them with pride.

On our way to the roundhouse we passed through the freight yards where long trains of boxcars lay on their sidings. My father said that the cars belonged to different railroads and came from various parts of the country, being coupled together here because all those in one train were bound for the same destination. This was getting too complicated but there was nothing complicated about my father's emotion when he said, "Working for a railroad is like living everywhere in the country at once!" A characteristic enchantment came into his eyes and voice, a contagious exhilaration which meant that anything it attached to was good. Living everywhere was something that even a child could grasp vaguely and pleasantly.

My father and I made other trips and best were the ones to the blast furnaces. He explained how the iron ore from the boats was mixed with coal and carried in little cars to the top of the chimney above the furnace. It was dumped in, and as it fell down "a special kind of very hot air" was blown into it. The coal and iron ore caught fire, and below they fell into great tubs as melting metal, a pinkish gold liquid, incandescent as the sun is when it is starting to set. The man and child were allowed to go rather near the vats, to feel the scorching heat and to drown their gaze in the glowing boil. All the rest of the building was dark; the silhouettes of the men who worked at the vats were black shadows. Wearing long leather aprons, they moved about the vats ladling off the slag. That was very skilled work, my father said; the men had to know just how much of the worthless slag to remove. For years afterwards, when we could no longer spend Sunday afternoons on these expeditions, we used to go out of our house at night to see the pink reflections from the blast furnaces on the clouds over Cleveland. We could remember that we had watched the vatfuls of heavily moving gold, and those events from the past were an unspoken bond between us.

Someone once said, "Your father must have been trying to turn you into a boy. He'd probably wanted his first child to be a son." Perhaps; but it was not strange to him to show a girl the achievements of men. He thought of women as human beings and assumed that they, even one very young, would be interested in anything that was interesting to him. He had absorbed that attitude from the women he'd grown up with, his mother and her four sisters, all of whom led adventurous lives. His favorite Aunt Chris had married a clipper captain and sailed with him all her life. When they retired, having seen the entire world, they chose to settle in Burma. Another aunt married one of the Morgan family, who established the famous breed of Morgan horses, and took up a homestead in Manitoba. Aunt Mary, a physician's wife, went with him out to

San Francisco during the Gold Rush and stayed there. The fourth aunt had married the inspector of ships' chronometers at Quebec; and my father's mother, of course, had married her skipper from Holland. In the winter when he was not on his ship he ran a factory for making barrel staves that he had established in western Kentucky—all this and the fathering of five children by the time he was twenty-eight, when he lost his life in a notorious Lake Erie storm. His wife, a musician, brought up her five without complaint, just as her mother, also an early widow, had reared her five gallant girls. With his memories of women like these it was not surprising that my father would wish, even somewhat prematurely, to show his daughter the things that were thrilling to him. I did not comprehend all his family history at four, but I did absorb the impression that girls and women reached out for life eagerly and that it was natural for them to be interested in absolutely everything.

VOCABULARY

paragraph 1: temperament
paragraph 4: contagious, exhilaration
paragraph 5: incandescent, slag
paragraph 6: chronometer

QUESTIONS

1. In paragraph 1 Carrighar develops her opening sentence—the main idea of the paragraph—with specific detail about her father. What is the main idea of paragraph 2, and how does she use the detail of the paragraph to develop it?

2. Paragraph 4 moves from specific detail to the main idea. What is that idea, and how does the author give it prominence?

3. Which of the subordinate ideas in paragraph 5 are in turn illustrated or developed?

4. Paragraphs 1–5 are subordinate to paragraph 6, which draws a conclusion from the experiences described and develops it through details of a different sort. What is this conclusion, and what new details develop it? How is this conclusion—the main

idea of the paragraph—restated later in the paragraph and made prominent?

SUGGESTIONS FOR WRITING

1. Write several paragraphs describing childhood experiences that taught you something about the adult world and about yourself. Begin with these truths, or build the paragraphs up to them, as Carrighar does.

2. Write several paragraphs about information you received or impressions you developed about women in your family. If you wish, contrast these impressions with those you received about boys and men. Use these impressions to develop a thesis.

DAVID HOLAHAN *attended Yale University, graduating in 1971. He published two Connecticut weekly newspapers until their sale in 1982, and since then has written for numerous magazines and newspapers throughout the United States. Holahan's essay is original and interesting because he writes about his football experiences from an unusual point of view. He makes the subject his own through concrete details that give insight into college football and the attitudes and feelings of the players.*

WHY DID I EVER PLAY FOOTBALL?

Coach kept running the halfback sweep through the projector, clicking the stop, rewind and forward buttons as he dwelled on each "individual breakdown" by our defense. Princeton had gained twenty yards on the play and our individual mistakes added up to a "total Yale breakdown." Gallagher and I sat with the other sophomores, savoring the embarrassment of the first-stringers.

The last individual to break down on the play was the defensive safety who started ahead of me. Yale's sports publicity department was touting him as a "pro prospect," but during the eleventh screening of his mistake, he protested that he was not sure how to defense a sweep. After three years on the varsity, our NFL-bound star didn't know how to play your everyday end run.

"The first rule," Gallagher said as loudly as he could, "is don't get hurt." Suppressed laughter spread through the room. Everyone knew "the films don't lie" and that "newspaper clippings don't make tackles"; that "you have to want it," even in the Ivy League.   3

I'm not entirely sure why I played football; it might have been because of those great clichés. I certainly didn't enjoy hitting people the way Gallagher did. He liked to bury his helmet into a quarterback's ribs and drive him into the turf. As he returned to the huddle, there would be a strange expression on his face, somewhere between a grimace and a smile. After a game he would be sore, bruised and bloodied, like the other linemen and linebackers, while I would feel about the same as I did after an uneventful mixer at Vassar.   4

Defensive safeties are not supposed to make a lot of tackles, especially when the people up front are good, which ours were, and that was just fine with me. Still, some of my most vivid memories are of moments of intense pain. Once in junior year I found myself in a dreaded position: one-on-one with a fullback charging as swiftly as his bulky legs would carry him. He was ten yards away and closing fast. He was also growling. "His S.A.T. scores must be beauts," flashed through my mind and the urge to flee became acute. Thousands of eyes were watching—including Coach's camera. If I blew it I would have to see the replay at least a dozen times.   5

Suddenly I was moving sideways through the air, pain jolting my body, the fullback forgotten. I hit the ground writhing, clutching my side and pulling my knees up to my chest. There was no air in my lungs. For a moment the world stopped at my skin. I wanted to stay crumpled up on the ground, but one of our linemen pulled me to my feet with one hand and half-carried me to the huddle. It must have been their end who hit me. I had seen him split out wide, then I forgot about him. He weighed over 200 pounds; I went about 160. What was I   6 thinking of, playing football? I didn't hear our captain call the defensive signals, but fear slowly returned as the pain subsided. If that quarterback were smart he would try a pass in my zone. The pass never came. Thank God we were playing Harvard.

Continuing to play football was not a particularly rational thing for me to do. In sixth grade I was as big and strong and fast as anyone our six-man team faced. And jocks were popular then. By college virtually everyone I played against was bigger and stronger, and the consensus on campus in the late 1960s was that we were a bunch of neofascists, at best. So much for "Boola, Boola." And when it wasn't a physically grinding ordeal, practice, too, could be as boring as Archeology 101.

Saturday's approach would turn my insides to mush, but the day I dreaded most was Sunday, film day. "Now I want everyone to watch the tackling technique on this play," Coach would say. "Holahan, I hope you squeeze your dates harder than this." Gallagher laughed the loudest.

Oh, I had my moments, usually when the people up front either played badly or were overmatched. Then I got a workout and there was no place to hide. Against Dartmouth, senior year, I turned positively vicious after watching their halfback gloat over one of our players lying injured on the field. I started burying my helmet into people even if they didn't have the ball. Once I made that halfback groan in pain. I also said some ugly things about his mother. I intercepted two passes. And the next day brought sweet soreness; so that's how Gallagher felt after every game.

There were other players who must have had a tougher time figuring out why they were playing football; high-school hotshots who couldn't crack the second string, but who hung on. Some who didn't play in games, never expected to, maybe never even wanted to, for blocking and tackling are clearly unpleasant experiences. A few were not in the least bit athletic. Who knows, they may have been doing it for their résumés, but I suppose they had their moments too, when things would happen that could never take place in

Archaeology 101. For me, Coach's films had something to do with why I continued to play.

Sunday afternoon was both a social and a moral occasion—funny, embarrassing, depressing or happy, depending on how the team had done and how each player had performed. Every fall Sabbath was a new Judgment Day. What was shown on the screen was often harsh, but always just. I could fool professors and pass courses without working very hard, but no one could slip anything past that camera. If I played well Saturday, I knew it; still, the camera confirmed it. There was no place to hide in that room, no big linemen up front to take the heat. Film immortalized shirking efforts.

I have often thought of driving forty minutes to New Haven and digging up that old Dartmouth game, going back fourteen years to see a younger, stronger, less cautious me. The temptation seems to grow each year, but I will never do it. It would be cheating the camera to look only at that one film.

VOCABULARY

paragraph 1: savoring, first-stringers
paragraph 2: touting, varsity
paragraph 4: clichés, grimace
paragraph 7: virtually, neofascists
paragraph 10: résumés
paragraph 11: shirking

QUESTIONS

1. Holahan might have opened the essay with the question asked in the title instead of building to it through the details of paragraphs 1–3. What does he gain through this buildup of details?
2. In paragraphs 5–6 Holahan describes an experience as a defensive safety in a college game with Harvard. Why does he present this experience before turning to earlier experiences as a football player?
3. Holahan builds to general conclusions through his experiences with football. How does he show that these conclusions are the main ideas of his essay?

4. What is the answer to the question that Holahan asks in the title of the essay and in paragraph 4, and where does he answer the question? What does Holahan gain in answering the question where he does?

SUGGESTIONS FOR WRITING

1. Illustrate your reasons for playing a sport or a musical instrument or for performing a similar activity. Don't state the reasons directly. Let your reader discover them through the details of your essay.

2. Write an essay on one of the following topics or on one of your own choosing. Give your thesis emphasis by introducing it in a prominent place in the essay—perhaps at the end of the opening paragraph, or in the final paragraph. If you begin the essay with your thesis, you can give it emphasis by repeating or restating it at key points:

   a. the art of keeping friends
   b. on not giving advice
   c. the art of persuading children
   d. on living away from home
   e. on waiting in line

3

Order of Ideas

The Paragraph

A unified paragraph develops one idea at a time and makes each idea relevant to the topic idea. You will keep a paragraph unified if, as you write and revise, you consider the order in which you want to present your ideas and details. This order is sometimes determined by the subject of the paragraph and sometimes by the audience you have in mind—and sometimes by both. For example, in describing parallel parking for people learning to drive, you probably would present each step as it occurs. But in describing the same process to driving instructors, you might present these steps in the order of their difficulty, to single out those steps needing the most practice.

An account of a process, or a narrative, is usually chronological. A description of a scene is generally spatial in organization—the details are presented as the eye sees them. The details or ideas can also be ordered in other ways, for example:

- from the easy to the difficult, as in the paragraph written for driving instructors
- from the less to the more important
- from the less to the more interesting or exciting
- from the general to the specific—for example, from the theory of combustion to the details of the process
- from the specific to the general—for example, from simple effects of gravity, like falling off a bike, to a definition of gravity or comment on these effects.

When ideas move from the less to the more important, the sense of importance is sometimes our own. We need to show this to the reader, perhaps through a simple transition like the words *more importantly* (p. 79). We can dispense with such transitions when the sense of rising importance is expressed directly, as in the famous statement of Julius Caesar—"I came, I saw, I conquered"—or in the details themselves:

50

A furious gale attacks him like a personal enemy, tries to grasp his limbs, fastens upon his mind, seeks to ro his very spirit out of him. (Joseph Conrad, *Typhoon*)

As in this sentence, we can achieve climax by making one idea seem to anticipate another and by giving weight to the final idea (in Conrad's sentence, through the word *very*). The terminal position in a sentence or paragraph is a position of natural emphasis because of its prominence—a fact that we can take advantage of in giving weight to ideas or details.

A paragraph may combine two or more orders of ideas. For instance, a paragraph written for driving instructors may move from the easy to the difficult steps of parallel parking, and at the same time from the less to the more important or even interesting.

Alan Cowell

Chief of the New York Times *Rome bureau*, ALAN COWELL *reported on the Iran-Iraq war and the Persian Gulf War, and on other wars in the Middle East and Africa. He received the George Polk Award for his reports on South Africa. In the opening paragraphs of his July 7, 1994,* Times *article on motorcycling in Kenya, South Africa, and Rome, Cowell tells us that seeing Rome through motorcycle goggles is one way of discovering the city: "To the uninitiated, it might appear that the traffic is just chaos—a snarling, honking beast whose only aim is to prevent any pedestrian from ever crossing the street. That, of course, is one of its prime functions. But within this apparent mayhem, there are actually rules—or at least battle lines—that only the foolhardy ignore. And rule one is: motorcyclists have no friends. Not even among other motorcyclists." In the concluding paragraphs reprinted here, Cowell tells us why. Earlier in the article, Cowell tells us that the British Ariel 600 was his first motorbike.*

ROME, ON TWO WHEELS

The first thing that happens when you ride a motorcycle in Rome is that you wish you hadn't. Forget any notion of two-wheeled solidarity, Harley-hogger style. You teeter into the traffic. The motorini buzz you like swarms of irate bees, cutting across your path, appearing from nowhere, darting from side roads with the insouciance that the city demands of its young. (Being "cool" in the American sense is as nothing compared to the sense of bella figura requiring that, beneath that Yankee baseball hat and behind those Ray-Ban shades, you must behave as if you are the only person on the entire planet.)

If you survive the motorini, you cope with the cars. All   2
Italian drivers, with no exception, drive as if they learned the craft from the video game called Tetris where the object is to fit as many objects as possible into a defined area without leaving a single space between them. That means motorcycle sandwich unless you manage to dart between the closing jaws of the Lancias and Fiats before they close on you.

And, if you survive the cars, you deal with your fellow motor-   3
cyclists, who live with a permanent sense of affront that you might think your motorcycle to be faster, louder, more muscular or more macho than theirs. In practical terms, this means that every traffic light is a drag race, every sliver of open road a challenge to change down through three howling gears, twist the throttle and head for the moon—or the intensive care unit. (The only exception is the small but highly visible group of female bikers on Harleys and Harley look-alikes, who ride with such overwhelming panache that they've won already.)

It is only after this initiation that you begin to discern   4
the rules.

Some rules are negative. For instance, because many mo-   5
torini have no license plates and therefore cannot be traced by the police, there are no red lights for motorini riders, just as there are no one-way streets, no pedestrian precincts and no distinctions between the road and the sidewalk.

Some rules are positive. If, for instance, you manage to get   6
your motorcycle's front tire a hair's breadth ahead of a motorino, motorcycle or car, you enjoy right of way—but only until that driver senses you will lose your nerve first.

Some rules fall between the two. A red light, for instance, 7
is only red if there's a policeman watching. And only foreign
visitors believe that white markings on the street denoting a
pedestrian crossing actually require anyone to slow the flow
of two-wheeled madness that eddies and swirls round obstacles like the Tiber in flood.

One rule is immutable: Buses always win. 8

So why do it?, friends ask. 9

I ride this monstrous motorcycle because, for one thing, I 10
can get across town with minimum delay, park without hin-
drance outside restaurants and thus give myself more time for
the really important aspects of life in Rome, such as the pasta.

But beyond those arguments, there's a rose-tinting that 11
goes on with motorcycles that has nothing to do with goggles. Sometimes, I ride motorcycles because it makes me feel
(though no one else is fooled) that I am, again, that 16-year-
old athwart the stuttering British BSA 250.

Perhaps there is a kind of continuity that starts for all bikers 12
with the equivalent of the Ariel 600 and runs through the present. The Via del Corso may not be the Rift Valley, and the traffic cops may not be soldiers telling you to go away from the
coup but the motorcycle provides a linear succession between
all those places and events. On two wheels, even the mundane
can be adventurous; and on two wheels, we can dream the
Easy Rider dreams of youth.

For that, even the battle with the motorini is worthwhile. 13

VOCABULARY

paragraph 1: teeter, insouciance
paragraph 3: affront, panache
paragraph 8: immutable
paragraph 12: mundane

QUESTIONS

1. In paragraph 1 Cowell describes Roman *motorini* or motorbikes.
   What is the order of details in the paragraph? Why is a *bella figura*
   or "looking good" necessary in motorcycling?

2. How is the "Harley-hogger style" referred to in paragraph 1 different from the experience of motorcycling in Rome traffic?

3. What experiences does Cowell describe in paragraphs 2 and 3? What does he gain by describing these before discussing the rules of the road in paragraphs 4–8?

4. To what topic does he turn in paragraphs 9–13? What does he gain by concluding with this topic?

SUGGESTIONS FOR WRITING

1. Discuss what Cowell's experiences and observations suggest about Italian drivers generally.

2. Describe your own experiences motorcycling or biking on American streets. Like Cowell, use your experiences to comment on American driving habits.

The Essay

The subject of a paragraph or essay often suggests how to organize it, as in the step-by-step, chronological description of a process. So does the intended audience. If the audience is unfamiliar with the subject, it may be preferable to build from simple to more difficult steps, details, and ideas, instead of presenting these chronologically. In a persuasive essay, for example, you might introduce the thesis at the beginning if you believe the audience will understand it without explanation; if the thesis requires explanation or is controversial, you might build to it through explanatory details and ideas.

The essay of personal experience usually follows a freer course than a formal essay of ideas. In her book *Pilgrim at Tinker Creek*, a description of her life in the Blue Ridge Mountains of Virginia, Annie Dillard divides an essay on winter into sections, each presenting diverse experiences and reflections that capture feelings of the moment inspired by the season. Here are the sentences that introduce the opening sections:

> It is the first of February, and everyone is talking about starlings.

> It is winter proper; the cold weather, such as it is, has come to stay.

Some weather's coming; you can taste on the sides of your tongue a quince tang in the air.

This is the sort of stuff I read all winter.

By contrast, an expository or persuasive essay will show the logical relationships of ideas, as the opening sentences of the first five paragraphs of Margaret Mead and Rhoda Metraux's essay on discipline (p. 152) show:

In the matter of childhood discipline there is no absolute standard.

The Mundugumor, a New Guinea people, trained their children to be tough and self-reliant.

The Arapesh, another New Guinea people, had a very different view of life and personality.

Even very inconsistent discipline may fit a child to live in an inconsistent world.

There are also forms of discipline that may be self-defeating.

The order of ideas in an essay may reveal a writer's characteristic way of expressing ideas. Expository and argumentative essays, too, may reveal an organization of ideas favored by a writer—perhaps a characteristic building to the thesis.

E. B. White

E. B. WHITE (1899–1985) *was one of America's most distinguished writers—an essayist, a poet, a writer of books for children. His long association with* The New Yorker *magazine began in 1926. The columns that appeared in* Harper's *magazine under the title "One Man's Meat" were collected in 1942 in a book of the same name. Other essays are found in* The Second Tree from the Corner (1954), The Points of My Compass (1962), *and* Essays of E. B. White (1977). *In all of these books there is much about Maine, where White lived for many years. But the city of New York was never far from his thoughts, as you can see in his profile of the city later in this book (p. 147).*

IN AN ELEVATOR

In an elevator, ascending with strangers to familiar heights, the breath congeals, the body stiffens, the spirit marks time. These brief vertical journeys that we make in a common lift, from street level to office level, past the missing thirteenth floor—they afford moments of suspended animation, unique and probably beneficial. Passengers in an elevator, whether wedged tight or scattered with room to spare, achieve in their perpendicular passage a trancelike state: each person adhering to the unwritten code, a man descending at five in the afternoon with his nose buried in a strange woman's back hair, reducing his breath to an absolute minimum necessary to sustain life, willing to suffocate rather than allow a suggestion of his physical presence to impinge; a man coming home at one A.M., ascending with only one other occupant of the car, carefully avoiding any slight recognition of joint occupancy. What is there about elevator travel that induces this painstaking catalepsy? A sudden solemnity, perhaps, which seizes people when they feel gravity being tampered with—they hope successfully. Sometimes it seems to us as though everyone in the car were in silent prayer.

VOCABULARY

congeals, animation, perpendicular, adhering, impinge, catalepsy, solemnity

QUESTIONS

1. What kind of tensions build in elevator rides, according to White?

2. How does White suggest this buildup of tension through the details of various rides?

3. Why do you think he concluded his description of elevator rides with a ride at one A.M.?

4. To what idea or reflection does White build the paragraph? Would the paragraph have the same effect if White had begun with this idea?

5. How well does White describe your own feelings riding an elevator?

SUGGESTIONS FOR WRITING

1. White asks the following question:

   What is there about elevator travel that induces this painstaking catalepsy?

   Write your own answer to this question or another suggested by an elevator ride you have taken recently.

2. Describe an experience similar to those described by White, and build the details to a climax as he does. Conclude with your own comment or reflection on the experience as White does.

Leonard Kriegel

LEONARD KRIEGEL *contracted polio at the age of* 11. *"I spent the next two years of my life in an orthopedic hospital, appropriately called a reconstruction home. By 1946, when I returned to my native Bronx, polio had reconstructed me to the point that I walked very haltingly on steel braces and crutches." Kriegel describes this and later experiences in* Working Through (1972) *and* Falling into Life (1991), *from which the following essay is taken.*

THE PURPOSE OF LIFTING

I began lifting weights in May, 1949, a few weeks before my sixteenth birthday. My closest friend and next-door neighbor, Frankie, had quit school—no one used the phrase "high school dropout" back then—to prepare himself for the Marine Corps. He had already enlisted, and he was bound for boot camp at Parris Island at the end of September. He had five months of life as a civilian in which to get his body into the shape the marines demanded.

Frankie bought a used York barbell set and then constructed a pressing bench from a slatted wooden cocktail table left unclaimed in the cellar of the Bronx apartment building in which we both lived. As a cripple, I was certainly not bound for the marines. But the door to Frankie's apartment was only a few feet from the door to our apartment. Curiously enough, losing the use of my legs to polio had served only to intensify the natural physical sense of oneself that preoccupies all adolescent boys. I might walk into Frankie's apartment on braces and crutches, but in my mind I saw myself as not only physically "normal" but the quintessence of health. And like any other male adolescent, I was already a sucker for anything that promised to test my strength and endurance. And so it was I found myself in Frankie's brightly lit room, lying on the cocktail table that had been thrust into service as a pressing bench, my brace-bound legs carefully straddling the bench, surrounded by steel bars, red-metal screw collars, and black cast-iron weights. On the light blue wall across from the converted cocktail table Frankie had taped a crayoned chart so that we could trace the growth of muscles and mass. The smell of our sweat mingled with the smells of cooking lasagna and baking apple pies that came from Frankie's mother's kitchen. An unexpected by-product of lifting was the sense I quickly had that even muscular power and definition were olfactory.

Assuming the role of mentor—he was, after all, a year 3
older and had already invested himself with the proxy authority of the marine he would soon become—Frankie stood above me, urging me on, as I pressed one hundred pounds up and down, up and down. The strength surging through my shoulders and chest was electric, as much with anticipation as with performance. Frankie and I would take turns on the pressing bench, encouraging each other. Then we would sit opposite one another on two hardwood kitchen chairs, vigorously performing set after set of bicep curls.

Until Frankie left for the marines, our lives were structured 4
by that bedroom gym. Both of us were conscious of the bodies we were remolding. Where we had once passed the time by speaking of the books we were reading or the ballplayers we admired or how the girls who filed out of the subway on the corner of 206th Street looked, we now talked about the

geometry of muscularity, our conversation knowingly sprinkled with references to "lats" and "pecs" and "trapezius." The world of male adolescents has always been curiously hermetic and insular. Lifting weights fit it like a tight glove, serving to make it even more secretive.

More than anything else I did then, lifting existed beyond 5 the boundaries established by my confrontation with the polio virus. When I first began lifting in Frankie's apartment, I told myself I was doing it to make walking on crutches easier by strengthening my arms and shoulders. But immediately after that first workout, I knew that lifting had as little to do with my need to build up strength in my arms in order to walk on the crutches as it did with Frankie's forthcoming life in the Marine Corps. The passion for working out, a passion each of us felt immediately, was shared by hundreds of thousands of young men throughout the country who were grunting and sweating as we were. All of us were lifting—no one called it "pumping iron" then—in hopes of molding our bodies into some Platonic vision of the ideal male form. Lifting was simply an act of male vanity. And we did it because we wanted to look good.

Of course, I wouldn't admit that in 1949. And neither 6 would Frankie. I don't think anyone who lifted back in 1949 could admit to so flagrant a male vanity. The aspirations we might confess to were limited to bigger biceps, a firmer chest—and, of course, the admiration of the women we knew and the women we wanted to know.

There were other rationalizations for lifting, and at one time 7 or another I probably used them all. I liked to tell myself, for instance, that my private ceremony endowed the world with order and proportion. As I grew older and began a doctorate in American studies, I would try to get myself to believe that by demanding effort, discipline, and patience of my body I was acting in pragmatic American fashion. I was making myself "better." Like the figure in the Charles Atlas ads in comic books I remembered from my childhood, I was making myself strong enough that no one could kick sand in my face.

As I grew less and less concerned with how I looked, I would 8
find myself trying to break myself of the passion for working
out with weights. Lifting, I now insisted in debates with an
imaginary self, was narcissistic and self-indulgent. It was
childish, an attempt to make the body into something greater
than it was. And it lacked dignity. I was no longer an adolescent preening for others. I had become a husband, a father, a
teacher. Orwell, Mann, Twain, Faulkner—I couldn't even imagine the writers I discussed with the students I taught sweating
and straining beneath a burden so mundane as cast-iron
weights. A man should learn to make do with the body he had
been given. Or so, at least, I tried to convince myself.

But try as I might, I never fully succeeded in breaking the 9
habit. Months would sometimes pass and I would refrain
from lifting. And then a morning would arrive and I would
suddenly find myself, like a reformed alcoholic trying to
maintain his virtue as he stares at the window of a liquor
store, staring at the dumbbells I kept stored beneath the bed.
And on a day when the world threatened to overwhelm me,
when it was simply too much with me, I would find myself
seeking refuge in one or another gym laced with the vapors of
sweat and Ben-Gay.

For a while, it was as if lifting alone promised to keep me 10
sane. During the 1970s, I would flee the rhetorical excess that
came to characterize the profession of college teaching for
the very repetitive motions that I had tried to convince myself
were senseless. The prospect of a good workout was sometimes the only thing enabling me to swim through that sea of
words about "standards" and "relevance" we academics had
unleashed upon ourselves and the nation.

It was also in the 1970s that I, along with others who had 11
been weaned on free weights, began to use those high-tech
machines with names such as Nautilus and Universal. The
lush, carpeted spas of chrome and mirrors were a far cry from
Frankie's bedroom with its makeshift pressing bench. But in
one crucial respect the machines made the purpose of lifting
clearer. In my mid-forties, strapped to the chrome and steel

and vinyl of a Nautilus double chest machine, I finally came to accept the idea that lifting had little to do with any kind of vanity, either that of how I looked or that of how I performed. To strap oneself into these gleaming machines was to affirm the surety of habit, to remove the burden of time. It had nothing to do with the virus that had cut me down and it had nothing to do with an adolescent's hunger for a physical sense of his own body. It had to do, rather, not with what I had lost but with what I had gained—an ease of motion that, having been done, could be done over and over and over again. Repetition, concentration, endurance: it was with these I had to concern myself. And it was these that promised to carry me to the idea of a body stripped of any needs other than its own.

I still lift—light weights now. But still lifting. And I no longer need any other kind of justification when I feel the urge to do what I first began doing at the age of sixteen. I am neither looking better nor growing particularly stronger. And I have no burning desire to stay in shape. All I want is to lock myself into the sweetness of motion and repetition. I want to continue, one movement following another. How grateful one can become for doing just that. 12

VOCABULARY

paragraph 2: quintessence, olfactory
paragraph 3: mentor, proxy
paragraph 4: hermetic, insular
paragraph 5: Platonic
paragraph 7: rationalizations, pragmatic
paragraph 8: narcissistic, mundane
paragraph 10: rhetorical

QUESTIONS

1. What is the central topic of the essay, and how does Kriegel introduce it through the details of the opening paragraphs?
2. In what order does he present his experiences with weight lifting?
3. What is the order of ideas in the whole essay?
4. What is Kriegel's chief point or thesis, and where does he state it?

SUGGESTIONS FOR WRITING

1. Kriegel shows how a childhood illness shaped later attitudes and interests. Discuss how an illness or another important experience in childhood shaped your own attitudes and interests. Present these in the order of their importance or seriousness or some other order of ideas and details.

2. Use your own experiences and observations to test Kriegel's statement that "the world of male adolescents has always been curiously hermetic and insular," or use them to make a statement about male or female adolescence and illustrate it. Organize your experiences and observations clearly and consistently.

Joan Didion

> JOAN DIDION *established her reputation as a magazine columnist and editor (for publications including* Vogue, The Saturday Evening Post, *and* National Review) *and later as a short story and screen writer and novelist. Her nonfictional writings include* Salvador *(1983), a report on the Central American country, and* Miami *(1988), a report on the Cuban-American community. Her essays are collected in* Slouching Towards Bethlehem *(1968),* The White Album *(1979), and* After Henry *(1992). In her novels* Play It As It Lays *(1970) and* The Book of Common Prayer *(1977) and in her many essays Didion depicts personal and social values often imperceptible to the people who live by them. She explores such values in her essay on the marriage business in Las Vegas.*

MARRYING ABSURD

To be married in Las Vegas, Clark County, Nevada, a bride must swear that she is eighteen or has parental permission and a bridegroom that he is twenty-one or has parental permission. Someone must put up five dollars for the license. (On Sundays and holidays, fifteen dollars. The Clark County Courthouse issues marriage licenses at any time of the day or night except between noon and one in the afternoon, between eight and nine in the evening, and between four and five in the morning.) Nothing else is required. The State of Nevada, alone among these United States, demands neither a premarital blood test nor a waiting period before or after the issuance of a marriage license. Driving in across the Mojave from Los Angeles, one sees the signs way out on the desert, looming up from the moonscape of rattlesnakes and mesquite, even before the Las Vegas lights appear like a mirage on the horizon: "GETTING MARRIED? Free License Information First Strip Exit." Perhaps the Las Vegas wedding industry achieved its peak operational efficiency between 9:00 P.M. and midnight of August 26, 1965, an otherwise unremarkable Thursday which happened to be, by Presidential order, the last day on which anyone could improve his draft status merely by getting married. One hundred and seventy-one couples were pronounced man and wife in the name of Clark County and the State of Nevada that night, sixty-seven of them by a single justice of the peace, Mr. James A. Brennan. Mr. Brennan did one wedding at the Dunes and the other sixty-six in his office, and charged each couple eight dollars. One bride lent her veil to six others. "I got it down from five to three minutes," Mr. Brennan said later of his feat. "I could've married them *en masse*, but they're people, not cattle. People expect more when they get married."

What people who get married in Las Vegas actually do expect—what, in the largest sense, their "expectations" are— strikes one as a curious and self-contradictory business. Las Vegas is the most extreme and allegorical of American settlements, bizarre and beautiful in its venality and in its devotion to immediate gratification, a place the tone of which is set by mobsters and call girls and ladies' room attendants with amyl nitrite poppers in their uniform pockets. Almost everyone notes that there is no "time" in Las Vegas, no night and no day and no past and no future (no Las Vegas casino, however, has taken the obliteration of the ordinary time sense quite so far as Harold's Club in Reno, which for a while issued, at odd intervals in the day and night, mimeographed "bulletins" carrying news from the world outside); neither is there any logical sense of where one is. One is standing on a highway in the middle of a vast hostile desert looking at an eighty-foot sign which blinks "STARDUST" or "CAESAR'S PALACE." Yes, but what does that explain? This geographical implausibility reinforces the sense that what happens there has no connection with "real" life; Nevada cities like Reno and Carson are ranch towns, Western towns, places behind which there is some historical imperative. But Las Vegas seems to exist only in the eye of the beholder. All of which makes it an extraordinarily stimulating and interesting place, but an odd one in which to want to wear a candlelight satin Priscilla of Boston wedding dress with Chantilly lace insets, tapered sleeves and a detachable modified train.

And yet the Las Vegas wedding business seems to appeal   3
to precisely that impulse. "Sincere and Dignified Since 1954," one wedding chapel advertises. There are nineteen such wedding chapels in Las Vegas, intensely competitive, each offering better, faster, and, by implication, more sincere services than the next: Our Photos Best Anywhere, Your Wedding on A Phonograph Record, Candlelight with Your Ceremony, Honeymoon Accommodations, Free Transportation from Your Motel to Courthouse to Chapel and Return to Motel, Religious or Civil Ceremonies, Dressing Rooms, Flowers, Rings, Announcements, Witnesses Available, and Ample Parking. All of these services, like most others in Las Vegas (sauna baths, payroll-check cashing, chinchilla coats for sale or rent) are offered twenty-four hours a day, seven days a week, presumably on the premise that marriage, like craps, is a game to be played when the table seems hot.

But what strikes one most about the Strip chapels, with   4
their wishing wells and stained-glass paper windows and their artificial bouvardia, is that so much of their business is by no means a matter of simple convenience, of late-night liaisons between show girls and baby Crosbys. Of course there is some of that. (One night about eleven o'clock in Las Vegas I watched a bride in an orange minidress and masses of flame-colored hair stumble from a Strip chapel on the arm

of her bridegroom, who looked the part of the expendable nephew in movies like *Miami Syndicate*. "I gotta get the kids," the bride whimpered. "I gotta pick up the sitter, I gotta get to the midnight show." "What you gotta get," the bridegroom said, opening the door of a Cadillac Coupe de Ville and watching her crumple on the seat, "is sober.") But Las Vegas seems to offer something other than "convenience"; it is merchandising "niceness," the facsimile of proper ritual, to children who do not know how else to find it, how to make the arrangements, how to do it "right." All day and evening long on the Strip, one sees actual wedding parties, waiting under the harsh lights at a crosswalk, standing uneasily in the parking lot of the Frontier while the photographer hired by The Little Church of the West ("Wedding Place of the Stars") certifies the occasion, takes the picture: the bride in a veil and white satin pumps, the bridegroom usually in a white dinner jacket, and even an attendant or two, a sister or a best friend in hot-pink *peau de soie*, a flirtation veil, a carnation nosegay. "When I Fall in Love It Will Be Forever," the organist plays, and then a few bars of Lohengrin. The mother cries; the stepfather, awkward in his role, invites the chapel hostess to join them for a drink at the Sands. The hostess declines with a professional smile; she has already transferred her interest to the group waiting outside. One bride out, another in, and again the sign goes up on the chapel door: "One moment please—Wedding."

I sat next to one such wedding party in a Strip restaurant 5 the last time I was in Las Vegas. The marriage had just taken place; the bride still wore her dress, the mother her corsage. A bored waiter poured out a few swallows of pink champagne ("on the house") for everyone but the bride, who was too young to be served. "You'll need something with more kick than that," the bride's father said with heavy jocularity to his new son-in-law; the ritual jokes about the wedding night had a certain Panglossian character, since the bride was clearly seven months pregnant. Another round of pink champagne, this time not on the house, and the bride began to cry. "It was just as nice," she sobbed, "as I hoped and dreamed it would be."

VOCABULARY

paragraph 1: mesquite
paragraph 2: allegorical, bizarre, venality, implausibility
paragraph 4: bouvardia, liaisons, expendable, facsimile, nosegay
paragraph 5: jocularity

QUESTIONS

1. One principle of order in Didion's essay is spatial: we see Las Vegas as a visitor would see it from the highway. From what other viewpoints do we see Las Vegas?
2. At the same time, the essay moves to increasingly bizarre episodes, culminating in the wedding party of the final paragraph. What is bizarre about the episode? What sentences indicate this organization?
3. In Voltaire's satirical novel *Candide* the philosopher Pangloss explains the evils and imperfections of the world in the statement, "All is for the best in the best of all possible worlds." Does Didion agree? What is her attitude to the world she describes? What is the dominant tone of or attitude expressed by the essay, and how does Didion establish it?
4. Does Didion state a thesis, or is she concerned only with giving a picture of Las Vegas and the people who marry there? Does Didion imply ideas or attitudes rather than state them?

SUGGESTIONS FOR WRITING

1. Compare Didion's way of revealing her attitude toward Las Vegas with James Stevenson's way of revealing his attitude toward Los Angeles (p. 11–12) or Eric Sevareid's way of revealing his attitude toward Velva, North Dakota (p. 29–34).
2. Characterize another city through an activity typical of its way of life and values. Let your details reveal this way of life and these values.

4

Beginning, Middle, and Ending

To make your ideas convincing, you need to capture the attention of your readers and hold it. You will lose their attention if, in beginning the essay, you describe in too much detail how you intend to proceed. Sometimes you need to indicate a point of view and suggest how you will develop the essay. The following is an ineffective way of doing so:

> I am going to describe my home town as I saw it on a recent visit. I will illustrate the changes and discuss their causes.

Compare these sentences with the opening paragraph of Eric Sevareid's essay on Velva, North Dakota. Sevareid states his subject and suggests how he will develop his essay—engaging the reader by appealing to common interests:

> My home town has changed in these thirty years of the American story. It is changing now, will go on changing as America changes. Its biography, I suspect, would read much the same as that of all other home towns. Depression and war and prosperity have all left their marks; modern science, modern tastes, manners, philosophies, fears and ambitions have touched my town as indelibly as they have touched New York or Panama City.

If you do need to state your purpose and outline the discussion to follow, you can do so with a minimum of personal reference and without sounding stuffy. Here is a paragraph that states the purpose and outlines the discussion to follow:

> The aim of this book is to delineate two types of clever schoolboy: the converger and the diverger. The earlier chapters offer a fairly detailed description of the intellectual abilities, attitudes and personalities of a few hundred such boys. In the later chapters, this

67

description is then used as the basis for a more speculative discussion—of the nature of intelligence and originality and of the ways in which intellectual and personal qualities interact. Although the first half of the book rests heavily on the results of psychological tests, and the last two chapters involve psychoanalytic theory, I have done my best to be intelligible, and, wherever possible, interesting to everyone interested in clever schoolboys: parents, school-teachers, dons, psychologists, administrators, clever schoolboys. (Liam Hudson, *Contrary Imaginations*)

This author directly challenges the interest of his reader. The bonus, this introductory paragraph promises, will be the wit of the author, evident in the humorous announcement of a seemingly dry subject.

By contrast, the author of the following paragraph eases his readers into the subject without an immediate statement of purpose. But he does make an immediate appeal to an important concern of his readers—the problem of how to deal with their own failures and those of friends and family members:

The administration of criminal justice and the extent of individual moral responsibility are among the crucial problems of a civilized society. They are indissolubly linked, and together they involve our deepest emotions. We often find it hard to forgive ourselves for our own moral failures. All of us, at some time or other, have faced the painful dilemma of when to punish and when to forgive those we love—our children, our friends. How much harder it is, then, to deal with the stranger who transgresses. (David L. Bazelon, "The Awesome Decision")

Notice that personal references are not out of place in an opening paragraph—or anywhere else in an essay. The risk of too many such references is that they can divert the reader from the subject of the essay to the author. For this reason they should be kept to a minimum.

The opening paragraphs build the expectations of the reader. The middle paragraphs develop ideas introduced at the beginning. They ought not to introduce new ideas without preparing the reader for a new turn of thought, as Eric Sevareid does:

The people have not changed, but the *kinds of* people have changed. . . .

They eat differently in Velva now. . . .

An effective ending will not let the discussion drop: The reader should not finish the essay with a sense of loose ends, of lines of thought left uncompleted. In the formal essay, the ending may restate the thesis or perhaps even state it for the first time—if you build to the thesis through explanation and details. One of the most effective conclusions, the reference back to ideas that opened the essay, gives the reader a sense of completion:

> It is personal freedom that makes us better persons, and they are freer in Velva now. There is no real freedom without privacy, and a resident of my home town can be a private person much more than he could before. People are able to draw at least a little apart from one another. In drawing apart, they gave their best human instincts room for expansion. (Eric Sevareid, "Velva, North Dakota")

Susan Allen Toth

> SUSAN ALLEN TOTH *teaches literature and creative writing at Macalester College, in St. Paul, Minnesota. In* Blooming: A Small-Town Girlhood *(1981),* Toth *describes growing up in Ames, Iowa, and in* Ivy Days: Making My Way Out East *(1984), her experiences at Smith College, in Northampton, Massachusetts. In the following excerpt from* Ivy Days, *she describes these two worlds, then gives an account of a fall event at Smith that she looked forward to each year.*

MOUNTAIN DAY

At first I was so overwhelmed by the Smith campus itself that I did not much wonder what lay beyond it. I concentrated on learning the campus pathways, exploring the labyrinth of the library, finding my gym locker and the geology lab. I tried to make myself as much at home as possible. In some ways, I succeeded. But I never fully conquered, or even understood, a kind of constriction, a tightness in my chest, that only eased for a time when I took the train home to Iowa at Christmas. Even then I wasn't sure what the feeling was. For four years, I now believe, I lived with a kind of deep claustrophobia, a sense of being closed in. It was part of the price I paid for going "out East."

The town I grew up in was not large. By the time I was a 2
teenager, I knew almost all its streets and connections, its stores and parks and schools. Bicycling everywhere or cruising in cars with my friends, I had the security of moving freely in a wholly known world. More important, I knew what lay beyond the town. Iowa's peaceful countryside, open fields, and sweeping skies were part of my unconscious landscape, lying in the back of my mind like a stage setting no one ever changed. Although I never lived in the actual country, it was the context in which Ames existed, the sea in which our small town was an important island. Smaller towns were smaller islands, Des Moines a large one. But the land surrounded them all. Driving Highway 30, straight through Ames, one left the endless fields of corn for perhaps ten minutes of houses, gas stations, and stores, and then plunged into the ocean of corn again.

In winter and early spring, stubbled fields revealed the 3
contours of the land, rippling toward the horizon in broken rhythms of bent brown cornstalks or ridged black furrows. By summer, all one saw was waves of green. The corn stood so tall on either side of the highway that it was as if Moses had struck his staff on the sunbaked ground and the green sea had opened a narrow path.

Even when I couldn't see beyond the first few rows of giant 4
stalks, I knew the fields rolled on for miles. Whatever direction we drove from Ames, we passed through the same landscape, black earth, plowed fields, and large clean skies. The farms themselves were tidy dots of house, barn, and sheds, far enough from the road to seem more like Monopoly buildings than real homes with real people. My Iowa landscape was mostly earth and air, plants and sky. Seven miles to the Nevada liquor store, fifteen miles to the park in Boone, thirty miles to shop in Des Moines, fifty or sixty miles to basketball or football games in Newton, Grinnell, Marshalltown: everywhere my mother drove me I absorbed the same sense of

space. Outside the towns was a reassuring repetition of fields and farm, fields and farm.

That unconscious assumption of space was part of what made my confinement in Northampton difficult. I didn't have time, or awareness, to ask myself why I sometimes felt almost smothered in Lawrence House, with its fifty-seven girls; why a walk around the artfully landscaped campus didn't always make me feel better; why I spent so much time lying on my bed looking out my small window at a patch of sky.

But I did instinctively know that I longed each year for Mountain Day. Mountain Day was a special Smith holiday, set aside so that students could admire the New England fall foliage. No one ever knew exactly when Mountain Day would fall, but early one crisp October morning, the loud ringing of the carillon signaled the cancellation of all classes. A few determined students remained on campus to study, some fled on buses to see their boyfriends an hour or two away, but most of us scurried about to find bicycles and food for picnic lunches. Soon a flood of girls streamed on their bicycles down the main street of Northampton, like a fall parade, heading to the highways out of town.

All Mountain Days blend into my first one that fall of my freshman year. I was curious about whether I could indeed find a mountain close to this Eastern campus. Another freshman across the hall, Meg, who lived in nearby Greenfield, said sure, we could bike to Mount Tom, easily, it wasn't very far; and so, with our roommates, we started off. I am amazed now that we made it. Flabby, out of condition, but high-spirited, we donned sweatshirts, mounted our secondhand, one-speed bikes, and headed for the mountain. On we bicycled, singing loudly, along the edge of a well-traveled highway, through straggling towns that seemed almost continuous, past occasional tobacco fields and vegetable stands. Ahead and behind us, we could see other lines of Smith girls, sometimes waving to us, passing us, or turning onto the Amherst exit.

The sun was high, warming our backs until we had to take off our sweatshirts and tie them around our waists. I looked at everything as hard as I could, every peeling farmhouse, heap of squash, white board fence, to see if I could discern a pattern. It was nice to see people going about ordinary tasks, shopping, working in gardens, trimming hedges. Closed in since my arrival at Smith, I felt miraculously released. The first few miles I scarcely noticed the heaviness of my bike or the unaccustomed strain on my muscles. Stopping occasionally to rest, we plugged onward, puffing and laughing, until finally in early afternoon we found the turnoff to the Mount Tom Lookout Tower. After we climbed the tower ladder, we sank gratefully onto the plank floor in the hot midday sun and decided to go no farther.

Though I recall few details about the surrounding country- 9
side, I know I gasped at the view. We were high above the ground, looking out on a panorama of hills, with fiery masses of leaves everywhere. The fall colors seemed more profuse and vivid than ours at home, probably because my part of Iowa had few hills to provide this sweep of reds, yellows, and golds. "This is it," I thought to myself with an assurance I hadn't had before. "This is New England, just like the pictures." I had foresightedly brought my Brownie, and I took my own pictures. Turning the pages of my photograph album today, I can see us still, rumpled but happy, with the hills behind us, sweatshirts tied around our waists, Coke bottles on the plank floor, and victorious grins on our faces. That afternoon, while we picnicked and talked and napped for a while on the rough boards, happiness flooded over me with the warm sunshine.

The distance to Mount Tom had been much farther than 10
we'd imagined, or than Meg remembered, and so we didn't dare stay too long. After an hour or so, Meg looked at her watch and warned us we'd have to start back. Pedaling home, we were all tired. We didn't talk much, and we didn't want to sing. My roommate, Alice, who'd been doing ski exercises, tried to start "One Hundred Bottles of Beer on the Wall," but no one joined in. My bottom was blistered, and my muscles ached. I began to think of tomorrow, lessons undone, art slides unstudied.

When we dragged in the front door, it was almost time for 11
dinner. As I hurried upstairs to change into a skirt, I brushed
by Lee Anderson, an ambitious, competitive girl who was in
my Art History class. "Boy, did you get sunburned," she said,
stopping to stare. "We went to Mount Tom," I said proudly.
"We bicycled all the way. Where did you go?"

"I decided to stay here," Lee said, with more than a trace of 12
self-satisfaction. "It was just great. There was absolutely no
one in the art library, so I had yesterday's slides all to myself.
I just got caught up a few minutes ago, and am I relieved.
Yesterday's lecture was really important, didn't you think?" I
didn't answer, except with a kind of grunt. I hurried past Lee
toward my room. At least, I thought to myself, now I have
seen New England.

QUESTIONS

1. Toth opens her account of her first Mountain Day at Smith with
   a comment on the Smith campus, then describes the very different world of Ames, Iowa. How do these comments help to
   explain why she later looked forward to Mountain Day?
2. Why does she mention in paragraph 6 the various ways Smith
   students spent the special day?
3. What feelings does she highlight in describing the bike ride to
   Mount Tom and the time spent at the lookout tower?
4. What does the encounter with the classmate tell us about her
   feelings at the end of the day?
5. Is Toth making a point or developing a thesis in describing this
   particular Mountain Day?

SUGGESTIONS FOR WRITING

1. Describe an annual high school event that you especially looked
   forward to, and at some point in your description explain why
   you did. Describe your feelings in the course of it, letting your
   details reveal them.
2. Toth describes the experience of returning to the college town in
   later years:

Though sometimes I bicycled to a professor's house or to a nearby city park, I really never saw the working side of Northampton, with its factories, commercial developments, and modest residential areas. If I saw, I didn't notice. For me, the East was typified by Smith. Years later, returning for the first time to the college, I was appalled at my ignorance of the town that enclosed it. I didn't even know what streets to take or how far Northampton extended. It was bigger, and less unusual, than I'd ever realized.

Expand your essay on p. 35 to describe your feelings on returning to the town or neighborhood where you once lived. You may wish to describe features that you noticed for the first time.

Nicolette Toussaint

NICOLETTE TOUSSAINT *has worked in media advertising and as a graphic designer and communications consultant and manager. She is founder of Public Relations for Social Change and works with many organizations and projects concerned with clean air, ethical advertising, adolescent AIDS prevention, violence toward women, and related environmental and social issues. Her articles have appeared in* Business Woman *and other periodicals. The article reprinted here appeared in* Newsweek *on May 23, 1994.*

HEARING THE SWEETEST SONGS

Every year when I was a child, a man brought a big, black, squeaking machine to school. When he discovered I couldn't hear all his peeps and squeaks, he would get very excited. The nurse would draw a chart with a deep canyon in it. Then I would listen to the squeaks two or three times, while the adults—who were all acting very, very nice—would watch me raise my hand. Sometimes I couldn't tell whether I heard the squeaks or just imagined them, but I liked being the center of attention. 1

My parents said I lost my hearing to pneumonia as a baby; but I knew I hadn't *lost* anything. None of my parts had dropped off. Nothing had changed: if I wanted to listen to 2

Beethoven, I could put my head between the speakers and turn the dial up to 7. I could hear jets at the airport a block away. I could hear my mom when she was in the same room—if I wanted to. I could even hear my cat purr if I put my good ear right on top of him.

I wasn't aware of *not* hearing until I began to wear a hearing aid at the age of 30. It shattered my peace: shoes creaking, papers crackling, pencils tapping, phones ringing, refrigerators humming, people cracking knuckles, clearing throats and blowing noses! Cars, bikes, dogs, cats, kids all seemed to appear from nowhere and fly right at me. ₃

I was constantly startled, unnerved, agitated—exhausted. I felt as though inquisitorial Nazis in an old World War II film were burning the side of my head with a merciless white spotlight. Under that onslaught, I had to break down and confess: I couldn't hear. Suddenly, I began to discover many things I couldn't do. ₄

I couldn't identify sounds. One afternoon, while lying on my side watching a football game on TV, I kept hearing a noise that sounded like my cat playing with a flexible-spring doorstop. I checked, but the cat was asleep. Finally, I happened to lift my head as the noise occurred. Heard through my good ear, the metallic buzz turned out to be the referee's whistle. ₅

I couldn't tell where sounds came from. I couldn't find my phone under the blizzard of papers on my desk. The more it rang, the deeper I dug. I shoveled mounds of paper onto the floor and finally had to track it down by following the cord from the wall. ₆

When I lived alone, I felt helpless because I couldn't hear alarm clocks, vulnerable because I couldn't hear the front door open and frightened because I wouldn't hear a burglar until it was too late. ₇

Then one day I missed a job interview because of the phone. I had gotten off the subway 20 minutes early, eager and dressed to the nines. But the address I had written down didn't exist! I must have misheard it. I searched the street, ₈

becoming overheated, late and frantic, knowing that if I confessed that I couldn't hear on the phone, I would make my odds of getting hired even worse.

For the first time, I felt unequal, disadvantaged and disabled. Now that I had something to compare, I knew that I *had* lost something: not just my hearing, but my independence and my sense of wholeness. I had always hated to be seen as inferior, so I never mentioned my lack of hearing. Unlike a wheelchair or a white cane, my disability doesn't announce itself. For most of my life, I chose to pass as abled, and I thought I did it quite well. 9

But after I got the hearing aid, a business friend said, "You know, Nicolette, you think you get away with not hearing, but you don't. Sometimes in meetings you answer the wrong question. People don't know you can't hear, so they think you're daydreaming, eccentric, stupid—or just plain rude. It would be better to just tell them." 10

I wondered about that then, and I still do. If I tell, I risk being seen as *un*able rather than *dis*abled. Sometimes, when I say I can't hear, the waiter will turn to my companion and say, "What does she want?" as though I have lost my power of speech. 11

If I tell, people may see *only* my disability. Once someone is labeled "deaf," "crippled," "mute" or "aged," that's too often all they are. I'm a writer, a painter, a slapdash housekeeper, a gardener who grows wondrous roses; my hearing is just part of the whole. It's a tender part, and you should handle it with care. But like most people with a disability, I don't mind if you ask about it. 12

In fact, you should ask, because it's an important part of me, something my friends see as part of my character. My friend Anne always rests a hand on my elbow in parking lots, since several times, drivers who assume that I hear them have nearly run me over. When I hold my head at a certain angle, my husband, Mason, will say, "It's a plane" or "It's a siren." And my mother loves to laugh about the times I *thought* I heard: last week, I was told that "the Minotaurs in the garden are getting 13 out of hand." I imagined capering bullmen and I was disappointed to learn that all we had in the garden were overgrown "baby tears."

Not hearing can be funny, or frustrating. And once in a while, it can be the cause of something truly transcendent. One morning at the shore I was listening to the ocean when Mason said, "Hear the bird?" What bird? I listened hard until I heard a faint, unbirdlike, croaking sound. If he hadn't mentioned it I would never have noticed it. As I listened, slowly I began to hear—or perhaps imagine—a distant song. Did I *really* hear it? Or just hear in my heart what he shared with me? I don't care. Songs imagined are as sweet as songs heard, and songs shared are sweeter still. 14

That sharing is what I want for all of us. We're all just temporarily abled, and every one of us, if we live long enough, will become disabled in some way. Those of us who have gotten there first can tell you how to cope with phones and alarm clocks. About ways of holding a book, opening a door and leaning on a crutch all at the same time. And what it's like to give up in despair on Thursday, then begin all over again on Friday, because there's no other choice—and because the roses are beginning to bud in the garden. 15

These are conversations we all should have, and it's not that hard to begin. Just let me see your lips when you speak. Stay in the same room. Don't shout. And ask what you want to know. 16

VOCABULARY

paragraph 4: inquisitorial, onslaught
paragraph 13: capering
paragraph 14: transcendent

QUESTIONS

1. How did Toussaint discover she was deaf? Did she immediately understand that she was also disabled? Once she understood and accepted her disability, how did her life change?

2. How do paragraphs 1–3 introduce the topic of the essay and suggest what is to follow? What does Toussaint discuss in the middle paragraphs?

3. Where does she state her central point or thesis? What does she gain by presenting it where she does?

4. To what particular experience does the title refer, and where does Toussaint present it?

5. The essay is expository in telling us how Toussaint discovered her deafness and how it affected her life. Is the essay also persuasive—perhaps, in seeking to change attitudes toward the deaf?

SUGGESTIONS FOR WRITING

1. Toussaint states: "We're all just temporarily abled, and every one of us, if we live long enough, will become disabled in some way." Write an essay about a personal disability, how you discovered it, and how the discovery changed your life. Your opening paragraphs should establish a point of view and indicate your subject and your purpose in writing.

2. Write about your discovery of a special talent or interest and how this discovery changed your life. Use your discussion to develop a thesis and perhaps to persuade your readers to change their thinking or seek to make a discovery about themselves.

5

Transitions

Transitional words and phrases help us connect ideas and details in our paragraphs and essays. We especially need them when we change the subject or course of discussion, as in the following sentence by James Stevenson:

> In some places, tons of concrete have been poured like icing over a section of hillside to hold it back—and the concrete has even been painted green—but the earth has begun to slip away beneath that, too, leaving edges of concrete sticking out against the sky.

The transitional words *even* and *too* show the course of Stevenson's thinking in the sentence: *even* tells us he is adding a detail to intensify his description of the street; *too* shows he is comparing the slipping earth to other sections of the road.

Words like *after* and *since* express relationships of time; words like *above* and *below*, relationships of space. Here are some important transitions that show the relationship of ideas:

- sequence: *first, second, third*
- qualification: *but, however, nevertheless, nonetheless*
- illustration and explanation: *for example, for instance, so, thus*
- comparison: *similarly, in the same way, by comparison, likewise*
- contrast: *by contrast, on the one hand, on the other hand*
- consequence: *thus, so, as a result, consequently, therefore*
- concession: *but, admittedly, nevertheless, however*
- amplification: *and, moreover, furthermore, also, in addition, indeed*
- summation: *in conclusion, to sum up, all in all, finally*

Punctuation also shows us how ideas are related. A colon tells us that an expansion, explanation, or illustration follows; a semicolon, that the ideas joined are closely related or of the same importance.

Lewis Thomas

In the course of his long career in medicine, LEWIS THOMAS (1913–1993) served as dean of the medical schools of Yale and New York University and president of Memorial Sloan-Kettering Cancer Center. His first collection of essays, The Lives of a Cell, received the National Book Award in 1974. Later collections on medicine, language, and other topics include The Medusa and the Snail (1979), Late Night Thoughts on Listening to Mahler's Ninth Symphony (1983), and Et Cetera, Et Cetera (1990). Thomas gives an account of his professional life in The Youngest Science (1983). The paragraphs reprinted here introduce an essay on human language in The Fragile Species (1992). An essay by Lewis Thomas appears on pp. 565–573.

COMMUNICATION

Other creatures, most conspicuously from our point of view the social insects, live together in dense communities in such interdependence that it is hard to imagine the existence of anything like an individual. They are arranged in swarms by various genetic manipulations. They emerge in foreordained castles, some serving as soldiers for defending the anthill or beehive; some as workers, bringing in twigs of exactly the right size needed for whatever the stage of construction of the nest; some as the food-gatherers tugging along the dead moth toward the hill; some solely as reproductive units for the replication of the community; even some specialized for ventilating and cleaning the nest and disposing of the dead. Automatons, we call them, tiny genetic machines with no options for behavior, doing precisely what their genes instruct them to do, generation after mindless generation. They communicate with each other by chemical signals, unambiguous molecules left behind on the trail to signify all sorts of news items of interest to insects: the dead moth is on the other side of the hill behind this rock, the intruders are approaching from that direction, the queen is upstairs and asking after you, that sort of news.

Bees, the earliest and greatest of all geometricians, dance in darkness to tell where the sun is and where it will be in exactly twenty minutes.

We, of course, are different. We make up our minds about the world as individuals, we look around at the world and plan our next move, we remember what happened last week when we made a mistake and got in trouble, and we keep records for longer memories, even several generations back. Also we possess what we call consciousness, awareness, which most of us regard as a uniquely human gift: we can even think ahead to dying, and we cannot imagine an insect, much less a wolf or a dolphin or even a whale, doing *that*. So we are different. And marvelously higher.

Nonetheless, we are a social species. We gather in communities far denser and more complex than any termite nest or beehive, and we depend much more on each other for individual survival than any troupe of army ants. We are compulsively, biologically, obsessively social. And we are the way we are because of language.

Of all the acts of cooperative behavior to be observed anywhere in nature, I can think of nothing to match, for the free exchange of assets and the achievement of equity and balance in the trade, human language. When we speak to each other, it is not like the social insects laying out chemical trails; it contains the two most characteristic and accommodating of all human traits, ambiguity and amiability. Almost every message in human communication can be taken in two or more ways. There are choices to be made all over the place, in the sending of messages and in their reception. We are, in this respect, unlike the ants and bees. We are obliged to listen more carefully, to edit whatever we hear, and to recognize uncertainty when we hear it, or read it.

Another difference is that the communication systems of animals much older than our species are fixed in place and unchangeable. Our system, language, is just at its beginning, only a few thousand years old, still experimental and flexible. We can change it whenever we feel like, and have been doing

2

3

4

5

so right along. How many of us can speak Chaucerian English, or Anglo-Saxon, or Indo-European, or Hittite? Or read them?

But it is still a genetically determined gift, no doubt about it. We speak and write and listen because we have genes for language. Without such genes, we might still be the smartest creatures on the block, able to make tools and outthink any other animal in combat, even able to think and plan ahead, but we would not be human.   6

VOCABULARY

paragraph 1: genetic, manipulations, foreordained, replication
paragraph 4: ambiguity, amiability, edit

QUESTIONS

1. What relationships do *even* and *we call them* express in connecting ideas in sentences 3 and 4 of paragraph 1?

2. What idea does the transitional *of course* express in the opening sentence of paragraph 2? What other transitional words occur in paragraph 2, and what relationships do they establish?

3. What relationships do *nonetheless* and *and* (sentences 1 and 4, paragraph 3), *in this respect* (sentence 5, paragraph 4), and *but* (sentence 1, paragraph 6) express? Could any of these transitions be omitted without loss of coherence or clarity?

4. What other transitional words or phrases might Thomas have substituted for the transitions just cited?

5. If we humans are "compulsively, biologically, obsessively social," how are we different from army ants and other social insects?

SUGGESTION FOR WRITING

Write a paragraph illustrating from personal experience one of the following ideas or another related to human communication:

Almost every message in human communication can be taken in two or more ways.

There are choices to be made all over the place, in the sending of messages and in their reception.

Restate the idea in light of your own experience and observation, qualifying or disagreeing with it, if you wish, and giving one or more examples. Use transitional words and phrases where needed to connect your ideas and examples.

Mary E. Mebane

> Born in 1993 in Durham, North Carolina, MARY E. MEBANE *grew up on a farm—the world she describes in her autobiography,* Mary *(1981), and in* Mary, Wayfarer *(1983). Following her graduation from college in Durham, she taught in public schools and took graduate degrees at the University of North Carolina. She has taught at various schools, including the University of South Carolina and the University of Wisconsin at Milwaukee. Like Sally Carrighar and Eudora Welty, Mebane immerses us in the sights, sounds, and smells of childhood in this portrait of her mother.*

NONNIE

Nonnie led a structured, orderly existence. Before six o'clock in the morning, she was up, starting her day. First she turned on WPTF and listened to the news and the weather and the music. Later, when WDNC in Durham hired Norfleet Whitted, the first black announcer in the area, she listened first to one station, then to the other. Some mornings it would be "They Traced Her Little Footprints in the Snow," and other mornings it would be black gospel-singing and rhythm-and-blues. Then she would make a fire in the wood stove and start her breakfast. She prepared some meat—fried liver pudding or fatback, or a streak-of-fat streak-of-lean—and made a hoecake of bread on top of the stove, which she ate with either Karo syrup or homemade blackberry preserves, occasionally with store-bought strawberry preserves, or sometimes with homemade watermelon-rind preserves that she had canned in the summer. Then she would drink her coffee, call me to get up, and leave the house in her blue uniform, blue apron, and blue cap—it would still be dark when she left on winter mornings—and go to catch her ride to the tobacco factory (with Mr. Ralph Baldwin at first, and then, when he retired, with Mr. James Yergan). When Miss Delilah still lived in Wildwood, before she and Mr. Leroy separated, she would come by and call from the road and the two of them would walk together to the end of the road near the highway and wait for Mr. Ralph there.

My job after she left was to see that the fire didn't go out in 2
the wood stove, to see that the pots sitting on the back didn't burn—for in them was our supper, often pinto beans or black-eyed peas or collard greens or turnip salad. Occasionally there was kale or mustard greens or cressy salad. The other pot would have the meat, which most often was neck bones or pig feet or pig ears, and sometimes spareribs. These would cook until it was time for me to go to school; then I would let the fire die down, only to relight it when I came home to let the pots finish cooking.

After Nonnie left, I also had the task of getting Ruf Junior up 3
so that he could get to school on time. This presented no problem to me until Ruf Junior was in high school and started playing basketball. Often he would travel with the team to schools in distant towns, sometimes getting home after midnight, and the next morning he would be tired and sleepy and wouldn't want to get up. I sympathized, but I had my job to do. If I let him oversleep, I knew that Nonnie would fuss when she got home. But on the other hand, no matter how often I called to him, he would murmur sleepily, "All right, all right," then go back to sleep. I solved this problem one bitter-cold winter morning. I jerked all the covers off his bed and ran. I knew that the only place he could get warm again would be in the kitchen. (The only fire was in the wood stove.) The fire was already out, so he'd have to make one. After that, I didn't have such a hard time getting him up.

My mother worked as a cutter, clipping the hard ends of 4
each bundle of tobacco before it was shredded to make cigarettes. At noon she ate the lunch she had brought from

home in a brown paper bag: a biscuit with meat in it and a sweet potato or a piece of pie or cake. Some of the women ate in the cafeteria, but in her thirty years at the Liggett and Myers factory, she never once did. She always took her lunch. Then she worked on until closing time, caught her ride back to Wildwood, and started on the evening's activities. First she had supper, which I had finished preparing from the morning. After I got older we sometimes had meat other than what had to be prepared in a "pot." It would be my duty to fry chicken or prepare ham bits and gravy.

After supper, she'd read the Durham *Sun* and see to it that 5 we did the chores if we hadn't done them already: slop the hogs, feed the chickens, get in the wood for the next day. Then we were free. She'd get her blue uniform ready for the next day, then listen to the radio. No later than nine o'clock, she would be in bed. In the morning she would get up, turn on the radio, and start frying some fatback. Another day would have started.

Saturdays were work days, too, the time for washing, iron- 6 ing, going to the garden, preparing Sunday dinner (no one was supposed to work on the Sabbath, so we ran the chicken down in the yard and Nonnie wrung its neck or chopped its head off with the ax). Sometimes we went to town on Saturday but not often, for Nonnie went to town every day. Sometimes, at lunchtime, she'd go down to Belk's, and always on Friday she went to the A&P on Mangum Street and bought her groceries; then she'd stop at the Big Star in Little Five Points if she had heard that there was a particularly good buy on something. So the Saturday-in-town ritual that is so much a part of the lives of most country children was not mine at all. I myself sometimes went to Brookstown several times a week when my father was alive, because that is where he went to get trash, sell vegetables, and visit his relatives.

Sunday afternoons she would go to see her friends or they 7 would come to see her. She would say, "I believe I'll go up to Miss Angeline's a little while." Or it would be Miss Pauline's or Claudia's. And she would stay until about dusk and come home, listen to the radio, then go to bed, ready to start Monday morning again.

In the spring and summer after work, my mother would plant in her garden: tomatoes, string beans, okra, and she'd sow a turnip patch. Then, every day after work, she'd go over to the garden on the hill to see how it was doing. On Saturdays she'd get her buckets if it was time for us to go berrypicking. And on hot summer evenings, if the peaches man had been around, she'd can them after work because they wouldn't keep until Saturday, the day she did most of her canning. ₈

This was her routine—fixed, without change, unvarying. And she accepted it. She more than accepted it, she embraced it; it gave meaning to her life, it was what she had been put here on this earth to do. It was not to be questioned. ₉

To Nonnie this life was ideal; she saw nothing wrong with it. And she wondered in baffled rage why her daughter didn't value it but rather sought something else, some other rhythm, a more meaningful pattern to human life. ₁₀

Nonnie Mebane was not political. However, a special awe would come into her voice when she said, "And Lee *surrendered*." She was from Virginia, and I realize now that she probably would have been imbued with Virginia history in her eight years of schooling there. I myself never heard Robert E. Lee's name mentioned in any class at Wildwood School. But my mother loved to say, "And Lee *surrendered*." She also liked to say sometimes that the Yankee soldiers rode up and said, "Come on out. Y'all are free this morning." ₁₁

The way she said it, I could see the men on horseback—the Yankees—coming around to the fields and to the cabins and saying to the blacks who had been slaves for centuries, "Come on out. Ya'll are free this morning." That was a magical moment. I used to get cold chills when she said it, for, I now realize, in her voice I heard the voice of my mother's mother as she told Nonnie and her other children how the Yankees came early one morning and what they had said. My mother's grandmother had heard them. ₁₂

Nonnie was a good plain cook, but she couldn't sew very well, couldn't fix hair—her own or her daughter's—and, though dutiful, was an indifferent housekeeper. She was thrifty and paid all of her bills on time. Work at the tobacco factory was her life.

QUESTIONS

1. How does the opening sentence—"Nonnie led a structured, orderly existence"—organize the paragraphs that follow?

2. Many of the transitional words are chronological, showing how the events of the day were connected in time. What examples of such transitions do you find in paragraphs 1, 4, and 8?

3. What transitional ideas do *often, but,* and *on the other hand* express in paragraph 3? What about *too* and *so* in paragraph 6, *however* in paragraph 11, and *for* in paragraph 12? Might Mebane have omitted any of these without loss of coherence—that is, without losing the sense of connection between ideas?

4. Does Mebane imply more about her mother's life than she states? What does she reveal about her own feelings or attitudes?

SUGGESTIONS FOR WRITING

1. Mebane describes the work she performed as a member of the family. Describe jobs that you similarly performed, and use this description to say something about the general attitude in your family toward everyday life or the role of children in the family.

2. Mebane refers in paragraph 10 to "some other rhythm, a more meaningful pattern to human life." She is suggesting here the values that children sometimes discover they possess. Discuss a conflict in values between yourself and another member of your family and the origin of this conflict as you see it.

Alice Walker

ALICE WALKER, *the youngest of eight children in a family of Georgia sharecroppers, was educated at Spelman College and Sarah Lawrence College. Her novel about the life of a black*

Georgia woman, The Color Purple (1982), *received the Pulitzer Prize and the American Book Award in 1983. Walker's other writings include the novels* Meridian (1976) *and* The Temple of My Familiar (1989), *and several collections of stories and essays, including* In Search of Our Mothers' Gardens (1983) *and* Living by the Word (1988).

IN SEARCH OF OUR MOTHERS' GARDENS

I described her own nature and temperament. Told how they needed a larger life for their expression. . . . I pointed out that in lieu of proper channels, her emotions had overflowed into paths that dissipated them. I talked, beautifully I thought, about an art that would be born, an art that would open the way for women the likes of her. I asked her to hope, and build up an inner life against the coming of that day. . . . I sang, with a strange quiver in my voice, a promise song. (Jean Toomer, "Avey," *Cane*)

The poet speaking to a prostitute who falls asleep while he's talking—   1

When the poet Jean Toomer walked through the South in   2
the early twenties, he discovered a curious thing: black women whose spirituality was so intense, so deep, so *unconscious*, that they were themselves unaware of the richness they held. They stumbled blindly through their lives: creatures so abused and mutilated in body, so dimmed and confused by pain, that they considered themselves unworthy even of hope. In the selfless abstractions their bodies became to the men who used them, they became more than "sexual objects," more even than mere women: they became "Saints." Instead of being perceived as whole persons, their bodies became shrines: what was thought to be their minds became temples suitable for worship. These crazy Saints stared out at the world, wildly, like lunatics—or quietly, like suicides; and the "God" that was in their gaze was as mute as a great stone.
Who were these Saints? These crazy, loony, pitiful women?   3

Some of them, without a doubt, were our mothers and 4
grandmothers.

In the still heat of the post-Reconstruction South, this is 5
how they seemed to Jean Toomer: exquisite butterflies trapped
in an evil honey, toiling away their lives in an era, a century,
that did not acknowledge them, except as "the *mule* of the
world." They dreamed dreams that no one knew—not even
themselves, in any coherent fashion—and saw visions no one
could understand. They wandered or sat about the countryside
crooning lullabies to ghosts, and drawing the mother of Christ
in charcoal on courthouse walls.

They forced their minds to desert their bodies and their 6
striving spirits sought to rise, like frail whirlwinds from the
hard red clay. And when those frail whirlwinds fell, in scattered particles, upon the ground, no one mourned. Instead,
men lit candles to celebrate the emptiness that remained, as
people do who enter a beautiful but vacant space to resurrect
a God.

Our mothers and grandmothers, some of them: moving to 7
music not yet written. And they waited.

They waited for a day when the unknown thing that was in 8
them would be made known; but guessed, somehow in their
darkness, that on the day of their revelation they would be
long dead. Therefore to Toomer they walked, and even ran, in
slow motion. For they were going nowhere immediate, and
the future was not yet within their grasp. And men took our
mothers and grandmothers, "but got no pleasure from it." So
complex was their passion and their calm.

To Toomer, they lay vacant and fallow as autumn fields, with 9
harvest time never in sight: and he saw them enter loveless
marriages, without joy; and become prostitutes, without resistance; and become mothers of children, without fulfillment.

For these grandmothers and mothers of ours were not 10
Saints, but Artists; driven to a numb and bleeding madness
by the springs of creativity in them for which there was no
release. They were Creators, who lived lives of spiritual waste,
because they were so rich in spirituality—which is the basis

of Art—that the strain of enduring their unused and un-wanted talent drove them insane. Throwing away this spiritu-ality was their pathetic attempt to lighten the soul to a weight their work-worn, sexually abused bodies could bear.

What did it mean for a black woman to be an artist in our 11 grandmothers' time? In our great-grandmothers' day? It is a question with an answer cruel enough to stop the blood.

Did you have a genius of a great-great-grandmother who 12 died under some ignorant and depraved white overseer's lash? Or was she required to bake biscuits for a lazy backwa-ter tramp, when she cried out in her soul to paint watercolors of sunsets, or the rain falling on the green and peaceful pas-turelands? Or was her body broken and forced to bear chil-dren (who were more often than not sold away from her) —eight, ten, fifteen, twenty children—when her one joy was the thought of modeling heroic figures of rebellion, in stone or clay?

How was the creativity of the black woman kept alive, year 13 after year and century after century, when for most of the years black people have been in America, it was a punishable crime for a black person to read or write? And the freedom to paint, to sculpt, to expand the mind with action did not exist. Consider, if you can bear to imagine it, what might have been the result if singing, too, had been forbidden by law. Listen to the voices of Bessie Smith, Billie Holiday, Nina Simone, Roberta Flack, and Aretha Franklin, among others, and imag-ine those voices muzzled for life. Then you may begin to comprehend the lives of our "crazy," "Sainted" mothers and grandmothers. The agony of the lives of women who might have been Poets, Novelists, Essayists, and Short-Story Writers (over a period of centuries), who died with their real gifts stifled within them.

And, if this were the end of the story, we would have cause 14 to cry out in my paraphrase of Okot p'Bitek's great poem:

> O, my clanswomen
> Let us all cry together!
> Come,

Let us mourn the death of our mother,
The death of a Queen
The ash that was produced
By a great fire!
O, this homestead is utterly dead
Close the gates
With *lacari* thorns,
For our mother
The creator of the Stool is lost!
And all the young women
Have perished in the wilderness!

But this is not the end of the story, for all the young 15
women—our mothers and grandmothers, *ourselves*—have not
perished in the wilderness. And if we ask ourselves why, and
search for and find the answer, we will know beyond all efforts
to erase it from our minds, just exactly who, and of what, we
black American women are.

One example, perhaps the most pathetic, most misunder- 16
stood one, can provide a backdrop for our mothers' work:
Phillis Wheatley, a slave in the 1700s.

Virginia Woolf, in her book A *Room of One's Own*, wrote that 17
in order for a woman to write fiction she must have two
things, certainly: a room of her own (with key and lock) and
enough money to support herself.

What then are we to make of Phillis Wheatley, a slave, who 18
owned not even herself? This sickly, frail black girl who required a servant of her own at times—her health was so precarious—and who, had she been white, would have been
easily considered the intellectual superior of all the women
and most of the men in the society of her day.

Virginia Woolf wrote further, speaking of course not of our 19
Phillis, that "any woman born with a great gift in the sixteenth
century [insert "eighteenth century," insert "black woman,"
insert "born or made a slave"] would certainly have gone
crazed, shot herself, or ended her days in some lonely cottage
outside the village, half witch, half wizard [insert "Saint"],
feared and mocked at. For it needs little skill and psychology

to be sure that a highly gifted girl who had tried to use her gift for poetry would have been so thwarted and hindered by contrary instincts [add "chains, guns, the lash, the ownership of one's body by someone else, submission to an alien religion"], that she must have lost her health and sanity to a certainty."

The key words, as they relate to Phillis, are "contrary   20
instincts." For when we read the poetry of Phillis Wheatley— as when we read the novels of Nella Larsen or the oddly false-sounding autobiography of that freest of all black women writers, Zora Hurston—evidence of "contrary instincts" is everywhere. Her loyalties were completely divided, as was, without question, her mind.

But how could this be otherwise? Captured at seven, a   21
slave of wealthy, doting whites who instilled in her the "savagery" of the Africa they "rescued" her from . . . one wonders if she was even able to remember her homeland as she had known it, or as it really was.

Yet, because she did try to use her gift for poetry in a world   22
that made her a slave, she was "so thwarted and hindered by . . . contrary instincts, that she . . . lost her health. . . ." In the last years of her brief life, burdened not only with the need to express her gift but also with a penniless, friendless "freedom" and several small children for whom she was forced to do strenuous work to feed, she lost her health, certainly. Suffering from malnutrition and neglect and who knows what mental agonies, Phillis Wheatley died.

So torn by "contrary instincts" was black, kidnapped,   23
enslaved Phillis that her description of "the Goddess"—as she poetically called the Liberty she did not have—is ironically, cruelly humorous. And, in fact, has held Phillis up to ridicule for more than a century. It is usually read prior to hanging Phillis's memory as that of a fool. She wrote:

> The Goddess comes, she moves divinely fair,
> Olive and laurel binds her *golden* hair.
> Wherever shines this native of the skies,
> Unnumber'd charms and recent graces rise. [italics added]

It is obvious that Phillis, the slave, combed the "Goddess's" 24 hair every morning; prior, perhaps, to bringing in the milk, or fixing her mistress's lunch. She took her imagery from the one thing she saw elevated above all others.

With the benefit of hindsight we ask, "How could she?" 25

But at last, Phillis, we understand. No more snickering 26 when your stiff, struggling, ambivalent lines are forced on us. We know now that you were not an idiot or a traitor; only a sickly little black girl, snatched from your home and country and made a slave; a woman who still struggled to sing the song that was your gift, although in a land of barbarians who praised you for your bewildered tongue. It is not so much what you sang, as that you kept alive, in so many of our ancestors, *the notion of song*.

Black women are called, in the folklore that so aptly identi- 27 fies one's status in society, "the *mule* of the world," because we have been handed the burdens that everyone else—*everyone else*—refused to carry. We have also been called "Matriarchs," "Superwomen," and "Mean and Evil Bitches." Not to mention "Castraters" and "Sapphire's Mama." When we have pleaded for understanding, our character has been distorted; when we have asked for simple caring, we have been handed empty inspirational appellations, then stuck in the farthest corner. When we have asked for love, we have been given children. In short, even our plainer gifts, our labors of fidelity and love, have been knocked down our throats. To be an artist and a black woman, even today, lowers our status in many respects, rather than raises it: and yet, artists we will be.

Therefore we must fearlessly pull out of ourselves and look 28 at and identify with our lives the living creativity some of our great-grandmothers were not allowed to know. I stress *some* of them because it is well known that the majority of our great-grandmothers knew, even without "knowing" it, the reality of their spirituality, even if they didn't recognize it beyond what happened in the singing at church—and they never had any intention of giving it up.

How they did it—those millions of black women who were 29
not Phillis Wheatley, or Lucy Terry or Frances Harper or Zora
Hurston or Nella Larsen or Bessie Smith; or Elizabeth Catlett,
or Katherine Dunham, either—brings me to the title of this
essay, "In Search of Our Mothers' Gardens," which is a personal
account that is yet shared, in its theme and its meaning, by all
of us. I found, while thinking about the far-reaching world of
the creative black woman, that often the truest answer to a
question that really matters can be found very close.

In the late 1920s my mother ran away from home to marry 30
my father. Marriage, if not running away, was expected of
seventeen-year-old girls. By the time she was twenty, she had
two children and was pregnant with a third. Five children
later, I was born. And this is how I came to know my mother:
she seemed a large, soft, loving-eyed woman who was rarely
impatient in our home. Her quick, violent temper was on view
only a few times a year, when she battled with the white
landlord who had the misfortune to suggest to her that her
children did not need to go to school.

She made all the clothes we wore, even my brothers' over- 31
alls. She made all the towels and sheets we used. She spent
the summers canning vegetables and fruits. She spent the
winter evenings making quilts enough to cover all our beds.

During the "working" day, she labored beside—not be- 32
hind—my father in the fields. Her day began before sunup,
and did not end until late at night. There was never a moment
for her to sit down, undisturbed, to unravel her own private
thoughts; never a time free from interruption—by work or the
noisy inquiries of her many children. And yet, it is to my
mother—and all our mothers who were not famous—that I
went in search of the secret of what has fed that muzzled and
often mutilated, but vibrant, creative spirit that the black
woman has inherited, and that pops out in wild and unlikely
places to this day.

But when, you will ask, did my overworked mother have 33
time to know or care about feeding the creative spirit?

The answer is so simple that many of us have spent years 34 discovering it. We have constantly looked high, when we should have looked high—and low.

For example: in the Smithsonian Institution in Wash- 35 ington, D.C., there hangs a quilt unlike any other in the world. In fanciful, inspired, and yet simple and identifiable figures, it portrays the story of the Crucifixion. It is considered rare, beyond price. Though it follows no known pattern of quilt-making, and though it is made of bits and pieces of worthless rags, it is obviously the work of a person of powerful imagi-nation and deep spiritual feeling. Below this quilt I saw a note that says it was made by "an anonymous Black woman in Alabama, a hundred years ago."

If we could locate this "anonymous" black woman from 36 Alabama, she would turn out to be one of our grandmoth-ers—an artist who left her mark in the only materials she could afford, and in the only medium her position in society allowed her to use.

As Virginia Woolf wrote further, in A *Room of One's Own*: 37

> Yet genius of a sort must have existed among women as it must have existed among the working class. [Change this to "slaves" and "the wives and daughters of sharecroppers."] Now and again an Emily Brontë or a Robert Burns [change this to "a Zora Hurston or a Richard Wright"] blazes out and proves its pres-ence. But certainly it never got itself on to paper. When, how-ever, one reads of a witch being ducked, of a woman possessed by devils [or "Sainthood"], of a wise woman selling herbs [our root workers], or even a very remarkable man who had a mother, then I think we are on the track of a lost novelist, a sup-pressed poet, of some mute and inglorious Jane Austen. . . . Indeed, I would venture to guess that Anon, who wrote so many poems without signing them, was often a woman. . . .

And so our mothers and grandmothers have, more often 38 than not anonymously, handed on the creative spark, the seed of the flower they themselves never hoped to see: or like a sealed letter they could not plainly read.

And so it is, certainly, with my own mother. Unlike "Ma" [39] Rainey's songs, which retained their creator's name even while blasting forth from Bessie Smith's mouth, no song or poem will bear my mother's name. Yet so many of the stories that I write, that we all write, are my mother's stories. Only recently did I fully realize this: that through years of listening to my mother's stories of her life, I have absorbed not only the stories themselves, but something of the manner in which she spoke, something of the urgency that involves the knowledge that her stories—like her life—must be recorded. It is probably for this reason that so much of what I have written is about characters whose counterparts in real life are so much older than I am.

But the telling of these stories, which came from my [40] mother's lips as naturally as breathing, was not the only way my mother showed herself as an artist. For stories, too, were subject to being distracted, to dying without conclusion. Dinners must be started, and cotton must be gathered before the big rains. The artist that was and is my mother showed itself to me only after many years. This is what I finally noticed:

Like Mem, a character in *The Third Life of Grange Copeland*, my [41] mother adorned with flowers whatever shabby house we were forced to live in. And not just your typical straggly country stand of zinnias, either. She planted ambitious gardens—and still does—with over fifty different varieties of plants that bloom profusely from each March until late November. Before she left home for the fields, she watered her flowers, chopped up the grass, and laid out new beds. When she returned from the fields she might divide clumps of bulbs, dig a cold pit, uproot and replant roses, or prune branches from her taller bushes or trees—until night came and it was too dark to see.

Whatever she planted grew as if by magic, and her fame as [42] a grower of flowers spread over three counties. Because of her creativity with her flowers, even my memories of poverty are seen through a screen of blooms—sunflowers, petunias, roses, dahlias, forsythia, spirea, delphiniums, verbena . . . and on and on.

And I remember people coming to my mother's yard to be given cuttings from her flowers; I hear again the praise showered on her because whatever rocky soil she landed on, she turned into a garden. A garden so brilliant with colors, so original in its design, so magnificent with life and creativity, that to this day people drive by our house in Georgia—perfect strangers and imperfect strangers—and ask to stand or walk among my mother's art. 43

I notice that it is only when my mother is working in her flowers that she is radiant, almost to the point of being invisible—except as Creator: hand and eye. She is involved in work her soul must have. Ordering the universe in the image of her personal conception of Beauty, 44

Her face, as she prepares the Art that is her gift, is a legacy of respect she leaves to me, for all that illuminates and cherishes life. She has handed down respect for the possibilities—and the will to grasp them. 45

For her, so hindered and intruded upon in so many ways, being an artist has still been a daily part of her life. This ability to hold on, even in very simple ways, is work black women have done for a very long time. 46

This poem is not enough, but it is something, for the woman who literally covered the holes in our walls with sunflowers: 47

> They were women then
> My mama's generation
> Husky of voice—Stout of
> Step
> With fists as well as
> Hands
> How they battered down
> Doors
> And ironed
> Starched white

Shirts
How they led
Armies
Headragged Generals
Across mined
Fields
Booby-trapped
Kitchens
To discover books
Desks
A place for us
How they knew what we
Must know
Without knowing a page
Of it
Themselves.

Guided by my heritage of a love of beauty and a respect for   48
strength—in search of my mother's garden, I found my own.

And perhaps in Africa over two hundred years ago, there was   49
just such a mother; perhaps she painted vivid and daring dec-
orations in oranges and yellows and greens on the walls of her
hut; perhaps she sang—in a voice like Roberta Flack's—*sweetly*
over the compounds of her village; perhaps she wove the most
stunning mats or told the most ingenious stories of all the village storytellers. Perhaps she was herself a poet—though only
her daughter's name is signed to the poems that we know.

Perhaps Phillis Wheatley's mother was also an artist.   50

Perhaps in more than Phillis Wheatley's biological life is   51
her mother's signature made clear.

VOCABULARY

paragraph 2: selfless abstractions, mute
paragraph 5: post-Reconstruction South, coherent
paragraph 6: resurrect
paragraph 14: paraphrase
paragraph 21: doting

paragraph 22: thwarted
paragraph 23: ironically
paragraph 26: snickering, ambivalent
paragraph 27: matriarchs, appellations
paragraph 32: muzzled, mutilated
paragraph 39: counterparts

QUESTIONS

1. What is the main topic of the essay, and how does Walker present it in the epigraph (the opening statement of Jean Toomer) and in her opening paragraphs?

2. Walker marks major divisions or subtopics by spacing between paragraphs. What are these subtopics, and how does each lead into the next?

3. Many of Walker's paragraphs consist of one or two sentences. Which of these paragraphs are transitional, marking turns in the discussion and introducing new topics? Which of these paragraphs are used to emphasize key ideas or conclusions?

4. In what ways did Afro-American mothers and grandmothers express their lives? How does Walker help the reader experience these lives?

5. What are the "contrary instincts" that Walker stresses in paragraph 20? What point is she making about these instincts?

6. Does Walker agree with Virginia Woolf that a successful woman writer must have "a room of one's own" and sufficient money? Is she saying that Phillis Wheatley requires a qualification of Woolf's statement?

7. What effect did the discoveries Walker made about her mother and other Afro-American women have on her life?

8. What is Walker's thesis, and where does she first state it? How does she restate it in the course of the essay?

SUGGESTIONS FOR WRITING

1. Walker shows how she made discoveries about her mother and other Afro-American women and how these affected her life. Discuss a discovery you made about a member of your family and the effect of this discovery on your own life.

2. Walker shows that artistic expression can take many forms. Illustrate this idea from your own experience and observation. Like Walker, be specific in your detail.

3. Listen to the songs of one of the singers named in paragraph 13. Then discuss what recurrent feelings, attitudes, and ideas you find expressed in these songs.

Part 2

DESCRIPTION, NARRATION, EXPOSITION

INTRODUCTION: DESCRIPTION, NARRATION, EXPOSITION

In exposition, we explain ideas and processes through example, classification and division, definition, comparison and contrast, analogy, process, and cause and effect—methods of analysis discussed in this part of the book. In explaining how to repair a car engine, for example, we might define key terms, trace the process, make comparisons with other kinds of engine repair, and discuss the causes of engine failure. Description and narration often combine with exposition, as in George Orwell's "Shooting an Elephant" (pp. 14–22). The methods named are not used just in exposition—they also occur in persuasive and other kinds of writing, as some of the following readings show.

The kind and number of examples and other methods you use depends on how much information your readers need. Keep in mind that you know more about the subject than your readers do: You are illustrating and analyzing ideas and process for their benefit. And the more explanation you give, the more attention you need to give to organization and transitions. Your readers should understand at every point in the essay what method of analysis you are using and why. How you organize the essay depends also on the readers. Some expository essays, like on the causes of a war, often contain a thesis; others, like an essay on repairing an engine, may not. If the essay does contain a thesis, where you place it may depend on how much information readers need to understand it. We shall see that where you place the thesis in the persuasive essay depends on how disposed readers are to accept it.

6

Description

In describing a person, place, or thing, we create a picture. George Orwell does so in describing a quarter of the Burmese town where as a police officer he had been called to deal with an elephant:

> It was a very poor quarter, a labyrinth of squalid bamboo huts, thatched with palm-leaf winding all over a steep hillside. ("Shooting an Elephant")

How much detail the writer gives depends on the purpose of the description. Orwell might have given more details of the town quarter. But additional details would have diverted us from the purpose of the description—to show that the impoverished life of the townspeople made them want to see the elephant shot.

In a descriptive paragraph or essay, the spatial arrangement of details must be clear, the physical point of view obvious and consistent. The writer must be careful to specify the place from which the observation is made. Orwell is careful to do so in describing the shooting of the elephant, and so is James Stevenson in describing a steep road:

> Partway down the long, very steep slope of Loma Vista Drive, descending through Beverly Hills, with the city of Los Angeles spread out far below the houses of sparkling opulence on either side, there is a sign warning "Use Lowest Gear" and, shortly after that, a sign that says "Runaway Vehicle Escape Lane 600 Feet Ahead." ("Loma Vista Drive")

Something more than the physical point of view is suggested in this opening sentence: We discover a dominant mood or attitude. This psychological point of view may be stated directly or conveyed by the details of the description. Orwell does both in describing the crowd of excited spectators:

But at that moment I glanced round at the crowd that had followed me. It was an immense crowd, two thousand at the least and growing every minute. It blocked the road for a long distance on either side. . . . And suddenly I realized that I should have to shoot the elephant after all. The people expected it of me and I had got to do it; I could feel their two thousand wills pressing me forward, irresistibly. ("Shooting an Elephant")

If the writer fails to clarify the point of view or changes it without preparing the reader, details will seem blurred. Abrupt or unexpected shifts in mood or attitude can also be confusing. Brief transitions that bridge these changes are the remedy.

Ray A. Williamson

RAY A. WILLIAMSON *is the editor of* Archaeoastronomy in the Americas (1981) *and the author of* Living the Sky: The Cosmos of the American Indian (1984). *A visit in 1972 to Pueblo ruins in New Mexico awakened his interest in the cosmology or worldview of Native Americans. "The remains of this civilization in Chaco Canyon and elsewhere in the Southwest pose an extraordinary, compelling puzzle for modern interpreters. What were these people doing there? What guided their lives? How did they organize their daily affairs? What was their view of the cosmos?" Williamson compared his findings with studies of other North American Indians. In the following section from* Living the Sky, *he describes the universe of the Pawnee Indians. The opening sentence refers to Coyote, the trickster in Native American lore, who "introduces disorder into the heavens by upsetting the intended orderly arrangement of the stars."*

THE PAWNEE UNIVERSE

In Native American thought, it is often the trickster, Coyote, or some other animal who brings a chaotic element into the otherwise orderly world. Ruled entirely by his passions, both cunning and credulous, and forever getting into trouble, Coyote often acts entirely counter to social and sacred order. In that role, he makes it possible to experience in speech actions that are not permitted to humans. The trickster, however, though he looses disorder upon the world, is not evil or a devil. He is truly a necessary figure for understanding the sacred. As the Chumash, and indeed the Hopi, stories about Coyote and Sun illustrate, not only does the trickster by his contrary actions illuminate the proper way by indirection, he also reflects an awareness of the nature of the chaotic element.

Opposed to the chaos represented by Coyote are the ordered motions of the sky. In fact, one important reason that traditional societies developed a deep interest in the sky was that it was the source of quite obvious and predictable regularities. They were principles the traditional society, with its limited technology, could depend upon. In the midst of varied and chaotic sense impressions, the regularity of the heavens must have seemed a comfort. The heavens also provided an ordering principle for humans. The nearness of the moon's synodic period to a woman's menstrual cycle may have suggested direct connections between the celestial realm and the earthly human sphere. The cycle of the seasons, following predictably (or nearly so) upon the motions of the sun, moon, and stars, provided another close and obvious tie. What better way to bring order and structure into our own life on earth than to model the regularities of the heavens in daily life? Virtually every Native American tribe or social group developed models of the celestial realm that were part of their everyday patterns of life.

In his famous treatise on the author of the *Odyssey*, Samuel Butler opined that "art is only interesting as it reveals an artist."[1] The Pawnee's artful response to the heavens reveals the structure of their world view and the complexity of their notions about space and time. In many respects their example serves as a paradigm of Native American cosmology in general. The earth lodge is of particular interest since it was a conscious and deliberate reflection of the cosmos, structured to incorporate the essential features of the sacred celestial realm.

---

[1] Samuel Butler, *The Authoress of the Odyssey* (Chicago: University of Chicago Press, 1967), 6.

As such, it served as a continual reminder of the essential underlying order of the world. Pawnee concepts of time and space meet in the earth lodge. This cosmic structure gave the Pawnee the foundation on which to model the rest of their world. For example, not only did the lodge and its central fire reflect the celestial realm, it also served as an image of a turtle.

> You see our fireplace. It is the Morning Star. That is where our sun comes from. It is also the picture of a turtle where really it is the Morning Star. You see the head of the turtle is towards the east. That is where the gods do their thinking in the east. While in the west all things are created and you see the hind end of the turtle in the west. The four legs are the four world quarter gods [that] uphold the heavens.[2]

The structure of the Pawnee earth lodge was dictated by the god Paruxti, the Wonderful Being, who was the spokesman of the creator Tirawahat. The circular floor of the Pawnee earth lodge was a symbol of the earth that meets the sky in a circle. The roof, supported by four posts, represented the sky. Each major roof post represented one of the four world-quarter stars, which, according to the origin myths of the Pawnee, were to be painted the colors associated with the stars. The stars themselves told the people, "You must see how I am painted, and you must paint the posts in the lodge as you see me. The posts must be yellow, white, red, and black," in accordance with the colors of the pillars of the sky.[3]   4

As astronomer Von Del Chamberlain has explicated in detail, everything in the Pawnee earth lodge represented a portion of the natural world outside. The two posts on either side of the entranceway represented the stars of day and night. The south post represented Morning Star and the day. It was the protector of humans. By the same token, the north post, which represented Big Black Meteoritic Star and night,   5

---

[2] George Dorsey, unpublished notes, quoted in Von Del Chamberlain, *When Stars Came Down to Earth* (Los Altos, CA: Ballena Press, 1982), 160–61.
[3] Alice Fletcher, unpublished notes, quoted in Chamberlain, *When Stars Came Down*, 100.

was the protector of animals. Thus, to walk into a Pawnee earth lodge was to come under the protection of these two stars and the ordering principles of night and day.

As a model of the abode of the gods, the entire earth lodge 6 was sacred. However, the west end of the lodge was especially sacred, for it held the sacred bundle. When not in use, the bundle hung from a roof pole. However, when opened and spread out, the bundle became an altar representing the garden of the Evening Star. On the altar rested a buffalo skull whose spirit still lived and conferred benefits upon the occupants of the lodge. As the anthropologist George Dorsey explained, "Upon this rectangular space, or garden, the sun descends and gives light and understanding to all men, for it is in this garden that the sun goes to renew its magic potency."[4]

Imagine what it must have been like to grow up and live in 7 such a model of the universe, in which every part had a symbolic sacred meaning. Virtually every act, whether deliberately sacred or merely mundane, would take on special meaning in such a structure. Just after a Pawnee child was born, he or she was dedicated to Morning Star, and placed in a cradleboard decorated with an image of Morning Star. The baby was physically secure while bound up in the cradleboard, and its spiritual state was watched over by the star whose representation was found on the head of the board. The baby's earliest impressions inside the lodge were of a highly structured, spatially oriented environment in which every element was charged with supernatural meaning. Safe in its immediate surroundings, when the child looked up, it saw the rounded dome of the lodge, which mimics the dome of the sky. When it looked around, it saw the supporting poles painted as the stars they represented. When it looked through the smoke hole at night, it could see the brighter stars of the celestial sphere shining down through the smoky haze. Because the doorway pointed east, the entire structure was oriented to the cosmic plan. This also meant that the family that resided within was oriented to

---

[4] George Dorsey, unpublished notes, quoted in Chamberlain, *When Stars Came Down*, 157.

the east and to the influence of Morning Star as well as to the rest of the celestial influences. Finally, the circular shape of the lodge's floor reflected the horizon circle outside.

As important as were the spatial, structural elements of the   8
lodge to the Pawnee, and to the education of the child, they constituted only a small part of its total exposure to the Pawnee view of the world. Because the lodge had only one room, even before the child could fully comprehend the significance of what transpired around it, the child witnessed the yearly ritual cycle and heard the stories of the beginning. Thus he or she grew up in a context of looking to the mythic past for guidance, for the proper patterns of behavior. For the attentive child, this was easy to do, because the spatial elements of the lodge, which represented the celestial sphere, also reflected sacred time in which the beginning recurred again and again as the ritual year played itself out. And in another image that was implicitly, if never explicitly, stated, the Pawnee astronomers, who were also medicine men and priests, sat within a model of the cosmos in order to witness through the smoke hole above the play of time displayed in the stars.

VOCABULARY

paragraph 1: credulous
paragraph 2: synodic period
paragraph 3: paradigm, cosmology
paragraph 5: explicated
paragraph 7: mimics
paragraph 8: transpired, context, mythic, implicitly, explicitly

QUESTIONS

1. From what vantage point is the earth lodge described in paragraphs 3–6? As the viewer, are you standing inside or outside the lodge?

2. How are these views different from the view of the lodge presented in paragraph 7?

3. In what ways did the lodge symbolize what the American Indian saw in looking up at the sky? What did the floor and the doorway

and roof posts of the lodge signify? Why was the western end of the lodge particularly significant?

4. Why was it important to the American Indian to make the structure of the lodge symbolic of the sky?

SUGGESTIONS FOR WRITING

1. As Williamson shows, buildings can reflect the values and even the worldview of the people who live in them. Describe a building you are familiar with—perhaps your own house, or a building on campus, or a church, synagogue, or mosque—that reflects certain values and possibly a worldview comparable to the Pawnee. Describe the building from a specific vantage point, or from several, from the outside as well as the inside. You may wish to comment on the building as you describe it or following your description.

2. Describe a city, town, or region you are familiar with from more than one physical vantage point to give the reader a sense of its size. For example, you might describe the place from a high building or a bridge, then from a moving vehicle.

3. Expand your description to include a view at one or more times of day or seasons of the year. Choose details that distinguish the place. You may wish to create a dominant impression.

N. Scott Momaday

Poet, artist, and novelist, N. SCOTT MOMADAY *is descended from the Kiowan Indians of Oklahoma on his father's side and an Anglo-American pioneer family on his mother's. Momaday describes these contemporary worlds in his novel* House Made of Dawn— *awarded the Pulitzer Prize for Fiction in 1969. "When I was growing up on the reservations of the Southwest," Momaday states in an interview, "I saw people who were deeply involved in their traditional life, in the memories of their blood. They had, as far as I could see, a certain strength and beauty that I find missing in the modern world at large. I like to celebrate that involvement in my writing." Momaday does so in* The Way to Rainy Mountain (1968), *a memoir introduced by the essay reprinted here.*

RAINY MOUNTAIN

A single knoll rises out of the plain in Oklahoma, north and west of the Wichita Range. For my people, the Kiowas, it is an old landmark, and they gave it the name Rainy Mountain. The hardest weather in the world is there. Winter brings blizzards, hot tornadic winds arise in the spring, and in summer the prairie is an anvil's edge. The grass turns brittle and brown, and it cracks beneath your feet. There are green belts along the rivers and creeks, linear groves of hickory and pecan, willow and witch hazel. At a distance in July or August the steaming foliage seems almost to writhe in fire. Great green and yellow grasshoppers are everywhere in the tall grass, popping up like corn to sting the flesh, and tortoises crawl about on the red earth, going nowhere in the plenty of time. Loneliness is an aspect of the land. All things in the plain are isolate; there is no confusion of objects in the eye, but *one* hill or *one* tree or *one* man. To look upon that landscape in the early morning, with the sun at your back, is to lose the sense of proportion. Your imagination comes to life, and this, you think, is where Creation was begun.

I returned to Rainy Mountain in July. My grandmother had died in the spring, and I wanted to be at her grave. She had lived to be very old and at last infirm. Her only living daughter was with her when she died, and I was told that in death her face was that of a child.

I like to think of her as a child. When she was born, the Kiowas were living the last great moment of their history. For more than a hundred years they had controlled the open range from the Smoky Hill River to the Red, from the headwaters of the Canadian to the fork of the Arkansas and Cimarron. In alliance with the Comanches, they had ruled the whole of the southern Plains. War was their sacred business, and they were among the finest horsemen the world has ever known. But warfare for the Kiowas was preeminently a matter of disposition rather than of survival, and they never understood the grim, unrelenting advance of the U.S. Cavalry. When at last, divided and ill-provisioned, they were driven onto the Staked Plains in the cold rains of autumn, they fell into panic. In Palo Duro Canyon they abandoned their crucial stores to pillage and had nothing then but their lives. In order to save themselves, they surrendered to the soldiers at Fort Sill and were imprisoned in the old stone corral that now stands as a military museum. My grandmother was spared the humiliation of those high gray walls by eight or ten years, but she must have known from birth the affliction of defeat, the dark brooding of old warriors.

Her name was Aho, and she belonged to the last culture to ₄ evolve in North America. Her forebears came down from the high country in western Montana nearly three centuries ago. They were a mountain people, a mysterious tribe of hunters whose language has never been positively classified in any major group. In the late seventeenth century they began a long migration to the south and east. It was a journey toward the dawn, and it led to a golden age. Along the way the Kiowas were befriended by the Crows, who gave them the culture and religion of the Plains. They acquired horses, and their ancient nomadic spirit was suddenly free of the ground. They acquired Tai-me, the sacred Sun Dance doll, from that moment the object and symbol of their worship, and so shared in the divinity of the sun. Not least, they acquired the sense of destiny, therefore courage and pride. When they entered upon the southern Plains they had been transformed. No longer were they slaves to the simple necessity of survival; they were a lordly and dangerous society of fighters and thieves, hunters and priests of the sun. According to their origin myth, they entered the world through a hollow log. From one point of view, their migration was the fruit of an old prophecy, for indeed they emerged from a sunless world.

Although my grandmother lived out her long life in the ₅ shadow of Rainy Mountain, the immense landscape of the continental interior lay like memory in her blood. She could tell of the Crows, whom she had never seen, and of the Black Hills, where she had never been. I wanted to see in reality what she had seen more perfectly in the mind's eye, and traveled fifteen hundred miles to begin my pilgrimage.

Yellowstone, it seemed to me, was the top of the world, a ₆
region of deep lakes and dark timber, canyons and waterfalls.
But, beautiful as it is, one might have the sense of confinement there. The skyline in all directions is close at hand, the
high wall of the woods and deep cleavages of shade. There is
a perfect freedom in the mountains, but it belongs to the
eagle and the elk, the badger and the bear. The Kiowas reckoned their stature by the distance they could see, and they
were bent and blind in the wilderness.

Descending eastward, the highland meadows are a stair- ₇
way to the plain. In July the inland slope of the Rockies is luxuriant with flax and buckwheat, stonecrop and larkspur. The
earth unfolds and the limit of the land recedes. Clusters of
trees, and animals grazing far in the distance, cause the
vision to reach away and wonder to build upon the mind. The
sun follows a longer course in the day, and the sky is
immense beyond all comparison. The great billowing clouds
that sail upon it are shadows that move upon the grain like
water, dividing light. Farther down, in the land of the Crows
and Blackfeet, the plain is yellow. Sweet clover takes hold of
the hills and bends upon itself to cover and seal the soil.
There the Kiowas paused on their way; they had come to the
place where they must change their lives. The sun is at home
on the plains. Precisely there does it have the certain character of a god. When the Kiowas came to the land of the Crows,
they could see the dark lees of the hills at dawn across the
Bighorn River, the profusion of light on the grain shelves, the
oldest deity ranging after the solstices. Not yet would they
veer southward to the caldron of the land that lay below; they
must wean their blood from the northern winter and hold the
mountains a while longer in their view. They bore Tai-me in
procession to the east.

A dark mist lay over the Black Hills, and the land was like ₈
iron. At the top of a ridge I caught sight of Devil's Tower
upthrust against the gray sky as if in the birth of time the core
of the earth had broken through its crust and the motion of

the world was begun. There are things in nature that engender an awful quiet in the heart of man; Devil's Tower is one of them. Two centuries ago, because they could not do otherwise, the Kiowas made a legend at the base of the rock. My grandmother said:

> Eight children were there at play, seven sisters and their brother. Suddenly the boy was struck dumb; he trembled and began to run upon his hands and feet. His fingers became claws, and his body was covered with fur. Directly there was a bear where the boy had been. The sisters were terrified; they ran, and the bear after them. They came to the stump of a great tree, and the tree spoke to them. It bade them climb upon it, and as they did so it began to rise into the air. The bear came to kill them, but they were just beyond its reach. It reared against the tree and scored the bark all around with its claws. The seven sisters were borne into the sky, and they became the stars of the Big Dipper.

From that moment, and so long as the legend lives, the Kiowas have kinsmen in the night sky. Whatever they were in the mountains, they could be no more. However tenuous their well-being, however much they had suffered and would suffer again, they had found a way out of the wilderness.

My grandmother had a reverence for the sun, a holy regard that now is all but gone out of mankind. There was a wariness in her, and an ancient awe. She was a Christian in her later years, but she had come a long way about, and she never forgot her birthright. As a child she had been to the Sun Dances; she had taken part in those annual rites, and by them she had learned the restoration of her people in the presence of Tai-me. She was about seven when the last Kiowa Sun Dance was held in 1887 on the Washita River above Rainy Mountain Creek. The buffalo were gone. In order to consummate the ancient sacrifice—to impale the head of a buffalo bull upon the medicine tree—a delegation of old men journeyed into Texas, there to beg and barter for an animal from the

Goodnight herd. She was ten when the Kiowas came together for the last time as a living Sun Dance culture. They could find no buffalo; they had to hang an old hide from the sacred tree. Before the dance could begin, a company of soldiers rode out from Fort Sill under orders to disperse the tribe. Forbidden without cause the essential act of their faith, having seen the wild herds slaughtered and left to rot upon the ground, the Kiowas backed away forever from the medicine tree. That was July 20, 1890, at the great bend of the Washita. My grandmother was there. Without bitterness, and for as long as she lived, she bore a vision of deicide.

Now that I can have her only in memory, I see my grand- 10
mother in the several postures that were peculiar to her: standing at the wood stove on a winter morning and turning meat in a great iron skillet; sitting at the south window, bent above her beadwork, and afterwards, when her vision failed, looking down for a long time into the fold of her hands; going out upon a cane, very slowly as she did when the weight of age came upon her; praying. I remember her most often at prayer. She made long, rambling prayers out of suffering and hope, having seen many things. I was never sure that I had the right to hear, so exclusive were they of all mere custom and company. The last time I saw her she prayed standing by the side of her bed at night, naked to the waist, the light of a kerosene lamp moving upon her dark skin. Her long, black hair, always drawn and braided in the day, lay upon her shoulders and against her breasts like a shawl. I do not speak Kiowa, and I never understood her prayers, but there was something inherently sad in the sound, some merest hesitation upon the syllables of sorrow. She began in a high and descending pitch, exhausting her breath to silence; then again and again—and always the same intensity of effort, of something that is, and is not, like urgency in the human voice. Transported so in the dancing light among the shadows of her room, she seemed beyond the reach of time. But that was illusion; I think I knew then that I should not see her again.

Houses are like sentinels in the plain, old keepers of the 11
weather watch. There, in a very little while, wood takes on the
appearance of great age. All colors wear soon away in the wind
and rain, and then the wood is burned gray and the grain
appears and the nails turn red with rust. The windowpanes are
black and opaque; you imagine there is nothing within, and
indeed there are many ghosts, bones given up to the land.
They stand here and there against the sky, and you approach
them for a longer time than you expect. They belong in the distance; it is their domain.

Once there was a lot of sound in my grandmother's house, 12
a lot of coming and going, feasting and talk. The summers
there were full of excitement and reunion. The Kiowas are a
summer people; they abide the cold and keep to themselves,
but when the season turns and the land becomes warm and
vital they cannot hold still; an old love of going returns upon
them. The aged visitors who came to my grandmother's house
when I was a child were made of lean and leather, and they
bore themselves upright. They wore great black hats and
bright ample shirts that shook in the wind. They rubbed fat
upon their hair and wound their braids with strips of colored
cloth. Some of them painted their faces and carried the scars
of old and cherished enmities. They were an old council of
warlords, come to remind and be reminded of who they were.
Their wives and daughters served them well. The women
might indulge themselves; gossip was at once the mark and
compensation of their servitude. They made loud and elaborate talk among themselves, full of jest and gesture, fright and
false alarm. They went abroad in fringed and flowered shawls,
bright beadwork and German silver. They were at home in the
kitchen, and they prepared meals that were banquets.

There were frequent prayer meetings, and great nocturnal 13
feasts. When I was a child I played with my cousins outside,
where the lamplight fell upon the ground and the singing of
the old people rose up around us and carried away into the
darkness. There were a lot of good things to eat, a lot of

laughter and surprise. And afterwards, when the quiet returned, I lay down with my grandmother and could hear the frogs away by the river and feel the motion of the air.

Now there is a funeral silence in the rooms, the endless 14 wake of some final word. The walls have closed in upon my grandmother's house. When I returned to it in mourning, I saw for the first time in my life how small it was. It was late at night, and there was a white moon, nearly full. I sat for a long time on the stone steps by the kitchen door. From there I could see out across the land; I could see the long row of trees by the creek, the low light upon the rolling plains, and the stars of the Big Dipper. Once I looked at the moon and caught sight of a strange thing. A cricket had perched upon the handrail, only a few inches away from me. My line of vision was such that the creature filled the moon like a fossil. It had gone there, I thought, to live and die, for there, of all places, was its small definition made whole and eternal. A warm wind rose up and purled like the longing within me.

The next morning I awoke at dawn and went out on the dirt 15 road to Rainy Mountain. It was already hot, and the grasshoppers began to fill the air. Still, it was early in the morning, and the birds sang out of the shadows. The long yellow grass on the mountain shone in the bright light, and a scissortail hied above the land. There, where it ought to be, at the end of a long and legendary way, was my grandmother's grave. Here and there on the dark stones were ancestral names. Looking back once, I saw the mountain and came away.

VOCABULARY

paragraph 3: preeminently, disposition, corral
paragraph 6: cleavage
paragraph 7: billowing, lee, profusion, solstice, caldron, wean
paragraph 8: engender, tenuous
paragraph 11: opaque, domain
paragraph 12: enmities
paragraph 15: hied

QUESTIONS

1. What details in paragraphs 1, 2, and 5 establish the time and place of Momaday's return to Rainy Mountain? What additional information does paragraph 7 give about the setting?

2. What features of the southern Plains does Momaday highlight in explaining the values of the Kiowas and the life and values of his grandmother?

3. How does the legend reported by his grandmother add to your understanding of these values?

4. In the description of his grandmother at prayer (paragraph 11), what details increase your understanding of her values and world? Is Momaday implying in these details a personal conflict in values and beliefs?

5. What is Momaday showing about the Kiowas in paragraphs 12 and 13, in describing their life and world? How is this description related to his final view of his grandmother's house, the surrounding land, and Rainy Mountain?

6. What is the central idea or thesis of the essay? Does Momaday state it directly, or is it implicit in his description of his grandmother and the Kiowan world?

SUGGESTIONS FOR WRITING

1. "Now that I can have her only in memory, I see my grandmother in the several postures that were peculiar to her," Momaday writes. Describe a relative or friend in various postures that you associate with him or her. Then describe one of these postures in more detail, as Momaday does in describing his grandmother at prayer.

2. Describe a social or religious ceremony—perhaps a holiday celebration, a wedding, a memorial service, or a funeral—that you once participated in. Give details of the setting, the participants, and the ceremony itself. Then discuss how the ceremony reveals something about the beliefs and values of those who perform it.

Ronald Takaki

RONALD TAKAKI, *professor of Ethnic Studies at the University of California, Berkeley, is the grandson of Japanese immigrant plantation workers in Hawaii. Takaki writes about their world in* Pau Hana: Plantation Life and Labor in Hawaii (1983). *His other books include* Iron Cages: Race and Culture in Nineteenth-Century America (1982), Strangers from a Different Shore (1990), *and* A Different Mirror: A History of Multicultural America (1993). *A selection from Ernesto Galarza's* Barrio Boy, *referred to in the essay, appears on pp. 553–557.*

THE BARRIO:
COMMUNITY IN THE COLONY

For many Mexicans, the border was only an imaginary line— one that could be crossed and recrossed at will. Unlike the migrants from Europe, Africa, and Asia, they came from a country touching the United States. Standing on the border, migrants had difficulty knowing where one country began and the other ended. Mexicans had been in the Southwest long before the Anglos, and they would continue to emigrate despite repatriation programs. In El Norte, there were jobs and also communities.

Indeed, over the years, Chicanos had been creating a Mexican-American world in the barrios of El Norte. In their communities, they did not feel like aliens in a foreign land as they did whenever they crossed the railroad tracks and ventured uptown into the Anglo World. Though their neighborhood was a slum, a concentration of shacks and dilapidated houses, without sidewalks or even paved streets, the barrio was home to its residents. The people were all compatriots. They had come from different places in Mexico and had been here for different lengths of time, but together they formed "the *colonia mexicana.*" "We came to know families from Chihuahua, Sonora, Jalisco, and Durango," remembered one of them. "Some had come to the United States even before the revolution, living in Texas before migrating to California. Like ourselves, our Mexican neighbors had come this far moving step by step, working and waiting. . . ."[1]

In El Norte, Chicanos were recreating a Mexican commu-   3
nity and culture. They celebrated national holidays like the Sixteenth of September, Mexican Independence Day. "We are Mexicans," declared a speaker at one of the celebrations, "almost all of us here . . . by our fathers or ancestors, although we are now under a neighboring nation's flag to which we owe respect. Notwithstanding, this respect does not prevent us from remembering our Mexican anniversary." The celebrations, Ernesto Galarza recalled, "stirred everyone in the *barrio*" and gave them the feeling that they were "still Mexicans." At these festive occasions, there were parades in the plazas attended by city and county officials as well as Mexican consuls. The entire town became a *fandango*. Colorful musicians strolled, and people danced in the streets. Excited crowds shouted, "*Viva* Mexico!" and sang Mexican songs as fireworks exploded and *muchachos* (kids) listened to stories about Mexico told by the *viejitos* (old ones). Bands played the national anthems of both countries. The flags and the colors of the United States and Mexico were displayed together— red, white, and blue as well as red, white, and green.[2]

The religion of the Chicanos was a uniquely Mexican ver-   4
sion of Catholicism, a blending of a faith brought from the Old World and beliefs that had been in the New World for thousands of years before Columbus. For the Mexicans, God was deeply personal, caring for each of them through their saints. In their homes, they decorated their altars with *santitos*, images of saints dear to them. They had a special relationship with the Virgen de Guadalupe: according to their account, she had visited a poor Indian and felt a particular

---

[1] Ernesto Galarza, *Barrio Boy: The Story of a Boy's Acculturation* (Notre Dame, IN, 1971), p. 200.
[2] Albert Camarillo, *Chicanos in a Changing Society: From Mexican Pueblos to American Barrios in Santa Barbara and Southern California, 1848–1930* (Cambridge, MA, 1979), p. 62; Galarza, *Barrio Boy*, p. 206; Arnold De Leon, *The Tejano Community, 1836–1900* (Albuquerque, NM, 1982), pp. 180–181.

concern for the people of Mexico. "I have with me an amulet which my mother gave to me before dying," a Mexican told an interviewer. "This amulet has the Virgin of Guadalupe on it and it is she who always protects me." Their Virgin Mary was Mexican: many paintings and statues represented her as dark in complexion.[3]

What bound the people together was not only ethnicity but also class. "We were all poor," a Mexican said, "we were all in the same situation." The barrio was a "grapevine of job information." A frequently heard word was *trabajo* (work), and "the community was divided in two—the many who were looking for it and the few who had it to offer." Field hands, railroad workers, cannery workers, construction laborers, and maids came back to the barrio after work to tell one another where the jobs were and how much they paid and what the food and living quarters were like.[4]

In the colony, unskilled workers from Mexico were welcomed, for they had come from the homeland. "These Mexicans are hired on this side of the Rio Grande by agents of the larger farms, and are shipped in car load lots, with windows and doors locked, to their destination," a local newspaper reported. "After the cotton season the majority will work their way back to the border and into Mexico." But the barrio offered these migrant workers a place to stay north of the border. "Beds and meals, if the newcomers had no money at all, were provided—in one way or another—on trust, until the new *chicano* found a job." Aid was given freely, for everyone knew what it meant to be in need. "It was not charity or social welfare," Ernesto Galarza explained, "but something my mother called *asistencia*, a helping given and received on trust, to be repaid because those who had given it were themselves in need of what they had given. *Chicanos* who had found work on farms or in railroad camps came back to pay us a few dollars for *asistencia* we had provided weeks or months before."[5]

---

[3] Manuel Gamio, *The Mexican Immigrant: His Life Story* (Chicago, 1931), p. 28; De Leon, *Tejano Community*, p. 160.
[4] Camarillo, *Chicanos in a Changing Society*, p. 169; Galarza, *Barrio Boy*, p. 201.
[5] De Leon, *Tejano Community*, p. 65; Galarza, *Barrio Boy*, p. 201.

In the barrio, people helped each other, for survival 7 depended on solidarity and mutual assistance. For example, Bonifacio Ortega had dislocated his arm while working in Los Angeles. "I was laid up and had to be in the hospital about three months," he recalled. "Fortunately my countrymen helped me a lot, for those who were working got something together every Saturday and took it to me at the hospital for whatever I needed. They also visited me and made me presents." Ortega's arm healed, and he returned to work at a brickyard. "We help one another, we fellow countrymen. We are almost all from the same town or from the nearby farms. The wife of one of the countrymen died the other day and we got enough money together to buy a coffin and enough so that he could go and take the body to Jalisco."[6]

Moreover, the barrio was a place where Mexicans could 8 feel at home in simple, day-to-day ways. Women wearing rebozos, or traditional shawls, were seen everywhere, just as in Mexico. There were Mexican plays and *carpas*—acrobats and traveling sideshows. Stands and cafés offered tamales and other favorites such as frijoles, tortillas, *menudo* (tripe stew), and *dulces* made with *piloncillo* (Mexican sugar). Cantinas and bars were places to hang out and drink beer. *Mercados* stocked Mexican foods like *chorizo* (sausage), while *panderias* baked fresh bread. Shopping in the *tiendas* was familiar. "In the secondhand shops, where the *barrio* people sold and bought furniture and clothing, there were Mexican clerks who knew the Mexican ways of making a sale."[7]

In the early evenings, as the sun began to set, the people 9 sat outside their homes, as they had on the other side of the border in their Mexican villages. The air still carried the smells of suppertime—"tortillas baking, beans boiling, chile roasting, coffee steaming, and kerosene stenching." The men "squatted on the ground, hunched against the wall of the house and smoked. The women and the girls . . . put away the kitchen things, the *candiles* turned down to save kerosene.

---

[6] Gamio, *Mexican Immigrant*, p. 26.
[7] Galarza, *Barrio Boy*, p. 239.

They listened to the tales of the day if the men were in a talking mood." They spoke in two languages—"Spanish and with gestures." An old man talked about a time called "Before the Conquest." The Indian tribes had their "own kings and emperors," he said. "Then the Spaniards [came], killing the Indians and running them down with hunting dogs. The conquerors took the land along the rivers where there was water and rich soil, flat and easy to farm. On these lands the Spaniards set up their haciendas, where the Indians were forced to labor for nothing or were paid only a few centavos for a hard day's work."[8]

Feeling homesick, the people sometimes took out their cedar boxes to display memorabilia from Mexico—a butterfly serape worn to celebrate the Battle of Puebla, tin pictures of grandparents, and "bits of embroidery and lace" made by aunts still in the homeland. They "took deep breaths of the aroma of *puro cedro*, pure Jalcocotan mixed with camphor." A song in Spanish floated in the air:

> I loved a little country girl
> She was so shy
> She couldn't even talk to me
> I would take her hand
> And she would sadly cry
> Now go away
> My mother will be scolding me.[9]

As darkness descended, the people complained about how they were not allowed to feel at home north of the border: "They [Anglos] would rant at public meetings and declare that this was an American country and the Mexicans ought to be run out." "You can't forget those things. You try to forget because . . . you should forgive and forget, but there is still a pain in there that another human being could do that to you." Someone argued: "I haven't wanted to, nor do I want to learn English, for I am not thinking of living in this country all my

---

[8] Ibid., pp. 12, 19, 23, 42.
[9] Ibid., pp. 237, 49.

life. I don't even like it here." A voice agreed: "They talk to us about becoming citizens, but if we become citizens we are still Mexicans. They look at our hair, and listen to our speech and call us Mexicans." Rejection in the new country reinforced a return mentality.[10]

An old man insisted on keeping his Mexican ties: "I have always had and now have my home in El Paso, but I shall never change my [Mexican] citizenship in spite of the fact that [here] I have greater opportunities and protection." Another admitted ambivalence: "I want to go back to Leon because it is my country and I love Mexico. But I like it better here for one can work more satisfactory. No one interferes with one and one doesn't have to fear that there will be or won't be revolutions."[11]

As the night air became chilly, the barrio people pulled their serapes and rebozos around their shoulders. They talked about this land as "occupied" Mexico and the nearness of the border. After arriving in Nogales, Arizona, a young Mexican boy was happy to be finally in the United States. "Look at the American flag," his mother said. As he watched it flying over a building near them, he noticed a Mexican flag on a staff beyond the depot down the street. "We are in the United States," his mother explained. "Mexico is over there." But no matter where they were in the United States, the border was always close to their hearts. Mexican Americans who were citizens by birth were often reminded that they were still Mexicans. By "nationality" my son is "American," a father explained, but he is "Mexicano" "by blood." A local Mexican newspaper criticized some Mexican Americans for not celebrating the Sixteenth of September: "To those 'Agringados' [Americanized Mexicans] who negate that they are Mexicans because they were born in the United States, we ask: what blood runs through their veins? Do they think they are members of the Anglo-Saxon race who only happen to have dark

[10] David Montejano, *Anglos and Mexicans in the Making of Texas*, 1836–1986 (Austin, TX, 1987), p. 31; Gamio, *Mexican Immigrant*, p. 13; Mark Reisler, *By the Sweat of Their Brow: Mexican Immigrant Labor in the United States*, 1900–1940 (Westport, CT, 1976), p. 113.
[11] Gamio, *Mexican Immigrant*, pp. 182, 104.

skins because they were born on the border! What nonsense! (Que barbaridad!)" A song chimed:

> . . . *he who denies his race*
> *Is the most miserable creature. . . .*
> *A good Mexican*
> *Never disowns*
> *The dear fatherland*
> *Of his affections.*[12]

Soon night fell, and the hunched figures blended into the darkness. But no one was sleepy yet, so the people continued to sit in front of their homes. The stars were brighter above Mexico, someone commented, and there were more of them. Sí, yes, another added, and there were coyotes howling nearby. Much was different in El Norte. But as in their old villages, the streets in the barrio had no lights, and now only their voices could be heard. "When they pulled on their cigarettes, they made ruby dots in the dark, as if they were putting periods in the low-toned conversation. The talk just faded away, the men went indoors, the doors were shut . . . there was nothing on the street but the dark. . . ."[13]   14

VOCABULARY

paragraph 2: barrio, compatriot
paragraph 3: fandango
paragraph 5: ethnicity
paragraph 8: frijole, tortilla, cantina
paragraph 9: hacienda, centavo
paragraph 10: serape
paragraph 13: rebozo, negate

QUESTIONS

1. How detailed is the description of the celebration of Mexican Independence Day in paragraph 3? Does Takaki describe the beginning of the celebration and its end?

---

[12] Galarza, *Barrio Boy*, p. 183; Camarillo, *Chicanos in a Changing Society*, p. 149; Mario T. Garcia, *Desert Immigrants: The Mexicans of El Paso, 1880–1920* (New Haven, CT, 1981), pp. 228–229; Gamio, *Mexican Immigrant*, p. 94.

[13] Galarza, *Barrio Boy*, p. 12.

2. By comparison, does the description of the barrio in paragraphs 9–14 begin and end at a certain time? Is the description continuous? To what details of barrio life does Takaki give special emphasis?
3. In the course of the essay, what Chicano attitudes and values does Takaki identify? Which of these does he highlight?
4. What is Takaki's thesis or central idea, and where does he first state it? Where does he restate it?

SUGGESTIONS FOR WRITING

1. Takaki states that "what bound the people together was not only ethnicity but also class." Explain what he means and show how he illustrates these bonds.
2. Many first- and second-generation Americans, even third- and fourth-generation ones, retain features of the language and culture of their family's origin. Like the Mexican Americans described by Takaki, many are multilingual or retain many of the names and expressions of a language other than American English. Food, art, music, religious practices may also be multicultural. Describe the multicultural world of your own family or neighborhood or another you have observed. Like Takaki, give a picture of this world, focusing on a particular time and place.

7

Narration

Description shows a person, place, or thing at a particular time; the ordering of details is spatial—proceeding from left to right or top to bottom or in some other way. The order of details in narration is temporal. Narration shows change occurring—a series of events, personal experiences, and the like presented chronologically, sometimes supported with descriptive details:

> I marched down the hill, looking and feeling a fool, with the rifle over my shoulder and an ever-growing army of people jostling at my heels. At the bottom, when you got away from the huts, there was a metalled road and beyond that a miry waste of paddy fields a thousand yards across, not yet ploughed but soggy from the first rains and dotted with coarse grass. The elephant was standing eight yards from the road, his left side toward us. He took not the slightest notice of the crowd's approach. He was tearing up bunches of grass, beating them against his knees to clean them, and stuffing them into his mouth. (George Orwell, "Shooting an Elephant")

Narration is often found in exposition. In explaining why the Spanish Armada came to defeat or why England survived heavy bombing at the beginning of World War II, the writer may give an account of a decisive event—the wind that blew the Armada off course, the discovery of radar—and subsequent events. Though narration is usually chronological, the writer may have reason to present events in a different order. Transitions are essential in preparing the reader for this change.

Paul Theroux

PAUL THEROUX'S *many novels include* The Family Arsenal (1976), Picture Palace (1978), *and* The Mosquito Coast (1982). *Theroux writes about his travels in South America, the*

128

Far East, and other parts of the world in The Great Railway Bazaar (1975), The Old Patagonian Express (1979), The Kingdom by the Sea (1983), *and* The Imperial Way (1985). *In his essay* Sunrise with Seamonsters, *Theroux describes several attempts to row a small boat in the rough waters off Cape Cod. On the evening of a second day of rowing, he is comforted by his mother and teased by his brothers: "My face was burned, the blisters had broken on my hands and left them raw, my back ached and so did the muscle strings in my forearms; there was sea salt in my eyes." One of his brothers "made a face at me, then silently mimicked a laugh at the absurdity of a forty-two year old man taking consolation from his mother." The following excerpt describes his third venture on the ocean, the next day.*

ROWING ON THE OCEAN

It had all been harmless ridicule, and yet the next morning I got into the skiff at Rock Harbor and felt my morale rising as I rowed away. I thought about the oddness of the previous day: I had ignored a Small Craft Advisory and had been tossed about in a difficult sea; and then I had gone home and had a family dinner. I had not been able to describe my rowing experience to them—anyway, what was the point? It had been private. And in poking fun at me, Alex had come crudely close to the truth—all risk-taking has a strong element of self-dramatization in it: daredevils are notorious egomaniacs. Of course it was foolish to be home eating and bumping knees with the aged parents after such a day! So, the next day, which was perfect—sunny and still—I went out farther than I ever had and I rowed twenty-two miles.

It was my reaction to home, or rather to the bewildering juxtaposition of this boat and that house. The absurdity of it all! I was self-sufficient and private in the boat, but from this protection at sea I had gone ashore and been half-drowned by the clamor and old jokes and nakedness at home. Now it was satisfying to be going—like running away. It was wonderful at last to be alone; and if I had courage and confidence it was because I had become attached to my boat.

"See you named it after a duck," a lobsterman called out as ³ I passed him that day. He was hauling pots out of the soupy water.

Goldeneye was carved on my transom and shining this sunny ⁴ morning, gold on mahogany.

"Killed plenty of them right here!" he shouted. "What with ⁵ this hot weather we probably won't see any until January!"

He went back to emptying his pots—the lobsterman's ⁶ habitual hurry, fueled by the anxiety that the poor beasts will die and deny him his $2.70 a pound at the market in Barnstable.

But even in his frenzy of work he glanced up again and ⁷ yelled, "Nice boat!"

It was a beautiful boat, an Amesbury skiff with dory lines, ⁸ all wood, as well-made and as lovely as a piece of Victorian furniture, with the contours and brasswork and bright finish of an expensive coffin. Every plank, every separate piece of wood in a wooden boat, has its own name. What you take to be a single part, say, the stem, is actually the false stem, the stem piece and the breasthook; and the frame is not merely a frame but a collection of supports called futtocks and gussets and knees. We can skip this nomenclature. *Goldeneye* is pine on oak, with mahogany lockers and thwarts, and a transom like a tombstone. It is fifteen feet long.

Mine is the deluxe model. It has a sliding seat for sculling, ⁹ out-rigger oarlocks, and three rowing stations. It is equipped to sail, with a dagger-board, a rudder and a sprit rig. I have three pairs of oars and two spare thwarts. It is a very strong boat, with a flat and markedly rockered bottom and the most amazing stern, tucked high to prevent drag and steeply raked, tapering at the bottom, which makes it extremely seaworthy for its size. The high waves of a following sea don't smash over it and swamp it but rather lift it and help it escape the swell.

"We used to make those for $35 each in Marblehead," an ¹⁰ old man told me in Harwichport. "That was years ago."

That certainly was years ago. This skiff cost me $4,371 at 11
Lowell's Boat Shop in Amesbury. I could have had it made for
half that, or less, but I wanted the extras. Most good wooden
boats are custom-made—no two are strictly alike. They are
made for particular coasts, for a certain number of people, for
the size and shape of the owner, for specific purposes. "If you
were sea-mossing you'd say, 'Put on an extra plank,'" I was
told by John Carter, curator of the Maine Maritime Museum.
It was Mr Carter who told me that this sort of boat had no
business on Cape Cod. It is a North Shore boat, made for the
waters off Cape Ann, where a shoal draft and a flat bottom are
helpful in the tidal rivers. The dory style of boat wasn't a suitable fishing boat for the Cape; here, people fish farther out
and often in very rough water.

Lowell's Boat Shop originated this skiff's design in the 12
1860's and made thousands of them. It was a working boat—
for hauling pots, handline fishing, and ferrying; and it was for
river rowing on the Merrimack and also in protected harbors,
like Salem. Rowing was one of the great American recreations,
and the rowing age stretched roughly from the end of the Civil
War until the invention of the outboard motor, in the 1920's.
The outboard motor, which is one of the ugliest and most
bad-tempered objects ever made, changed the shape of boats
and made them also ugly and furiously turbulent. It is not very
difficult for the average twin-engine cabin cruiser to swamp a
thirty-foot sailboat. Motorboats are the rower's nightmare
because the shoebox-shape creates a pitiless wake. I tend to
think that only a motorboat can swamp a skiff.

My skiff had an old pedigree. It was based on the dory that 13
was designed by Simeon Lowell in the early eighteenth century, and it is related to the French-Canadian *bateaux*. There are
family resemblances—and certainly connections—between it
and the flat-bottomed boats you see in India, and the skiffs
depicted in Dürer engravings. There are sampans on the
Karnafuli River at Chittagong in Bangladesh which are certainly skiff-like. John Gardner, who wrote a history of this style

of boat, found an Amesbury skiff in "Big Fish Eat Little Ones" (1556) by Brueghel the Elder.

The shore had begun to look as featureless as the sea had once 14
done. The sea seemed passionate and enigmatic and the charts showed the sea bottom to be almost comically irregular—here, at Billingsgate Shoal, miles from Rock Harbor, I could stand up; and farther on I could lean out of the skiff and poke crabs scuttling along the sand. I saw the shore as something shrunken and impenetrable. I had never expected to be indifferent to it, but I had grown impatient. It was the result of that awkwardness I had felt at going home. I rowed, and I stared at the receding shore as I had once stared at the brimming ocean. The shoreline was a smudged stripe: tiny boats, frail houses, timid swimmers—small-scale monotony.

A mile or so southwest of Billingsgate Light there was a 15
large rusty ship in the water. This was the *James Longstreet*, a Second World War Liberty Ship that had been scuttled here to be used as a target ship. I was told in Orleans to look for it. A few Cape Codders set themselves up in successful scrap businesses by sneaking out to the ship at night in the early days and stripping it of its copper and brass. During the Vietnam War, ARVN pilots flew up from Virginia and dropped sand bombs on it. It was big and broken, russet-colored this bright day, and listing from the weight of its barnacles.

I shipped my oars off Great Island—the Wellfleet shore— 16
and ate lunch. And then I made a little nest in the bow and lay there and went to sleep. It was hot and dead still and pleasant—like dozing in a warm bath, with a little liquid chuckle at the waterline. I was two miles out. I woke up refreshed, put my gloves on and continued, occasionally glancing at the long empty beaches and wooded dunes. My destination had been the Pamet River, but it was only two-thirty and I could see the dark tower of the Pilgrim Memorial where the top of Cape Cod hooked to the west.

Excited by the prospect of rowing so far in a single day, I 17
struck out for Provincetown. I found Pamet Creek and Corn

Hill on my chart and calculated that I had only about seven or eight miles to go. A light breeze came up from the west and helped me. But water distorts distance: after an hour I was still off Pamet Creek and Corn Hill, and Provincetown looked no closer. I may have been about three miles from shore. I began to suspect that I had not made much progress, and that gave me a lonely feeling that I tried to overcome by rowing faster.

Just about four o'clock a chill swept over me. The sun still 18 burned in the sky, but the breeze had freshened to a steady wind. It was not the gust I experienced yesterday that pushed me back and forth; this was a ceaselessly rising wind that lifted the sea in a matter of minutes from nothing to about a foot, and then to two feet, and whitened it, and kept it going higher, until it was two to four, and so steep and relentless that I could not keep the boat straight for Provincetown. I thought of Alex saying: *The wind and the murderous waves! Please pass the spaghetti, mother.*

I could only go in one direction—the way the wind was 19 blowing me. But when I lost concentration or rested on my oars the boat slipped aside and I was drenched. I had no doubt that I would make it to shore—the wind was that strong—but I expected to be swamped, I assumed I would go over and be left clinging to my half-drowned boat, and I knew that it would take hours to get to the beach that way.

The discouraging thing was that I was nearer to Prov- 20 incetown than to the Truro shore. So I was turning away. I rowed for an hour, pulling hard, and at times I was so tired I just yanked the oars, keeping the high sea behind me. Every six seconds I was smacked by an especially high wave—but even the sea's crude clockwork didn't sink me, and it gave me a special admiration for the boat's agility. The wind had beaten all the Sunfish and the windsurfers to the beach at North Truro, but there were children dodging waves and little dogs trotting along the sand, and people preparing barbeques. I pulled the boat up the beach and looked out to sea. Nothing was visible. That unpredictable place where an hour ago I was afraid I might drown now looked like no more than a frothy mockery of the sky, with nothing else on it.

VOCABULARY

paragraph 1: egomaniac
paragraph 2: juxtaposition
paragraph 4: transom
paragraph 8: skiff, dory, contour, nomenclature, thwart
paragraph 9: sculling, out-rigger oarlock, sprit rig
paragraph 12: shoal draft, flat bottom, wake
paragraph 13: pedigree, sampan
paragraph 14: enigmatic
paragraph 15: barnacle

QUESTIONS

1. What details of Cape Cod and the Amesbury skiff in paragraphs 8–13 help you visualize the experience Theroux describes in paragraphs 14–20?
2. What hazards does the ocean present to the rower? How does Theroux help the reader visualize these hazards?
3. How specific is Theroux in narrating how he dealt with them?
4. Is Theroux giving instructions on how to row on the ocean, or warning about these hazards? Is he making a point or developing a thesis, or does he wish only to narrate an experience?

SUGGESTIONS FOR WRITING

1. Narrate your own first experience with an outdoor activity or sport, explaining how you trained for it, what happened in first performing it, and what you felt in doing so. Like Theroux, give details of the setting and equipment. You may wish to discuss a discovery you made about yourself or about the activity or place.
2. Theroux states that "all risk-taking has a strong element of self-dramatization." Explain what he means, illustrating from the essay. Then discuss how true this statement is of professional athletes in a particular sport.

EUDORA WELTY *was born and raised in Jackson, Mississippi. Her mother was a West Virginian; her father, an Ohioan and the president of a Jackson insurance company. Welty worked at a number of jobs after college before beginning her career as a photographer and writer. She is the author of numerous short stories, novels, and essays, chiefly about Mississippi life. Her novel* The Optimist's Daughter *won the Pulitzer Prize for Fiction in 1973. Welty describes her Jackson girlhood and early career in* One Writer's Beginnings (1984), *from which this account of a summer trip north is taken.*

A SUMMER TRIP

When we set out in our five-passenger Oakland touring car on our summer trip to Ohio and West Virginia to visit the two families, my mother was the navigator. She sat at the alert all the way at Daddy's side as he drove, correlating the AAA Blue Book and the speedometer, often with the baby on her lap. She'd call out, "All right, Daddy: '86-point-2, crossroads. Jog right, past white church. Gravel ends.'—And there's the church!" she'd say, as though we had scored. Our road always became her adversary. "This doesn't surprise me at all," she'd say as Daddy backed up a mile or so into our own dust on a road that had petered out. "I could've told you a road that looked like that had little intention of going anywhere."

"It was the first one we'd seen all day going in the right direction," he'd say. His sense of direction was unassailable, and every mile of our distance was familiar to my father by rail. But the way we set out to go was popularly known as "through the country."

My mother's hat rode in the back with the children, suspended over our heads in a pillowcase. It rose and fell with us when we hit the bumps, thumped our heads and batted our ears in an authoritative manner when sometimes we bounced as high as the ceiling. This was 1917 or 1918; a lady couldn't expect to travel without a hat.

Edward and I rode with our legs straight out in front of us   4
over some suitcases. The rest of the suitcases rode just outside the doors, strapped on the running boards. Cars weren't
made with trunks. The tools were kept under the back seat
and were heard from in syncopation with the bumps; we'd
jump out of the car so Daddy could get them out and jack up
the car to patch and vulcanize a tire, or haul out the tow rope
or the tire chains. If it rained so hard we couldn't see the road
in front of us, we waited it out, snapped in behind the rain
curtains and playing "Twenty Questions."

My mother was not naturally observant, but she could   5
scrutinize; when she gave the surroundings her attention, it
was to verify something—the truth or a mistake, hers or
another's. My father kept his eyes on the road, with glances
toward the horizon and overhead. My brother Edward periodically stood up in the back seat with his eyelids fluttering
while he played the harmonica, "Old Macdonald had a farm"
and "Abdul the Bulbul Amir," and the baby slept in Mother's
lap and only woke up when we crossed some rattling old
bridge. *"There's* a river!" he'd crow to us all. "Why, it certainly
is," my mother would reassure him, patting him back to sleep.
I rode as a hypnotic, with my set gaze on the landscape that
vibrated past at twenty-five miles an hour. We were all
wrapped by the long ride into some cocoon of our own.

The journey took about a week each way, and each day had   6
my parents both in its grip. Riding behind my father I could
see that the road had him by the shoulders, by the hair under
his driving cap. It took my mother to make him stop. I inherited his nervous energy in the way I can't stop writing on a
story. It makes me understand how Ohio had him around the
heart, as West Virginia had my mother. Writers and travelers
are mesmerized alike by knowing of their destinations.

And all the time that we think we're getting there so fast,   7
how slowly we do move. In the days of our first car trip,

Mother proudly entered in her log, "Mileage today: 161!" with an exclamation mark.

"A Detroit car passed us yesterday." She always kept those 8 logs, with times, miles, routes of the day's progress, and expenses totaled up.

That kind of travel made you conscious of borders; you 9 rode ready for them. Crossing a river, crossing a country line, crossing a state line—especially crossing the line you couldn't see but knew was there, between the South and the North—you could draw a breath and feel the difference.

The Blue Book warned you of the times for the ferries to 10 run; sometimes there were waits of an hour between. With rivers and roads alike winding, you had to cross some rivers three times to be done with them. Lying on the water at the foot of a river bank would be a ferry no bigger than somebody's back porch. When our car had been driven on board— often it was down a roadless bank, through sliding stones and runaway gravel, with Daddy simply aiming at the two-plank gangway—father and older children got out of the car to enjoy the trip. My brother and I got barefooted to stand on wet, sun-warm boards that, weighted with your car, seemed exactly on the level with the water; our feet were the same as in the river. Some of these ferries were operated by a single man pulling hand over hand on a rope bleached and frazzled as if made from cornshucks.

I watched the frayed rope running through his hands. I 11 thought it would break before we could reach the other side.

"No, it's not going to break," said my father. "It's never bro- 12 ken before, has it?" he asked the ferry man.

"No sirree." 13

"You see? If it never broke before, it's not going to break 14 this time."

His general belief in life's well-being worked either way. If 15 you had a pain, it was "Have you ever had it before? You have? It's not going to kill you, then. If you've had the same thing before, you'll be all right in the morning."

My mother couldn't have more profoundly disagreed with that. [16]

"You're such an optimist dear," she often said with a sigh, as she did now on the ferry. [17]

"You're a good deal of a pessimist, sweetheart." [18]

"I certainly *am*." [19]

And yet I was well aware as I stood between them with the water running over my toes, he the optimist was the one who was prepared for the worst, and she the pessimist was the daredevil: he the one who on our trip carried chains and a coil of rope and an ax all upstairs to our hotel bedroom every night in case of fire, and she the one—before I was born—when there *was* a fire, had broken loose from all hands and run back—on crutches, too—into the burning house to rescue her set of Dickens which she flung, all twenty-four volumes, from the window before she jumped out after them, all for Daddy to catch. [20]

"I make no secret of my lifelong fear of the water," said my mother, who on ferry boats remained inside the car, clasping the baby to her—my brother Walter, who was destined to prowl the waters of the Pacific Ocean in a minesweeper. [21]

As soon as the sun was beginning to go down, we went more slowly. My father would drive sizing up the towns, inspecting the hotel in each, deciding where we could safely spend the night. Towns little or big had beginnings and ends, they reached to an edge and stopped, where the country began again as though they hadn't happened. They were intact and to themselves. You could see a town lying ahead in its whole, as definitely formed as a plate on a table. And your road entered and ran straight through the heart of it; you could see it all, laid out for your passage through. Towns, like people, had clear identities and your imagination could go out to meet them. You saw houses, yards, fields, and people busy in them, the people that had a life where they were. You could hear their bank clocks striking, you could smell their bakeries. You would know those towns again, recognize the salient detail, seen so close up. Nothing was blurred, and in [22] passing along Main Street, slowed down from twenty-five to twenty miles an hour, you didn't miss anything on either side. Going somewhere "through the country" acquainted you with the whole way there and back.

My mother never fully gave in to her pleasure in our trip— for pleasure every bit of it was to us all—because she knew we were traveling with a loaded pistol in the pocket on the door of the car on Daddy's side. I doubt if my father fired off any kind of gun in his life, but he could not have carried his family from Jackson, Mississippi to West Virginia and Ohio through the country, unprotected. 23

QUESTIONS

1. What do the details of the summer trip tell you about motoring in 1917 or 1918? Does Welty highlight any features of the trip or travel generally?

2. What do these and other details reveal about her mother and father? What characteristics does Welty comment on?

3. Is the purpose of the narrative to give a picture of her mother and father and comment on them, or does Welty have another purpose in writing?

SUGGESTIONS FOR WRITING

1. Discuss what the narrative reveals about Eudora Welty as a person and writer. Explain how the narrative reveals these qualities.

2. Narrate a travel experience in which you made an unexpected discovery about yourself, about a place, or about people you were traveling with. You need not give the full details of the trip to let your reader experience what you did and make a point about it.

Esmeralda Santiago

ESMERALDA SANTIAGO, *the oldest in a family of 11 children, lived most of her childhood in rural Puerto Rico, in "a rectangle of rippled metal sheets on stilts hovering in the middle of a circle of red dirt."* When Santiago was 13, her mother moved the family to New York City—her father remaining in Puerto Rico. Following high school in Brooklyn, Santiago attended Harvard University and later Sarah Lawrence College. She describes her childhood and adolescence in Puerto Rico and the United States in When I Was Puerto Rican (1993). In the section reprinted here, she tells us what happened when American nutritionists came to instruct the women of her Puerto Rican village.

THE AMERICAN INVASION OF MACÚN

Lo que no mata, engorda.

What doesn't kill you, makes you fat.

> *Pollito*, chicken
> *Gallina*, hen
> *Lápiz*, pencil
> *y Pluma*, pen.
> *Ventana*, window
> *Puerta*, door
> *Maestra*, teacher
> *y Piso*, floor.

Miss Jiménez stood in front of the class as we sang and, with her ruler, pointed at the chicks scratching the dirt outside the classroom, at the hen leading them, at the pencil on Juanita's desk, at the pen on her own desk, at the window that looked out into the playground, at the door leading to the yard, at herself, and at the shiny tile floor. We sang along, pointing as she did with our sharpened pencils, rubber end out.   1

"¡*Muy bien!*" She pulled down the map rolled into a tube at the front of the room. In English she told us, "Now gwee estody about de Jun-ited Estates gee-o-graphee."   2

It was the daily English class. Miss Jiménez, the second- and third-grade teacher, was new to the school in Macún. She looked like a grown-up doll, with high rounded cheekbones, a freckled *café con leche* complexion, black lashes, black curly hair pulled into a bun at the nape of her neck, and the prettiest legs in the whole *barrio*. Doña Ana said Miss Jiménez had   3 the most beautiful legs she'd ever seen, and the next day, while Miss Jiménez wrote the multiplication table on the blackboard, I stared at them.

She wore skirts to just below the knees, but from there 4 down, her legs were shaped like chicken drumsticks, rounded and full at the top, narrow at the bottom. She had long straight hair on her legs, which everyone said made them even prettier, and small feet encased in plain brown shoes with a low square heel. That night I wished on a star that someday my scrawny legs would fill out into that lovely shape and that the hair on them would be as long and straight and black.

Miss Jiménez came to Macún at the same time as the com- 5 munity center. She told us that starting the following week, we were all to go to the *centro comunal* before school to get breakfast, provided by the Estado Libre Asociado, or Free Associated State, which was the official name for Puerto Rico in the Estados Unidos, or in English, the Jun-ited Estates of America. Our parents, Miss Jiménez told us, should come to a meeting that Saturday, where experts from San Juan and the Jun-ited Estates would teach our mothers all about proper nutrition and hygiene, so that we would grow up as tall and strong as Dick, Jane, and Sally, the A*mericanitos* in our primers.

"And Mami," I said as I sipped my afternoon *café con leche*, 6 "Miss Jiménez said the experts will give us free food and toothbrushes and things . . . and we can get breakfast every day except Sunday . . ."

"Calm down," she told me. "We'll go, don't worry." 7

On Saturday morning the yard in front of the *centro comunal* 8 filled with parents and their children. You could tell the experts from San Juan from the ones that came from the Jun-ited Estates because the A*mericanos* wore ties with their white shirts and tugged at their collars and wiped their foreheads with crumpled handkerchiefs. They hadn't planned for children, and the men from San Juan convinced a few older girls to watch the little ones outside so that the meeting could proceed with the least amount of disruption. Small children refused to leave their mothers' sides and screeched the minute one of the white-shirted men came near them. Some women sat on the folding chairs at the rear of the room nursing, a cloth draped over their baby's face so that the experts would not be upset at the sight of a bare breast. There were no fathers. Most of them worked seven days a week, and anyway, children and food were women's work.

"Negi, take the kids outside and keep them busy until this is over."   9

"But Mami . . ."   10

"Do as I say."   11

She pressed her way to a chair in the middle of the room and sat facing the experts. I hoisted Edna on my shoulder and grabbed Alicia's hand. Delsa pushed Norma out in front of her. They ran into the yard and within minutes had blended into a group of children their age. Héctor found a boy to chase him around a tree, and Alicia crawled to a sand puddle where she and other toddlers smeared one another with the fine red dirt. I sat at the door, Edna on my lap, and tried to keep one eye on my sisters and brother and another on what went on inside.   12

The experts had colorful charts on portable easels. They introduced each other to the group, thanked the Estado Libre Asociado for the privilege of being there, and then took turns speaking. The first expert opened a large suitcase. Inside there was a huge set of teeth with pink gums.   13

"Ay, Dios Santo, qué cosa tan fea," said a woman as she crossed herself. The mothers laughed and mumbled among themselves that yes, it was ugly. The expert stretched his lips into a smile and pulled a large toothbrush from under the table. He used ornate Spanish words that we assumed were scientific talk for teeth, gums, and tongue. With his giant brush, he polished each tooth on the model, pointing out the proper path of the bristles on the teeth.   14

"If I have to spend that much time on my teeth," a woman whispered loud enough for everyone to hear, "I won't get anything done around the house." The room buzzed with giggles,   15 and the expert again spread his lips, took a breath, and continued his demonstration.

"At the conclusion of the meeting," he said, "you will each 16 receive a toothbrush and a tube of paste for every member of your family."

"*¿Hasta pa' los mellaos?*" a woman in the back of the room 17 asked, and everyone laughed.

"If they have no teeth, it's too late for them, isn't it," the 18 expert said through his own clenched teeth. The mothers shrieked with laughter, and the expert sat down so that an *Americano* with red hair and thick glasses could tell us about food.

He wiped his forehead and upper lip as he pulled up the 19 cloth covering one of the easels to reveal a colorful chart of the major food groups.

"*La buena* nutrition is *muy importante para los niños.*" In heav- 20 ily accented, hard to understand Castilian Spanish he described the necessity of eating portions of each of the foods on his chart every day. There were carrots and broccoli, iceberg lettuce, apples, pears, and peaches. The bread was sliced into a perfect square, unlike the long loaves Papi brought home from a bakery in San Juan, or the round *pan de manteca* Mami bought at Vitín's store. There was no rice on the chart, no beans, no salted codfish. There were big white eggs, not at all like the small round ones our hens gave us. There was a tall glass of milk, but no coffee. There were wedges of yellow cheese, but no balls of cheese like the white *queso del país* wrapped in banana leaves sold in bakeries all over Puerto Rico. There were bananas but no plantains, potatoes but no *batatas*, cereal flakes but no oatmeal, bacon but no sausages.

"But, *señor*," said Doña Lola from the back of the room, 21 "none of the fruits or vegetables on your chart grow in Puerto Rico."

"Then you must substitute our recommendations with 22 your native foods."

"Is an apple the same as a mango?" asked Cirila, whose 23 yard was shaded by mango trees.

"Sí," said the expert, "a mango can be substituted for an
apple."   24

"What about breadfruit?"   25

"I'm not sure . . ." The Americano looked at an expert from   26
San Juan who stood up, pulled the front of his guayabera down
over his ample stomach, and spoke in a voice as deep and
resonant as a radio announcer's.

"Breadfruit," he said, "would be equivalent to potatoes."   27

"Even the ones with seeds?" asked Doña Lola, who roasted   28
them on the coals of her fogón.

"Well, I believe so," he said, "but it is best not to make sub-   29
stitutions for the recommended foods. That would throw the
whole thing off."

He sat down and stared at the ceiling, his hands crossed   30
under his belly as if he had to hold it up. The mothers asked
each other where they could get carrots and broccoli, iceberg
lettuce, apples, peaches, or pears.

"At the conclusion of the meeting," the Americano said, "you   31
will all receive a sack full of groceries with samples from the
major food groups." He flipped the chart closed and moved
his chair near the window, amid the hum of women asking
one another what he'd just said.

The next expert uncovered another easel on which there   32
was a picture of a big black bug. A child screamed, and a
woman got the hiccups.

"This," the expert said scratching the top of his head, "is   33
the magnified image of a head louse."

Following him, another Americano who spoke good Spanish   34
discussed intestinal parasites. He told all the mothers to boil
their water several times and to wash their hands frequently.

"Children love to put their hands in their mouths," he said,   35
making it sound like fun, "but each time they do, they run the
risk of infection." He flipped the chart to show an enlargement of a dirty hand, the tips of the fingernails encrusted
with dirt.

"Ugh! That's disgusting!" whispered Mami to the woman   36
next to her. I curled my fingers inside my palms.

"When children play outside," the expert continued, "their 37
hands pick up dirt, and with it, hundreds of microscopic parasites that enter their bodies through their mouths to live
and thrive in their intestinal tract."

He flipped the chart again. A long flat snake curled from 38
the corner at the top of the chart to the opposite corner at the
bottom. Mami shivered and rubbed her arms to keep the
goose bumps down.

"This," the *Americano* said "is a tapeworm, and it is not 39
uncommon in this part of the world."

Mami had joked many times that the reason I was so 40
skinny was that I had a *solitaria*, a tapeworm, in my belly. But
I don't think she ever knew what a tapeworm looked like, nor
did I. I imagined something like the earthworms that crawled
out of the ground when it rained, but never anything so ugly
as the snake on the chart, its flat body like a deck of cards
strung together.

"Tapeworms," the expert continued, "can reach lengths of 41
nine feet." I rubbed my belly, trying to imagine how long nine
feet was and whether I had that much room in me. Just thinking about it made my insides itchy.

When they finished their speeches, the experts had all the 42
mothers line up and come to the side of the room, where
each was given samples according to the number of people
in their household. Mami got two sacks of groceries, so Delsa
had to carry Edna all the way home while I dragged one of the
bags full of cans, jars, and bright cartons.

At home Mami gave each of us a toothbrush and told us 43
we were to clean our teeth every morning and every evening.
She set a tube of paste and a cup by the door, next to Papi's
shaving things. Then she emptied the bags.

"I don't understand why they didn't just give us a sack of rice 44
and a bag of beans. It would keep this family fed for a month."

She took out a five-pound tin of peanut butter, two boxes 45
of cornflakes, cans of fruit cocktail, peaches in heavy syrup,
beets, and tuna fish, jars of grape jelly and pickles and put
everything on a high shelf.

"We'll save this," she said, "so that we can eat like *Americanos*   46
cuando el hambre apriete." She kept them there for a long time but
took them down one by one so that, as she promised, we ate
like Americans when hunger cramped our bellies.

QUESTIONS

1. How does Santiago characterize the Americans who come to the
   Puerto Rican village from San Juan? Does she tell us anything
   about them through how they dress and look?

2. What is the attitude of the Americans toward the Puerto Rican
   women who attend the Saturday meeting at the community
   center?

3. How does Santiago characterize the Puerto Rican women? Why
   do they come to the meeting? What is their attitude toward the
   Americans and what they see and hear, and how does Santiago
   reveal it?

4. What is her purpose in narrating the episode?

SUGGESTIONS FOR WRITING

1. Narrate a similar episode in which two groups, different in culture and perhaps language, meet. Let the differences between
   these groups emerge in the details of their dress and appearance
   and what they say. Let your attitude and the point of the episode
   emerge in these details.

2. Cultural differences often lead to misunderstanding between
   friends. Write an account of a misunderstanding you experienced, giving details of how it came about and ended.

8

Example

The word *example* originally referred to a sample or a typical instance. The word still has this meaning, and for many writers it is an outstanding instance—even one essential to the idea under discussion, as in the following explanation of right- and left-handedness in the world:

> The world is full of things whose right-hand version is different from the left-hand version: a right-handed corkscrew as against a left-handed, a right snail as against a left one. Above all, the two hands; they can be mirrored one in the other, but they cannot be turned in such a way that the right hand and the left hand become interchangeable. That was known in Pasteur's time to be true also of some crystals, whose facets are so arranged that there are right-hand versions and left-hand versions. (J. Bronowski, *The Ascent of Man*)

Examples are essential in presenting ideas. Those that seem clear to us may not be clear to our readers. Concrete instances like those Bronowski gives help to make our ideas understood.

E. B. White

In this excerpt from a profile of New York City, first published in Holiday Magazine *in April, 1949, E. B. WHITE writes from the point of view of an inhabitant who knows the city well. White conveys the special excitement of the city through a series of examples. Compare this general characterization of New York with the specific picture of a New York street presented by Jane Jacobs (pp. 527–533).*

NEW YORK

It is a miracle that New York works at all. The whole thing is implausible. Every time the residents brush their teeth, millions of gallons of water must be drawn from the Catskills and the hills of Westchester. When a young man in Manhattan writes a letter to his girl in Brooklyn, the love message gets blown to her through a pneumatic tube—*pfft*—just like that. The subterranean system of telephone cables, power lines, steam pipes, gas mains and sewer pipes is reason enough to abandon the island to the gods and the weevils. Every time an incision is made in the pavement, the noisy surgeons expose ganglia that are tangled beyond belief. By rights New York should have destroyed itself long ago, from panic or fire or rioting or failure of some vital supply line in its circulatory system or from some deep labyrinthine short circuit. Long ago the city should have experienced an insoluble traffic snarl at some impossible bottleneck. It should have perished of hunger when food lines failed for a few days. It should have been wiped out by a plague starting in its slums or carried in by ships' rats. It should have been overwhelmed by the sea that licks at it on every side. The workers in its myriad cells should have succumbed to nerves, from the fearful pall of smoke-fog that drifts over every few days from Jersey, blotting out all light at noon and leaving the high offices suspended, men groping and depressed, and the sense of world's end. It should have been touched in the head by the August heat and gone off its rocker.

VOCABULARY

implausible, pneumatic tube, subterranean, incision, ganglia, labyrinthine, myriad

QUESTIONS

1. What examples show that "the whole thing is implausible"?
2. White explicitly compares New York City to a human being. What

are the similarities, and how does the comparison help to emphasize the "miracle" he is describing?

3. What is the tone or attitude expressed, and how does White convey it?

SUGGESTIONS FOR WRITING

1. In a well-developed paragraph state an idea about your hometown or city and develop it by a series of short examples. Make your examples vivid and lively.

2. Develop one of the following statements by example:

   a. "The insupportable labor of doing nothing." (Sir Richard Steele)

   b. "The first blow is half the battle." (Oliver Goldsmith)

   c. "Ask yourself whether you are happy, and you cease to be so." (John Stuart Mill)

   d. "All the modern inconveniences." (Mark Twain)

   e. "He had been kicked in the head by a mule when young and believed everything he read in the Sunday papers." (George Ade)

Tom Wolfe

TOM WOLFE, *perhaps best recognized for his novel* The Bonfire of the Vanities *and his non-fiction epic* The Right Stuff, *has written much about American life in the 1960s and 1970s, particularly about the "youth culture" of this period. His articles in* New York Magazine *and other periodicals have been collected in a number of books, including* The Electric Kool-Aid Acid Test (1968), The Pump House Gang (1968), *and* The Kandy-Kolored Tangerine-Flake Streamline Baby (1965), *from which the following excerpt is taken. Wolfe's ironic view of urban life is nowhere better illustrated than in his portrait of New York teenagers at a subway station at rush hour. Wolfe here develops one of his favorite themes, the "generation gap," and says something about New York life generally.*

THURSDAY MORNING IN
A NEW YORK SUBWAY STATION

Love! Attar of libido in the air! It is 8:45 A.M. Thursday morn-   1
ing in the IRT subway station at 50th Street and Broadway
and already two kids are hung up in a kind of herringbone
weave of arms and legs, which proves, one has to admit, that
love is not *confined* to Sunday in New York. Still, the odds! All
the faces come popping in clots out of the Seventh Avenue
local, past the King Size Ice Cream machine, and the turnstiles start whacking away as if the world were breaking up on
the reefs. Four steps past the turnstiles everybody is already
backed up haunch to paunch for the climb up the ramp and
the stairs to the surface, a great funnel of flesh, wool, felt,
leather, rubber and steaming alumicron, with the blood
squeezing through everybody's old sclerotic arteries in
hopped-up spurts from too much coffee and the effort of sur-
facing from the subway at the rush hour. Yet there on the
landing are a boy and a girl, both about eighteen, in one of
those utter, My Sin, backbreaking embraces.

He envelops her not only with his arms but with his chest,   2
which has the American teen-ager concave shape to it. She
has her head cocked at a 90-degree angle and they both have
their eyes pressed shut for all they are worth and some incredibly feverish action going with each other's mouths. All round
them, ten, scores, it seems like hundreds, of faces and bodies
are perspiring, trooping and bellying up the stairs with arte-
riosclerotic grimaces past a showcase full of such novel items
as Joy Buzzers, Squirting Nickels, Finger Rats, Scary Tarantulas
and spoons with realistic dead flies on them, past Fred's bar-
bershop, which is just off the landing and has glossy photographs of young men with the kind of baroque haircuts one
can get in there, and up onto 50th Street into a madhouse of
traffic and shops with weird lingerie and gray hair-dyeing displays in the windows, signs for free teacup readings and a
pool-playing match between the Playboy Bunnies and

Downey's Showgirls, and then everybody pounds on toward the Time-Life Building, the Brill Building or NBC.

The boy and the girl just keep on writhing in their embroil- 3 ment. Her hand is sliding up the back of his neck, which he turns when her fingers wander into the intricate formal gardens of his Chicago Boxcar hairdo at the base of the skull. The turn causes his face to start to mash in the ciliated hull of her beehive hairdo, and so she rolls her head 180 degrees to the other side, using their mouths for the pivot. But aside from good hair grooming, they are oblivious to everything but each other. Everybody gives them a once-over. Disgusting! Amusing! How touching! A few kids pass by and say things like "Swing it, baby." But the great majority in that heaving funnel up the stairs seem to be as much astounded as anything else. The vision of love at rush hour cannot strike anyone exactly as romance. It is a feat, like a fat man crossing the English Channel in a barrel. It is an earnest accomplishment against the tide. It is a piece of slightly gross heroics, after the manner of those knobby, varicose old men who come out from some place in baggy shorts every year and run through the streets of Boston in the Marathon race. And somehow that is the gaffe against love all week long in New York, for everybody, not just two kids writhing under their coiffures in the 50th Street subway station; too hurried, too crowded, too hard, and no time for dalliance.

QUESTIONS

1. Wolfe illustrates "the gaffe against love all week long in New York." What precisely is the "gaffe"? What do the details suggest about the Thursday morning mood of New Yorkers?

2. What does the description of the showcase and of 50th Street imply about the world of the lovers? Would they stand out in any setting? Does Wolfe find the lovers comical, or is he sympathetic and admiring?

3. How similar is Wolfe's view of New York to White's, in the quality of life or its pace?

SUGGESTIONS FOR WRITING

1. Every piece of writing suggests something about the personality, interests, and ideas of the author, even when he or she speaks to us through a narrator. Discuss the impression you receive of the author of this selection.

2. Describe one or two people in a situation made comical by the setting. Allow your reader to visualize the setting as well as the situation through your choice of examples.

Margaret Mead and Rhoda Metraux

MARGARET MEAD (1901–1978) *was for more than 40 years an ethnologist at the Museum of Natural History in New York City. She taught at numerous universities, mostly at Columbia, and wrote some of the most influential books in the field of social anthropology—including* Coming of Age in Samoa (1928), Growing Up in New Guinea (1930), *and* Male and Female (1949). RHODA METRAUX, *an anthropologist also associated with the Museum of Natural History, collaborated with Mead on the writing of several books and a series of magazine essays, later collected in* A Way of Seeing (1970) *and* Aspects of the Present (1980). *Mead and Metraux look at parents and children from the point of view of the anthropologist. Their ideas on how children can be encouraged to develop an independent judgment might be compared with those of John Holt (pp. 158–163).*

DISCIPLINE: TO WHAT END?

In the matter of childhood discipline there is no absolute standard. The question is one of appropriateness to a style of living. What is the intended outcome? Are the methods of discipline effective in preparing the child to live in the adult world into which he is growing? The means of discipline that are very effective in rearing children to become headhunters and cannibals would be most ineffective in preparing them to become peaceful shepherds.

The Mundugumor, a New Guinea people, trained their children to be tough and self-reliant. Among these headhunters, when one village was preparing to attack another and wanted to guard itself against attack by a third village, the first village sent its children to the third to be held as hostages. The children knew that they faced death if their own people broke this temporary truce. Mundugumor methods of child-rearing were harsh but efficient. An infant sleeping in a basket hung on the wall was not taken out and held when it wakened and cried. Instead, someone scratched on the outside of the basket, making a screeching sound like the squeak of chalk on a blackboard. And a child that cried with fright was not given the mother's breast. It was simply lifted and held off the ground. Mundugumor children learned to live in a tough world, unfearful of hostility. When they lived among strangers as hostages, they watched and listened, gathering the information they would need someday for a successful raid on this village. 2

The Arapesh, another New Guinea people, had a very different view of life and human personality. They expected their children to grow up in a fairly peaceful world, and their methods of caring for children reflected their belief that both men and women were gentle and nurturing in their intimate personal relations. Parents responded to an infant's least cry, held him and comforted him. And far from using punishment as a discipline, adults sometimes stood helplessly by while a child pitched precious firewood over a cliff. 3

Even very inconsistent discipline may fit a child to live in an inconsistent world. A Balinese mother would play on her child's fright by shouting warnings against nonexistent dangers: "Look out! Fire! . . . Snake! . . . Tiger!" The Balinese system required people to avoid strange places without inquiring why. And the Balinese child learned simply to be afraid of strangeness. He never learned that there are no bears under the stairs, as American children do. We want our children to test reality. We teach our children to believe in Santa Claus and later, without bitter disappointment, to give 4 up that belief. We want them to be open to change, and as they grow older, to put childhood fears and rewards aside and be ready for new kinds of reality.

There are also forms of discipline that may be self-defeating. Training for bravery, for example, may be so rigorous that some children give up in despair. Some Plains Indians put boys through such severe and frightening experiences in preparing them for their young manhood as warriors that some boys gave up entirely and dressed instead as women.

In a society in which many people are socially mobile and may live as adults in a social or cultural environment very different from the one in which they grew up, old forms of discipline may be wholly unsuited to new situations. A father whose family lived according to a rigid, severe set of standards, and who was beaten in his boyhood for lying or stealing, may still think of beatings as an appropriate method of disciplining his son. Though he now lives as a middle-class professional man in a suburb, he may punish his son roughly for not doing well in school. It is not the harshness as such that then may discourage the boy even more, but his bewilderment. Living in a milieu in which parents and teachers reward children by praise and presents for doing well in school—a milieu in which beating is not connected with competence in schoolwork—the boy may not be able to make much sense of the treatment he receives.

There is still another consideration in this question about discipline. Through studies of children as they grow up in different cultures we are coming to understand more about the supportive and the maiming effects of various forms of discipline. Extreme harshness or insensitivity to the child may prepare him to survive in a harsh environment. But it also may cripple the child's ability to meet changing situations. And today we cannot know the kind of world the children we are rearing will live in as adults. For us, therefore, the most important question to ask about any method of discipline is: How will it affect the child's capacity to face change? Will it give the child the kind of strength necessary to live under new and unpredictable conditions?

An unyielding conscience may be a good guide to success- 8 ful living in a narrow and predictable environment. But it may become a heavy burden and a cruel scourge in a world in which strength depends on flexibility. Similarly, the kind of discipline that makes a child tractable, easy to bring up and easy to teach in a highly structured milieu, may fail to give the child the independence, courage and curiosity he will need to meet the challenges in a continually changing situation. At the same time, the absence of forms of discipline that give a child a sense of living in an ordered world in which it is rewarding to learn the rules, whatever they may be, also may be maiming. A belief in one's own accuracy and a dependable sense of how to find the patterning in one's environment are necessary parts of mature adaptation to new styles of living.

There is, in fact, no single answer to the problem of child- 9 hood discipline. But there is always the central question: For what future?

VOCABULARY

paragraph 1: appropriateness
paragraph 3: nurturing
paragraph 6: mobile, environment, milieu
paragraph 8: scourge, maiming

QUESTIONS

1. Do Mead and Metraux give examples of all kinds of childhood discipline, or just of kinds that work well?
2. What thesis do their examples support, and where do Mead and Metraux first state it? Where do they restate it?
3. How do the examples in paragraph 6 help us to understand the kind of society that is "socially mobile"?
4. Would the exposition be as clear if Mead and Metraux had discussed the Arapesh of New Guinea before discussing the Mundugumor? Or does the order of discussion not matter?

5. How do the opening sentences of the nine paragraphs state the relationship of ideas in the whole essay?

SUGGESTION FOR WRITING

State why you agree or disagree with one of the following statements, supporting your ideas with examples from your own experience and observation:

a. "Even very inconsistent discipline may fit a child to live in an inconsistent world."

b. "There are also forms of discipline that may be self-defeating."

c. "In a society in which many people are socially mobile and may live as adults in a social or cultural environment very different from the one in which they grew up, old forms of discipline may be wholly unsuited to new situations."

d. "Extreme harshness or insensitivity to the child may prepare him to survive in a harsh environment. But it also may cripple the child's ability to meet changing situations."

e. "At the same time, the absence of forms of discipline that give a child a sense of living in an ordered world in which it is rewarding to learn the rules, whatever they may be, also may be maiming."

9

Classification and Division

There are times when you want to show what various objects have in common. To do so, you engage in the process of classification—grouping objects, persons, or ideas that share significant qualities. To show the range of cars manufactured in the United States, you might classify Chevrolets, Dodges, and Fords with other American cars. To illustrate the importance of General Motors in the manufacture of cars, you can classify Chevrolets with Buicks, Oldsmobiles, and other GM cars. The number of classes to which an object can be fitted is obviously wide.

The process of division begins with a class and shows its subclassifications or divisions. The class may be a broad one, as in the following division of American cars according to manufacturer:

By *manufacturer*: GM cars, Chrysler cars, Ford cars, etc.

The same class of American cars may be divided in another way:

By *transmission*: cars with manual transmission, cars with automatic transmission

Any one of the subclasses or divisions may be divided by the same or by another principle—GM cars may be subdivided according to size, engine, color, or place of manufacture, to cite only a few ways:

By *size*: small, compact, medium, large GM cars

By *engine*: (GM cars with) four-cylinder, six-cylinder, eight-cylinder engines

Again the basis or principle of division you choose depends on the purpose of the analysis. Here is an example of division in a scientific discussion of meteorites:

purpose of analysis	For the investigator of meteorites, the basic challenge is deducing the history of the *meteorites* from a bewildering abundance of evidence. The richness of the problem is indicated by the sheer variety of types of meteorite. The two main classes are the *stony meteorites* and the *iron meteorites*. The stony meteorites consist mainly of silicates, with an admixture of nickel and iron. The iron meteorites consist mainly of nickel and iron in various proportions. A smaller class is the *stony-iron meteorites*, which are intermediate in composition between the other two. Stony meteorites are in turn divided into two groups: the chrondites and the achrondites, according to whether or not they contain chondrules, spherical aggregates of magnesium silicate. With each group there are further subdivisions based on mineralogical and chemical composition. (I. R. Cameron, "Meteorites and Cosmic Radiation" [italics added])
class: *meteorites*	
division or subclassification according to constituent material	
first type: *stony*	
second type: *iron*	
third type: *stony-iron*	
subdivision of stony meteorites according to presence or absence of chondrules	
further subdivisions	

John Holt

JOHN HOLT (1923–1985) *widely influenced ideas on the teaching of children in the 1960s and 1970s—through such books as* How Children Fail (1964), How Children Learn (1967), Escape from Childhood (1974), *and* Freedom from Beyond (1972), *based on his experience as a high school teacher in Colorado and Massachusetts. Holt believed that teachers do their job best when they help students teach themselves. His discussion of the various disciplines that guide our learning reveals other assumptions and beliefs.*

KINDS OF DISCIPLINE

A child, in growing up, may meet and learn from three differ- 1
ent kinds of disciplines. The first and most important is what
we might call the Discipline of Nature or of Reality. When he
is trying to do something real, if he does the wrong thing or
doesn't do the right one, he doesn't get the result he wants.
If he doesn't pile one block right on top of another, or tries to
build on a slanting surface, his tower falls down. If he hits the
wrong key, he hears the wrong note. If he doesn't hit the nail
squarely on the head, it bends, and he has to pull it out and
start with another. If he doesn't measure properly what he is
trying to build, it won't open, close, fit, stand up, fly, float,
whistle, or do whatever he wants it to do. If he closes his eyes
when he swings, he doesn't hit the ball. A child meets this
kind of discipline every time he tries to *do* something, which
is why it is so important in school to give children more
chances to do things, instead of just reading or listening to
someone talk (or pretending to). This discipline is a great
teacher. The learner never has to wait long for his answer; it
usually comes quickly, often instantly. Also it is clear, and
very often points toward the needed correction; from what
happened he can not only see that what he did was wrong,
but also why, and what he needs to do instead. Finally, and
most important, the giver of the answer, call it Nature, is
impersonal, impartial, and indifferent. She does not give
opinions, or make judgments; she cannot be wheedled, bul-
lied, or fooled; she does not get angry or disappointed; she
does not praise or blame; she does not remember past failures or hold grudges; with her one always gets a fresh start,
this time is the one that counts.

The next discipline we might call the Discipline of Culture, 2
of Society, of What People Really Do. Man is a social, a cultural animal. Children sense around them this culture, this
network of agreements, customs, habits, and rules binding
the adults together. They want to understand it and be a part
of it. They watch very carefully what people around them are
doing and want to do the same. They want to do right, unless

they become convinced they can't do right. Thus children rarely misbehave seriously in church, but sit as quietly as they can. The example of all those grownups is contagious. Some mysterious ritual is going on, and children, who like rituals, want to be part of it. In the same way, the little children that I see at concerts or operas, though they may fidget a little, or perhaps take a nap now and then, rarely make any disturbance. With all those grownups sitting there, neither moving nor talking, it is the most natural thing in the world to imitate them. Children who live among adults who are habitually courteous to each other, and to them, will soon learn to be courteous. Children who live surrounded by people who speak a certain way will speak that way, however much we may try to tell them that speaking that way is bad or wrong.

The third discipline is the one most people mean when they speak of discipline—the Discipline of Superior Force, of sergeant to private, of "you do what I tell you or I'll make you wish you had." There is bound to be some of this in a child's life. Living as we do surrounded by things that can hurt children, or that children can hurt, we cannot avoid it. We can't afford to let a small child find out from experience the danger of playing in a busy street, or of fooling with the pots on the top of a stove, or of eating up the pills in the medicine cabinet. So, along with other precautions, we say to him, "Don't play in the street, or touch things on the stove, or go into the medicine cabinet, or I'll punish you." Between him and the danger too great for him to imagine we put a lesser danger, but one he can imagine and maybe therefore want to avoid. He can have no idea of what it would be like to be hit by a car, but he can imagine being shouted at, or spanked, or sent to his room. He avoids these substitutes for the greater danger until he can understand it and avoid it for its own sake. But we ought to use this discipline only when it is necessary to protect the life, health, safety, or well-being of people or other living creatures, or to prevent destruction of things that people care about. We ought not to assume too long, as we usually do, that a child cannot understand the real nature of the danger from which we want to protect him. The sooner he avoids the danger, not to escape our punishment, but as a matter of good sense, the better. He can learn that faster than we think. In Mexico, for example, where people drive their cars with a good deal of spirit, I saw many children no older than five or four walking unattended on the streets. They understood about cars, they knew what to do. A child whose life is full of the threat and fear of punishment is locked into babyhood. There is no way for him to grow up, to learn to take responsibility for his life and acts. Most important of all, we should not assume that having to yield to the threat of our superior force is good for the child's character. It is never good for *anyone's* character. To bow to superior force makes us feel impotent and cowardly for not having had the strength or courage to resist. Worse, it makes us resentful and vengeful. We can hardly wait to make someone pay for our humiliation, yield to us as we were once made to yield. No, if we cannot always avoid using the Discipline of Superior Force, we should at least use it as seldom as we can.

There are places where all three disciplines overlap. Any 4
very demanding human activity combines in it the disciplines of Superior Force, of Culture, and of Nature. The novice will be told, "Do it this way, never mind asking why, just do it that way, that is the way we always do it." But it probably *is* just the way they always do it, and usually for the very good reason that it is a way that has been found to work. Think, for example, of ballet training. The student in a class is told to do this exercise, or that; to stand so; to do this or that with his head, arms, shoulders, abdomen, hips, legs, feet. He is constantly corrected. There is no argument. But behind these seemingly autocratic demands by the teacher lie many decades of custom and tradition, and behind that, the necessities of dancing itself. You cannot make the moves of classical ballet unless over many years you have acquired, and renewed every day, the needed strength and suppleness in scores of muscles and joints. Nor can you do the difficult motions, making them look easy, unless you have learned hundreds of easier ones first.

Dance teachers may not always agree on all the details of teaching these strengths and skills. But no novice could learn them all by himself. You could not go for a night or two to watch the ballet and then, without any other knowledge at all, teach yourself how to do it. In the same way, you would be unlikely to learn any complicated and difficult human activity without drawing heavily on the experience of those who know it better. But the point is that the authority of these experts or teachers stems from, grows out of, their greater competence and experience, the fact that what they do *works*, not the fact that they happen to be the teacher and as such have the power to kick a student out of the class. And the further point is that children are always and everywhere attracted to that competence, and ready and eager to submit themselves to a discipline that grows out of it. We hear constantly that children will never do anything unless compelled to by bribes or threats. But in their private lives, or in extracurricular activities in school, in sports, music, drama, art, running a newspaper, and so on, they often submit themselves willingly and wholeheartedly to very intense disciplines, simply because they want to learn to do a given thing well. Our Little-Napoleon football coaches, of whom we have too many and hear far too much, blind us to the fact that millions of children work hard every year getting better at sports and games without coaches barking and yelling at them.

QUESTIONS

1. Does Holt divide discipline according to source or to the uses of discipline in education—or according to some other principle? Is Holt's division exhaustive?

2. Holt states in paragraph 4 that the kinds of discipline distinguished overlap. How do they?

3. Holt's principle of division might have been the effects of discipline on the personality of the young person. Is Holt concerned with effects in the course of his discussion?

4. How else might discipline be analyzed in a discussion of it, and to what purpose?

5. Do you agree with Holt that people learn best when they are not coerced? Do you agree with him about coercive sports coaches?

SUGGESTIONS FOR WRITING

1. Divide discipline according to a principle different from Holt's. Make your divisions exclusive of one another and indicate how exhaustive you think they are.
2. Write an essay on jobs or hobbies, developing the topic by division. If you divide by more than one principle, keep each breakdown and discussion separate and consistent.
3. Discuss why you think Holt would agree or disagree with Margaret Mead and Rhoda Metraux on effective and ineffective kinds of discipline (pp. 152–155). Analyze key statements in the two essays to support your answer.

Allan Nevins

> One of America's most important historians, ALLAN NEVINS (1890–1971) wrote important biographies of many famous Americans, including John D. Rockefeller and Henry Ford, and won Pulitzer Prizes in 1933 and 1937 for his lives of Grover Cleveland and Hamilton Fish. His discussion of newspapers shows one important use of division in exposition and also tells us something important about the interpretation of evidence—a subject we will consider later in this book.

THE NEWSPAPER

Obviously, it is futile to talk of accuracy or inaccuracy, authority or lack of authority, with reference to the newspaper as a whole. The newspaper cannot be dismissed with either a blanket endorsement or a blanket condemnation. It cannot be used as if all its parts had equal value or authenticity. The first duty of the historical student of the newspaper is to discriminate. He must weigh every separate department, every article, every writer, for what the department or article or writer seems to be worth. Clearly, a great part of what is printed in every newspaper is from official sources, and hence may be relied upon to be perfectly accurate. The weather report is accurate; so are court notices, election notices, building permits, lists of marriage licenses, bankruptcy lists. Though unofficial, other classes of news are almost totally free from error. The most complete precautions are taken to keep the stock market quotations minutely accurate, both by stock exchange authorities and by the newspaper staffs. An error in stock quotations may have the most disastrous consequences, and mistakes are hence excluded by every means within human power. So with shipping news, news of deaths, and a considerable body of similar matter—sports records, registers of Congressional or legislative votes, and so on.

Thus one great division of material in newspapers can be 2 treated as completely authentic. There is another large division which may in general be treated as trustworthy and authoritative. This is the news which is prepared by experts under conditions exempt from hurry and favorable to the gathering of all the significant facts. The weekly review of a real estate expert is a case in point. The sporting news of the best newspapers, prepared by experts under conditions which make for accuracy, is singularly uniform, and this uniformity is the best evidence that it is truthful and well proportioned. Society news, industrial news, and similar intelligence, especially when it appears in the form of weekly surveys written by known specialists, is worthy of the utmost reliance.

But in dealing with news which contains a large subjective 3 element, and which is prepared under conditions of hurry and strain, the critical faculty must be kept constantly alert. Every conscientious correspondent at an inauguration, or a battle, or a political rally, or in an interview, tries to report the facts. But not one of them can help reporting, in addition to the facts, the impression that he has personally received of them. The most honest and careful observer ordinarily sees a little of what he wishes to see. It is through failure to make critical allowance for this fact that the historical student of newspapers is most likely to be led astray. Beveridge in his life of Lincoln remarks upon the striking difference between the Democratic reports and the Republican reports of the Lincoln–Douglas debates. At Ottawa, Illinois, for example, these two great leaders held their first joint debate on August 21, 1858. Lincoln came on a special train of fourteen cars crowded with shouting Republicans. It arrived at Ottawa at noon and, according to the Republican papers, when Lincoln alighted a shout went up from a dense and enthusiastic crowd which made the bluffs of the Illinois River and the woods along it ring and ring again. Lincoln entered a carriage; according to the *Chicago Tribune* men with evergreens, mottoes, fair young ladies, bands of music, military companies, and a dense mass of cheering humanity followed him through the streets in a scene of tumultuous excitement. But according to the *Philadelphia Press* and other Douglas papers, Lincoln had only a chilly and lackadaisical reception. "As his procession passed," stated the *Philadelphia Press*, "scarcely a cheer went up. They marched along silently and sorrowfully, as if it were a funeral cortege following him to the grave." On the other hand, the Democratic papers declared that the reception of Douglas was perfectly tremendous; the cheers were so thundering, said the *Philadelphia Press*, that they seemed to rend the very air. But the *Chicago Tribune* said that Douglas had no reception of consequence; that the only cheers he got came from the Irish Catholics. Yet both reporters were probably fairly honest. They saw what they wished to see.

VOCABULARY

paragraph 1: endorsement, discriminate
paragraph 2: authentic, authoritative, exempt
paragraph 3: conscientious, tumultuous, lackadaisical, cortege

QUESTIONS

1. On what basis does Nevins divide his paragraphs on material in newspapers? What are the three divisions he distinguishes?

2. What point is he making through these divisions?

3. In referring to the "large subjective element" of certain newspaper accounts, is Nevins referring to bias or prejudice in the reporters? What does his example of the Lincoln–Douglas debates show?

4. What is the order of ideas in the three paragraphs? Why does Nevins save "news which contains a large subjective element" for last?

5. Newspapers might be classified generally with sources of information, as in "Newspapers are one of the many sources of information on how government works. . . ." How many other classes can you think of? What purposes might these classifications serve?

SUGGESTIONS FOR WRITING

1. In one or two paragraphs of your own, divide materials in newspapers by another principle of division and use your division to make a point, as Nevins does.

2. Analyze the front page stories of an issue of a newspaper according to the degree of their reliability. Discuss the "subjective element" of one of the stories, as Nevins discusses the account of the Lincoln–Douglas debates.

Garrison Keillor

Humorist and essayist GARRISON KEILLOR worked as a radio announcer following graduation from the University of Minnesota in 1966. In his radio program A Prairie Home Companion, *begun in 1974, Keillor made famous a fictional midwestern town he called Lake Wobegon. Keillor received the George Foster Peabody Broadcasting Award in 1980, and in 1985 the Edward R. Murrow Award of the Corporation for Public Broadcasting for service to public radio. His novels and story collections include* The Book of Guys (1993), WLT: A Radio Romance (1991), and We Are Still Married (1989), *in which his essay "Hoppers" appears. Keillor uses both classification and division in describing people on a New York City street.*

HOPPERS

A hydrant was open on Seventh Avenue above 23rd Street last   1
Friday morning, and I stopped on my way east and watched
people hop over the water. It was a brilliant spring day. The
water was a nice clear creek about three feet wide and ran
along the gutter around the northwest corner of the intersection. A gaggle of pedestrians crossing 23rd went *hop hop hop hop
hop* over the creek as a few soloists jaywalking Seventh performed at right angles to them, and I got engrossed in the
dance. Three feet isn't a long leap for most people, and the
ease of it permits a wide range of expression. Some hoppers
went a good deal higher than necessary.

Long, lanky men don't hop, as a rule. The ones I saw hardly   2
paused at the water's edge, just lengthened one stride and
trucked on across—a rather flatfooted approach that showed
no recognition of the space or occasion. Tall men typically
suffer from an excess of cool, but I kept hoping for one of
them to get off the ground. Most of the tall men wore top-
coats and carried briefcases, so perhaps their balance was
thrown off. One tall man in a brown coat didn't notice the
water and stepped off the curb into the fast-flowing Hydrant
Creek and made a painful hop, like a wounded heron: a
brown heron with a limp wing attached to a briefcase bulging
full of dead fish. He crossed 23rd looking as though his day
had been pretty much shot to pieces.

Short, fat men were superb: I could have watched them all   3
morning. A typical fat man crossing the street would quicken
his step when he saw the creek and, on his approach, do a little shuffle, arms out to the sides, and suddenly and with great
concentration *spring*—a nimble step all the more graceful for
the springer's bulk. Three fairly fat men jiggled and shambled
across 23rd together, and then one poked another and they saw
the water. They stepped forward, studying the angle, and just
before the point man jumped for the curb his pals said something, undoubtedly discouraging, and he threw back his head
and laughed over his shoulder and threw himself lightly, boy-
ishly, across the water, followed—*boing boing*—by the others.

The women who hopped the water tended to stop and   4
study the creek and find its narrows and measure the distance and then lurch across. They seemed dismayed that the
creek was there at all, and one, in a beige suit, put her hands
on her hips and glared upstream, as if to say, "Whose water *is*
this? This is utterly unacceptable. I am *not* about to jump over
this." But then she made a good jump after all. She put her
left toe on the edge of the curb, leaned forward with right arm
outstretched—for a second, she looked as if she might take
off and zoom up toward the Flatiron Building—and pushed
off, landing easily on her right toe, her right arm raised. The
longest leap was made by a young woman in a blue raincoat
carrying a plastic Macy's bag and crossing west on Seventh.
She gathered herself up in three long, accelerating strides
and sailed, her coat billowing out behind her, over the water
and five feet beyond, almost creaming a guy coming out of
Radio Shack. He shrank back as she loped past, her long
black hair and snow-white hands and face right *there*, then
gone, vanished in the crowd.

And then it was my turn. I waited for the green light,   5
crossed 23rd, stopped by the creek flowing around the bend of
curb and heard faint voices of old schoolmates ahead in the
woods, and jumped heavily across and marched after them.

VOCABULARY

paragraph 1: gaggle
paragraph 3: jiggle, shamble
paragraph 4: lurch, billowing, creaming, lope

QUESTIONS

1. By what principle does Keillor divide the class *male hoppers*? How
   do the characteristics shared by "long, lanky men" influence the
   way they cross the water? How do the characteristics of "short,
   fat men" influence the way they do?

2. How do most of the women differ from men in how they cross
   the water?

3. In what class does Keillor put himself in paragraph 5? How does this class differ from the other classes described?

4. Is Keillor making a point or developing a thesis in the essay? Or is his essay descriptive only?

SUGGESTIONS FOR WRITING

1. Like Keillor, identify classes of people on the basis of how they act on the street or at home—for example, how they cross a busy intersection, get up in the morning, or prepare for bed.

2. Like Keillor, who divides the men hopping the stream, divide one of the classes identified according to a single principle. And, like Keillor, put yourself in a separate class or, if appropriate, in one of the classes you identify. If you wish, use your classification to make a point, perhaps an observation about human nature or differences in age groups or genders.

10

Definition

There are many ways of defining something, and the way we choose depends on our purpose and audience. If we are in a store that advertises "Hero Sandwiches" and a visitor asks what these are, we can point to one on the counter. But pointing may not be enough: we may have to "denote" what a hero sandwich is—that is, distinguish the "hero" from other things like it. In a denotative definition we can start with a classification of things like food and single the hero out from all other kinds. But since the visitor knows a hero is something to eat, we can narrow our class to sandwiches.

A dictionary definition usually gives us a denotative definition of this sort—identifying first the class or genus of objects to which the word belongs and then distinguishing the word by its specific difference. As we noted, the class or genus may be broad (*food*) or it may be narrow (*sandwich*). The following dictionary definition of *hero* chooses a narrow genus:

> *hero* U.S. A sandwich [*genus*] made with a loaf of bread cut lengthwise [*specific difference*]. (*Standard College Dictionary*)

Sometimes we want to do more than merely name or identify an object: we want to present ideas and impressions, the emotional aura we associate with it. The word *rose* has a precise denotation—a particular flower with describable properties. It also has a range of connotations or associations. Thus roses are often associated with success or happiness, and we recognize this association in the popular expression "a rosy future." Connotations may be positive in their implication, or negative. Though the words *inexpensive* and *cheap* both mean low price, *cheap* for many people carries the connotation of poor quality or of something contemptible. *Inexpensive* is an emotionally neutral word; *cheap* is not.

Denotative and connotative definitions tell us how words are used currently. Sometimes we find it helpful to give the original meaning, or etymology, to clarify the current meaning—for example, to explain that the word *gravity* comes from the Latin *gravitas* meaning weight or heaviness. But we must be careful not to assume that a current word possesses, or should be limited to, its original meaning. We would certainly be misunderstood if we used *sinister*, a word of Latin derivation originally meaning *left* and *left-handed*, to refer to a left-handed person.

We can also use definitions to fix words that have become indefinite or confused in popular usage. We sometimes call this kind of definition *precising*. Judicial decisions are often of this kind, as in decisions that define obscenity in books and films. Another use of definition is to stipulate or propose a name or term for a newly discovered phenomenon so that we can refer to it. An example is the term *quasar*, proposed in the 1960s for newly discovered "quasi-stellar" sources of light in the sky that seem not to be stars. *Stipulative* definitions are proposed with the understanding that the term may change later as more is discovered. By contrast, *theoretical* definitions propose an explanation or theory of the phenomenon: they do not merely propose a term for discussion and further research. Most textbook definitions of democracy and similar ideas are theoretical. In giving definitions, we should be clear about the use we are making of them. It will matter to the reader whether we are trying to make a commonly used word more exact in its usage or proposing a definition without claiming to know the whole truth about it.

Catherine Caufield

CATHERINE CAUFIELD *has written articles for* The New Scientist *and other periodicals. Her book* In the Rainforest (1985) *is a report on the destruction of rainforest in Central and South America and other parts of the world. She writes the following in her May 14, 1990,* New Yorker *magazine article, "The Ancient Forest"— a report on the old-growth forests of the Pacific Northwest:*

Originally, the Pacific forest covered seventy thousand square miles of Canada and the United States. About sixty per cent of Canada's Pacific forest has by now been destroyed, mostly in the past forty years. In the United States, less than ten per cent survives. Almost all that remains is on public lands, and it is scheduled to be cut for lumber, plywood, and pulp, much of it for export to Japan.

In the following excerpt Caufield defines the old-growth forest. In the course of her definition, she refers to David Kelly, author of Secrets of the Old Growth Forest *(1988), and Jerry Franklin, a U.S. Forest Service scientist and the main author of a 1981 report on the Douglas fir forest.*

OLD-GROWTH FORESTS

Forests, like human beings, have a natural life span. Once they reach maturity, at about two hundred years, growth slows down considerably, and most of their energy goes into sustaining themselves. Eventually, though it may take several centuries more, decay sets in, and the trees die and fall down. To a logger, leaving trees in the ground beyond their point of maximum annual wood production makes no sense. Since the Pacific forest consists of trees that tend to live for centuries beyond that point, it has been regarded by loggers and foresters alike as decadent. The professional forester's view is that such forests should be cleared and replanted with healthy young trees as quickly as possible. Franklin and his colleagues, however, found that this post-mature phase, now generally called old-growth, is the richest, most complex stage of the forest's life. For the first few decades after a patch of forest is cleared—by fire, wind, or logging—it is an open, grassy area, a good feeding ground for wildlife such as deer, bears, and elk. During severe winters, though, when these open areas are blanketed with several feet of snow, the animals take refuge in old-growth stands, where the ground is protected from snow, and food is still available. At about thirty years, the young stand enters an almost sterile period that lasts for up to a hundred years. This occurs because the trees, all the same age, have formed a dense, unbroken canopy, which blocks the sun and shades out understory growth. As the stand ages, trees die and fall, allowing sunlight to penetrate to the forest floor and stimulate another layer of growth. When the stand achieves a certain complexity of structure—shrubs, herbs, and trees of varying heights creating a multistoried canopy—it has become old-growth.

It is impossible to come up with a description of old-growth 2 forest that fits the whole Pacific region, since, as Franklin points out, "nature is just too complex and variable to fit into neat conceptual boxes." Still, there is general agreement that true old-growth forests are characterized by large, old living trees; a multilayered canopy; large standing dead trees, called snags; and large dead trees on the ground and in streams. The dead trees are essential to the health of the forest, and are the basis of its astonishing productivity. The nutrients that the forest needs are not mainly in the soil but in the living and dead plant material itself. As leaves and branches fall to the forest floor, as trees and plants die and decay, this material is recycled to the living forest. With this highly efficient and almost closed system, the forest feeds itself, wasting nothing.

Though the great old giants of the forest may be beyond 3 their wood-producing prime, they are at their prime for many other functions. Scientists have lately discovered that there are lichens that grow only on the canopies of the old-growth trees and can capture nitrogen from the atmosphere. A steady, barely noticeable rain of these lichens constantly enriches the layer of nutrients on the forest floor. A single old-growth tree may have sixty to seventy million needles, and a total of forty-three thousand square feet of leaf surface. The needles are astonishingly successful at collecting moisture and chemical nutrients from the atmosphere. When forests were cut around the Bull Run watershed, from which Portland, Oregon, gets some of its water supply, Forest Service scientists expected more water to enter the reservoir, because of reduced evaporation and transpiration. Instead, water levels in the reservoir dropped. Surprised researchers found that almost a third of the water in the Bull Run reservoir has never come from rain. Rather, the tall trees in old-growth forests collect it from passing clouds and fog banks. When the trees are cut down, the moisture banks waft by without depositing the water they hold. Old-growth trees also protect the soil and the wildlife from the extreme effects of the region's wet, cold winters and dry summers: first, the dense canopy breaks the impact of the intense rain and snow, helping to prevent disastrous floods, landslides, and soil erosion, and providing a sheltered environment for wildlife in winter; second, the huge trunks can store thousands of gallons of water for the trees' own use and that of other species in the dry season.

One of the most important features of the old-growth forest is the variety of habitats it provides for wildlife. More than a hundred and fifty species of mammals live in such forests, and as many as fifteen hundred invertebrate species may live in a single stand. So far, according to Kelly's book, scientists have found a hundred and eighteen vertebrate species (mammals, birds, reptiles, amphibians, and fishes) whose primary habitat is old-growth. The large old trees, merely by virtue of their great height, create a continuum of climatic conditions, from the cool, dark, moist forest floor to the harsher environment of the canopy, exposed to the sun, rain, snow, fog, and wind. Every part of the tree—living or dead, including the roots—is home to a whole community of plants, insects, birds, and mammals. The plants and the animals that dwell in the canopy are different from those which nest in a snag, live halfway down a tree trunk, or stay on the forest floor. One species, the tiny red tree vole, which is found only in these forests, spends its entire life high up in a Douglas fir. It makes its nest there, eats almost nothing but Douglas-fir needles, and gets its water by licking rain from the needles.

A tree that is killed by fire, lightning, insects, or disease may remain standing for two hundred years or more. These huge snags are colonized by many types of insects, birds, and mammals. Several species of bats and birds breed under patches of loose bark. Ospreys and bald eagles use the snags as lookout posts. But the most valuable feature of the snags is the cavities that develop in their trunks and branches. At least forty-five vertebrate species, from the northern flying squirrel to the rare and beautiful northern spotted owl, will nest or feed only in the cavities of old-growth trees. These animals eat the mosses, lichens, and insects that invade dead or dying trees, and they in turn are eaten by animals higher up the food chain—animals like black bears, pine martens, and bobcats, all of which take shelter in snags.

In the very act of falling, a tree contributes to forest diversity in several ways. Its fall creates a light gap—a hole in the canopy through which sunlight can penetrate to the forest floor and stimulate the growth of plants, such as Western hemlock, that have survived for years in the deep shade but needed this burst of light to grow to full size. A tree that is uprooted creates two new wildlife habitats: the pit where its roots used to be, and the exposed roots themselves. A walk through any old-growth forest will take one past several fallen trees, their huge but shallow roots sticking ten or fifteen feet into the air and overgrown with mosses, lichens, ferns, and shrubs. The wresting of the roots from the ground allows organic matter to mix in with the mineral soil—an essential ecological service in the Sitka-spruce forests of Alaska, where the soil has a tendency to harden and form an impervious pan.

A thousand-year-old tree that falls to the forest floor may take four hundred years more to decay completely. During those centuries, it contributes in many ways to the life and the balance of the forest. Downed logs reduce soil erosion by creating a natural terracing effect on hillsides. They contain enormous amounts of water—enough to see many forest creatures through the dry season. A fallen tree supports an amazing, though still not entirely charted, variety of wildlife—at least a hundred and sixty-three species of birds, mammals, reptiles, and amphibians, and more invertebrates than have yet been counted. Most old-growth forests contain more than fifty tons of downed wood per acre. As much as a third of the forest's soil organic matter comes from these decaying logs; hemlock seedlings and other shade-tolerant plants take root in them as if in a rich plot of soil. In some areas, these "nurse logs" are the primary sites for tree reproduction.

Perhaps the most important and interesting aspect of the 8
decay cycle is the interplay between certain fungi, which grow
on decaying trees, and the roots of living trees. These fungi,
called mycorrhizae, infect the root tips of many tree species,
including all the conifers in the Pacific Northwest forest. In
doing so, they promote the growth of tiny root hairs that
spread across the forest floor searching for nutrients, and so
help trees absorb nutrients that are unavailable to uninfected
roots. Without mycorrhizae, trees cannot obtain the phospho-
rus, the nitrogen, and the water they need to survive and grow.
An experiment that was conducted in Oregon's Siskiyou
National Forest by Oregon State University in cooperation
with the Forest Service found that Douglas-fir seedlings died
within two years of planting when they were deprived of mycorrhizae. In turn, mycorrhizae, which cannot photosynthesize, obtain their food from trees.

VOCABULARY

paragraph 1: decadent, understory
paragraph 2: conceptual
paragraph 3: lichen
paragraph 4: invertebrate, vertebrate, vole
paragraph 6: ecological
paragraph 8: fungi, photosynthesize

QUESTIONS

1. Is Caufield's definition of "old-growth forest" in paragraph 1
   denotative, connotative, stipulative, or theoretical?
2. What benefits do standing old-growth trees confer on the forest?
   What benefits do fallen trees confer?
3. In what order does Caufield discuss these benefits in paragraphs
   3–8?
4. In what order does Caufield discuss aspects of the decay cycle in
   paragraphs 6–8?

SUGGESTIONS FOR WRITING

1. Summarize the case made by the ecologists cited by Caufield for
   preserving old-growth forests.

2. Using the resources of your college library, investigate the case for clearing old-growth forests and replanting, or the arguments for and against restricting logging on public lands in the Pacific Northwest and other parts of the United States. Write a summary of your findings.

3. Use the Oxford English Dictionary and other historical and special dictionaries to discover the etymology and distinguishing properties of one of the following words. In other reference books and special studies find information on its history and effects. Organize your information in one or more well-organized paragraphs.

   a. aspirin

   b. DDT

   c. insulin

   d. nitroglycerin

   e. radar

Lawrence M. Friedman

LAWRENCE M. FRIEDMAN, Professor of Law at Stanford University, is the author of A History of American Law (1986), The Republic of Choice (1990), and other books. In Crime and Punishment in American History (1993), Friedman discusses the social response to crime from colonial times to the present. The definition of crime reprinted here appears in the introduction.

CRIME

There is no real answer to the question, What is crime? There are popular ideas about crime: crime is bad behavior, antisocial behavior, blameworthy acts, and the like. But in a very basic sense, crime is a *legal* concept: what makes some conduct criminal, and other conduct not, is the fact that some, but not others, are "against the law."*

---

* Most criminologists, but not all, would agree with this general formulation; for an exception see Michael R. Gottfredson and Travis Hirschi, A General Theory of Crime (1990). [Friedman's note]

Crimes, then, are forbidden acts. But they are forbidden in   2
a special way. We are not supposed to break contracts, drive
carelessly, slander people, or infringe copyrights; but these
are not (usually) criminal acts. The distinction between a *civil*
and a *criminal* case is fundamental in our legal system. A civil
case has a life cycle entirely different from that of a criminal
case. If I slander somebody, I might be dragged into court, and
I might have to open my checkbook and pay damages; but I
cannot be put in prison or executed, and if I lose the case, I do
not get a criminal "record." Also, in a slander case (or a negligence case, or a copyright–infringement case), the injured
party pays for, runs, and manages the case herself. He or she
makes the decisions and hires the lawyers. The case is entirely
voluntary. Nobody forces anybody to sue. I can have a good
claim, a valid claim, and simply forget it, if I want.

In a criminal case, in theory at least, society is the victim,   3
along with the "real" victim—the person robbed or assaulted
or cheated. The crime may be punished without the victim's
approval (though, practically speaking, the complaining witness often has a crucial role to play). In "victimless crimes"
(gambling, drug dealing, certain sex offenses), there is nobody
to complain; both parties are equally guilty (or innocent).
Here the machine most definitely has a mind of its own. In
criminal cases, moreover, the state pays the bills. It should be
pointed out, however, that the further back in history one
goes, the more this pat distinction between "civil" and "criminal" tends to blur. In some older cultures, the line between
private vengeance and public prosecution was indistinct or
completely absent. Even in our own history, we shall see some
evidence that the cleavage between "public" and "private"
enforcement was not always deep and pervasive.

All sorts of nasty acts and evil deeds are not against the law,   4
and thus not crimes. These include most of the daily events
that anger or irritate us, even those we might consider totally
outrageous. Ordinary lying is not a crime; cheating on a wife or
husband is not a crime in most states (at one time it was,

almost everywhere); charging a huge markup at a restaurant or store is not, in general, a crime; psychological abuse is (mostly) not a crime.

Before some act can be isolated and labeled as a crime, there must be a special, solemn, social and *political* decision. In our society, Congress, a state legislature, or a city government has to pass a law or enact an ordinance adding the behavior to the list of crimes. Then this behavior, like a bottle of poison, carries the proper label and can be turned over to the heavy artillery of law for possible enforcement.

We repeat: crime is a *legal* concept. This point, however, can lead to a misunderstanding. The law, in a sense, "creates" the crimes it punishes; but what creates criminal law? Behind the law, and above it, enveloping it, is society; before the law made the crime a crime, some aspect of social reality transformed the behavior, culturally speaking, into a crime; and it is the social context that gives the act, and the legal responses, their real meaning. Justice is supposed to be blind, which is to say impartial. This may or may not be so, but justice *is* blind in one fundamental sense: justice is an abstraction. It cannot see or act on its own. It cannot generate its own norms, principles, and rules. Everything depends on society. Behind every *legal* judgment of criminality is a more powerful, more basic *social* judgment, a judgment that this behavior, whatever it is, deserves to be outlawed and punished.

VOCABULARY

paragraph 2: infringe, civil, slander, negligence case, valid
paragraph 6: concept, context

QUESTIONS

1. What distinguishes a criminal case from a civil case?
2. Why is Friedman's definition of crime theoretical, as he implies in paragraph 3, and not denotative or stipulative?
3. What misunderstanding may arise in stating that crime is a "legal concept"? How does Friedman clarify this idea?

4. Friedman states that careless driving and copyright infringement are not usually defined as crimes. Under what circumstances might they be?

SUGGESTION FOR WRITING

Examine the definition of the following terms in your collegiate dictionary to determine whether it is denotative, connotative, stipulative, or theoretical. You may find that the dictionary lists more than one kind; for example, it may list connotations of the word, in addition to its denotation. Write a brief paragraph on each word, discussing your findings:

a. comedy

b. democracy

c. fascism

d. filibuster

e. liberal

f. neutron star

g. unicorn

h. witty

Philip Hamburger

A *native of* Wheeling, West Virginia, PHILIP HAMBURGER *has been a staff member of* The New Yorker *magazine since* 1939, *except for two years of government service during* World War II *in the Office of Facts and Figures (later the Office of War Information). On his return to* The New Yorker *in* 1943, *he served as a war correspondent in Europe for the magazine. Hamburger has written for most sections of* The New Yorker. *His many contributions include pieces in "Talk of the Town" and "Notes and Comments," "Reporter at Large" articles, film and music criticism, and columns on television. His most recent book is* Curious World: A New Yorker at Large (1987). *He received the George Polk Career Award in* 1994. *In* An American Notebook *he shows a particular city through the eyes of its inhabitants; this excerpt is taken from his profile of Oklahoma City.*

THE SOONERS

No higher compliment can be paid to an Oklahoma City man these days than to call him a Sooner. Call an Oklahoma City man a Sooner, and his chest puffs out and his eyes light up. It means that you appreciate the chap—his vigor, his vitality, his civic pride, his alliance with the tall white buildings that, first glimpsed from miles away and across long stretches of land, appear to be a mirage but turn out, upon a closer approach, to be Oklahoma City. Call a man a Sooner, and you identify him with, among other things, the University of Oklahoma football team—the Sooners—and what man could ask for more? Oklahoma City's most fashionable hotel, the Skirvin (Perle Mesta owns part of the Skirvin; her daddy was a Skirvin), has a Sooner Room, which constitutes semiofficial recognition that the word "Sooner" has reached an impeccable social plateau. The use of "Sooner" as an accolade represents a mellowing process. Up to seventy years ago, to call a man a Sooner was to risk being hit over the head with the spare wheel of a covered wagon, kicked in the stomach, or worse. It all goes back to April 22, 1889, the day of The Run, when the Oklahoma Territory (then called the Indian Territory) was opened to settlers, and when the settlers, poised and in natural Technicolor, awaited the sound of the gun that would permit them to race pell-mell for new land and new homes. There is many a man in Oklahoma City today who remembers The Run, and millions of moviegoers feel that they, too, made The Run, as a result of the numerous cinema epics that have glorified it. When dawn broke on that April 22nd, what was to become Oklahoma City was a sleepy little railroad stop sitting out on the lonely grass. Nothing much to be said about it, really—a few wooden houses, a water tower, some railroad tracks, the usual complement of early-rising roosters, perhaps a barefoot boy with a can of worms, and the West stretching as far as the eye could see. There were also on hand some people called Sooners. These were people who had shown up too soon—who weren't taking any chances on losing out in the race for land, and who had crossed the line before the starting gun. To the thousands of law-abiding citizens who waited patiently behind the line, the Sooners were beneath contempt. "They were chisellers, that's what they were," an old-time Oklahoma City resident said not long ago. He was in the Sooner Room at the time, sipping a brandy. "The organized Sooners, who were sooner than the Sooners, were known as Boomers, and it is hard to say which were worse. They were all mean, dirty, low-life chisellers." By nightfall, after the gun had gone off and The Run had been accomplished, Oklahoma City was a city of ten thousand souls, many of them out looking for the Sooners and the Boomers. Time heals many wounds.

VOCABULARY

mirage, impeccable, social plateau, pell-mell, complement

QUESTIONS

1. What is the denotative definition of *Sooner*, and where in the paragraph does Hamburger present it?
2. What positive and negative connotations does the word *Sooner* have? Why does Hamburger give us information about the Boomers?
3. What do these connotations tell you about Oklahomans and changes in Oklahoma life since 1889?
4. What is the tone of the paragraph—the voice of the writer that you hear in reading it? Specifically, is the tone admiring or sarcastic or amused? Or does Hamburger express no attitude toward the people and the world he describes?

SUGGESTIONS FOR WRITING

1. First give the denotative meaning of a name like the one Hamburger describes—perhaps the name associated with your city or town or with your high school and its teams. Then give its connotations and, if you can, explain their origin. Use your definition to make a point.
2. Advertisers depend on connotative meanings to sell their products. Discuss differences in the connotations of similar products

—for example, automobiles with names like "Cougar" and "Charger." Use your discussion to make a point.

Casey Miller and Kate Swift

CASEY MILLER *has worked in publishing and as a free-lance writer and editor.* KATE SWIFT *is also a free-lance writer and editor and has been a science writer for the* American Museum of Natural History *and a news director for the* Yale School of Medicine. *The discussion reprinted here is taken from* Words and Women (1976) —*a book concerned with the influence of language on the lives of women.*

"MANLY" AND "WOMANLY"

Webster's Third New International Dictionary (1966) defines *manly* as "having qualities appropriate to a man: not effeminate or timorous; bold, resolute, open in conduct or bearing." The definition goes on to include "belonging or appropriate in character to a man" (illustrated by "manly sports" and "beer is a manly drink"), "of undaunted courage: gallant, brave." The same dictionary's definition of *womanly* is less specific, relying heavily on phrases like "marked by qualities characteristic of a woman"; "possessed of the character or behavior befitting a grown woman"; "characteristic of, belonging to, or suitable to a woman's nature and attitudes rather than to a man's." Two of the examples provided are more informative: "convinced that drawing was a waste of time, if not downright womanly . . ." and "her usual womanly volubility."

In its definition of *manly* the Random House Dictionary of the English Language (1967) supplies the words "strong, brave, honorable, resolute, virile" as "qualities usually considered desirable in a man" and cites "feminine; weak, cowardly," as antonyms. Its definitions of *womanly* are "like or befitting a woman; feminine; not masculine or girlish" and "in the manner of, or befitting, a woman." The same dictionary's synonym essays for these words are worth quoting in full because of the contrasts they provide:

MANLY, MANFUL, MANNISH mean possessing the qualities of a man. MANLY implies possession of the most valuable or desirable qualities a man can have, as dignity, honesty, directness, etc., in opposition to servility, insincerity, underhandedness, etc.: *A manly foe is better than a weak friend.* It also connotes courage, strength, and fortitude: *manly determination to face what comes.* MANFUL stresses the reference to courage, strength, and industry: *manful resistance.* MANNISH applies to that which resembles man: *a boy with a mannish voice.* Applied to a woman, the term is derogatory, suggesting the aberrant possession of masculine characteristics: *a mannish girl; a mannish stride.*

WOMANLY, WOMANLIKE, WOMANISH, mean resembling a woman. WOMANLY implies resemblance in appropriate, fitting ways: *womanly decorum, modesty.* WOMANLIKE, a neutral synonym, may suggest mild disapproval or, more rarely, disgust: *Womanlike, she (he) burst into tears.* WOMANISH usually implies an inappropriate resemblance and suggests weakness or effeminacy; *womanish petulance.*

What are these parallel essays saying? That we perceive 3 males in terms of human qualities, females in terms of qualities—often negative—assigned to them as females. The qualities males possess may be good or bad, but those that come to mind when we consider what makes "a man" are positive. Women are defined circularly, through characteristics seen to be appropriate or inappropriate to women—not to human beings. In fact, when women exhibit positive attributes considered typical of men—dignity, honesty, courage, strength, or fortitude—they are thought of as aberrant. A person who is "womanlike" may (although the term is said to be "neutral") prompt a feeling of disgust.

The broad range of positive characteristics used to define 4 males could be used to define females too, of course, but they are not. The characteristics of women—weakness is among the most frequently cited—are something apart. At its entry for *women* Webster's *Third* provides this list of "qualities considered distinctive of womanhood": "Gentleness, affection, and domesticity or on the other hand fickleness, superficiality, and folly." Among the "qualities considered distinctive of manhood" listed in the entry for *man*, no negative attributes detract from the "courage, strength, and vigor" the definers associate with males. According to this dictionary, *womanish* means "unsuitable to a man or to a strong character of either sex."

Lexicographers do not make up definitions out of thin air. Their task is to record how words are used, it is not to say how they should be used. The examples they choose to illustrate meanings can therefore be especially revealing of cultural expectations. The *American Heritage Dictionary* (1969), which provides "manly courage" and "masculine charm," also gives us "Woman is fickle," "brought out the woman in him," "womanly virtue," "feminine allure," "feminine wiles," and "womanish tears." The same dictionary defines *effeminate*, which comes from the Latin *effeminare*, meaning "to make a woman out of," as "having the qualities associated with women; not characteristic of a man; unmanly" and "characterized by softness, weakness, or lack of force; not dynamic or vigorous." For synonyms one is referred to *feminine*.

Brother and *sister* and their derivatives have acquired similar features. A columnist who wrote that "the political operatives known as 'Kennedy men' and 'Nixon men' have been sisters under their skins" could not possibly have called those adversaries "brothers," with all the mutual respect and loyalty that word implies. As the writer explained, "Like the colonel's lady and Judy O'Grady, their styles were different but their unwavering determination to win was strikingly similar." Other kinds of sisters for whom no comparable male siblings exist include the sob sister, the weak sister, and the plain ordinary sissy, whose counterpart in the brotherhood is the buddy, a real pal. Like *effeminate*, these female-related words and phrases are applied to males when a cutting insult is intended.

Masculine, manly, manlike, and other male-associated words used to compliment men are frequently also considered complimentary when applied to women: thus a woman may be said to have manly determination, to have a masculine mind, to take adversity like a man, or to struggle manfully against overwhelming odds. The one male-associated word sometimes used to insult her is mannish, which may suggest she is too strong or aggressive to be a true woman, or that she is homosexually oriented, in which case mannish can become a code word.

Female-associated words, on the other hand, must be hedged, as in "He has almost feminine intuition," if they are used to describe a man without insulting him. He may be praised for admirable qualities defined as peculiar to women, but he cannot be said to have womanly compassion or womanlike tenderness. In exceptions to this rule—for example, when a medic on the battlefield or a sports figure in some postgame situation of unusual drama is said to be "as gentle as a woman"—the life-and-death quality of the circumstances makes its own ironic and terrible commentary on the standards of "masculinity" ordinarily expected of men.

The role expectations compressed into our male-positive-important and female-negative-trivial words are extremely damaging, as we are beginning to find out. The female stereotypes they convey are obvious, but the harm doesn't stop there. The inflexible demands made on males, which allow neither for variation nor for human frailty, are dehumanizing. They put a premium on a kind of perfection that can be achieved only through strength, courage, industry, and fortitude. These are admirable qualities, but if they are associated only with males, and their opposites are associated only with females, they become sex-related demands that few individuals can fulfill.

VOCABULARY

paragraph 1: effeminate, timorous, undaunted, volubility
paragraph 2: virile, antonym, servility, derogatory, aberrant, decorum, synonym, petulance
paragraph 4: fickleness, superficiality
paragraph 5: lexicographer, wiles

paragraph 6: sibling
paragraph 8: intuition
paragraph 9: stereotype, dehumanizing, fortitude

QUESTIONS

1. Miller and Swift state that "Women are defined circularly, through characteristics seen to be appropriate or inappropriate to women—no to human beings." How is the definition of women circular?

2. What attitudes toward men and women underlie the dictionary definition—and current uses—of *manly* and *womanly*? What change in attitude toward men and women do Miller and Swift favor? Do they say what change they favor, or do you infer their beliefs from their analysis?

3. To what extent do Miller and Swift describe your own use of *manly* and *womanly* and your conceptions of manhood and womanhood?

SUGGESTIONS FOR WRITING

1. Miller and Swift state that language today makes "sex-related demands that few individuals can fulfill." Explain what they mean. Then state your reasons for agreeing or disagreeing with them.

2. Analyze your own conception of manliness and womanliness, comparing your use of *manly* and *womanly* with those discussed by Miller and Swift.

3. Miller and Swift suggest that the words we commonly use create "role expectations"—attitudes and behavior society looks for in men and women. Discuss "role expectations" promoted in advertisements for a particular product, such as sports equipment.

Herbert J. Gans

HERBERT J. GANS *is* Robert S. Lynd Professor of Sociology at Columbia University in New York City. In his article on the word "underclass" published in The Washington Post September 10,

1990, *Gans shows how a widely accepted word can create an unfair stereotype and influence thinking on issues of welfare and poverty. In exploring the connotations of the term, Gans is also considering the implications of what is for journalists and sociologists a theoretical definition.*

THE UNDERCLASS

Sticks and stones may break my bones, but names can never 1 hurt me goes the old proverb. But like many old proverbs, this one is patent nonsense, as anyone knows who has ever been hurt by ethnic, racist or sexist insults and stereotypes.

The most frequent victims of insults and stereotypes have 2 been the poor, especially those thought to be undeserving of help because someone decided—justifiably or not—that they had not acted properly. America has a long history of insults for the "undeserving" poor. In the past they were bums, hoboes, vagrants and paupers; more recently they have been culturally deprived and the hard-core poor. Now they are "the underclass."

Underclass was originally a 19th-century Swedish term for 3 the poor. In the early 1960s, the Swedish economist Gunnar Myrdal revived it to describe the unemployed and unemployables being created by the modern economy, people who, he predicted, would soon be driven out of that economy unless it was reformed. Twenty years later, in Ronald Reagan's America, the word sprang to life again, this time not only to describe but also to condemn. Those normally consigned to the underclass include: women who start their families before marriage and before the end of adolescence, youngsters who fail to finish high school or find work, and welfare "dependents"—whether or not the behavior of any of these people is their own fault. The term is also applied to low-income delinquents and criminals—but not to affluent ones.

"Underclass" has become popular because it seems to grab 4 people's attention. What grabs is the image of a growing horde of beggars, muggers, robbers and lazy people who do not carry their part of the economic load, all of them threatening nonpoor Americans and the stability of American society. The image may be inaccurate, but then insults and pejoratives don't have to be accurate. Moreover, underclass sounds technical, academic, and not overtly pejorative, so it can be used without anyone's biases showing. Since it is now increasingly applied to blacks and Hispanics, it is also a respectable substitute word with which to condemn them.

There are other things wrong with the word underclass. For 5 one, it lumps together in a single term very diverse poor people with diverse problems. Imagine all children's illnesses being described with the same word, and the difficulties doctors would have in curing them.

For example, a welfare recipient often requires little more 6 than a decent paying job—and a male breadwinner who also has such a job—to make a normal go of it, while a high school dropout usually needs both a better-equipped school, better teachers and fellow students—and a rationale for going to school when he or she has no assurance that a decent job will follow upon graduation. Neither the welfare recipient nor the high school dropout deserves to be grouped with, or described by, the same word as muggers or drug dealers.

Labeling poor people as underclass is to blame them for 7 their poverty, which enables the blamers to blow off the steam of self-righteousness. That steam does not, however, reduce their poverty. Unfortunately, underclass, like other buzzwords for calling the poor undeserving, is being used to avoid starting up needed antipoverty programs and other economic reforms.

Still, the greatest danger of all lies not in the label itself but 8 in the possibility that the underclass is a symptom of a possible, and dark, American future: that we are moving toward a "post-post-industrial" economy in which there may not be enough decent jobs for all. Either too many more jobs will move to Third World countries where wages are far lower or they will be performed by ever more efficient computers and other machines.

If this happens, the underclass label may turn out to be 9 a signal that the American economy, and our language, are preparing to get ready for a future in which some people are going to be more or less permanently jobless—and will be blamed for their joblessness to boot.

Needless to say, an American economy with a permanently $\quad$ 10 jobless population would be socially dangerous, for all of the country's current social problems, from crime and addiction to mental illness would be sure to increase considerably. America would then also become politically more dangerous, for various kinds of new protests have to be expected, not to mention the rise of quasi-fascist movements. Such movements can already be found in France and other European countries. $\quad$ 11

Presumably, Americans—the citizenry and elected officials both—will not let any of this happen here and will find new sources of decent jobs, as they have done in past generations, even if today this requires a new kind of New Deal. Perhaps there will be another instance of what always saved America in the past: new sources of economic growth that cannot even be imagined now. $\quad$ 12

The only problem is that in the past, America ruled the world economically, and now it does not—and it shows in our lack of economic growth. Consequently, the term underclass could become a permanent entry in the dictionary of American pejoratives.

VOCABULARY

paragraph 1: stereotype
paragraph 2: hoboes, vagrants, paupers
paragraph 4: pejoratives
paragraph 6: rationale
paragraph 8: symptom
paragraph 10: quasi-fascist

QUESTIONS

1. Gans shows that the economist Gunnar Myrdal introduced a precising definition for the nineteenth-century Swedish word *underclass*. What was the original meaning of the word, and how did Myrdal make the meaning precise?

2. To what extent has Myrdal's meaning been adopted by Americans, according to Gans? What additional meanings has the word acquired since the early 1960s?

3. Why does Gans consider *underclass* an inaccurate term or label for the poor? What additional danger does he see in the widespread acceptance of the term?

4. Does Gans believe that poverty is irremediable? Or does he believe that remedies exist in America today?

SUGGESTIONS FOR WRITING

1. Define one of the following words or another word descriptive of an attitude or behavior by stating what it is and what it is not. Comment on the significance of its etymology.

   a. gluttony

   b. greed

   c. intolerance

   d. laziness

   e. stinginess

2. Discuss the various meanings of a descriptive term like *cool* or *tacky*, illustrating these meanings by your use of them.

11

Comparison and Contrast

Comparison shows the similarities between people, things, or ideas; contrast shows the differences. The word *comparison* sometimes refers to both kinds of analysis, as in this block comparison of President Franklin Roosevelt with Great Britain's wartime prime minister, Winston S. Churchill:

> Roosevelt, as a public personality, was a spontaneous optimistic, pleasure-loving ruler who dismayed his assistants by the gay and apparently heedless abandon with which he seemed to delight in pursuing two or more totally incompatible policies, and astonished them even more by the swiftness and ease with which he managed to throw off the cares of office during the darkest and most dangerous moments. Churchill too loves pleasure, and he too lacks neither gaiety nor a capacity for exuberant self-expression, together with the habit of blithely cutting Gordian knots in a manner which often upset his experts; but he is not a frivolous man. His nature possesses a dimension of depth—and a corresponding sense of tragic possibilities—which Roosevelt's light-hearted genius instinctively passed by. (Sir Isaiah Berlin, "Mr. Churchill")

Block comparisons present the details of the first subject as a whole and then the details of the second. But the author may choose to develop the comparison point by point, as in this succeeding paragraph on Roosevelt and Churchill:

> Roosevelt played the game of politics with virtuosity, and both his successes and his failures were carried off in splendid style; his performance seemed to flow with effortless skill. Churchill is acquainted with darkness as well as light. Like all inhabitants and even transient visitors of inner worlds, he gives evidence of seasons of agonized brooding and slow recovery. Roosevelt might have spoken of sweat and blood, but when Churchill offered his people tears, he spoke a

word which might have been uttered by Lincoln or Mazzini or Cromwell, but not Roosevelt, great-hearted, generous and perceptive as he was.

Both paragraphs build from similarities to differences. Were the similarities more important, the author would probably have built up to them instead. Notice also that the purpose of the comparison is to arrive at a relative estimate of the two men as leaders. We discover the qualities of Roosevelt through Churchill, and those of Churchill through Roosevelt.

Relative estimates aid in explaining something strange or new, as in the following extended comparison of a concentration camp inmate of Nazi Germany or the Soviet Union with other kinds of prisoners.

> Forced labor as a punishment is limited as to time and intensity. The convict retains his rights over his body; he is not absolutely tortured and he is not absolutely dominated. Banishment banishes only from one part of the world to another part of the world, also inhabited by human beings; it does not exclude from the human world altogether. Throughout history slavery has been an institution within a social order; slaves were not, like concentration-camp inmates, withdrawn from the sight and hence the protection of their fellow-men; as instruments of labor they had a definite price and as property a definite value. The concentration-camp inmate has no price, because he can always be replaced; nobody knows to whom he belongs, because he is never seen. From the point of view of normal society he is absolutely superfluous, although in times of acute labor shortage, as in Russia and in Germany during the war, he is used for work. (Hannah Arendt, *The Origins of Totalitarianism*)

Though the author is concerned with defining the status of the concentration camp inmate, she does so through a relative estimate that illuminates the special situation of each kind of prisoner.

Marie Winn

MARIE WINN *is the author of numerous articles and books on parents and children—including* Children Without Childhood (1983) *and* Unplugging the Plug-In Drug (1987). *Her book on children and television,* The Plug-In Drug (1977), *is based on interviews with parents and children, social workers, teachers, and child psychologists in Denver and New York City. Winn is concerned about our experience with television and about what happens to children when it takes the place of reading. She believes that "a disposition toward 'openness,'" acquired through years of television viewing "has influenced adversely viewers' ability to concentrate, to read, to write clearly—in short, to demonstrate any of the verbal skills a literate society requires." Her comparison between reading and television viewing tells us why.*

READING AND TELEVISION

A comparison between reading and viewing may be made in respect to the pace of each experience, and the relative control a person has over that pace, for the pace may influence the ways one uses the material received in each experience. In addition, the pace of each experience may determine how much it intrudes upon other aspects of one's life.

The pace of reading, clearly, depends entirely upon the reader. He may read as slowly or as rapidly as he can or wishes to read. If he does not understand something, he may stop and reread it, or go in search of elucidation before continuing. The reader can accelerate his pace when the material is easy or less than interesting, and slow down when it is difficult or enthralling. If what he reads is moving, he can put down the book for a few moments and cope with his emotions without fear of losing anything.

The pace of the television experience cannot be controlled by the viewer; only its beginning and end are within his control as he clicks the knob on and off. He cannot slow down a delightful program or speed up a dreary one. He cannot "turn back" if a word or phrase is not understood. The program moves inexorably forward, and what is lost or misunderstood remains so.

Nor can the television viewer readily transform the material he receives into a form that might suit his particular emotional needs, as he invariably does with material he reads. The images move too quickly. He cannot use his own imagination to invest the people and events portrayed on television with the personal meanings that would help him understand and resolve relationships and conflicts in his own life; he is under the power of the imagination of the show's creators. In the television experience the eyes and ears are overwhelmed with the immediacy of sights and sounds. They flash from the television set just fast enough for the eyes and ears to take them in before moving on quickly to the new pictures and sounds . . . so as *not to lose the thread.*

Not to lose the thread . . . it is this need, occasioned by the irreversible direction and relentless velocity of the television experience, that not only limits the workings of the viewer's imagination, but also causes television to intrude into human affairs far more than reading experiences can ever do. If someone enters the room while one is watching television—a friend, a relative, a child, someone, perhaps, one has not seen for some time—one must continue to watch or one will lose the thread. The greetings must wait, for the television program will not. A book, of course, can be set aside, with a pang of regret, perhaps, but with no sense of permanent loss.

VOCABULARY

paragraph 2: elucidation, accelerate, enthralling
paragraph 3: inexorably
paragraph 5: irreversible, velocity

QUESTIONS

1. What is the purpose of the comparison, according to paragraph 1?
2. What are the differences? In what order does Winn present them?
3. Does Winn say that we should give up television, or is she making no recommendation?
4. Do you agree with her description of reading and watching television? Is reading ever as compelling an experience as television for you?
5. Is the experience of watching a sports event on television much the same as reading about the event? If not, what are the

differences? Do these similarities give support to Winn, or do they provide contrary evidence?

SUGGESTIONS FOR WRITING

1. In a few well developed paragraphs, make a comparison between one of the following pairs. State the purpose of your comparison somewhere in your essay, and draw conclusions as you discuss the similarities or differences.

   a. playing baseball (or another sport) and watching baseball

   b. listening to a particular kind of music and dancing to it

   c. reading a book and seeing the movie made from it

   d. riding a bicycle and driving a car on a busy highway

2. Compare the experience of reading a newspaper or newsmagazine with that of reading a novel or a textbook. Draw conclusions from your comparison at the end of your discussion.

3. The following activities require similar skills. First discuss these similarities, and then discuss the different skills also required:

   a. parallel parking and backing into a garage

   b. pruning a hedge and pruning a tree

   c. learning to ride a bike and learning to drive

   d. painting a chair and painting a room

Jacob Bronowski

A *mathematician, scientist, and writer* (JACOB BRONOWSKI, 1908–1974) *taught at various universities and did scientific research at the Salk Institute of Biological Studies in San Diego. "We are a scientific civilization," he states in his book (and television series)* The Ascent of Man; *"that means, a civilization in which knowledge and its integrity are crucial. Science is only a Latin word for knowledge." Bronowski argues that we cannot afford to be ignorant or unconcerned about the values of science: "Knowledge is not a loose-leaf notebook of facts. Above all, it is a responsibility for the integrity of what we are, primarily of what we are as ethical creatures." Bronowski's comparison of the athlete and the gazelle, in* The

Ascent of Man, *illustrates how facts of nature can help us under-stand ourselves as human beings.*

THE ATHLETE AND THE GAZELLE

Every human action goes back in some part to our animal ori- 1
gins; we should be cold and lonely creatures if we were cut off
from that blood-stream of life. Nevertheless, it is right to ask
for a distinction: What are the physical gifts that man must
share with the animals, and what are the gifts that make him
different? Consider any example, the more straightforward the
better—say, the simple action of an athlete when running or
jumping. When he hears the gun, the starting response of the
runner is the same as the flight response of the gazelle. He
seems all animal in action. The heartbeat goes up; when he
sprints at top speed the heart is pumping five times as much
blood as normal, and ninety percent of it is for the muscles.
He needs twenty gallons of air a minute now to aerate his
blood with the oxygen that it must carry to the muscles.

The violent coursing of the blood and intake of air can be 2
made visible, for they show up as heat on infra-red films
which are sensitive to such radiation. (The blue or light zones
are hottest; the red or dark zones are cooler.) The flush that we
see and that the infra-red camera analyzes is a by-product that
signals the limit of muscular action. For the main chemical
action is to get energy for the muscles by burning sugar there;
but three-quarters of that is lost as heat. And there is another
limit, on the runner and the gazelle equally, which is more
severe. At this speed, the chemical burn-up in the muscles is
too fast to be complete. The waste products of incomplete
burning, chiefly lactic acid, now foul up the blood. This is what
causes fatigue, and blocks the muscle action until the blood
can be cleansed with fresh oxygen.

So far, there is nothing to distinguish the athlete from the 3
gazelle—all that, in one way or another, is the normal metabolism of an animal in flight. But there is a cardinal difference: the runner was not in flight. The shot that set him off was
the starter's pistol, and what he was experiencing, deliberately,

was not fear but exaltation. The runner is like a child at play; his actions are an adventure in freedom, and the only purpose of his breathless chemistry was to explore the limits of his own strength.

Naturally there are physical differences between man and the other animals, even between man and the apes. In the act of vaulting, the athlete grasps his pole, for example, with an exact grip that no ape can quite match. Yet such differences are secondary by comparison with the overriding difference, which is that the athlete is an adult whose behavior is not driven by his immediate environment, as animal actions are. In themselves, his actions make no practical sense at all; they are an exercise that is not directed to the present. The athlete's mind is fixed ahead of him, building up his skill; and he vaults in imagination into the future.

Poised for that leap, the pole-vaulter is a capsule of human abilities: the grasp of the hand, the arch of the foot, the muscles of the shoulder and pelvis—the pole itself, in which energy is stored and released like a bow firing an arrow. The radical character in that complex is the sense of foresight, that is, the ability to fix an objective ahead and rigorously hold his attention on it. The athlete's performance unfolds a continued plan; from one extreme to the other, it is the invention of the pole, the concentration of the mind at the moment before leaping, which give it the stamp of humanity.

VOCABULARY

paragraph 1: aerate
paragraph 2: infra-red, gazelle
paragraph 3: metabolism, cardinal
paragraph 5: capsule, pelvis

QUESTIONS

1. What similarities between humans and animals does Bronowski develop through his example?
2. What are the differences between the pole-vaulter and the gazelle and other animals discussed in these paragraphs?

3. In general, what are the physical traits that humans share with animals, and what gifts make humans different?

4. What other comparison between humans and animals could Bronowski have used to distinguish human from animal qualities?

SUGGESTIONS FOR WRITING

1. Compare and contrast one of the following pairs of activities, or a similar pair to arrive at a relative estimate of them and to make a point:

   a. softball and hardball

   b. football and touch football

   c. jogging and running

   d. tennis and badminton

   e. checkers and chess

2. Do the same for one of the following pairs, or a similar pair, of activities:

   a. studying for examinations in different subjects

   b. repairing or changing an automobile tire and a bicycle tire

   c. driving in a small town and in a large city

Edward T. Hall

EDWARD T. HALL, *professor of anthropology at Northwestern University from 1967 to 1977, has studied the cultures of many peoples of the world, especially that of the Pueblo Indians of the Southwest. His books include* The Silent Language *(1959) and* Beyond Culture *(1976). In* The Hidden Dimension *(1966) Hall states a major theme of his many writings on culture and the nonverbal forms of language: "Contrary to common belief, the many diverse groups that make up our country have proved to be surprisingly persistent in maintaining their separate identities. Superficially, these groups may all look alike and sound somewhat alike but beneath the surface there lie manifold unstated, unformulated differences in the structuring of time, space, materials, and relationships. It is these very things that, though they give significance to our lives,*

*so often result in the distortion of meaning regardless of good inten-
tions when peoples of different cultures interact." In this section Hall
combines contrast with other methods of analysis in discussing how
people perceive space in different ways. The word* proxemics *is a
term coined by Hall for "the interrelated observations and theories of
man's use of space as a specialized elaboration of culture."*

THE ENGLISH AND THE AMERICANS

It has been said that the English and the Americans are two
great people separated by one language. The differences for
which language gets blamed may not be due so much to
words as to communications on other levels beginning with
English intonation (which sounds affected to many Americans) and continuing to ego-linked ways of handling time,
space, and materials. If there ever were two cultures in which
differences of the proxemic details are marked it is in the educated (public school) English and the middle-class Americans. One of the basic reasons for this wide disparity is that in
the United States we use space as a way of classifying people
and activities, whereas in England it is the social system that
determines who you are. In the United States, your address is
an important cue to status (this applies not only to one's
home but to the business address as well). The Joneses from
Brooklyn and Miami are not as "in" as the Joneses from New-
port and Palm Beach. Greenwich and Cape Cod are worlds
apart from Newark and Miami. Businesses located on Madison and Park avenues have more tone than those on Seventh
and Eighth avenues. A corner office is more prestigious than
one next to the elevator or at the end of a long hall. The
Englishman, however, is born and brought up in a social system. He is still Lord—no matter where you find him, even if it
is behind the counter in a fishmonger's stall. In addition to
class distinctions, there are differences between the English
and ourselves in how space is allotted.

The middle-class American growing up in the United States
feels he has a right to have his own room, or at least part of a
room. My American subjects, when asked to draw an ideal

room or office, invariably drew it for themselves and no one else. When asked to draw their present room or office, they drew only their own part of a shared room and then drew a line down the middle. Both male and female subjects identified the kitchen and the master bedroom as belonging to the mother or the wife, whereas Father's territory was a study or a den, if one was available; otherwise, it was "the shop," "the basement," or sometimes only a workbench or the garage. American women who want to be alone can go to the bedroom and close the door. The closed door is the sign meaning "Do not disturb" or "I'm angry." An American is available if his door is open at home or at his office. He is expected not to shut himself off but to maintain himself in a state of constant readiness to answer the demands of others. Closed doors are for conferences, private conversations, and business, work that requires concentration, study, resting, sleeping, dressing, and sex.

The middle- and upper-class Englishman, on the other hand, is brought up in a nursery shared with brothers and sisters. The oldest occupies a room by himself which he vacates when he leaves for boarding school, possibly even at the age of nine or ten. The difference between a room of one's own and early conditioning to shared space, while seeming inconsequential, has an important effect on the Englishman's attitude toward his own space. He may never have a permanent "room of his own" and seldom expects one or feels he is entitled to one. Even Members of Parliament have no offices and often conduct their business on the terrace overlooking the Thames. As a consequence, the English are puzzled by the American need for a secure place in which to work, an office. Americans working in England may become annoyed if they are not provided with what they consider appropriate enclosed work space. In regard to the need for walls as a screen for the ego, this places the Americans somewhere between the Germans and the English.

The contrasting English and American patterns have some remarkable implications, particularly if we assume that man, like other animals, has a built-in need to shut himself off from others from time to time. An English student in one of my seminars typified what happens when hidden patterns clash. He was quite obviously experiencing strain in his relationships with Americans. Nothing seemed to go right and it was quite clear from his remarks that we did not know how to behave. An analysis of his complaints showed that a major source of irritation was that no American seemed to be able to pick up the subtle clues that there were times when he didn't want his thoughts intruded on. As he stated it, "I'm walking around the apartment and it seems that whenever I want to be alone my roommate starts talking to me. Pretty soon he's asking 'What's the matter?' and wants to know if I'm angry. By then I am angry and say something."

It took some time but finally we were able to identify most of the contrasting features of the American and British problems that were in conflict in this case. When the American wants to be alone he goes into a room and shuts the door—he depends on architectural features for screening. For an American to refuse to talk to someone else present in the same room, to give them the "silent treatment," is the ultimate form of rejection and a sure sign of great displeasure. The English, on the other hand, lacking rooms of their own since childhood, never developed the practice of using space as a refuge from others. They have in effect internalized a set of barriers, which they erect and which others are supposed to recognize. Therefore, the more the Englishman shuts himself off when he is with an American the more likely the American is to break in to assure himself that all is well. Tension lasts until the two get to know each other. The important point is that the spatial and architectural needs of each are not the same at all.

VOCABULARY

paragraph 1: intonation, ego-linked, fishmonger

QUESTIONS

1. What is Hall's thesis, and where does he first state it? Where does he restate it later in the essay?

2. How does he organize the contrast between the English and the Americans? Does he contrast the English and American patterns point by point or in blocks? Or does he mix these methods of organization?

3. How does he illustrate these patterns? Does he illustrate all of them?

4. Hall traces cause-and-effect relations through contrast of living patterns. What are the chief relations he traces?

5. How do the examples explain the phrase *internalized a set of barriers*, in the concluding paragraph? What does Hall mean by *screening*?

6. What use does he make of classification in the whole essay? On what basis does he divide the English and the Americans?

7. To what extent does Hall clarify a misunderstanding you have had with a roommate or friend?

SUGGESTIONS FOR WRITING

1. Discuss the extent to which your study habits fit the English or the American pattern. Use your analysis to comment on the accuracy of Hall's thesis.

2. Contrast two of your friends or relatives on the basis of their attitudes toward space and architecture or toward privacy. State the similarities before commenting on the differences. Notice that the differences may be slight ones, and even slight differences may be revealing of people.

Dorothy Noyes

DOROTHY NOYES *wrote a column, "Your Child," for the* Chicago Daily News *and other newspapers (1958–1961) and is the author of* Your Child: Step by Step Toward Maturity *(1963) and other books. From 1969 to 1972 she was Director of Environmental Studies at Southern Connecticut State College, in New Haven. In this essay, published in* Newsweek *on September 5, 1994, she makes comparisons between teenagers and seniors like herself.*

SENIOR-TEENER. A NEW HYBRID

Come next May, there's no denying the fact that I'll have 1
racked up 89 years as an inhabitant of planet earth. One
glance and you'd know I'm a Senior. The hair on my head is
white, and although my face is not overly lined, it's obvious
that I'm past 50 or 60 or even 70. While I work at standing
erect, my shoulders slouch a bit. And, despite regular swim
sessions and frequent brisk walks, I have difficulty hiding my
protruding belly. But the *inner* me, the *emotional* me, is so frequently a Teener. I feel much as I did 75 years ago: alone,
tremulous and fearful about my future.

Were Charles Darwin to arise from the dead, I'd say to him, 2
"There's a new subspecies abroad today, sir." And I'd tell him
about its evolution during the latter part of the 20th century
when humankind—particularly womankind—was living
longer and longer in an amazing state of physical health. But
I'd have to come clean as to the emotional downside: the
sense of queasiness that from time to time overtakes an otherwise reasonably fit body. For today I'm often jittery and "out
of it" as in long-ago days—no special boyfriend or agemates.
Three husbands have predeceased me, and my longtime
female intimates have also made their final exits.

At the start of my adolescence, my self-confidence was on 3
the low side. Because I was born a southpaw, conventional
wisdom forced me to learn to write with the "right" hand. Even
now, my friends' exhortations to "type, don't write" can be
amusing but far from uplifting. That I was clumsy was dinned
into me time and again. Well, I still feel clumsy.

Transplant shock also took its toll. When I was 12, and for 4
the next several years, we lived in cities in three different
states. This meant four high schools. I've never succeeded in
blocking out the memory of that sense of desolation when
I was 13½ and a sophomore in Montclair High School in New
Jersey—far from the kids I knew as a freshman in Evanston, Ill.
That unforgettable moment when I saw the spot on my
white skirt: I was a child no longer. How to blot it out? Where
to go?

This is somewhat comparable to one of Seniors' embar- 5
rassing problems: the need for protective garments to cope
with the unexpected lack of control over failing body parts.
While Senior and Teener are not *look*-alikes, they're so often
act-alikes.

Obviously, the female bodily changes of Teener and Senior 6
are not the same. Teener's route is onward and upward,
though it doesn't always seem so to her as she deplores some
of the external blemishes. For Senior it's mostly downhill,
obliged as she is to spend more and more time in body-repair
shops to compensate for eyes and ears and other organs that
malfunction. Our commonality lies in our need to face up to
the inevitable biologic changes with equanimity—to learn the
art of self-mastery, of peaceful acceptance of the inevitable
and of our own self-worth as the life cycle spirals on. Living
comfortably with one's own body with its limitations and
defects is no easy assignment.

One of our most difficult challenges comes from the out- 7
side world. It's another factor that makes our struggle to
mature so alike: coping with those numerous unsympathetic,
contemptuous and sometimes outright hostile others. Like
those folk who accuse Teeners of being too self-absorbed,
irresponsible, sex-driven, booze-drinking, "no good"; and for
those who look upon Seniors with much disdain, not as
national treasures.

Virtually from the first moment last spring when I was intro- 8
duced to the about-to-be-15-year-old stepdaughter of my
godson, I remembered how, long ago, I cherished the com-
panionship of an elderly spinster who paid special attention
to insecure young me. This probably prompted me to issue a
spur-of-the-moment invitation to Christine. She seemed
ecstatic at the thought of spending part of a holiday weekend
with me. All during the first day as we meandered through
Central Park and again at dinner and at the dance theater, I
was struck by her apparent maturity—fascinated as she was in
studying people's faces. "What do you suppose they're thinking about, Dorothy?" But this confidence—this absorption

with others—was not to last. Christine was pondering her trip home the next day: alone in a taxi and the crowd at Penn Station! She hated to bother me, but would I mind coming along as a pal, just in case . . . ? Of course I went. Her scary moment of panic came when she couldn't find the platform for the train's departure. (I experience comparable panicky self-doubt when I'm under pressure.)

In the early '60s, when Doubleday was about to publish my first book, there was great discussion as to the title of this parental "how to" guide. It was understandable that it should be called "Your Child," based as it was in part on my syndicated newspaper column with that title. The big question was: should we add "from birth to maturity"? Not *to* maturity, I insisted, but rather *toward* maturity. For who knows when maturity has been reached? And, besides, what kind of maturity are we thinking about?

For Teener, maturity means graduation from kid-dom—the search for personhood in her own right, the freedom to find her own worth and her own place. For Senior, maturity means greater acceptance of waning physical powers and the ability to continue to grow in understanding and, yes, in wisdom—to accept death as part of life. Neither Teener nor Senior can control biological maturity, but each can have much effect over psychological and philosophical maturity.

Many times, the Teener part of this hybrid is thrown by what she feels must be grasped to gain self-mastery and to appreciate what life is all about. So, too, the Senior is frequently nonplussed by how much more there is to discover about our universe. And time is running short—gotta crowd in as much as possible as fast as possible! Each of us must deal with continuing bodily changes and our reactions to them as well as with our changing relationships with our fellow earthlings. Both of us long for many of those Others to appreciate what seems to be the professional consensus that Teeners and Seniors both are almost *over*endowed with heartfelt compassion for all humankind.

VOCABULARY

paragraph 2: queasiness
paragraph 3: exhortations
paragraph 6: equanimity
paragraph 11: hybrid, consensus

QUESTIONS

1. What similarities does Noyes cite between Seniors and Teeners?
2. What differences does she also cite? Do the similarities outweigh the differences, or are both of equal importance to her thesis?
3. How does Noyes introduce her thesis? Where does she restate it?
4. Does Noyes develop her comparison and contrast in blocks or point by point?
5. Noyes leads from comments about herself to comments on people generally. What does she gain from organizing her essay in this way?

SUGGESTIONS FOR WRITING

1. Discuss a recent decision that affected your own "search for personhood." Explain how the decision arose and how you dealt with it.
2. Noyes compares adolescents and older people. Compare two other age groups—for example, 13- and 14-year-olds with older adolescents—citing similarities and differences. Use your comparison to develop a thesis of your own.

Richard Selzer

> For many years a surgeon and member of the faculty of the Yale School of Medicine, RICHARD SELZER *has written on medicine and the art of surgery in* Mortal Lessons (1976), Letters to a Young Doctor (1982), Confessions of a Knife (1986), *and*

Taking the World in for Repairs (1986). *He is also the author of collections of stories,* Rituals of Surgery (1974) *and* Imagine a Woman and Other Tales (1990). *In the following essay, published in* The New York Times Magazine *August 21, 1988, Selzer describes his two vocations of writing and medicine.*

THE PEN AND THE SCALPEL

I had been a general surgeon for 15 years when, at the age of 40, the psychic energy for writing inexplicably appeared. It was an appearance that was to knock over my life. For 15 years I had studied, practiced and taught surgery at the Yale School of Medicine, all the while enjoying the usefulness and *handsomeness* of the craft. For the next 16 years, until my recent retirement, I would practice both surgery and writing. But where to fit in the writing when all of my days and half of my nights were fully engaged? Certainly not evenings. In the evening, one visits with one's next-of-kin; in the evening one helps with homework; in the evening, if one is so inclined, one has a martini. Instead, I became the first adult in the state of Connecticut to go to bed in the evening. Having slept from 8:30 P.M. to 1 in the morning, I rose, went down to the kitchen, put on a pot of tea and wrote in longhand (a typewriter would disturb the household) until precisely 3 o'clock. Then it was back upstairs and to sleep until 6 in the morning, when I began the day's doctoring. Plenty of sleep, only divided by two hours, when I was alone with my pen, and all the light in the world gathered upon a sheet of paper. In this way, I wrote three collections of stories, essays and memoirs.

Time was when in the professions—medicine and law—to patronize the arts was respectable; to practice them was not. For a surgeon it was even more questionable. Who wants to know, after all, what a surgeon does in his spare time? When it became known how I was spending my wild nights, my colleagues at the hospital were distressed. "Come, come" they coaxed in (more or less) the words of the poet Richard Wilbur, "Forsake those roses of the mind, and tend the true, the moral flower." But because the subject of my writings was my work as a doctor, the two seemed inseparable. The one fertilized the other. Why, I wondered, doesn't every surgeon write? A doctor walks in and out of a dozen short stories a day. It is irresistible to write them down. When, at last, the time came to make a choice between my two passions, it had already been made for me. Listen:

In the operating room, the patient must be anesthetized in order that he feel no pain. The surgeon too must be "anesthetized" in order to remain at some distance from the event: when he cuts the patient, his own flesh must not bleed. It is this seeming lack of feeling that gives the surgeon the image of someone who is out of touch with his humanity, a person wanting only to cut, to perform. I assure you that it is the image only. A measure of insulation against the laying open of the bodies of his fellow human beings is necessary for the well-being of both patient and doctor. In surgery, if nowhere else, dispassion is an attribute. But the surgeon-writer is not anesthetized. He remains awake; sees everything; censors nothing. It is his dual role to open and repair the body of his patient and to report back to the waiting world in the keenest language he can find. By becoming a writer, I had stripped off the protective carapace. It was time to go. A surgeon can unmake himself; a writer cannot.

A Faustian bargain, you say? Perhaps, but, truth to tell, New Haven had begun to seem rather like the Beast With a Thousand Gallbladders. And where is it graven in stone that, once having been ordained, a surgeon must remain at the operating table until the scalpel slips from his lifeless fingers? Nor had I any wish to become like the old lion whose claws are long since blunt but not the desire to use them. Still, one does not walk away from the workbench of one's life with a cheery wave of the hand. In the beginning, I felt a strange sense of dislocation. As though I were standing near a river whose banks were flowing while the stream itself stood still. Only now, after two years, have I ceased to have attacks of longing for the labor that so satisfied and uplifted my spirit. Then, too, there was the risk that by withdrawing from the hospital, with its rich cargo of patients and those who tend them, I would be punished as a writer, suffer from impotence of the pen. A writer turns his back upon his native land at his own peril. Besides, to begin the life of a writer at the age of 56 is to toil under the very dart of death. As did another doctor-writer, John Keats, I too "have fears that I may cease to be before my pen has gleaned my teeming brain."

In medicine, there is a procedure called transillumination. 5 If, in a darkened room, a doctor holds a bright light against a hollow part of the body, he will see through the outer tissues to the structures within that cavity—arteries, veins, projecting shelves of bone. In such a ruby gloom he can distinguish among a hernia, a hydrocele of the scrotum and a tumor of the testicle. Or he can light up a sinus behind the brow. Unlike surgery, which opens the body to direct examination, transillumination gives an indirect vision, calling into play the simplest perceptions of the doctor. To write about a patient is like transillumination. You hold the lamp of language against his body and gaze through the covering layers at the truths within.

At first glance, it would appear that surgery and writing 6 have little in common, but I think that is not so. For one thing, they are both sub-celestial arts; as far as I know, the angels disdain to perform either one. In each of them you hold a slender instrument that leaves a trail wherever it is applied. In one, there is the shedding of blood; in the other it is ink that is spilled upon a page. In one, the scalpel is restrained; in the other, the pen is given rein. The surgeon sutures together the tissues of the body to make whole what is sick or injured; the writer sews words into sentences to fashion a new version of human experience. A surgical operation is rather like a short story. You make the incision, rummage around inside for a bit, then stitch up. It has a beginning, a middle and an end. If I were to choose a medical specialist to write a novel, it would be a psychiatrist. They tend to go on and on. And on.

Despite that I did not begin to write until the middle of my 7 life, I think I must always have been a writer. Like my father who was a general practitioner during the Depression in Troy, N.Y., and who wrote a novel. It was all about a prostitute with a heart of gold (her name was Goldie!) and the doctor who first saves her life, then falls in love with her. Mother read it and told him: "Keep it away from the children."

Father's office was on the ground floor of an old brown- 8 stone, and we lived upstairs. At night, after office hours, my brother Billy and I (we were 10 and 9 years old) would sneak downstairs to Father's darkened consultation room and there, shamefaced, by the light of a candle stub, we would take down from the shelves his medical textbooks. Our favorite was "The Textbook of Obstetrics and Gynecology."

It was there that I first became aware of the rich language of 9 medicine. Some of the best words began with the letter C. *Carcinoma*, I read, and thought it was that aria from "Rigoletto" that mother used to sing while she washed and dried the dishes. *Cerebellum.* I said the word aloud, letting it drip off the end of my tongue like melted chocolate. And I read *choledochojejunostomy*, which I later was to learn was the name of an operation. All those syllables marching off in my mind to that terminal *y*! If that was the way surgeons talked, I thought, I would be one of them, and live forever in a state of mellifluous rapture. I do not use these words in my writing, but I do try to use the language that evokes the sounds of the body—the *lub-dup*, *lub-dup* of the garrulous heart, the gasp and wheeze of hard breathing, all the murmur and splash of anatomy and physiology. And I have tried to make use of the poetic potential in scientific language. Here, from my diary, this specimen:

How gentle the countryside near Troy, with much farming 10 everywhere. Farming gives a sense of health to the land. It is replenishing to watch at dusk as a herd of cattle flows like a giant amoeba toward the barn. First one cow advances. She pauses. Another pseudopodium is thrust ahead, pulling the others behind it until all of the cytoplasm, trailing milk, is inside the barn. All along the banks of the Hudson River, oak, elm and locust trees have grown very tall. The bark of the locust is thrown into deep folds coated with lichen and moss.

So old are these trees that, without the least wind, one will drop off a quite large branch as if to shed a part of its burden. This letting-fall doesn't seem to do the tree any harm. It is more an anatomical relinquishment of a part so that the whole might remain healthy. Much as a diabetic will accept amputation of a gangrenous toe in order that he might once again walk on his foot. How clever of these locust trees to require no surgeon for their trimmage, only their own corporeal wisdom.

VOCABULARY

paragraph 1: psychic, inexplicably
paragraph 2: patronize
paragraph 3: insulation, dispassion, attribute, carapace
paragraph 4: Faustian, ordained, blunt, dislocation
paragraph 5: hernia
paragraph 6: sub-celestial, suture
paragraph 8: obstetrics, gynecology
paragraph 9: mellifluous, evoke, garrulous, specimen
paragraph 10: replenishing, amoeba, pseudopodium, cytoplasm, relinquishment, gangrenous, corporeal

QUESTIONS

1. How did his work as a surgeon prepare Selzer to become a writer?
2. Does Selzer compare surgery and writing in blocks or point by point? How many similarities and differences does Selzer discuss?
3. In what sense of the word must the surgeon be "anesthetized"? Why must the surgeon-writer not be anesthetized?
4. Is the reader referring to surgery or writing in asking about a "Faustian bargain" in paragraph 4?
5. What is transillumination, and how is writing similar to it? Why does Selzer introduce this comparison in paragraph 5?
6. How did childhood experiences prepare Selzer to become a writer? Why does Selzer conclude the essay with these experiences, instead of opening the essay with them?
7. What does the sample from Selzer's diary show?

SUGGESTIONS FOR WRITING

1. Discuss experiences in your own childhood or adolescence that generated interest in a type of work or career. Discuss later decisions and acts that resulted from these experiences.

2. Selzer discusses two different occupations, surgery and writing, each of which nurtured the other. Discuss two interests or occupations with which you have had a similar experience. In the course of your discussion, cite similarities as well as differences, developing your comparison in blocks or point by point.

12

Analogy

Illustrative *analogy* is a special kind of example, a comparison, usually point by point, between two quite different things or activities for the purpose of explanation—a child growing like a tender plant and needing sun, water, and a receptive soil as well as proper care from a skilled gardener. But there are differences also, and if there is danger of the analogy being carried too far (children are not so tender that they need as much protection as plants from the hazards of living), the writer may state these differences to limit the inferences readers may draw. The writer has chosen the analogy for the sake of vivid illustration and nothing more. We will see later that analogy is often used in argument: children *should* be fully protected from various hazards because they are tender plants. The argument will stand or fall depending on how convinced we are of the similarities and of the unimportance of the differences.

Analogy is often used in explanations of scientific ideas. One of the most famous is Fred Hoyle's analogy between the moving apart of the galaxies in the universe and an expanding raisin cake:

> Suppose the cake swells uniformly as it cooks, but the raisins themselves remain of the same size. Let each raisin represent a cluster of galaxies, and imagine yourself inside one of them. As the cake swells, you will observe that all the other raisins move away from you. Moreover, the farther away the raisin, the faster it will seem to move. When the cake has swollen to twice its initial dimensions, the distance between all the raisins will have doubled itself—two raisins that were initially an inch apart will now be two inches apart; two raisins that were a foot apart will have moved two feet apart. Since the entire action takes place within the same time interval, obviously the more distant raisins must move apart faster than those close at hand. So it happens with the clusters of galaxies.

And Hoyle draws a further conclusion from his analogy:

> No matter which raisin you happen to be inside, the others will always move away from you. Hence the fact that we observe all the

other galaxies to be moving away from us does not mean that we are situated at the center of the universe. Indeed, it seems certain that the universe has no center. A cake may be said to have a center only because it has a boundary. We must imagine the cake to extend outward without any boundary, an infinite cake, so to speak, which means that however much cake we care to consider there is always more. ("When Time Began")

Hoyle points out the limits of the analogy in these final sentences. One advantage of the raisin analogy is the disparity of size between a raisin and a galaxy—a system of sometimes billions of stars occupying an enormous amount of space. The disparity in size provides a relative estimate of size in the universe.

Loren Eiseley

LOREN EISELEY (1907–1977) *was Benjamin Franklin Professor of Anthropology at the University of Pennsylvania. His many books on human origins and society and other topics include* The Immense Journey (1957), The Firmament of Time (1960), The Unexpected Universe (1969), The Night Country (1971), *and* The Innocent Assassins (1973). *In his autobiography,* All the Strange Hours (1975), *Eiseley describes his Nebraska boyhood and later experiences that shaped him as an anthropologist and writer. In the following excerpt, he uses an extended analogy and a childhood experience to comment on the resources the personal essayist draws upon.*

WHAT MAKES A WRITER

In all the questioning about what makes a writer, and especially perhaps the personal essayist, I have seen little reference to this fact; namely, that the brain has become a kind of unseen artist's loft. There are pictures that hang askew, pictures with outlines barely chalked in, pictures torn, pictures the artist has striven unsuccessfully to erase, pictures that only emerge and glow in a certain light. They have all been teleported, stolen, as it were, out of time. They represent no longer the sequential flow of ordinary memory. They can be pulled about on easels, examined within the mind itself. The act is not one of total recall like that of the professional mnemonist. Rather it is the use of things extracted from their context in such a way that they have become the unique possession of a single life. The writer sees back to these transports alone, bare, perhaps few in number, but endowed with a symbolic life. He cannot obliterate them. He can only drag them about, magnify or reduce them as his artistic sense dictates, or juxtapose them in order to enhance a pattern. One thing he cannot do. He cannot destroy what will not be destroyed; he cannot determine in advance what will enter his mind.

By way of example, I cannot explain why, out of many forgotten childhood episodes, my mind should retain as bright as yesterday the peculiar actions of a redheaded woodpecker. I must have been about six years old, and in the alley behind our house I had found the bird lying beneath a telephone pole. Looking back, I can only assume that he had received in some manner a stunning but not fatal shock of electricity. Coming upon him, seemingly dead but uninjured, I had carried him back to our porch and stretched him out to admire his color.

In a few moments, much to my surprise, he twitched and jerked upright. Then in a series of quick hops he reached the corner of the house and began to ascend in true woodpecker fashion—a hitch of the grasping feet, the bracing of the tail, and then, wonder of wonders, the knock, knock, knock, of the questing beak against our house. He was taking up life where it had momentarily left him, somewhere on the telephone pole. When he reached the top of the porch he flew away.

So there the picture lies. Even the coarse-grained wood of the porch comes back to me. If anyone were to ask me what else happened in that spring of 1913 I would stare blindly and be unable to answer with surety. But, as I have remarked, somewhere amidst the obscure lumber loft of my head that persistent hammering still recurs. Did it stay because it was my first glimpse of unconsciousness, resurrection, and time lapse presented in bright color? I do not know. I have never

chanced to meet another adult who has a childhood woodpecker almost audibly rapping in his skull.

VOCABULARY

paragraph 1: teleported, mnemonist, transports, obliterate,
juxtapose, enhance
paragraph 4: obscure, resurrection

QUESTIONS

1. What are the similarities between the brain of the writer and the
   "artist's unseen loft"?
2. Would the analogy be more or less exact if Eiseley had compared
   the writer's mind to the basement of the artist's house?
3. To what extent could a diary or journal serve as another analogy
   for the special qualities Eiseley is illustrating? Are the differences significant enough to weaken the analogy?
4. What idea is Eiseley illustrating in paragraphs 2–4?

SUGGESTION FOR WRITING

Use an analogy to explain the sensation of being alone in a car
in heavy traffic or a storm or to explain a similar experience that
requires comparison. At some point in your explanation, comment on the differences between the things you are comparing.

Loren Eiseley

LOREN EISELEY *had the gift of explaining highly complex ideas to
the general reader. In this section from* The Invisible Pyramid
(1972), *he uses brief, revealing analogies to help the reader understand a series of ideas related to space travel.*

THE COSMIC PRISON

This, then, is the secret nature of the universe over which the
ebullient senator so recklessly proclaimed our absolute mastery. Time in that universe is in excess of ten billion years. It

recedes backward into a narrowing funnel where, at some inconceivable point of concentration, the monobloc containing all the matter that composes the galaxies exploded in the one gigantic instant of creation.

Along with that explosion space itself is rushing outward. Stars and the great island galaxies in which they cluster are more numerous than the blades of grass upon a plain. To speak of man as "mastering" such a cosmos is about the equivalent of installing a grasshopper as Secretary General of the United Nations. Worse, in fact, for no matter what system of propulsion man may invent in the future, the galaxies on the outer rim of visibility are fleeing faster than he can approach them. Moreover, the light that he is receiving from them left its source in the early history of the planet earth. There is no possible way of even establishing their present existence. As the British astronomer Sir Bernard Lovell has so appropriately remarked, "At the limit of present-day observations our information is a few billion years out of date." 2

Light travels at a little over one hundred and eighty-six thousand miles a second, far beyond the conceivable speed of any spaceship devised by man, yet it takes light something like one hundred thousand years just to travel across the star field of our own galaxy, the Milky Way. It has been estimated that to reach the nearest star to our own, four light-years away, would require, at the present speed of our spaceships, a time equivalent to more than the whole of written history, indeed one hundred thousand earthly years would be a closer estimate—a time as long, perhaps, as the whole existence of *Homo sapiens* upon earth. And the return, needless to state, would consume just as long a period. 3

Even if our present rocket speeds were stepped up by a factor of one hundred, human generations would pass on the voyage. An unmanned probe into the nearer galactic realms would be gone so long that its intended mission, in fact the country which sent it forth, might both have vanished into the mists of history before its messages began to be received. All this, be it noted, does not begin to involve us in those intergalactic 4 distances across which a radio message from a cruising space-ship might take hundreds of years to be received and a wait of other hundreds before a reply would filter back.

We are, in other words, truly in the position of the blood cell exploring our body. We are limited in time, by analogy a miniature replica of the cosmos, since we too individually ascend from a primordial atom, exist, and grow in space, only to fall back in dissolution. We cannot, in terms of the time dimension as we presently know it, either travel or survive the interstellar distances.

Two years ago I chanced to wander with a group of visiting scholars into a small planetarium in a nearby city. In the dark in a remote back seat, I grew tired and fell asleep while a lecture was progressing. My eyes had closed upon a present-day starry night as represented in the northern latitudes. After what seemed in my uneasy slumber the passage of a long period of time, I started awake in the dark, my eyes fixed in amazement upon the star vault overhead. All was quiet in the neighboring highbacked seats. I could see no one. Suddenly I seemed adrift under a vast and unfamiliar sky. Constellations with which I was familiar had shifted, grown minute, or vanished. I rubbed my eyes. This was not the universe in which I had fallen asleep. It seemed more still, more remote, more enormous, and inconceivably more solitary. A queer sense of panic struck me, as though I had been transported out of time.

Only after some attempt to orient myself by a diminishing pole star did the answer come to me by murmurs from without. I was not the last man on the planet, far in the dying future. My companions had arisen and left, while the lecturer had terminated his address by setting the planetarium lights forward to show the conformation of the heavens as they might exist in the remote future of the expanding universe. Distances had lengthened. All was poised, chill, and alone.

I sat for a moment experiencing the sensation all the more intensely because of the slumber which left me feeling as though ages had elapsed. The sky gave little sign of movement. It seemed drifting in a slow indeterminate swirl, as though the forces of expansion were equaled at last by some monstrous tug of gravity at the heart of things. In this remote night sky of the far future I felt myself waiting upon the inevitable, the great drama and surrender of the inward fall, the heart contraction of the cosmos.

I was still sitting when, like the slightest leaf movement   9
on a flooding stream, I saw the first faint galaxy of a billion suns race like a silverfish across the night and vanish. It was enough: the fall was equal to the flash of creation. I had sensed it waiting there under the star vault of the planetarium. Now it was cascading like a torrent through the ages in my head. I had experienced, by chance, the farthest reach of the star prison. I had similarly lived to see the beginning descent into the maelstrom.

VOCABULARY

paragraph 1: ebullient, monobloc
paragraph 4: intergalactic
paragraph 5: primordial, interstellar
paragraph 7: orient
paragraph 9: maelstrom

QUESTIONS

1. In paragraph 2 Eiseley depends on the simple comparison or analogy of blades of grass to suggest how many stars and galaxies exist. What other such analogies does he use in paragraphs 1 and 9 for explanation?

2. What are the points of similarity in the analogy in paragraph 5? Does the difference in size between humankind and the cosmos increase the effectiveness of the analogy or diminish it?

3. What point is Eiseley making through the experience described in paragraphs 6–9? How is the experience analogous to that of the space traveler as well as to the human being on Earth?

4. Eiseley is arguing against the view that humans have attained or will attain "absolute mastery" over the universe. Is he also implying that exploration of far space is a useless enterprise, given the enormous space between stars and galaxies?

SUGGESTION FOR WRITING

Eiseley states in a later section of *The Invisible Pyramid* that "there are other confinements . . . than that imposed by the enormous distances of the cosmos." Our senses, he suggests, confine us through their limitations. Write an essay developing this point through your own experiences. Focus on one or two of the senses.

Michio Kaku

> MICHIO KAKU, *Professor of Theoretical Physics at the City College of the City University of New York, is the author of several books on quantum physics and the theory of higher dimensional space, and (with Jennifer Trainer)* Beyond Einstein *(1987). In this section from* Hyperspace *(1994), Kaku uses an illustrative analogy to explain how his interest in higher dimensional space began. He then describes how interest in the ideas of Albert Einstein led to scientific experiments of his own.*

THE EDUCATION OF A PHYSICIST

Two incidents from my childhood greatly enriched my understanding of the world and sent me on a course to become a theoretical physicist.

I remember that my parents would sometimes take me to visit the famous Japanese Tea Garden in San Francisco. One of my happiest childhood memories is of crouching next to the pond, mesmerized by the brilliantly colored carp swimming slowly beneath the water lilies.

In these quiet moments, I felt free to let my imagination wander; I would ask myself silly questions that only a child might ask, such as how the carp in that pond would view the world around them. I thought, What a strange world theirs must be!

Living their entire lives in the shallow pond, the carp would believe that their "universe" consisted of the murky water and the lilies. Spending most of their time foraging on the bottom of the pond, they would be only dimly aware that an alien world could exist above the surface. The nature of my world was beyond their comprehension. I was intrigued that I could sit only a few inches from the carp, yet be separated from them by an immense chasm. The carp and I spent our lives in two distinct universes, never entering each other's world, yet were separated by only the thinnest barrier, the water's surface.

I once imagined that there may be carp "scientists" living 5 among the fish. They would, I thought, scoff at any fish who proposed that a parallel world could exist just above the lilies. To a carp "scientist," the only things that were real were what the fish could see or touch. The pond was everything. An unseen world beyond the pond made no scientific sense.

Once I was caught in a rainstorm. I noticed that the pond's 6 surface was bombarded by thousands of tiny raindrops. The pond's surface became turbulent, and the water lilies were being pushed in all directions by water waves. Taking shelter from the wind and the rain, I wondered how all this appeared to the carp. To them, the water lilies would appear to be moving around by themselves, without anything pushing them. Since the water they lived in would appear invisible, much like the air and space around us, they would be baffled that the water lilies could move around by themselves.

Their "scientists," I imagined, would concoct a clever inven- 7 tion called a "force" in order to hide their ignorance. Unable to comprehend that there could be waves on the unseen surface, they would conclude that lilies could move without being touched because a mysterious invisible entity called a force acted between them. They might give this illusion impressive, lofty names (such as action-at-a-distance, or the ability of the lilies to move without anything touching them).

Once I imagined what would happen if I reached down and 8 lifted one of the carp "scientists" out of the pond. Before I threw him back into the water, he might wiggle furiously as I examined him. I wondered how this would appear to the rest of the carp. To them, it would be a truly unsettling event. They would first notice that one of their "scientists" had disappeared from their universe. Simply vanished, without leaving a trace. Wherever they would look, there would be no evidence of the missing carp in their universe. Then, seconds later, when I threw him back into the pond, the "scientist" would abruptly reappear out of nowhere. To the other carp, it would appear that a miracle had happened.

After collecting his wits, the "scientist" would tell a truly 9 amazing story. "Without warning," he would say, "I was some- how lifted out of the universe (the pond) and hurled into a mysterious nether world, with blinding lights and strangely shaped objects that I had never seen before. The strangest of all was the creature who held me prisoner, who did not re- semble a fish in the slightest. I was shocked to see that it had no fins whatsoever, but nevertheless could move without them. It struck me that the familiar laws of nature no longer applied in this nether world. Then, just as suddenly, I found myself thrown back into our universe." (This story, of course, of a journey beyond the universe would be so fantastic that most of the carp would dismiss it as utter poppycock.)

I often think that we are like the carp swimming contentedly 10 in that pond. We live out our lives in our own "pond," confi- dent that our universe consists of only those things we can see or touch. Like the carp, our universe consists of only the familiar and the visible. We smugly refuse to admit that parallel universes or dimensions can exist next to ours, just beyond our grasp. If our scientists invent concepts like forces, it is only because they cannot visualize the invisible vibrations that fill the empty space around us. Some scientists sneer at the mention of higher dimensions because they cannot be conveniently measured in the laboratory.

Ever since that time, I have been fascinated by the possibil- 11 ity of other dimensions. Like most children, I devoured adven- ture stories in which time travelers entered other dimensions and explored unseen parallel universes, where the unusual laws of physics could be conveniently suspended. I grew up wondering if ships that wandered into the Bermuda Triangle mysteriously vanished into a hole in space; I marveled at Isaac

Asimov's Foundation Series, in which the discovery of hyper-space travel led to the rise of a Galactic Empire.

A second incident from my childhood also made a deep, 12 lasting impression on me. When I was 8 years old, I heard a story that would stay with me for the rest of my life. I remember my schoolteachers telling the class about a great scientist who had just died. They talked about him with great reverence, calling him one of the greatest scientists in all history. They said that very few people could understand his ideas, but that his discoveries changed the entire world and everything around us. I didn't understand much of what they were trying to tell us, but what most intrigued me about this man was that he died before he could complete his greatest discovery. They said he spent years on this theory, but he died with his unfinished papers still sitting on his desk.

I was fascinated by the story. To a child, this was a great 13 mystery. What was his unfinished work? What was in those papers on his desk? What problem could possibly be so difficult and so important that such a great scientist would dedicate years of his life to its pursuit? Curious, I decided to learn all I could about Albert Einstein and his unfinished theory. I still have warm memories of spending many quiet hours reading every book I could find about this great man and his theories. When I exhausted the books in our local library, I began to scour libraries and bookstores across the city, eagerly searching for more clues. I soon learned that this story was far more exciting than any murder mystery and more important than anything I could ever imagine. I decided that I would try to get to the root of this mystery, even if I had to become a theoretical physicist to do it.

I soon learned that the unfinished papers on Einstein's 14 desk were an attempt to construct what he called the unified field theory, a theory that could explain all the laws of nature, from the tiniest atom to the largest galaxy. However, being a child, I didn't understand that perhaps there was a link between the carp swimming in the Tea Garden and the unfinished papers lying on Einstein's desk. I didn't understand that higher dimensions might be the key to solving the unified field theory.

Later, in high school, I exhausted most of the local libraries and often visited the Stanford University physics library. There, I came across the fact that Einstein's work made possible a new substance called antimatter, which would act like ordinary matter but would annihilate upon contact with matter in a burst of energy. I also read that scientists had built large machines, or "atom smashers," that could produce microscopic quantities of this exotic substance in the laboratory. 15

One advantage of youth is that it is undaunted by worldly constraints that would ordinarily seem insurmountable to most adults. Not appreciating the obstacles involved, I set out to build my own atom smasher. I studied the scientific literature until I was convinced that I could build what was called a betatron, which could boost electrons to millions of electron volts. (A million electron volts is the energy attained by electrons accelerated by a field of a million volts.) 16

First, I purchased a small quantity of sodium-22, which is radioactive and naturally emits positrons (the antimatter counterpart of electrons). Then I built what is called a cloud chamber, which makes visible the tracks left by subatomic particles. I was able to take hundreds of beautiful photographs of the tracks left behind by antimatter. Next, I scavenged around large electronic warehouses in the area, assembled the necessary hardware, including hundreds of pounds of scrap transformer steel, and built a 2.3-million-electron-volt betatron in my garage that would be powerful enough to produce a beam of antielectrons. To construct the monstrous magnets necessary for the betatron, I convinced my parents to help me wind 22 miles of copper wire on the high-school football field. We spent Christmas vacation on the 50-yard line, winding and assembling the massive coils that would bend the paths of the high-energy electrons. 17

When finally constructed, the 300-pound, 6-kilowatt betatron consumed every ounce of energy my house produced. When I turned it on, I would usually blow every fuse, and the 18 house would suddenly become dark. With the house plunged periodically into darkness, my mother would often shake her head. (I imagined that she probably wondered why couldn't have a child who played baseball or basketball, instead of building these huge electrical machines in the garage.) I was gratified that the machine successfully produced a magnetic field 20,000 times more powerful than the earth's magnetic field, which is necessary to accelerate a beam of electrons.

VOCABULARY

paragraph 2: mesmerized
paragraph 9: nether
paragraph 15: antimatter
paragraph 16: electron volt
paragraph 17: cloud chamber

QUESTIONS

1. In the analogy developed in paragraphs 5–10, to whom does Kaku compare the carp in the Tea Garden pond, and to whom does he compare the carp scientists? To what does he compare the rainstorm that disturbs the pond?

2. In stating that the carp scientist disappears from the pond, then suddenly reappears, is Kaku suggesting that something similar can occur in our world? Or is what happens to the scientist merely fanciful?

3. What is the point of the analogy?

4. What is the link between the unfinished papers on Einstein's desk and the carp in the pond?

5. Is Kaku making a general point, explicitly or implicitly, in describing how his interest in physics developed and what experiments he performed while in high school?

SUGGESTIONS FOR WRITING

1. Describe how your interest in a particular science or art developed. Be specific in describing personal experiences.

2. Develop an analogy that you might use to explain to a child why the sun rises and sets, or to explain a similar phenomenon.

13

Process

A process is a series of connected actions, each developing from the preceding and leading to a result of some kind: a product, an effect, even a decision. Mechanical processes are probably the kind we deal with most, like the first example in this section—the process of cooking over an outdoor fire. A mechanical process is one that we create. By contrast, a natural process such as Bronowski describes (pp. 196–199) in his description of the athlete is one we may initiate but do not create:

> He seems all animal in action. The heartbeat goes up, when he sprints at top speed the heart is pumping five times as much blood as normal, and ninety per cent of it is for the muscles. ("The Athlete and the Gazelle")

Both mechanical and natural processes are repeatable. A particular historical process—the events that led to the Great Depression of the 1930s—is not, though the general circumstances that lead to economic depression may repeat themselves at another time.

Though we are committed in describing a process to present the steps chronologically—in the order they occur—we may interrupt the account to discuss its implications or details. In describing a complex process, we need to distinguish the main stages and steps and procedures contained in each. Process and causal analysis, discussed in the next section, are closely related and often combined.

Jearl Walker

JEARL WALKER, *Professor of Physics at Cleveland State University, is the author of* The Flying Circus of Physics (1977) *and* Roundabout: The Physics of Rotation in the Everyday World (1985). *In this excerpt from an article on outdoor cooking*

227

in the August 1985 issue of Scientific American, Walker *explains the physical basis of various mechanical cooking processes. Proceeding step by step, he allows his readers to visualize each of the processes. In the course of his explanation, he describes the necessary implements.*

OUTDOOR COOKING

Outdoor cooking can be a pleasant part of camping or a key to   1
survival in an emergency. It can also provide a study in thermal physics: how heat can be transferred from a heat source to food. This month I analyze several ways of cooking food with flames, coals or charcoal briquettes. The techniques require little or no equipment.

A few fundamental concepts of thermal physics underlie all   2
cooking procedures. One concept involves what is meant by heat and temperature. The atoms and molecules of a substance move randomly at any temperature above absolute zero. In a solid the motion consists in rotation and vibration. In a gas or a liquid the phenomenon also includes the random motion of atoms and molecules that are traveling in straight lines, colliding and then again traveling in straight lines.

When a substance is heated, the heat represents the addi-   3
tional energy imparted to the random motion. Temperature is a measure of the amount of energy in the random motion. Thus when the substance is heated, its temperature increases and the substance is said to be hotter. The heat of cooking increases the energy of the random motion of the atoms and molecules in the food, and the food thereupon cooks by undergoing certain chemical and physical changes.

Conduction, convection and radiation are the three primary   4
ways of transferring heat energy. In conduction the heat is conveyed through some intermediate material such as a metal pan or foil by means of atomic collisions. As the outside surface of the metal warms, the energy in the random motion of the atoms there increases. They collide with atoms somewhat deeper in the metal, giving those atoms some of the kinetic energy derived from the heat source. Eventually atoms on the

inside surface receive the energy and collide with atoms on the surface of the food, heating the food. Conduction continues for as long as the temperature of the heat source is above the temperature of the food.

Convection involves the ascent of a heated fluid, either air 5 or a liquid. Heat increases the energy in the random motion of the fluid and decreases the density of the fluid. The surrounding cooler and denser fluid then pushes the heated fluid upward. As the hot fluid passes the food, the atoms and molecules in the fluid collide with those on the surface of the food and transfer energy to them.

Radiation involves the emission and absorption of electro- 6 magnetic waves. In cooking the source is light. The surface of a heat source such as burning coal emits light in the infrared and visible parts of the electromagnetic spectrum. Since light has energy, this emission is a radiation of energy. When the light is absorbed by atoms and molecules on the surface of the food, the energy of their random motion increases, as does the temperature of the surface. Heating by radiation therefore requires that the food absorb some of the light (primarily the infrared) emitted by the heat source.

Many campfire-cooking techniques draw on more than one 7 of these primary means of transferring heat. For example, a fire might heat a metal pan by both convection of hot air and radiation of light. As the metal warms, energy is conducted through it to the food. As the surface of the food then heats up, conduction brings the heat into the food.

One of the easiest ways to cook food such as meat is to 8 spear it with a stick or wrap it around the stick and then suspend it over the fire or coals. The food is heated by the convection of rising hot air and by the radiation from the heated surfaces of the wood and from the hot regions in the flame. You can save work by propping the stick over the fire or suspending it across the fire by means of two forked sticks driven into the ground on opposite sides of the campfire.

A large piece of meat suspended over the fire must be 9 turned frequently, because only the side toward the fire gets the effect of the rising hot air and the radiation. The rig known as a dingle fan, probably from the logging-camp shed called a dingle, is helpful in this task. To make the apparatus attach a short chain to the upper end of a stick that is angled upward over the perimeter of the campfire. Suspend the meat from the chain by a string attached to a hook in one end of the meat. Tie a short stick to the string. One end of the stick holds a fan made of wire or branches wrapped in aluminum foil or leaves. To the other end attach a small rock to serve as a counterweight to the fan. Orient the plane of the fan some-what off the vertical and arrange the entire assembly so that the fan is in the hot air rising from the campfire. The meat is not in that convection current but is exposed to the radiation from the fire.

The rising hot air pushes against the underside of the fan. 10
The force moves the fan to one side, twisting the chain and rotating the meat. Once the fan is out of the convection cur-rent the chain untwists, rotating the meat in the opposite direction. It overshoots the original position, again twisting the chain. The cycle continues indefinitely, exposing about half of the meat to the radiation. After a while invert the roast and hang it from a hook on the other end to expose the other half of the meat to the radiation.

To fry food you can make a stove from an empty No. 10 can. 11
Remove one end plate of the can and cut a flap at the open end. Bend the flap outward. Push the loose end plate into the can and against the other end plate. With a can opener (the kind that punches triangular holes) or a knife, cut flaps in the can in several places near the closed end. Push the flaps into the can and against the loose end plate to hold it near the fixed end one. Place the open end of the can over a heat source. The upper end plate serves as a surface on which eggs, bacon and other items can be fried.

The can functions as a chimney because cool air is sucked 12
in through the open flap at the bottom to replace the hot air rising to the top and out through the holes there. The strong

flow of air through the can fans the fire and keeps it burning briskly.

You could make the stove without the loose end plate held 13 near the top. That plate, however, helps to produce a nearly uniform temperature over the entire cooking surface. Without this plate the part of that surface directly above the heat source would be hotter than the rest of the surface because it receives more radiation from the source. The loose plate is intended to heat the small layer of air above it, transferring heat to the cooking surface evenly by the conduction and convection through the air.

A popular heat source for the stove is a "buddy burner," a 14 small can filled with corrugated cardboard over which hot paraffin has been poured. When the can is brought out for cooking, the paraffin is solid. A match melts and vaporizes some of it, and thereafter the vapor burns. The flame melts more paraffin, which is drawn to the top of the cardboard, where it vaporizes and burns. The cardboard also burns, but slowly, like the wick of a candle. A damper can be placed over part of the burner to slow things down if the stove gets too hot. Make the damper by folding the lid from the can over a doubled piece of wire.

VOCABULARY

paragraph 3: atoms, molecule
paragraph 4: kinetic energy
paragraph 5: ascent, density
paragraph 6: infrared spectrum, electromagnetic spectrum
paragraph 9: vertical
paragraph 10: paraffin

QUESTIONS

1. What are the differences between conduction, convection, and radiation? How do the three sometimes work together in the process described in paragraph 7?

2. In the process described in paragraphs 8–10, what aspects does Walker describe in most detail? How do his earlier definitions help him in explaining the process?

3. What devices used in the same process does Walker describe? Does he give a full description of each device, or does he describe only those parts needed in cooking?

4. What devices used in frying food does Walker describe in paragraphs 11–14? How detailed is his description of each device?

5. Is Walker writing to readers unfamiliar with laws of physics and cooking techniques? Or does he assume that his readers vary in knowledge and experience?

SUGGESTION FOR WRITING

Describe one of the following processes or another that you have performed often enough to explain thoroughly. Explain your terms and steps of the process in nontechnical language that readers who are unfamiliar with it will understand:

a. seeding and tending a lawn or garden

b. growing tomatoes or another fruit or vegetable

c. cutting down a dead tree

d. carving a turkey

e. mastering a difficult technique in learning to play a musical instrument or to draw or paint

f. repairing a small motor or other equipment

John Richards

Trained as an engineer, the English nature writer JOHN RICHARDS *brings a keen eye to his description of the workings of nature—in the excerpt reprinted here from* The Hidden Country *(1973), the intricate natural process of spinning orb-webs. Richards is describing the web-spinning of the Diadem spider, a brown spider with a large white cross on its abdomen. Richards states: "These web-building spiders have eight eyes, yet in spite of this their sight is not good. Unlike the spiders which hunt and catch their prey by watching for them or by chasing, they do not need to see well; what is much more important is their ability to interpret the meaning of the various tensions in the threads of their webs." The drawing Richards refers to has been omitted.*

HOW THE SPIDER SPINS ITS WEB

I have shown the garden spider in the center of its web, but you will rarely find one there during the daytime. This would be a dangerous situation for the spider when birds are about, and it would be unlikely to stay there for long. Instead, it spends the day in a lair by the side of the web, coming out to the center only in the evening, and staying there for the night, unless otherwise engaged.

The orb-webs, as they are called, from their circular shape, are masterpieces of construction, and yet are relatively short-lived. They are usually built in the late evening, and may in some cases be virtually demolished and rebuilt each night. The webs vary considerably in size, and the one which I have drawn, for the sake of convenience, is one of the smallest.

The spider constructs these webs using two different kinds of silk, which it produces from spinnerets at the end of the abdomen. A more or less horizontal thread is needed as a start for the web, and the spider produces this in one of several ways, depending on the circumstances.

If the wind direction is right, it may be enough to stand on one point and to put out a long thread into the wind, so that this eventually becomes fouled on a twig or other projection on the far side of the chosen gap. The spider can walk across this thread, anchor the other end firmly, and then reinforce the thread with one or more additional strands.

In other cases, as for example when the web is to be made across a window frame, it may be possible for the spider to walk from one point to the other, trailing a line as it goes, which can subsequently be tightened as necessary. Yet again, it will sometimes drop on a thread to the bottom of the window, and then walk up to the required spot, taking the thread with it.

Once this starting line is established, the rest of the outer ₆
frame of the web is built in much the same way, until the size
and basic outline has been settled. A couple of radii can now
be dropped from points along the top thread, and when these
are crossed over, they locate the point which is to be the center of the web.

The rest of the radii are now laid in, so that when finished ₇
they are all at very nearly the same angle to their neighbors.
The spider does this by walking along one thread as it spins
the adjacent one, and it appears to be able to determine the
appropriate distance at which to keep it with considerable
accuracy. This is quite surprising, because as the web does not
have a circular outline, the radii cannot be evenly spaced along
the outer threads.

Once the radii are in position, the spider constructs a ₈
flat non-sticky platform at the center of the web, and then
uses this same kind of silk to lay down a spiral, starting
from the center and working outwards until it comes to the
outer frame.

This thread serves only as a form of scaffolding, to establish ₉
finally how the spiral will go, and to secure the radial threads
firmly at the correct distances apart, ready for the next stage.
In his last step, the sticky spiral will be placed in position.

Starting at the outer end of the scaffolding spiral, the ₁₀
spider begins to work inwards, spinning a new sticky thread,
anchoring this firmly to the radii, and destroying the temporary thread as it goes. The real purpose of the temporary
spiral now becomes apparent. The sticky thread, when it first
comes from the spinnerets, is smooth, and the spider tenses
and relaxes it repeatedly as it is laid down. In doing this, it
breaks up the gummy material on the silk from a continuous
film into strings of small droplets at intervals along the
silk thread. Had the spider not first fixed the radial threads
firmly in the required position with the temporary spiral
thread, this stretching and relaxing would pull them badly
out of line.

VOCABULARY

paragraph 1: lair
paragraph 2: orb-webs
paragraph 3: spinnerets
paragraph 6: radii
paragraph 9: scaffolding

QUESTIONS

1. When must the spider take account of the place or setting and the weather in spinning the web?
2. How does the spider spin a temporary spiral, and what is its purpose?
3. What details does Richards stress to show that the orb-webs are "masterpieces of construction"?
4. At which points in his description does Richards pause to give additional information or comment on the process?

SUGGESTION FOR WRITING

Make several observations of a natural process similar to the one Richards describes—for example, a bird building a nest, a grasshopper leaping through the grass, a dog swimming, or an ant moving a grain of sand. Then write a description of the process, explaining your terms and the steps of the process for readers unfamiliar with it.

Ian Frazier

IAN FRAZIER *writes frequently for* The New Yorker. *His essays for that magazine are collected in the humorous* Dating Your Mom (1986) *and* Nobody Better, Better Than Nobody (1987). *In* Family (1994), *he touches upon mortality and history through a look at his own family's roots. His* Great Plains (1989) *describes changes in towns he visited in Kansas, the Dakotas, and other midwestern and western states. Frazier's essay on retrieving balloons from trees appeared in* The New Yorker *on May 23, 1994.*

BAGS IN TREES

Last year in this space I talked about the phenomenon of plastic bags stuck in trees. I did not mention one fact: I don't like plastic bags stuck in trees. Maybe it was a mistake to notice them in the first place; now I notice them everywhere. The trees on my street in Brooklyn are old for city trees, and have grown toward the light and away from the buildings, so that now they lean over the street and nearly meet. In a high branch just across from my window, a cluster of plastic party balloons and ribbons on a stick became lodged in the late nineteen-eighties. I watched it go from sort of festive to unrecognizable as it persisted like a debt. Storms that strewed branches all over the street did not budge it. One day, I told my friend Tim about it, and we considered what to do.

At Space Surplus Metals, on Church Street, downtown, we bought one eight-and-a-half-foot and one seven-foot length of stout aluminum tube about an inch across. One length of tube just fit inside the other. Tim is a jeweller, and he took both tubes to his shop and drilled holes in them so they could be held together by a bolt and nut, and he made a device to fit into the other end of the narrower length. This device was a configuration of short, bendable steel rods soldered to a piece of brass pipe. It looked, very roughly, like a hand with crooked and spread fingers, the middle finger longer, upright, and sharpened into a cutting hook. Assembled, the snagger (as we called it) was about sixteen feet long. Tim brought it to my house early one morning, and we put it together. It lacked about two feet of reaching the party balloons. I went back inside and got a kitchen stool. Tim is tall, and he stood on the stool on tiptoe. The hook end of the snagger made contact. A few twists, a few pulls, and the ancient remnants fell to the sidewalk. The tree seemed to shiver like an unsaddled horse.

We walked all over my neighborhood plucking bags. The snagger worked great—a twist of the crooked metal fingers would inveigle the bag, then the sharpened hook would cut it free. In just a few hours, we had removed scores of bags. Old, shredded ones took a lot of monkeying around with, but new, fresh ones sometimes came free in a single motion. The sensation was like having your arm suddenly extended sixteen feet, and the satisfaction like getting something out of your eye. Dangling above traffic makes the bags sooty, and they soon turned our hands a graphite color. A woman passed by, looked at us, and said, "Oh, it's the bag-removal guys." Then she asked us to go to her house and remove some bags from the trees in front. She carefully gave us her address. After she walked on, Tim said, "She doesn't know there *are* no bag-removal guys."

Recently, Tim made another length for the snagger. Now we can insinuate it more than twenty-five feet through the airy upper realms of ginkgos and lindens and oaks to snatch bags that had eluded us before and had assumed that they had tenure. Last weekend, we were snagging at Collect Pond Park, a bestrewn square plot of pavement and scuffed dirt and benches surrounded by court buildings downtown. Tim's brother, Bill, came, too, and we spelled each other. Holding your arms up that long is tiring. Tim climbed on a "Don't Walk" sign to reach a very high pink plastic bag. We also removed a leather belt, a pair of sneakers, an electrical cord and plug, and some tulle. We spent an hour on a bunch of unidentifiable plastic—a drop cloth, maybe—draping the branches like an exploded fright wig. People stared at us in uneasy incomprehension. The next day, there were nine new bags in two of the trees we had cleaned.

In the Ohio town where I grew up, only the church steeples were higher than the trees. Trees occupied the region between us and the sky, and we spent a lot of time looking up into them to see how strong the wind was, or daydreaming. Plastic bags did not get stuck in them, but I did. Once, I climbed an elm in our back yard and wedged my leg between the trunk and a nearly parallel branch. I could not get my arms around the tree to hold on, and so dangled by my leg and yelled. My mother ran to the house being built across the street, and workmen came with a long two-by-four and pried me free.

QUESTIONS

1. How does the snagger work generally? How does Frazier use it to retrieve rubber balloons, the pair of sneakers, and the other objects mentioned in paragraph 4?

2. Is Frazier's purpose in writing to give instructions on how to use the snagger to help clean up the city? Or does he have another purpose in writing—perhaps to express his pleasure in making an unusual tool or in finding a way to get foreign objects out of trees? How do you know?

SUGGESTIONS FOR WRITING

1. Frazier tells us how he dealt with a particular annoyance encountered in the city where he lives. Describe how you dealt with a similar annoyance encountered in your own town or city.

2. Describe a tool that you invented to perform a difficult job. Explain how you constructed the tool and put it to use. You may wish to use your explanation to instruct others in its use, or perhaps to express an interest, or share your pleasure with your readers, or persuade them to take action of some sort.

14

Cause and Effect

There is not just one kind of causal analysis. In explaining why you missed a chemistry exam, you may say that you overslept. In explaining an event like a steep decline in stock prices, a market analyst may cite an event occurring immediately before the decline—for example, the announcement of a rise in interest rates. These are the *immediate* (or *proximate*) causes. Asked why you overslept, you trace the prior events that made you so tired; the market analyst traces the events that led to the rise in interest rates. These are the *mediate* (or *remote*) causes. What one points to as the "cause" depends on the purpose of the analysis. In analyzing an event like a decline in the stock market, an explanation that satisfies a person untrained in economics may not satisfy the professional economist.

Objects, too, have more than one cause. One useful and traditional kind of analysis distinguishes four related ones. Consider a dictionary. Its *material cause* is the paper, ink, and other materials used in its manufacture. The *formal cause* is its shape—the alphabetic arrangement of words, and the arrangements of definitions according to a plan. The *efficient cause* is the dictionary writer, and the *final cause*, the use intended for the dictionary. The analysis of a chemical compound is more rigorous, requiring an account of substances that form the compound as well as the process by which the formation occurs. Process analysis is often an essential part of causal analysis because we want to understand both the how and the why of objects and events. Later in this book we will consider another, more technical kind of causal explanation.

John Brooks

JOHN BROOKS *has written about American business for* The New Yorker *since* 1949. *His books include* The Go-Go Years

(1973) The Games Players (1980), Showing Off in America (1981), *and* The Takeover Game (1987). *In the following
paragraph from* The Telephone (1976), *a history of* AT&T,
Brooks *refers to the idea of Marshall McLuhan that the telephone is
a "cool" medium—one requiring full participation because, unlike
print, it is empty of content. The user supplies this content, unlike
the reader of a book. Brooks says later in his book: "In the uneasy
postwar world, people seemed to be coming to associate the telephone
with their frustrations, their fears, and their sense of powerlessness
against technology."*

THE TELEPHONE

What has the telephone done to us, or for us, in the hundred   1
years of its existence? A few effects suggest themselves at
once. It has saved lives by getting rapid word of illness, injury,
or famine from remote places. By joining with the elevator to
make possible the multistory residence or office building, it
has made possible—for better or worse—the modern city. By
bringing about a quantum leap in the speed and ease with
which information moves from place to place, it has greatly
accelerated the rate of scientific and technological change
and growth in industry. Beyond doubt it has crippled if not
killed the ancient art of letter writing. It has made living alone
possible for persons with normal social impulses; by so
doing, it has played a role in one of the greatest social
changes of this century, the breakup of the multigenerational
household. It has made the waging of war chillingly more efficient than formerly. Perhaps (though not provably) it has prevented wars that might have arisen out of international
misunderstanding caused by written communication. Or perhaps—again not provably—by magnifying and extending
irrational personal conflicts based on voice contact, it has
caused wars. Certainly it has extended the scope of human
conflicts, since it impartially disseminates the useful knowledge of scientists and the babble of bores, the affection of
the affectionate and the malice of the malicious.

But the question remains unanswered. The obvious effects ₂ just cited seem inadequate, mechanistic; they only scratch the surface. Perhaps the crucial effects are evanescent and unmeasurable. Use of the telephone involves personal risk because it involves exposure; for some, to be "hung up on" is among the worst of fears; others dream of a ringing telephone and wake up with a pounding heart. The telephone's actual ring—more, perhaps, than any other sound in our daily lives—evokes hope, relief, fear, anxiety, joy, according to our expectations. The telephone is our nerve-end to society.

In some ways it is in itself a thing of paradox. In one sense ₃ a metaphor for the times it helped create, in another sense the telephone is their polar opposite. It is small and gentle—relying on low voltages and miniature parts—in times of hugeness and violence. It is basically simple in times of complexity. It is so nearly human, recreating voices so faithfully that friends or lovers need not identify themselves by name even when talking across oceans, that to ask its effects on human life may seem hardly more fruitful than to ask the effect of the hand or the foot. The Canadian philosopher Marshall McLuhan—one of the few who have addressed themselves to these questions—was perhaps not far from the mark when he spoke of the telephone as creating "a kind of extra-sensory perception."

QUESTIONS

1. Why does Brooks consider the effects he discusses in paragraph 1 less significant than those in paragraph 2? What does he mean by the statement, "Perhaps the crucial effects are evanescent and unmeasurable"?

2. In what ways is the telephone a paradox? Does the author show it to be a paradox in paragraphs 1 and 2?

3. Has Brooks stated all the effects of the telephone, or has he identified only a few? What central point is he making?

SUGGESTIONS FOR WRITING

1. Develop one of the ideas in the essay from your personal experience. You might discuss your own positive and negative

attitudes toward the telephone, and the reasons for them, or you might develop the statement, "In some ways it is in itself a thing of paradox."

2. Write an essay describing what it would be like to live without a telephone, or discuss the impact of the telephone on life in your home. Distinguish the various uses and effects of the telephone for various members of your family.

Marvin Harris

> MARVIN HARRIS, *Graduate Research Professor of Anthropology at the University of Florida, writes about American life from the point of view of the anthropologist in* Cannibals and Kings: The Origins of Culture (1977) *and* America Now: The Anthropology of a Changing Culture (1981). *Other books include* Good to Eat (1986) *and* The Sacred Cow and the Abominable Pig (1985), *both concerned with "riddles of food and culture." Harris gives in this excerpt from* America Now *an interesting illustration of Murphy's Law. Notice that he combines many of the types of exposition discussed in this section of the book, including definition, process, and example. Later in this book, Edward Tenner gives another explanation for similar happenings (pp. 262–272).*

WHY NOTHING WORKS

According to a law attributed to the savant known only as Murphy, "if anything can go wrong, it will." Corollaries to Murphy's Law suggest themselves as clues to the shoddy goods problem: If anything can break down, it will; if anything can fall apart, it will; if anything can stop running, it will. While Murphy's Law can never be wholly defeated, its effects can usually be postponed. Much of human existence consists of efforts aimed at making sure that things don't go wrong, fall apart, break down, or stop running until a decent interval has elapsed after their manufacture. Forestalling Murphy's Law as applied to products demands intelligence, skill, and commitment. If these human inputs are assisted by special quality-control instruments, machines, and scientific sampling procedures, so much the better. But gadgets and sampling alone will never do the trick since these items are also subject to Murphy's Law. Quality-control instruments need maintenance; gauges go out of order; X rays and laser beams need adjustments. No matter how advanced the technology, quality demands intelligent, motivated human thought and action.

Some reflection about the material culture of prehistoric and preindustrial peoples may help to show what I mean. A single visit to a museum which displays artifacts used by simple preindustrial societies is sufficient to dispel the notion that quality is dependent on technology. Artifacts may be of simple, even primitive design, and yet be built to serve their intended purpose in a reliable manner during a lifetime of use. We acknowledge this when we honor the label "handmade" and pay extra for the jewelry, sweaters, and handbags turned out by the dwindling breeds of modern-day craftspeople.

What is the source of quality that one finds, let us say, in a Pomo Indian basket so tightly woven that it was used to hold boiling water and never leaked a drop, or in an Eskimo skin boat with its matchless combination of lightness, strength, and seaworthiness? Was it merely the fact that these items were handmade? I don't think so. In unskilled or uncaring hands a handmade basket or boat can fall apart as quickly as baskets or boats made by machines. I rather think that the reason we honor the label "handmade" is because it evokes not a technological relationship between producer and product but a social relationship between producer and consumer. Throughout prehistory it was the fact that producers and consumers were either one and the same individuals or close kin that guaranteed the highest degree of reliability and durability in manufactured items. Men made their own spears, bows and arrows, and projectile points; women wove their own baskets and carrying nets, fashioned their own clothing from animal skins, bark, or fiber. Later, as technology advanced and material culture grew more complex, different members of the band or village adopted craft specialties such as pottery-making, basket-weaving, or canoe-building. Although many items were obtained through barter and trade, the connection between producer and consumer still remained intimate, permanent, and caring.

A man is not likely to fashion a spear for himself whose point will fall off in midflight; nor is a woman who weaves her own basket likely to make it out of rotted straw. Similarly, if one is sewing a parka for a husband who is about to go hunting for the family with the temperature at sixty below, all stitches will be perfect. And when the men who make boats are the uncles and fathers of those who sail them, they will be as seaworthy as the state of the art permits.

In contrast, it is very hard for people to care about strangers or about products to be used by strangers. In our era of industrial mass production and mass marketing, quality is a constant problem because the intimate sentimental and personal bonds which once made us responsible to each other and to our products have withered away and been replaced by money relationships. Not only are the producers and consumers strangers but the women and men involved in various stages of production and distribution—management, the worker on the factory floor, the office help, the salespeople—are also strangers to each other. In larger companies there may be hundreds of thousands of people all working on the same product who can never meet face-to-face or learn one another's names. The larger the company and the more complex its division of labor, the greater the sum of uncaring relationships and hence the greater the effect of Murphy's Law. Growth adds layer on layer of executives, foremen, engineers, production workers, and sales specialists to the payroll. Since each new employee contributes a diminished share to the overall production process, alienation from the company and its product are likely to increase along with the neglect or even purposeful sabotage of quality standards.

QUESTIONS

1. What role does Murphy's Law play in Harris's explanation of why nothing works? Does he say or imply that the law is irreversible and that things inevitably break down?

2. How does Harris attempt to prove that quality is not dependent on technology?

3. Does Harris provide the same kind of evidence for his explanation of the source of quality in the handmade products he discusses in paragraphs 3–5?

4. We can test the evidence Harris presents in paragraph 2 by examining the museum objects discussed. Can you think of a way to test the explanation in paragraphs 3–5 if the evidence cannot be tested directly? How convincing do you find his explanation of these paragraphs?

SUGGESTIONS FOR WRITING

1. Write your own explanation of why something you own does not work. In the course of your analysis, discuss the extent to which the ideas of Harris offer an explanation.

2. Write an essay on succeeding in a sport or another topic of your choosing, using causal analysis and examples to develop a thesis. The more limited your focus and discussion, the stronger your thesis will be.

James Trefil

JAMES TREFIL, *Professor of Physics at George Mason University, is the author of* Meditations at Sunset (1986), Scientist at the Seashore (1987), The Dark Side of the Universe (1988), *and other books on science. In* A Scientist in the City (1994), *he discusses "how energy shapes a city," first when people walk or depend on horses and other animals: "Julius Caesar got around in Rome pretty much the same way that the young Queen Victoria got around London. All of these famous figures had only one way to move from one point to another—they had to use muscles, either their own or those of some animal." In the sections reprinted here,*

Trefil traces technological changes from the age of "muscle power" to the age of petroleum. The "Rule of 45" that restricts the size of cities is that "most people will not travel more than 45 minutes to work or shop."

THE GROWTH OF CITIES

Mass Transportation in the Age of Muscle Power

Cities grow. This is the clear message of several centuries of experience. So what can be done to deal with the transportation problems that growth brings? One approach, exemplified by the broad boulevards of Paris and modern eight-lane freeways, is to build bigger roads and more bridges. Another approach is to make the movement of traffic more efficient by grouping travelers together in one vehicle. Bus lines, trams, and trains are examples of this approach. Finally, we can finesse the geometrical constraints completely by moving traffic to a plane different from the city surface. Elevated railways (like Chicago's El) lift traffic above the ground; subways move it below. A recent variation on this theme is found in many cities today: keep vehicular traffic on the ground and build a new "surface" of walkways, parks, and buildings above it. Except for mass transportation, all of these methods of dealing with congestion have obvious limits. There is, after all, only so much space in a central city that can be used for freeways and tunnels.

But mass transportation needn't necessarily wait for breakthroughs in energy technology. In fact, in the nineteenth century, cities developed their first systems based on the use of one of mankind's oldest suppliers of energy: the horse.

As far as I can tell, the first public mass transit system in the world was inaugurated by a man named Henri Baudry in Nantes, France, in 1826. A retired army officer who owned a resort outside of town, he thought he could help business by running a short, regularly scheduled stagecoach line from town to his establishment. The stages left from a location in front of a hatmaker named Omnes, so it quickly acquired the name "omnibus."

Baudry noticed that most of his passengers seemed to be 4 getting off before they got to his place. He must have been a good businessman because instead of getting upset and trying to restrict the use of his stage, he realized that this represented an opportunity and began running stages all over town. His fleet of omnibuses was so successful that it was quickly copied in Paris, London, and New York, which by 1853 had over 600 licensed coaches.

But just putting people in horse-drawn wagons didn't 5 improve transportation all that much. For one thing, the roads were full of potholes and puddles, so the rides tended to be on the bumpy side. For another, there was already so much congestion in the streets that travel was slow—in most places, it was quicker to walk than to ride. The combination of uncomfortable ride and slow progress was probably what the *New York Herald* had in mind when it commented in 1864 that "modern martyrdom may be succinctly described as riding in a New York omnibus."

The development of the horsecar in the mid-nineteenth 6 century eased this burden somewhat. Also called the street railway, the horsecar ran on metal wheels over tracks laid in the street—think of it as a horse-drawn trolley. The ride was smoother and the progress a little more rapid than was possible with an omnibus; horsecars typically moved at speeds of 6 to 8 miles per hour, or about as fast as a jogger. They caught on quickly, particularly in American cities, where they provided transportation to what were then outlying suburbs. In New York, for example, lines on Second and Sixth avenues reached to what is now Central Park, and well-to-do people could commute downtown to work in less than 45 minutes. In the words of one Philadelphian in 1859:

> These passenger cars, which are street railroads with horse power, are a great convenience. Though little more than a year old, they have almost displaced the heavy, jolting, slow and uncomfortable omnibus. . . . They are roomy, their motion smooth and easy, they are clean, well cushioned and handsome, low to the ground so that it is convenient to get on and

off, and are driven at a rapid pace. They offer great facility for traversing the city, now grown so large that the distances are very considerable from place to place.

Nor were horsecars confined to large cities on the East Coast. I was very surprised to learn from my father-in-law, for example, that the town of Billings, Montana—hardly a major metropolis—had a horsecar line connecting the downtown to the railroad yards. He can remember the tracks still being in the street when he was a boy (although the cars no longer ran at that time). Many scholars credit the horsecar with beginning the explosive dispersion of American cities by making it possible for people to live far from their place of work. 7

The organization of mass transportation systems was an important step forward in urban social organization, but it hardly marked a major breakthrough in technology. Horses, after all, had been used to pull wagons from time immemorial. Aside from the rather mundane development that saw rails put in city streets, there was very little to distinguish the early-nineteenth-century transportation engineer from his Roman (or even Sumerian) counterpart. 8

Mass Transportation in the Age of Steam

We usually think of the steam engine as the great driver of change in transportation systems. The first steam railroads were built at mineheads in England in the early nineteenth century. (Some of these early freight lines also offered a passenger service—using, oddly enough, horse-drawn cars.) The first railroad line in the United States, the beginning of the Baltimore & Ohio Railroad, opened in Baltimore in 1830. Long before this time, improvements in the steam engine had made it small enough to be portable and powerful enough to run not only railroads but ships as well. 9

In fact, that quintessentially American phenomenon, the flight to the suburbs, began in 1814, when the first steam ferry started operating between New York (what we would call 10

Manhattan today) and the small farm town of Brooklyn across the East River. By 1860, the population of the town had grown from less than 5000 to 250,000 as people who worked in New York sought quiet, tree-shaded homes for their families. No less a personage than Walt Whitman, writing for the *Brooklyn Eagle,* talked of "Brooklyn the Beautiful," where "men of moderate means may find homes of moderate rent, whereas in New York City there is no median between a palatial mansion and a dilapidated hovel." He also cast a sardonic eye on the behavior of passengers when the ferry docked. His description will seem familiar to anyone who has ever negotiated a subway during rush hour:

> It is highly edifying to see the phrenzy exhibited by certain portions of the younger gentlemen when the bell (signifying the arrival of the ferry) strikes. They rush forward as if for dear life, and woe to the fat woman or unwieldy person of any kind, who stands in their way.

But it was the steam railroad that really shaped American urban areas. Its effect on cities was governed by one simple fact: a steam locomotive takes a mile or more to get up to its running speed. This means that the most efficient way for a railroad-driven transportation system to operate is to have towns strung every few miles along the railroad track. In this kind of situation, people in the "railroad suburbs" walk or ride to the station, then take the train into town. A typical string of such suburbs are towns along the Main Line near Philadelphia. 11

Not everyone was happy with the growth of suburbs. In 1849, the *New York Tribune* sounded a complaint that can still be heard in American cities today when it said: 12

> Property is continually tending from our city to escape the oppressiveness of our taxation. . . . While every suburb in New York is rapidly growing, and villages twenty and thirty miles distant are sustained by incomes earned here and expended

there, our City has no equivalent rapidity of growth, and unimproved property here is often unsalable at a nominal price.

When the first urban transportation systems were built— 13
London's Underground and New York's Elevated, for example—they used steam locomotives because there wasn't anything else available. But this form of steam technology just didn't fit naturally into city life and was quickly dropped. Some way had to be found to harness the power of steam in a form where energy was generated in a fixed spot, then sent out to be used on the streets.

For a brief period in the 1880s and '90s, cable car networks 14
were built in a number of American cities. Today, we associate them with San Francisco, but Chicago, New York, and Philadelphia all used them at one time or another. A cable car works like this: A steam engine is used to turn a large cylinder that, in turn, pulls a long cable through a groove between tracks in a city street. The operator of the car pulls a lever that causes a pair of grippers under the car to grab the cable, and the car then moves along.

In San Francisco, such a system has obvious advantages. 15
You don't have to lift the motor to get the car over a hill. On flat stretches of land such as are found in most eastern and midwestern cities, however, the cable system has proved remarkably inefficient. Up to 90 percent of the energy generated by the steam engine may go to pulling the cable, and only 10 percent to the cars themselves. Obviously, there has to be a better way to get the job done.

Mass Transportation in the Age of Electricity

That "better way" was demonstrated by a man named Frank 16
Sprague in 1887. Working in Richmond, Virginia, he built the first electrically operated street railroad system—the first trolley. In this system, steam turbines generated electricity at a central location, and the electricity was run out to the cars through wires above the streets. A flexibly mounted pole on top of the car maintained contact with these wires and fed the

electricity to the car's motor. (The word "trolley" is a corruption of "troller," the technical word for a little wheel at the end of the pole.)

Sprague installed some 12 miles of track in the Richmond 17 system, but he never really cleared a profit on it. His demonstration was such a technical success, however, that cities all over the country began buying his equipment and taking out licenses on his patents. By 1893, there were no fewer than 250 electric railway companies in the United States; by 1903, there were some 30,000 miles of electrified street railways. Even in our own age of rapid change, when new subdivisions seem to spring up overnight, it's a little hard to envision such a massive revolution in transportation taking place in just 15 years.

The streetcars accelerated the explosion of American cities. 18 "Streetcar suburbs" grew up around every major city, connected to the city by steel tracks and overhead wires. There were even interurban trolleys; for example, you could go from New York to Philadelphia on the streetcar. The "interurbans" also ran to small farm towns outside of cities. I can recall my grandfather talking about how he used to ride them out from Chicago to buy farm produce. Many of what are now established city neighborhoods and close suburbs got their start from the streetcars.

Like the steam railroad, streetcars produced a characteris- 19 tic pattern of city growth. If a typical ride downtown is 20 minutes, then the Rule of 45 tells us that most people will live within a 25-minute walk (a mile or so) of the track. In this situation, growth will be along a series of fingers spreading away from the city center. This pattern will, in fact, by typical of any system that depends on public transportation built around a central city hub.

Mass Transportation in the Age of Petroleum

It was the development of the automobile that filled in the 20 spaces between the urban fingers created by trolleys. It is a product of the most recent change of energy source, from coal to petroleum products. The internal combustion engine, which burns gasoline and uses the resulting energy to turn a shaft that runs wheels, is ubiquitous today. It runs cars, trucks, and buses, of course, but we hear its high-pitched drone on summer afternoons when people are cutting their lawns; in the woods, where chain saws cut down trees; and at construction sites, where a variety of machines are used to excavate and shape the land. The first vehicle powered by an internal combustion engine was built in Germany in 1885 by Karl Benz (whose name survives on one of that country's more upscale products). In 1903, Henry Ford formed the company that bears his name and soon began producing the Model T.

The great advantage of the internal combustion engine was   21
its use of energy derived directly from burning fossil fuels. Thus, all the messy apparatus connected with the use of steam could be eliminated. Both the engine and the fuel in the automobile were compact, so that it was economical to build a vehicle that would carry only a few people at a time.

The "automobilization" of America is a story too well   22
known and too well told to be repeated here. Suffice it to say that it didn't take long for Americans to adopt the automobile. Not long after World War II, there was one car per family in this country; and in the 1970s, one car per worker. By 1985, the number of cars in the United States actually exceeded the number of registered drivers, and it now hovers at about 20 percent more than that number. (I didn't believe this figure, but experts I talked to pointed out that many cars are owned by corporations and rental companies, and many families own seldom-used machines like recreational vehicles in addition to their working cars.)

With the growth of car ownership—with almost all individ-   23
uals now having a vehicle at their disposal—a new pattern of city growth has developed. Cities now grow in rings, with all the land a given distance from the city center being used before land farther out is built up. This is, of course, the familiar pattern of "urban sprawl." As we pointed out earlier, cities took this shape when individuals controlled their own travel

by walking. It's not surprising to find it repeated today, when we control our own travel by driving.

At first, this kind of uniform concentric growth produced a 24 metropolitan area that consisted of a central city full of jobs, surrounded by bedroom suburbs full of commuting workers. Books like *The Lonely Crowd* and *The Organization Man* decried the spiritual aridity of the suburbs and helped create a stereotype of the suburbs that persists to this day.

But whether such sociological views are valid or not, from 25 a technological standpoint there is no question that the modern suburb owes its existence and its organization to the internal combustion engine. This engine has one important use, however, that tends to get overlooked in the story of suburban growth: it can drive trucks as well as automobiles. This means that, like automobiles, trucks can "fill in the blanks" between rail lines in the urban growth ring. Consequently, almost as soon as people started migrating to the suburbs, factories and warehouses started migrating with them. From the very beginnings of urban expansion, there were jobs available in the suburbs.

VOCABULARY

paragraph 1: finesse, constraints
paragraph 5: succinctly
paragraph 7: dispersion
paragraph 8: mundane, Sumerian
paragraph 10: quintessential, median, dilapidated, hovel, sardonic
paragraph 20: ubiquitous
paragraph 24: aridity

QUESTIONS

1. How did horse-drawn vehicles influence the growth of New York City in the nineteenth century?

2. How did the steam railroad and steamboat later influence its growth and that of other cities?

3. Why was the cable car an efficient means of transportation in San Francisco but not in other cities like Chicago?

4. Why was the electrically operated vehicle more efficient than the steam-powered vehicle? Did the electrically operated streetcar influence city growth in the same way as earlier steam-powered vehicles?

5. Why was the internal combustion engine more efficient than steam-powered vehicles? What influence did it have on the growth and life of cities?

6. What is Trefil's thesis, and does he state it explicitly? How do the changes in mass transportation discussed illustrate it?

SUGGESTIONS FOR WRITING

1. James Trefil explains how various kinds of transportation have influenced the social life of people in cities—in particular, where they live and work. Describe how the means of transportation that became available to you where you grew up changed your life.

2. As Alan Cowell shows in his account of motorcycling in Rome (pp. 51–53), the layout and design of city streets influences the driving habits and attitudes of bikers, cyclists, and motorists. Explain how the streets in a particular town or city influence driving habits and attitudes, giving examples from your own experience.

Part 3

ARGUMENT AND PERSUASION

15

Inductive Reasoning

Part 2 discussed descriptive, narrative, and expository writing—writing that describes, gives an account of events, defines, explains or illustrates, traces causes and effects, and so on. Part 3 discusses how we argue, or seek to prove our ideas, and how we use argument and other means to make our ideas persuasive. The essays in this and the following section of Part 3 show how we reason from various kinds of evidence. The process by which we generalize from personal experience, observation, and other factual evidence is called *induction*. The process by which we show what truths beliefs and long–established generalizations imply or entail is called *deduction*.

We reason inductively every day, for example in drawing the conclusion that a painful, red, and swollen finger is probably infected, or predicting that an unusual number of car accidents will probably follow an icestorm. Inductive reasoning often generalizes or makes predictions about a whole class of people or things by observing some of its members. An example is the generalization that drivers in a particular age group will have a higher than average number of car accidents—based on observation of a number of drivers in the particular group over a ten-month period, or the accident history of the group statewide or nationwide gathered statistically from police reports and insurance claims. In this kind of reasoning, no prediction can be made about any single member of the group, nor can the prediction about the group as a whole be made with absolute certainty.

The problem in inductive reasoning is to choose particular instances that truly represent the group or class about which we are generalizing or making predictions. But, as in the sample precincts that pollsters use to predict the outcome of elections, it is impossible to guarantee that the limited number of people sampled are actually typical or representative. We also may be unaware of special

257

circumstances that, if known, would weaken the generalization. These are important reasons for not claiming certainty.

A "hasty generalization" is a judgment made on the basis of insufficient evidence or on the basis of special cases. Thus someone might argue that, because a large number of drivers 70 years of age or older had car accidents during a three-month period, all drivers in this age group will have a higher than average number of accidents in the future, and therefore should pay higher insurance premiums. The argument might be worth considering if the behavior of sample drivers and the conditions under which they were driving could be shown to be typical. It might have been the case, however, that most of the drivers in these accidents proved to have impaired vision (by no means a characteristic of older people) or that the accidents occurred in a harsh winter month. The generalization in question would then have been based both on special cases and on special circumstances.

Many beliefs arise from hasty generalizations like the one just cited: small towns are safer than large cities; redheaded people have short tempers; New Yorkers are rude. Consider the last of these generalizations: the New Yorkers who prompted the statement may have been observed on a crowded, stalled bus on the hottest day of the year. We will consider some special forms of inductive reasoning in the discussions that follow.

Experience and Observation

The process of reasoning from experience and observation requires careful qualification and repeated testing. Scientists engage in a continuous process of testing promising explanations or hypotheses derived from previous experiments and observations in the laboratory and in the field. They test anew conclusions that seem well established. New hypotheses arise that also require testing; if confirmed, these may lead to a questioning of earlier conclusions.

Reasoning from everyday experience and observation requires the same care taken in reasoning from scientific evidence. But this process of reasoning is perhaps even more difficult, for many ideas originate in attitudes and prejudices that we adopt unknowingly. The more deep-rooted the idea, the less likely we are to test it by experience. Indeed, we are more likely to look for evidence that confirms it. So the advice to think "objectively" about people and the world is not easily followed. We can, however, learn to treat with caution the ideas that we derive from what we hear and read. In writing about ideas, we do best to pause and ask where an idea came from before committing it to paper.

Vicki Hearne

VICKI HEARNE *is a fellow at the Yale University Institute for Social and Policy Studies. In 1992 she received an award from the American Academy and Institute of Arts and Letters for distinguished literary achievement.* Adam's Task: Calling Animals by Name (1986) *and* Bandit: Dossier of a Dangerous Dog (1991) *describe her experiences as an animal trainer. A collection of essays,* Animal Happiness (1994), *is an account of "the mysteries of connection between different kinds of mind," animal and human. These kinds of mind are evident in Hearne's description in the following essay of an unusual seeing-eye dog and the woman he serves.*

MAX INTO MAXIMILIAN

Mary Stockstill has long put her trust in the Good Book. The two great Braille volumes beside the chair in which she might be found knitting a multicolored blanket or entertaining her grandchildren are a source of light in her life. There is also her dog Max, in whom she believes, and the typewriter in which she has come to believe, the Braille one I used to ask her questions about Max when I went nosing over to her house. Max, a chocolate Labrador, her eyes and ears.

Not just her eyes. Her eyes and ears. Mary Stockstill is both deaf and blind.

Max is in "limited service." Most of the blind who use dogs can communicate through the harness about what they hear in the way of dangers, especially traffic dangers—a matter of some moment, since a dog who is concentrating on avoiding obstacles, particularly obstacles a dog is not naturally given to worrying about, such as overhanging branches, is distracted from auditory cues. Hence, normally, handler and dog guide each other. Guide dogs are justly famous for their "disobedience"; a good guide dog should refuse to obey a command that will take the handler into danger. Similarly, the blind handler should refuse to follow the dog if he or she hears danger. Since Mary Stockstill can't hear, she and Max cannot negotiate traffic, hence the expression "limited service."

But this is some kind of limited service. I watched Stockstill   4
work Max at night, alone on a residential street. He took her safely down the street—skirting a pile of weeds and branches left carelessly on the sidewalk, which could have meant a nasty fall—and stopped at the curb. He also glanced back nervously at me. Stockstill didn't know why he was hesitating, only that his halt wasn't the usual firm halt that signals the presence of a curb. He continued looking back at me each time she urged him forward.

When we got back to the house and could talk again   5
through her Braille typewriter, she wondered if Max had been distracted by barking dogs—if, that is, he had not worked responsibly while I watched.

I thought he had worked beautifully. There had been some-   6
thing suspicious for him to worry about: me, following the two of them in the dark as I scribbled in my notebook and muttered into my tape recorder. Not many young dogs would have kept their cool with such conflicting messages. How would you feel if the person you were supposed to be guiding and watching out for was being trailed by a dubious-looking stranger talking into a tape recorder? I would want to call my mother, or the cops—or Max.

Instead of calling his mother, Max just kept doing his job,   7
which at that point had entailed keeping Stockstill out of the street, not letting her get lost, and watching me. She, deciding to trust Max, asked him to guide her home, which he did, still keeping a wary eye on me.

So Max thinks for himself, but his human handlers don't   8
always appreciate his wisdom. There was the time, for example, out shopping, when Max decided it was too warm in the store and simply led Stockstill out, without being requested to do so. Her husband, Chuck, panicked, then found them

outside the door. He said in the somewhat cross relief one feels under such circumstances, "I wasn't through shopping!"

Mary said, "Well, Max decided you were." 9

Stockstill became blind in 1939 at the age of ten. Her deaf- 10 ness "bottomed out" in 1959, which was also the year she thought she had to give up on having a dog, because there were no facilities then that trained dogs to deal with people who were both deaf and blind. It was nearly three decades before she got Max—years of I don't know what grief, frustration, and despair that go with being housebound and pretty much cut off. I don't know about all that because Mary Stockstill wouldn't tell me about it. "Just make Max look good."

Well, that isn't hard. He used to be, as Stockstill said, "just 11 a puppy named Max. Now he's Maximilian."

QUESTIONS

1. Under what circumstances is a guide dog in "limited service," and by implication, in full service?

2. How does Hearne illustrate this kind of service in paragraph 4? What explanation does Hearne give for Max's hesitation at the curb? How did she reach an understanding of his behavior?

3. What idea about animal behavior does Max confirm? What further confirmation does Hearne provide? How has she reasoned inductively?

4. Why does she emphasize in the title of the essay and the concluding paragraph that Max is now Maximilian?

SUGGESTIONS FOR WRITING

1. Describe an experience with a particular breed of dog or cat that led you to generalize about the breed. You may wish to discuss other experiences with the breed that confirmed or led you to question your generalization or reject it.

2. We often generalize about people observed in a city or part of the country we have visited. Alan Cowell does so in generalizing about Italian drivers on the basis of experiences on Roman streets (pp. 51–53). Discuss what you would consider a fair generalization

about drivers in your own town or city or part of the country. Explain what circumstances would make a generalization unfair.

Edward Tenner

EDWARD TENNER *attended Princeton University and received his Ph.D. in European history from the University of Chicago. He has been a junior fellow in the Harvard Society of Fellows, has worked in scientific and trade publishing, and has held visiting positions at Princeton and the Institute for Advanced Study. Tenner's description of how mechanical devices take revenge upon the user deserves comparison with Marvin Harris's explanation of "why nothing works" (p. 242).*

REVENGE THEORY

Why are the lines at automatic cash dispensers longer in the evening than those at tellers' windows used to be during banking hours? Why do helmets and other protective gear help make football more dangerous than rugby? Why do filter-tip cigarettes usually fail to reduce nicotine intake? Why are today's paperback prices starting to overtake yesterday's clothbound prices? Why has the leisure society gone the way of the leisure suit?

The world we have created seems to be getting even, twisting our cleverness against us. Or we may be the ones who are unconsciously twisting. Either way, wherever we turn we face the ironic unintended consequences of mechanical, chemical, medical, social, and financial ingenuity—revenge effects, they might be called.

Revenge effects don't require space-age technology. As the humorist Will Cuppy observed of the first pyramids, "Imhotep the Wise originated the idea of concealing the royal corpse and his treasure in a monument so conspicuous that it could not possibly be missed by body snatchers and other thieves." At Elizabethan hangings of cutpurses, their surviving colleagues worked the distracted throngs.

Cognizance of revenge effects is much more recent. Craft-   4
workers and farmers before the nineteenth century, as far as I
can tell, didn't seem to blame their tools or materials when
things went wrong. They recognized providence and luck, and
some of them (notably miners) discerned malicious spirits,
but not ornery ordinary *things*. For all the prophecy of Mary
Shelley and the insight of Henry David Thoreau, the critic
Friedrich Theodor Vischer (1807–1887) probably deserves the
honor of propelling revenge theory into common speech in a
novel, *Auch Einer* (*Another*), published in 1867. His eccentric—
critics say, autobiographical—hero is convinced that everyday
objects, like pencils, pens, inkwells, and cigars, harbor a perverse and demonic spirit. Although not quite in today's literary
canon even in his native Germany, Vischer did achieve immortality through the phrase *die Tücke des Objekts*—the malice of
things.

In 1878 Thomas Edison, possibly echoing telegraphers'   5
slang, first wrote of a *bug* as a hidden problem to be removed
from a design. According to a later article in *The Pall Mall Gazette*,
he was implying "that some imaginary insect has secreted
itself inside and is causing all the trouble." It appears that by
the mid-1930s, "ironing the bugs out" had become American
engineering slang.

By the 1940s the complexity of technological systems   6
raised the consciousness of troops and civilians alike about
how many things could go wrong. The London *Observer* acknowledged in 1942 that the behavior of machines "couldn't
always be explained by . . . laws of aerodynamics. And so,
lacking a Devil, the young fliers . . . invented a whole hierarchy
of devils. They called them Gremlins. . . ."

In 1949 revenge theory took a giant step when Col. P. J.   7
Stapp of Edwards Air Force Base referred to (his colleague
Captain Ed) Murphy's Law—that if something can go wrong, it
will—in a press conference. Aeronautical manufacturers soon
were exploiting it in their advertising, and it passed into folklaw, that vast body of free-form theorizing. Only a year later
the British humorist Paul Jennings published, as a parody of

the Paris avant-garde, an essay on "Resistentialism," a movement supposedly sweeping the Left Bank with the watchword, "*Les choses sont contre nous.*" Our growing "illusory domination over Things," the Resistentialists believed, "has been matched . . . by the increasing hostility (and greater force) of the Things arrayed against [us]."

In 1955 C. Northcote Parkinson (an expatriate historian then   8
as obscure as Murphy himself) began an article in *The Economist* with the "commonplace observation that work expands so as to fill the time available for its completion. Thus, an elderly lady of leisure can spend the entire day in writing and dispatching a postcard to her niece at Bognor Regis." He pointed out that there were nearly 68 percent fewer ships in the Royal Navy in 1928 than in 1914, but more than 78 percent more Admiralty officials.

What all this speculation had in common was a sense that   9
technology and the bureaucracies that sustained it had sometimes amusing and sometimes troubling sides. There probably is no single way to classify the tendencies that these and others have seen—whole books of folklaw principles have been compiled—but at least five are noteworthy. They might be called *repeating, recomplicating, recongesting, regenerating,* and *rearranging.*

Repeating is the most universal. When a chore becomes eas-   10
ier or faster, people assume they will be able to spend less time on it and more on important matters. Instead, they may have to or want to do it more often, or to do new things. The historian of technology Ruth Schwartz Cowan has shown in *More Work for Mother* that while vacuum cleaners, washing machines, and other "labor-saving" appliances did gradually improve the working-class standard of living, they saved no time for middle-class housewives. Women who had sent soiled clothing to a commercial laundry began to do more and more loads of washing. And as laundries and other services went out of business, fewer choices remained.

Much computing is information housekeeping. The billions 11
of dollars of microcomputers installed in the 1980s replaced
batch processing and mainframes, just as home appliances
had defeated the laundries. If this unprecedented power had
performed as advertised, productivity in services should have
soared. Instead, it increased only 1.3 percent a year between
1982 and 1986. In 1989–90 it grew by only 0.5 percent. The
largely precomputer postwar average growth had been fully
2.3 percent.

Experts disagree about the reasons for what *Fortune* called 12
"the puny payoff from office computers," but repeating effects
are surely involved. When spreadsheets were laborious, people did them as seldom and as cautiously as possible. Now
recalculations can be done much more easily, but at the cost
of having to do them much more often, and of learning to use
the software. Meanwhile, competitors have their own spreadsheets (and faxes and cellular telephones), so there isn't even
a relative advantage. Likewise, the time spent revising a com-
puterized letter or memo may cancel the advantage of not
having to retype. And of course mass-produced "personal" letters and memos eat into the time of the recipients.

Computers also force repeating, because often at least 13
some essential data aren't on line. Patrons at libraries with
electronic catalogues usually have to search the old printed
catalogue too, probably increasing total search time. And they
may discover that precious data are almost inaccessible in
tapes in obsolete formats.

Even the body rebels against repeating. According to the 14
U.S. Bureau of Labor Statistics, repetitive motion disorders
(including hand injuries related to computer keyboards)
accounted for fully 147,000 of 284,000 occupational illnesses
in 1989.

Recomplicating is another ironic consequence of the simplify- 15
ing abilities of computers. Wands, bar codes, on-screen displays, have failed to demystify the operations of video
cassette recorders. Touch-tone telephones began as a small

saving in dialing time for gadget-minded subscribers. By now the time savings of punching rather than dialing has been more than consumed by the elaborate systems built to take advantage of it. When the carrier access code and credit card number are added to the number itself, a single call may require thirty digits. And a voice mail system may then take over, demanding still more digits and waiting.

Powerful mainframes have allowed airlines to maximize income with fare structures that are ever more difficult to understand. A single carrier routinely makes tens of thousands of fare changes each day. The Airline Tariff Publishing Company, the industry cooperative, has processed as many as 600,000 changes in 24 hours. Dozens of fares may apply on the same route. The system may benefit the airlines or the public, but it makes it almost impossible for either to understand without tying into the computer networks that make it possible.

16

Even safety devices can recomplicate fatally. In *Normal Accidents* the sociologist Charles Perrow mentions, among other merchant marine perils, "radar-assisted collisions" caused in part by difficulties of plotting multiple and moving targets. One study even determined that as many vessels changed course *toward* a radar-detected target as went in the other direction.

17

Recomplicating may be political rather than technological or economic. The 1986 tax code, introduced as fairer and simpler, has relieved some taxpayers of itemizing, but the cost of preparing a tax return may now be as much as 2 percent of a small company's revenue. *The Wall Street Journal* points out that the rules on passive-loss deductions alone take 196 pages to define *activity*. In 1988 the Business Council on the Reduction of Paperwork estimated an average time of 18.6 hours to complete Form 1040, as opposed to the 2.6 hours claimed by the Internal Revenue Service.

18

In *recongesting*, the system doesn't necessarily become harder to understand. It's just slower and less comfortable.

19

Technological change opens new frontiers but soon clogs them up again.

The automobile-based suburb once seemed to show that [20] new machines could break the stranglehold of grasping railroads and monopolistic center-city landlords. Only decades later did rapid traffic flow turn out to be a mirage. As Parkinson observed of bureaucrats and budgets, cars and car trips have multiplied to saturate the roads built for them, and even the hours of the day. The lunchtime rush hour in the Washington, D.C., area is now as congested as those in the morning and evening. Traffic approaching New York City between 4 and 7 A.M. grew 60 percent from 1967 to 1987. Average travel speed in Los Angeles is projected to slow from 35 miles per hour to under twenty in the next twenty years. Daniel Patrick Moynihan predicts that at present rates, Interstate 95 between Fort Lauderdale and Miami will need 44 lanes in another thirty years.

The historian and critic Ivan Illich estimates that the average [21] American now spends a combined 1,600 hours either driving or earning the money to support automotive costs "to cover a year total of 6,000 miles, four miles per hour. This is just as fast as a pedestrian and slower than a bicycle."

It's no longer unusual to spend more time on transportation [22] to and from airports, waiting and connection times, and flight delays, than on actual time in the air. Congestion continues even within the aircraft cabin, as coach seats have shrunk from the formerly standard 22 inches to nineteen inches, and pitch (front-to-back spacing) from 34 to 31 inches.

Space itself is not immune. Between 30,000 and 70,000 [23] pieces of space debris, each measuring a centimeter or more in diameter and capable of shattering a spacecraft, now clutter the earth's orbit, endangering future missions. Over 6,600 pieces are the size of a softball, or larger. Donald Kessler of the Johnson Space Center in Houston told *The Washington Post* that by 2050, space junk might reach "critical density" and "grind itself to dust," making low earth orbit unusable.

Regenerating, unlike recongesting, usually appears after a   24
problem seems to have been solved. Instead, the solution
turns out to have revived or amplified the problem. Some
teachers reinforce the traditional European preference for
pencils with plain, painted ends, banning built-in rubber tips
as encouragements to sloppy work—a revenge hypothesis, of
course. Their pupils respond by finding great big erasers that
can rub out entire lines with ease.

More seriously, pest control regenerates pests. In the 1950s   25
and 1960s the pesticides heptachlor and later Mirex devas-
tated wildlife and endangered human health when the U.S.
Department of Agriculture deployed them over more than 130
million acres of the South. These tragic costs were tradeoffs,
not revenge effects. The revenge effect was that the chemicals
also killed the natural ant predators of the targets of the spraying, fire ants, which were able to move into their rivals' territory. Likewise in the 1950s, application of DDT wiped out
natural wasp predators of Malaysian caterpillars, bringing
defoliation until spraying was stopped. And it should hardly be
news that anti-rattlesnake drives in the United States are leading to a surge in reported rattlesnake bites—after a period
when there were so few that the Red Cross had discontinued
snakebite courses.

Bacteria have a hydralike way of multiplying in response to   26
bathing and even surgical scrubbing, possibly because heat
and moisture split large colonies into smaller ones. Michael
Andrews reports in *The Life That Lives on Man* that "tests on volunteers who have showered and soaped for ten minutes
showed a marked increase in the number of bacteria floating
in the air on their rafts of shed skin when they were dressing."

Insects and bacteria that resist pesticides and drugs are an   27
even more alarming regenerating effect, the products of nature's own genetic engineering. Excessive use of antibiotics in
livestock feed and over-the-counter drugs has made the problem urgent in the Third World, where resistant strains of bacteria causing ear infections, pneumonia, tuberculosis, and
gonorrhea are now common. Even in the United States,

antimicrobials in animal feed have helped select and promote resistant strains of salmonella. In 1987 the University of Illinois entomologist Robert Metcalf declared that "we may be rushing headlong back into the agricultural and medical dark ages that existed before the discovery of modern insecticides and antibiotics."

Finally, *rearranging* is the revenge effect that shifts a problem in time or space. To be a true revenge effect it must, of course, fall on the same population. For example, if air conditioning raises the ambient temperature of city dwellers who lack it, the result may be uncomfortable and possibly unjust, but it is no revenge effect. But air conditioning in subway systems may be a different story. A spokesman for the New York Transit Authority recently acknowledged that air-conditioned subway cars may provide a cooler ride, "but the stations and the tunnels themselves have become a lot hotter. We seem to be averaging about ten degrees warmer than the outside temperature, so on a day when it's 92 outside, it can be over 100 inside the stations." In fact, heat can actually damage the train air-conditioning units themselves. Then the train windows can't be opened, or opened much—a form of compound revenge.

As heat is pushed around beneath the cities, disaster is deferred in the countryside and suburbs. The Caltech geologist W. Barclay Kamb, in John McPhee's *The Control of Nature*, describes efforts to channel debris flow from the San Gabriel Mountains with crib structures. "You're not changing the source of the sediment," says Kamb. "Those cribworks are less strong than nature's own constructs. . . . Sooner or later, a flood will wipe out those small dams and scatter the debris. Everything you store might come out in one event."

The environmental historian Stephen J. Pyne points out in *Fire in America* that suppressing forest fires may promote long-term accumulation of combustible materials, leading to even larger conflagrations, just as water control projects may make still heavier flooding possible by blocking off a river's normal channels. And of course all forms of disaster control and relief (including deposit insurance) risk increasing the casualties of disaster by encouraging people to move into and remain in risk-prone areas.

Problems are rearranged above the earth as well as in and on it. The 1970 Clean Air Act, by requiring high smokestacks to protect the surroundings of Midwestern coal-burning plants, ensured the windborne transport of sulfur dioxide, spreading acid rain to woodlands and waters hundreds of miles away. 31

Do revenge effects teach a political and social lesson? Scholars of unintended consequences draw different conclusions. The historian William H. McNeill points out that Chinese engineers managing the Yellow River in 600 B.C. faced the same cycle as the Army Corps of Engineers does today on the lower Mississippi: levees concentrating sediment and raising water levels, requiring higher levees. The prosperity of the industrial West after World War II, he says, has depended in part on its ability to transfer much of the cost of fluctuations in the business cycle to the loosely organized raw materials producers and immigrant workers of less developed countries. He suggests that "every gain in precision in the coordinating of human activity and every heightening of efficiency in production" may be matched by "a new vulnerability to breakdown," and (while rejecting fatalism) wonders whether "the conservation of catastrophe may indeed be a law of nature like the conservation of energy." 32

The economist Albert O. Hirschman suggests in his new book, *The Rhetoric of Reaction* (Harvard University Press), that right-wing critics of social and economic reforms exaggerate the seriousness of unintended consequences. He labels the argument that change is counterproductive the "perversity thesis," the assertion that it is useless the "futility thesis," and the claim that it endangers already achieved reforms the "jeopardy thesis." And he shows how closely related the neoconservative critique of the welfare state is to the earlier conservative polemics against the French Revolution and, later, against the spread of the right to vote. 33

While McNeill sees what I call revenge effects as serious   34
consequences probably fated by increasing economic and
technological scale, Hirschman regards them as second-order
problems magnified by the smug and self-interested. But the
fact that all reactionaries invoke unintended consequences
doesn't mean that all who take them seriously have been
friends of the status quo ante or even the status quo. Consider
George Orwell's observation in *The Road to Wigan Pier* (1937): "If
the unemployed learned to be better managers they would be
visibly better off, and I fancy it would not be long before the
dole was docked correspondingly."

Fifty years later, liberals are as likely as conservatives to   35
invoke revenge effects. Some cite them in arguing that new
road construction may increase traffic congestion, others in
insisting that increasing police and prisons actually promotes
criminality, and still others in arguing that advanced medical
technology may be unhealthy, that pesticides and fertilizers
endanger food production in the long run, and that new
weapons systems make nations less secure. As the Right took
over technological optimism from the Left in the 1970s and
1980s, liberal social critics (Hirschman does not deny this)
countered with perversity and futility theories of their own. It
is Ivan Illich who first suggested the tormented mythological
figure of Tantalus as a symbol of the frustrations of modern
life in his book *Medical Nemesis*.

Can there be a strategy against revenge effects? Observers of   36
ironies have been better at posing paradoxes than at resolving
them. But that might be because they haven't paid enough
attention to how revenge effects have been overcome or at
least managed successfully. Think back to the gremlins of
World War II aviation. Human ingenuity overcame them. The
very jokes about gremlins must have done wonders for morale.
And the Axis had gremlins (or Vischerian treacherous objects)
of its own.

After the war, Murphy's Law entered the dictionary only   37
because Captain Murphy and his technician finally managed

to get the strain gauge bridges wired to assure operation of the balky strap transducer that inspired his law in the first place. Despite tragic episodes, both aircraft design and air traffic control show how engineering practice is able to ensure a remarkably high level of safety in apparently fragile and complex systems. Entire textbooks deal with reliability engineering, though Charles Perrow has argued that nuclear weapons and nuclear power have risks that are inherently and unacceptably high.

Clarity about our expectations also helps. There's nothing wrong with wanting to use higher productivity to repeat some activities, like washing clothing, instead of having more free time. Nor is it wicked or foolish to print out three or four drafts of a document or to withdraw cash at all hours from bank accounts. The pleasure of a cool ride, especially for longer-distance subway travelers, may more than offset the discomfort of a hotter platform. The point is to understand choices. 38

Manufacturers and programmers probably should think more about designing products that can be switched easily among different levels of difficulty. There would be nothing wrong with a complex airline fare system if computer interfaces gave travel agents and eventually the public a clearer overview of alternatives. And individuals could learn to avoid revenge effects by developing their abilities to work without technology. People who can do rapid mental and back-of-the-envelope calculations are most likely to catch costly spreadsheet errors. Those who can write fluently with pencil and paper are best able to use the computer's powers of revision. People who can work with constraint are able to get the most out of power. 39

Revenge theory doesn't oppose change. It just favors preventive pessimism. As the computer pioneer John Presper Eckert wrote: "If you have a radical idea . . . for God's sake don't be a radical in how you carry it out. . . . Become a right-wing conservative in carrying out a left-wing idea." 40

VOCABULARY

paragraph 4: cognizance, discerned, malicious, perverse
paragraph 6: aerodynamics, hierarchy
paragraph 7: avant-garde
paragraph 8: expatriate
paragraph 11: batch processing, mainframe, unprecedented, productivity
paragraph 12: spreadsheet, fax, cellular phone
paragraph 13: obsolete, format
paragraph 23: immune, debris, critical density
paragraph 26: hydralike
paragraph 27: genetic engineering, resistant
paragraph 28: ambient
paragraph 29: cribwork
paragraph 30: conflagration, casualty
paragraph 32: levee, fluctuations, coordinating
paragraph 33: neoconservative, polemics
paragraph 34: reactionary, status quo, ante
paragraph 35: Tantalus
paragraph 36: paradox
paragraph 39: interface, constraint

QUESTIONS

1. In what order does Tenner present the five "folklaw principles" discussed?

2. What is "repeating," and what kind of evidence does Tenner present for it?

3. How is "recomplicating" different from "recongesting," and what evidence does Tenner present for these?

4. What evidence does Tenner present for "regenerating," and how is this process different from "recongesting"?

5. How is "rearranging" different from the other folklaws, and what evidence does Tenner present for it?

6. What kinds of inductive evidence—personal experience, observation, statistical studies, for example—does Tenner present in support of his thesis?

7. What thesis concerning technological progress does Tenner develop, and where does he first state it? Does he argue that

technological progress is a myth? Does he accept the view of the Left or the Right toward technological progress, or does he reject both views?

SUGGESTIONS FOR WRITING

1. Present personal experiences and observations that lead you to agree with Tenner's analysis about one of the five folklaws, or lead you to doubt or qualify his analysis.

2. State your own view of technological progress, and explain why you hold it. In the course of the discussion, explain why your view of technological progress is the same as or different from Tenner's.

William Zinsser

> WILLIAM ZINSSER *has had wide opportunity to study American culture as a journalist and teacher. His long career includes experience as a film critic, a feature writer for* The New York Herald Tribune, *and a columnist for* Life *magazine and* The New York Times. *He has published several collections of essays on life in America, including* The Lunacy Boom (1970). *Zinsser taught writing at Yale for a number of years and gives valuable advice on the subject in his book* On Writing Well (*Fifth Edition*, 1994), *a chapter from which appears later in this book (pp. 591–596).*

THE RIGHT TO FAIL

I like "dropout" as an addition to the American language because it's brief and it's clear. What I don't like is that we use it almost entirely as a dirty word.

We only apply it to people under twenty-one. Yet an adult who spends his days and nights watching mindless TV programs is more of a dropout than an eighteen-year-old who quits college, with its frequently mindless courses, to become, say, a VISTA volunteer. For the young, dropping out is often a way of dropping in.

To hold this opinion, however, is little short of treason in America. A boy or girl who leaves college is branded a failure—

and the right to fail is one of the few freedoms that this country does not grant its citizens. The American dream is a dream of "getting ahead," painted in strokes of gold wherever we look. Our advertisements and TV commercials are a hymn to material success, our magazine articles a toast to people who made it to the top. Smoke the right cigarette or drive the right car— so the ads imply—and girls will be swooning into your deodorized arms and caressing your expensive lapels. Happiness goes to the man who has the sweet smell of achievement. He is our national idol, and everybody else is our national fink.

I want to put in a word for the fink, especially the teen-age 4 fink, because if we give him time to get through his finkdom— if we release him from the pressure of attaining certain goals by a certain age—he has a good chance of becoming our national idol, a Jefferson or a Thoreau, a Buckminster Fuller or an Adlai Stevenson, a man with a mind of his own. We need mavericks and dissenters and dreamers far more than we need junior vice-presidents, but we paralyze them by insisting that every step be a step up to the next rung of the ladder. Yet in the fluid years of youth, the only way for boys and girls to find their proper road is often to take a hundred side trips, poking out in different directions, faltering, drawing back, and starting again.

"But what if we fail?" they ask, whispering the dreadful word 5 across the Generation Gap to their parents, who are back home at the Establishment, nursing their "middle-class values" and cultivating their "goal-oriented society." The parents whisper back: "Don't!"

What they should say is "Don't be afraid to fail!" Failure 6 isn't fatal. Countless people have had a bout with it and come out stronger as a result. Many have even come out famous. History is strewn with eminent dropouts, "loners" who followed their own trail, not worrying about its odd twists and turns because they had faith in their own sense of direction. To read their biographies is always exhilarating, not only because they beat the system, but because their system was better than the one that they beat.

Luckily, such rebels still turn up often enough to prove that 7
individualism, though badly threatened, is not extinct. Much
has been written, for instance, about the fitful scholastic
career of Thomas P. F. Hoving, New York's former Parks Com-
missioner and now director of the Metropolitan Museum of
Art. Hoving was a dropout's dropout, entering and leaving
schools as if they were motels, often at the request of the
management. Still, he must have learned something during
those unorthodox years, for he dropped in again at the top of
his profession.

His case reminds me of another boyhood—that of Holden 8
Caulfield in J. D. Salinger's *The Catcher in the Rye*, the most
popular literary hero of the postwar period. There is nothing
accidental about the grip that this dropout continues to hold
on the affections of an entire American generation. Nobody
else, real or invented, has made such an engaging shambles
of our "goal-oriented society," so gratified our secret belief
that the "phonies" are in power and the good guys up the
creek. Whether Holden has also reached the top of his chosen
field today is one of those speculations that delight fanciers
of good fiction. I speculate that he has. Holden Caulfield, incidentally, is now thirty-six.

I'm not urging everyone to go out and fail just for the sheer 9
therapy of it, or to quit college just to coddle some vague discontent. Obviously it's better to succeed than to flop, and in
general a long education is more helpful than a short one.
(Thanks to my own education, for example, I can tell George
Eliot from T. S. Eliot, I can handle the pluperfect tense in
French, and I know that Caesar beat the Helvetii because he
had enough frumentum.) I only mean that failure isn't bad in
itself, or success automatically good.

Fred Zinnemann, who has directed some of Hollywood's 10
most honored movies, was asked by a reporter, when *A Man for
All Seasons* won every prize, about his previous film *Behold a Pale
Horse*, which was a box-office disaster. "I don't feel any obligation to be successful," Zinnemann replied. "Success can be
dangerous—you feel you know it all. I've learned a great deal

from my failures." A similar point was made by Richard Brooks about his ambitious money loser, *Lord Jim*. Recalling the three years of his life that went into it, talking almost with elation about the troubles that befell his unit in Cambodia, Brooks told me that he learned more about his craft from this considerable failure than from his many earlier hits.

It's a point, of course, that applies throughout the arts. 11 Writers, playwrights, painters, and composers work in the expectation of periodic defeat, but they wouldn't keep going back into the arena if they thought it was the end of the world. It isn't the end of the world. For an artist—and perhaps for anybody—it is the only way to grow.

Today's younger generation seems to know that this is true, 12 seems willing to take the risks in life that artists take in art. "Society," needless to say, still has the upper hand—it sets the goals and condemns as a failure everybody who won't play. But the dropouts and the hippies are not as afraid of failure as their parents and grandparents. This could mean, as their elders might say, that they are just plumb lazy, secure in the comforts of an affluent state. It could also mean, however, that they just don't buy the old standards of success and are rapidly writing new ones.

Recently it was announced, for instance, that more than 13 two hundred thousand Americans have inquired about service in VISTA (the domestic Peace Corps) and that, according to a Gallup survey, "more than three million American college students would serve VISTA in some capacity if given the opportunity." This is hardly the road to riches or to an executive suite. Yet I have met many of these young volunteers, and they are not pining for traditional success. On the contrary, they appear more fulfilled than the average vice-president with a swimming pool.

Who is to say, then, if there is any right path to the top, or 14 even to say what the top consists of? Obviously the colleges don't have more than a partial answer—otherwise the young would not be so disaffected with an education that they consider vapid. Obviously business does not have the answer—

otherwise the young would not be so scornful of its call to be an organization man.

The fact is, nobody has the answer, and the dawning aware- 15 ness of this fact seems to me one of the best things happening in America today. Success and failure are again becoming individual visions, as they were when the country was younger, not rigid categories. Maybe we are learning again to cherish this right of every person to succeed on his own terms and to fail as often as necessary along the way.

VOCABULARY

paragraph 3: swooning, fink
paragraph 4: mavericks, dissenters
paragraph 6: exhilarating
paragraph 7: extinct, unorthodox
paragraph 8: shambles, fanciers
paragraph 9: coddle, frumentum
paragraph 12: affluent
paragraph 14: vapid

QUESTIONS

1. Zinsser develops his thesis in paragraphs 1–4. What is his thesis, and where does he state it? What kinds of evidence support it?

2. Paragraphs 5–8 provide support for the thesis by *defending* the right to fail. What form does this defense take? What does Zinsser gain by citing the hero of *The Catcher in the Rye*?

3. Paragraphs 9–12 *qualify* what has been said earlier: Zinsser tells us what he does not mean by "the right to fail." What does he not mean, and how does he qualify his idea of failure through discussion of success and failure in the arts, the film art specifically?

4. Paragraphs 13–15 provide additional supporting evidence that the maverick has a role to play in American society (Zinsser's point in paragraphs 6 and 7) and restate the thesis to conclude the essay. What is that evidence, and how is the thesis restated?

5. Do you agree with Zinsser that parents and society provide teenagers with rigid standards of success? Do you agree with his belief that failure is a means to growth?

SUGGESTIONS FOR WRITING

1. Discuss your agreement or disagreement with Zinsser about the demands made on teenagers today, drawing on your own experiences and ideas of success and failure. Do not try to speak for all teenagers. Limit yourself to your own experience and personal goals.

2. Discuss the value of two or three different courses you took in high school, with attention to their effect on your choice of a college or a college major, or on the development of long-term goals (or all of these).

3. Write an essay on one of the following topics. In the course of your essay, state a thesis and explain it, defend it with supporting evidence, qualify it (explaining what you do not mean and limiting your generalizations), provide additional evidence for one or more of your supporting ideas, and restate your thesis in conclusion:

   a. unintended lessons taught in high school classes

   b. lessons that cannot be taught in school

   c. discovering the nature of prejudice

   d. "rules" that work at home or at school

   e. "rules" that do not work

Ellen Goodman

ELLEN GOODMAN *worked for* Newsweek *and the* Detroit Free Press *before joining the* Boston Globe *in 1967 as feature writer and columnist. In 1980 she received the Pulitzer Prize for Commentary. Her columns on a wide range of social and political issues appear regularly in the* Globe *and other newspapers in the United States. They are collected in* At Large *(1981),* Keeping in Touch *(1985),* Making Sense *(1989), and* Value Judgments *(1993). The column reprinted here first appeared on June 19, 1990.*

WAIT A MINUTE

The cop and the rap singer went on the air together last   1
Wednesday. It's the American way. One minute you're arresting

a guy and the next minute you're in the greenroom with him. One day he's putting cuffs on you, the next day he's your co-guest.

When the lights went on at *Geraldo*, the Florida sheriff, Nick Navarro, and the leader of 2 Live Crew, Luther Campbell, played their parts like polished performers assigned the role of enemies. Navarro portrayed himself as a lawman and Campbell as his obscene lawbreaker. Campbell cast himself as the rap singer and Navarro as his "Communist and racist."

Then the two parted company and Campbell went on to *Donahue* and then to *Live at Five*. Another opening, another show. That's entertainment.

The scene wasn't much more heartening in Congress, where the players are feeling the dramatic heat of flag burning. Those who were for and against a constitutional amendment to ban the desecration of the flag were worrying about the reviews. Some, like Nebraska senator Bob Kerrey, imagined bleakly how they would look: "Bob Kerrey votes for gun control and he won't vote to protect the flag. It's a great thirty-second spot."

These days, it seems every issue becomes instant theater. Every advocate worries about how his act will play. Every conflict becomes a Punch and Judy show. Are you in favor of Robert Mapplethorpe's photographs? Are you against censors?

In public, people swing beliefs at each other like fists. The audience is expected to identify a hero and a villain. Which do you prefer: the First Amendment or pornography, the Bill of Rights or the flag, freedom of speech or obscenity?

What is so appalling about these one-acts is that they lead the audience to assume that every issue must be equally polarized. Like guests on a talk show, we either have to buy *Me So Horny* or ban it. We must favor the flag or the flag burners. We have to choose between license and crackdown. Now.

Indeed, at the ends of the American spectrum there are people who can only scream at each other across a stage. Americans do feel differently about symbols and speech.

Over the years, the passion to crack down on dissent or on speech has come from those who believe there's a natural human drift down to the lowest common denominator of behavior. Unchecked, they say, the human heart of darkness grows.

Those who have defended free speech have put their faith in reason, persuasion, what was once called enlightenment. In the free marketplace of ideas, they wager, the 2 Live Crew will lose and the flag burners will simmer down.

Over the course of American history, the value of free speech has outlasted both its abusers and its attackers. Over time, the Bill of Rights has been shielded from those who want to express their outrage by repressing outrageousness. But I wonder if these days, we have the time.

Out of the limelight, most Americans are not as certain as talk-show guests or as polarized as attack ads. There are First Amendment absolutists who would like to throttle Andrew Dice Clay and be there when Luther Campbell's daughter asks him to explain his work. There are people who neither want a Mapplethorpe on their wall nor want to dine with his censors.

But today public debate has been pared down to its speed-racing form, a sleek and simplistic shape. Even the Senate now pushes for an amendment with the urgency of a television host trying to wrap things up before the political commercial break.

When asked about the flag amendment, Arkansas senator Dale Bumpers said, "I belong to the wait-just-a-minute club." It's a club with a shrinking membership.

I don't think we need to imprison a rap singer to express our abhorrence of sexual assault songs. Like profanity on *Geraldo*, 2 Live Crew is a bleep in time. Nor do I think we need to singe the Constitution to punish the few who torch a symbol. Flag burning isn't even a fad.

How do you defend a two-hundred-year-old principle in the era of the thirty-second spot? How do you wait-a-minute, and listen-a-while, in the passionate and polarizing ethic of the moment?

The Bill of Rights is on the political entertainment schedule now. And, it appears, the producers are only worried about today's show.

VOCABULARY

paragraph 6: pornography, obscenity
paragraph 12: polarized, absolutists
paragraph 13: simplistic

QUESTIONS

1. How does Goodman support her generalization in paragraph 5 that "These days, it seems every issue becomes instant theater"?
2. What is "instant" about this kind of theater?
3. Does Goodman believe that most Americans are at one end or the other of the American political spectrum—the far left or far right?
4. Does Goodman propose a remedy for instant theater and the polarization of public issues? How should the country deal with offensive song lyrics and photographs and with flag burning?
5. How does she connect her discussion of censorship to that of political discourse in America today? Does she give both problems equal attention?
6. What is Goodman's thesis, and where does she state it?

SUGGESTIONS FOR WRITING

1. Discuss your experience in trying to debate a controversial issue with a friend or a member of your family. To what extent does your personal experience confirm the views Goodman presents in her essay?
2. In the course of a classroom debate on a current issue, one of the students engages in name calling, using language and stereotypes offensive to others in the class. Discuss how you would deal with this situation as the instructor. Would you impose limits on the discussion at the beginning of the debate, telling the class what terms, references, and topics are not permissible? Would you encourage the class to impose its own limits, or would you discourage—and refuse to impose—any limits whatever? State your reasons and defend them.

Analogy

We discussed earlier the use of analogy, or point-by-point comparison of two things, for the purpose of illustration (p. 214). In reasoning about everyday decisions and choices you often use analogy, as in deciding to buy a book similar in subject and setting to an author's earlier book you enjoyed. Since arguments from analogy make predictions only, the fact that you enjoyed the earlier book does not guarantee that you will enjoy the author's new one. But you can increase the probability by noting similarities with other enjoyable books of the same author.

The greater the number of relevant similarities, the stronger the argument. A candidate for governor may argue that she has the same record and personal characteristics as a much admired former governor; her case becomes stronger if she cites several similarities and not just one, and it becomes even stronger if she makes the comparison with several former governors instead of one. Thus she may point out that, like them, she was a mayor of a large city, held office in years of economic hardship, had a successful career as a state legislator, and served for several years in Congress.

Dissimilarities between the candidate and former governors cited must not be significant enough to weaken the argument. Differences in height or in color of hair are obviously insignificant and irrelevant to the conclusion. But the candidate may have to persuade some members of her audience that her being a woman is an insignificant difference, too. She may even use dissimilarities to strengthen her case. If the governors cited have the same record of service as she yet are different in gender, race, or background—some coming from small towns and some from large cities—the probability increases that the similarities she has cited support her claim to be qualified, despite these differences.

The points of similarity must be relevant to the conclusion: the similarities noted do support the claim of the candidate that she has the experience needed to deal intelligently with unemployment and the state budget deficit. However, they would not support the claim that she had the same kind of education as previous governors. A limited conclusion may be drawn from a limited analogy if the points of similarity are clearly specified or agreed upon, if these points are relevant to the conclusion, and if inferences are drawn from these points only.

Brooks Atkinson

BROOKS ATKINSON (1894–1984) *was associated throughout his long career as a journalist with the* New York Times, *as war correspondent, dramatic critic, and essayist. In 1947 he received the Pulitzer Prize for Foreign Correspondence. His books include* Henry Thoreau: The Cosmic Yankee (1927), East of the Hudson (1931), *and* Brief Chronicles (1966). *Atkinson wrote often about environmental issues. The essay reprinted here first appeared in the* New York Times *on November 23, 1968. The essay, one of Atkinson's finest on this subject, is particularly effective in its use of analogy.*

THE WARFARE IN THE FOREST IS NOT WANTON

After thirty-five years the forest in Spruce Notch is tall and sturdy. It began during the Depression when work gangs planted thousands of tiny seedlings in abandoned pastures on Richmond Peak in the northern Catskills. Nothing spectacular has happened there since; the forest has been left undisturbed.

But now we have a large spread of Norway spruces a foot thick at the butt and 40 or 50 feet high. Their crowns look like thousands of dark crosses reaching into the sky.

The forest is a good place in which to prowl in search of wildlife. But also in search of ideas. For the inescapable fact is that the world of civilized America does not have such a clean record. Since the seedlings were planted the nation has fought three catastrophic wars, in one of which the killing of combatants and the innocent continues. During the lifetime of the forest 350,000 Americans have died on foreign battlefields.

Inside America civilized life is no finer. A President, a Senator, a man of God have been assassinated. Citizens are murdered in the streets. Riots, armed assaults, looting, burning, outbursts of hatred have increased to the point where they have become commonplace.

Life in civilized America is out of control. Nothing is out of ₅ control in the forest. Everything complies with the instinct for survival—which is the law and order of the woods.

Although the forest looks peaceful it supports incessant ₆ warfare, most of which is hidden and silent. For thirty-five years the strong have been subduing the weak. The blueberries that once flourished on the mountain have been destroyed. All the trees are individuals, as all human beings are individuals; and every tree poses a threat to every other tree. The competition is so fierce that you can hardly penetrate some of the thickets where the lower branches of neighboring trees are interlocked in a blind competition for survival.

Nor is the wildlife benign. A red-tailed hawk lived there last ₇ summer—slowly circling in the sky and occasionally drawing attention to himself by screaming. He survived on mice, squirrels, chipmunks and small birds. A barred owl lives somewhere in the depth of the woods. He hoots in midmorning as well as at sunrise to register his authority. He also is a killer. Killing is a fundamental part of the process. The nuthatches kill insects in the bark. The woodpeckers dig insects out. The thrushes eat beetles and caterpillars.

But in the forest, killing is not wanton or malicious. It is for ₈ survival. Among birds of equal size most of the warfare consists of sham battles in which they go through the motions of warfare until one withdraws. Usually neither bird gets hurt.

Nor is the warfare between trees vindictive. Although the ₉ spruces predominate they do not practice segregation. On both sides of Lost Lane, which used to be a dirt road, maples, beeches, ashes, aspens and a few red oaks live, and green curtains of wild grapes cover the wild cherry trees. In the depths of the forest there are a few glades where the spruces stand aside and birches stretch and grow. The forest is a web of intangible tensions. But they are never out of control. Although they are wild they are not savage as they are in civilized life.

For the tensions are absorbed in the process of growth, ₁₀ and the clusters of large cones on the Norway spruces are certificates to a good future. The forest gives an external impression of discipline and pleasure. Occasionally the pleasure is rapturously stated. Soon after sunrise one morning last summer when the period of bird song was nearly over, a solitary rose-breasted grosbeak sat on the top of a tall spruce and sang with great resonance and beauty. He flew a few rods to another tree and continued singing: then to another tree where he poured out his matin again, and so on for a half hour. There was no practical motive that I was aware of.

After thirty-five uneventful years the spruces have created 11 an environment in which a grosbeak is content, and this one said so gloriously. It was a better sound than the explosion of bombs, the scream of the wounded, the crash of broken glass, the crackle of burning buildings, the shriek of the police siren.

The forest conducts its affairs with less rancor and malevo- 12 lence than civilized America.

VOCABULARY

paragraph 8: wanton, malicious
paragraph 9: segregation, intangible
paragraph 10: discipline, resonance, matin
paragraph 12: rancor, malevolence

QUESTIONS

1. One sometimes hears the argument that violence is natural to human beings, since we are a part of a warring world. How does Atkinson implicitly reject this analogy? More specifically, what are the points of dissimilarity between the world of the forest and the world of humans?

2. How might the world of the forest be used to challenge the argument that competition in the world of humans need be destructive as some of those competing—as the argument that only the "fit" survive in the world of business implies?

3. How does Atkinson strengthen his argument through the details he marshals in support of it?

SUGGESTION FOR WRITING

Each of the following statements suggests analogy. Write on one of them, discussing points of similarity and dissimilarity and using this discussion to argue a thesis.

a. The family is a small nation.

b. The nation is a large family.

c. College examinations are sporting events.

d. Choosing a college is like buying a car.

John Henry Newman

JOHN HENRY NEWMAN (1801–1890), *one of the influential English religious leaders of the nineteenth century, entered the Catholic Church in 1845 and two years later was ordained as priest. In 1879 he was appointed cardinal of the Church. Rector of the Catholic University of Dublin from 1851 to 1858,* Newman *delivered a series of lectures on university education—published in 1873 as* The Idea of a University. *The chief purpose of a university is to develop the power to think, Newman argues. Though knowledge is a means to "material and moral advancement," it is "an end in itself," and should be valued for its own sake. Newman argues this point by analogy in this section from a discourse late in the book,* Knowledge Viewed in Relation to Professional Skill.

THE END OF EDUCATION

You will see what I mean by the parallel of bodily health. [1] Health is a good in itself, though nothing came of it, and is especially worth seeking and cherishing; yet, after all, the blessings which attend its presence are so great, while they are so close to it and so redound back upon it and encircle it, that we never think of it except as useful as well as good, and praise and prize it for what it does, as well as for what it is, though at the same time we cannot point out any definite and distinct work or production which it can be said to effect. And so as regards intellectual culture, I am far from denying utility in this large sense as the end of Education, when I lay it down, that the culture of the intellect is a good in itself and its own end; I do not exclude from the idea of intellectual culture what it cannot but be, from the very nature of things; I only deny that we must be able to point out, before we have any right to call it useful, some art, or business, or profession, or trade, or work, as resulting from it, and as its real and complete end. The parallel is exact: As the body may be sacrificed to some manual or other toil, whether moderate or oppressive, so may the intellect be devoted to some specific profession; and I do not call *this* the culture of the intellect. Again, as some member or organ of the body may be inordinately used and developed, so may memory, or imagination, or the reasoning faculty; and *this* again is not intellectual culture. On the other hand, as the body may be tended, cherished, and exercised with a simple view to its general health, so may the intellect also be generally exercised in order to its perfect state; and this *is* its cultivation.

Again, as health ought to precede labor of the body, and as ²a man in health can do what an unhealthy man cannot do; and as of his health the properties are strength, energy, agility, graceful carriage and action, manual dexterity, and endurance of fatigue, so in like manner general culture of mind is the best aid to professional and scientific study, and educated men can do what illiterate cannot; and the man who has learned to think and to reason and to compare and to discriminate and to analyze, who has refined his taste, and formed his judgment, and sharpened his mental vision, will not indeed at once be a lawyer, or a pleader, or an orator, or a statesman, or a physician, or a good landlord, or a man of business, or a soldier, or an engineer, or a chemist, or a geologist, or an antiquarian, but he will be placed in that state of intellect in which he can take up any one of the sciences or callings I have referred to, or any other for which he has a taste or special talent, with an ease, a grace, a versatility, and a success, to which another is a stranger. In this sense then, and as yet I have said but a very few words on a large subject, mental culture is emphatically *useful.*

If then I am arguing, and shall argue, against Professional or Scientific knowledge as the sufficient end of a University Education, let me not be supposed, Gentlemen, to be disrespectful towards particular studies, or arts, or vocations, and those who are engaged in them. In saying that Law or Medicine is not the end of a University course, I do not mean to imply that the University does not teach Law or Medicine. What indeed can it teach at all, if it does not teach something particular? It teaches *all* knowledge by teaching all *branches* of knowledge, and in no other way. I do but say that there will be this distinction as regards a Professor of Law, or of Medicine, or of Geology, or of Political Economy, in a University and out of it, that out of a University he is in danger of being absorbed and narrowed by his pursuit, and of giving Lectures which are the Lectures of nothing more than a lawyer, physician, geologist, or political economist; whereas in a University he will just know where he and his science stand, he has come to it, as it were, from a height, he has taken a survey of all knowledge, he is kept from extravagance by the very rivalry of other studies, he has gained from them a special illumination and largeness of mind and freedom and self-possession, and he treats his own in consequence with a philosophy and a resource, which belongs not to the study itself, but to his liberal education.

This then is how I should solve the fallacy, for so I must call it, by which Locke and his disciples would frighten us from cultivating the intellect, under the notion that no education is useful which does not teach us some temporal calling, or some mechanical art, or some physical secret. I say that a cultivated intellect, because it is a good in itself, brings with it a power and a grace to every work and occupation which it undertakes, and enables us to be more useful, and to a greater number. There is a duty we owe to human society as such, to the state to which we belong, to the sphere in which we move, to the individuals towards whom we are variously related, and whom we successively encounter in life; and that philosophical or liberal education, as I have called it, which is the proper function of a University, if it refuses the foremost place to professional interests, does but postpone them to the formation of the citizen, and, while it subserves the larger interests of philanthropy, prepares also for the successful prosecution of those merely personal objects, which at first sight it seems to disparage.

VOCABULARY

paragraph 1: utility, inordinately
paragraph 2: dexterity, culture, antiquarian
paragraph 3: extravagance
paragraph 4: grace, philanthropy

QUESTIONS

1. What analogy does Newman employ in paragraphs 1 and 2 to argue his thesis, and how does he develop it?

2. In saying that law, medicine, and other professional studies are not the "sufficient end" of university education, is Newman saying that these studies do not develop the mind? What does he mean by the word *sufficient*?

3. How does the university teach *"all* knowledge by teaching all *branches* of knowledge? Is Newman saying that students need to study all branches, including law and medicine, to be fully educated?

4. According to the *Oxford English Dictionary*, what is the origin of the word *liberal* with reference to education? What does Newman mean by *liberal education* in the final sentence of paragraph 3?

SUGGESTIONS FOR WRITING

1. Discuss how Newman probably would answer the objection that we value physical exercise and a healthy diet, not as ends in themselves, but as means to keeping alive and working efficiently.

2. Develop your discussion by explaining why you agree or disagree with Newman's analogy.

Deborah Tannen

DEBORAH TANNEN, *Professor of Linguistics at Georgetown University, discusses the "talking voices" of men and women in her books* That's Not What I Mean (1986), You Just Don't Understand (1990), *and* Talking 9 to 5 (1994). *Tannen shows how different conversational styles create misunderstanding and conflict. In her essay in* The New York Times, *January 14, 1994, she discusses another source of misunderstanding and conflict in public discourse. Ellen Goodman discusses the same problem in her essay on pp.* 279–281).

THE TRIUMPH OF THE YELL

I put the question to a journalist who had written a vitriolic   1
attack on a leading feminist researcher: "Why do you need to make others wrong for you to be right?" Her response: "It's an argument!"

That's the problem. More and more these days, journalists,   2
politicians and academics treat public discourse as an argument—not in the sense of *making* an argument, but in the sense of *having* one, of having a fight.

When people have arguments in private life, they're not try-   3
ing to understand what the other person is saying. They're listening for weaknesses in logic to leap on, points they can distort to make the other look bad. We all do this when we're angry, but is it the best model for public intellectual interchange? This breakdown of the boundary between public and private is contributing to what I have come to think of as a culture of critique.

Fights have winners and losers. If you're fighting to win, the   4
temptation is great to deny facts that support your opponent's views and present only those facts that support your own.

At worst, there's a temptation to lie. We accept this style of   5
arguing because we believe we can tell when someone is lying. But we can't. Paul Ekman, a psychologist at the University of

California at San Francisco, has found that even when people are very sure they can tell whether or not some one is dissembling, their judgments are as likely as not to be wrong.

If public discourse is a fight, every issue must have two 6 sides—no more, no less. And it's crucial to show "the other side," even if one has to scour the margins of science or the fringes of lunacy to find it.

The culture of critique is based on the belief that opposition 7 leads to truth: when both sides argue, the truth will emerge. And because people are presumed to enjoy watching a fight, the most extreme views are presented, since they make the best show. But it is a myth that opposition leads to truth when truth does not reside on one side or the other but is rather a crystal of many sides. Truth is more likely to be found in the complex middle than in the simplified extremes, but the spectacles that result when extremes clash are thought to get higher ratings or larger readership.

Because the culture of critique encourages people to attack 8 and often misrepresent others, those others must waste their creativity and time correcting the misrepresentations and defending themselves. Serious scholars have had to spend years of their lives writing books proving that the Holocaust happened, because a few fanatics who claim it didn't have been given a public forum. Those who provide the platform know that what these people say is, simply put, not true, but rationalize the dissemination of lies as showing "the other side." The determination to find another side can spread disinformation rather than lead to the truth.

The culture of critique has given rise to the journalistic prac- 9 tice of confronting prominent people with criticism couched as others' views. Meanwhile, the interviewer has planted an accusation in readers' or viewers' minds. The theory seems to be that when provoked, people are spurred to eloquence and self-revelation. Perhaps some are. But others are unable to say what they know because they are hurt, and begin to sputter when their sense of fairness is outraged. In those cases, opposition is not the path to truth.

When people in power know that what they say will be scru- 10
tinized for weaknesses and probably distorted, they become
more guarded. As an acquaintance recently explained about
himself, public figures who once gave long, free-wheeling
press conferences now limit themselves to reading brief statements. When less information gets communicated, opposition
does not lead to truth.

Opposition also limits information when only those who are 11
adept at verbal sparring take part in public discourse, and
those who cannot handle it, or do not like it, decline to participate. This winnowing process is evident in graduate schools,
where many talented students drop out because what they
expected to be a community of intellectual inquiry turned out
to be a ritual game of attack and counterattack.

One such casualty graduated from a small liberal arts col- 12
lege, where she "luxuriated in the endless discussions." At the
urging of her professors, she decided to make academia her
profession. But she changed her mind after a year in an art history program at a major university. She felt she had fallen into
a "den of wolves." "I wasn't cut out for academia," she concluded. But does academia have to be so combative that it
cuts people like her out?

In many university classrooms, "critical thinking" means 13
reading someone's life work, then ripping it to shreds. Though
critique is surely one form of critical thinking, so are integrating ideas from disparate fields and examining the context out
of which they grew. Opposition does not lead to truth when we
ask only "What's wrong with this argument?" and never "What
can we use from this in building a new theory, and a new
understanding?"

Several years ago I was on a television talk show with a rep- 14
resentative of the men's movement. I didn't foresee any problem, since there is nothing in my work that is anti-male. But in
the room where guests gather before the show I found a man
wearing a shirt and tie and a floor-length skirt, with waist-
length red hair. He politely introduced himself and told me he
liked my book. Then he added: "When I get out there, I'm going

to attack you. But don't take it personally. That's why they invite me on, so that's what I'm going to do."

When the show began, I spoke only a sentence or two before 15 this man nearly jumped out of his chair, threw his arms before him in gestures of anger and began shrieking—first attacking me, but soon moving on to rail against women. The most disturbing thing about his hysterical ranting was what it sparked in the studio audience: they too became vicious, attacking not me (I hadn't had a chance to say anything) and not him (who wants to tangle with someone who will scream at you?) but the other guests: unsuspecting women who had agreed to come on the show to talk about their problems communicating with their spouses.

This is the most dangerous aspect of modeling intellectual 16 interchange as a fight: it contributes to an atmosphere of animosity that spreads like a fever. In a society where people express their anger by shooting, the result of demonizing those with whom we disagree can be truly demonic.

I am not suggesting that journalists stop asking tough ques- 17 tions necessary to get at the facts, even if those questions may appear challenging. And of course it is the responsibility of the media to represent serious opposition when it exists, and of intellectuals everywhere to explore potential weaknesses in others' arguments. But when opposition becomes the overwhelming avenue of inquiry, when the lust for opposition exalts extreme views and obscures complexity, when our eagerness to find weaknesses blinds us to strengths, when the atmosphere of animosity precludes respect and poisons our relations with one another, then the culture of critique is stifling us. If we could move beyond it, we would move closer to the truth.

VOCABULARY

paragraph 1: vitriolic
paragraph 3: critique
paragraph 8: Holocaust, dissemination, disinformation
paragraph 11: winnowing
paragraph 12: luxuriated
paragraph 16: demonizing

QUESTIONS

1. What is the "boundary between public and private," referred to in paragraph 3, and how does its breakdown contribute to the culture of critique?

2. On what analogy is the culture of critique based? What reasons does Tannen give for rejecting the analogy?

3. What are the effects of the culture of critique on print and television journalism, academia, and public discourse generally? What examples does Tannen give of these effects?

4. What solution does she propose?

SUGGESTIONS FOR WRITING

1. Both Ellen Goodman (see pp. 279–281) and Deborah Tannen consider the debate of current issues on television talk shows. Discuss the extent to which they agree on what happens in these debates, on the reasons for what happens, and on ways to improve public discourse.

2. Describe a debate on a current issue on a recent televised news program or talk show, or in one of your classes. Discuss what took place in light of Tannen's comments on "the culture of critique."

Cause and Effect

Earlier we discussed some ways of analyzing cause and effect in paragraphs and essays. These include tracing an effect to its recent or immediate cause (death because of famine) and to its more distant or remote causes (drought, soil erosion, ignorance, indifference, neglect). We also discussed the "four causes" of an object —the materials of its manufacture (material cause), the shape given it (formal cause), its maker (efficient cause), and use (final cause).

Cause may also be analyzed through the words *necessary* and *sufficient*, as when we say that getting an "A" on the final exam is necessary but not sufficient for an "A" in the course: an "A" on the final would be sufficient only if the exam solely determined the course grade. A necessary condition is one that must be present for something to happen. The condition is sufficient if the event must happen. When scientists say that a necessary condition of getting a cold is exposure to a virus, they mean that a virus of some kind must be present—not that the virus always produces a cold. Other conditions obviously need to be present, but scientists do not now claim to know what all of these are. If all necessary conditions of the cold were known, we would consider their joining sufficient to produce the cold.

In reasoning about cause in this way, we implicitly recognize that events, like the reasons for our actions, are complex. Yet this is not what some of our statements show. Statements that generalize about *the* cause of a cold, or some other complex physical or social or political ill, often mistakenly assume that a single cause can be identified. Another hasty generalization arises from the idea that one event must be the cause of another because it precedes it: I caught the cold "because" I was soaked in a rainstorm. Temporal sequence does not necessarily make one event the cause of the next. Clearly we might have caught the cold even if we had not been soaked, and we cannot know whether getting soaked will always give one a cold—even if it has always in the past. This kind of reasoning (discussed by George F. Will, "The Not-So-Mighty Tube") is given a Latin name—the *post hoc* fallacy, from the expression *"post hoc, ergo propter hoc"* ("after this, therefore because of this").

Norman Cousins

The name of NORMAN COUSINS (1915–1990) *is inseparably linked with the* Saturday Review, *which he edited from 1940 to 1977. Cousins won numerous awards for his journalism and his work on behalf of world peace, including the Peace Medal of the United Nations in 1971. His columns, collected in a number of books, provide a continuous commentary on postwar America and the world. His essay on Benny Paret raises important questions about boxing and spectator sports generally—and also about the responsibility of the public for the violence encouraged in them. Emile Griffith knocked out Paret in the twelfth round of a world championship welterweight bout at Madison Square Garden on March 25, 1962. Paret died on April 3, still in a coma, at the age of 24. The essay first appeared in* Saturday Review *on May 5, 1962.*

WHO KILLED BENNY PARET?

Sometime about 1935 or 1936 I had an interview with Mike   1
Jacobs, the prize-fight promoter. I was a fledgling newspaper
reporter at that time; my beat was education, but during the
vacation season I found myself on varied assignments, all the
way from ship news to sports reporting. In this way I found
myself sitting opposite the most powerful figure in the boxing
world.

There was nothing spectacular in Mr. Jacobs's manner or   2
appearance; but when he spoke about prize fights, he was no
longer a bland little man but a colossus who sounded the way
Napoleon must have sounded when he reviewed a battle. You
knew you were listening to Number One. His saying something made it true.

We discussed what to him was the only important element   3
in successful promoting—how to please the crowd. So far as
he was concerned, there was no mystery to it. You put killers
in the ring and the people filled your arena. You hire boxing
artists—men who are adroit at feinting, parrying, weaving,
jabbing, and dancing, but who don't pack dynamite in their
fists—and you wind up counting your empty seats. So you

searched for the killers and sluggers and maulers—fellows who could hit with the force of a baseball bat.

I asked Mr. Jacobs if he was speaking literally when he said people came out to see the killer.   4

"They don't come out to see a tea party," he said evenly. "They come out to see the knockout. They come out to see a man hurt. If they think anything else, they're kidding themselves."   5

Recently a young man by the name of Benny Paret was killed in the ring. The killing was seen by millions; it was on television. In the twelfth round he was hit hard in the head several times, went down, was counted out, and never came out of the coma.   6

The Paret fight produced a flurry of investigations. Governor Rockefeller was shocked by what happened and appointed a committee to assess the responsibility. The New York State Boxing Commission decided to find out what was wrong. The District Attorney's office expressed its concern. One question that was solemnly studied in all three probes concerned the action of the referee. Did he act in time to stop the fight? Another question had to do with the role of the examining doctors who certified the physical fitness of the fighters before the bout. Still another question involved Mr. Paret's manager; did he rush his boy into the fight without adequate time to recuperate from the previous one?   7

In short, the investigators looked into every possible cause except the real one. Benny Paret was killed because the human fist delivers enough impact, when directed against the head, to produce a massive hemorrhage in the brain. The human brain is the most delicate and complex mechanism in all creation. It has a lacework of millions of highly fragile nerve connections. Nature attempts to protect this exquisitely intricate machinery by encasing it in a hard shell. Fortunately, the shell is thick enough to withstand a great deal of pounding. Nature, however, can protect man against everything except man himself. Not every blow to the head will kill a man—but there is always the risk of concussion and damage to the brain. A prize fighter may be able to survive   8 even repeated brain concussions and go on fighting, but the damage to his brain may be permanent.

In any event, it is futile to investigate the referee's role and 9 seek to determine whether he should have intervened to stop the fight earlier. This is not where the primary responsibility lies. The primary responsibility lies with the people who pay to see a man hurt. The referee who stops a fight too soon from the crowd's viewpoint can expect to be booed. The crowd wants the knockout; it wants to see a man stretched out on the canvas. This is the supreme moment in boxing. It is nonsense to talk about prize fighting as a test of boxing skills. No crowd was ever brought to its feet screaming and cheering at the sight of two men beautifully dodging and weaving out of each other's jabs. The time the crowd comes alive is when a man is hit hard over the heart or the head, when his mouthpiece flies out, when blood squirts out of his nose or eyes, when he wobbles under the attack and his pursuer continues to smash at him with poleax impact.

Don't blame it on the referee. Don't even blame it on the 10 fight managers. Put the blame where it belongs—on the prevailing mores that regard prize fighting as a perfectly proper enterprise and vehicle of entertainment. No one doubts that many people enjoy prize fighting and will miss it if it should be thrown out. And that is precisely the point.

VOCABULARY

paragraph 1: fledgling
paragraph 2: colossus
paragraph 3: adroit, feinting, parrying
paragraph 8: hemorrhage
paragraph 9: poleax

QUESTIONS

1. Cousins distinguishes between the immediate and the remote causes of Paret's death (see p. 296). What does he show to be the immediate cause, and why can this cause be stated with near certainty?

2. Cousins is concerned chiefly with the remote cause of Paret's death. How is this concern basic to his purpose in writing the essay? What are the chief indications of that purpose?

3. How would a different purpose have required Cousins to focus instead on the immediate cause?

4. How does Cousins establish the remote cause? Is his evidence statistical—based on a sample of statements of boxing fans? Is it theoretical—based on a discussion of "human nature"? Is he concerned with the psychology of the crowd or the sociology of boxing? Is his analysis of the event intended to offer a complete explanation?

SUGGESTIONS FOR WRITING

1. Analyze two or more pro football or hockey games to determine the extent of their appeal to violent emotions.

2. Discuss the immediate and remote (or mediate) causes of an important event in your life, for example, your decision to attend a particular college, to enter a particular field, or to play a sport. Highlight the causes you consider the most, and explain why you do.

George F. Will

GEORGE F. WILL *taught political science and served as a senatorial aide before turning to journalism. From 1972 to 1976, he served as Washington editor of the* National Review *and began his political column for* Newsweek *in 1975. Will is also a columnist for* The Washington Post *and appears regularly on ABC news programs. His numerous books include* Soulcraft as Statecraft *(1983) and* Restoration *(1992), as well as* The Morning After *(1986),* Suddenly *(1990), and* The Leveling Wind *(1994), collections of his newspaper and magazine columns. In 1977 Will received the Pulitzer Prize for Commentary. In the following essay he discusses an interesting example of "post hoc" reasoning about the effects of television.*

THE NOT-SO-MIGHTY TUBE

In simpler days it was said that the hand that rocked the cra- 1
dle ruled the world. Today, says Professor Michael J. Robinson
of Catholic University (in *The Public Interest*), the rule of television rocks the world: "In the 1950s television was a *reflection* of
our social and political opinions, but by the 1960s it was an
important *cause* of them." He insists that television journalism
did "engender" fundamental changes, "moving us" toward conservatism, and entertainment programming is a "fomenter" of
social liberalism, "fostering" and "pushing us toward" change.

"Mary Tyler Moore and 'Mary Tyler Mooreism' seem to have 2
been unusually effective in 'consciousness raising.' Between
1958 and 1969, the percentage of women accepting the idea
that a woman could serve effectively as President actually
declined by 3 percent. But between 1969 and 1972, the proportion of women who came to accept the idea of a female President *increased* by 19 percent. . . . During those first two seasons
in which Mary Richards and Rhoda Morgenstern came to television, the level of public support among women for a female
President increased more than among any other two-year—or
ten-year—period since the 1930s."

The *post hoc, ergo propter hoc* fallacy involves mistaking mere 3
antecedents for causes: the cock crows and then the sun rises,
so the crowing caused the sunrise. Did prim Mary cause consciousness to rise? Does the water wheel move the river? Television conforms entertainment to market research, struggling
to paddle as fast as the current. Robinson finds it ironic that
entertainment programing, the servant of commerce, is supportive of "social liberalism," which he identifies with "hedonism and libertarianism" (and "Maude"). But commerce,
which profits from the sovereignty of appetites, has never
been a conservative force.

Television is not always benign or even innocuous. When 4
vacuous or violent it is enervating and desensitizing; and it has
influenced, often unfortunately, the way Americans campaign
for office and for change. But it is more mirror than lever.

Robinson believes the "audio-visual orgy of the 1960s" 5
shifted "power" upward toward the President and downward
toward "have-nots" such as the civil-rights movement, and
other "groups wretched or angry or clever enough to do what
was needed to become photogenic." But Kennedy, constantly
on television and consistently stymied by Congress, learned
that conspicuousness is not power. Jimmy Carter, who uses
television even more assiduously than Kennedy did, is learning that television does not make governing easier. Americans
have developed fine filters for what they consider static, commercial and political, so Carter's media blitz about the energy
crisis was like water thrown on sand: it left little trace. Thanks
in part to broadcasting, political rhetoric has become like
advertising, audible wallpaper, always there but rarely
noticed.

Robinson notes that the 1963 "March on Washington" ("the 6
greatest public-relations gambit ever staged") capped five
months of intense civil-rights coverage, during which the percentage of Americans regarding civil rights as "the most
important problem facing America" soared from 4 to 52. But it
is unhistorical to say that this means the networks had begun
"to define our political agenda."

Television did not give civil rights leaders the idea of a 7
March on Washington or make the idea effective. In 1941 the
mere threat (by A. Philip Randolph) of a march frightened FDR
into important policy changes. The civil rights movement did
not start with television, but with the moral and social
changes wrought by the Second World War. The movement's
first great victory was the Supreme Court's 1954 desegregation
decision, when television was in its infancy. (During the two
television decades the least "photogenic" branch of government, the judiciary, has grown in importance relative to the
other branches.) The movement had on its side great leaders,
centuries of grievances, the Constitution, and justice. It benefited from television, but did not depend upon it. Television
hastened change a bit, but probably did not determine the
direction or extent of change. What television did on its own

(for example, manufacturing Stokely Carmichael as a "black leader") was as evanescent as most shoddy fiction.

When Robinson says, "Nixon would have lost in 1968 had it not been for network news coverage of politics between 1964 and his election," he must mean either that LBJ would have been re-elected but for disintegration at home and defeat abroad; or that without television Americans would not have minded disintegration and defeat; or that without television there would not have been disintegration and defeat. The first idea is true but trivial; the last two are false. [8]

The United States has never had national newspapers, so the focus of news was local. But network news is "national news." So, Robinson says, television has shifted frustrations toward the national government. But the centralization of power in Washington began well before television and would have "nationalized" news, and frustrations, with no help from television. Robinson believes that television journalism, although accused of liberal bias, has recently stimulated political conservatism. But the limitations of government would have become apparent, and the conservative impulse would have had its day, even if television had developed only as an entertainment industry. [9]

To represent situation-comedy shows as shapers of the nation's consciousness is to portray the public as more passive and plastic than it is. To represent television journalism as a fundamentally transforming force is to make the nation's politics seem less purposeful, more mindless, more a matter of random causes than is the case. The contours of history are not determined by communications technology, however much it pleases people to think that history is what, and only what, can be seen at home. To see the rise of blacks, or the fall of LBJ, as primarily a consequence of television is to hollow out history. It discounts the noble and ignoble ideas and passions, heroes and villains and common people who make history. [10]

In the silly movie *Network*, millions of Americans are prompted by a deranged anchor man to sprint to their windows to shout, "We're mad as hell and we won't take it any [11] more." Modern man, proudly sovereign beneath a blank heaven, is prone to believe that "they" (evil persons, irresistible impulses, impersonal forces) control the world. Astrology, vulgar Marxism and Freudianism, and other doctrines nourish this need. So does the exaggeration of media influence. Journalists and perhaps even serious scholars, such as Robinson, who study television, are prone to believe that it turns the world. But the world is not that easy to turn.

VOCABULARY

paragraph 1: engender, fomenter
paragraph 3: antecedents, ironic, hedonism, libertarianism
paragraph 4: benign, innocuous, vacuous, enervating
paragraph 5: orgy, rhetoric
paragraph 10: plastic, contours, ignoble
paragraph 11: deranged

QUESTIONS

1. What in the reasoning that Will disputes illustrates the *post hoc* fallacy?
2. What evidence does Will present to show that television may not have created the civil rights movement and other social movements or influenced national politics to the extent that some people believe?
3. What alternative influences does he propose?
4. Does Will say or imply that television exerts no influence on our society and political life and thinking or that the media in general exert greater influence than they should?
5. Where does Will first state his thesis, and where does he restate it?
6. Do you agree with Will that media blitzes, like the one discussed in paragraph 5, exert less influence than some believe? On what evidence do you base your opinion?

SUGGESTIONS FOR WRITING

1. Trace an idea you hold about energy conservation or drug testing or nuclear power or a similar social or political issue today

to its sources—family, friends, school, church, the media, or your own thinking on the issue. State which of these influences was the greatest, and present evidence for your reasons.

2. Discuss the extent to which television influences your attitude toward thinking about a current social or political issue—the power of the presidency or the Supreme Court, for example. Build your discussion to a general assessment of the influence of television on your thinking on social and political issues.

Alan Wertheimer

ALAN WERTHEIMER, *Professor of Political Science at the University of Vermont, writes often on issues of public policy. His essay, reprinted here, first published in the* New York Times *on April 25, 1980, explores the dilemma that he believes underlies much discussion about government spending—the choice between "helping identifiable lives and saving statistical lives." Knowing that a large segment of his audience supports what he refers to as "welfare-state humanitarianism," Wertheimer uses the dilemma to force a recognition that the issue is complex, does not present a simple choice between right and wrong, and demands an examination of basic assumptions.*

STATISTICAL LIVES

Suppose the following were true: 1

At least some money spent on open-heart surgery could be   2
used to prevent heart disease. True, patients in need of such surgery might die, but many more lives would be saved.

Some money spent treating tooth decay among low-   3
income children might be used on fluoridation and dental hygiene. True, some decay would go untreated, but fewer children would ever need such treatment.

We could prohibit ransom payments to kidnappers. True,   4
kidnapped children might die, but by lowering the incentive to kidnap, fewer children would be taken.

We could drastically reduce unemployment compensation. 5 True, the unemployed would suffer, but by converting the money saved to private investment and by lowering the incentive to stay jobless, there would be substantially less unemployment.

These cases exhibit a similar structure. All involve choosing 6 between a policy designed to help specific persons and one that seeks to prevent the need for such help. These choices are especially difficult because we know who needs help. The patient requiring open-heart surgery, the kidnapped child, the unemployed auto worker—they have names and faces; they are "identifiable" lives. On the other hand, we do not know whose lives will be saved or who will benefit from the prevention of heart disease, tooth decay, kidnappings, or creation of new jobs. Some people will, and we may be able to estimate their numbers with precision. These are real lives, but they are only "statistical" lives.

We might say we do not have to choose between helping 7 those in need and preventing future needs. After all, we could do both. But resources are scarce, and even when resources are not at issue (as in the kidnapping case), we often must choose between competing persons or goals. We cannot do everything we might like to the extent we might like. We must often choose between helping identifiable lives and saving statistical lives.

I wish to make three points about these dilemmas. First we 8 do seem to favor the interests of identifiable lives (saving the kidnapped child) and it may not be irrational to do so. Second, we nevertheless do see the need to attend to the interests of statistical lives, even if this injures identifiable lives. Thus it is now common to hear people advocating directing more medical resources to primary prevention of disease and fewer to treatment. Israel's policy of refusing to negotiate with terrorists may risk the lives of some hostages, but we do see the point. Third, welfare-state policies focus on identifiable lives, whereas conservative economists prefer to focus on statistical lives.

Monetary theory and other technical issues aside, the new 9
Adam Smith tells us that however well-intentioned, welfare-
state policies have not (always) worked—on the policies' own
terms. Minimum-wage laws, unemployment compensation,
consumer protection, occupational safety, Medicaid, Social
Security—by interfering with market efficiency, by discouraging individual initiative, by impeding private-capital formation, by incurring large-scale expenditures on governmental
bureaucracies—all these policies (and others) have been self-
defeating. They argue that liberal economics, filled with concern for the genuine needs of identifiable lives, has swelled
the future ranks of statistical lives in need. Welfare-state humanitarianism is shortsighted, they say, and is thus less
humanitarian than we may believe.

We need not dwell on the accuracy of this account. Conser- 10
vative economists may be wrong about the facts. We certainly
need not assume that market choices and private-capital formation always serve the interests of all social groups, that regu-
lation always does more harm than good. But suppose
conservative economists are (sometimes) right about the facts.
Suppose that attempts to serve the needs of identifiable lives
do end up harming future statistical lives. Should we turn our
back on the needs that we see in order to prevent those that we
cannot see? Regrettably, the answer may sometimes be yes.

VOCABULARY

paragraph 4: incentive
paragraph 6: statistical
paragraph 8: dilemmas
paragraph 9: impeding, incurring, humanitarianism

QUESTIONS

1. Wertheimer's argument is in part inductive in showing that well-
   established facts and expert testimony make the dilemma real,
   not fictitious. What are these facts and testimony? What in the
   wording of paragraphs 9–10 shows that Wertheimer considers
   this evidence highly probable and not certain?

2. If we choose to save specific persons, what would be the consequences? What would they be if we choose to save "statistical" lives?

3. One way of refuting a dilemma is to "grasp the horns" and show that at least one of the alternatives is false or would not lead to the alleged consequences. Another way is to "go between the horns" and show that a third alternative exists—a policy that would save specific persons and "statistical" lives both. In paragraphs 7–8, how does Wertheimer anticipate refutation of the dilemma and answer it?

4. Do you agree with Wertheimer's response to the dilemma in paragraph 10? On what evidence do you base your agreement or disagreement—facts, expert testimony, or assumptions that you regard as self-evident?

SUGGESTIONS FOR WRITING

1. Present examples of your own of the dilemma Wertheimer presents, and use them to explore their implications for your own beliefs and conclusions.

2. Present a dilemma that you believe should concern Americans today. Introduce facts or expert testimony to show that the dilemma is a real one, anticipate a refutation of your dilemma and answer it, and state your own views on what can or should be done.

Roger D. Stone

ROGER D. STONE *worked for* Time *magazine from 1955 to 1970, serving in the 1960s as bureau chief in San Francisco, Rio de Janeiro, and Paris. He was vice-president of Chase Manhattan Bank until 1975, and in 1976 he joined the World Wildlife Fund—becoming vice-president in 1982. Stone is author of* Dreams of Amazonia *(1985), a history of the Brazilian rain forest. Stone's article on saving the world's jungles appeared in* The New York Times *on November 11, 1986.*

WHY SAVE TROPICAL FORESTS?

Many Americans feel that saving the world's tropical forests   1
warrant about as much concern as the snail darter. In Europe
and the United States, they say, deforestation was the inevitable and desirable consequence of economic progress;
why, therefore, should it be any different in the largely under-
developed nations where the world's tropical forests are to
be found?

It *is* different, and our failure to appreciate the difference   2
stems largely from our inability to distinguish between temperate and tropical conditions. The rich soils and relative biological simplicity of the temperate world enhances forest
conversion and eventual reforestation. In tropical forest regions, soils tend to be poor. Life supporting nutrients are
stored not in soils but in the trees. Remove them and the
whole fragile system collapses. History is littered with examples of failed efforts to convert large areas of tropical forest to
agriculture, cattle ranching or other "modern" uses.

People and nature both end up losers when the tropical for-   3
est is clumsily invaded. To begin with, such forests supply the
world with goods—hardwoods, rubber, fruits and nuts, drugs
and medicines and fragrances and spices—that often cannot
be successfully raised in any but natural conditions. Harvest-
ing beyond sustainable limits has already brought some of
the tropical forests' best hardwoods—Brazilian rosewood for
example—close to extinction.

The tropical forest is also a biological warehouse. Estimates   4
of the total number of species on the planet range up to 30
million, of which only 1.6 million have been identified. It is further estimated that tropical forests, while occupying only 7
percent of the earth's surface, may contain as many as half of
all the earth's forms of life. This means that only a tiny fraction
of all tropical forest species has so far been studied, and
despite the drug industry's increasing reliance on computer
modeling, genetic engineering and other laboratory devices,
concerned biologists regard the heedless squandering of the

tropical forests' known and unknown resources as a major tragedy.

Similarly, we depend on a small group of plants—corn, rice, wheat and the like—for a large part of our sustenance. From time to time, plant pathologists have found, the commonly used strains of these plants require genetic fortification from the wild to protect them from blight and disease. Since many such plants originated in tropical areas and only later were cultivated elsewhere, the primeval forests of the tropics represent a vast genetic storehouse of great potential value to everyone.

Left untouched, tropical forests also contribute to the stability of the world's climate. But when the forests are burned, the carbon released plays an important role in the buildup of atmospheric gases producing the "greenhouse effect," which is causing a warming trend on the planet. The consequences of this trend could be profound. America's corn belt could become a subtropical region, while the melting of the polar ice cap could cause sea levels to rise and lead to drastic losses of coastal land.

In view of all these factors, one might ask why the attack against the tropical forest continues so relentlessly. The answer is that even the infertile tropical forest is often capable of providing short-term economic benefits to individuals and corporations. Given the human propensity to enjoy one last meal if the alternative seems to be no meal at all, the present defoliation will probably continue unless a revolution in public and official attitudes—equivalent to the dramatic change of the 1980's in how smoking is perceived and handled—comes to the rescue at the 11th hour.

VOCABULARY

paragraph 1: deforestation
paragraph 4: computer modeling, genetic engineering, squandering
paragraph 5: plant pathologists, blight
paragraph 6: "greenhouse effect"
paragraph 7: defoliation

QUESTIONS

1. Why must we distinguish between temperate and tropical conditions in discussing deforestation and its consequences for the planet? What argument in defense of tropical deforestation is Stone refuting in making this distinction?

2. What causes of tropical deforestation does Stone cite? Does he claim to have cited all of them?

3. What would be the short-range effects of tropical deforestation—those that would immediately change our lives? What would be the remote or long-range effects that would change our lives in the future or speed a process now occurring? In what order does Stone present these effects?

4. Is Stone addressing a general audience—some of whom are unfamiliar with the issues and the scientific facts of tropical deforestation? Or is he addressing a special audience—all of whom are familiar with the issues and facts? In addressing a different audience, would he need to argue in a different way?

SUGGESTION FOR WRITING

Analyze the causal arguments for and against a current policy that affects the environment—for example, allowing fires in national forests to burn out of control. In the course of your analysis, discuss how people who are for or against an issue distinguish these effects and use them in making their case.

Herbert Hendin

HERBERT HENDIN, *Professor of Psychiatry at New York Medical College, is the author of* Black Suicide (1969), The Age of Sensation (1975), *and* Wounds of War: The Psychological Aftermath of Combat in Vietnam (1984), *and other psychosocial studies. Hendin states the basic assumptions of his study of drug users in his preface to* The Age of Sensation: *"Social facts are empty numbers unless translated into psychosocial facts that reflect the dynamism of life, the emotion behind the fact, the cause for the statistic. Culture is a two-way street, a flow between individuals*

*and institutions, single minds and collective forces." In this section
from the book, Hendin identifies conditions present in the lives of particular users, without trying to suggest that these are necessary—
that is, are always present.*

STUDENTS AND DRUGS

No more dramatic expression of the dissatisfaction students   1
feel with themselves can be found than students abusing
drugs. Students often become drug abusers, that is, heavy and
habitual users, in an attempt to alter their emotional lives, to
transform themselves into the people they wish they could be,
but feel they never could be without drugs. What they crave is
to restructure their own emotions, not to be themselves, but to
live as some "other." What this "other" is like and how it can be
achieved cut to the center of the changing American psyche.

The turmoil over performance, achievement, and success,   2
the increasing terror of becoming "too" involved with anyone;
the attempt to find in fragmentation the means of effecting
a pervasive change in one's total relation to life—all these are
everywhere prevalent on campus. Students abusing drugs
are often attempting to cure themselves of the malaise they
see everywhere around them and in themselves.

Why do some students take LSD or heroin while others take   3
marijuana or amphetamines? Why do still others take anything
and everything? Students who are intrigued by drugs can learn
through trial and error and from other students to find and
favor the drugs which most satisfy their particular emotional
needs. They rapidly become expert psychopharmacologists,
able to locate the specific drug cure for what disturbs them.
One student who by seventeen had tried just about everything
and had become a daily, intravenous heroin user, had rejected
LSD early in his drug career, explaining, "I can't see what anyone gets out of it. It just sort of makes you schizy—quiet one
minute and freaked out the next."

Some students were initially drawn to the "cops-and-   4
robbers" quality of drug abuse. While they were clearly out to
defy their parents and the whole structure of authority, they

were often unaware that their abuse had anything to do with their families, so profoundly had they pushed their rage at them out of their consciousness. Such students were invariably unable to deal with their parents directly and were bound in a need to defy them and a simultaneous need to punish themselves for their rebellion.

Drugs provided these students with both crime and punishment, while removing their defiance out of the direct presence of their parents. One student would "let his mind float away" and concentrate on music he liked whenever his father berated him. Afterward he went out and took whatever drugs he could buy. While he never connected his drug abuse with his anger toward his father, he often dreamed of it as a crime for which he would be punished. He had a dream in which a riot was going on in another part of town while he was shooting heroin. He was afraid that somehow he would be arrested along with the rioters. Drugs were clearly his way of rioting, of diverting the crime of rebellion to the crime of drug abuse and focusing his destructive potential on himself. The expectation this student had that he would be arrested was typical, and revelatory of the appeal of drugs for him. Jail signified to such students a concrete way of locking up their rage. Drugs permitted them to both contain their rage and to express it in a way that gave them a sense of defiance, however self-damaging that defiance may be. Often, students who are most in trouble with the police over drugs are those for whom the need for crime and punishment was more significant than the need for drugs.

For most of the students who abused them, drugs also provided the illusion of pleasurable connection to other people while serving to detach them from the emotions real involvement would arouse. Drugs were, for these students, the best available means of social relations. Heroin abusers found in the junkie underworld a sense of security, belonging, and acceptance derived from the acknowledgement and the shared need for heroin. LSD abusers felt their most intimate experiences involved tripping with another person. Marijuana abusers felt that drugs "took the edge off their personality" enough to permit them to be gentle and to empathize with other people. Amphetamine abusers were pushed into the social round on amphetamine energy, often being enabled to go through sexual experience they would otherwise have found unendurable.

For many students drug abuse is the means to a life without drugs. Such students take drugs to support the adaptation they are struggling to make. Once it is established, they are often able to maintain it without drugs. The period of heavy drug abuse often marks the crisis in their lives when they are trying to establish a tolerable relation to the world and themselves. Appealing, tumultuous, sometimes frighteningly empty, the lives of students who turn to drugs are an intense, dramatic revelation of the way students feel today, what they are forced to grapple with not only in the culture, but in themselves.

7

VOCABULARY

paragraph 1: psyche
paragraph 2: fragmentation, malaise
paragraph 3: amphetamines, psychopharmacologists, intravenous
paragraph 5: berated, revelatory
paragraph 6: illusion, empathize
paragraph 7: tumultuous

QUESTIONS

1. Does Hendin single out a sufficient cause of drug use among students, or instead identify a number of related (or unrelated) necessary causes?

2. Does he distinguish psychological from social causes, or does he assume these are one and the same?

3. Is Hendin generalizing about all students—even those who do not use drugs—or is he commenting merely on student drug users?

4. How does drug use foster "fragmentation" in the drug user? How can "fragmentation" provide a solution to the problems Hendin identifies in paragraph 2?

5. What does Hendin mean by the statement, "For many students drug abuse is the means to a life without drugs"?

SUGGESTIONS FOR WRITING

1. Describe tensions you have observed in yourself or in fellow students, and discuss the extent to which these tensions resemble those that Hendin identifies. Suggest some of the causes for those you have experienced or observed.

2. Hendin's book appeared in 1975. Investigate recent studies of drug use in a particular class of people—for example, children sixteen and younger—and compare the causes identified by the authors.

16

Deductive Reasoning

Induction, as we saw, sometimes reasons from particular instances to a general conclusion or truth:

> I studied the equations but didn't do the practice problems, and I failed algebra. I studied French but skipped the language lab and did poorly on the exam. I studied the formulas and performed the experiments carefully and passed Chemistry [*three particular instances*]. Learning seems to depend on practice as well as study [*probable truth*].

Deduction, by contrast, is the process of inference—of reasoning from a general truth to another general truth or a particular instance:

The act of learning is an act that depends on study and practice.
The mastery of French is an act of learning.
Therefore, the mastery of French is an act that depends on study and practice.

Usually the argument is shortened and worded less formally:

> Learning depends on study and practice, and therefore so does mastery of French.

In shortened arguments such as this, the major premise, or minor premise (as in the example), or conclusion may be implied. A shortened argument is called an *enthymeme*. In ordinary conversation we may say, in different words, "I passed French because I studied and went to the language lab."

Where inductive arguments depend on the weight of factual evidence beyond the premises, deductive arguments depend on the premises alone as evidence for the conclusion. No other evidence is required because the premises are regarded to be true—as in the *Declaration of Independence*:

316

> We hold these truths to be self-evident: that all men are created equal;
> that they are endowed by their creator with certain unalienable rights;
> that among these are life, liberty, and the pursuit of happiness.

From truths such as these—long-held beliefs, generalizations established by long experience, scientific "laws" confirmed by repeated observation and laboratory experiments—we draw conclusions, make inferences, as in our original example. Thus, if it is true that learning depends on study and practice and true also that mastery of French is an act of learning, it must be true that mastering French depends on study and practice. In a deductive argument, we look to see what other truths such premises imply or entail.

Though no other evidence but the premises *need* be provided, we may decide to illustrate or back up one or both. Most arguments in fact contain illustration and backing of some kind. For a true statement is not always obvious to everyone. In one kind of argument we may cite the experimental data that supports a scientific truth. In another we may cite laws, statutes, precedents, and judicial rulings. How detailed or technical the backing is depends on the audience being addressed. A trial lawyer shares with the judge and other lawyers certain assumptions, standards, and legal knowledge that usually need to be presented to a jury unacquainted with the applicable law.

The deductive argument must satisfy two requirements: the propositions that form the premises must be true, and the process of reasoning must be correct, or to use the technical term, must be valid.

Note that "valid" does not mean "true": an argument may be false in its premises, but still be valid if the process of inference from these premises is correct. Here is a valid argument, both of whose premises are false:

All Texans are taxpayers.
All property owners are Texans.
Therefore, all property owners are taxpayers.

We ask of an argument that it be valid in its reasoning and true in its premises. A valid argument whose premises are true is called sound. The argument just cited would be sound, if, in fact, all Texans do pay taxes, and all property owners (everywhere) are Texans. The argument is, of course, unsound. Logicians have complex techniques for testing the validity of the many kinds of syllogism; we cannot review them here. But we need to keep in mind a few characteristics that invalidate deductive arguments:

Someone says to us: "My neighbors must all be property owners because they all pay taxes." Something strikes us as wrong with the statement, but what is it? We can construct the whole argument as follows:

All property owners are taxpayers.
My neighbors are taxpayers.
Therefore, my neighbors are property owners.

The trouble is with the middle term, taxpayers. The major term of a syllogism is the predicate term of its conclusion; the minor term is the subject. The term that appears in the premises but not in the conclusion is called the middle term.

All	$\underline{\text{A}}$	is	$\underline{\text{B}}$
	middle		MAJOR
All	$\underline{\text{C}}$	is	$\underline{\text{A}}$
	MINOR		middle
All	$\underline{\text{C}}$	is	$\underline{\text{B}}$
	MINOR		MAJOR

A valid argument may not have more than these three terms. The middle term must also be "distributed" in at least one of the premises; that is, it must refer to—that is, be distributed among—all members of the class named. In the argument above, the middle term, *taxpayers*, is undistributed in both premises—referring in each to some members of the class taxpayers, but not necessarily to all:

All property owners are taxpayers.
My neighbors are taxpayers.

Though all property owners are taxpayers, not all taxpayers may own property. And though all my neighbors are taxpayers, not all taxpayers may be my neighbors. The argument is thus invalid.

Other invalid arguments can be analyzed more easily. The middle term must not be ambiguous, as in the following argument:

Whoever helps himself is helped by God.
A thief helps himself.
Therefore, a thief is helped by God.

And both premises must be affirmative if the conclusion is so: if one of the premises is negative, so must be the conclusion. And, if both premises are negative, no conclusion follows. The following argument is invalid for this reason:

No dogs are welcome visitors.
No children are dogs.
Therefore, children are welcome visitors.

In developing arguments of our own, we need to remember that an argument may seem "logical" because the process of reasoning is correct, and yet be unsound because the premises are questionable or false. In reading arguments, we need to consider both the premises that form it and the way the writer reasons from them.

H. L. Mencken

HENRY LOUIS MENCKEN (1880–1956) *wrote for Baltimore newspapers and other periodicals most of his life and was one of the founders and editors of the* American Mercury *magazine. His satirical essays on American life and politics were collected in six volumes under the title* Prejudices. *His three volumes of autobiography describe his youth in Baltimore and his later career in journalism. Mencken's interests were wide, and he wrote extensively about American democracy and American English, whose characteristics he describes in* The American Language (*Fourth Edition, 1936*). *His reflections on war were published in* Minority Report (1956).

REFLECTIONS ON WAR

The thing constantly overlooked by those hopefuls who talk of abolishing war is that it is by no means an evidence of decay but rather a proof of health and vigor. To fight seems to be as natural to man as to eat. Civilization limits and wars upon the impulse but it can never quite eliminate it. Whenever the effort seems to be most successful—that is, whenever man seems to be submitting most willingly to discipline, the spark is nearest to the powder barrel. Here repression achieves its inevitable work. The most warlike people under civilization are precisely those who submit most docilely to the rigid inhibitions of peace. Once they break through the bounds of their repressed but steadily accumulating pugnacity, their destructiveness runs to great lengths. Throwing off the chains of order, they leap into the air and kick their legs. Of all the nations engaged in the two World Wars the Germans, who were the most rigidly girded by conceptions of renunciation and duty, showed the most gusto for war for its own sake.

The powerful emotional stimulus of war, its evocation of   2
motives and ideals which, whatever their error, are at least more stimulating than those which impel a man to get and keep a safe job—that is too obvious to need laboring. The effect on the individual soldier of its very horror, filling him with a sense of the heroic, increases enormously his self-respect. This increase in self-respect reacts upon the nation, and tends to save it from the deteriorating effects of industrial discipline. In the main, soldiers are men of humble position and talents—laborers, petty mechanics, young fellows without definite occupation. Yet no one can deny that the veteran shows a certain superiority in dignity to the average man of his age and experience. He has played his part in significant events; he has been a citizen in a far more profound sense than any mere workman can ever be. The effects of all this are plainly seen in his bearing and his whole attitude of mind. War may make a fool of man, but it by no means degrades him; on the contrary, it tends to exalt him, and its net effects are much like those of motherhood on women.

That war is a natural revolt against the necessary but ex-   3
tremely irksome discipline of civilization is shown by the difficulty with which men on returning from it re-adapt themselves to a round of petty duties and responsibilities. This was notably apparent after the Civil War. It took three or four years for the young men engaged in that conflict to steel themselves to

the depressing routine of everyday endeavor. Many of them, in fact, found it quite impossible. They could not go back to shovelling coal or tending a machine without intolerable pain. Such men flocked to the West, where adventure still awaited them and discipline was still slack. In the same way, after the Franco-Prussian War, thousands of young German veterans came to the United States, which seemed to them one vast Wild West. True enough, they soon found that discipline was necessary here as well as at home, but it was a slacker discipline and they themselves exaggerated its slackness in their imagination. At all events, it had the charm of the unaccustomed.

We commonly look upon the discipline of war as vastly more rigid than any discipline necessary in time of peace, but this is an error. The strictest military discipline imaginable is still looser than that prevailing in the average assembly-line. The soldier, at worst, is still able to exercise the highest conceivable functions of freedom—that is, he is permitted to steal and to kill. No discipline prevailing in peace gives him anything even remotely resembling this. He is, in war, in the position of a free adult; in peace he is almost always in the position of a child. In war all things are excused by success, even violations of discipline. In peace, speaking generally, success is inconceivable except as a function of discipline.

The hope of abolishing war is largely based upon the fact that men have long since abandoned the appeal to arms in their private disputes and submitted themselves to the jurisdiction of courts. Starting from this fact, it is contended that disputes between nations should be settled in the same manner, and that the adoption of the reform would greatly promote the happiness of the world.

Unluckily, there are three flaws in the argument. The first, which is obvious, lies in the circumstances that a system of legal remedies is of no value if it is not backed by sufficient force to impose its decisions upon even the most powerful litigants—a sheer impossibility in international affairs, for even if one powerful litigant might be coerced, it would be plainly impossible to coerce a combination, and it is precisely a combination of the powerful that is most to be feared. The second lies in the fact that any legal system, to be worthy of credit, must be administered by judges who have no personal interest in the litigation before them—another impossibility, for all the judges in the international court, in the case of disputes between first-class powers, would either be appointees of those powers, or appointees of inferior powers that were under their direct influence, or obliged to consider the effects of their enmity. The third objection lies in the fact, frequently forgotten, that the courts of justice which now exist do not actually dispense justice, but only law, and that this law is frequently in direct conflict, not only with what one litigant honestly believes to be his rights, but also with what he believes to be his honor. Practically every litigation, in truth, ends with either one litigant or the other nursing what appears to him as an outrage upon him. For both litigants to go away satisfied that justice has been done is almost unheard of.

In disputes between man and man this dissatisfaction is not of serious consequence. The aggrieved party has no feasible remedy; if he doesn't like it, he must lump it. In particular, he has no feasible remedy against a judge or a juryman who, in his view, has treated him ill; if he essayed vengeance, the whole strength of the unbiased masses of men would be exerted to destroy him, and that strength is so enormous, compared to his own puny might, that it would swiftly and certainly overwhelm him. But in the case of first-class nations there would be no such overwhelming force in restraint. In a few cases the general opinion of the world might be so largely against them that it would force them to acquiesce in the judgment rendered, but in perhaps a majority of important cases there would be sharply divided sympathies, and it would constantly encourage resistance. Against that resistance there would be nothing save the counter-resistance of the opposition—*i.e.*, the judge against the aggrieved litigant, the twelve jurymen against the aggrieved litigant's friends, with no vast and impersonal force of neutral public opinion behind the former.

VOCABULARY

paragraph 1: repression, docilely, inhibitions, pugnacity, girded, gusto
paragraph 2: stimulus, evocation, impel, deteriorating, profound
paragraph 3: endeavor
paragraph 6: litigants, coerced
paragraph 7: feasible, aggrieved, essayed, puny

QUESTIONS

1. In paragraphs 1–4, Mencken argues that war will not be easily abolished, and he states his major premise explicitly: "To fight seems to be as natural to man as to eat." How do the wording of his statement and the wording of others in these paragraphs show that Mencken regards these premises as certain and decisive evidence for his conclusions? What conclusions does he reach based on these premises?

2. Though he regards his premises as certain, Mencken explains and illustrates them. What examples does he present? Does he discuss one civilization or instead generalize about "warlike people" on the basis of observations made over a period of time?

3. Paragraph 1 of the Mencken essay contains the making of several syllogisms. In the first of these, the major premise may be stated in these words: "The expression of a natural instinct is evidence of health and vigor." What are the minor premise and conclusion?

4. In paragraph 1 Mencken argues that repression of a natural instinct leads to increased destructiveness. What are the minor premise and the conclusion.

5. L. A. White, in *Science of Culture*, argues that the need for military conscription refutes the assumption that people are naturally warlike. Given his assumptions and evidence, how might Mencken answer this objection? What do paragraphs 5–7 suggest?

6. In paragraphs 5–7 Mencken challenges "the hope of abolishing war," a hope based on the assumption that people have long since "submitted themselves to the jurisdiction of courts." What flaws does Mencken find in the argument, and what kind of evidence does he present in refutation? Does he deal with particular instances or instead generalize from observations made over a period of time?

7. Decide whether the following arguments are sound (review p. 317). It may be necessary to reword the premises:

   a. Since all voters are citizens and I am a voter, I am a citizen.

   b. Since all voters are citizens and I am a citizen, I am a voter.

   c. Since the Irish are vegetarians and Bernard Shaw was Irish, Shaw was a vegetarian.

   d. Those who made 93 or better on the exam will receive an A in the course. Seven of us received an A in the course and therefore must have made 93 or better on the exam.

   e. Since beneficent acts are virtuous and losing at poker benefits others, losing at poker is virtuous.

8. An *enthymeme* is a condensed syllogism (see p. 316). In the following enthymemes, reconstruct the original syllogism by supplying the missing premise, and then evaluate the argument. The premises and conclusion may need rewording:

   a. John F. Kennedy was a good President because he supported the space program and other kinds of scientific research.

   b. Capital punishment protects society from depraved individuals.

   c. I am successful at business because I once had a paper route.

   d. I am an independent voter, just as my father and grandfather were.

SUGGESTION FOR WRITING

Write an argument for or against one of the following. In an additional paragraph identify one or more assumptions that underlie your argument, and explain why you hold these assumptions:

a. setting the drinking age at 21

b. a ban on smoking in restaurants

c. retaining the 55-mile-per-hour speed limit

d. periodic examination of licensed drivers

e. required attendance in college classes

Kenneth B. Clark

KENNETH B. CLARK, Distinguished Professor of Psychology at City College of New York from 1970 to 1975, began teaching at City College in 1942. His writings have exerted wide influence on social legislation and judicial thinking about civil rights. His many influential books include Dark Ghetto (1965) and Pathos of Power (1974), from which this section on "relevance" in education is taken.

THE LIMITS OF RELEVANCE

As one who began himself to use the term "relevant" and to insist on its primacy years ago, I feel an obligation to protest the limits of relevance or to propose a redefinition of it to embrace wider terms.

Definitions of education that depend on immediate relevance ignore a small but critical percentage of human beings, the individuals who for some perverse reason are in search of an education that is not dominated by the important, socially and economically required pragmatic needs of a capitalist or a communist or a socialist society. Such an individual is not certain what he wants to be; he may not even be sure that he wants to be successful. He may be burdened with that perverse intelligence that finds the excitement of life in a continuous involvement with ideas.

For this student, education may be a lonely and tortuous process not definable in terms of the limits of course requirements or of departmental boundaries, or the four- or six-year span of time required for the bachelor's or graduate degree. This student seems unable to seek or to define or to discuss relevance in terms of externals. He seems somehow trapped by the need to seek the dimensions of relevance in relation to an examination and re-examination of his own internal values. He may have no choice but to assume the burden of seeking to define the relevance of the human experience as a reflection of the validity of his own existence as a value-seeking, socially sensitive, and responsive human being. He is required to deny himself the protective, supporting crutch of accepting and clutching uncritically the prevailing dogmatisms, slogans, and intellectual fashions.

If such a human being is to survive the inherent and proba-   4
bly inevitable aloneness of intellectual integrity, he must balance it by the courage to face and accept the risks of his individuality; by compassion and empathetic identification with the frailties of his fellow human beings as a reflection of his own; by an intellectual and personal discipline which prevents him from wallowing in introspective amorphousness and childlike self-indulgence. And, certainly, he must demonstrate the breadth of perspective and human sensitivity and depth of affirmation inherent in the sense of humor which does not laugh at others but laughs with man and with the God of Paradox who inflicted upon man the perpetual practical joke of the human predicament.

American colleges, with few notable exceptions, provide lit-   5
tle room for this type of student, just as American society provides little room for such citizens. Perhaps it is enough to see that institutions of higher education do not destroy such potential. One could hope wistfully that our colleges and even our multiuniversities could spare space and facilities to serve and to protect those students who want to experiment without being required to be practical, pragmatic, or even relevant.

Is it possible within the complexity and cacophony of our   6
dynamic, power-related, and tentatively socially sensitive institutions for some few to have the opportunity to look within, to read, to think critically, to communicate, to make mistakes, to seek validity, and to accept and enjoy this process as valid in itself? Is there still some place where relevance can be defined in terms of the quest—where respect for self and others can be taken for granted as one admits not knowing and is therefore challenged to seek?

May one dare to hope for a definition of education which   7
makes it possible for man to accept the totality of his humanity without embarrassment? This would be valuable for its own

sake, but it might also paradoxically be the most pragmatic form of education—because it is from these perverse, alone-educated persons that a practical society receives antidotes to a terrifying sense of inner emptiness and despair. They are the font of the continued quest for meaning in the face of the mocking chorus of meaninglessness. They offer the saving reaffirmation of stabilizing values in place of the acceptance of the disintegration inherent in valuelessness. They provide the basis for faith in humanity and life rather than surrender to dehumanization and destruction. From these impracticals come our poets, our artists, our novelists, our satirists, our humorists. They are our models of the positives, the potentials, the awe and wonder of man. They make the life of the thinking human being more endurable and the thought of a future tolerable.

VOCABULARY

paragraph 2: relevance, pragmatic, perverse
paragraph 3: dimensions, dogmatisms
paragraph 4: empathetic, introspective, amorphousness, paradox
paragraph 5: wistfully
paragraph 6: cacophony, validity
paragraph 7: antidotes, font, reaffirmation, dehumanization, satirists, humorists

QUESTIONS

1. How does Clark explain the meanings of the term *relevant*? Why does he briefly review these meanings?

2. What assumptions does Clark make about the educational needs of people?

3. What conclusions does he derive from his assumptions?

4. Do you agree that American colleges have little room for the kind of student described in paragraph 4? What is your answer to the questions Clark asks in paragraph 6?

5. Does Clark seek to refute those who argue the "pragmatic needs" of education? Or does he present confirming arguments only?

6. To what extent does Clark describe your goals in seeking an education?

SUGGESTION FOR WRITING

Evaluate one of the following statements on the basis of your experience and observation:

a. "American colleges, with few notable exceptions, provide little room for this type of student, just as American society provides little room for such citizens."

b. ". . . [I]t is from these perverse, alone-educated persons that a practical society receives antidotes to a terrifying sense of inner emptiness and despair."

Ellen Goodman

ELLEN GOODMAN's *column on pornography and the First Amendment was first published in January of 1984. The proposed ordinance described in the column was vetoed by the mayor of Minneapolis; a similar Indianapolis ordinance was later ruled invalid by the United States Court of Appeals in Chicago.*

WHEN PORNOGRAPHY
AND FREE SPEECH COLLIDE

Just a couple of months before the pool-table gang rape in   1
New Bedford, Massachusetts, *Hustler* magazine printed a photo feature that reads like a blueprint for the actual crime. There were just two differences between *Hustler* and real life. In *Hustler*, the woman enjoyed it. In real life, the woman charged rape.

There is no evidence that the four men charged with this   2
crime had actually read the magazine. Nor is there evidence that the spectators who yelled encouragement for two hours had held previous ringside seats at pornographic events.

But there is a growing sense that the violent pornography   3
being peddled in this country helps to create an atmosphere in which such events occur. As recently as last month, a study done by two University of Wisconsin researchers suggested that even "normal" men, prescreened college students, were changed by their exposure to violent pornography.

After just ten hours of viewing, reported researcher Edward   4
Donnerstein, "the men were less likely to convict in a rape trial,
less likely to see injury to a victim, more likely to see the victim
as responsible." Pornography may not cause rape directly, he
said, "but it maintains a lot of very callous attitudes. It justifies
aggression. It even says you are doing a favor to the victim."

If we can prove that pornography is harmful, then shouldn't   5
the victims have legal rights? This, in any case, is the theory
behind a city ordinance that recently passed the Minneapolis
City Council. Vetoed by the mayor last week, it is likely to be
back at the council for an overriding vote, likely to appear in
other cities, other towns.

What is unique about the Minneapolis approach is that for   6
the first time it attacks pornography, not because of nudity or
sexual explicitness, but because it degrades and harms women.
It opposes pornography on the basis of sex discrimination.

University of Minnesota Law professor Catharine   7
MacKinnon, who coauthored the ordinance with feminist
writer Andrea Dworkin, says that they chose this tactic because they believe that pornography is central to "creating
and maintaining the inequality of the sexes. . . . Just being a
woman means you are injured by pornography."

They defined pornography carefully as, "the sexually explicit   8
subordination of women, graphically depicted, whether in pictures or in words." To fit their legal definition it must also include one of nine conditions that show this subordination, like
presenting women who "experience sexual pleasure in being
raped or . . . mutilated. . . ."

Under this law, it would be possible for a pool-table rape   9
victim to sue *Hustler.* It would be possible for a woman to sue
if she were forced to act in a pornographic movie. Indeed, since
the law describes pornography as oppressive to all women, it
would be possible for any woman to sue those who traffic in
the stuff for violating her civil rights.

In many ways, the Minneapolis ordinance is an appealing   10
attack on an appalling problem. The authors have tried to resolve a long and bubbling conflict among those who have both

a deep aversion to pornography and a deep loyalty to the value of free speech.

"To date," says Professor MacKinnon, "people have identi- 11 fied the pornographer's freedom with everybody's freedom. But we're saying that the freedom of the pornographer is the subordination of women. It means one has to take a side."

But the sides are not quite as clear as Professor MacKinnon 12 describes them. Nor is the ordinance.

Even if we accept the argument that pornography is harmful 13 to women—and I do—then we must also recognize that anti-Semitic literature is harmful to Jews and racist literature is harmful to blacks. For that matter, Marxist literature may be harmful to government policy.

It isn't just women versus pornographers. If women win the 14 right to sue publishers and producers, then so could Jews, blacks, a long list of people who may be able to prove they have been harmed by books, movies, speeches, or even records. The Manson murders, you may recall, were reportedly inspired by the Beatles.

We might prefer a library or bookstore or lecture hall with- 15 out *Mein Kampf* or the Grand Whoever of the Ku Klux Klan. But a growing list of harmful expressions would inevitably strangle freedom of speech.

This ordinance was carefully written to avoid problems of 16 banning and prior restraint, but the right of any woman to claim damages from pornography is just too broad. It seems destined to lead to censorship.

What the Minneapolis City Council has before it is a very 17 attractive theory. What MacKinnon and Dworkin have written is a very persuasive and useful definition of pornography. But they haven't yet resolved the conflict between the harm of pornography and the value of free speech. In its present form, this is still a shaky piece of law.

QUESTIONS

1. What distinguishes the Minneapolis definition of pornography from earlier definitions?

2. If the major premise of the ⬛
   violates their legal rights, what ⬛
   conclusion?

3. What does Goodman mean by "free⬛
   conclusion does she draw about the Min⬛
   her belief?

4. If Goodman opposes banning or censorship⬛
   books and opposes the prior restraint of speech t⬛
   censorship entail, is she therefore in favor of unrestr⬛
   sion of ideas? Or is it impossible to know from the ess⬛

5. Do you agree or disagree with Goodman that the Minneso⬛
   nance is flawed? Do you believe censorship is ever justified?⬛

SUGGESTIONS FOR WRITING

1. Write a letter to another city council, supporting the ordinance or opposing it. In the course of your letter, summarize Goodman's argument against the ordinance and explain why you agree or disagree with Goodman. State your own beliefs and defend them.

2. Goodman agrees with the Minneapolis City Council's definition of pornography but disagrees with the ordinance. Discuss an ordinance with which you similarly disagree and explain why you do. State whether or not a need exists for the ordinance and whether you would favor a better ordinance or none at all.

Jane Goodall

JANE GOODALL *began her studies of animal behavior as assistant and secretary to the distinguished paleontologist Dr. Louis Leakey, curator of the National Museum of Natural History in Nairobi, Kenya. Goodall began her study of chimpanzees under natural conditions in 1960 at Gombe Stream Research Centre, Tanzania, East Africa. Her numerous books and articles include* In the Shadow of Man *(1971),* The Chimpanzees of Gombe *(1986), and* Through a Window *(1990), in which the essay reprinted here appears. Goodall discusses an issue under fierce debate in Great Britain and the United States—the use of animals in biomedical research, product testing, and other experimental studies. From lusions perti-*

E

ANIMALS

ıman animals, 1
ɔrrespondingly
erns are raised
ther this be in
aboratories or
. This concern
ds to intense
with regard to

.iving animals 2
began in an era when the man in the street, while believing that animals felt pain (and other emotions) was not, for the most part, much concerned by their suffering. Subsequently, scientists were much influenced by the Behaviorists, a school of psychologists which maintained that animals were little more than machines, incapable of feeling pain or any human-like feelings or emotions. Thus it was not considered important, or even necessary, to cater to the wants and needs of experimental animals. There was, at that time, no understanding of the effect of stress on the endocrine and nervous systems, no inkling of the fact that the use of a stressed animal could affect the results of an experiment. Thus the conditions in which animals were kept—size and furnishings of cage, solitary versus social confinement—were designed to make the life of the caretaker and experimenter as easy as possible. The smaller the cage the cheaper it was to make, the easier to clean, and the simpler the task of handling its inmate. Thus it was hardly surprising that research animals were kept in tiny sterile cages, stacked one on top of the other, usually one animal per cage. And ethical concern for the animal subjects was kept firmly outside the (locked) doors.

As time went on, the use of non-human animals in the lab- 3
oratories increased, particularly as certain kinds of clinical
research and testing on *human* animals became, for ethical reasons, more difficult to carry out legally. Animal research was
increasingly perceived, by scientists and the general public, as
being crucial to all medical progress. Today it is, by and large,
taken for granted—the accepted way of gaining new knowledge about disease, its treatment and prevention. And, too,
the accepted way of testing all manner of products, destined
for human use, before they go on the market.

At the same time, thanks to a growing number of studies 4
into the nature and mechanisms of animals' perceptions and
intelligence, most people now believe that all except the most
primitive of non-human animals experience pain, and that the
"higher" animals have emotions similar to the human emotions that we label pleasure or sadness, fear or despair. How is
it, then, that scientists, at least when they put on their white
coats and close the lab doors behind them, can continue to
treat experimental animals as mere "things"? How can we, the
citizens of civilized, western countries, tolerate laboratories
which—from the point of view of animal inmates—are not
unlike concentration camps? I think it is mainly because most
people, even in these enlightened times, have little idea as to
what goes on behind the closed doors of the laboratories,
down in the basements. And even those who do have some
knowledge, or those who are disturbed by the reports of cruelty that are occasionally released by animal rights organizations, believe that *all* animal research is essential to human
health and progress in medicine and that the suffering so often
involved is a *necessary* part of the research.

This is not true. Sadly, while some research is undertaken 5
with a clearly defined objective that could lead to a medical
breakthrough, a good many projects, some of which cause
extreme suffering to the animals used, are of absolutely no
value to human (or animal) health. Additionally, many experiments simply duplicate previous experiments. Finally, some
research is carried out for the sake of gaining knowledge for its

own sake. And while this is one of our more sophisticated intellectual abilities, should we be pursuing this goal at the expense of other living beings whom, unfortunately for them, we are able to dominate and control? Is it not an arrogant assumption that we have the *right* to (for example) cut up, probe, inject, drug and implant electrodes into animals of all species simply in our attempt to learn more about what makes them tick? Or what effect certain chemicals might have on them? And so on.

We may agree that the general public is largely ignorant of 6
what is going on in the labs, and the reasons behind the research there, rather as the German people were mostly uninformed about the Nazi concentration camps. But what about the animal technicians, the veterinarians and the research scientists, those who are actually working in the labs and who know exactly what is going on? Are all those who use living animals as part of standard laboratory apparatus, heartless monsters?

Of course not. There may be some—there are occasional 7
sadists in all walks of life. But they must be in the minority. The problem, as I see it, lies in the way we train young people in our society. They are victims of a kind of brainwashing that starts, only too often, in school and is intensified, in all but a few pioneering colleges and universities, throughout higher science education courses. By and large, students are taught that it is ethically acceptable to perpetrate, in the name of science, what, from the point of view of the animals, would certainly qualify as torture. They are encouraged to suppress their natural empathy for animals, and persuaded that animal pain and feelings are utterly different from our own—if, indeed, they exist at all. By the time they arrive in the labs these young people have been programed to accept the suffering around them. And it is only too easy for them to justify this suffering on the grounds that the work being done is for the good of humanity. For the good of one animal species which has evolved a sophisticated capacity for empathy, compassion and understanding, attributes which we proudly acclaim as the hallmarks of humanity.

I have been described as a "rabid anti-vivisectionist." But my own mother is alive today because her clogged aortic valve was removed and replaced by that of a pig. The valve in question— a "bioplasticized" one, apparently—came, we were told, from a commercially slaughtered hog. In other words, the pig would have died anyway. This, however, does not eliminate my feelings of concern for that particular pig—I have always had a special fondness for pigs. The suffering of laboratory pigs and those who are raised in intensive farming units has become a special concern of mine. I am writing a book, *An Anthology of the Pig*, which I hope, will help to raise public awareness regarding the plight of those intelligent animals. [8]

Of course I should like to see the lab cages standing empty. So would every caring, compassionate human, including most of those who work with animals in biomedical research. But if all use of animals in the laboratory was *abruptly* stopped there would probably, for a while anyway, be a great deal of confusion, and many lines of inquiry would be brought to a sudden halt. This would inevitably lead to an increase in human suffering. This means that, until alternatives to the use of live animals in the research labs are widely available and, moreover, researchers and drug companies are legally compelled to use them, society will demand—and accept—the continued abuse of animals on its behalf. [9]

Already, in many fields of research and testing, the growing concern for animal suffering has led to major advances in the development of techniques such as tissue culture, *in vitro* testing, computer simulation and so on. The day will eventually come when it will no longer be necessary to use animals at all. It must. But much more pressure should be brought to bear for the speedy development of additional techniques. We should put far more money into the research, and give due acknowledgement and acclaim to those who make new breakthroughs—at the very least a series of Nobel prizes. It is necessary to attract the brightest in the field. Moreover, steps should be taken to insist on the use of techniques already developed and proven. In the meantime, it is imperative that [10] the numbers of animals used be reduced drastically. Unnecessary duplication of research must be avoided. There should be more stringent rules regarding what animals may and may not be used for. They should be used only for the most pressing projects that have clear-cut health benefits for many people, and contribute significantly to the alleviation of human suffering. Other uses of animals in the labs should be stopped *immediately*, including the testing of cosmetics and household products. Finally, so long as animals are used in our labs, for any reason whatsoever, they should be given the most humane treatment possible, and the best possible living conditions.

Why is it that only relatively few scientists are prepared to 11 back those who are insisting on better, more humane conditions for laboratory animals? The usual answer is that changes of this sort would cost so much that all progress in medical knowledge would come to an end. This is not true. Essential research would continue—the cost of building new cages and instigating better care-giving programmes would be considerable, but negligible, I am assured, when compared with the cost of sophisticated equipment used by research scientists today. Unfortunately, though, many projects are poorly conceived and often totally unnecessary. They might indeed suffer if the costs of maintaining the research animals are increased. People making their living from them would lose their jobs.

When people complain about the cost of introducing 12 humane living conditions, my response is: "Look at your lifestyle, your house, your car, your clothes. Think of the administrative buildings in which you work, your salary, your expenses, the holidays you take. And, after thinking about those things, *then* tell me that we should begrudge the extra dollars spent in making a little less grim the lives of the animals used to reduce human suffering."

Surely it should be a matter of moral responsibility that we 13 humans, different from other animals mainly by virtue of our more highly developed intellect and, with it, our greater capacity for understanding and compassion, ensure that medical progress speedily detaches its roots from the manure of non-human animal suffering and despair. Particularly when this involves the servitude of our closest relatives.

In the United States, federal law still requires that every 14 batch of hepatitis B vaccine be tested on a chimpanzee before it is released for human use. In addition, chimpanzees are still used in some highly inappropriate research—such as the effect on them of certain addictive drugs. There are no chimpanzees in the labs in Britain—British scientists use chimpanzees in the United States, or at the TNO Primate Centre in Holland where EEC funding has recently gone into a new chimpanzee facility. (British scientists do, of course, make massive use of other non-human primates and thousands of dogs, cats, rodents, and so forth.)

The chimpanzee is more like us than is any other living 15 being. Physiological similarities have been enthusiastically described by scientists for many years, and have led to the use of chimpanzees as "models" for the study of certain infectious diseases to which most non-human animals are resistant. There are, of course, equally striking similarities between humans and chimpanzees in the anatomy of the brain and nervous system, and—although many have been reluctant to admit to these—in social behavior, cognition and emotionality. Because chimpanzees show intellectual abilities once thought unique to our own species, the line between humans and the rest of the animal kingdom, once thought to be so clear, has become blurred. Chimpanzees bridge the gap between "us" and "them."

Let us hope that this new understanding of the chim- 16 panzees' place in nature will bring some relief to the hundreds who presently live out their lives as prisoners, in bondage to Man. Let us hope that our knowledge of their capacity for affection and enjoyment and fun, for fear and sadness and suffering, will lead us to treat them with the same compassion that we would show towards fellow humans. Let us hope that while medical science continues to use chimpanzees for painful or psychologically distressing experiments, we shall have the honesty to label such research for what, from the chimpanzees' point of view, it certainly is—the infliction of torture on innocent victims.

And let us hope that our understanding of the chimpanzee 17 will lead also to a better understanding of the nature of other non-human animals, a new attitude towards the other species with which we share this planet. For, as Albert Schweitzer said, "We need a boundless ethic that includes animals too." And at the present time our ethic, where non-human animals are concerned, is limited and confused.

If we, in the western world, see a peasant beating an emaci- 18 ated old donkey, forcing it to pull an oversize load, almost beyond its strength, we are shocked and outraged. That is cruelty. But taking an infant chimpanzee from his mother's arms, locking him into the bleak world of the laboratory, injecting him with human diseases—this, if done in the name of Science, is not regarded as cruelty. Yet in the final analysis, both donkey and chimpanzee are being exploited and misused for the benefit of humans. Why is one any more cruel than the other? Only because science has come to be venerated, and because scientists are assumed to be acting for the good of mankind, while the peasant is selfishly punishing a poor animal for his own gain. In fact, much animal research is self-serving too— many experiments are designed in order to keep the grant money coming in.

And let us not forget that we, in the west, incarcerate mil- 19 lions of domestic animals in intensive farm units in order to turn vegetable protein into animal protein for the table. While this is usually excused on grounds of economic necessity, or even regarded by some as sound animal husbandry, it is just as cruel as the beating of the donkey, the imprisonment of the chimpanzee. So are the fur farms. So is the abandonment of pets. And the illegal puppy farms. And fox hunting. And much that goes on behind the scenes when animals are trained to perform for our entertainment. The list could get very long.

Often I am asked whether I do not feel that it is unethical to 20 devote time to the welfare of "animals" when so many human beings are suffering. Would it not be more appropriate to help starving children, battered wives, the homeless? Fortunately, there are hundreds of people addressing their considerable talents, humanitarian principles and fund-raising abilities to such causes. My own particular energies are not needed there. Cruelty is surely the very worst of human sins. To fight cruelty, in any shape or form—whether it be towards other human beings or non-human beings—brings us into direct conflict with that unfortunate streak of *inhumanity* that lurks in all of us. If only we could overcome cruelty with compassion we should be well on the way to creating a new and boundless ethic—one that would respect all living beings. We should stand at the threshold of a new era in human evolution—the realization, at last, of our most unique quality: humanity.

VOCABULARY

paragraph 2: biomedical, endocrine
paragraph 3: clinical
paragraph 4: mechanism
paragraph 5: arrogant, assumption
paragraph 7: sadist, empathy, hallmark
paragraph 8: rabid
paragraph 10: *in vitro*, simulation, stringent
paragraph 11: sophisticated, negligible
paragraph 13: servitude
paragraph 15: cognition, emotionality
paragraph 18: venerated
paragraph 19: incarcerate, husbandry
paragraph 20: threshold, evolution

QUESTIONS

1. According to paragraph 1, what is the central moral issue in the debate over the use of non-human animals in biomedical research?

2. What misconceptions about the use of animals in biomedical research does Goodall discuss in her review of the issue in paragraphs 2–7?

3. What personal experiences, attitudes, and ideas does she discuss in paragraphs 8 and 9?

4. How does she use her opening review in paragraphs 2–7 and the discussion that follows in paragraphs 8 and 9 to develop her point about biochemical research?

5. What objections to humane treatment of animals does she answer in paragraphs 11–13? How does she use chimpanzees to confirm the need for humane treatment?

6. What use does she make of analogy in further supporting her thesis in paragraph 18?

7. Goodall states that "cruelty is surely the very worst of human sins" (paragraph 20). What conclusions does she draw from this belief about the use of animals in biomedical research? Where does she first refer to the ethic that should govern such research and policy decisions generally?

8. Goodall states that "until alternatives to the use of live animals in the research labs are widely available and, moreover, researchers and drug companies are legally compelled to use them, society will demand—and accept—the continued abuse of animals on its behalf" (paragraph 9). Does she believe that the use of animals in biomedical research has been ethical in the absence of alternatives? Would the use of animals be ethical if no other alternatives were to be found?

9. In your view, what policy should govern the use of animals in research of any kind? What beliefs govern your thinking on the issue?

SUGGESTIONS FOR WRITING

1. Though many will agree with Goodall that "cruelty is surely the very worst of human sins," they may not agree on how to define cruelty. For example, those who agree with the constitutional ban on "cruel and unusual punishment" may disagree on whether capital punishment is in fact cruel. Using the *New York Times Index* and other indexes available in your college library, discuss the role the word *cruelty* played in the public and judicial debate over capital punishment in 1973 and since. Focus on two or three judicial opinions issued in a single court case or articles prompted by the case or a particular event.

2. Discuss which of the definitions of cruelty in the judicial opinions or articles examined best agrees with your own conception.

Explain how your conception guides your thinking on capital punishment or another issue of concern to you.

Karl L. Schilling and Karen Maitland Schilling

KARL L. SCHILLING *is director of the American Association for Higher Education's Assessment Program and associate dean of the Western College Program at Miami University, in Oxford, Ohio.* KAREN MAITLAND SCHILLING *is university director of liberal education at the same university. Their article on university examinations appeared in the* Chronicle of Higher Education, *February 2, 1994.*

FINAL EXAMS DISCOURAGE TRUE LEARNING

While we were visiting another campus recently, a faculty member mentioned his bewilderment about what he saw happening to students as they moved from semester to semester. He frequently taught students in the "intro" course in his discipline during the fall semester and later, in the spring semester of the same academic year, taught many of the same students in the second course in his department's introductory students. He was dismayed at the blank stares he received in the spring when he'd say: "As you remember from last semester, we discussed. . . ." 1

Indeed, the ideas he was recalling had played an important role in the final exam that students had taken only three weeks before. Yet many looked at him as though he had started to speak a foreign language. Was he mistaken? Had he covered this material the year before but forgotten to talk about it this year? When he checked his syllabus, his notes, and his final exam, they all confirmed that he had covered the material and that the students had performed very well on the final-exam questions on the topic. What was happening? 2

Comprehensive final exams are one of the cherished tradi- 3
tions of higher education. Institutions stop teaching and set
aside entire weeks for these tests. Some even give students
extra days without classes before exam week to prepare. Leg-
ends of all-nighters during this period abound. Clearly, many
alumni hold fond memories of these academic hell weeks—of
having survived and proved themselves. Yet maybe this great
tradition is dysfunctional.

Thinking about the underlying symbolic communication in 4
the way we use final exams may provide an answer to our colleague's frustration. "Final" conveys a conclusion, a *terminus*. If
we faculty members think of the curriculum that our department offers as an educational program, as opposed to a collection of discrete courses, that exam at the end of a semester
is not really a terminus, but a pause to review and reflect
before moving onward.

However, students may mistake the pause as the end of 5
their need to know the material that they have just covered. To
students, our assessment practices may be unwittingly communicating the idea that they are finished with a particular set
of ideas and concepts. They will move on in the next semester
to discrete new chunks of material, they believe; recollection
or connection seems unnecessary.

Students may not understand that ideas and concepts run 6
through and connect courses, rather than falling neatly under
course titles. They may not realize that the way material is
"chunked" into courses is arbitrary. They probably haven't
guessed that the institution's bureaucratic need to organize
knowledge into billable units structures their courses more
than any compelling educational rationale does. They may not
realize, for example, that Freud did not separate his considerations of human psychology into separate topics such as personality development and abnormal psychology—although
students are exposed to his thought in courses that package
these topics into discrete one-week units.

Many of our current testing practices, particularly final 7
exams, encourage the development of academic bulimia:

binge-and-purge learning. If we were to graph the time that students spend studying, we would find a disappointingly low level of effort until the week or two before a major exam. (Most research shows that students spend less than an hour a day on academic work outside of the classroom.) Right before the exam, the graph would rise steeply, peaking the day before the exam, followed by a precipitous fall to near zero for the weeks following the exam. If we measured students' understanding and retention of material, we would find a similar curve—including the precipitous decline following the exam. Although objective tests, particularly multiple-choice final exams that rely heavily on superficial recall, may be the clearest perpetrator of this approach to learning, all forms of evaluation that communicate that the exam is a terminal event encourage it.

How might we signal students that education occurs in a continuum? Giving exams to students as they enter courses could serve this purpose, by providing an assessment of—and emphasis on—students' learning in previous courses. Indeed, one might imagine an "entrance-exam week" in which students would show that they had mastered the material necessary to enroll in subsequent courses. 8

A student would take an entrance exam (or undergo some other form of assessment) that would evaluate whether he or she had the knowledge and skills needed for the next class. Any student who failed to demonstrate the required competencies could take a short review course based on the material covered in the previous course. If a student failed the entrance test a second time, but had passed the previous course given as a prerequisite, he or she should be allowed to repeat the previous course, for no additional credit and at no financial cost. If a student insisted on taking the more-advanced course, he or she would be allowed to enroll, but "against educational advice." Clearly, if numerous students who had passed a course could not pass the entrance exam for the following class, the failure could be seen as that of the instructor or the curriculum. 9

Entrance exams would allow students who have been out of   10
school for a while or who have transferred from another institution to place themselves more accurately in the curriculum.
Indeed, one could imagine that if faculty members became
skilled enough at preparing these assessments, a first-year
student who was well-prepared might be able to go right into
more demanding, upper-level courses. Many institutions
already allow students to take tests in certain disciplines, such
as foreign languages, for advanced placement; the practice
deserves expansion.

Most important, entrance exams would help students see   11
the connections among courses within a major (or between
any upper-level course and the prerequisites that it requires).
Entrance exams also would signal that an instructor was not
going to re-teach material covered in the previous course. Having passed the entrance exam, the students should have the
earlier material fresh in mind and be ready to apply it in the
new course.

Instructors would have to be clear about their expectations   12
for students entering a particular course. The expectations
would need to be communicated to faculty members teaching
introductory courses and any other classes listed as prerequisites for upper-level courses. What better index of teaching
effectiveness could there be than one tied to students' mastery
of material needed in a subsequent course? Similarly, what
better corrective measure for grade inflation than having
another faculty member assess students' readiness to begin a
subsequent course?

Clear course goals would make both students and faculty   13
members more accountable for what goes on in the classroom.
They also would provide clear expectations about the level at
which students should be performing, which could help meet
the concerns of public officials about rampant grade inflation
and a lack of high educational standards.

Giving entrance exams would force faculty members to   14
talk with each other about what they do in their classes, what

the goals are for their majors, where in the curriculum the goals should be met, and maybe even what their courses have to offer to the liberal education of all students in the institution.

We have championed a "John Wayne" model for faculty members' behavior—a model of rugged individualists who, under a mistaken understanding of academic freedom, believe that what they do in their classrooms should not necessarily be subject to what happens in any other classroom. In doing so, we have conveyed the notion to students that they are performing for individual professors rather than developing themselves as learners. 15

Currently, students receive little encouragement to view their education as a continuous process, even if they are "traditional" students who graduate in four years and are not among those whose education is spread over 10 years or more. But the vision of a continuum of education is crucial if faculty members are to break the current cycle of having to repeat much of the same introductory material in course after course. We must signal students that they need to carry material forward, that we cannot continue to re-teach ideas as we do now. In short, we can change our educational system to promote a healthier way of thinking about learning. 16

VOCABULARY

paragraph 3: dysfunctional
paragraph 4: discrete
paragraph 7: bulimia, precipitous, perpetrator
paragraph 8: continuum

QUESTIONS

1. What is the specific problem that the authors wish to solve? How do they show in paragraphs 1–5 that the problem exists?

2. What do they assume is the purpose of education? Do they state this assumption directly and defend it, or do they instead imply it in discussing examination systems?

3. The authors state that education is a continuum, not independent "chunks of material" (paragraph 8). Do they offer proof for this assumption, or present it as a given truth?

4. How does the assumption that education is a continuum guide their reasoning on what should be done to solve the problem discussed in paragraphs 1–5?

5. What are the advantages of the solution they propose? What difficulties do they foresee in reforming the examination system? Do they suggest ways to overcome these difficulties?

6. Are the authors addressing their proposal to teachers, administrators, or students, or to some or all of these? How do you know? Do they take account of objections that might be made by each of these groups?

7. The authors organize their discussion in a persuasive way. To what extent does it contain the elements of the persuasive essay described on pp. 432–434?

SUGGESTIONS FOR WRITING

1. Describe your own study habits, including the amount of time you spend out of class on each subject. Comment on how adequate these habits and the time spent are.

2. State your own ideas on what education should be, and use these to judge how well these courses prepared you for college work. Explain how you came to hold these ideas.

3. Argue for or against entrance exams for prerequisites, based on your own ideas about education and your own educational experience.

William Raspberry

WILLIAM RASPBERRY *has written for the* Washington Post *since 1962, first as a reporter and editor, then as a columnist, commenting on urban and national affairs. Raspberry wrote the following article shortly before the November 3, 1992, referendum on capital punishment in Washington DC. In his article he asks his readers to consider how they think about criminal justice.*

WHO DESERVES THE DEATH PENALTY?

Capital punishment, which will be on the Nov. 3 ballot here, 1
defies reasonable argument. Produce statistics "proving" that
the prospect of capital punishment does not deter the crimes
that frighten us most, and proponents change their tack. Maybe it doesn't, they say, but certain kinds of behavior *earn* the
death penalty; it's a matter of just desserts. But are all offend-
ers who commit the same offense under the same circumstances deserving of the same punishment?

I put the question to a judicial conference a few years ago. 2
Most people, I said, no matter their views on standardized
testing, recognize that identical scores may not be equal. Take
the prep-school grandson of a physicist, whose parents are a
diplomat and a research scientist, who scores 1300 on the SAT.
Now take a youngster who is not sure what sort of work his
grandfather did and whose family income, for most of his life,
has consisted of his mother's AFDC check. He is a senior at the
drug-ridden and academically dreadful public school. And his
combined SAT score is 1300.

Not one of the judges would, given the disparity of oppor- 3
tunity afforded the two applicants, rate their identical scores
equal, I told them. Well, I reminded them, they *are* admissions
officers: not to Penn State but to the state pen. Should they
take account of the fact that the defendants before them for
sentencing, however comparable their offenses, had unequal
chances to avoid criminal involvement?

Should they deal with two "applicants" for a prison cell— 4
both 24-year-olds convicted of selling cocaine—when one is
a graduate student at Georgetown and the other a jobless
dropout from the ghetto? Are their identical offenses equal? Or
should they deny "admission" to the young man whose lack of
economic and social advantages makes it a snap for him to
pass the prison entrance test—and give admissions preference to the Georgetown student who had to overcome a background of social advantage to qualify?

But if it's common sense to acknowledge that identical 5
crimes may not be equal, doesn't it follow that ostensibly

identical punishments may also be unequal? Can a judge properly consider the fact that a youngster from the projects would be less likely to be destroyed by a stint in prison, while the kid from Georgetown might not survive the experience?

Is it unreasonable, for example, for a judge to look at one offender and conclude that, given his unhealthy background, the odds are overwhelming that he will commit new offenses unless he is properly punished? Or to look at the second and guess that the shock of being arrested (and putting at risk his career and social standing) has straightened him out? 6

Obviously judges cannot postpone the punishment of criminals until society learns what to do about the underclass. But just as obviously, they cannot ignore the social circumstances that predispose some young men to lawlessness. It's one thing to punish people for what they do; quite another to add to that punishment because they've got nothing to lose. 7

QUESTIONS

1. Raspberry believes that the judges he spoke to at a judicial conference would not have rated two applicants for college equal on the basis of identical scores on the SAT. Why not?

2. If the judges agree that they would not do so, what view must they then take of comparable crimes in sentencing two young men convicted of selling cocaine?

3. What then does Raspberry demonstrate in paragraphs 5 and 6 from what he has shown about identical crimes?

4. What general conclusion does he draw about punishment in paragraph 7? What is his thesis, and where does he first state it? Where does he restate it?

5. What part of Raspberry's argument is deductive, and what in the wording shows that it is?

SUGGESTIONS FOR WRITING

1. State whether you would rate two applicants for college equal on the basis alone of identical scores on the SAT. Explain why, identifying the assumptions that guide your reasoning.

2. Explain why judges should or should not take the background and the chances of surviving prison into account in determining a sentence. Identify the assumptions that guide your reasoning, and explain why you hold them.

17

Controversy

Inductive and deductive reasoning often work together, depending on the particular argument and the point at issue. Proponents of nuclear power plants may, for example, insist that the issue in making the decision to build a plant in a particular region is economic—the increasing power needs of industry. Opponents may argue that the issue is the danger of an accident or the difficulty of disposing of nuclear waste. The argument in such a debate probably will be inductive: statistical information on productivity and nuclear fuel, eyewitness accounts of nuclear plant operations, scientific reports on waste disposal, and the like. The argument will also be deductive in the inferences drawn from certain assumptions: that a high standard of living is a desirable goal in the community; that risk must be taken into account in making a decision about nuclear power; that high productivity depends on a dependable source of electrical power.

Sometimes both assumptions and conclusions are debated; sometimes the assumptions are accepted as "givens" and not debated. In all debate, fairness and sound argument ideally should prevail. It hardly needs to be said that they often do not. Here are a few important "logical fallacies" that a good argument avoids:

Arguing in a circle is closely related to begging the question, where we assume as true what we are trying to prove. "No person who cares about jobs would oppose the bill because it is one that those who care about jobs in Ohio can support." The speaker has not given a reason to support the bill, but has merely restated the opening assertion, arguing in a circle.

Non sequitur ("it does not follow"): The assertion, "I oppose nuclear power because my father does," contains a hidden premise or assumption—that father knows best. Since this assumption is hidden, the second part of the statement does not follow from the first part clearly. An assumption of this sort may be hidden because, once stated, it shows the statement to be questionable or absurd.

Irrelevant conclusion: If the point at issue is whether nuclear plants present a risk, the argument that they are needed is an irrelevant argument. It may, of course, be relevant later in the debate.

Ad hominem argument ("to the person"): I may attack my opponents rather than the issue—for example, by arguing that proponents of nuclear power are selfish and greedy. Even if they were people of bad character, their proposals must be judged on their merits. In other circumstances, such as an election campaign, the character of a person may be the issue.

Ad populum argument ("to the people"): I may also appeal to popular feeling or prejudice to gain support—suggesting that some highly revered and usually long-dead person would have favored (or opposed) nuclear power. Appeals to authority may also depend on fear. An appeal to authority is legitimate when the person cited is a recognized expert and has stated an opinion on the subject.

Either–or hypothesis: I may set up two alternatives—nuclear power or economic depression—without allowing for other solutions.

Complex question asks two questions in the guise of asking one. "Are you in favor of closing nuclear plants to remove an uncontrollable source of radiation?" The person answering no is forced to admit that nuclear power is in fact uncontrollable—a question that deserves to be debated separately.

Hasty generalization draws on a conclusion from an insufficient number of facts, sometimes even from a single fact (see p. 257). Even if one or more nuclear power plants have operated without an accident, we cannot draw the conclusion that all nuclear power plants are necessarily safe. Conversely, a large number of accidents, even a major one like that at Three Mile Island and at Chernobyl in the 1980s, does not prove conclusively that nuclear power plants cannot be operated safely. Numerous facts and possibilities including human and mechanical error need to be considered. Usually the greater number of instances cited, the more probable the generalization. But the probability may be qualified by unstated or unknown facts—for example, the risk presented by aging equipment. And, as in the example of Three Mile Island and Chernobyl, a single serious instance or fact may have great force in argument.

Argument from ignorance: We cannot draw the conclusion that something *must* exist because no evidence has been found to prove it does not. We can't assert that nuclear power is not a threat to the environment or is not the cause of increasing cancer on the ground that no evidence exists to prove it is a threat. Judgment on such questions must remain open in light of possible new evidence. However, we can make qualified judgments and recommendations on the basis of available scientific evidence.

Antonia Fraser

English historian ANTONIA FRASER *is the author of numerous historical and biographical studies, including* Mary, Queen of Scots *(1969), awarded the James Tait Black Prize for Biography in 1969, and* Cromwell, the Lord Protector *(1973). The* Warrior Queens *(1989) is a study of female military figures, prominent among them Boadicea, the British queen of the first century* A.D., *who is reputed to have led a revolt against the Roman occupiers of England, and, failing, died possibly by her own hand. In the excerpt reprinted here, Fraser analyzes attitudes toward women in combat, drawing upon primary and secondary sources. Her conclusions may be compared with those of David H. Hackworth, Elaine Tyler May, and others in the section that follows.*

UNBECOMING IN A WOMAN?

At the heart of the matter lies the feeling, almost if not entirely universal in history, that war itself is "conduct unbecoming" in a woman. When George Buchanan attacked female government, especially in time of war, in the late sixteenth century, he explicitly contrasted the established roles of the two sexes. " 'Tis no less unbecoming [in] a Woman," he wrote, "to levy Forces, to conduct an Army, to give a Signal to the Battle, than it is for a Man to tease Wool, to handle the Distaff, to Spin or Card, and to perform the other Services of the Weaker Sex." When a woman did take part in such unnatural (to her sex) procedures, the effects were dire: for that which was reckoned "Fortitude and Severity" in a man, was liable to turn to "Madness and Cruelty" in a woman.[1]

It is not difficult to see why this philosophy should be widely held. "The act of giving birth itself" has been considered

---

[1] Cit. James E. Phillips, Jr., "The Woman Ruler in Spenser's *Faerie Queen,*" *Huntington Library Quarterly* (1941–2), 220.

throughout history to be "profoundly incompatible with the act of dealing death"; thus wrote Nancy Huston in a 1986 symposium of "contemporary perspectives" entitled *The Female Body in Western Culture*.[2] Biology alone—or by extension let us call it chivalry—provides an obvious explanation: if women, as the mothers of the race, need physical protection which they in turn extend to their young, then surely it is unreasonable, even unkind, to expect them to take part in war as well. From women's weaker physical strength, a more or less universal estimate, springs the concept of their tenderness, again an almost if not entirely universally held opinion; an extension of this is their timidity. (Why not be timid if physically so much weaker than a potential aggressor? It is a reasonable reaction.) And from their tenderness in one sense is derived another sense of their tenderness: woman the nurse, the nurturer, the succorer. . . .

The epitaph to Pocahontas in St. George's churchyard, [3] Gravesend, on the outskirts of London, where she lies buried, is a perfect case in point: "Gentle and humane, she was the friend of the earliest struggling English colonists whom she boldly rescued, protected and helped." It was an early American feminist writer, Margaret Fuller, who commented on the universal appeal of the American Indian Princess: "All men love Pocahontas for the angelic impulse of tenderness and pity that impelled her to the rescue of Smith," she wrote in *The Great Lawsuit: Man v. Woman*, first published in *The Dial*, Boston, in 1843; while women pity her for "being thus made a main agent in the destruction of her own people."[3] Compared to Boadicea, with those threatening knives on the wheels of her chariot, Pocahontas is a heroine who fulfills the highest expectations concerning her sex in general.

The problems of "masculinity" in a woman—inevitable in [4] some sense in a woman who leads in war—were argued by Helene Deutsch, one of the first four women to be analyzed by

---

[2] Nancy Huston, "The Matrix of War: Mothers and Heroes" in *The Female Body in Western Culture: Contemporary Perspectives*, edited by Susan Rubin Suleiman (1986), 119–38.

[3] Frances Mossiker, *Pocahontas: The Life and the Legend* (1977), 225; Margaret Fuller Ossoli, *Women in the Nineteenth Century*, edited by Arthur B. Fuller (Boston, 1874), 307.

Freud. *The Psychology of Women* was a comprehensive study of the female life-cycle and emotional life, which extended and modified Freud's own postulates. In it, Helene Deutsch devoted considerable discussion to what she called "The Active Woman" and her "Masculinity Complex" which "originates in a surplus of aggressive forces that were not subjected to inhibition and that lack the possibility of an outlet such as is open to man. For this reason the masculine woman is also the aggressive woman." This view stretches back at least as far as the wild, untamed and basically anarchic conception of the female in Athenian drama, at a time when woman's physical nature was itself thought to be unstable (based on the demands of her reproductive system).[4]

Although *The Psychology of Women* was published in 1944 (in 5 the United States whither Helene Deutsch had fled in 1933), time and political events have not diminished the strong perceived connection between "masculinity"—activity—in a woman and an "aggression" felt by many to be unsuitable in one of her sex.

It is the leading role upon the stage which is felt to be 6 unnatural in a woman, as opposed to any role. Many men all through history have after all been content to accept and even approve the ambitions of Fulvia, wife to Antony, as described by Plutarch: "her desire was to govern those who governed or to command a commander-in-chief." Cleopatra the dominatrix (and the seducer) is another matter. Boadicea herself may have acted the Fulvia before the death of her husband Prasutagus: we cannot know, *pace* Judy Grahn's free-wheeling lesbian Celt.* When women have been compelled by circumstances to take a dominating role, they are expected to surrender it gracefully afterwards; the "natural" behavior is that of Spenser's Britomart, the chaste warrior–maid who finally dropped her shield when her purpose was fulfilled and became "a gentle courteous Dame." As for the unnatural Amazons whom Britomart

---

[4] Helene Deutsch, *The Psychology of Women: A Psychoanalytic Interpretation*, 2 vols. (New York, 1944), Vol. I, ch. 8, 279–324; see Helene B. Foley, "The Conception of Women in Athenian Drama" in *Reflections of Women in Antiquity* (New York, 1981), 134.

* The view of Boadicea developed by the poet Judy Grahn in an 1980 article. *Spare Rib,* referred to in the next paragraph, is a British feminist periodical—Ed.

subdued, "that liberty" being removed from them, which they as women had wrongfully usurped, they were returned to "men's subjection."[5]

The strong contention of many theorists of the Women's [7] Movement that war itself is the product of aggressive *masculine* values, and might even be eliminated if "the whole wide world" were under "a woman's hand" (one of the Sibylline prophecies linked to Cleopatra), meshes of course with these more primitive feelings.[6] *Spare Rib*'s denunciation of Mrs. Thatcher following the Falklands War for promoting such values will be recalled, but the point is inclined to emerge whenever women, outraged by the depredations of war, manage to find a voice.

Militarism versus Feminism was written in 1915, the anguished [8] product of feminist pacifism in response to the first terrible months of carnage in the First World War.[7] It was in effect a plea for internationalism—the Hague Women's Peace Conference of that year—in the cause of peace. The three authors, Mary Sargent Florence, Catherine E. Marshall and C. K. Ogden, argued not only that war was man's creation (as opposed to woman's) but also that man used war as a weapon in order to keep the other sex in perpetual subjection, since in time of war he was the manifest ruler. Catherine Marshall in particular, a prime mover behind the setting up of the conference, referred to the "deep horror of war" which had entered into the soul of the organized Women's Movement, adding her belief that "women's experience as mothers and heads of households" had given them "just the outlook on human affairs" which was needed in such a process of international and creative reconstruction. (This is the argument which Mrs. Thatcher, following the Falklands War, stood on its head by announcing that it was just her practical feminine abilities as a homemaker which had enabled her to keep going in the direction of military affairs.)

"But if woman climbed up to the clearer air above the battle- [9] field," wrote Catherine Marshall in 1915, "and cried aloud in her

---

[5] *Nine Lives by Plutarch*, "Makers of Rome," translated and with an Introduction by Ian Scott-Kilvert (1972 pbk reprint), 280.

[6] Michael Grant, *Cleopatra* (revised edn. 1974 pbk), 84.

[7] Catherine Marshall, C. K. Ogden, & Mary Sargent Florence, *Militarism versus Feminism*, edited by Margaret Kamester and Jo Vellacott (1987 pbk reprint), 40, 47, 96, 140.

anguish to her sisters afar off: 'These things must not be, they shall never be again!', would man indeed say, 'Down with her!' Would he not allow her prerogative? Would he not even wish to climb up, too?" Once again, the experience of women sixty or seventy years later protesting at Greenham Common against nuclear weapons in the cause of peace does not suggest that man necessarily allows woman her prerogative in this respect. Nor does it propose that all men (any more than all women) wish to climb up to the clearer air above the battlefield.

Nevertheless the sheer appalling magnitude of the disaster to humankind inherent in any actual use of nuclear weapons suggests an interesting possibility. John Keegan, at the end of *The Mask of Command* (1987), a study in heroic leadership, calls for a new "Post-heroic leadership"; he points out that the old inspiring "heroic" leader, at the forefront of the battle itself, has been rendered obsolete and even dangerous by the advent of nuclear weapons. "Today the best must find convictions to play the hero no more"; leaders should now be chosen for "intellectuality" and the capacity for making decisions.[8] Women might now make more suitable political leaders than men (being strong enough *not* to press the button), provided of course that the conventional view of woman the peacemaker is accepted.

Certainly for many feminists the connection between women and peace remains "some sort of 'given' "—the phrase is that of the more skeptical Lynne Segal. As Petra Kelly, for example, wrote in 1984 in *Fighting for Hope*: "Woman must lead the efforts in education for peace awareness, because only she can . . . go back to her womb, her roots, her natural rhythms, her inner search for harmony and peace. . . ." Woman's pacific nature can however only be taken as some sort of given so long as any outstanding woman who does not seem to suffer from conspicuously peaceful inclinations is treated as an honorary male. According to this argument, which has a circular quality, Tomyris, issuing her plea to Cyrus of Persia, "Rule your own

[8] John Keegan, *The Mask of Command* (New York, 1987), 345–346, 351.

people, and try to bear the sight of me ruling mine," is acting in accordance with her true feminist nature, whereas the same Queen Tomyris who had Cyrus put bloodily to death was acting as a man.[9] In the absence of an all-female-ruled state (with all-female-ruled neighbors) the thesis must remain unproved. But the importance of the argument from the point of view of a study of Warrior Queens is that it represents the meeting point of visionary feminism and its direct opposite: war is an unnatural occupation for a woman.

VOCABULARY

paragraph 1: explicitly, distaff, card, dire
paragraph 2: perspective, nurturer, succorer
paragraph 3: epitaph
paragraph 4: inhibition, anarchic
paragraph 6: dominatrix
paragraph 7: Sibylline

QUESTIONS

1. What biological evidence is sometimes presented for the view that war is unbecoming conduct to women? How does Fraser explain the reasoning of those who consider this evidence credible?

2. Does the historical evidence presented in paragraph 3 support the same view? Or is Fraser illustrating another view?

3. What psychological explanation does Fraser cite in paragraph 4 for female aggressiveness? Does Fraser accept this explanation?

4. Does the historical evidence cited in paragraph 6 further support the psychological explanation discussed earlier? Does the political evidence cited in paragraph 10?

5. What "interesting possibility" or thesis does Fraser discuss in paragraphs 10 and 11? How does this thesis represent "the meeting point of visionary feminism and its direct opposite: war is an unnatural occupation for a woman"?

[9] Lynne Segal, Is the Future Female? Troubled Thoughts on Contemporary Feminism (1987 pbk), 198; Petra Kelly, Fighting for Hope (1984), 104; Herodotus, The Histories, translated by Aubrey de Sélincourt, revised by A. R. Burn (1972 pbk), 123; Giovanni Boccaccio, Concerning Famous Women, translated with an Introduction by Guido A. Guarmio (1964), 104.

SUGGESTIONS FOR WRITING

1. Fraser discusses attitudes toward women in traditional male roles in literature of the past. Discuss what recent movies and television comedy and drama show to be conduct becoming or unbecoming to women in jobs they perform—for example, as police officers, private detectives, newscasters, teachers, or office workers. Explain how the movies or television programs make an explicit or implied judgment about one or more female characters.

2. Analyze a series of advertisements in one or more issues of a magazine published in the 1930s or 1940s to discover what conduct advertisers and editors assumed was becoming to women. Draw a limited conclusion on the stated or implied attitudes from the evidence you present. Describe the ads in sufficient detail to support your thesis.

Presidential Commission on the Assignment of Women in the Armed Forces

The Defense Authorization Act of December 5, 1991, established by amendment a presidential commission required, in the words of the enabling statute, to "assess the laws and policies restricting the assignment of female servicemembers." A second amendment, as described in the Commission report, "repealed the combat exclusionary provision relating to female Naval aviation officiers and the exclusion of women from assignment in the Air Force to duty in aircraft engaged in combat missions." Rules then in effect excluded women from Navy and Marine Corps vessels engaged in combat missions, except for aviation officers assigned to air wings and women on hospital ships and other Navy vessels not involved in combat. Each armed service separately interpreted a Risk Rule in deciding what noncombatant positions should be open to women. The Commission issued its report on November 15, 1992. One of its recommendations was that "military readiness should be the driving *concern regarding assignment policies; there are circumstances under which women might be assigned to combat positions." But the Commission recommended continued exclusion of women from ground combat and re-enacting the provision excluding women from air combat. Reprinted below is this specific recommendation on ground combat and a dissent by three of the commissioners.*

GROUND COMBAT

Should the existing service policies restricting the assignment of service-women with respect to ground combat MOS*/specialties be retained, modified, rescinded, or codified?

Recommendation: *The sense of the Commission is that women should be excluded from direct land combat units and positions. Further, the Commission recommends that the existing service policies concerning direct land combat exclusions be codified. Service Secretaries shall recommend to the Congress which units and positions should fall under the land combat exclusion.*

The issue of whether to retain, modify, rescind, or codify the policies restricting the assignment of women in ground combat specialties was statutorily required to be considered by the Commission. In addressing the issue, the Commission found the effectiveness of ground units to be the most significant criterion.

American military women are prohibited by Service policies that preclude them from serving in direct ground combat positions. Current policy excluding women from ground combat is based, in part, on Congressional intent to preclude women from serving in combat aircraft or on combatant ships. The specialties that fall under the exclusion may be grouped into four major areas: infantry, armor, artillery, and combat engineers, all of which require a soldier to be prepared to fight in direct, close-quarters combat.

* MOS: Military Operational Specialty. DoD: Department of Defense.

Through testimony and trips, the Commission heard and observed that the daily life of the ground soldier in combat circumstances is one of constant physical exertion, often in extreme climatic conditions with the barest of amenities and the inherent risks of injury, capture and death. The Commission learned that despite technological advances, ground combat has not become less hazardous and physically demanding.

The evidence before the Commission clearly shows distinct physiological differences between men and women. Most women are shorter in stature, have less muscle mass and weigh less than men. These physiological differences place women at a distinct disadvantage when performing tasks requiring a high level of muscular strength and aerobic capacity, such as hand-to-hand fighting, digging, carrying heavy loads, lifting and other tasks central to ground combat.

The Commission also heard from women of tremendous physical ability who expressed a desire to serve in the ground combat arms. There is little doubt that some women could meet the physical standards for ground combat, but the evidence shows that few women possess the necessary physical qualifications. Further, a 1992 survey of 900 Army servicewomen showed that only 12 percent of enlisted women and 10 percent of the female noncommissioned officers surveyed said they would consider serving in the combat arms.

The Commission considered the effects that women could have on the cohesion of ground combat units. Cohesion is defined as the relationship that develops in a unit or group where: (1) members share common values and experiences; (2) individuals in the group conform to group norms and behavior in order to ensure group survival and goals; (3) members lose their personal identity in favor of a group identity; (4) members focus on group activities and goals; (5) members become totally dependent on each other for the completion of their mission or survival; and (6) members must meet all standards of performance and behavior in order not to threaten group survival. The evidence clearly shows that unit cohesion can be negatively affected by the introduction of any element that detracts from the need for such key ingredients as mutual confidence, commonality of experience, and equitable treatment. There are no authoritative military studies of mixed-gender ground combat cohesion, since available cohesion research has been conducted among male-only ground combat units.

One research study reviewed by the Commission indicates   9
that the following are areas where cohesion problems might develop:

1. Ability of women to carry the physical burdens required of each combat unit member. This entails an ability to meet physical standards of endurance and stamina.

2. Forced intimacy and lack of privacy on the battlefield (e.g. washing, bathing, using latrine facilities, etc.).

3. Traditional Western values where men feel a responsibility to protect women.

4. Dysfunctional relationships (e.g. sexual misconduct).

5. Pregnancy.

Of these, the prospect of sexual relationships in land units in direct combat with the enemy was considered to be dysfunctional and would encumber small unit ground combat leaders, noncommissioned officers, lieutenants and captains, in carrying out their military missions.

Ground combat incurs a high risk of capture by the enemy.   10
The Commission's review of our nation's recent wars with respect to POWs suggests that potential enemies may not

accord respect for the Geneva Convention and customary rules related to protection of prisoners. During our nation's major wars in this century, except Vietnam, the number of POWs has been greatest from the ground forces, the next largest number from downed aircraft and the least number from Navy ships. The Commission heard testimony from DoD representatives and POWs who indicated that the mistreatment of women taken as POWs could have a negative impact on male captives.

The Commission's enabling statute required examination of 11 public attitudes toward the assignment of women in the military. Several surveys were conducted to determine what the American public and military attitudes were toward women in ground combat. The results of these surveys indicate that members of the military are strongly against women serving in all branches of ground combat, while the public has mixed views on service in different ground combat specialties. The Roper survey of the American public showed that 57 percent of the American public polled said that women should not be assigned to the infantry, and 52 percent were against women in Marine infantry. However, 58 percent of the public surveyed were in favor of assigning women to both artillery and armor positions.

The Roper military poll reported that 74 percent of the mil- 12 itary members surveyed did not think women should serve in the infantry, 72 percent rejected the idea of women in Marine infantry, 59 percent opposed women in tank crews, and 54 percent did not want women to serve in the artillery. When the same question was asked of military personnel who had actually served in the ground combat arms, the numbers increased to 83 percent against women in the infantry, 83 percent against women serving in Marine infantry, 71 percent against women in armor, and 64 percent against women in artillery.

Several countries have placed women in ground combat 13 units with little success. Historically, those nations that have permitted women in close combat situations (the Soviet Union, Germany and Israel) have done so only because of grave threats to their national survival. After the crisis passed, each nation adopted policies which excluded the employment of women in combat. In more current times, the Commission learned that countries that have tested integrating women in ground combat units have found those tests unsuccessful.

The Commission also considered the effect on registration and conscription if women were allowed in ground combat units. In 1981, the Supreme Court upheld the male-only registration provision of the Military Selective Service Act, 50 U.S.C. App. 453, against a due process equal protection challenge from men who claimed that it was discriminatory because it required men, but not women, to register for the draft. The Court's opinion rested on the following argument: the purpose behind the registration requirement is to create a pool of individuals to be called up in the event of a draft; a draft is used to obtain combat troops; women are prevented, through law and policy, from serving in combat positions in any of the four Services; therefore, men and women are dissimilarly situated in regard to the registration requirement and it is permissible to treat them differently. 14

The Commission reviewed the assignment of draftees in our most recent conflicts, and according to statistics provided by DoD, 98 percent of draftees went to the Army during Vietnam, 95 percent during Korea and 83 percent during World War II. Because a draft is used to obtain combat troops and historically most draftees go into the Army, it can be deduced that the draft is used primarily to obtain a pool of ground combat troops. The Commission considered the possibility that lifting the ground combat exclusion pertaining to women may undermine the justification used by the Supreme Court to uphold the constitutionality of the all-male draft, because women would be eligible to serve in the positions which are filled through conscription. 15

The case against women in ground combat is compelling 16 and conclusive. The physiological differences between men and women are most stark when compared to ground combat tasks. This is underscored by the evidence that there are few women, especially enlisted women, interested in serving in ground combat specialties. The overriding importance of small unit cohesion to ground military success, and the unknown but probably negative effect that the presence of women would have in those units were of critical concern to most Commissioners. Several polls revealed in most convincing terms that the public and military, especially the military people most familiar with its rigors, were fundamentally opposed to women in ground combat. The weight of international experience with women in ground combat units provides no conclusive evidence supporting the assignment of women in ground combat units. Finally, the legal implications of lifting the ground combat exclusion policy for the possible registration and conscription of women for ground combat were considered. The current ground combat exclusion policies, which are derived from Congressional intent to restrict the assignment of women in other Services, would be vulnerable if the remaining statute was repealed. The Commission therefore recommends that the ground exclusion policies be enacted into law for consistency and as sound public policy.

DISSENT ON GROUND COMBAT

We, the undersigned Commissioners, do not concur with the 1 Commission recommendation to retain and codify existing Army policies as they relate to the assignment of servicewomen to Army Aviation, Field Artillery, Air Defense Artillery and Combat Engineers.

Combat power is a function of fire and maneuver, time and 2 position, judgement and luck, and the leader: a whole that is greater than the sum of its parts. These are factors that transcend gender, Service and branch.

A military organization that puts any factor at higher value   3
than the national defense is derelict in its duty. A military organization that allows its combat power to erode or denies itself
combat power multipliers does its duty incompletely.

There are four factors that must be addressed regarding   4
the exclusion of women from Army Aviation, Field Artillery, Air
Defense Artillery and Combat Engineers. These factors are cohesion, living conditions, fighting as infantry in case of emergency, and the possibility for a combatant becoming a prisoner
of war (POW).

Aviation

Women pilots are now in combat. They fly in the same airspace   5
and are shot at with the same anti-aircraft weapons the same
as combat helicopter pilots. The only difference is that they
can't shoot back. Women should be allowed to fly attack helicopters. Aviation should be open to the best soldiers available,
regardless of gender. Women military aviators have been
trained according to male standards. They have measured up
in every respect. Why hold women aviators back and keep
them from operationally flying all aircraft? It is not a matter of
capability but it is a matter of male attitude.

Field Artillery

Few women currently serve in the Field Artillery as most posi-   6
tions and all weapons systems previously opened to women
have been phased out in recent years. Women served effectively in some specialties of the Field Artillery, but the very
restrictive assignment policies which they were subjected to
have made a viable career path impossible; many were
removed and retrained into other occupational specialties.
There was no evidence that the women were not contributing,
but rather that the convoluted and arbitrary nature of the
Army's assignment policy prevented their effective utilization.

The Field Artillery branch should be reopened to women and there should be no restrictions on their assignment within the branch. Gender neutral, performance-based physical strength and endurance standards for Army specialties should be adopted as recommended in the full Commission report.

Air Defense Artillery

Women currently play a limited role in the Air Defense Artillery. They attend the same initial training as their male counterparts, but then are restricted to rocket units. These rocket units are located further to the rear areas than the Short Range Air Defense Systems from which women are restricted. This rear area would have the supposed effect of limiting the risk of death to women. In reality, the long range weapons systems to which women are assigned are a high priority target for the enemy aircraft and Air Defense Systems and are less mobile; therefore, they are more susceptible to enemy attack. These assignment restrictions limit women's professional development within their branch and hence, their ability to contribute, while not giving them any greater protection from risk. The Air Defense Artillery should be totally open to women. Gender neutral strength/endurance and performance-based standards should be adopted as recommended in the full Commission report.

Combat Engineers

Women currently serve in 24 of 29 enlisted Military Occupational Specialties and all of the officer and warrant officer specialties. They undergo the same training and can demonstrate the same skills as their male counterparts, but are restricted from serving in certain units. Although Combat Engineers have a secondary mission of infantry support, testimony highlighted that combat engineers only receive weapons firing training once a year. This, of course, places a tremendous artificial burden on the personnel system. Despite a demonstrated ability to carry out the tasks expected of them in their specialty, they are not allowed to be assigned to many positions in that specialty.

All engineer positions at brigade level and above should be open to women. By doing so, positions at battalion level and below, which would require women engineers to collocate with infantry and armor units, should remain closed, but all other positions should be opened. As Major General Christman, Commanding General of the U.S. Army Engineer Center, said: "Female soldiers are already versed in each of these areas and have clearly demonstrated their tactical and professional competence in engineer positions currently open to both sexes. Why ignore this tremendous resource?" 9

Relevant Issues

Cohesion
Cohesion is a function of individual and group confidence, self confidence, confidence in peers, and confidence in leaders. Individual and group confidence is engendered in military organizations by team building, close association, mutual experience and, ultimately, proven success. The large number of mixed gender organizations that habitually associate, undergo stressful mutual experience, and are proven successes is a matter of public record in every police force, hospital, and mixed-gender military organization in the United States. Cohesion is not a single gender experience, it is a function of good leadership, trust, competence and shared experience. 10

Prisoners of War
Since U.S. military women have already been POWs, this issue is a question of degree. Undeniably, there will be more women POWs if the exclusion policy is lifted; however, the treatment of POWs is the real issue, not the marginal percentage increase in women POWs. As with our current national policy, we hold our enemies responsible for the 11

treatment of our imprisoned servicemen and women. We will continue to do so. Recent events have reiterated that American memories are long regarding POWs. They are slow to forgive mistreatment, and they never forget. In the Gulf War, two American servicewomen were taken prisoner by the enemy. They have both experienced the risks all servicewomen take by membership in the military. Although neither of these women were in combat specialties, they were still not protected from the risk, of becoming a prisoner. Servicewomen understand and accept such risks.

Additionally, U.S. military personnel are protected under 12
the Geneva Convention relative to the treatment of Prisoners of War (August 12, 1949). History is full of the abuse and atrocities visited on non-combatants, in uniform and out. If we do not treat our military women as combatants, we can not expect our enemies to do so.

Living Conditions
War is brutalizing, and one of the most brutalizing aspects 13
are the living conditions. The lack of privacy, cleanliness, and fresh clothing are inconveniences compared to the loss of respect for humanity and the discounted value of human life that is the result of grinding exposure to prolonged combat.

Women currently train and fight under these conditions. 14
Dropping combat exclusion policies for Army Aviation, Field Artillery, Air Defense Artillery, and Combat Engineers would not change this situation.

Acting as Infantry in Case of Emergency
One of the arguments used to maintain the combat exclusion 15
policies in Army Aviation, Field Artillery, Air Defense Artillery and Combat Engineers is that if these positions were to fall under attack, all personnel would have to fight as infantry soldiers. This is already true for both men and women, and is not made less true by combat exclusion policies. If anything,

it creates a false expectancy in women soldiers that, as non-combatants, they can neglect basic soldier skills. Such false expectations increase the degree of risk to themselves and others, while making our forces less capable.

Mary E. Clark
Major General, USA (Ret.)

Mary M. Finch
Captain, USA

Meredith A. Neizer

QUESTIONS

1. The Commission states in an earlier section of the report that "under some circumstances, American society not only allows, but actually encourages and approves the further integration of women into combat roles," and the Commission agrees that "there are circumstances in which women might be assigned to combat roles." From which combat roles does it specifically exclude women? Does it state what roles should be open to them?

2. In addition to physical ability, what other evidence did the Commission consider in deciding whether to exclude women from ground combat?

3. Does the recommendation state or imply that the Commission gave equal weight to each kind of evidence? If it did not, does the recommendation show that it gave greater weight to one or more kinds?

4. Do the dissenting commissioners answer each of the objections of the majority recommendation? Do they present other kinds of evidence for their own views?

SUGGESTIONS FOR WRITING

1. State which of the majority or the dissenting arguments you find the most and the least persuasive, and why. Give your reasons, citing beliefs you hold as well as experiences and observations, perhaps in the military.

2. Young women occasionally participate in male-centered sports like football and hockey. Discuss your reasons for supporting their participation or opposing it.

David H. Hackworth

COL. DAVID H. HACKWORTH *served with the* U.S. *Army in Korea and Vietnam, retiring in* 1971. *In his memoir* About Face (1989), *he describes his eight years of combat experience. A contributing editor to* Newsweek, *Hackworth wrote an account of women in combat in the Persian Gulf War for the issue of August* 5, 1991. *The point at issue in the debate over women in combat, Hackworth states in* Newsweek, *is not courage or heroism:*

> Equality and opportunity are noble ideals, but they have little to do with the battlefield, where the issues are living and dying. The question is: what if it turns out that equality and opportunity hurt combat readiness? The issue is not female bravery; the gulf war proved that patriotism and heroism are not gender-dependent. It isn't professionalism. The women troops I met during and after the war are smart, dedicated and technically competent. They are also better educated than their male counterparts.

Hackworth raises the same concern in an article in the Washington Post, *reprinted here. In the article Hackworth raises other concerns and makes a recommendation to legislators considering a revision of the federal Combat Exclusion Act of 1948 and army policies that exclude women from combat aircraft and ships and from infantry and armored combat.*

WOMEN AND COMBAT

Congress will decide very soon whether to set up a commission on women in combat. 1

I believe such a commission is essential. It is needed to determine whether women could be drafted and whether combat assignments for women could be kept voluntary when they aren't voluntary for men. More than that, though, the commission is needed to take stock of what we've learned so far about women in the military, and to look ahead. 2

As a *Newsweek* reporter assigned to the Persian Gulf during the war, I watched firsthand as American servicewomen 3 performed splendidly there. A few years before that, I was a proud papa when my own daughter received three commendations for valor for her work on Coast Guard choppers plucking people from the sea. I understand America's sense of gratitude to its women warriors, and I know how important our nation's ideals, such as equality and opportunity, are to the whole sense of why we fight.

But as an experienced combat soldier, I have to say that in direct combat there's something more important than gratitude, more important even than equality and opportunity. It's life and death. Often, life and death for dozens of soldiers can come down to how fast a pace you can maintain with a hundred-pound pack on your back, to a split-second command to the fighter aircraft at your wingtip, to whether the grunt next to you is strong enough to carry you off the battlefield if your leg's been blown apart, to whether your platoon is operating at full fighting strength or is three soldiers short, and to whether your unit is moving faster than the enemy. Under modern conditions of fast-maneuver warfare, stamina and speed matter even more than they did a generation ago.

It's not that "women can't do it." It's rather that our information isn't good enough yet to risk lives on. Double standards for judging the physical strength and stamina of servicemen and -women have become pervasive.

At West Point, for example, women practice handling an M-14 rifle whose spring has been modified to make it easier for them. The obstacle course has been eased for them. Running shoes are used because female cadets were getting too many foot injuries running in Army boots. Army physical fitness standards call for men to be able to do 80 pushups; women must do 56. Men 17 to 25 years of age must run two miles in 17 minutes, 55 seconds, or better; women are allowed 22 minutes, 14 seconds. Marine men must climb 20 feet of rope in 30 seconds; Marine women are given 50 seconds.

In the thousand-plus interviews of service men and women that I did for a *Newsweek* story on women in combat, these double standards were the No. 1 complaint. With women excluded from combat, such double standards were "only" morale-busters; in battle, they'll cost women and men their lives.

8 We need to know the truth about how many women would be capable and qualified under genuinely equal standards—and we need to know before we start assigning women to combat specialties and before bullets start flying.

9 A commission should also help the military accurately project how many soldiers would be available for combat in a future conflict.

10 How many soldiers deployed to the gulf were out of action—and for how long—because of noncombat-related accidents and pregnancies? What percentage of the men and women called up had custody of young children they couldn't leave? Such information tells us a lot about how many active and reserve personnel we'll need, and how fast, to keep the front lines at full strength. If we don't know or we're seriously wrong, we're going to lose battles and lives.

11 The biggest unknown, though, is what the soldiers who will be most affected by the proposed changes think.

12 The soldiers I interviewed, from buck privates to generals, raised detailed concerns that no one in Washington seems to be publicly discussing. And the closer one gets to the soldiers who will do the bleeding and dying, the more concerns they raise. Our country's leaders have a high moral responsibility to talk to these soldiers, to hear them out and to consider their views carefully.

13 Incidentally, these issues have not been "studied to death." I asked senators and representatives, Pentagon officials, think tanks, service medical and training commands, and 45 years' worth of military contacts for any studies they had. What I got was anecdotes, opinions about what the facts show and random statistics. But no studies.

14 The achievements women have made in the armed services will not be lost or forgotten if we reserve judgment on women's roles in the military until all the facts are in. Women themselves will see to that.

The greater danger is that mistakes made now, in a haste to   15
get women into combat, could lead to needless fatalities. If
that happens, there will be hell to pay politically and militarily.
The backlash could set military women back decades.

Let a commission of civilian and military leaders bring as   16
much expertise as possible to these decisions. Now is not the
time for our political leaders to duck and weave, but to look
this issue dead in the eye and act responsibly.

QUESTIONS

1. Does Hackworth support or oppose women in combat? Or does
   he reserve judgment on the issue?

2. Is there a single overriding issue for Hackworth in the debate?
   How do you know?

3. Do you support or oppose women in combat? What beliefs and
   experiences guide your thinking on the issue?

SUGGESTION FOR WRITING

Write an argumentative essay on a current issue of concern to
you. Assume you are addressing an audience unfamiliar with the
issue and therefore in need of facts. You might begin your essay
by introducing the issue and then presenting the facts or background and stating your thesis—your position on the issue. Next,
you might argue in support of your position, then introduce and
answer objections or counterarguments (see p. 433). An alternate
method is to begin with these objections and state your position
in answering them. To conclude your essay, you might restate
your arguments and affirm your thesis.

Elaine Tyler May

ELAINE TYLER MAY, *Professor of History at the University of
Minnesota, is the author of* Great Expectations: Marriage and
Divorce in Post-Victorian America (1983) *and* Homeward
Bound: American Families in the Cold War Era (1988). In

examining the issue of women in combat, May employs the popular
form of debate described on p. 433, using her narrative or back-
ground of the case to present the opposing arguments. May is par-
ticularly interested in assumptions that guide thinking on the issue,
for example, the assumption that "the only good fighting force is one
in which heterosexual men pursue their mission free from sexual
temptation." Her article appeared in the New York Times *on*
August 7, 1991.

WOMEN IN THE WILD BLUE YONDER

Now that Congress has opened the door for women to enter   1
the ranks of combat pilots, many Americans find themselves
uncomfortable with the idea. Why do so many people cringe at
the thought of women in combat? Full access to the military is
a logical next step on the road to equal opportunity for
women. Perhaps the real question is why it has taken so long
for women to enter battle.

The combat barrier somehow seems different, more omi-   2
nous than other rights gained by women. Not because it marks
the invasion of women into one of the few remaining bastions
of masculinity, but because it threatens what is perhaps the
sole surviving gender myth of the twentieth century: that
women are the world's nurturers. Can a nurturer also be a
destroyer?

Those opposed to sending women into combat sidestep the   3
issue. Some claim that women are not physically strong
enough to serve as fighter pilots. That argument collapses at a
time when strength and endurance are as readily developed in
women as in men. Besides, these women would be flying
planes, not lifting them. And with sophisticated weaponry,
women can push the buttons to drop the bombs as easily as
men can.

Others argue that men should protect women, not the other   4
way around. That chivalry might make some sense if it operated anywhere else in our society. But women are at risk in
other occupations, where hazards to their safety abound. It is
disingenuous to hear calls for their protection in battle when

they are not even protected at home, where domestic abuse and violence against women are widespread.

Still, maybe war is different. Since our War of Independence, women have participated in warfare. They have provided supplies and medical care, even on the front lines. During World War I, men were urged to fight for mothers, wives and sweethearts back home.

In World War II, sentimental views of women were replaced by other images. Rosie the Riveter became a national icon, doing "men's work" in war industries. These female workers were glorified, though they were expected to relinquish their well-paying, physically demanding jobs after the war. At the same time, symbols of female sexuality entered the iconography of war. Pinups appeared in military barracks; the noses of thousands of bombers were decorated with erotic portraits.

If the U.S. hires women as professional killers, allowing them into the cockpit, what remains of the sentimental ideal of women as pure and gentle creatures might vanish. It is not so much that women might get killed; it is that they might kill.

The ability to kill is the ultimate equalizer. Indeed, the integration of combat units after World War II signaled a major change in the nation's racial relations. The symbolic impact of women fighting in combat cannot be overlooked.

Power, of course, is intimately connected to sex. It is no accident that another policy under discussion bans homosexuals from the armed forces. In World War II and the cold war, women and gays were barred from combat, in part because they were believed to be security risks.

We now know that in spite of the ban, many gay men and women served heroically in World War II. Still, military policies are based on the theory that the only good fighting force is one in which heterosexual men pursue their mission free from sexual temptation. Since no such force has ever existed, it is difficult to know if there is any truth to the myth.

There are those on the other side of the debate who argue that women are really less warlike than men and that bringing them fully into the military would humanize the armed services.

Perhaps. But we won't know, at least not until women fill the leadership ranks of the military establishment—from running major defense industries and the Pentagon to serving as the Commander in Chief herself.

VOCABULARY

paragraph 2: ominous, bastion, nurturer
paragraph 3: sophisticated
paragraph 4: chivalry
paragraph 6: sentimental, icon, iconography
paragraph 8: symbolic

QUESTIONS

1. Is May addressing a general audience that varies in knowledge and interest in the controversy over women in combat, or is she addressing a special audience that knows the facts, is interested, and perhaps has special concerns? How do you know?

2. What is a "gender myth," and what gender myth does May challenge? How do the objections to women in combat discussed in paragraphs 3 and 4 illustrate this myth, and how does May answer them?

3. What additional answer does May give to the gender myth in paragraphs 5–7?

4. What explanation does May present in paragraphs 9 and 10 for male opposition to women in combat? What supporting evidence does she present?

5. Why does she conclude the essay by considering the argument that women are "really less warlike than men"?

6. Where does May first state her thesis? Where does she restate it?

7. Is the point at issue over women in combat the same for May and Hackworth, or are they concerned with different issues?

SUGGESTIONS FOR WRITING

1. Discuss the extent to which Antonia Fraser's survey of attitudes and opinions (pp. 352–357) supports May's analysis of male opposition to women in combat.

2. Using magazine and newspaper articles and editorials, analyze other opinions on women in combat, focusing on contrasting statements or exchanges that vary sharply on problems and solutions. Don't try to cover all opinions on the issue. Focus on ones that represent major positions and disagreements.

Mark H. Moore

> Analogies with past historical events are popular in dealing with current issues. The Munich Pact, signed by Great Britain, Germany, Italy, and France in September of 1938, is commonly cited in discussions on dealing with dictatorial regimes; but, Peter McGrath argues, "It is not at all clear that the 'lessons of Munich' are easily translated to other contexts" (Newsweek, October 3, 1988). To cite Munich, McGrath suggests "is inevitably to suggest that nothing has really changed since the world of the late 1930s, that if it was proper to risk war then, it is proper to do so now."
> MARK H. MOORE, Professor of Criminal Justice at Harvard University's Kennedy School of Government, warns against another popular analogy in discussions of the current drug war. His article appeared in the New York Times on October 16, 1989.

PROHIBITION AND DRUGS

History has valuable lessons to teach policy makers but it reveals its lessons only grudgingly. Close analyses of the facts and their relevance is required lest policy makers fall victim to the persuasive power of false analogies and are misled into imprudent judgments. Just such a danger is posed by those who casually invoke the "lessons of Prohibition" to argue for the legalization of drugs.

What everyone "knows" about Prohibition is that it was a failure. It did not eliminate drinking; it did create a black market. That in turn spawned criminal syndicates and random violence. Corruption and widespread disrespect for law were incubated and, most tellingly, Prohibition was repealed only 14 years after it was enshrined in the Constitution.

The lesson drawn by commentators is that it is fruitless to   3
allow moralists to use criminal law to control intoxicating substances. Many now say it is equally unwise to rely on the law
to solve the nation's drug problem.

But the conventional view of Prohibition is not supported by   4
the facts.

First, the regime created in 1919 by the 18th Amendment   5
and the Volstead Act, which charged the Treasury Department
with enforcement of the new restrictions, was far from all-
embracing. The amendment prohibited the commercial manufacture and distribution of alcoholic beverages; it did not
prohibit its use, nor production for one's own consumption.
Moreover, the provisions did not take effect until a year after
passage—plenty of time for people to stockpile supplies.

Second, alcohol consumption declined dramatically during   6
Prohibition. Cirrhosis death rates for men were 29.5 per 100,000
in 1911 and 10.7 in 1929. Admissions to state mental hospitals
for alcoholic psychosis declined from 10.1 per 100,000 in 1919
to 4.7 in 1928.

Arrests for public drunkenness and disorderly conduct   7
declined 50 percent between 1916 and 1922. For the population as a whole, the best estimates are that consumption of
alcohol declined by 30 percent to 50 percent.

Third, violent crime did not increase dramatically during   8
Prohibition. Homicide rates rose dramatically from 1900 to
1910 but remained roughly constant during Prohibition's 14
year rule. Organized crime may have become more visible and
lurid during Prohibition, but it existed before and after.

Fourth, following the repeal of Prohibition, alcohol con-   9
sumption increased. Today, alcohol is estimated to be the
cause of more than 23,000 motor vehicle deaths and is impli-
cated in more than half of the nation's 20,000 homicides. In
contrast, drugs have not yet been persuasively linked to highway fatalities and are believed to account for 10 percent to 20
percent of homicides.

Prohibition did not end alcohol use. What is remarkable,   10
however, is that a relatively narrow political movement, relying

on a relatively weak set of statutes, succeeded in reducing, by one-third, the consumption of a drug that had wide historical and popular sanction.

This is not to say that society was wrong to repeal Pro- 11 hibition. A democratic society may decide that recreational drinking is worth the price in traffic fatalities and other consequences. But the common claim that laws backed by morally motivated political movements cannot reduce drug use is wrong.

Not only are the facts of Prohibition misunderstood, but the 12 lessons are misapplied to the current situation.

The U.S. is in the early to middle stages of a potentially 13 widespread cocaine epidemic. If the line is held now, we can prevent new users and increasing casualties. So this is exactly *not* the time to be considering a liberalization of our laws on cocaine. We need a firm stand by society against cocaine use to extend and reinforce the messages that are being learned through painful personal experience and testimony.

The real lesson of Prohibition is that society can, indeed, 14 make a dent in the consumption of drugs through laws. There is a price to be paid for such restrictions, of course. But for drugs such as heroin and cocaine, which are dangerous but currently largely unpopular, that price is small relative to the benefits.

VOCABULARY

paragraph 2: spawned, syndicates, random, incubated
paragraph 3: moralist
paragraph 6: psychosis
paragraph 8: lurid
paragraph 13: epidemic, liberalization

QUESTIONS

1. Moore warns against "persuasive power of false analogies" in discussing legalization of drugs and other issues. What analogy is often cited in favor of legalization of drugs, and why does Moore consider it false?

2. What kind of evidence does Moore present to show that the analogy is false?

3. Does Moore believe that society was right to repeal Prohibition? How do you know?

4. What is the thesis of the essay, and where does Moore state it?

SUGGESTIONS FOR WRITING

1. Explain why, in your view, society was right or wrong to repeal Prohibition or is right or wrong to prohibit heroin and cocaine.

2. Moore states that, contrary to popular opinion, restrictions on alcohol and drugs can work, but "there is a price to be paid for such restrictions." Explain what price would be paid for restrictions on the use of alcohol, tobacco, or firearms. Then explain why, in your opinion, the price would or would not be too high for society to pay.

Alan M. Dershowitz

ALAN M. DERSHOWITZ, *Professor of Law at Harvard University, writes about civil liberties and other contemporary issues in* The Best Defense *(1982),* Taking Liberties *(1988),* The Abuse Excuse *(1994), and* Contrary to Popular Opinion *(1992), in which the following proposal to legalize heroin appears. The call for legalization of heroin and other addictive drugs has come from many quarters, as the rate of addiction and drug-related crime has risen in the United States. Opposition to legalization is equally strong, as the statement that follows by Congressman Charles B. Rangel of New York shows.*

THE CASE FOR MEDICALIZING HEROIN

When *Time* magazine has a cover story on the legalization of drugs, and when Oprah Winfrey devotes an entire show to that "unthinkable" proposition, you can be sure that this is an issue whose time has come—at least for serious discussion.

But it is difficult to get politicians to *have* a serious discussion about alternatives to our currently bankrupt approach to drug abuse. Even thinking out loud about the possibility of decriminalization is seen as being soft on drugs. And no elected official can afford to be viewed as less than ferocious and uncompromising on this issue. 2

Any doubts about that truism were surely allayed when Vice President Bush openly broke with his president and most important supporter over whether to try to make a deal with Panamanian strongman Manuel Noriega, whom the United States has charged with drug-trafficking. 3

I was one of the guests on the recent Oprah Winfrey show that debated drug decriminalization. The rhetoric and emotions ran high, as politicians and audience members competed over who could be tougher in the war against drugs. 4

"Call out the marines," "bomb the poppy fields," "execute the drug dealers"—these are among the "constructive" suggestions being offered to supplement the administration's simpleminded "just say no" slogan. 5

Proposals to medicalize, regulate, or in another way decriminalize any currently illegal drug—whether it be marijuana, cocaine, or heroin—were greeted by derision and cries of "surrender." Even politicians who *in private* recognize the virtues of decriminalization must continue to oppose it when the cameras are rolling. 6

That is why it is so important to outline here the politically unpopular case for an alternative approach. 7

Ironically, the case is easiest for the hardest drug—heroin. There can be no doubt that heroin is a horrible drug: It is highly addictive and debilitating; taken in high, or unregulated, doses, it can kill; when administered by means of shared needles, it spreads AIDS; because of its high price and addictive quality, it makes acquisitive criminals out of desperate addicts. Few would disagree that if we could rid it from the planet through the passage of a law or the invention of a plant-specific herbicide, we should do so. 8

But since we can neither eliminate heroin nor the demand for 9 it, there is a powerful case for medicalizing as much of the problem as is feasible. Under this proposal, or one of its many variants, the hard-core addict would receive the option of getting his fix in a medical setting, administered by medical personnel.

The setting could be a mobile hospital van or some other 10 facility close to where the addicts live. A doctor would determine the dosage for each addict—a maintenance dosage designed to prevent withdrawal without risking overdose. And the fix would be injected in the medical facility so the addict could not sell or barter the drug or prescription.

This will by no means solve all the problems associated with 11 heroin addiction, but it would ameliorate some of the most serious ones. The maintained heroin addict will not immediately become a model citizen. But much of the desperation that today accounts for the victimization of innocent home-dwellers, store employees, and pedestrians—primarily in urban centers—would be eliminated, and drug-related crime would be significantly reduced.

Today's addict is simply not deterred by the law. He will get 12 his fix by hook or by crook, or by knife or by gun, regardless of the risk. That is what heroin addiction means. Giving the desperate addict a twenty-four-hour medical alternative will save the lives of countless innocent victims of both crime and AIDS.

It will also save the lives of thousands of addicts who now 13 kill themselves in drug shooting galleries by injecting impure street mixtures through AIDS-infected needles.

There will, of course, always be a black market for heroin, 14 even if it were medicalized. Not every addict will accept a medically administered injection, and even some of those who do will supplement their maintenance doses with street drugs. But much of the desperate quality of the constant quest for the fix will be reduced for at least some heroin addicts. And this will have a profound impact on both the quantity and violence of inner-city crime.

Nor would new addicts be created by this medical approach. 15 Only long-term adult addicts would be eligible for the program. And the expenses would be more than offset by the extraordinary savings to our society in reduced crime.

If this program proved successful in the context of heroin 16 addiction, variants could be considered for other illegal drugs such as cocaine and marijuana. There is no assurance that an approach which is successful for one drug will necessarily work for others. Many of the problems are different.

We have already decriminalized two of the most dangerous 17 drugs known to humankind—nicotine and alcohol. Decriminalization of these killers, which destroy more lives than all other drugs combined, has not totally eliminated the problems associated with them.

But we have come to realize that criminalization of nicotine 18 and alcohol causes even more problems than it solves. The time has come to consider whether that is also true of heroin and perhaps of other drugs as well.

QUESTIONS

1. What reasons does Dershowitz give for legalizing heroin? Does he give these reasons equal weight?

2. How does he answer objections to legalization? Does he cite differing attitudes and concerns among those opposed?

3. To what extent does his statement of the case and answer to objections fit the pattern of the persuasive essay described on p. 433?

SUGGESTIONS FOR WRITING

1. Compare the case Dershowitz makes for legalization with that of Louis Nizer in the June 8, 1986, issue of the *New York Times*, or Frederick B. Campbell in the January 23, 1990, issue of the same newspaper, or another writer in a book or periodical. Discuss points on which they agree as well as differences in approach as well as argument: One writer may focus on addiction in children; another on addiction in adults. Comment on similarities and differences in kinds of evidence presented—personal experience, testimony of drug users, analogies, statistical studies, authoritative studies, and the like—as well as in the arguments presented.

2. Discussion of legalization in the United States sometimes centers on drug policies in Holland and other European countries. Report on several studies of drug use and addiction rates in one or more of these countries, commenting on what support these studies provide for or against legalization.

Charles B. Rangel

> A *graduate of New York University and St. John's College of Law,* Congressman CHARLES B. RANGEL *has represented the 16th District of New York since 1970. Between 1976 and 1994 he was chairman of the House Select Committee on Narcotics Abuse and Control. Representing a large metropolitan area, he has long been involved in efforts to curb drug use in city neighborhoods. His article opposing legalization of drugs appeared in the* New York Times *on May 17, 1988.*

LEGALIZE DRUGS?

The escalating drug crisis is beginning to take its toll on many   1
Americans. And now growing numbers of well-intentioned officials and other opinion leaders are saying that the best way to fight drugs is to legalize them. But what they're really admitting is that they're willing to abandon a war that we have not even begun to fight.

For example, the newly elected and promising Mayor of Bal-   2
timore, Kurt Schmoke, at a meeting of the United States Conference of Mayors, called for a full-scale study of the feasibility of legalization. His comments could not have come at a worse time, for we are in the throes of the worst drug epidemic in our history.

Here we are talking about legalization, and we have yet to   3
come up with any formal national strategy or any commitment from the Administration on fighting drugs beyond mere words. We have never fought the war on drugs like we have fought other legitimate wars—with all the forces at our command.

Just the thought of legalization brings up more problems 4 and concerns than already exist.

Advocates of legalization should be reminded, for example, 5 that it's not as simple as opening up a chain of friendly neighborhood pharmacies. Press them about some of the issues and questions surrounding this proposed legalization, and they never seem to have any answers. At least not any logical, well thought out ones.

Those who tout legalization remind me of fans sitting in the 6 cheap seats at the ballpark. They may have played the game, and they may think they know all the rules, but from where they're sitting they can't judge the action.

Has anybody ever considered which narcotic and psy- 7 chotropic drugs would be legalized?

Would we allow all drugs to become legally sold and used, 8 or would we select the most abused few, such as cocaine, heroin and marijuana?

Who would administer the dosages—the state or the 9 individual?

What quantity of drugs would each individual be allowed 10 to get?

What about addicts: Would we not have to give them more 11 in order to satisfy their craving, or would we give them enough to just whet their appetites?

What do we do about those who are experimenting? Do we 12 sell them the drugs, too, and encourage them to pick up the habit?

Furthermore, will the Government establish tax-supported 13 facilities to sell these drugs?

Would we get the supply from the same foreign countries 14 that support our habit now, or would we create our own internal sources and "dope factories," paying people the minimum wage to churn out mounds of cocaine and bales of marijuana?

Would there be an age limit on who can purchase drugs, as 15 exists with alcohol? What would the market price be and who would set it? Would private industry be allowed to have a stake in any of this?

What are we going to do about underage youngsters—the 16
age group hardest hit by the crack crisis? Are we going to give
them identification cards? How can we prevent adults from
purchasing drugs for them?

How many people are projected to become addicts as a 17
result of the introduction of cheaper, more available drugs
sanctioned by government?

Since marijuana remains in a person's system for weeks, 18
what would we do about pilots, railroad engineers, surgeons,
police, cross-country truckers and nuclear plant employees
who want to use it during off-duty hours? And what would be
the effect on the health insurance industry?

Many of the problems associated with drug abuse will not 19
go away just because of legalization. For too long we have
ignored the root cause, failing to see the connection between
drugs and hopelessness, helplessness and despair.

We often hear that legalization would bring an end to the 20
bloodshed and violence that has often been associated with
the illegal narcotics trade. The profit will be taken out of it, so
to speak, as will be the urge to commit crime to get money to
buy drugs. But what gives anybody the impression that legalization would deter many jobless and economically deprived
people from resorting to crime to pay for their habits?

Even in a decriminalized atmosphere, money would still be 21
needed to support habits. Because drugs would be cheaper
and more available, people would want more and would commit more crime. Does anybody really think the black market
would disappear? There would always be opportunities for
those who saw profit in peddling larger quantities, or
improved versions, of products that are forbidden or restricted.

Legalization would completely undermine any educational 22
effort we undertake to persuade kids about the harmful effects
of drugs. Today's kids have not yet been totally lost to the drug
menace, but if we legalize these substances they'll surely get
the message that drugs are O.K.

Not only would our young people realize that the threat of 23
jail and punishment no longer exists. They would pick up the

far more damaging message that the use of illegal narcotics does not pose a significant enough health threat for the Government to ban its use.

If we really want to do something about drug abuse, let's 24 end this nonsensical talk about legalization right now.

Let's put the pressure on our leaders to first make the drug 25 problem a priority issue on the national agenda, then let's see if we can get a coordinated national battle plan that would include the deployment of military personnel and equipment to wipe out this foreign-based national security threat. Votes by the House and more recently the Senate to involve the armed forces in the war on drugs are steps in the right direction.

Finally, let's take this legalization issue and put it where it 26 belongs—amid idle chit-chat as cocktail glasses knock together at social events.

QUESTIONS

1. In what order does Rangel ask questions about legalization of drugs in paragraphs 7–17? Does he proceed from less damaging effects to more damaging ones? Or from lesser costs to greater costs of making drugs available? Or from difficulties in making the system work to moral objections to legalization? Or does he ask questions in another order?

2. Rangel might have stated his objections in declarative sentences, for example, "Nobody has yet considered which narcotic and psychotropic drugs would be legalized." What does he gain by presenting his objections in the form of questions?

3. What shows that Rangel is addressing a general audience—readers of a large metropolitan newspaper—and not a special audience or segment of that readership? Were he addressing a city police force, what objections might he have highlighted? What if he were addressing health care and social workers?

4. Does Rangel assume that the majority of his readers are willing to consider legalization, or instead are opposed, or have not made up their minds? How do you know?

SUGGESTION FOR WRITING

The "war" against drugs, still in progress, is controversial. Some observers consider it a success; others, a failure. Compare two articles that present opposite views on an aspect of the drug war—for example, efforts by the federal government to reduce entry of drugs into the United States, cooperative efforts with foreign countries, penalties for drug possession.

18

Interpretation of Evidence

In explaining your ideas or beliefs, or in debating an issue, you usually draw on personal experience and observation for illustration and evidence. And sometimes you must turn to other sources of information. Opinions need the support of facts.

In investigating an event, you may find evidence in primary sources—firsthand accounts by participants and observers—and in secondary sources—reports and interpretations by those not present. An eyewitness account is a different kind of evidence from the reconstruction of the event by a historian in later years. Though primary evidence might seem the more reliable, it may be contradictory in itself or be contradicted by other eyewitnesses. At the time of the killing of President John F. Kennedy, eyewitnesses disagreed on what they saw and heard. More than thirty years after the event, researchers continue to disagree on what evidence to consider and how to interpret the evidence they do accept.

Secondary sources are often indispensable in deciding how to use primary sources and in determining their reliability. But establishing the reliability of secondary sources can also be difficult. For evidence seldom speaks for itself, and no presentation can be totally neutral or objective, even when the writer seeks to present the evidence fairly; all interpretations are shaped by personal and cultural attitudes. In judging a secondary source, you need to consider the weight given to various kinds of evidence, and need to be alert to special circumstances or biases that limit the usefulness of the source or make it unreliable. Primary and secondary sources both are necessary in the search for facts, and both must be used with care.

Peter H. Rossi

PETER H. ROSSI *is Professor of Sociology at the University of Massachusetts in Amherst.* In *his book* Down and Out in America: The Origins of Homelessness (1989) *he gives a history of homelessness in America, describes sampling methods he and associates used to determine the number of homeless in Chicago, and reaches some conclusions about causes.* Rossi *states:*

> The social welfare system has never been very attentive to unattached, disaffiliated men, and now it appears to be as unresponsive to unattached females. Likewise, the social welfare system does little to help families support their dependent adult members. Many of the homeless of the 1950s and early 1960s were pushed out or thrown away by their families when they passed the peak of adulthood; many of the new homeless are products of a similar process.

In *the following section from* Down and Out in America, Rossi *describes the homeless of the 1970s and the 1980s. In his account he draws on authoritative studies by other sociologists and demographers, among them Donald B. Bogue (see list of references) who recommended that scattered housing and social services for the disabled and alcoholics replace flophouses in the Chicago central business district—to be subsidized by the city.*

THE NEW HOMELESS
OF THE 1970S AND 1980S

By the middle of the seventies, striking changes had taken place in city after city. Indeed, it looked as if at least part of Bogue's advice to Chicago had been followed in every large city. Many of the flophouse cubicle hotels had been demolished, replaced initially by parking lots and later by office buildings and apartment complexes for young professionals. The collection of cheap SRO hotels, where the more prosperous of the old homeless had lived, also had been seriously diminished.

Although the long-established Skid Rows had shrunk and in 2
some cases had been almost obliterated, urban Skid Rows did
not disappear altogether: in most places the missions still
remained,[1] and smaller Skid Rows sprouted in several places
throughout the cities where the remaining SRO hotels and
rooming houses still stood.

In the 1960s and 1970s the need for very cheap accommo- 3
dations for old age pensioners documented by Bogue and by
Caplow and Bahr diminished. The number of elderly extremely
poor had declined as the coverage of the Social Security old
age pension system increased to include more of the labor
force and Congress in the 1960s voted more generous benefits
for those who had been working all their lives under its coverage. In 1974 Social Security old age benefits were pegged to
the cost-of-living index, ensuring that the high inflation rates
of the 1970s would not wipe out their value. In addition, subsidized senior citizens' housing, our most popular public housing program, began to provide affordable accommodations to
the elderly. This increase in the economic well-being of the
aged is most dramatically shown in the remarkable decline in
the proportion of those sixty-five and over who were below the
poverty line: from 25% in 1968 to less than 13% in 1985, with
the most precipitous decline of 9% in the three-year period
between 1970 and 1973. The consequence of these changes
was that a large portion of those who might otherwise have
been residents of the 1950s-style Skid Row disappeared in the
1970s into the more general housing stock.[2] Higher benefits
and subsidized housing made it possible for the aged pensioners successfully to obtain modest housing. In addition,
more generous benefits were available for the physically
disabled and the chronic mentally ill through an expanded

---

[1] Pacific Garden Mission, one of Chicago's oldest and largest missions, is still at the same address as in 1958. When studied by Bogue, it was surrounded by exceedingly shabby buildings
housing cubicle hotels, pawnshops, and cheap restaurants and bars. When I visited there in
1987, it was in the midst of a considerably upgraded neighborhood with only one of the SROs
still functioning.
[2] The age structure of the 1950s and 1960s Skid Rows made changes rapidly evident. The elderly
residents of those times were mostly dead by the end of the 1970s. The changes in the Social
Security system primarily benefited those who retired after 1970.

Supplemental Security Income (SSI) and Social Security Disability Insurance (SSDI) program, enabling this group to move up in the housing market.

The "old" homeless may have blighted some sections of the central cities, but from the perspective of urbanites they had the virtue of being concentrated on Skid Row, which one could avoid and hence ignore. Also, most of the old homeless had some shelter, although inadequate by any standards, and very few were literally sleeping on the streets.

Indeed, in those earlier years, if people had tried to bed down on steam grates or in doorways and vestibules anywhere in the city, police patrols would have bundled them off to jail. The subsequent decriminalization of many status crimes, such as public inebriation and vagrancy—and the decreased emphasis on charges such as loitering has enlarged the turf homeless persons can claim.

Homelessness began to take on new forms by the end of the 1970s. Although all the researchers found some homeless people sleeping out on the streets or in public places in the 1950s and 1960s, the homeless by and large were familyless persons living in very inexpensive (and often inadequate) housing, mainly cubicle and SRO hotels. Toward the end of the next decade, what had been a minor form of homelessness became more prevalent: literal homelessness began to grow and at the same time to become more visible to the public. It became more and more difficult to ignore the evidence that some people had no shelter and lived on the streets. The "new" homeless could be found resting or sleeping in public places such as bus or railroad stations, on steam grates, in doorways and vestibules, in cardboard boxes, in abandoned cars, or in other places where they could be seen by the public.

With the decriminalization of public drunkenness and relaxed enforcement of ordinances concerning many status crimes, police patrols no longer picked up people sleeping out on the streets or warned them away from downtown streets or places with nighttime public access. In addition, whatever bizarre behavior may have characterized the old homeless of the 1950s and 1960s, that behavior was acted out on Skid Row.[3] Now the public could observe first-hand shabbily dressed persons acting in bizarre ways, muttering, shouting, and carrying bulky packages or pushing supermarket carts filled with junk and old clothes.

Even more striking was the appearance of significant numbers of women among the homeless. Shabby and untidy women could now be seen shuffling along the streets with their proverbial shopping bags or nodding sleepily in bus stations. What few homeless women there were in the 1950s and 1960s must have kept out of sight. 8

Although homeless families rarely were seen walking streets, they started to appear at welfare offices asking for help in obtaining shelter. When homeless families began to come to the attention of the mass media and to show up in television clips and news articles, public attention grew even stronger and sharper. 9

Reminiscent of the Dust Bowl migration of the Great Depression, stories began appearing in the newspapers about families migrating from the Rust Belt cities to the Sun Belt. The resemblances were striking. The family breadwinner had lost his job in a factory and, after weeks of fruitless search for employment in one or another mid-American city, had loaded household possessions and family into an old car, driving to Houston or Phoenix in search of the employment reputed to be found in the booming Sun Belt. 10

Popular response to the new homeless grew with the evidence of homelessness. In a celebrated 1979 New York case,[4] public interest lawyers sued the city, claiming that New York had an obligation to provide shelter to homeless men. Their 11

---

[3] Bahr and Caplow mention that 1960s bus tours of New York advertised as visiting New York's famous "sights" regularly included a visit to the Bowery, with the tour guide pointing out the "scenes of depravity" that could be viewed safely from the bus.

[4] The case in question, *Callahan v. Carey*, was filed in the New York State Supreme Court in 1979 by Robert Hayes, then director of the New York Coalition for the Homeless. The suit claimed that the state constitution and municipal charter stated that shelter was an entitlement. Shortly after the case was filed, the court issued a temporary injunction requiring the city to expand the capacity of municipal shelters. When the case came to trial in 1981, it was settled by a consent decree in which the city agreed to provide shelter upon demand.

victory in New York led to an expansion of a network of "emergency" municipal shelters in that city, which currently provides 6,000 beds nightly, almost entirely in dormitory quarters. Subsequent court decisions have extended New York City's shelter obligations to include homeless women.

The new "emergency shelters" that have been provided in 12 city after city are certainly better than having no roof at all over one's head, but a case can be made that in some respects the cubicle hotels were better. The men's shelters established in New York in the past decade resemble in physical layout the dormitory accommodations provided by the missions in the old Skid Row, which the homeless regarded as last-resort alternatives to sleeping outside. In social organization these shelters most closely resemble minimum-security prisons whose gates are open during the day.

As reported in a survey of New York shelter clients (Crystal 13 and Goldstein 1982), the shelter residents rated prisons *superior* to shelters in safety, cleanliness, and food quality. The shelters were regarded clearly superior only in freedom—meaning the right to leave at any time. The new homeless were clearly worse off in regard to shelter than the old homeless.

The housing for homeless single women was somewhat better 14 than that supplied to men. The single-women's shelters most closely resembled the cubicle flophouses with their cramped individual accommodations.

New York is exceptional in that the municipal government 15 has directly provided most of the shelters for the homeless. In most cities, private charities with government subsidies usually provide the shelters. The long-established religious missions—for example, the Salvation Army, the Volunteers of America, and the Society of Saint Vincent de Paul—expanded their existing shelters and in some instances undertook to run shelters under contract to municipalities or states. Other charities provided shelters for the first time.

In Bogue's 1958 study, the four or five mission shelters provided 16 only 975 beds for the homeless of Chicago, in contrast to the forty-five shelters we found in that city in the winter of

1985–86, providing a total of 2,000 beds. Several commentators have observed that the shelters provided by private charities are superior in many respects to those run by municipalities.[5]

To accommodate the influx of family groups into the homeless population, new types of shelter arrangements have come into being. Some specialize in quasi-private quarters for family groups, usually one or two rooms per family with shared bathrooms and cooking facilities. In many cities welfare departments have provided temporary housing for families by renting rooms in hotels and motels: for example, in 1986 New York City housed 3,500 homeless families a month in "welfare hotels" (Bach and Steinhagen 1987).[6]   17

On a scale that was inconceivable earlier, considerable funds for the new homeless have been allocated out of local, state, and federal funds. Private charity has also been generous; most of the "emergency" shelters for the homeless are organized and run by private groups with subsidies from public funds. Foundations have given generous grants. For example, the Robert Wood Johnson Foundation in association with the Pew Memorial Trust supports medical clinics for the homeless persons in nineteen cities. The states have provided funds through existing programs and special appropriations.   18

In the spring of 1987, after a prelude media event in which congressmen and advocates for the homeless slept overnight on the Capitol steps, Congress passed the McKinney Homeless Assistance Act, which appropriated $442 million for the homeless in fiscal 1987 and $616 million in 1988. The money was channeled through a group of agencies, providing some housing for the homeless, subsidies for existing shelters, and subsidies for a variety of rehabilitation programs including   19

---

[5] At least part of the difference in quality arises because most privately run shelters restrict whom they admit, usually excluding those who are drunk, appear aggressive or behave bizarrely. Municipal shelters ordinarily have to admit everyone and hence find it difficult to exclude anyone on such grounds.

[6] An ironic feature of the use of welfare hotels is that the rents paid by the welfare departments for these accommodations are clearly far greater than current rents at the lowest end of the housing market. Welfare payments are not enough to pay market rents for apartments, but the welfare departments find it possible to pay much higher hotel rents for homeless clients!

vocational training, medical care, and services for the chronically mentally ill. The funds authorized in the McKinney Act were in addition to those available from existing programs that have supported homeless persons through welfare benefit programs and federally supported medical services.

Reversing the decline discerned in the 1960s, there can be little doubt that homelessness has increased over the past decade and that the composition of the homeless population has changed dramatically. There are ample signs of these changes. In the few cities where data over time exist, there is clear evidence that the number of homeless people is increasing in at least some localities. In New York City, shelter capacity has increased from 3,000 beds to 6,000 over a five-year period. In the same city, the number of families in the welfare hotels has increased from a few hundred to the 3,500 of today. In addition there are many homeless people who do not use the shelters, though the number is not known with any precision.

Nevertheless, for the country as a whole no one knows for sure how much of an increase there has been over the past decade, let alone how many homeless people there are in the United States today. There are many obstacles to obtaining this knowledge. Some of the major obstacles are technical. For example, conventional censuses and surveys proceed on the assumption that nearly everyone in the United States can be reached through an address, an assumption that is clearly violated in the case of the homeless. Hence we cannot look to the 1980 census (or likely to the 1990 census)[7] or the Current Population Survey for credible estimates of homelessness. Other obstacles are more ideological; a central one centers on whether the concept of homelessness should be restricted to those who are without conventional housing or extended to

---

[7] Current plans for the 1990 census include enumerations late at night in public places, such as bus stations, where homeless persons are known to congregate, as well as full coverage of emergency shelters. If carried through as currently (1988) planned, the 1990 census will provide a better count of the literally homeless than now exists. Nevertheless, the improved tally will still not include homeless people in locations other than those best known to the local experts on whom the census will rely for information on where to count.

cover all who are inadequately housed. Depending on whether one adopts a narrow or a more inclusive definition, the number of homeless will differ by several magnitudes.

These difficulties notwithstanding, several estimates have been made of the size of the homeless population. The National Coalition for the Homeless, an advocacy group, "guesstimates" anywhere between 1.5 and 3 million. A much maligned report of the United States Department of Housing and Urban Development (1984), using four different estimation approaches, put the national figure at somewhere between 250,000 and 300,000 in 1983. A more recent estimate by Freeman and Hall (1986) comes closer to the HUD figures with an estimate of 350,000 in 1986. All the existing estimates are vulnerable to criticism, since they all rest on heroic assumptions that challenge credibility. 22

Although the issue of how many homeless people there are in the United States is a contentious one, it does not really matter which of these estimates is most accurate: homelessness is obviously a major social problem. By any standards, all the estimates point to a national disgrace, clearly unacceptable in a rich, humane society. 23

Since 1980, there have been approximately forty reasonably well-conducted social science studies of the homeless whose results are available to the diligent and patient researcher.[8] As in the late 1950s and 1960s, the purpose of funding and carrying out these studies is to provide information on which to base policies and programs to alleviate the pitiful condition of the American homeless. Research funds have been provided by private foundations and government agencies, among which the National Institute of Mental Health has been a major contributor. 24

The cities studied range across all regions of the country, including all the major metropolises as well as more than a score of smaller cities. One study even attempted to study the rural homeless but had little success in locating them. The 25

---

[8] Many of these studies are privately published in reports that are not circulated through the publications market.

cumulative knowledge about the new homeless that can be acquired through these studies is impressive and hardly contentious. Despite wide differences in the definitions of homelessness used,[9] approaches taken, methods, and degree of technical sophistication, there is considerable convergence among their findings. A fairly clear understanding is now emerging concerning who the new homeless are, how they contrast with the general population, and how they differ from the homeless of the 1950s.

Some of the important ways the current homeless differ from the old homeless have already been mentioned. Bogue estimated that in 1958 only about 100 homeless men slept out on the streets of Chicago. Caplow and Bahr make some passing mention of the Bowery homeless sleeping out on the streets or in public places in 1964, but their lack of attention to this feature implies that the number was small. Blumberg's study of Philadelphia uncovered only 64 homeless persons living on the streets in 1960. In contrast, my own studies of homelessness in Chicago found close to 1,400 homeless persons out on the streets in the fall of 1985 and 528 in that condition in the dead of winter in early 1986. Comparably large numbers of street homeless, proportionate to community size, have been found over the past five years in studies of, among other cities, Los Angeles, New York, Nashville, Austin, Detroit, Baltimore, and Washington, D.C. A major difference between the old and the new homeless is that the old homeless routinely managed somehow to find shelter indoors, while a majority of the new homeless in most studies are out on the streets. As far as shelter goes, the new homeless are clearly worse off. In short, *homelessness today means more severe basic shelter deprivation*.

There is also some evidence that those housed in emergency shelters may be worse off than the homeless who lived in the cubicle hotels of the 1960s. Whatever the deficiencies of the cubicle hotels, they were a step above the dormitory

26

27

---

[9] The definitional differences are mainly on the nominal level. Although many of the studies include the precariously housed as homeless in principle, in practice almost all deal with the literally homeless.

arrangements of the 1980s and considerably better than sleeping on the streets or in public places.

Furthermore, the new homeless, sheltered or out on the streets, are no longer concentrated in Skid Row. They can be encountered more widely throughout the downtown areas of our cities. Homelessness today cannot be easily ignored as in the past. In the expectation that homeless were on the decline, the traditional Skid Row areas were demolished and homelessness was decentralized. In addition, the liberalization of police patrol practices in many cities has meant that the homeless can wander more freely through our downtown areas. Thus the public receives more direct exposure to the sight of destitution.

A second major contrast is the presence of women among the homeless. In Chicago's Skid Row, Bogue estimated that women may have constituted up to 3% of the residents, and he thought that many were not homeless but were simply living in the Skid Row areas.[10] As reported by Bahr and Garrett (1976), homeless women on the Bowery in the 1960s constituted only a handful—64 over a period of a year—of alcoholics housed in a special shelter for homeless women.[11]

In contrast, we found that women constituted 25% of the 1985–86 Chicago homeless population, close to the average of 21% for studies of the homeless conducted during the 1980s. All the studies undertaken in the 1980s have found that women constitute a much larger proportion of the homeless than in research done before 1970. The proportion female among the homeless varies somewhat from place to place: if women living in the New York welfare hotels are counted as homeless, then women constitute close to one-third of the homeless population of New York. In contrast, a study of the homeless of Austin, Texas, found that only 7% were

28

29

30

[10] Bogue did not interview any women in his sample of cubicle hotel and SRO residents. His estimate of 3% comes from a special tabulation from the 1950 census of persons living outside households in Skid Row census tracts. Bogue believed some of the women were live-in employees of the hotels and others were simply renting rooms in households that lived in conventional dwellings in the Skid Row areas.

[11] In their study of homeless women, they took as subjects every person admitted to a Bowery treatment center for alcoholic women. It took an entire year's set of admissions to supply sixty-four subjects for their study.

women, certainly a smaller proportion than in New York, but clearly greater than was found in any of the older Skid Row studies.

A third contrast with the old homeless is in age composi- 31 tion. There are very few persons over sixty among today's homeless and virtually no Social Security pensioners. Instead, today's homeless are concentrated in their twenties and thirties, the early years of adulthood. This is clearly shown in the median age of today's Chicago homeless, thirty-nine, in comparison with the median age of fifty found in Bogue's study. In the forty studies of the homeless conducted in the past few years, the average median age recorded was thirty-six, with a range running from twenty-eight through forty-six. Among the homeless populations throughout the country, most people are in the middle and lower thirties. Where we have data over time, as in the New York City men's shelters, the median age has been dropping rapidly over the past decade.

A fourth contrast is in employment status and income: 32 except for aged pensioners, over half of the Chicago homeless studied in 1958 were employed in any given week, either full time (28%) or intermittently (25%), and almost all worked for some period during a year's time. In contrast, among the new Chicago homeless, only 3% reported having a study job, and only 39% had worked for some time during the previous month.

Correspondingly, the new homeless have less income than 33 the old. Bogue estimated that the median annual income of the 1958 homeless was $1,058. Our Chicago finding was a median annual income of $1,198. Correcting for inflation, the income of the current homeless is equivalent to only $383 in 1958 dollars. The new homeless are clearly farther out on the fringe of the American economy: their income level is less than one-third that of the old homeless! Similar levels—average median was $1,127—were found in the nine other studies that attempted to measure income.

A final contrast is presented by the ethnic composition of 34 the old and new homeless populations. The old homeless were predominantly white—70% on the Bowery and 82% on

Chicago's Skid Row. But the new homeless are recruited heavily from among ethnic minorities: in Chicago 54% were black, and in New York's shelters more than 75% were black, a proportion that has been increasing since the early 1980s. Similar patterns are shown in other American cities, with the minority group in question changing according to the ethnic mix of the general population. In short, we can generalize that minorities are consistently overrepresented among the new homeless in ratios that are some multiple of their presence in the community. The old homelessness was more blind to color and ethnicity than the new homelessness.[12]

There are also some continuities from the old to the new homeless. First of all, they share the condition of extreme poverty. Although the new homeless are lower on the economic ladder, there can be little doubt that both groups' incomes are far too low to support any reasonable standard of living. In Chicago in 1985 and 1986, we found abysmally low incomes among the homeless. With median incomes of less than $100 per month or about $3.25 per day, even trivial expenditures loom as major expenses: for example, a round trip on Chicago's bus system in 1986 cost $1.80, more than half a day's income. A night's lodging at even the cheapest hotel costs $5.00 and up, more than a day's income. And of course, a median income figure simply marks the income received by persons right at the midpoint of the income distribution: half of the homeless live on less than the median, and close to one-fifth (18%) report no income at all. In addition, the income of the homeless is not a steady stream of $3.25 every day; it is intermittent and unpredictable, meaning that for many days in the week, weeks in the month, and months in the year many homeless people have no income at all.

Given these income levels, it is no mystery why the homeless are without shelter; their incomes simply do not allow

---

[12] Blumberg speculated that the black homeless men in the Philadelphia of 1960 were kept out of Skid Row by the discriminatory practices of cubicle hotel landlords and had to be absorbed into the black ghetto areas in rented rooms and boardinghouses. He predicted that the proportion black would rise.

them to enter effectively into the housing market. Indeed, the only way they can get by is to look to the shelters for a place to sleep, to the food kitchens for meals, to the free clinics and emergency rooms for medical care, and to the clothing distribution depots for something to put on their backs.

The new and the old homeless also are alike in having high levels of disability. The one change from the 1950s to the 1980s is that fewer have the disability of age. As I mentioned earlier, few of the new homeless are over sixty. The current homeless suffer from much the same levels of mental illness, alcoholism, and physical disability as the old homeless. 37

Much has been written asserting that the deinstitutionalization of the chronically mentally ill during the 1960s and 1970s is a major cause of the recent rise in homelessness. Almost as much has been written denying it. At this time it is almost pointless to try to determine which side in this controversy is correct, largely or in part. The decanting of the mental hospital population occurred throughout the 1960s, so its current effects have in any event long since been diluted by time. What is important right now are the current admissions policies of our mental hospitals. Many of the chronically mentally ill homeless would have been admitted two decades ago under then-existing practices. The shelters and the streets now substitute in part for the hospitals of the past.[13] 38

Remember also that the old Skid Rows were not free of the chronically mentally ill. All the researchers of the 1950s and 1960s remark on the presence of clearly psychotic persons in the flophouses of Chicago and New York. Bogue estimated that about 20% of Skid Row inhabitants were mentally ill. Blumberg found that among the 1960 Philadelphia homeless, 16% had been hospitalized at least once in a mental institution. 39

---

[13] In 1958 the municipal court that had jurisdiction over Chicago's Skid Row area had a psychiatrist on its staff whose function was to recommend commitment to mental hospitals for Skid Row residents judged psychotic who were brought before the court. Bogue suggests that this screening process lowered the proportion of Skid Row residents he found to be psychotic. A 1934 study by Sutherland and Locke of emergency municipal shelters for homeless men describes a psychiatric screening process in admission that shunted the clearly psychotic men to mental hospitals. Shelters in Chicago now often refuse admission to persons who behave bizarrely. The clearly psychotic are left to sleep on the streets.

Chronic mental illness seemingly has always been a significant presence among the homeless. Skid Row, with its easy acceptance of deviance of all sorts, certainly did not draw the line at chronic mental illness.

Because of the attention paid to deinstitutionalization as a possible contributory factor in homelessness, research on the new homeless almost invariably attempts to estimate the prevalence of chronic mental illness among them. A variety of measures have been employed, with the surprising outcome that they tend to converge: a fair summary is represented by the following averages: 25% of the homeless report previous episodes as mental hospital patients, and 33% show signs of current psychosis or affective disorders. Although the reported current prevalence of chronic mental illness appears to be more than 50% higher among the new homeless than among the old, measurement procedures may account for that difference. In any event, compared with the general population both levels are extremely high.

Physical disabilities also are prevalent among the new homeless. The best evidence on this score comes from the records of medical clinics for the homeless supported by the Robert Wood Johnson Foundation, which document high levels of both chronic conditions, such as hypertension, diabetes, and circulatory disorders, and acute conditions, some integrally related to homelessness, such as lice infestation, trauma, and leg ulcers. The few studies that looked into mortality rates among the new homeless reported rates ten to forty times those found in the general population. Unfortunately, none of the studies of the older homeless give comparable detail on medical conditions, although all the researchers remark on the presence of severe disabilities. Bogue did judge that close to half of the 1958 Skid Row inhabitants had moderate to severe disabilities that would substantially reduce their employability. His studies found much the same mortality levels as have been found among the new homeless—more than ten times higher than among comparable age groups in the domiciled population.

All the studies of the old homeless stress how widespread 42
alcoholism was. Bogue found that 30% were heavy drinkers,
defined as persons spending 25% or more of their income on
alcoholic beverages and drinking the equivalent of six or more
pints of whiskey a week. Using a comparable measure, Bahr
and Caplow found 36% to be heavy drinkers. Similar proportions were found in Minneapolis and Philadelphia about the
same time.

Studies of the new homeless show similar degrees of 43
prevalence of alcoholism. In our Chicago study, 33% had been
in a detoxification unit, indicating that one in three had had
serious problems with alcohol. Studies in other cities produced estimates of current alcoholism averaging 33%, with a
fairly wide range. The consensus of the studies is that about
one in three of the new homeless are chronic alcoholics.

A new twist is drug abuse. None of the studies of the 1980 44
homeless has attempted to measure drug abuse in any satisfactory way, but all point to the significant presence of drug
abuse, past and present, among the new homeless. Recent
studies of the homeless in New York men's shelters claim that
about 20% of the homeless men were current hard drug users
or had been addicted in the past.

Although only large minorities of the new homeless are 45
afflicted with any one of the disabilities of chronic mental illness, debilitating physical conditions, or chronic alcoholism,
their effects are additive. A substantial majority have at least
one and sometimes several disabling conditions. About two-
thirds of the Chicago homeless had physical health problems,
mental health problems, substance abuse problems, or some
combination of them.

Another point of comparability between the old and the 46
new homeless concerns the heterogeneity of both populations. Both comprised some persons who remained homeless
for only short periods and others who were homeless for a
long time. The Skid Rows were points of entry for poor
migrants to urban centers, who rented cubicles until they had
established themselves and could afford conventional

dwellings. The short-term new homeless are somewhat different—poor persons whose fortunes have temporarily taken a turn for the worse and who find the shelters a good way to cut back on expenses until they can reestablish themselves.[14] A large portion of the temporary new homeless population consists of young female-headed households in transition from one household (often their parents') to another, using the shelters as a resting place until they can establish a new home on their own, often while waiting for certification as AFDC recipients.

A final point of comparability between the old and the new   47
homeless is that both are relatively isolated socially. The new homeless report few friends and intimates and little contact with relatives and family. There are also signs of some friction between the homeless and their relatives. So extensive was the absence of social ties with kin and friends among the old homeless that Caplow and Bahr define homelessness as essentially a state of *disaffiliation*, without enduring and supporting ties to family, friends, and kin. Disaffiliation also characterizes the new homeless, marking this group off from other extremely poor persons.

The contrasts between the homeless of the 1950s and   48
1960s and the homeless of the 1980s offer some strong clues to why homelessness has become defined as a social problem. First, there can be no doubt that more Americans are exposed to the sight of homelessness because homeless persons are less spatially concentrated today. Second, homelessness has shifted in meaning: the old homeless were sheltered in inadequate accommodations, but they were not sleeping out on the streets and in public places in great numbers. Literal on-the-street homelessness has increased from virtually

---

[14] In many housing markets a prospective renter must have enough cash to put down a month's rent in advance plus a security deposit in order to rent an apartment. Thus one may need as much as $800 simply to make an offer for an apartment renting for $400 a month. If we also consider that some minimum of furniture is necessary, setting up a new household in a rental apartment may take more than $1,000 in cash. Although few researchers have provided any firm numbers, several have remarked on shelter dwellers who are employed full time and using the cheap accommodations while they accumulate the cash necessary to enter the conventional rental market.

negligible proportions to more than half of the homeless population. Third, homelessness now means greater deprivation. The homeless men living on Skid Row were surely poor, but their average income from casual and intermittent work was three to four times that of the current homeless. The emergency shelter housing now available is at best only marginally better than the cubicle rooms of the past.

Finally, the composition of the homeless has changed dramatically. Thirty years ago old men were the majority among the homeless, with only a handful of women in that condition and virtually no families. The current homeless are younger and include a significant proportion of women. Finally, advocate organizations and groups have arisen to speak on behalf of the homeless and to raise public consciousness of the problem. 49

This combination of changes helps explain why there is so much interest in the homeless today compared with a few decades ago. 50

References

Bach, Victor, and Renée Steinhagen. 1987. *Alternatives to the welfare hotel.* New York: Community Service Society.

Bahr, Howard M., and Theodore Caplow. 1974. *Old men: Drunk and sober.* New York: New York University Press.

Bahr, Howard M., and Gerald Garrett. 1976. *Women alone.* New York: New York University Press.

Blumberg, Leonard, Thomas E. Shipley, Jr., and Irving W. Shandler. 1973. *Skid Row and its alternatives.* Philadelphia: Temple University Press.

Bogue, Donald B. 1963. *Skid Row in American cities.* Chicago: Community and Family Study Center, University of Chicago.

Crystal, Stephen, and Merv Goldstein. 1982. *Chronic and situational dependency: Long-term residents in a shelter for men.* New York: Human Resources Administration.

Freeman, Richard B., and Brian Hall. 1986. "Permanent homelessness in America." Unpublished manuscript, National Bureau of Economic Research, Cambridge, Mass.

Sutherland, Edwin H., and Harvey J. Locke. 1936. *Twenty thousand homeless men*: A *study of unemployed men in Chicago shelters*. Chicago: J. B. Lippincott.

United States Department of Housing and Urban Development (HUD). 1984. A report to the secretary on the homeless and emergency shelters. Office of Policy Development and Research, Washington, DC.

VOCABULARY

paragraph 1: flophouse, cubicle
paragraph 2: obliterated
paragraph 3: precipitous
paragraph 4: blighted, perspective, urbanite
paragraph 5: vestibule, decriminalization, inebriation, vagrancy
paragraph 17: influx, quasi-private
paragraph 19: subsidy
paragraph 22: heroic assumption
paragraph 25: cumulative, contentious, technical sophistication, convergence
paragraph 31: median age
paragraph 34: ethnic composition
paragraph 35: intermittent
paragraph 38: deinstitutionalization
paragraph 39: psychotic
paragraph 43: detoxification
paragraph 47: disaffiliation

QUESTIONS

1. What differences does Rossi cite between the new homeless of the 1970s and 1980s and the homeless of earlier times?
2. What characteristics or conditions do they share?
3. How does Rossi explain these differences? Does he explain all of them? Does he single out any cause as dominant?
4. Does Rossi base his conclusions on one kind of evidence—for example, interviews with the homeless, statistical studies, the testimony of social workers and psychologists—or does he base them on more than one kind?
5. What degree of probability does Rossi claim for his conclusions? Does he qualify his evidence or conclusion in any way?

SUGGESTIONS FOR WRITING

1. Drawing on the *New York Times Index,* the *Washington Post Index,* or the index to another metropolitan newspaper, compile a list of recent articles on homelessness in New York, Washington, DC, or another city. In reading the articles, note whether the authors state or imply any causes for homelessness or for its rise or decline. Then summarize your findings, noting similarities and differences in the evidence presented.

2. As an alternate topic, investigate action taken to deal with homelessness or a related social problem in the same city or area. Note differences of opinion on policies and their effects.

Leanne G. Rivlin

> LEANNE G. RIVLIN *is Professor of Environmental Psychology at the Graduate School and University Center, City University of New York. She (with M. Wolfe) is the author of* Institutional Settings in Children's Lives *(1985). Her essay on homelessness was adapted from an invited address to the Society for the Psychological Study of Social Issues, presented at the American Psychological Association meeting in August, 1985. In discussing the causes of homelessness, Rivlin draws on her own research and that of other social psychologists.*

A NEW LOOK AT THE HOMELESS

The problem of homelessness has escalated into a critical contemporary social issue. Repeatedly, we hear the phrase, "not since the Great Depression of the 30s" have we faced such numbers of people without stable shelter, yet the efforts to deal with this tidal wave of miseries have been limited, at best.

In the last few years it has been difficult, if not impossible, to open the daily newspaper and fail to find at least one article on the homeless. Although attention to the problem declines in mild weather, it does not disappear. Accounts of suffering and deaths, reports of insufficient and brutal shelters, and deaths on the streets are commonplace. The problem is especially grave for homeless families who are housed in sleazy hotels in the Times Square area of New York City, where streets that are crowded with tourists, pimps, prostitutes, and drug pushers are the children's playgrounds.

Other homeless persons have been observed in public 3 transportation stations such as Grand Central Terminal and the Port Authority Bus Terminal in New York. These are the homeless who find temporary havens in public places subject to the changing policies of the public officials who administer these sites and the private individuals who manage them. Open spaces such as parks, plazas, and the entrances of public buildings uncover other homeless persons who find a temporary perch in mild weather as these locations become public hotels for the needy.

By now most of us have had some contact with the home- 4 less, especially but not exclusively in cities. Even if we have not seen or recognized homeless persons, we are familiar with accounts of the problem. However, many may not be aware of the extensiveness of homelessness and the numbers of persons involved.

Incidences of Homelessness

Accurate statistics on homelessness are impossible to obtain 5 since the very nature of being homeless makes people difficult to count, unless they come into contact with an official agency. According to the U.S. Department of Housing and Urban Development (1984), in the winter of 1983–1984, there were between 250,000 and 350,000 homeless per night. These statistics have been criticized as inaccurate by many, among them the research team of the Community Service Society of New York, a group that has done some landmark work on the homeless. They prefer to use an estimate of the *total numbers* of people homeless over the course of a year (Hopper and Hamburg, 1984), which might extend well beyond two million. They also raise the question of the definition of a homeless person, offering Caro's view—a person "without an address which assures them of at least the following 30 days of sleeping quarters which meet minimal health and safety standards" (Caro, 1981). While governmental guidelines are more restrictive, they are based largely on emergency needs, although a month of assured residence does not constitute the security of a home. Since many of the homeless persons today are children, especially minority children, this criterion becomes even more questionable.

Homelessness exists in many different forms and degrees 6 based on the time period involved, the alternative shelter available, and the nature of the person's social contacts. The stereotypic "Bowery bum" is a *chronic, marginal* kind associated with alcoholism and drug abuse, with life on the street most of the day, and with just enough money for a "flophouse" bed. These people may have consistent social contacts and many have a social network or support system of persons like themselves. In some cases they form small communities of persons with similar life styles.

Another kind is *periodic* homelessness—persons who leave 7 home when pressures become intense, leading them to the shelter or the streets, but the home is still available when the tensions subside. A form of periodic homelessness occurs when migrant workers must move with or without their families to the seasonal work that is the source of their livelihoods. This homelessness is time-limited and fairly predictable, with alternative shelter provided, however inadequate it may be. Still, it does involve periodic uprooting and temporary loss of home-based social and emotional needs.

Temporary homelessness is more time-limited than the other 8 forms and is usually a response to a crisis that arises—a fire, hospitalization, a move from one community to another. The assumption here is that the ability to create a home has not been threatened and that once the person leaves the hospital, returns to the damaged home, or reaches a new one the home-building will continue. Their roots are damaged but not destroyed.

The most catastrophic form of homelessness may be the 9 *total* form involving the sudden and complete loss of home and roots through natural, economic, industrial, or interpersonal disasters. Beds may be provided in city shelters, gymnasiums, or church basements, but there is no home left and the physical and psychological process of home-building must begin anew. Although the prospects for the future will differ across individuals and families, the trauma of the total devastation of social and physical supports seriously threatens the recuperative powers of the people involved. It is this group that we see increasing in catastrophically huge numbers.

Sources of Homelessness

There are many assumptions as to why people are homeless, which influence the ways they are perceived and dealt with, ultimately shaping the policies of various levels of governmental agencies. This raises the question of how much we really know about why people are homeless.

Most people move over the course of a lifetime, sometimes voluntarily, sometimes forced by circumstances over which they have little power. In fact, statistics indicate that one in five persons in the United States moves each year. But as Peter Rossi (1980) has described it, once the realization that one must move occurs, it is followed by a search for a new home, the assessment of an alternative or alternatives, and the selection of the place. Rossi has examined what he calls an "accounting scheme" that leads to the moving process. Although the scheme acknowledges that some families have very limited opportunities—in some cases a single alternative—the homeless have less than that one choice. Given the present housing market, all but the affluent have had their options seriously reduced, although usually not totally removed.

Studies such as those of the Community Service Society of New York have laid to rest many unwarranted myths about the homeless (Baxter and Hopper, 1981). One such myth is that people are homeless by choice, that they prefer a nomadic existence. Thus, the term "urban nomad" that often is applied to them. This is a dangerous view, one that can give us license *not* to address the problems that lead to homelessness and fail to search out the root causes and take appropriate measures. Very few people choose to be homeless. Most are forced into this existence by poverty, the elimination of services, fires that demolish homes, and evictions that have resulted from the difficult economic circumstances in which people are finding themselves today.

Another myth relates to family responsibility: all homeless 13 persons have relatives who should take care of them. This view shifts the burden away from agencies and ordinary citizens, denying the needs that exist, and failing to recognize the devastation and pain that separate homeless persons from their families and friends, if, indeed, they exist.

Who are the homeless? In truth, many different kinds of 14 persons are affected: single men and women and poor elderly who have lost their marginal housing, ex-offenders, single-parent households, runaway youths, "throwaway" youths (abandoned by their families or victims of family abuse), young people who have moved out of foster care, women escaping from domestic violence, undocumented and legal immigrants, Native Americans leaving the reservation after federal cutbacks and unemployment, alcoholics and drug abusers, ex-psychiatric patients, and the so-called "new poor," who are victims of unemployment and changes in the job market (Hopper and Hamburg, 1984). Minorities are among the most affected groups (Mercado-Llorens and West, 1985), and there is persistent evidence that the homeless are getting younger and younger (Hopper and Hamburg, 1984; Salerno, Hopper and Baxter, 1984; U.S. Department of Housing and Urban Development, 1984).

Deinstitutionalization has been accused of being the major 15 contributor to the ranks of the homeless. In fact, many assume that *most* of the homeless are formerly hospitalized mental patients since they often are quite conspicuous. But this is another myth. Again, statistics are inadequate, but it is now estimated that the deinstitutionalized make up 20 to 30 percent of the total numbers of homeless. There is no question that emptying hospitals and failing to provide adequate back-up services led many ex-patients to the streets. Lacking the necessary skills for daily life after years of institutionaliza-tion, unable to maintain their fragile hold on housing and nourishment, many end up homeless. These victims of years of deprivation are likely to suffer in a situation where housing is costly and difficult to locate and maintain.

However, the major victims of homelessness are not ex- 16 patients but children, who are forced to live with their families under the most desperate conditions—in overcrowded shelters or welfare hotels. In some parts of the country families search-ing for employment have been living in their automobiles.

On an international scale the problem of homeless chil- 17 dren is remarkably widespread. Their numbers, estimated at 90 million in 1983, have been increasing—with a 90 percent increase anticipated for Brazil (Jupp, 1985). There are children without their families who roam the streets in many countries, but we hear most about them in South and Central America, Africa, India, Bangladesh, Thailand, and the Philippines.

A widely used typology makes the distinction among "chil- 18 dren *on* the street," "children *of* the street," and "abandoned" children (Jupp, 1985). Children on the street, over 60 percent of the total according to Felsman (1981; 1984), are children who work on the streets while still maintaining contacts with their families. Children of the streets (over 30 percent of the group) are those living independently with occasional con-tacts with families. The final group, perhaps 7 percent of the total, are "throwaway" children, abandoned by their families and lacking stable long-term housing and the security of a home.

Basic to most homelessness, in this country and elsewhere, 19 is the critical shortage of low-cost housing created by a com-bination of factors. One factor is the shrinking housing pic-ture—each year about 2.5 million persons in this country lose the places where they live. Over half-a-million low-rental housing units are burned out, demolished, or upgraded and priced out of the market for low-income people. When this depressing loss of housing is placed against other changes—

deindustrialization and loss of unskilled and semiskilled jobs, a rise in the poorly paid service economy, the feminization of poverty and persistent unemployment, reduction of benefits due to tightened eligibility requirements (Hopper and Hamburg, 1984)—a disaster scenario emerges. The single-room occupancy hotels, rooming and boarding houses, and other inexpensive, marginal housing that were used by low-income people in the past have all but disappeared, leaving few alternatives. There is little doubt that housing policies and resulting housing shortages are at the base of much of the homelessness we see.

Most homeless persons do try to find places to live—with 20 families, friends, or housing offered by municipal agencies. In most cases these arrangements break down, in time, as families and friends become taxed by the additional burdens, forcing the extra members to leave. But there is no low-cost housing to turn to. Public housing has waiting lists years long. In many cities like New York, the homeless end up in shelters or hotels. Federal funds pay exorbitant monthly rates—generally well over $1,000 and often more than $2,000 for families—for a single substandard hotel room. Those going to municipal shelters find huge dormitories of hundreds of beds, impersonal service, unsanitary conditions, and threats to their person and belongings that may drive them back to the streets and total homelessness.

At a recent meeting on homelessness, a mother with two 21 young children described her shelter experiences—being shifted from one unfamiliar neighborhood to another while city agencies were trying to locate a replacement for her condemned apartment. She was appalled at the dirt, the closeness of the shelter beds, the mixture of people who, from her view, were threats to herself and her children. Coping with her four-year-old son's toileting needs made an ordinary activity into a major obstacle, since she had been warned against letting him use the men's room alone and the child was terrified of getting lost. It was a calamity every time the toilet had to be used.

Other homeless persons are victims of various kinds of dis-   22
asters that are as painful as fires, loss of income, or gentrification. Tidal waves and floods in Bangladesh is one such
natural catastrophe, leaving thousands in a state of homelessness. The drought in Africa created another group of wan-
derers looking for food with many dying in the process,
especially the children. In some cases the disaster is far from
natural: the result of pollution, contamination, or nuclear
accidents. The victims of Three Mile Island or Buffalo Creek
are no less homeless than the tidal wave or drought survivor.
So, too, the refugees of war, the boat people from Vietnam,
the thousands of Central Americans who have fled their
homes as a result of war, poverty, or political conflict are
examples of the homeless. These victims share the fate of the
burned-out or evicted families in their search for a haven,
although the conditions and the needs may differ.

Although the homelessness that results from fire, floods,   23
famine, or political conditions that redefine national boundaries or wars that scatter populations can occur almost anywhere, there is evidence that in some societies the homeless
are quickly absorbed, taken in and helped by friends, neighbors, and family. There are places and times in history where
all participate in the reconstruction of the home. However, if
the catastrophe affects a large enough area, rendering all residents victims, few resources or people may remain to provide
help. The so-called "safety net" of the present Administration
in Washington has great gashes that permit many to drop
through.

We might suspect that some people are more vulnerable   24
than others for various reasons. For some, social or cultural
supports may be strong, providing resources that others lack.
Clearly, those with financial ability can find housing substitutes that are not available to the poor. Illness can exacerbate
the condition of loss of home. Minority status offers both economic and social disadvantages in finding shelter and starting
over. But we really know little about the contribution of
people's past to their management of homelessness. Before

decisions are made about what to do and where to direct resources, we need to know much more about homelessness.

The Homeless Existence

Wherever we find the homeless their days are filled with constant battles to find places to rest or sleep, to keep clean, to find food, to be safe, to retain personal belongings, and, for some, to fill up the empty hours that stretch ahead. A woman describes the effort to find places where she can wash her hair. Men in a small voluntary shelter launder their clothing in a tiny washroom, drying garments over radiators. The hunger of the homeless is overwhelming as is their eagerness and gratitude for white bread and peanut butter, for hot coffee and oranges. The children play in huge armories around lines and lines of cots or in the plazas near welfare hotels dominated by drug pushers and alcoholics. This is the "life world" of homeless citizens:

> the taken-for-granted pattern and context of everyday life in which people routinely conduct their daily affairs without having to bring each gesture, behavior, and event to conscious attention. (Seamon, 1984, p. 124)

For the homeless person, little can be taken for granted: the lifeworld is threatened at the core. The struggle to satisfy the very basic needs taken for granted by most of us—for food, rest, protection from the elements, and safety—must be constantly and consciously negotiated. Life in the public shelters or welfare hotels can be as precarious and difficult as the streets. In the welfare hotels in New York, a parent must prepare meals on a limited daily food allowance in a room with no refrigerator and a single hotplate, difficult, indeed, when there are a number of persons to feed.

The public shelters for single persons and families are enormous barrack-like structures allowing no privacy and few comforts. The meals that are provided may be unfamiliar foods served at odd hours. The number of personal possessions that can be maintained is sorely limited since storage is non-existent and the loss of belongings persistent. These places share many of the qualities of other institutions— impersonality, routine, and lack of privacy and control (Rivlin, Bogert and Cirillo, 1981).

The challenges to daily life activities come from many 28 sources—criminals who prey on the homeless, space managers who want them out of places, and others who find it uncomfortable to be around homeless persons. But the resourcefulness of many of the homeless is impressive. Some are able to "pass"—to cloak themselves in sufficiently ordinary ways so as to look like the people they are not. Others are able to find safe places for themselves, where there is warmth and some measure of security against the array of threats to their well-being.

There is also a great deal of supportiveness within home- 29 less groups: the sharing of survival tips, of job possibilities, where to go to keep warm, as well as cigarettes, reading material, food, and clothing. It would be well to identify these strengths and build on them in the process of dealing with homelessness. There is cleverness and street-wisdom in the woman who found a place to shampoo her hair and clean herself or the man in Grand Central Terminal who converted an old wardrobe trunk into a portable earth station, neatly filled with an array of life-sustaining possessions—clothing, cleaning materials, and dishes. These are capable survivors, whose coping strategies and the competence that supports them need to be documented, rather than their weaknesses and needs alone.

Attitudes Toward the Homeless

Some of the challenges faced by homeless persons come from 30 the attitudes of those around them. Mobile people tend to be mistrusted by governments that want to count, tax, and control those living within their boundaries. Indeed, over the years there have been direct and indirect measures taken to sedentarize nomadic groups, to keep them in defined areas, often in the name of economic development. If governments have been unsympathetic toward mobile persons, there also is a long history of mixed reactions toward all kinds of strangers, especially destitute ones. Homeless strangers have been the object of pity, charity, and hospitality, but they also have been feared, rejected, and abused.

In literature the stranger is often the subject of suspicion, 31 at the very least. The Torah speaks of the "ger" (resident strangers), non-Israelites who were unable to rely on their tribes for protection (Union of American Hebrew Congregations, 1981). The kindness that was extended to these strangers derived from the Biblical injunction "You shall not wrong a stranger or oppress him for you were strangers in the land of Egypt" (Exodus 22,20). These were not homeless persons, in the sense that we have today. Our homeless were made strangers by their loss of permanent shelter and community connections. However, the concept of "resident stranger" is a useful one.

In many ways homeless people have become "resident 32 strangers," people who have lost their roles within society, along with their homes. Evidence for this can be found in the generic term "homeless": an undifferentiated form rather than mothers, children, fathers, sons, and daughters whose misfortunes and society's failures have led them to the streets, the welfare hotels, or the shelters. The label serves to obscure their heterogeneity. By depersonalizing them, the impact of their plight is blunted; we distance them from our own lives and fail to address the serious and complex social problems that have produced them in the numbers we see today. It is critical that the psychological, economic, and political dimensions of homelessness be understood and that the distorted, romantic, and inaccurate images of homeless life be disabused.

The current social context becomes apparent when we look 33 *historically* at homelessness and how it defines a relationship between people and environments. There has been a long history of prejudice toward strangers, mobile people, and the poor. The most prevalent homeless persons were paupers, a term that included the indigent, sick or aged, widows and orphans, and also the insane. For example, in colonial times there was concern with the financial consequences of "all adverse conditions, not their idiosyncratic attributes" (Rothman, 1971, p. 5). Although there was some concern for "needy neighbors" there was none for "needy outsiders" (Rothman, 1971). The bases for these attitudes were the religious and social traditions of the colonists that reflected, in part, their English heritage. Almshouses and workhouses for the most "suspect" among the poor, a model adapted from English forms, along with various benevolent societies, became the means of dealing with poverty. The presence of the poor was seen as a way for people "to do good" (Rothman, 1971).

Paupers were some of this country's earliest homeless citizens and seen from afar the manner of dealing with them may seem to reflect different policies than we have today. However, there are some uncomfortable similarities in the generalizing, the victimization of children, and the ambivalence reflected in the attitudes of the community. 34

Today, our most powerful images of homelessness come from the media with their emphasis on the most visible homeless—usually the mentally disturbed—and from stereotypes of homeless life—gypsies, hoboes, and bag ladies, people who have been portrayed either as vagabonds with carefree lives or secret millionaires hoarding and hiding their affluence. But the homeless also have been greeted with suspicion and contempt and viewed as non-persons since they defy the largely middle-class moral order of the city, a moral order that frequently views homelessness as vagrancy (Duncan, 1975). 35

In his study of hoboes the British writer Kenneth Allsop (1967) looked for an explanation of mobility in this country and found considerable ambivalence in our attitudes. "My starting point was not the belief that mobility is unique to America, only that America has a unique kind of mobility." He goes on to a broad, admittedly risky generalization: 36

To the European impermanence and change are bad, restlessness reveals the flaw of instability; whereas to an American restlessness is pandemic; entrenchment means fossilization, a poor spirit. (Allsop, 1967, p. 31)

He sees a prizing of "fluidity," mobile executives (as Toffler would later describe them in *Future Shock*, 1970) and millions on the road in automobiles, vans, trailers, and campers, using supermarket plazas, malls, drive-in banks, fast-food and open-air restaurants. Allsop suggests that there is a certain amount of official support for this migratory style especially for unemployed workers.

> Mobility is unarguably an indispensable component in an economy of the American character and in a nation of America's size, and so is justifiably prized and commended. But the idea itself has come to be qualified by a cluster of subordinate clauses. Mobility with money is, of course, laudable and desirable—you are then a tourist or envoy of business. Mobility between firms and cities is proof of a professional man's initiative and ambition. Mobility is also proof of a workless working man's grit, of his determination to hunt down the breach in the wall and find readmission to the commonwealth. Finally, mobility without these objectives or rationalizations— therefore, mobility for its own feckless sake—must be held to be bad, for it is the act of a renegade and puts in jeopardy the American declaration of intent. (Allsop, 1967, p. 436)

Although there is ambivalence about mobility, in fact, we know little about specific attitudes toward homeless persons. It is clear, however, that people are not happy about having shelters in their neighborhoods. Public shelters tend to be concentrated in marginal areas, places where local residents have little political influence or the organization to resist.

A *Newsweek* article on the homeless in Arizona describes one kind of local resistance that seems to be working (Alter, 1984). A "fight back" campaign mounted by Phoenix community leaders to "wipe out the 'unacceptable behavior' of the area's 1,500 street-people" features an ad campaign that has an illustration of a man on a bench, sleeping. A red line is "drawn through it like an international traffic sign." Intended to discourage "outsiders" and abolish soup kitchens and other homeless hangouts, the effort to maintain an image of a clean and conventional community persists even as homelessness increases in the Southwest.

Significance of Homelessness

What does it mean to be homeless? On a practical level it   38
means loss of the right to vote, to receive regular social services, to maintain contacts through mail and telephone. It includes loss of roles, loss of being a neighbor and having neighbors, of hosting visitors, of being a worker, a provider of shelter and nurturance. The homeless are perpetual guests and often unwelcome ones.

Loss of a home must be considered one of life's most pro-   39
found traumas (Dohrenwend and Dohrenwend, 1974; Marris, 1975). Although residential mobility often is a response to stress (Shumaker and Stokols, 1982), it also is a producer of stress even when the decision to relocate is a voluntary one and a sign of upward mobility (Rossi, 1980). The slum clearance projects of the 50s and 60s have left us with vivid descriptions of "grieving for a lost home" (Fried, 1963), after the destruction of a neighborhood for urban renewal.

A home may be viewed as a slum by city officials and urban   40
planners, but it is a place rich with social connections, familiar people, and deep personal meanings. When the uprooted residents of the West End of Boston were interviewed, the sadness that they felt for the loss of their old homes, and neighborhood was of major proportions. In fact, half of the 566 men and women studied described severe depression or other disturbances ("It was like a piece being taken from me." "Something of me went with the West End").

This pattern also has been documented by Michael Young   41
and Peter Willmott for the relocation of families from the East End of London (1957; 1966), by Marris for Lagos, Nigeria (Marris, 1961; 1975), and Kai Erikson (1976) for the Buffalo Creek Dam disaster. In some cases grief can result from local changes that render a home geography unfamiliar. Nora

Rubinstein's (1983) study of the Pine Barrens of New Jersey, a semi-rural area near Atlantic City, identified people deeply troubled by changes happening around them. A number of residents could make enormous profits from the sale of their homes and property, but for many the transformation of the area is a painful reminder of a lost past and, most of all, their own limited power to control their immediate environment. Although the grief over the loss of a home and neighborhood, or profound changes to it, may subside over time and be replaced by attachment to the new setting (Willmott, 1963), it is useful to ask why the deep emotion over places exists and how it develops.

We are accustomed to discussions of attachment to people—parents, families, friends—or even attachment to pets. In fact, the developmental literature from infancy through the later years defines growth largely in terms of social experiences. We are less likely to find the context, or setting, of this growth the subject of serious concern, although this is changing (Rivlin and Wolfe, 1985). The recognition that settings and objects within them are components of growth and development, in interactive participation with social experiences, provides a good deal of the answer of why people grieve for lost places and why homelessness is so profoundly painful. As we explore the meaning of home to people, we are learning about the attachments to place and the significance of change and loss (Marris, 1975).

We are beginning to appreciate the contribution of environmental experiences to a person's identity (Proshansky, Fabian and Kaminoff, 1983), the power of enduring memories of home, and their effects on both the course of development and on the ability to make a home (see, for example, Cooper Marcus, 1978a;b; Hester, 1978; Horwitz and Klein, 1978; Horwitz and Tognoli, 1982; Rowles, 1978; 1980; 1981). The restorative qualities of a home as "a place to rest, whose familiarity and security permit the person to recuperate for future ventures away from home" (Seamon, 1984, p. 758) are being recognized. These are affective ties to place that the geographer

Yi-Fu Tuan has described as *topophilia*, "love of place" (Tuan, 1974), giving people a sense of roots and a feeling of security (Tuan, 1980).

It is essential to question the impact of a homeless experi- 44 ence for anyone, but especially for children. Robert Coles (1970) has provided some powerful descriptions of periodic homelessness in the lives of migrant farm workers' children. Whether by accident, poverty, or corruption, large numbers of urban children today lack permanent homes, live in temporary shelters and hotel rooms, in neighborhoods ill-equipped to support healthy childhood activities. Their education often is interrupted until emergency arrangements can be set up. In New York City, school buses now circulate among the welfare hotels and shelters, transporting children to schools. But it took a long time to set this system in place, and few children receive continuous schooling.

There is recent evidence that homelessness has serious 45 consequences for children. Some preliminary data from a study conducted by Dr. Ellen Bassuk, of Harvard University Medical School, found that 78 children (from 51 families) living in shelters had signs of anxiety, severe depression, and serious developmental lags (Bassuk, 1985). Some of the symptoms were severe enough to be considered a state of "acute psychiatric crisis." Emotional difficulties were only part of the problems—there were physical and learning disabilities, as well.

Attachments to place are strongest when large portions of 46 a person's life are laid down in an area (Rivlin, 1982). This occurs when a person resides in an area over an extended time and when a person uses the area for purposes central to life—working, shopping, raising children, playing, socializing, and attending religious services. The greater the *number* of domains of life that take place in an area and the more concentrated these domains are within an area, "the deeper the roots are likely to be in the place" (Rivlin, 1982, p. 89). Although it might be argued that the quality of life today does not encourage the development of roots, that people move widely over their geographies with few deep connections to place, the impact of each setting and the enduring memories of home that parallel these experiences must be acknowledged. Home as an ideal image or a real place acts to anchor, shelter, and personally define an individual to herself or himself.

Rootedness and place attachment do not depend on the quality of a place, its amenities, its services, or the housing stock. Rootedness can occur in places defined as slums, as well as in modest and affluent areas. Although victims of urban homelessness are likely to come from poorer areas, their roots and attachments are as strong and their losses no less painful than victims of floods and fires. The young, disabled, and elderly are particularly vulnerable. For them uprooting means loss of familiar objects, possessions, people, and places and the need to adjust to a series of alternatives under difficult conditions over which they have little or no control. 47

Conclusion

Homelessness takes many forms, in terms of chronic, temporary, periodic and total types. They involve people who may be victims of poverty, many of them ill, or old, or very young, some alcoholic or with severe psychological problems. These are people caught in a reality in which programs developed to enable them to survive intact in their homes have been systematically dismantled by the current Administration, widening the possibility of who can become homeless. Homelessness itself creates a plethora of problems and personal risks, not the least of which is a severe threat to the person's identity and sense of self. 48

We can do something about this epidemic in personal, political, and professional ways and we must do it soon, before the homeless become resigned to their state and other people become desensitized to the problems. We can identify the ecology of homelessness, how it happens, the series of stages that exist in the progress to the streets, in order to catch the 49 problem before it escalates. We also need to know what happens to these people over time and determine how many are able to escape from the shelters, hotels, and streets and re-establish themselves. We can help to define the varied needs of the different types of homeless persons—for housing, food, jobs, vocational training. We can recognize their capabilities and provide resources for self-help efforts wherever possible. We need to document coping strategies and competence, not just pathology. Most critically, we must recognize the most threatened among the group—the children.

We must work with communities to have them accept shelters and other housing for the homeless, politic for affordable housing, and educate the public about the enormity of the problem. We have had emergency measures for dealing with acute homeless situations for some time. The Red Cross and Salvation Army have long histories of stepping in and offering assistance to victims of floods, fires, and the like. But there is a totally different condition today: an enormous pool of homeless persons largely created by contemporary social policies. We require new policies to deal with these numbers.

Temporary shelters are a small move toward resolving the problem of homeless people. But unless people consider other alternatives to accommodate the homeless within their neighborhoods, we will end up with enormous shelter-institutions removed from communities and more and more families in hotels. Action research is needed to work with communities toward accepting diversity within their boundaries and to work with the homeless to provide housing and services.

In the end the images of homeless individuals, particularly people that we see or read about, provide the strongest motivation to do something. I am reminded of a character in *The Street*, a novel by Israel Rabon, published in 1928 but recently translated from the Yiddish language. It describes the experiences of a veteran of World War I, a man without family who goes to the city of Lodz in Poland when discharged and ends up penniless and on the street. There is a brief passage that is the essence of the homeless experience:

In the several weeks since I had been hanging around town, I had become acquainted with—and made only too much use of—the places where one could hope to get in out of the rain, or where one might run into somebody one knew. In the waiting rooms of the town's two train stations I was already well known as a bad penny. To the women who kept the buffet counters and to the people at the newspaper kiosks, I was a suspicious character. I did not leave those places because anyone threatened me in any way but because I felt myself overwhelmed by pity—self-pity.

How could a healthy, vigorous person like me be down and out?

In those weeks of knocking about in Lodz, I had grown accustomed to the pathetic silence of my life. I felt my soul being swallowed up in the rhythms of idleness, of futility. There is something about wandering the strange streets of a large industrial city, trying to warm oneself by the light of a chilly sun, turning weaker and weaker with hunger—there is something in all this that separates, alienates one from the entire world.

Our efforts now must be directed toward preventing this alienation, and the bitter loss that goes with it. 53

References

K. Allsop, *Hard Travellin': The Hobo and His History* (New York: The New American Library, 1967).

J. Alter, "Homeless in America," *Newsweek* (Jan. 2, 1984), pp. 20–28.

E. L. Bassuk, *The Feminization of Homelessness: Homeless Families in Boston's Shelters.* Keynote address at the yearly benefit of Shelter, Inc. Cambridge, MA (July 11, 1985).

E. Baxter, and K. Hopper, *Private Lives/Public Spaces* (New York: Community Service Society of New York, 1981).

F. Caro, *Estimating Numbers of Homeless Families* (New York: Community Service Society of New York, 1981).

R. Coles, *Uprooted Children: The Early Life of Migrant Farmworkers* (Pittsburgh: University of Pittsburgh Press, 1970).

C. Cooper Marcus, "Remembrance of Landscapes Past," *Landscape*, Vol. 22, No. 3 (1978), pp. 34–43.

———— , "Environmental Autobiography," *Childhood City Newsletter* (Dec. 1978), pp. 3–5.

B. P. Dohrenwend, and B. S. Dohrenwend, *Stressful Life Events: Their Nature and Effects* (New York: John Wiley, 1974).

J. S. Duncan, *Men Without Property: The Tramp's Classification and Uses of Urban Space*. Unpublished manuscript, Syracuse University, Department of Geography (1975).

K. T. Erikson, *Everything in Its Path* (New York: Simon and Schuster, 1976).

J. K. Felsman, "Street Urchins of Colombia," *Natural History* (April 1981).

———— , "Abandoned Children: A Reconsideration," *Children Today* (May–June 1984), pp. 13–18.

M. Fried, "Grieving for a Lost Home," in L. J. Duhl (ed.), *The Urban Condition* (New York: Basic Books, 1963).

R. Hester, "Favorite Spaces," *Childhood City Newsletter* (Dec. 1978), pp. 15–17.

K. Hopper, and J. Hamburg, *The Making of America's Homeless: From Skid Row to New Poor* (New York: Community Service Society of New York, 1984).

J. Horwitz, and S. Klein, "An Exercise in the Use of Environmental Autobiography for Programming and Design of a Day Care Center," *Childhood City Newsletter* (Dec. 1984), pp. 18–19.

J. Horwitz, and J. Tognoli, "The Role of Home in Adult Development," *Journal of Family Relations* (July 1982), pp. 134–140.

M. Jupp, "From Needs to Rights: Abandoned/Street Children," *Ideas Forum* (1985).

P. Marris, *Family and Social Change in an African City* (London: Routledge & Kegan Paul, 1961).

———— , *Loss and Changes* (Garden City, NY: Anchor Books, 1975).

S. Mercado-Llorens, and S. L. West, "The New Grapes of Wrath: Hispanic Homelessness in the Urban Highland," U.S. *Hispanic Affairs Magazine* (Summer 1985).

H. M. Proshansky, A. K. Fabian, and R. Kaminoff, "Place Identity: Physical World Socialization of the Self," *Journal of Environmental Psychology* (1983), pp. 57–83.

I. Rabon, *The Street* (New York: Schocken, 1985).

L. G. Rivlin, "Group Membership and Place Meanings in an Urban Neighborhood," *Journal of Social Issues*, Vol. 38, No. 3 (1982), pp. 75–93.

L. G. Rivlin, V. Bogert, and R. Cirillo, "Uncoupling Institutional Indicators," in A. E. Osterberg, C. P. Tiernan and R. A. Findlay (eds.), *Design Research Interactions: Proceedings of the Twelfth International Conference of the Environmental Design Research Association*, Ames, IA (1981).

L. G. Rivlin, and M. Wolfe, *Institutional Settings in Children's Lives* (New York: John Wiley, 1985).

P. H. Rossi, *Why Families Move*, 2nd ed. (Beverly Hills, CA: Sage Publications, 1980).

D. Rothman, *The Discovery of the Asylum: Social Order and Disorder in the New Republic* (Boston: Little, Brown, 1971).

G. D. Rowles, *Prisoners of Space? Exploring the Geographical Experience of Older People* (Boulder, CO: Westview Press, 1978),

——— , "Toward a Geography of Growing Old," in A. Buttimer and D. Seamon (eds.), *The Human Experience of Space and Place* (New York: St. Martin's Press, 1980).

——— , "Geographical Perspectives on Human Development," *Human Development* (1981), pp. 67–76.

N. Rubinstein, A *Psycho-social Impact Analysis of Environmental Change in New Jersey's Pine Barrens.* Unpublished doctoral dissertation, City University of New York (1983).

D. Salerno, K. Hopper, and E. Baxter, *Hardship in the Heartland: Homelessness in Eight American Cities* (New York: Community Service Society, 1984).

D. Seamon, "Emotional Experience of the Environment," *American Behavioral Scientist*, Vol. 27, No. 6 (1984), pp. 757–770.

S. A. Shumaker, and D. Stokols, "Residential Mobility As a Social Issue and Research Topic," *Journal of Social Issues*, Vol. 38, No. 3 (1982), pp. 1–19.

A. Toffler, *Future Shock* (New York: Random House, 1970).

Y. Tuan, *Topophilia: A Study of Environmental Perceptions, Attitudes and Values* (Englewood Cliffs, NJ: Prentice Hall, 1974).

_____ , "Rootedness versus Sense of Place," *Landscape*, Vol. 24, No. 1 (1980), pp. 3–8.

Union of American Hebrew Congregations, *The Torah: A Modern Commentary* (1985).

U. S. Department of Housing and Urban Development, *Report to the Secretary on the Homeless and Emergency Shelters* (1984).

P. Willmott, *Evolution of a Community* (London: Routledge & Kegan Paul, 1963).

P. Willmott, and M. Young, *Family and Class in a London Suburb* (London: Routledge & Kegan Paul, 1966).

M. Young, and P. Willmott, *Family and Kinship in East London* (London: Routledge & Kegan Paul, 1957).

VOCABULARY

paragraph 6: chronic
paragraph 9: trauma
paragraph 11: affluent
paragraph 12: nomadic
paragraph 15: deinstitutionalization
paragraph 18: typology
paragraph 19: deindustrialization, feminization
paragraph 22: gentrification
paragraph 24: exacerbate
paragraph 30: sedentarize
paragraph 32: heterogeneity, depersonalizing
paragraph 33: idiosyncratic
paragraph 36: ambivalence, pandemic, entrenchment, fossilization, feckless
paragraph 38: nurturance
paragraph 48: plethora
paragraph 49: ecology, pathology

QUESTIONS

1. By what principle does Rivlin distinguish types of homelessness in paragraphs 6–9? Why does she stress that there are different types?

2. Which type is of most concern to Rivlin? In the remainder of the essay, does she discuss this type only, or does she give attention to other types?

3. Rivlin states that "Homelessness exists in many different forms and degrees based on the time period involved, the alternative shelter available, and the nature of the person's social contacts" (paragraph 6). What kind of evidence does she present to support this statement? To what extent does she depend on the testimony of the homeless? On statistical evidence? On studies by psychiatrists and sociologists?

4. What popular views of homelessness does Rivlin reject? How do these views impede a solution to the problem?

5. Why does Rivlin give particular attention to Kenneth Allsop's view of American life (paragraph 36)? Does she accept or reject his view? Does his view illuminate the causes of homelessness, or present a mistaken analysis, or suggest a solution?

6. Why does Rivlin give attention to "rootedness and place attachment" (paragraph 47)? Does her discussion bear on causes or solutions?

7. To what extent does the solution depend for Rivlin on a change in perception or understanding of the causes, or on sympathy for the homeless? How do you know?

8. Does Rivlin suggest a single social or political remedy—for example, restoration of government programs, increase in state and federal spending on the homeless? Or does she suggest various remedies?

SUGGESTIONS FOR WRITING

1. In seeking to persuade the audience, a writer may appeal to emotion as well as to reason. The character of the writer displayed—in the reasoned judgment and the concern and sympathy shown—also makes an ethical appeal. What evidence do you find of these kinds of appeal in Rivlin's essay?

2. Rivlin discusses the condition of the homeless and causes of homelessness in the 1980s. Discuss an important recent development relating to one of the following topics or a related one. Include discussion of differing attitudes or alternate proposals.

Base your discussion on newspapers, magazines, journal articles, and government publications available in your college library.

a. "throwaway" children on American streets

b. educating homeless children

c. housing homeless families

d. homeless women and their problems

e. removing homeless people from public places

f. medical care of the homeless

g. improving homeless shelters

h. public attitudes toward the homeless

19

Methods of Persuasion

How you develop an essay depends on your purpose and audience. The demands of exposition and persuasion are not the same. Your major concern in exposition is to be clear; clarity is important in a persuasive essay, but your major concern is to present your ideas in an honest and convincing way. In describing how to conserve fuel by driving properly, for example, you need to make the process clear; if your purpose is also to persuade drivers to change their driving habits, you need to choose the best means of doing so, given what you know about your audience. If most are hostile or indifferent to the idea of conservation, you might discuss conservation of fuel and make various appeals—for example, to conscience, public spirit, practical concerns—before turning to the matter of driving. If most are friendly to the idea, you probably need only remind them of the importance of conservation.

Persuasive arguments present additional challenges. You must construct a sound argument, arouse the interest of the audience through a legitimate appeal to their emotions, and show that you are well informed on the issue and honest in your presentation and therefore deserve a hearing. Though some writers seek to avoid emotional appeals in the belief that the soundness of the argument guarantees its persuasiveness, few arguments are entirely free of emotion or need to be free of it. The problem is not how to rid the argument of emotion but how to balance emotion and reason so that the aroused reader considers the argument fully, gives rational assent to it, and is free to disagree with it in whole or in part.

Persuasive arguments are based on facts that the reader can verify. The facts alone may generate emotion without a direct appeal, as in the following description of homeless people in New York City:

432

Many homeless people, unable to get into shelters, or frightened of disease or violence, or intimidated by the regulations, look for refuge in such public places as train stations and church doorways. Scores of people sleep in the active subway tunnels of Manhattan, inches from six-hundred-volt live rails. Many more sleep on the ramps and the station platforms. Go into the subway station under Herald Square on a December night at twelve o'clock and you will see what scarce accommodations can mean. Emerging from the subway, walk along Thirty-third Street to Eighth Avenue. There you will see another form of scarce accommodations: hot-air grates outside the buildings on Eighth Avenue are highly prized. Homeless people who arrive late often find there is no vacancy, even for a cardboard box over a grate. (Jonathan Kozol, "The Homeless")

The author may build to even more shocking facts—homeless people stabbed and set on fire, or crushed to death as they sleep in trash compactors heated by rotting food. The author knows that some facts challenge belief:

Even phone-booth vacancies are scarce in New York City: as in public housing, people are sometimes obliged to double up. One night, I saw three people—a man, a woman, and a child—jammed into a single booth. All three were asleep.

Kozol does make direct comments on the situation of the homeless, but he usually lets the facts make their own appeal. Anna Quindlen and Hilary de Vries, in the essays on the homeless that follow, express their personal feelings, but ground them in fact and their reliability as witnesses.

Order of Ideas in Persuasive Essays

Argumentative essays have a traditional organization that is easy to learn and to put to use. This organization, derived from the oration of the law courts and legislatures of ancient Greece and Rome, shaped the varieties of essay that we have been considering—in particular the division of the essay into an introduction that states the purpose and gives pertinent background, the main discussion or body, and the conclusion. The persuasive essay today, like the oration of ancient times, often contains these divisions but expands them to meet the needs of the argument. These divisions can be illustrated by David H. Hackworth's essay on pp. 370–373:

introduction, or what was called the exordium or exhortation to the audience, appealing to their interest and good will, and stating the subject of the oration or essay (Hackworth: paragraphs 1–2);

narration or background, stating the facts of the case (paragraphs 3–4);

division of proofs, stating the thesis partly or fully, and summarizing the evidence and arguments to be presented (paragraph 5: Hackworth's statement of thesis; summary of evidence and proof omitted);

confirmation or proof, arguing the thesis (paragraphs 6–12);

refutation, answering opponents (paragraph 13);

conclusion, reinforcing and summarizing the main argument, and reinforcing the original appeal to the audience (paragraphs 14–16, restating the thesis and calling for study of the issue).

These parts may be combined or arranged in a different order—the narration or background perhaps combined with the confirming arguments, or the refutation coming before the confirmation. Often the division or outline of the arguments is omitted, and instead of coming early in the argument, the thesis may be delayed until the conclusion for reasons discussed earlier. Jane Goodall, earlier in this book (see pp. 331–339), follows the same plan as Hackworth's but omits a summary of her evidence and main arguments and reverses her confirming arguments and her refutation.

Hilary de Vries

HILARY DE VRIES *graduated from Ohio Wesleyan University in 1976. In 1981 she received an M.A. in creative writing from Boston University. In 1983, she was named Magazine Writer of the Year by the New England Women's Press Association. Her essay describing a visit to a Boston shelter for the homeless was published in* The Christian Science Monitor *on September 17, 1987. Like Anna Quindlen, de Vries gives a face to the homeless and in this way urges the reader to reject a stereotype.*

"I THINK I WILL NOT FORGET THIS"

I never learned her name. But she spotted me across the room—the common area of the shelter for the homeless which served as her living room. If I wasn't exactly a guest in her house, then I was just another reporter doing another story on the homeless. She was the one who lived here. She was the one with a story to tell.

I arrived at the shelter in the early evening. Just before supper. Just in time to catch the nightly intake of the hundreds of men and women who, through alcoholism, or mental illness, or just plain hard times, had nowhere to call home but this shelter. It was one of a dozen in dozens of cities, tucked away in a commercial part of town where warehouses and loading docks didn't form neighborhood coalitions against the housing of the homeless. 2

I was here to put a face on what I thought was an all-too-faceless social problem. I had stepped around my share of breathing bodies lying on the sidewalk in front of department stores. I had argued with myself over whether to feel anger or pity or simply gratitude that it wasn't me lying there gloveless and filthy. Mostly, I wondered how people could live like that. 3

That's where the woman came in. The woman with neatly filed nails and beautiful skin who didn't wait for me but simply walked across the room and asked me if I was from a newspaper. Her breath smelled faintly of mint and she wore a yellow sweater. I thought at first she was a staff member, and told her I was touring the facility. Come back and talk to me, she said. I'll tell you what it's like to live here. 4

I was taken first to the men's side of the shelter, to their front door where I watched them being frisked, a man in a black baseball jacket running his hands lightly down their sides as the men stood silently in the first of many lines—a line for admittance, a line for supper, a line for bed. Here, there are only two rules: no guns, no violence. The men had only to get across the threshold to get a bed for the night. If they came late, they joined the 200 others lying on benches or the floor of the day room or the lobby. Every night it was the same. No one was turned away. 5

One man was lying in the doorway with a pink electric blanket wrapped around him, cradling a boom box. The man next to him was snoring. His coat was greasy with dirt and served as 6 a pillow for both of them. Neither of them noticed me stepping over them, or the officer who stood a few feet away. A policeman was posted here 24 hours. Just in case. Overhead fluorescent lights blazed. They stay on all night, I am told. All night someone will be awake—awake and walking, awake and talking to someone or to themselves. All night the phone will ring.

Upstairs in the painted cement block rooms, I walk by rows 7 of twin beds with rounded edges—nothing sharp here—and plastic-covered mattresses. Three hundred men on secondhand designer sheets and under donated blankets. Each bed is made up for the night. Outside in the hall, someone's heels click by, and the low rumble from the men standing downstairs, crowded and jostling, rises up the stairwell.

It must be easier to be a woman here, I think. It is less 8 crowded for them. They are neater. No torn bread crusts and spilled cups of soup in the corners. No loud bursts of laughter.

When I am taken to their side of the shelter, a woman pushes 9 open the door wearing a rabbit fur coat and suede boots. For a minute I think she works here, until I am told that the donations here are good ones, that the bulging sacks under the stairwell belong to the bag ladies, that the women do not steal from one another, that some of them do arts and crafts here. There are homemade paintings hanging on the wall.

Now, it is dinner time for the women. They sit on benches 10 alongside a wall waiting for an empty chair. It is almost like a restaurant, I think, but not quite. Women from a local church are serving the meal, cafeteria-style. The handwritten menu is posted at the head of the line: three kinds of sandwiches, pea soup, and fruit. At the plastic-covered picnic tables, the women eat neatly. They do not talk, only peel back the wax paper from the sandwiches and take small bites. They do not look at one another or anyone else.

Soon it will be time for bed. Lights here go out at 9 p.m. No 11 exceptions. The women will go upstairs, stand in line, put their clothes in a bin, put a rubberized band around their wrist. The band has a metal tab with a number on it. It is the number for their bed. In the middle of the night, if someone should call, the woman can be located by number. Next, a woman staff member takes their clothes, hands them a nightgown and a towel. Both are clean and folded. There is some lace on one of the nightgowns. The women's own clothes are put into the "oven," where they bake all night. This is to dry them and to kill lice. Then they take a shower. No exceptions. The women's showers are stalls fitted with curtains, not like the men's, a bare room with a guard posted. "No more than 5 minutes in the shower," says a sign taped to the wall. It is almost like being back in gym class, I think. But it isn't. It isn't a school. It isn't even a home. And I still wonder how people can live like this.

I make my way down the stairs, under the cold fluorescent 12 lights and with the smell of antiseptic all around me. Now the woman in the yellow sweater finds me again, corners me here in the common room. She doesn't wait for my questions, but starts to tell me that all the women here are unique, that it is not easy or right to categorize them. That is her word, categorize. She tells me that the women are divorced or displaced or just couldn't deal with the life they were dealt. She tells me that it is hard to get stabilized when you do not have a job. She has lived here 3½ weeks; this is her address. She tells me she is going back to school, that she is working on her secretarial skills. She tells me she is from Cleveland, has a job here now but not the $600 a month for an apartment. "You know they give foot soaks here every night," she says. "Some of the women really need them."

Outside it has begun to snow. I would like to go home. Or 13 sit down, just for a minute. But the woman hasn't finished. She hands me a scrap of paper she took from the bulletin board that morning. "This says it for a lot of us," she says, looking right at me. She is not smiling. Someone yells for her to come pick up her things from the floor. I look down at the paper. The handwriting is in faint blue ink: "These times remind me of a situation I never want to realize again."

I look up at the woman. She is not smiling. Remember, she 14 says, everyone here is different, everyone here is an individual. I think I will not forget this, when I am out walking and see a woman pulling bottles from a trash can with dirty, ungloved hands and I start to wonder how can people live like this.

I think I will remember this when I am tired and want to go 15 home or sit down, just for a minute. I will remember the woman with no home, the woman with the neatly filed nails practicing her typing skills. I think I will remember that persistence does not have any particular address or wear any specific outfit; that courage can be found in a gnarled hand gripping the lip of a garbage can.

But mostly I think I will remember that compassion is not 16 limited to those who can write checks or their representative or articles for newspapers, that empathy might be most easily found among those with their heads bowed over bowls of donated soup, and that concern for one's fellow human beings, as in the case of this one woman, does not even have to come with a name.

QUESTIONS

1. De Vries says of the woman who showed her the shelter: "I never learned her name." Why does she stress this fact at the beginning of the essay and return to it at the end?

2. What details does she give us about the woman? What point is she making through these details? Is she arguing a thesis?

3. Does the visit to the shelter change her image of homeless people or of how they live? Does the visit change her attitude and feelings toward them?

4. Is de Vries contrasting the men's shelter with the women's or merely giving us a picture of both? What does she gain by focusing on a single shelter and homeless person?

5. A writer may appeal to our reason, our feelings, and our respect for qualities of the writer's character evident in the essay (ethical appeal). What appeals does de Vries make in her essay? How successful do you find the appeal that de Vries makes to you?

SUGGESTION FOR WRITING

Report an experience that changed your thinking and feelings about a group of people or a current social problem. Build your discussion to a judgment or a comment, as de Vries does in her essay.

Anna Quindlen

ANNA QUINDLEN *reported for the* New York Post *before becoming a reporter and columnist for the* New York Times. *In her column "About New York" and the later "Life in the 30s" Quindlen described daily life in New York City. From 1990 to 1994 she wrote an op-ed column, "Public and Private"—awarded the Pulitzer Prize for Commentary in 1992. Quindlen's novels include* Object Lessons *(1991) and* One True Thing *(1994). Her columns for the* Times *are collected in* Thinking Out Loud *(1993) and* Living Out Loud *(1988), in which the following essay on her encounter with a homeless woman in New York City appears.*

HOMELESS

Her name was Ann, and we met in the Port Authority Bus Terminal several Januarys ago. I was doing a story on homeless people. She said I was wasting my time talking to her; she was just passing through, although she'd been passing through for more than two weeks. To prove to me that this was true, she rummaged through a tote bag and a manila envelope and finally unfolded a sheet of typing paper and brought out her photographs.

They were not pictures of family, or friends, or even a dog or cat, its eyes brown-red in the flashbulb's light. They were pictures of a house. It was like a thousand houses in a hundred towns, not suburb, not city, but somewhere in between, with aluminum siding and a chain-link fence, a narrow driveway running up to a one-car garage and a patch of backyard. The house was yellow. I looked on the back for a date or a name, but neither was there. There was no need for discussion. I knew what she was trying to tell me, for it was something I had often felt. She was not adrift, alone, anonymous, although her bags and her raincoat with the grime shadowing its creases had made me believe she was. She had a house, or at least once upon a time had had one. Inside were curtains, a couch, a stove, potholders. You are where you live. She was somebody.

I've never been very good at looking at the big picture, tak- 3 ing the global view, and I've always been a person with an over-active sense of place, the legacy of an Irish grandfather. So it is natural that the thing that seems most wrong with the world to me right now is that there are so many people with no homes. I'm not simply talking about shelter from the elements, or three square meals a day or a mailing address to which the welfare people can send the check—although I know that all these are important for survival. I'm talking about a home, about precisely those kinds of feelings that have wound up in cross-stitch and French knots on samplers over the years.

Home is where the heart is. There's no place like it. I love my 4 home with a ferocity totally out of proportion to its appearance or location. I love dumb things about it: the hot-water heater, the plastic rack you drain dishes in, the roof over my head, which occasionally leaks. And yet it is precisely those dumb things that make it what it is—a place of certainty, stability, predictability, privacy, for me and for my family. It is where I live. What more can you say about a place than that? That is everything.

Yet it is something that we have been edging away from 5 gradually during my lifetime and the lifetimes of my parents and grandparents. There was a time when where you lived often was where you worked and where you grew the food you ate and even where you were buried. When that era passed, where you lived at least was where your parents had lived and where you would live with your children when you became enfeebled. Then, suddenly, where you lived was where you lived for three years, until you could move on to something else and something else again.

And so we have come to something else again, to children 6 who do not understand what it means to go to their rooms because they have never had a room, to men and women whose fantasy is a wall they can paint a color of their own choosing, to old people reduced to sitting on molded plastic chairs, their skin blue-white in the lights of a bus station, who pull pictures of houses out of their bags. Homes have stopped being homes. Now they are real estate.

People find it curious that those without homes would 7 rather sleep sitting up on benches or huddled in doorways than go to shelters. Certainly some prefer to do so because they are emotionally ill, because they have been locked in before and they are damned if they will be locked in again. Others are afraid of the violence and trouble they may find there. But some seem to want something that is not available in shelters, and they will not compromise, not for a cot, or oatmeal, or a shower with special soap that kills the bugs. "One room," a woman with a baby who was sleeping on her sister's floor, once told me, "painted blue." That was the crux of it; not size or location, but pride of ownership. Painted blue.

This is a difficult problem, and some wise and compassion- 8 ate people are working hard at it. But in the main I think we work around it, just as we walk around it when it is lying on the sidewalk or sitting in the bus terminal—the problem, that is. It has been customary to take people's pain and lessen our own participation in it by turning it into an issue, not a collection of human beings. We turn an adjective into a noun: the poor, not poor people; the homeless, not Ann or the man who lives in the box or the woman who sleeps on the subway grate.

Sometimes I think we would be better off if we forgot about 9 the broad strokes and concentrated on the details. Here is a woman without a bureau. There is a man with no mirror, no wall to hang it on. They are not the homeless. They are people who have no homes. No drawer that holds the spoons. No window to look out upon the world. My God. That is everything.

QUESTIONS

1. What appeal is Quindlen making to her readers? Is she asking them to take action to reduce homelessness, or to change their thinking about its causes, or to change their attitude toward the homeless? Or does she have another purpose in writing?

2. How is a "global view" of homelessness different from the view Quindlen takes? How does she justify this view?

3. How is this view of the homeless different from the view Hilary de Vries presents? Is her view a global one?

SUGGESTIONS FOR WRITING

1. Describe an encounter with a stranger that aroused your concern or changed your thinking on a particular issue. Like Quindlen, be specific in your detail, but select it carefully so that each detail is pertinent to your thesis.

2. Quindlen says that home is "something that we have been edging away from gradually during my lifetime and the lifetimes of my parents and grandparents." Explain what she means, then discuss whether or not the statement applies to you and your family. Be specific in your detail without turning your essay into a narrative or story.

Anonymous

> The anonymous writer of this essay makes a direct appeal to the reader, like Anna Quindlen and Hilary de Vries grounding it in facts. The essay illustrates the traditional ethical appeal of the speech maker—in the words of Edward P. J. Corbett, "the persuasive value of the speaker's or writer's character." "The whole discourse," Corbett states, "must maintain the 'image' that the speaker or writer seeks to establish. The ethical appeal, in other words, must be pervasive throughout the discourse." The anonymous writer is highly successful in meeting this test.

WHO AM I?

After I tell you who I am you may not know me. You may not recognize me. You may deny that I exist. Who am I? I'm a product of myself. I'm a product of you and of my ancestors.

Now, one half of my ancestors were the Spanish who were Western European, but who were also part African and part Middle Eastern. They came to this country and met with the other side of my family—the Indians. The Indians also were a great race—people of a great culture. There were many kinds of Indians, as there were many kinds of Spaniards. They mixed, they married, they had children. Their children were called Mestizos, and this is what I am.

We came to California long before the Pilgrims landed at Plymouth Rock. We settled California and all of the south-western part of the United States, including the states of Arizona, New Mexico, Colorado, and Texas. We built the missions, and we cultivated the ranches. We were at the Alamo in Texas, both inside and outside. You know, we owned California—that is, until gold was found there.

I think it was a mistake to let you into the southwestern states, because eventually you took away our lands. When we fought to retain what was ours, you used the vigilantes to scare us away, to hang us, and to take away our lands. We became your slaves. Now we cook your food, we build your railroads, we harvest your crops, we dig your ditches, we stand in your unemployment lines—and we receive more than 20 percent of your welfare. But we've done some good things, too: We won more Medals of Honor during World War II than any other ethnic group. We've never had a turncoat, even during the Korean War. Yes, we have had outstanding war records. But, you know, we don't complain. By the same token, we don't get much attention, either.

We don't live in your neighborhoods unless we let you call us Spanish, French, or something else, but not what we are. We usually attend our own schools at the elementary or junior high level; and if we get to high school, we may go to school with you. However, even before we finish high school, more than 50 percent of us drop out, and you know we don't go to college. We make up less than 1 percent of the college students, yet we are 12 percent of the total school population. We don't use government agencies because our experiences with them have been rather poor; they haven't been very friendly or helpful. The Immigration Department has never really been our friend. The land offices help to take away our lands—we couldn't exactly call them friendly. The Farm Labor Bureau has never truly served us. The schools haven't really lifted us educationally. The police—well, they haven't been the most cooperative agency in the government either. You accept our Spanish words as long as we don't speak them, because if we do, you say they're "poor" Spanish—not Castilian; so our language can't be very good—it's almost like swearing. We are usually Catholics and sometimes Protestants, but in either case we have our own churches. You say we can leave our *barrios* to live near you—that is, only if we stay in our own place. When we attend your parties to meet your friends, you usually introduce us as being Spanish or something else that we are not. You are ashamed of what we are, and your attitude makes us feel that we, too, should be ashamed of what we are. When we go to school, we don't take part in your school activities; we don't think we're wanted. We seldom participate in sports; we don't run for student offices; we don't go to your school dances; we aren't valedictorians at graduations; we seldom win recognition as students, even in Spanish; we seldom receive scholarships; we are seldom given consideration in school plans; we are seldom given lead parts in school plays. The higher in education we go, the more obvious are the double standards; yet, we haven't given up.

Who are we? Some call us the forgotten people; others call us chili snappers, tacos, spics, mexs, or greasers. Some ignore us and pretend that we don't exist. Some just wish that we would go away. The late U.S. Senator Chavez from New Mexico once said, "At the time of war we are called 'the great patriotic Americans,' and during elections politicians call us 'the great Spanish-speaking community of America.' When we ask for jobs, we are called 'those damn Mexicans.'" 6

Who am I? I'm a human being. I have the same hopes that you have, the same fears, same drives, same desires, same concerns, and same abilities. I want the same chance that you have to be an individual. Who am I? In reality, I am who you want me to be. 7

VOCABULARY

paragraph 5: Castilian, barrios, valedictorians

QUESTIONS

1. How does the author create an image of the class of people described? What defining qualities or facts does the author delay in presenting, and why?
2. What is the purpose of the essay, and what audience is the author addressing? Is the author seeking to persuade readers to change their thinking and possibly take action on discrimination or federal policies?
3. How do the persuasive means employed serve this purpose?
4. What does the author gain in persuasiveness by remaining anonymous?
5. How persuasive do you find the essay, and why?

SUGGESTION FOR WRITING

Write your own persuasive essay on who you are. Use the information you give about yourself and your ethnic, racial, religious, professional, or age group to persuade your readers to change their image of the group and possibly take action on a related issue.

Wendell Berry

WENDELL BERRY, *long associated with the environmental movement in the United States, has written much about the need to preserve wilderness and eliminate pollution. Berry has also written about his native Kentucky in poems, essays, and novels. His novels include* Nathan Coulter *(1960) and* The Memory of Old Jack *(1969). Collections of his essays include* The Long-Legged House *(1969),* The Unsettling of America *(1977),* Home Economics *(1987), and* What Are People For? *(1990). In his essay "The Rise," Berry comments on the pollution of the American continent:*

We haven't accepted—we can't really believe—that the most characteristic product of our age of scientific miracles is junk, but that is so. And we still think and behave as though we face an unspoiled continent, with thousands of acres of living space for every man. We still sing "America the Beautiful" as though we had not created in it, by strenuous effort, at great expense, and with dauntless self-praise, an unprecedented ugliness.

WASTE

As a country person, I often feel that I am on the bottom end of the waste problem. I live on the Kentucky River about ten miles from its entrance into the Ohio. The Kentucky, in many ways a lovely river, receives an abundance of pollution from the Eastern Kentucky coal mines and the central Kentucky cities. When the river rises, it carries a continuous raft of cans, bottles, plastic jugs, chunks of styrofoam, and other imperishable trash. After the floods subside, I, like many other farmers, must pick up the trash before I can use my bottomland fields. I have seen the Ohio, whose name (*Oyo* in Iroquois) means "beautiful river," so choked with this manufactured filth that an ant could crawl dryfooted from Kentucky to Indiana. The air of both river valleys is seriously polluted. Our roadsides and roadside fields lie under a constant precipitation of cans, bottles, the plastic-ware of fast food joints, soiled plastic diapers, and sometimes whole bags of garbage. In our county we now have a "sanitary landfill" which daily receives, in addition to our local production, fifty to sixty large truckloads of garbage from Pennsylvania, New Jersey, and New York.

Moreover, a close inspection of our countryside would reveal, strewn over it from one end to the other, thousands of derelict and worthless automobiles, house trailers, refrigerators, stoves, freezers, washing machines, and dryers; as well as thousands of unregulated dumps in hollows and sink holes, on streambanks and roadsides, filled not only with "disposable" containers but also with broken toasters, television sets, toys of all kinds, furniture, lamps, stereos, radios, scales, coffee makers, mixers, blenders, corn poppers, hair dryers, and micro-wave ovens. Much of our waste problem is to be accounted for by the intentional flimsiness and unrepairability of the labor-savers and gadgets that we have become addicted to.

Of course, my sometime impression that I live on the receiv-ing end of this problem is false, for country people contribute their full share. The truth is that we Americans, all of us, have become a kind of human trash, living our lives in the midst of a ubiquitous damned mess of which we are at once the victims and the perpetrators. We are all unwilling victims, perhaps; and some of us even are unwilling perpetrators, but we must count ourselves among the guilty nonetheless. In my house-hold we produce much of our own food and try to do without as many frivolous "necessities" as possible—and yet, like everyone else, we must shop, and when we shop we must bring home a load of plastic, aluminum, and glass containers de-signed to be thrown away, and "appliances" designed to wear out quickly and be thrown away.

I confess that I am angry at the manufacturers who make these things. There are days when I would be delighted if cer-tain corporation executives could somehow be obliged to eat their products. I know of no good reason why these containers and all other forms of manufactured "waste"—solid, liquid, toxic, or whatever—should not be outlawed. There is no sense and no sanity in objecting to the desecration of the flag while tolerating and justifying and encouraging as a daily business the desecration of the country for which it stands.

But our waste problem is not the fault only of producers. It is the fault of an economy that is wasteful from top to bottom—a symbiosis of an unlimited greed at the top and a lazy, passive, and self-indulgent consumptiveness at the bottom—and all of us are involved in it. If we wish to correct this economy, we must be careful to understand and to demonstrate how much waste of human life is involved in our waste of the material goods of Creation. For example, much of the litter that now defaces our country is fairly directly caused by the massive secession or exclusion of most of our people from active participation in the food economy. We have made a social ideal of minimal involvement in the growing and cooking of food. This is one of the dearest "liberations" of our affluence. Nevertheless, the more dependent we become on the *industries* of eating and drinking, the more waste we are going to produce. The mess that surrounds us, then, must be understood not just as a problem in itself but as a symptom of a greater and graver problem: the centralization of our economy, the gathering of the productive property and power into fewer and fewer hands, and the consequent destruction, everywhere, of the local economies of household, neighborhood, and community.

This is the source of our unemployment problem, and I am 6
not talking just about the unemployment of eligible members of the "labor force." I mean also the unemployment of children and old people, who, in viable household and local economies, would have work to do by which they would be useful to themselves and to others. The ecological damage of centralization and waste is thus inextricably involved with human damage. For we have, as a result, not only a desecrated, ugly, and dangerous country in which to live until we are in some manner poisoned by it, and a constant and now generally accepted problem of unemployed or unemployable workers, but also classrooms full of children who lack the experience and discipline of fundamental human tasks, and various institutions full of still capable old people who are useless and lonely.

I think that we must learn to see the trash on our streets and 7
roadsides, in our rivers, and in our woods and fields, not as the side effects of "more jobs" as its manufacturers invariably insist that it is, but as evidence of good work *not* done by people able to do it.

VOCABULARY

paragraph 1: styrofoam, precipitation
paragraph 2: derelict
paragraph 3: ubiquitous, perpetrator
paragraph 5: symbiosis, affluence
paragraph 6: viable, desecrated

QUESTIONS

1. How does Berry try to persuade us that waste is an environmental problem? What other damage does waste create?

2. What causes of waste does Berry identify? Which cause does he discuss in most detail?

3. What is Berry's central point or thesis, and where does he state it? Where does he restate it? What does he gain by stating the idea where he does?

4. How persuasive do you find the essay?

SUGGESTIONS FOR WRITING

1. Discuss your own habits of consumption. Then state whether they give support to Berry's charge that consumption in America is "self-indulgent."

2. State your agreement or disagreement with the following statement or another in the essay, supporting your discussion from your own experience and observation:

> We have made a social ideal of minimal involvement in the growing and cooking of food.

Jonathan Swift

JONATHAN SWIFT (1667–1745), *the son of English Protestant parents, was born and educated in Ireland. In 1688 he went to England to seek a career in literature. Swift wrote satirical poems, essays, pamphlets, and tracts on the major issues of the day and became involved in many of its political and religious controversies. During his stay, Swift was ordained in the Church of England. In 1713 he became Dean of St. Patrick's Cathedral in Dublin and in the succeeding years wrote widely on various questions bearing on Ireland and England. His most famous satirical work,* Gulliver's Travels, *was published in 1726. Swift was deeply concerned about the sufferings that he had observed in his country from boyhood. Ireland, under the control of the British government, was an impoverished country—restricted in selling its goods and incapable of producing enough food to feed the population. Most of the poor were*

Catholic, a point Swift emphasizes in his "modest proposal"—written in 1729 to suggest a remedy for the widespread starvation and misery of the country. Swift writes as a disinterested observer, anxious to perform a service to both the English and the Irish with his proposal. The persuasive means that Swift uses deserves the closest study.

A MODEST PROPOSAL

For Preventing the Children of Poor People in Ireland from Being a Burden to Their Parents or Country, and for Making Them Beneficial to the Public

It is a melancholy object to those who walk through this great ₁ town, or travel in the country, when they see the streets, the roads, and cabin-doors crowded with beggars of the female sex, followed by three, four, or six children, all in rags, and importuning every passenger for an alms. These mothers, instead of being able to work for their honest livelihood, are forced to employ all their time in strolling to beg sustenance for their helpless infants: who, as they grow up, either turn thieves for want of work, or leave their dear native country to fight for the Pretender in Spain, or sell themselves to the Barbadoes.

I think it is agreed by all parties, that this prodigious num- ₂ ber of children in the arms, or on the backs, or at the heels of their mothers, and frequently of their fathers, is in the present deplorable state of the kingdom, a very great additional grievance; and, therefore, whoever could find out a fair, cheap, and easy method of making these children sound and useful members of the commonwealth, would deserve so well of the public, as to have his statue set up for a preserver of the nation.

But my intention is very far from being confined to provide ₃ only for the children of professed beggars; it is of a much greater extent, and shall take in the whole number of infants at a certain age, who are born of parents in effect as little able to support them as those who demand our charity in the streets.

As to my own part, having turned my thoughts for many 4
years upon this important subject, and maturely weighed the
several schemes of other projectors, I have always found them
grossly mistaken in their computation. It is true, a child, just
dropped from its dam, may be supported by her milk for a solar
year with little other nourishment; at most, not above the
value of two shillings, which the mother may certainly get, or
the value in scraps, by her lawful occupation of begging; and it
is exactly at one year old that I propose to provide for them in
such a manner, as, instead of being a charge upon their parents or the parish, or wanting food and raiment for the rest of
their lives, they shall, on the contrary, contribute to the feeding, and partly to the clothing, of many thousands.

There is likewise another great advantage in my scheme, 5
that it will prevent those voluntary abortions, and that horrid
practice of women murdering their bastard children, alas, too
frequent among us, sacrificing the poor innocent babes, I
doubt more to avoid the expense than the shame, which would
move tears and pity in the savage and inhuman breast.

The number of souls in this kingdom being usually reckoned 6
one million and a half, of these I calculate there may be about
two hundred thousand couple whose wives are breeders; from
which number I subtract thirty thousand couple, who are able
to maintain their own children (although I apprehend there
cannot be so many, under the present distresses of the kingdom); but this being granted, there will remain an hundred
and seventy thousand breeders. I again subtract fifty thousand
for those women who miscarry, or whose children die by accident or disease within the year. There only remain a hundred
and twenty thousand children of poor parents annually born.
The question therefore is how this number shall be reared and
provided for? which, as I have already said, under the present
situation of affairs, is utterly impossible by all methods hith-
erto proposed. For we can neither employ them in handicraft
or agriculture; we neither build houses (I mean in the country)
nor cultivate land: they can very seldom pick up a livelihood by
stealing until they arrive at six years old, except where they are

of towardly parts; although I confess they learn the rudiments much earlier; during which time they can, however, be properly looked upon only as probationers; as I have been informed by a principal gentleman in the county of Cavan, who protested to me, that he never knew above one or two instances under the age of six, even in a part of the kingdom so renowned for the quickest proficiency in that art.

I am assured by our merchants that a boy or a girl before 7 twelve years old is no salable commodity; and even when they come to this age they will not yield above three pounds or three pounds and half-a-crown at most, on the exchange; which cannot turn to account either to the parents or kingdom, the charge of nutriment and rags having been at least four times that value.

I shall now, therefore, humbly propose my own thoughts, 8 which I hope will not be liable to the least objection.

I have been assured by a very knowing American of my 9 acquaintance in London, that a young healthy child, well nursed, is, at a year old, a most delicious, nourishing, and wholesome food, whether stewed, roasted, baked, or boiled; and I make no doubt that it will equally serve in a fricassee or a ragout.

I do therefore humbly offer it to public consideration, that of 10 the hundred and twenty thousand children already computed, twenty thousand may be reserved for breed, whereof only one-fourth part to be males; which is more than we allow to sheep, black cattle, or swine; and my reason is, that these children are seldom the fruits of marriage, a circumstance not much regarded by our savages, therefore one male will be sufficient to serve four females. That the remaining hundred thousand may, at a year old, be offered in sale to the persons of quality and fortune through the kingdom; always advising the mother to let them suck plentifully in the last month, so as to render them plump and fat for a good table. A child will make two dishes at an entertainment for friends; and when the family dines alone, the fore or hind quarter will make a reasonable dish, and, seasoned with a little pepper or salt, will be very good boiled on the fourth day, especially in winter.

I have reckoned, upon a medium, that a child just born will weigh twelve pounds, and in a solar year, if tolerably nursed, increaseth to twenty-eight pounds. 11

I grant this food will be somewhat dear, and therefore very proper for landlords, who, as they have already devoured most of the parents, seem to have the best title to the children. 12

Infants' flesh will be in season throughout the year, but more plentifully in March, and a little before and after: for we are told by a grave author, an eminent French physician, that fish being a prolific diet, there are more children born in Roman Catholic countries about nine months after Lent than at any other season; therefore, reckoning a year after Lent, the markets will be more glutted than usual, because the number of popish infants is at least three to one in this kingdom; and therefore, it will have one other collateral advantage, by lessening the number of papists among us. 13

I have already computed the charge of nursing a beggar's child (in which list I reckon all cottagers, labourers, and four-fifths of the farmers) to be about two shillings per annum, rags included; and I believe no gentleman would repine to give ten shillings for the carcass of a good fat child, which, as I have said, will make four dishes of excellent nutritive meat, when he has only some particular friend, or his own family, to dine with him. Thus, the squire will learn to be a good landlord, and grow popular among his tenants; the mother will have eight shillings net profit, and be fit for work till she produces another child. 14

Those who are more thrifty (as I must confess the times require) may flay the carcass; the skin of which artificially dressed, will make admirable gloves for ladies, and summer-boots for fine gentlemen. 15

As to our city of Dublin, shambles[1] may be appointed for this purpose in the most convenient parts of it, and butchers 16

---

[1] *Shambles: butcher shops.*

we may be assured will not be wanting; although I rather recommend buying the children alive, and dressing them hot from the knife, as we do roasting pigs.

A very worthy person, a true lover of this country, and whose   17
virtues I highly esteem, was lately pleased, in discoursing on this matter, to offer a refinement upon my scheme. He said, that many gentlemen of this kingdom, having of late destroyed their deer, he conceived that the want of venison might be well supplied by the bodies of young lads and maidens, not exceeding fourteen years of age, nor under twelve; so great a number of both sexes in every county being now ready to starve for want of work and service; and these to be disposed of by their parents, if alive, or otherwise by their nearest relations. But, with due deference to so excellent a friend, and so deserving a patriot, I cannot be altogether in his sentiments; for as to the males, my American acquaintance assured me from frequent experience, that their flesh was generally tough and lean, like that of our schoolboys, by continual exercise, and their taste disagreeable; and to fatten them would not answer the charge. Then as to the females, it would, I think, with humble submission, be a loss to the public, because they soon would become breeders themselves: and besides, it is not improbable that some scrupulous people might be apt to censure such a practice (although indeed very unjustly) as a little bordering upon cruelty; which, I confess hath always been with me the strongest objection against any project, how well soever intended.

But in order to justify my friend, he confessed that this ex-   18
pedient was put into his head by the famous Psalmanazar,[2] a native of the island Formosa, who came from thence to London above twenty years ago; and in conversation told my friend, that in his country, when any young person happened to be put to death, the executioner sold the carcass to persons of quality as a prime dainty; and that in his time the body of a plump girl of fifteen, who was crucified for an attempt to

---

[2] *Psalmanazar:* A French writer, George Psalmanazar, who posed as a native of Formosa in a fake book he published about that country in 1704, in England.

poison the emperor, was sold to his Imperial Majesty's prime minister of state, and other great mandarins of the court, in joints from the gibbet, at four hundred crowns. Neither indeed can I deny, that if the same use were made of several plump young girls in this town, who, without one single groat to their fortunes, cannot stir abroad without a chair, and appear at playhouse and assemblies in foreign fineries which they never will pay for, the kingdom would not be the worse.

Some persons of a desponding spirit are in great concern 19 about that vast number of poor people who are aged, diseased, or maimed; and I have been desired to employ my thoughts what course may be taken to ease the nation of so grievous an encumbrance. But I am not in the least pain upon that matter, because it is very well known, that they are every day dying, and rotting, by cold and famine, and filth and vermin, as fast as can be reasonably expected. And so to the younger labourers, they are now in almost as hopeful a condition: they cannot get work, and consequently pine away for want of nourishment, to a degree, that if at any time they are accidentally hired to common labour, they have not strength to perform it; and thus the country and themselves are happily delivered from the evils to come.

I have too long digressed, and therefore shall return to 20 my subject. I think the advantages by the proposal which I have made are obvious and many, as well as of the highest importance.

For first, as I have already observed, it would greatly lessen 21 the number of papists, with whom we are yearly overrun, being the principal breeders of the nation as well as our most dangerous enemies; and who stay at home on purpose with a design to deliver the kingdom to the Pretender, hoping to take their advantage by the absence of so many good Protestants, who have chosen rather to leave their country than stay at home and pay tithes against their conscience to an idolatrous Episcopal curate.[3]

---

[3] Swift is attacking the prejudice against Irish Catholics in his time, and also the motives of a number of Protestant dissenters from the Church of England.

Secondly, the poorer tenants will have something valuable 22 of their own, which by law may be made liable to distress, and help to pay their landlord's rent; their corn and cattle being already seized, and money a thing unknown.

Thirdly, whereas the maintenance of an hundred thousand 23 children, from two years old and upwards, cannot be computed at less than ten shillings a piece per annum, the nation's stock will be thereby increased fifty thousand pounds per annum; besides the profit of a new dish introduced to the tables of all gentlemen of fortune in the kingdom who have any refinement in taste. And the money will circulate among ourselves, the goods being entirely of our own growth and manufacture.

Fourthly, the constant breeders, besides the gain of eight 24 shillings sterling per annum by the sale of their children, will be rid of the charge of maintaining them after the first year.

Fifthly, this food would otherwise bring great custom to taverns; where the vintners will certainly be so prudent as to procure the best receipts for dressing it to perfection, and, consequently, have their houses frequented by all the fine gentlemen, who justly value themselves upon their knowledge in good eating: and a skillful cook, who understands how to oblige his guests, will contrive to make it as expensive as they please.

Sixthly, this would be a great inducement to marriage, 26 which all wise nations have either encouraged by rewards, or enforced by laws and penalties. It would increase the care and tenderness of mothers towards their children, when they were sure of a settlement for life to the poor babes, provided in some sort by the public, to their annual profit instead of expense. We should soon see an honest emulation among the married women, which of them could bring the fattest child to the market. Men would become as fond of their wives during the time of their pregnancy, as they are now of their mares in foal, their cows in calf, or sows when they are ready to farrow; nor offer to beat or kick them (as is too frequent a practice) for fear of a miscarriage.

Many other advantages might be enumerated. For instance, 27 the addition of some thousand carcasses in our exportation of barrelled beef; the propagation of swine's flesh, and improvement in the art of making good bacon, so much wanted among us by the great destruction of pigs, too frequent at our tables, which are no way comparable in taste or magnificence to a well-grown, fat yearling child, which, roasted whole, will make a considerable figure at a Lord Mayor's feast, or any other public entertainment. But this, and many others, I omit, being studious of brevity.

Supposing that one thousand families in this city would 28 be constant customers for infants' flesh, besides others who might have it at merry meetings, particularly weddings and christenings, I compute that Dublin would take off annually about twenty thousand carcasses; and the rest of the kingdom (where probably they will be sold somewhat cheaper) the remaining eighty thousand.

I can think of no one objection that will possibly be raised 29 against this proposal, unless it should be urged, that the number of people will be thereby much lessened in the kingdom. This I freely own, and it was indeed one principal design in offering it to the world. I desire the reader will observe that I calculate my remedy for this one individual kingdom of Ireland, and for no other that ever was, is, or I think ever can be, upon earth. Therefore let no man talk to me of other expedients: of taxing our absentees at five shillings a pound: of using neither clothes nor household-furniture except what is of our own growth and manufacture: of utterly rejecting the materials and instruments that promote foreign luxury: of curing the expensiveness of pride, vanity, idleness, and gaming in our women; of introducing a vein of parsimony, prudence, and temperance: of learning to love our country, wherein we differ even from Laplanders, and the inhabitants of Topinamboo:[4] of quitting our animosities and factions, nor act any longer like the Jews, who were murdering one another at the very moment

---

[4] *Topinamboo*: A district of Brazil notorious for its barbarism and ignorance.

their city was taken:[5] of being a little cautious not to sell our country and consciences for nothing: of teaching landlords to have at least one degree of mercy towards their tenants: lastly, of putting a spirit of honesty, industry, and skill into our shop-keepers; who, if a resolution could now be taken to buy only our native goods, would immediately unite to cheat and exact upon us in the price, the measure, and the goodness, nor could ever yet be brought to make one fair proposal of just dealing, though often and earnestly invited to it.

Therefore I repeat, let no man talk to me of these and the like expedients, till he hath at least some glimpse of hope that there will ever be some hearty and sincere attempt to put them in practice. 30

But, as to myself, having been wearied out for many years with offering vain, idle, visionary thoughts, and at length utterly despairing of success, I fortunately fell upon this pro-posal; which as it is wholly new, so it hath something solid and real, of no expense and little trouble, full in our own power, and whereby we can incur no danger in disobliging England. For this kind of commodity will not bear exportation, the flesh being of too tender a consistence to admit a long continuance in salt, although perhaps I could name a country which would be glad to eat up our whole nation without it. 31

After all, I am not so violently bent upon my own opinion as to reject any offer proposed by wise men which shall be found equally innocent, cheap, easy, and effectual. But before some-thing of that kind shall be advanced in contradiction to my scheme, and offering a better, I desire the author, or authors, will be pleased maturely to consider two points. First, as things now stand, how they will be able to find food and raiment for a hundred thousand useless mouths and backs? And, sec-ondly, there being a round million of creatures in human figure throughout this kingdom, whose whole subsistence put into a common stock would leave them in debt two millions of pounds sterling, adding those who are beggars by profession, 32

---

[5] Swift is referring to the fall of Jerusalem to the Romans in 70 A.D.

to the bulk of farmers, cottagers, and labourers, with the wives and children who are beggars in effect; I desire those politicians who dislike my overture, and may perhaps be so bold as to attempt an answer, that they will first ask the parents of these mortals, whether they would not at this day think it a great happiness to have been sold for food at a year old, in the manner I prescribe, and thereby have avoided such a perpetual scene of misfortunes as they have since gone through, by the oppression of landlords, the impossibility of paying rent without money or trade, the want of common sustenance, with neither house nor clothes to cover them from the inclemencies of weather, and the most inevitable prospect of entailing the like, or greater miseries, upon their breed for ever.

I profess, in the sincerity of my heart, that I have not the least personal interest in endeavouring to promote this necessary work, having no other motive than the public good of my country, by advancing our trade, providing for infants, relieving the poor, and giving some pleasure to the rich. I have no children by which I can propose to get a single penny; the youngest being nine years old, and my wife past child-bearing. 33

VOCABULARY

paragraph 1: importuning
paragraph 2: prodigious
paragraph 4: schemes, projectors, raiment
paragraph 6: apprehend, rudiments, probationers, renowned
paragraph 9: fricassee, ragout
paragraph 13: prolific, papists
paragraph 14: squire
paragraph 15: flay
paragraph 17: venison
paragraph 18: mandarins, gibbet
paragraph 19: encumbrance
paragraph 20: digressed
paragraph 21: tithes, idolatrous, Episcopal curate
paragraph 25: vintners
paragraph 26: emulation, foal, farrow
paragraph 27: yearling

paragraph 29: expedients, parsimony, animosities
paragraph 31: consistence
paragraph 32: effectual, entailing

QUESTIONS

1. How does Swift establish the basic character and motives of his proposer in the opening paragraphs?

2. How does Swift reveal his attitude toward the proposer? Is he in accord with his general view of the English and of absentee landlords? Are their motives stated directly or implied?

3. Is the proposer—and perhaps Swift himself—critical of the Irish, or does he exonerate them entirely?

4. Short of adopting the actual "modest proposal," is there another way of remedying the evils exposed in the course of the essay? In other words, does Swift suggest other policies that would reduce poverty and starvation in Ireland?

5. In general, what strategy does Swift employ to deal with English policies and motives and perhaps Irish attitudes too?

6. How persuasive do you find the essay? Is it an essay of historical interest or literary interest only, or does it have something to say to people today?

SUGGESTION FOR WRITING

Write your own "modest proposal" for dealing with a current social or political evil. You may wish to write as yourself or, like Swift, impersonate someone who wishes to make a modest proposal. Maintain a consistent tone throughout your essay, or at least make any shifts in tone consistent with the character of your speaker and his or her motives in writing.

Part 4

MATTERS OF STYLE:
DICTION

Introduction

The word *diction* refers to the choice of words we make in speaking and writing. The choice may be a matter of vocabulary—as in exposition, when we name a specific tool in performing a job, and in descriptive writing, when we choose concrete words or phrases and vivid images and suggestive metaphors to create a mental picture. In persuasive writing, we look for words that are exact but also move the reader to accept an idea or take action. Diction concerns both the use and the misuse of words. In all kinds of writing, we look for words that have appropriate connotations and seek also to avoid words that have misleading ones.

The first two sections of Part 4 discuss the matter of usage or appropriateness of words and phrases and show how writers control the tone of their essays to express their attitude toward the subject and audience. The sections that follow define and illustrate various kinds of images and common figurative language, such as simile, metaphor, and personification. The concluding section deals with inappropriate or inexpressive uses of words and singles out words that are meaningless and ugly.

Like earlier discussions and readings, those in this part of the book can serve in drafting essays and revising them. Finding the right tone and "level" of usage for an essay is a major concern in starting to write.

20

Usage

None of us speaks or writes in the same way on all occasions: the differences depend on how formal the occasion is. A letter of application for a job will be more formal than a letter to a friend; a graduation speech will sound different from a locker-room conversation.

Each of us has a formal and an informal language—and standards for judging their effectiveness. These standards come from the different groups we belong to—each group with its special idioms and vocabulary. Teenagers share a special dialect or spoken language. They may also share a special dialect with their families and with their friends. And at school they may share with their teachers a language different from the dialect they speak at home. Even a family may have its own private language—special words and expressions to describe acts and feelings.

Cutting across these differences is a standardized English we hear on television and read in newspapers—a language sometimes less colorful and personal than these other languages, but serving as a medium for communication among diverse groups of people, not only in the United States but in other English-speaking countries. This standard is of long growth, and it changes less than the informal language and slang of particular groups. This standard, represented in the readings in this book, falls between two extremes—one formal and abstract in its content and sentences, the other informal and concrete:

[*Formal*] It is simple enough to say that since books have classes—fiction, biography, poetry—we should separate them and take from each what it is right that each should give us. Yet few people ask from books what books can give us. Most commonly we come to books with blurred and divided minds, asking of fiction that it shall be true, of poetry that it shall be false, of biography that it shall be flattering, of history that it shall enforce our own prejudices. If we could banish all such preconceptions when we read, that would be an admirable beginning. (Virginia Woolf, "How Should One Read a Book?")

465

[Informal] Bryant's specializes in barbecued spareribs and barbecued beef—the beef sliced from briskets of steer that have been cooked over a hickory fire for thirteen hours. When I'm away from Kansas City and depressed, I try to envision someone walking up to the counterman at Bryant's and ordering a beef sandwich to go—for me. The counterman tosses a couple of pieces of bread onto the counter, grabs a half-pound of beef from the pile next to him, slaps it onto the bread, brushes on some sauce in almost the same motion, and then wraps it all up in two thicknesses of butcher paper in a futile attempt to keep the customer's hand dry as he carries off his prize. (Calvin Trillin, *American Fried*)

The abstract ideas of Woolf could be stated less formally. But usage is a matter of convention and occasion as well as personal choice, and if we would not be surprised to find her ideas stated informally, we probably would be surprised to find barbecue described in formal language.

As a rule, informal writing is closer to the patterns of everyday speech; formal writing seems impersonal if it departs widely from these patterns. Much standard writing today has both formal and informal features: we find colloquialisms (*grabs a half-pound of beef, slaps it onto*) in company with abstract or less familiar words (*envision*). We also find striking balance and antithesis—a feature of formal sentences—in company with looser, more familiar phrasing and expressions:

What I would like to know is: how should I feel about the earth, these days? Where has all the old nature gone? What became of the wild, writhing, unapproachable mass of the life of the world, and what happened to our old, panicky excitement about it? Just in fifty years, since I was a small boy in a suburban town, the world has become a structure of steel and plastic, intelligible and diminished. (Lewis Thomas, "A Trip Abroad")

William Least Heat-Moon

WILLIAM LEAST HEAT-MOON *states that the name "Least Heat-Moon" is Sioux in origin: "My father calls himself Heat-Moon, my elder brother Little Heat-Moon. I, coming last, am therefore Least." In 1978, he packed a 1975 Ford van that he called Ghost Dancing and began a search for his ancestors in rural America. Heat-Moon traveled east from Columbia, Missouri, to the Atlantic and then clockwise around the United States, on backroads marked blue on roadmaps. In* Blue Highways: A Journey into America *(1982), he tells us that he sought places where "change did not mean ruin and where time and men and deeds connected." In* PrairyErth *(1991), Heat-Moon describes later travels. The restaurant described in the following section from* Blue Highways *tells us much about the people and customs of rural Georgia.*

IN THE LAND OF "COKE-COLA"

In the land of "Coke-Cola" it was hot and dry. The artesian water   1
was finished. Along route 72, an hour west of Ninety-Six, I tried
not to look for a spring; I knew I wouldn't find one, but I kept
looking. The Savannah River, dammed to an unnatural wide-
ness, lay below, wet and cool. I'd come into Georgia. The sun
seemed to press on the roadway, and inside the truck, hot light
bounced off chrome, flickering like a torch. Then I saw what I
was trying not to look for: in a coppice, a long-handled pump.

I stopped and took my bottles to the well. A small sign: 2
WATER UNSAFE FOR DRINKING. I drooped like warm tallow. What
fungicide, herbicide, nematicide, fumigant, or growth regu-
lant—potions that rebuilt Southern agriculture—had seeped
into the ground water? In the old movie Westerns there is
commonly a scene where a dehydrated man, crossing the barren waste, at last comes to a water hole; he lies flat to drink
the tepid stuff. Just as lips touch water, he sees on the other
side a steer skull. I drove off thirsty but feeling a part of mythic
history.

The thirst subsided when hunger took over. I hadn't eaten   3
since morning. Sunset arrived west of Oglesby, and the air
cooled. Then a roadsign:

SWAMP GUINEA'S FISH LODGE

ALL YOU CAN EAT!

An arrow pointed down a county highway. I would gorge
myself. A record would be set. They'd ask me to leave. An
embarrassment to all.

The road through the orange earth of north Georgia passed ₄ an old, three-story house with a thin black child hanging out of every window like an illustration for "The Old Woman Who Lived in a Shoe"; on into hills and finally to Swamp Guinea's, a conglomerate of plywood and two-by-fours laid over with the smell of damp pine woods.

Inside, wherever an oddity or natural phenomenon could ₅ hang, one hung: stuffed rump of a deer, snowshoe, flintlock, hornet's nest. The place looked as if a Boy Scout troop had decorated it. Thirty or so people, black and white, sat around tables almost foundering under piled platters of food. I took a seat by the reproduction of a seventeenth-century woodcut depicting some Rabelaisian banquet at the groaning board.

The diners were mostly Oglethorpe County red-dirt farmers. ₆ In Georgia tones they talked about their husbandry in terms of rain and nitrogen and hope. An immense woman with a glossy picture of a hooked bass leaping the front of her shirt said, "I'm gonna be sick from how much I've ate."

I was watching everyone else and didn't see the waitress ₇ standing quietly by. Her voice was deep and soft like water moving in a cavern. I ordered the $4.50 special. In a few minutes she wheeled up a cart and began offloading dinner: ham and eggs, fried catfish, fried perch fingerlings, fried shrimp, chunks of barbecued beef, fried chicken, French fries, hush puppies, a broad bowl of cole slaw, another of lemon, a quart of ice tea, a quart of ice, and an entire loaf of factory-wrapped white bread. The table was covered.

"Call me if y'all want any more." She wasn't joking. I ₈ quenched the thirst and then—slowly—went to the eating. I had to stand to reach plates across the table, but I intended to do the supper in. It was all Southern fried and good, except the Southern-style sweetened ice tea; still I took care of a quart of it. As I ate, making up for meals lost, the Old-Woman-in-the-Shoe house flashed before me, lightning in darkness. I had no moral right to eat so much. But I did. Headline: STOMACH PUMP FAILS TO REVIVE TRAVELER.

The loaf of bread lay unopened when I finally abandoned 9 the meal. At the register, I paid a man who looked as if he'd been chipped out of Georgia chert. The Swamp Guinea. I asked about the name. He spoke of himself in the third person like the Wizard of Oz. "The Swamp Guinea only tells regulars."

"I'd be one, Mr. Guinea, if I didn't live in Missouri." 10

"Y'all from the North? Here, I got somethin' for you." He 11 went to the office and returned with a 45 rpm record. "It's my daughter singin'. A little promotion we did. Take it along." Later, I heard a husky north Georgia voice let go a down-home lyric rendering of Swamp Guinea's menu:

> That's all you can eat
> For a dollar fifty,
> Hey! The barbecue's nifty!

And so on through the fried chicken and potatoes.

As I left, the Swamp Guinea, a former antique dealer whose 12 name was Rudell Burroughs, said, "The nickname don't mean anything. Just made it up. Tried to figure a good one so we can franchise someday."

The frogs, high and low, shrilled and bellowed from the trees 13 and ponds. It was cool going into Athens, a city suffering from a nasty case of the sprawls. On the University of Georgia campus, I tried to walk down Swamp Guinea's supper. Everywhere couples entwined like moonflower vines, each waiting for the blossom that opens only once.

VOCABULARY

paragraph 1: artesian water, coppice
paragraph 2: fungicide, herbicide, nematicide, fumigant, tepid, mythic
paragraph 4: conglomerate
paragraph 5: phenomenon, Rabelaisian
paragraph 6: husbandry
paragraph 7: fingerlings
paragraph 9: chert

QUESTIONS

1. What expressions or grammatical characteristics mark the speech of the diner, the waitress, and the restaurant owner as regional or dialectal?

2. To what extent does Least Heat Moon depend on colloquial or everyday spoken expressions in writing about his experience? Is his sentence construction loose, or is he writing at a general or formal level?

3. Is he merely describing rural Georgia and the fish restaurant, or is he making a judgment about this world and developing a thesis?

4. Why does he conclude with the description of the couples on the Georgia campus?

SUGGESTION FOR WRITING

Describe a restaurant through its appearance, the food it serves, and the speech of its employees and possibly its owner. Let your details express a judgment or make a point about the restaurant. Don't state the judgment or the point explicitly.

Newsweek

> In its special fiftieth anniversary issue, NEWSWEEK *magazine traced the history of five families in Springfield, Ohio—typical of the life of Americans from 1933 to 1983. The description here is of Dick Hatfield, the "guru of cool" in Springfield in the 1950s. Hatfield illustrates an attitude and style that require concrete detail to be understood.*

BEING COOL

The time then ending had been one in which quietude had been elevated to national policy and a certain insouciance called *cool* became a personal style among the trendier young. The guru of cool in Springfield was Dick Hatfield, Catholic Central High class of '53, known as the Imperial Debubba of the Hort Club in tribute to two of the nonsense words he contributed to the nearly universal vocabulary of the city's cooler youth. Hatfield had been a precocious student, a high-school graduate at 15, which gave him a long run on the street—he hung out with the classes of '53 through '57—and a recognized seniority in the world of cool. When local advertisers dropped his word "hort" into their copy or bought little blocks of space that said DIGGEDY DIGGEDY DA BUSH BUSH, nothing more, it was a homage to Hatfield, his gift of unintelligible gab and his authority as an arbiter of cool taste.

Being cool, Hatfield remembers now, had to do first with how you looked and what you wore. Cool guys did not wear leather jackets or chinos and sweat socks, either. Cool guys wore pleated gray-flannel pants, custom pegged by a needle-woman named Ma Weiner for 75 cents a pair, with a skinny belt buckled on the side and a shirt with the billowing Mr. B collar popularized by the singer Billy Eckstine, who was *very* cool. Cool guys had cool walks, too, working at them till they had just the right hunch to the shoulders, just the right swing to the arms. "Sometimes," Hatfield recalls, "you would just *stand* there and be cool. Some chick would come by and say, 'He's cool,' just by the way you stood."

Cool guys did not sit home watching family sitcoms or the Mouseketeers. When they were home at all, cool guys watched "77 Sunset Strip" mostly for Kookie, the eighth avatar of cool, or Dick Clark's "American Bandstand"; it was the constant intention of Hatfield's crowd to go to Philly, where the Bandstand was produced, and really show them how to dance, but somehow they never saved up enough money. They did their stepping instead at El Som (for sombrero) dances at the Y on football and basketball Friday nights, or later, when they came of drinking age, at upscale clubs like the Melody Showbar—the Four Freshmen played there once—or funkier joints like the Frolics out on Lagonda Avenue. Hatfield, ultracool, preferred the Frolics for its ambience, which included a bouncer with a .357 magnum and featured a rhythm-and-blues band presided over by a large black man named H-Bomb Ferguson. You could do the dirty boogie at the Frolics, "a modified jitterbug," as

Hatfield remembered it, "with like more hips," and find out quickly which guys and chicks were truly cool.

Cool guys hung out, at Frisch's Big Boy for the burgers, or 4 under the clock at Woolworth's for the girl-watching, or at East High Billiards for the action; Hatfield was taking tickets there one March day in 1954 when the great Willie Mosconi came in and sank 526 straight balls for a world's record. But mostly cool guys cruised, customizing their cars and living an automotive life later imitated by art in the film "American Graffiti." Hatfield's wheels supported a mink-white Chevy with scallops in three colors, regatta blue, Bahama blue and Inca gray, and the what-me-worry likeness of Alfred E. Neuman hand-done on the gas cap by a local painter. For a final touch of style, he installed a dummy telephone with a real-sounding Ma Bell ring, activated by a push button under the dashboard. Sometimes he would set it off with his knee at Frisch's just as one of the carhop girls came over to take his order. "Hold on a second, will you, honey," he would say, picking up the receiver. "I got an important call here."

The cruising route favored by the cool guys was downtown 5 when it still *was* downtown, its streets alive with life; Hatfield figured he spent very nearly every evening for four years going around the core block in the heart of the city, so many times he imagined that his tire tracks must have been indelibly imprinted in the left-hand lane. You cruised for a while, checking out the happenings; then you did the joints, O'Brien's Tavern at 9, then the Savoy, and then, at 1 A.M., the Alibi or the Shady Lane Saloon.

But suddenly everything began changing, and the cool life 6 began to chill. Hatfield noticed it around the time he was called up into the Reserves in 1960, at 22. Guys were getting restless, itchy for something new; some were disappearing into the military, some into marriages. The music was changing; five white guys named the Beach Boys were bleaching out Chuck Berry's black sound, and the dirty boogie was washed under by the twist, the pony and the mashed potato. "It was like everybody knew how to do *our* dance," Hatfield recalls. "The dirty boogie was no longer new." Downtown was changing, too, emptying out and beginning to go seedy. The difference struck Hatfield one day in the early '60s when he pulled up at East High Billiards and found a parking space right across the street. There was nobody around; being cool wasn't cool anymore.

Hatfield grew up when he came home from the Reserves; he 7 went back to work with the railroad for a while, then spun records for Station WBLY for a while more and now sells steel for the Benjamin Steel Co. He sold the '53 Chevy with the tricolor scallops before he went away and bought a 1960 Plymouth Valiant when he came back, a car so square that it couldn't be customized. He restocked his record library with Percy Faith and retooled his nights out to consist of taking a nice girl to a nice dinner at the Holiday Inn.

But some of the cool guys of his day could never let go of 8 the rites of coolness. The world had changed under them; Kennedy had died, with all that diamond-bright promise; new tribes of the young had divided American politics, morals and popular culture across a void that came to be known as the generation gap; Chuck Berry's records were golden oldies, and Kookie was the answer to a trivia tease. Nothing remains now of the age of cool in Springfield except its last few survivors, baldish men in their middle and late 40s with two or three divorces behind them, still driving the old cruising routes as if in familiar motion they could catch up with the past and recover the last innocent time.

VOCABULARY

paragraph 1: quietude, insouciance, guru, arbiter
paragraph 3: magnum
paragraph 4: regatta
paragraph 8: trivia

QUESTIONS

1. How do the details help explain what the phrase "being cool" meant to teenagers in the late 1950s? Does *Newsweek* state the meaning directly?

2. What other slang does Newsweek identify? How do you discover the meaning of these words or expressions?

3. What does the language of these teenagers tell you about their world and values? Is the Newsweek account a sympathetic one? Or is Newsweek merely reporting what happened to teenagers in the 1950s?

4. How different is the voice of Newsweek from the voice of Hatfield and the other teenagers described? What words and sentences tell you that the voices are different?

5. How different are Hatfield's world and values from your own? What language expresses the values of teenagers today? What influence does popular music have on current teenager slang and values?

SUGGESTIONS FOR WRITING

1. Analyze the language of two sports columnists, noting the degree of informality in each and the extent to which each depends on sports jargon. Use your analysis to define the difference in the voice of each writer.

2. Describe a special jargon or slang that you share with friends or your family. Discuss the special meanings of these words and the values they express.

3. Every profession and trade has a special language or jargon that provides a "shorthand" or concise means of communicating. Examine a trade journal or popular magazine directed to a particular audience—*Popular Mechanics, Field and Stream, Stereo Review*—and identify particular words and phrases of this kind. Discuss the special meanings conveyed by several of these words or phrases.

21

Tone

By the tone of a piece of writing, we mean the reflection of the writer's attitude toward the subject or reader. The possibilities are many: A piece of writing may be sarcastic, bitter, angry, mocking, whimsical, facetious, joyful, admiring, or indifferent. And we can reveal this attitude in numerous ways—most commonly by stating it directly:

> There should be more sympathy for school children. The idea that they are happy is of a piece with the idea that the lobster in the pot is happy. (H. L. Mencken, "Travail")

Or we can express our attitude indirectly—perhaps by exaggerating, sometimes to the point of absurdity, for a humorous or satirical effect, as in this parody of a course description in a college bulletin:

> Rapid Reading—This course will increase reading speed a little each day until the end of the term, by which time the student will be required to read *The Brothers Karamazov* in fifteen minutes. (Woody Allen, "Spring Bulletin")

Or we can write sarcastically, intending to ridicule:

> He has occasional flashes of silence, that make his conversation perfectly delightful. (Sydney Smith, describing a famous nineteenth-century historian)

Sarcasm is a biting or sometimes angry form of irony. An ironic statement implies that something more is meant than is actually stated, as in Sydney Smith's statement. Irony may suggest that we mean the opposite of what we say and can be humorous:

> It has been known for years that prisons have been accepting a very low-class type of inmate, some without any education, others who are unstable, and some who are just plain anti-social. (Art Buchwald, "Upping Prison Requirements")

475

Understatement is another form of irony:

> The reports of my death have been greatly exaggerated. (Mark Twain, cable to the Associated Press)

Paradoxical statements can also be ironic:

> Trash has given us an appetite for art. (Pauline Kael, *Going Steady*)

And so can statements that prepare us for one conclusion and then turn around and surprise us with another:

> A little sincerity is a dangerous thing, and a great deal of it is absolutely fatal. (Oscar Wilde, *The Critic As Artist*)

As these examples suggest, the tone of a sentence, a paragraph, or an essay is conveyed by the *voice* we try to express in writing. Voice depends on the rhythms and nuances of speech, carried into the modulations and rhythms of the sentences and paragraphs. False starts in writing are often failures to discover the right voice or tone. Too formal a sentence or choice of words may create the impression of distance or unconcern; a highly informal style may suggest lack of seriousness or flippancy. Not surprisingly, we often find as we write that we need to adjust the tone. An essay need not express a single dominant tone; however, the expression of our attitude often changes as we turn to new ideas and details.

Mark Singer

> MARK SINGER *has written a number of talk pieces and profiles for* The New Yorker *magazine. He is also the author of* Funny Money (1985) *and* Mr. Personality (1988). *Singer's account of a karate birthday party in a New York suburb appeared in "The Talk of the Town"—a collection of short commentaries, profiles, and sketches in each issue of* The New Yorker. *The observer in the account at no point makes a personal reference or states an opinion about the party. The tone of the essay is therefore crucial in deciding whether the observer is satirizing the birthday party or sharing in the fun.*

OSU!

The karate-birthday-party concept occurred to Howard Fryd-   1
man because Howard Frydman is an acutely aware person. To
begin with, it was obvious to Howard and his partner, Tokey
Hill, who run the Karate Center of Champions, a martial-arts
academy that sits right next to the Long Island Rail Road station in Douglaston, Queens, that kids love karate. Then the
mother of one of the many fine eight-year-old boys in Nassau
County remarked to Howard that virtually every variety of
kid's-birthday-party idea you could think of had been done to
death. That was about three years ago. Since then, Howard
and Tokey—Howard was the captain of the American karate
team and a silver-medal winner at the 1981 Maccabiah Games,
in Israel, and Tokey has won even more medals than Howard,
and they both recently joined the Budweiser National Karate
Team and appeared on the cover of the première issue of
the magazine *American Karate*—have developed and refined the
karate-birthday-party concept. By now, they've done hundreds
of parties. For the basic fee—a hundred dollars—you get a
thirty-minute karate class for the entire party, plus fifteen minutes of professional kicking, punching, blocking, and board-
breaking. Maybe, for a little extra money, Howard and Tokey
will arrange for a ninja to come out and terrify the guests with
one of the magnificent steel-and-chrome ninja swords that you
see advertised in all the martial-arts magazines. After the kicking, punching, blocking, and board-breaking (and the ninja appearance, if that's in the package) come the pizza and cake and
ice cream and birthday presents. Howard and Tokey will stage
a karate birthday party either way—at your home or at the
Karate Center of Champions. They'll even do it in a restaurant;
Howard has done a couple of karate birthday parties at Beni-
hana. Another time, he went to New Jersey. For a karate birthday party in Jersey, though, he charges a pretty penny, because
of all the travel.

The Karate Center of Champions has about two thousand   2
square feet of classroom space, plywood floors, white walls,

some broad mirrors along the walls, and, just inside the front door, a desk, plenty of framed and mounted photographs and martial-arts-magazine covers, and a Karate Master video game. Howard Frydman has dark hair, a trim, muscular build, a thin, bony face, and twenty years of seniority over this particular Saturday's birthday boy—Joshua Feldman, son of Geoff and Jill, of Great Neck. Joshua has the standard dimensions of an eight-year-old, curly blond hair, freckles, and pouchy cheeks. He wears a white karate robe with a blue belt. The blue belt signifies that Joshua knows how to execute fifteen basic karate movements—low block, chest block, head block, knife-hand block, several kicks, and some other stuff. If you are going to execute any of the fifteen basic karate movements, you first have to spit out your bubble gum. Then you line up and do whatever the sensei (that's an honorific term accorded a senior martial-arts instructor; Tokey Hill is out of town, so Howard is the principal sensei today) tells you to do.

Always—*always*—Sensei Frydman starts things off with a ₃ formal Oriental bow and the Japanese greeting "O*su*!"—which sounds more like "Oos!" There are very few gestures in karate that do not seem nicer with a heartfelt "O*su*!" tacked on at the end.

Sensei Frydman (bowing): O*su*! ₄

Joshua and Invited Guests (Adam, Jason, Jeremy, Michael, ₅ etc., in chorus, bowing): O*su*!

S.F.: O.K., spread the feet a little bit. Hands on the hips. Left ₆ ear to the left shoulder. Now right ear to the right shoulder. And rotate. Rotate. O.K., rotate the entire head. That's it. Roll it around. Anybody tired yet?

I.G.s (faint chorus): No, Sensei. ₇

S.F. (loud enough to intimidate I.G.s): I CAN'T HEAR YOU! ₈

I.G.s (loud enough to compete with passing train): NO, SENSEI! ₉

S.F.: Good. O.K., shake it out. Now, as part of this demon- ₁₀ stration, we demand that Josh cut Adam in half with the sword. Are you ready? Hmm. All right, we'll do that later, after we cut the cake. Now I need some hips. Let's loosen it up. Come on,

Feldman. All right, everybody sit down. Heels together, head to toes. Loosen up the back, hold your breath. O.K. Legs apart. Nose to the knee. Come on, Blue Belts, lock those knees. Close it up, Silverman. Good. Shake it out. All right, who knows what "karate" means? (Silence.) The word "karate"—nobody knows what it means?

I.G. in back row: "Self-defense"? 11

S.F.: No, that's what karate *is*. What does it mean? 12

I.G. in front row (wearing white robe and blue belt): "Empty 13 hand."

S.F.: Empty hand. Right. Now, what is the main purpose of 14 karate?

A different Blue Belt: Self-defense. 15

S.F.: Good. So what does that mean? It means that after 16 class there will be no running around punching and kicking each other. When you leave here and go home and are playing with your friends, there will be no punching and kicking. If you want to punch or kick the air, that's fine. But otherwise no punching or kicking. Does everybody understand?

I.G.s: Yes, Sensei. 17

S.F. (painful to eardrums): I CAN'T HEAR YOU! 18

I.G.s (loud enough to compete with passing train plus low- 19 flying aircraft): YES, SENSEI!

S.F.: O.K., another thing. What is it you can't do if you can't 20 stand up? Come on, Blue Belts—Feldman, Teppel, Stock—you know the answer.

A Blue Belt: Fight. 21

S.F.: Right. Because if you're down, your opponent can do 22 *this* to you. (Demonstrates incapacitating maneuvers that op- ponent might, if provoked, consider doing.) O.K., stand up. Up! Too slow. Down again. Now up! Stand straight. Stand strong. Silverman, what happened to you? You're like chopped liver today. You— Stop smiling. You don't have any teeth. Your opponent sees that, you're open to attack. Nice suntan, Levy. O.K., punch-and-twist exercise. That's it, full speed, full power. We're all gonna count in Japanese. Count with me.

S.F. and I.G.s count together in Japanese. 23

S.F.: O.K. Anybody tired yet? Hey, Silverman, what you got   24
there? A gun? Give me that gun. Oh, a toy gun. Control yourself, Silverman. Relax.

At the conclusion of one exercise, Sensei Frydman says,   25
"What, no 'Osu'? Down. Everyone. Ten pushups." Ten pushups
ensue. Next, the sensei demonstrates a U-punch and an elbow
strike. Then he announces that Joshua Feldman will demonstrate a flying front kick, whereupon he lifts Joshua by the
lapels of his white robe and Joshua incapacitates the air with
his bare feet.

Any minute now, thumping sounds will come from the   26
stairway that leads to the basement, and then the door will
burst open and one of the other Karate Center of Champions
instructors, Sensei David Gonzalez, will appear wearing the
sort of black ninja uniform that you see advertised in all the
karate magazines: black jacket with hidden pocket, black
pants with leg ties, black hood, black hand wraps, the magnificent sword—the works. After Sensei Frydman has vanquished
the ninja, he will say, "All right, who wants to see the ninja
break a board?" Then Sensei Frydman will hold an inch-thick
board at eye level, and Sensei Gonzalez will try to break it with
his left foot, using a spinning-jump-hook kick. On the fifth
attempt, he will get it right. Everyone—the twenty birthday
celebrators, Sensei Frydman, Sensei Gonzalez—will pose for a
group picture, and then it will be time to go downstairs for
pizza and soft drinks and cake and ice cream. During the pizza
course, Joshua Feldman and some of the other Blue Belts will
get tomato-sauce stains on their white robes. After the pizza
and before the cake and ice cream (there's a drawing of Hulk
Hogan on the cake), the invited guests will suffer a collective
mental lapse and get up from the table and run around and
kick and punch and scream—all in self-defense. There will be
a crucial moment during which Joshua Feldman pauses to
catch his breath and to contemplate what he might like to do
at his ninth-birthday party: "Go bowling. *Osu!*"

QUESTIONS

1. Is the reporter chiefly concerned with Howard Frydman and the idea of the karate birthday party, or with the party itself and Howard's friends? How do you know?
2. What is the attitude of the reporter toward Howard Frydman and the karate party? Is he admiring, or critical, or amused, or is his account wholly neutral and objective?
3. Does the reporter hold the same attitude toward Joshua Feldman and the other eight-year-old boys? How do you know?
4. Does the tone of the report change?
5. Is the reporter making a point or arguing a thesis? Or is the reporter merely describing a birthday party?

SUGGESTIONS FOR WRITING

1. Describe an event like the karate party from two points of view— from that of a neutral observer and from that of an angry or critical or amused one. Make the tone of each description clear and consistent.
2. Analyze a speech in a recent issue of *Vital Speeches* or another periodical to discover the tone of the speaker. Does the speech have a single, dominant tone, or does it change in tone? Explain how you know.

William Finnegan

WILLIAM FINNEGAN, *staff writer for* The New Yorker *since 1987, is the author of three books about Africa*: Crossing the Line: A Year in the Land of Apartheid (1986), Dateline Soweto: Travels with Black African Reporters (1988; *updated edition*, 1995), *and* A Complicated War: The Harrowing of Mozambique (1992). *His description of surfing in northern California is excerpted from his two-part essay, "Surfing,"* in The New Yorker *on August 17 and August 24, 1992.*

SURFING

The rain puddles are like small powder-blue windows scattered on the muddy farm road as I hurry down to the beach at Four Mile. It's a soft, clear morning, with not a breath of wind, and a north swell looks to have sneaked in overnight. Remarkably, there's no one around. Four Mile is a reef break in a pristine cove between San Francisco and Santa Cruz. The break isn't visible from the highway, but it's a short walk from the road to a vantage point, and the spot is popular with surfers from Santa Cruz. I have caught Four Mile good before, but have never surfed it alone. When I pick my way across a creek behind the beach, I find myself listening anxiously for howls from the hillside behind me—other surfers arriving and seeing the swell. But the only sound is a tractor chugging down long rows of Brussels sprouts that stretch away to the south.

A deep, reliable channel runs out through the middle of the cove at Four Mile; the wave is on the north side. It's a quirky right, with sections that change with the tide or with any shift in the size and direction of the swell. It can get quite big, and very spooky, but the surf this morning looks benign. I paddle out through the channel, hands stinging, and my heart starts to pound when a good-sized wave hits the outside reef, stands up—bottle-green against the pale-blue sky—pitches out, explodes, and begins to wind down the reef in fine, peeling sections. This may be the best wave I've ever seen break at Four Mile. Two more nearly as good follow, and I take deep breaths to try to control a flurry of adrenaline. Carried on the back of a swift seaward current, I reach the lineup with my hair still dry. I move along a line of broad boils, paddling slowly, watching the horizon for a set, looking for a likely takeoff spot near the head of a chunk of reef, checking my position against a cypress tree on the bluff. Still nobody in sight on shore. Just one wave, I find myself praying, just one wave.

A wave comes. It swings silently through the kelp bed, a long, tapering wall, darkening upcoast. I paddle across the grain of the water streaming toward the wave across the reef, angling to meet the hollow of a small peak ghosting across the face. For a moment, in the gully just in front of the wave, my board loses forward momentum as the water rushing off the reef sucks it back up the face. Then the wave lifts me up—I've met the steepest part of the peak, and swerved into its shoreward track—and with two hard strokes I'm aboard. It's a clean takeoff: a sudden sense of height fusing with a deep surge of speed. I hop to my feet and drive to the bottom, drawing out the turn and sensing, more than seeing, what the wave plans to do ahead—the low sun is blinding off the water looking south. Halfway through the first turn, I can feel the wave starting to stand up ahead. I change rails, bank off the lower part of the face, and start driving down the line. The first section flies past, and the wave—it's slightly overhead, and changing angle as it breaks, so that it now blocks out the sun—stands revealed: a long, steep, satiny arc curving all the way to the channel. I work my board from rail to rail for speed, trimming carefully through two more short sections. Gaining confidence that I will in fact make this wave, I start turning harder, slicing higher up the face and, when a last bowl section looms beside the channel, stalling briefly before driving through in a half crouch, my face pressed close to the glassy, rumbling, pea-green wall. The silver edge of the lip's axe flashes harmlessly past on my left. A second later, I'm coasting onto flat water, leaning into a pullout, and mindlessly shouting "My God!"

VOCABULARY

paragraph 1: pristine
paragraph 2: quirky, benign, adrenaline
paragraph 3: kelp

QUESTIONS

1. What are Finnegan's thoughts and feelings as he walks to the beach at Four Mile? What is the tone of paragraph 1?
2. Is there a change in tone from paragraph 1 to paragraph 2?
3. Is there a further change in paragraph 3?
4. How much of the technique employed would Finnegan need to explain if he were instructing the reader how to surf?

SUGGESTIONS FOR WRITING

1. Compare Finnegan's essay with one of the earlier readings in this book, explaining how each author establishes a tone and perhaps changes to another.

2. Narrate an experience in the course of which your feelings changed. Let the details and tone of your narrative reveal your feelings and reflect the changes.

22

Imagery

Images convey sensory impressions: impressions of sight, hearing, smell, taste, or touch. The following passage from a story by James Joyce illustrates most of these:

> The cold air stung us and we played till our bodies glowed. Our shouts echoed in the silent street. The career of our play brought us through the dark muddy lanes behind the houses where we ran the gauntlet of the rough tribes from the cottages, to the back doors of the dark dripping gardens where odors arose from the ashpits, to the dark odorous stables where a coachman smoothed and combed the horse or shook music from the buckled harness. ("Araby")

We think in images constantly. Joyce could not have expressed his sense of a particular street on a particular night in abstract language. The more evocative our imagery when the situation calls for vivid impressions, the more directly will our words express experience. A passage will seem overwritten if a vivid representation of experience is not needed; so-called fine writing tries to be too evocative of sense experience. In the passage quoted above, Joyce selects only those details that give the reader an impression of the physical sensations experienced in the darkness. The imagery suggests the vitality of imagination, a theme of the story; Joyce probably could not have conveyed that vitality without it.

Rachel Carson

American biologist and conservationist RACHEL CARSON (1907–1964) worked at the Marine Biological Laboratory at Woods Hole, Massachusetts, and as editor-in-chief for the U. S. Fish and Wildlife Service. Carson wrote several books about the natural life of the Atlantic coast, including Under the Sea-Wind (1941) *and* The Edge of the Sea (1955). *The Sea Around Us received the National Book Award for* 1951. Silent Spring (1962), *probably the most influential book written in the United States on environmental issues, warned of the pollution of the environment by chemicals and insecticides. The following excerpt from* The Edge of the Sea *shows Carson's remarkable descriptive powers.*

THE ROCKY SHORES

When the tide is high on a rocky shore, when its brimming fullness creeps up almost to the bayberry and the junipers where they come down from the land, one might easily suppose that nothing at all lived in or on or under these waters of the sea's edge. For nothing is visible. Nothing except here and there a little group of herring gulls, for at high tide the gulls rest on ledges of rock, dry above the surf and the spray, and they tuck their yellow bills under their feathers and doze away the hours of the rising water. Then all the creatures of the tidal rocks are hidden from view, but the gulls know what is there, and they know that in time the water will fall away again and give them entrance to the strip between the tide lines.

When the tide is rising the shore is a place of unrest, with the surge leaping high over jutting rocks and running in lacy cascades of foam over the landward side of massive boulders. But on the ebb it is more peaceful, for then the waves do not have behind them the push of the inward pressing tides. There is no particular drama about the turn of the tide, but presently a zone of wetness shows on the gray rock slopes, and offshore the incoming swells begin to swirl and break over hidden ledges. Soon the rocks that the high tide had concealed rise into view and glisten with the wetness left on them by the receding water.

Small, dingy snails move about over rocks that are slippery with the growth of infinitesimal green plants; the snails scraping, scraping, scraping to find food before the surf returns.

Like drifts of old snow no longer white, the barnacles come into view; they blanket rocks and old spars wedged into rock crevices, and their sharp cones are sprinkled over empty mussel shells and lobster-pot buoys and the hard stipes of deep-water seaweeds, all mingled in the flotsam of the tide.

Meadows of brown rockweeds appear on the gently sloping 5 rocks of the shore as the tide imperceptibly ebbs. Smaller patches of green weed, stringy as mermaids' hair, begin to turn white and crinkly where the sun has dried them.

Now the gulls, that lately rested on the higher ledges, pace 6 with grave intentness along the walls of rock, and they probe under the hanging curtains of weed to find crabs and sea urchins.

In the low places little pools and gutters are left where the 7 water trickles and gurgles and cascades in miniature water-falls, and many of the dark caverns between and under the rocks are floored with still mirrors holding the reflections of delicate creatures that shun the light and avoid the shock of waves—the cream-colored flowers of the small anemones and the pink fingers of soft coral, pendent from the rocky ceiling.

In the calm world of the deeper rock pools, now undis- 8 turbed by the tumult of incoming waves, crabs sidle along the walls, their claws busily touching, feeling, exploring for bits of food. The pools are gardens of color composed of the delicate green and ocher-yellow of encrusting sponge, the pale pink of hydroids that stand like clusters of fragile spring flowers, the bronze and electric-blue gleams of the Irish moss, the old-rose beauty of the coralline algae.

And over it all there is the smell of low tide, compounded 9 of the faint, pervasive smell of worms and snails and jellyfish and crabs—the sulphur smell of sponge, the iodine smell of rockweed, and the salt smell of the rime that glitters on the sun-dried rocks.

One of my favorite approaches to a rocky seacoast is by a 10 rough path through an evergreen forest that has its own pecu-liar enchantment. It is usually an early morning tide that takes me along that forest path, so that the light is still pale and fog drifts in from the sea beyond. It is almost a ghost forest, for among the living spruce and balsam are many dead trees—some still erect, some sagging earthward, some lying on the floor of the forest. All the trees, the living and the dead, are clothed with green and silver crusts of lichens. Tufts of the bearded lichen or old man's beard hang from the branches like bits of sea mist tangled there. Green woodland mosses and a yielding carpet of reindeer moss cover the ground. In the quiet of that place even the voice of the surf is reduced to a whispered echo and the sounds of the forest are but the ghosts of sound—the faint sighing of evergreen needles in the moving air; the creaks and heavier groans of half-fallen trees resting against their neighbors and rubbing bark against bark; the light rattling fall of a dead branch broken under the feet of a squirrel and sent bouncing and ricocheting earthward.

But finally the path emerges from the dimness of the 11 deeper forest and comes to a place where the sound of surf rises above the forest sounds—the hollow boom of the sea, rhythmic and insistent, striking against the rocks, falling away, rising again.

Up and down the coast the line of the forest is drawn sharp 12 and clean on the edge of a seascape of surf and sky and rocks. The softness of sea fog blurs the contours of the rocks; gray water and gray mists merge offshore in a dim and vaporous world that might be a world of creation, stirring with new life.

VOCABULARY

paragraph 2: ebb
paragraph 3: infinitesimal
paragraph 4: barnacles, buoys, flotsam
paragraph 6: sea urchins
paragraph 7: anemones, pendent
paragraph 8: hydroids, coralline, algae
paragraph 9: rime
paragraph 10: lichen, ricocheting

QUESTIONS

1. How does Carson establish a place of observation or physical point of view in paragraphs 1–9? Does the place of observation change in the course of these paragraphs?

2. What changes from high tide to low does Carson focus on? What images of sight highlight these changes?

3. To what extent does she also depend on images of sound and smell? Do you also find images of touch?

4. How does Carson establish a physical point of view in paragraphs 10–12? Does this point of view change in the course of these paragraphs?

5. What kinds of imagery do you find? Does one or more kind of imagery dominate the description?

6. What feelings does Carson experience in observing the seacoast and walking toward it? Does she name these feelings, or express them through images?

7. Does she make a point or develop a thesis in paragraphs 1–9? Does she in paragraphs 10–12? Or is her purpose in writing descriptive and expressive?

SUGGESTIONS FOR WRITING

1. Show how one of the earlier writers in this book—for example, George Orwell in "Shooting an Elephant" (pp. 14–22) or Joan Didion in "Marrying Absurd" (pp. 62–66)—uses images to convey an idea or express an attitude.

2. Describe an experience that gave you an unexpected picture of the world and revealed a truth about it. Let your details convey the discovery and truth. Don't state these directly.

23

Concreteness

Writing is *concrete* when it makes an observation or impression perceptible to the senses. Eric Sevareid makes concrete the changes that occurred in his hometown in North Dakota:

> Sounds have changed; I heard not once the clopping of a horse's hoof, nor the mourn of a coyote. I heard instead the shriek of brakes, the heavy throbbing of the once-a-day Braniff airliner into Minot, the shattering sirens born of war, the honk of a diesel locomotive which surely cannot call to faraway places the heart of a wakeful boy like the old steam whistle in the night. ("Velva, North Dakota")

Complex ideas can be made concrete with vivid examples; indeed, examples are essential to our understanding:

> I have described the hand when it uses a tool as an instrument of discovery. . . . We see this every time a child learns to couple hand and tool together—to lace its shoes, to thread a needle, to fly a kite or to play a penny whistle. With the practical action there goes another, namely finding pleasure in the action for its own sake—in the skill that one perfects, and perfects by being pleased with it. This at bottom is responsible for every work of art, and science too: our poetic delight in what human beings do because they can do it. (J. Bronowski, *The Ascent of Man*)

Imagery and figurative language can increase the vividness of specific details.

Whatever the purpose of the writer, excessive detail will blur the focus and perhaps make the writing incoherent. Voltaire said, "The secret of being a bore is to tell everything." A boring movie may show everything in what seems like an endless stream of detail; a boring paragraph or essay does the same thing. To develop an idea or impression effectively, we must *select* the detail. Good writing is economical.

490

Bailey White

A graduate of Florida State University, BAILEY WHITE *teaches first grade in Thomasville, Georgia. Her commentaries on her life in the South are heard periodically on National Public Radio. Her essays are collected in* Mama Makes Up Her Mind and Other Dangers of Southern Living (1993), *in which the following appears.*

MORTALITY

It really makes you feel your age when you get a letter from your insurance agent telling you that the car you bought, only slightly used, the year you got out of college, is now an antique. "Beginning with your next payment, your insurance premiums will reflect this change in classification," the letter said.

I went out and looked at the car. I thought back over the years. I could almost hear my uncle's disapproving voice. "You should never buy a used car," he had told me the day I brought it home. Ten years later I drove that used car to his funeral. I drove my sister, Louise, to the hospital in that car to have her first baby, and I drove to Atlanta in that car when the baby graduated from Georgia Tech with a degree in physics.

"When are you going to get a new car?" my friends asked me.

"I don't need a new car," I said. "This car runs fine."

I changed the oil often, and I kept good tires on it. It always got me where I wanted to go. But the stuffing came out of the backseat and the springs poked through, and the dashboard disintegrated. At 300,000 miles the odometer quit turning, but I didn't really care to know how far I had driven.

A hole wore in the floor where my heel rested in front of the accelerator, and the insulation all peeled off the fire wall. "Old piece of junk," my friends whispered. The seat-belt catch wore out, and I tied on a huge bronze hook with a fireman's knot.

Big flashy cars would zoom past me. People would shake their fists out the windows. "Get that clunker off the road!" they would shout.

Then one day on my way to work, the car coughed, sput- 8
tered, and stopped. "This is it," I thought, and I gave it a pat.
"It's been a good car."

I called the mechanic. "Tow it in," I said. "I'll have to decide 9
what to do." After work I went over there. I was feeling very
glum. The mechanic laughed at me. "It's not funny," I said. "I've
had that car a long time."

"You know what's wrong with that car?" he said. "That car 10
was out of gas." So I slopped a gallon of gas in the tank and
drove ten more years. The gas gauge never worked again after
that day, but I got to where I could tell when the gas was low
by the smell. I think it was the smell of the bottom of the tank.

There was also a little smell of brake fluid, a little smell of 11
exhaust, a little smell of oil, and after all the years a little smell
of me. Car smells. And sounds. The wonderful sound when the
engine finally catches on a cold day, and an ominous *tick tick* in
July when the radiator is working too hard. The windshield
wipers said "Gracie Allen Gracie Allen Gracie Allen." I didn't
like a lot of conversation in the car because I had to keep listening for a little skip that meant I needed to jump out and
adjust the carburetor.

I kept a screwdriver close to hand—and a pint of brake fluid, 12
and a new roter, just in case. "She's strange," my friends whispered. "And she drives so slow."

I don't know how fast I drove. The speedometer had quit 13
working years ago. But when I would look down through the
hole in the floor and see the pavement, a gray blur, whizzing by
just inches away from my feet, and feel the tremendous heat of
internal combustion pouring back through the fire wall into my
lap, and hear each barely contained explosion just as a heart
attack victim is able to hear his own heartbeat, it didn't feel like
slow to me. A whiff of brake fluid would remind me just what a
tiny thing I was relying on to stop myself from hurtling along
the surface of the earth at an unnatural speed, and when I
finally arrived at my destination, I would slump back, unfasten
the seat belt hook with trembling hands, and stagger out. I

would gather up my things and give the car a last look. "Thank you, sir," I would say. "We got here one more time."

But after I got that letter, I began thinking about getting a new car. I read the newspaper every night. Finally I found one that sounded good. It was the same make as my car, but almost new. "Call Steve," the ad said.

I went to see the car. It was parked in Steve's driveway. It was a fashionable wheat color. There was carpet on the floor, and the seats were covered with a soft, velvety-feeling stuff. It smelled like acrylic and vinyl and Steve. The instrument panel looked like what you would need to run a jet plane. I turned a knob. Mozart's Concerto for Flute and Harp poured out of four speakers. "But how can you listen to the engine with music playing?" I asked Steve.

I turned the key. The car started instantly. No desperate pleadings, no wild hopes, no exquisitely paired maneuvers with the accelerator and the choke. Just instant ignition. I turned off the radio. I could barely hear the engine running, a low, steady hum. I fastened my seat belt. Nothing but a click.

Steve got in the passenger seat, and we went for a test drive. We floated down the road. I couldn't hear a sound, but I decided it must be time to shift gears. I stomped around on the floor and grabbed Steve's knee before I remembered it had automatic transmission. "You mean you just put it in 'Drive' and drive?" I asked.

Steve scrunched himself way over against his door and clamped his knees together. He tested his seat belt. "Have you ever driven a car before?" he asked.

I bought it for two thousand dollars. I rolled all the windows up by mashing a button beside my elbow, set the air-conditioning on "Recirc," and listened to Vivaldi all the way home.

So now I have two cars. I call them my new car and my real car. Most of the time I drive my new car. But on some days I go out to the barn and get in my real car. I shoo the rats out of the backseat and crank it up. Even without daily practice my hands and feet know just what to do. My ears perk up, and I sniff the air. I add a little brake fluid, a little water. I sniff again. It'll need gas next week, and an oil change.

I back it out and we roll down the road. People stop and look. They smile. "Neat car!" they say. 21

When I pull into the parking lot, my friends shake their heads and chuckle. They amble into the building. They're already thinking about their day's work. But I take one last look at the car and think what an amazing thing it is, internal combustion. And how wonderful to be still alive! 22

QUESTIONS

1. How does Bailey White make the differences between the old car and her new one concrete for the reader? How does she make her driving experiences concrete?

2. Is White making a point directly or indirectly in describing the physical differences and her driving experiences in the two cars?

3. What are the sources of humor in the essay? Is the essay satirical as well as humorous?

SUGGESTIONS FOR WRITING

1. Write about your own experiences with an old car, using these experiences to develop an idea. Make the idea concrete through the details you provide of the car and your experiences.

2. Compare the use Bailey White makes of her driving experiences with the use Alan Cowell makes of his (pp. 51–53) or Eudora Welty makes of hers (pp. 135–139). Discuss differences in tone as well as purpose.

Lillian Ross

LILLIAN ROSS *has written numerous profiles and sketches for the "Talk of the Town" column and as reporter at large for* The New Yorker. *Some of these writings are collected in* Reporting (1952), Portrait of Hemingway (1961), Talk Stories (1963), *and* Reporting Two (1969). Vertical and Horizontal (1963) *is a*

*collection of stories. The humorous essay reprinted here establishes
its tone and point of view through a parody of "The Night Before
Christmas." Ross saturates the reader in sounds, colors, sights. She
does not merely give us impressions.*

THE VINYL SANTA

Our lighted fireproof plastic Christmas bells are strung all
through the house, not a creature is stirring, and our mail-
order catalogues—now piled high on the back porch—have
been under surveillance since August, when they started coming in from Atlantic City, New Jersey; Oshkosh, Wisconsin;
Evanston, Illinois; Chicago, Illinois; Falls Church, Virginia;
Omaha, Nebraska; Vineland, New Jersey; Northport, New York;
New York, New York; and elsewhere, including points across
the seas. We did our shopping during Indian summer, without
leaving our chair. Our house is full. Our task is completed. We
are ready.

On our front door is a "Deck the Door Knob of red-and-
green felt with touches of glittering gold that has three jingly
bells to say 'Hi! and Merry Christmas!' to all comers." On our
windows are "Press-On Window Scenes" of snowmen and
reindeer, and the windows are further ornamented with
"Giant, 29-inch by 20-inch Personal Balls Artistically Hand-
Lettered with the Family Name." Mounted outside on the wall
of the house are "The Three Wise Men in Full Color in a Procession of Heavy Weatherproof Methyl-methacrylate Plastic."
Each Wise Man is three feet tall and illuminated. A "Life-Size
Climbing Vinyl Santa" is on the rooftop, and on the front lawn
we have "3-D Thirty-Inch High Full Color Carollers of Strong
Vinylite Carolling 'Oh, Come All Ye Faithful!'" In place of our
regular doorbell we have a "glowing, jingling Santa stamped
with the family name with a cord that visitors pull that raises
Santa's arms in welcome, jingling bright brass bells." The
garage door is covered with a "Giant Door Greeter Five Feet
High and Six Feet Wide, Reading 'Merry Christmas.'" Indoors,
all our rooms have been sprayed either with "Bayberry Mist,

1

2

the forest-fresh scent-of-Christmas" or with the "pungent, spicy, exotic, sweet and rare frankincense-and-myrrh spray— gift of the Magi to the newborn Babe." Each light switch is covered with a "Switchplate-Santa made of white felt with red bell-bedecked cap—the switch comes through his open mouth, the sight of which will make you feel jolly." The towels on the bathroom racks are hand-printed with designs of sleighs and candy canes. The rug next to the tub has "Jolly Old Santa centered in deep, soft, plushy, white pile, and he's wreathed in smiles and in cherries, too, for 'round his head is a gay, cherry wreath." All the mirrors in the house are plastered with red, green, and white pleated tissue cutouts of angels with self-adhesive backs. In the dining room, "Full Size Santa Mugs of Bright Red-and-White Glazed Ceramic are 'Ready' for a 'Spot' of Holiday Cheer." In the living room, we have a "giant holiday chandelier of metallic foil discs reflecting a rainbow of colors," and "giant four-foot electric candles in festive red-and-white candy stripes are glowing cheerfully from their rock-steady base to their dripping wax 'flame.'" On the hall table stands our "Electric Musical Church, five inches high, with inspirational strains of 'Silent Night' pealing reverently from behind lighted, colorfully stained windows."

The tree is trimmed, all the way from a "Perforated Golden Star Making the Sun Envious of Its Brilliance, as though the Blazing Star of Bethlehem Were Pausing in Its Orbit at Your Home," down to the "Christmas Tree Bib Covered with a Profusion of Christmas Designs and Colors" on the floor. Reflecting the light of the Perforated Golden Star, which is made of anodized aluminum with "Hundreds of Holes through which the Light Twinkles just like a Real Star," hang dozens of "Personalized Tree Balls with Names of the Family Nicely Applied in Shimmering, Non-Tarnishing Glitter." Bare spots on the tree are filled in with "Luminous Tree Icicles of Plastic," "Luminous, Plastic, Heavenly Angel Babes Who Have Left the Milky Way," "Handcarved Wooden Angels Holding Hymnals on Gilded Hanging Strings," "Frosty White Pine Cones Lit with Colored Bulbs," "Miniature Felt Money Bags Gayly Trimmed in Assorted

Designs of Yuletide," and "Yummy-Yum-Yum Santa Sweetest Holiday Lollipops."

On Christmas morning, there will be plenty of laughs when 4 everybody gets dressed. Dad will be wearing his "Personalized Holiday Ringing Bell Shorts of White Sanforized Cotton with Santa Claus Handpainted in All His Glory on One Side with a Tinkling Bell on the Tassle of His Cap and Dad's name embroidered in Contrasting Red on the Other." Big Sister will have on "Bright Red Holiday Stretch Socks of Bright Red Nylon Embossed with Contrasting White Holiday Motif." Little Sister and Mom will have on matching "Candy Striped Flannelette Housecoats." Brother will have on a "Clip-On Bow Tie of Red Felt in a Holly Pattern" and also "The Host with the Most Bright Red Felt Vest with Colorful Christmas Accent." Auntie will have on "Ringing Bell Panties Boasting a Ribbon Bedecked Candy Cane Handpainted in Brilliant Yuletide Colors with a Real Tinkling Bell for Extra Cheer." And Shep will have on his own "Personalized Dog Galoshes Embossed with Dog Claus on the Toes." Odds and ends under the tree will include a "Jingle Bell Apron that Plays a Merry Tune with Every Movement," "Donner and Blitzen Salt and Pepper Shakers," a set of "Holly Jewelry for the Holly-Days," a "Ten Commandments Bookmark of Ten Radiant Gold-Plated Squares that Look Like Ancient Scrolled Pages of the Old Testament with the Commandments Etched Upon Them," and "Hi-Fi Bible Stories on a Personalized Record." And our Christmas dinner will be prepared with the help of the "No Cooking Cookbook, with a Collection of Easy-To-Fix Recipes for Busy Mothers that Turns Canned and Frozen Foods into a Banquet of Gourmet Dishes."

QUESTIONS

1. What does the inventory of objects show about the meaning of Christmas to people? What people does Ross have in mind?
2. Is she satirizing practices and attitudes through her details, or is she merely deriving humor from them?
3. How does she organize these details? Does she build them to a climax, or does she present them at random?

SUGGESTION FOR WRITING

Write a description of the objects and slogans associated with another holiday, perhaps Thanksgiving or the Fourth of July. Let your point of view and tone emerge through your details. Be as specific as you can in describing these objects and slogans.

24

Figurative Language

A simile is an explicit comparison (using *like* or *as*) that usually develops or implies one or more simple points of resemblance:

> Will Brangwen ducked his head and looked at his uncle with swift, mistrustful eyes, like a caged hawk. (D. H. Lawrence, *The Rainbow*)

A metaphor is an implicit comparison in which an object is presented as if it were something else.

> Constant use had not worn ragged the fabric of their friendship. (Dorothy Parker, *The Standard of Living*)

Personification is the attribution of human qualities to abstract ideas or objects. Simile, metaphor, and personification unite in the following passage:

> Then Sunday light raced over the farm as fast as the chickens were flying. Immediately the first straight shaft of heat, solid as a hickory stick, was laid on the ridge. (Eudora Welty, *Losing Battles*)

One purpose of figures of speech is to evoke the qualities of experience and give shape or substance to an emotion or awareness that up to the moment of its expression may be indefinite. In exposition a writer will depend on metaphor because of its property of expressing an attitude as well as representing an idea:

> My parents' house had an attic, the darkest and strangest part of the building, reachable only by placing a stepladder beneath the trap-door and filled with unidentifiable articles too important to be thrown out with the trash but no longer suitable to have at hand. This mysterious space was the memory of the place. After many years all the things deposited in it became, one by one, lost to consciousness. But they were there, we knew, safely and comfortably stored in the tissues of the house. (Lewis Thomas, "The Attic of the Brain")

Figurative writing is particularly important in descriptive writing, as in the following paragraph which conveys an unusual experience and sensation through metaphor and other figures:

> Although I was still miles from the ocean, a heavy sea fog came in to muffle the obscure woods and lie over the land like a sheet of dirty muslin. I saw no cars or people, few lights in the houses. The wind-shield wipers, brushing at the fog, switched back and forth like cats' tails. I lost myself to the monotonous rhythm and darkness as past and present fused and dim things came and went in a staccato of moments separated by miles of darkness. On the road, where change is continuous and visible, time is not; rather it is something the rider only infers. Time is not the traveler's fourth dimension—change is. (William Least Heat Moon, *Blue Highways*)

K. C. Cole

> A *former editor of* Saturday Review *and* Newsday, K. C. COLE *has written articles for numerous periodicals, including the* New York Times *and* Psychology Today. *Her book* Between the Lines (1982) *discusses contemporary issues of feminism. Cole has also written about physics as a profession in* Sympathetic Vibrations: Reflections on Physics as a Way of Life (1985). *She draws on her knowledge of physics in this unusual essay on the literal and metaphorical meanings of resonance.*

RESONANCE

Metaphor is truly a marvelous thing. We speak of being in tune with the times or out of tune with each other. We speak of sympathetic vibrations and being on the same wavelength. We speak of going through phases, of ideas that resonate and descriptions that ring true. I wonder how many of us know that all the time we are talking physics?

Resonance is the physics lesson all children learn the first time they try to pump themselves on a swing. Pushing forward or leaning backward at the wrong place or time in the swing gets them nowhere. But pushing and pulling precisely in tune with the natural period of swing will get them as high as they want to go. Being in tune means pushing in the same direction that the swing naturally wants to go. It means going with the flow. Pushing at any other time goes against the swing and bucks the current. It saps energy instead of adding it. Eventually, it will bring the highest swinger to a halt.

Resonance is music to our ears. A violin bow slips along the string, imperceptibly catching it at precise intervals that push it at the proper time to keep it vibrating. The air in a flute resonates at many different frequencies, depending on how far the vibration can travel between lips and mouthpiece. But the stops in a flute are not spaced just anywhere. Beware the flute player who sets the air vibrating at a frequency not natural to the flute; the sound is not a note at all, only an amorphous, irritating hiss. 3

Being out of tune is always irritating because the energy we put into our efforts doesn't seem to get us anywhere. It goes against our grain instead of with it. It steals our harmony and leaves us noise. We can be in or out of tune with ourselves— like the flute and the violin—or in or out of tune with others. Two flutes played beautifully but slightly out of tune with each other can be just as unpleasant as one played badly. Partners in a marriage who are perfectly in tune with their professional or personal lives can be badly out of tune with each other too. 4

To resonate means to sound again, to echo. The trick is to have something that resounds again and again. Two can play this game much better than one because one can feed energy to the other. That's what sympathetic vibrations are all about. 5

Though almost everything—and everyone—can resonate to many different frequencies, it is rare to find ourselves exactly in resonance with something or someone else. When we do, it is the click of recognition that comes with finding a friend who laughs at your jokes and whose understanding goes without saying, who reads correctly the exact meaning of the tilt of your slightly raised eyebrow and who provides the ingredients that make the occasion. 6

It's like the car with the unbalanced wheel that starts to   7
shimmy at exactly 62 miles per hour. At other speeds the wheel
still wobbles but the springs of the car can't respond; only at
62 miles an hour do the two frequencies coincide and the
two vibrations become completely sympathetic. Then the car
shakes like mad. It's all a matter of timing.

With resonance, a small unnoticed vibration can add up to   8
large, often lovely effects. Lasers are the result of sympathetic
vibrations of light. The opera singer's aria is an ode to resonance. Each pure tone that fills the opera house is the tiny
vibration of a vocal cord amplified by the shape of chest and
throat. The same pure tone can shatter a crystal glass. Resonance can be dangerous. Soldiers marching in step across a
bridge can cause it to start swinging at its natural frequency,
straining its supports and making it collapse. A lot of little
pushes in an angry crowd can add up to a full-scale riot. A lot
of little digs over the dinner table can lead to a divorce.

Resonance can also be deceiving: a politician who senses   9
dissatisfaction over inflation and taxes can get a large resonant response with a very small input of energy or new ideas—
and winds up playing in a vacuum, with no result. A woman
who comes into a man's life at the moment he happens to be
looking for a wife (or vice versa) may find herself quickly, but in
the long run unhappily, married. Being in tune can easily be a
matter of superficial coincidence, not lasting harmony.

It is not easy, that is, to stay in tune even when we start up   10
that way. I am always unprepared for the precipitate ups and
downs in my marriage and my relations with friends. One week
we seem never to be together enough, seem never to have
enough time to say what we want to say, seem so closely
attuned to each other's needs and fancies that we are irrevocably inseparable. A week or month later the feelings of being
in tune evaporate as invisibly—but surely—as water from a dry
stream. Suddenly we seem to have nothing to say to each
other and everything we do say is misunderstood. Arguments
and hurt feelings lie beneath the surface like spikes, waiting to
trip us up.

Anything that resonates necessarily oscillates; it swings or 11 vibrates back and forth. Just because you start out swinging in the same direction doesn't mean you will reverse direction at the same time. Each part of the swing has its phases: ups and downs, stops and starts. If your timing is not right you will soon find yourself up when your partner is down, just starting when your partner has already stopped. Even flutes get out of tune as they warm up. People or things that make beautiful music together must continually be adjusted, fine-tuned. Resonance is a delicate thing.

Still, it is amazing how much of the world around us is col- 12 ored by resonance. Each atom resonates with one or, often, several natural frequencies. Sodium light is yellow because the sodium atom resonates with the frequency of radiation we see as the color yellow. Grass is green because all the colors of sunlight except green resonate within the grass and become stuck; green is the only color left to reflect to our eyes. Ultraviolet wavelengths of light become stuck within the molecules of a windowpane and prevent us from getting a suntan indoors. The ozone layer of the atmosphere, like suntan lotion, also absorbs resonant ultraviolet rays and protects us from potentially damaging light.

Resonance determines what is transparent, what is in- 13 visible, what we see and hear. Tuning into a radio or television station merely means putting your receiver on the same wavelength as the station's transmitter. In the process of tuning into one channel, of course, we ignore all the others. We do the same thing when we tune in to certain people and ideas. When a woman becomes pregnant she focuses on her condition and sometimes ceases to pay attention to anything else. Teenagers tune into teen-agers; kids into other kids.

It's important to have something around that responds 14 when you push against it, of course; a resounding board, so to speak. I never felt so lonely as when I was bringing up my son and all my friends, childless, were bringing up their careers. I'd throw out experiences and insights only to have them land with a thud. My friends had nothing to give back, nothing to reinforce my joys or help to lessen the sting of my sorrows. On the other hand, I felt just as isolated when I was surrounded by women whose lives were exclusively submerged in homes and children. They could not have commiserated with my conflicts even if they had wanted to.

My friend Alice, who is 73, joked that I would never find a 15 compatible neighborhood because I would never find neighbors who shared my eclectic collection of experiences. It reminded me of a middle-aged woman who was visiting a museum I work in and complained that people like herself probably couldn't relate to our teen-age guides. She had a good point. And yet I wonder how many teen-agers have been permanently put off museums by middle-aged guides like myself. And how much nicer it would be if we could vibrate to a large collection of resonances. How sad it would be if we could relate only to people exactly like ourselves.

Resonance determines what goes right through and what 16 sinks in. It even determines what we are. Particles of matter, it turns out, are really just resonances of energy. A certain frequency of vibration and presto! a proton. Change the frequency and presto! you have something else.

Fortunately, in addition to the sharp focus of single reso- 17 nance, we can have a rich spectrum of resonances called harmonics. Harmonics sounds the difference between a twanging string and a violin. Changing our tunes every now and then may not be such a bad idea.

VOCABULARY

paragraph 3: amorphous
paragraph 8: lasers
paragraph 10: precipitate
paragraph 14: commiserated
paragraph 15: eclectic

QUESTIONS

1. What is resonance, and where does Cole first define it? How does she develop this definition in the course of the essay?

2. Cole concludes with the statement that "changing our tunes every now and then may not be such a bad idea." How does she develop this metaphorical statement through the physical resonance of music?

3. What other metaphorical meanings of resonance does Cole discuss? How does she illustrate them?

4. Is the essay an account of the many uses of a single metaphor, or is Cole making a point about people or life through the metaphor of resonance?

SUGGESTIONS FOR WRITING

1. Through experiences and observations of your own, illustrate one of the points Cole makes about resonance. You might begin your essay by restating her definition of resonance and commenting on it.

2. Give the dictionary meaning of each of the following words, then discuss the various metaphorical meanings of one of the words in your own experience:
   a. resilience
   b. flexibility
   c. toughness
   d. tenacity

Diane Ackerman

DIANE ACKERMAN, *poet and essayist, has written numerous articles on natural history, some of which are collected in* The Moon by Whale Light *(1991). Her books of poetry include* Wife of Light *(1978),* Lady Faustus *(1983), and* Reverse Thunder *(1988).* On Extended Wings: An Adventure in Flight *(1985) is a memoir.* A Natural History of Love *(1994) is a companion to* A Natural History of the Senses *(1990), in which her essay on a night launching of the space shuttle appears. Ackerman writes: "We live on the leash of our senses. Although they enlarge us, they also limit and restrain us, but how beautifully."*

Figurative language is one means by which Ackerman helps the reader experience the sensations of the launch.

WATCHING A NIGHT LAUNCH
OF THE SPACE SHUTTLE

A huge glittering tower sparkles across the Florida marshlands. Floodlights reach into the heavens all around it, rolling out carpets of light. Helicopters and jets blink around the launch pad like insects drawn to flame. Oz never filled the sky with such diamond-studded improbability. Inside the cascading lights, a giant trellis holds a slender rocket to its heart, on each side a tall thermos bottle filled with solid fuel the color and feel of a hard eraser, and on its back a sharp-nosed space shuttle, clinging like the young of some exotic mammal. A full moon bulges low in the sky, its face turned toward the launch pad, its mouth open.

On the sober consoles of launch control, numbers count backward toward zero. When numbers vanish, and reverse time ends, something will disappear. Not the shuttle—that will stay with us through eyesight and radar, and be on the minds of dozens of tracking dishes worldwide, rolling their heads as if to relieve the anguish. For hours we have been standing on these Floridian bogs, longing for the blazing rapture of the moment ahead, longing to be jettisoned free from routine, and lifted, like the obelisk we launch, that much nearer the infinite. On the fog-wreathed banks of the Banana River, and by the roadside lookouts, we are waiting: 55,000 people are expected at the Space Center alone.

When floodlights die on the launch pad, camera shutters and mental shutters all open in the same instant. The air feels loose and damp. A hundred thousand eyes rush to one spot, where a glint below the booster rocket flares into a pinwheel of fire, a sparkler held by hand on the Fourth of July. White clouds shoot out in all directions, in a dust storm of flame, a gritty, swirling Sahara, burning from gray-white to an incandescent platinum so raw it makes your eyes squint, to a radiant gold so narcotic you forget how to blink. The air is full of bee stings, prickly and electric. Your pores start to itch. Hair stands up stiff on the back of your neck. It used to be that the launch pad would melt at lift-off, but now 300,000 gallons of water crash from aloft, burst from below. Steam clouds scent the air with a mineral ash. Crazed by reflection, the waterways turn the color of pounded brass. Thick cumulus clouds shimmy and build at ground level, where you don't expect to see thunderheads.

Seconds into the launch, an apricot *whoosh* pours out in spasms, like the rippling quarters of a palomino, and now out-bleaches the sun, as clouds rise and pile like a Creation scene. Birds leap into the air along with moths and dragonflies and gnats and other winged creatures, all driven to panic by the clamor: booming, crackling, howling downwind. What is flight, that it can take place in the fragile wings of a moth, whose power station is a heart small as a computer chip? What is flight, that it can groan upward through 4.5 million pounds of dead weight on a colossal gantry? Close your eyes, and you hear the deafening *rat-a-tat-tat* of firecrackers, feel them arcing against your chest. Open your eyes, and you see a huge steel muscle dripping fire, as seven million pounds of thrust pauses a moment on a silver haunch, and then the bedlam clouds let rip. Iron struts blow over the launch pad like newspapers, and shock waves roll out, pounding their giant fists, pounding the marshes where birds shriek and fly, pounding against your chest, where a heart already rapid begins running clean away from you. The air feels tight as a drum, the molecules bouncing. Suddenly the space shuttle leaps high over the marsh-lands, away from the now frantic laughter of the loons, away from the reedy delirium of the insects and the open-mouthed awe of the spectators, many of whom are crying, as it rises on a waterfall of flame 700 feet long, shooting colossal sparks as it climbs in a golden halo that burns deep into memory.

Only ten minutes from lift-off, it will leave the security blan-ket of our atmosphere, and enter an orbit 184 miles up. This is not miraculous. After all, we humans began in an early tantrum of the universe, when our chemical makeup first took form. We evolved through accidents, happenstance, near misses, and good luck. We developed language, forged cities, mustered nations. Now we change the course of rivers and move mountains; we hold back trillions of tons of water with cement dams. We break into human chests and heads; operate on beating hearts and thinking brains. What is defying gravity compared to that? In orbit, there will be no night and day, no up and down. No one will have their "feet on the ground." No joke will be "earthy." No point will be "timely." No thrill will be "out of this world." In orbit, the sun will rise every hour and a half, and there will be 112 days to each week. But then time has always been one of our boldest and most ingenious inventions, and, when you think about it, one of the least plausible of our fictions.

Lunging to the east out over the water, the shuttle rolls 6 slowly onto its back, climbing at three g's, an upshooting torch, twisting an umbilical of white cloud beneath it. When the two solid rockets fall free, they hover to one side like bright red quotation marks, beginning an utterance it will take four days to finish. For over six minutes of seismic wonder it is still visible, this star we hurl up at the star-studded sky. What is a neighborhood? one wonders. Is it the clump of wild daisies beside the Banana River, in which moths hover and dive without the aid of rockets? For large minds, the Earth is a small place. Not small enough to exhaust in one lifetime, but a compact home, cozy, buoyant, a place to cherish, the spectral center of our life. But how could we stay at home forever?

VOCABULARY

paragraph 1: Oz, trellis
paragraph 2: console, obelisk
paragraph 3: incandescent
paragraph 4: palomino, gantry, arcing, haunch, bedlam, reedy
paragraph 5: tantrum, happenstance, plausible
paragraph 6: umbilical, seismic

QUESTIONS

1. What similes and metaphors help to describe the launch pad in paragraph 1? What use does Ackerman make of personification?

2. What similes, metaphors, and personifications help her describe the launch in paragraphs 3 and 4?

3. How do these and other figures help Ackerman express her feelings about the launch?

4. What central idea or thesis does she develop? Where does she first state it? What images and figures help her to express it?

SUGGESTIONS FOR WRITING

1. Write several paragraphs describing an exciting event you once witnessed. Rewrite your description, heightening it through similes, metaphors, and other figures. Keep your audience in mind as you write.

2. Analyze the use Rachel Carson makes of figurative language in one or two paragraphs of her description of the Maine coast (pp. 485–488).

3. Analyze the figurative language in a series of automobile or cosmetic ads, or those for another product. Comment on the effectiveness of the language.

25

Euphemism and Jargon

We hear much today about the abuse of language—particularly about euphemism and equivocation like that cited by George Orwell in his classic essay "Politics and the English Language":

> Defenseless villages are bombarded from the air, the inhabitants driven out into the countryside, the cattle machine-gunned, the huts set on fire with incendiary bullets: this is called *pacification*. Millions of peasants are robbed of their farms and sent trudging along the roads with no more than they can carry: this is called *transfer of population* or *rectification of frontiers*.

Writing in 1946, Orwell bluntly tells his readers that "In our time, political speech and writing are largely the defense of the indefensible," and he adds that this language "has to consist largely of euphemism, question-begging, and sheer cloudy vagueness." We can guess what Orwell would have said about political language in our own time—about such phrases as "credibility gap" and "positive reference input" to describe the reputations of office holders and candidates, and in nonpolitical discourse, "learning resource centers" and "interfaces between student and teacher" to describe libraries and conferences. Such vague and pretentious language can be comical, as Russell Baker shows in his retelling of "Little Red Riding Hood" (see pp. 516–518), but as Orwell explains, the abuses of language have consequences: ". . . if thought corrupts language, language can also corrupt thought."

Every profession and trade has a special language—technical words and, as Perri Klass shows, sometimes coded expressions—making communication efficient and precise. "It would be well if *jargon* could be confined to the first sense," H.W. Fowler says in *Modern English Usage*, referring to this professional language. "There is plenty

510

of work for it there alone, so copiously does jargon of this sort breed nowadays, especially in the newer sciences such as psychology and sociology, and so readily does it escape from its proper sphere to produce popularized technicalities—words that cloud the minds alike of those who use them and those who read them."

Perri Klass

> PERRI KLASS *graduated from* Harvard Medical School *in* 1986. *She describes her experiences there in* A Not Entirely Benign Procedure (1987), *in which the following essay appears. Klass writes about her experiences as a Boston pediatrician in* Baby Doctor (1992). *She is also the author of* I Am Having an Adventure (1986), *a collection of stories, and a novel* Other Women's Children (1990).

LEARNING THE LANGUAGE

"Mrs. Tolstoy is your basic LOL in NAD, admitted for a soft rule-out MI," the intern announces. I scribble that on my patient list. In other words, Mrs. Tolstoy is a Little Old Lady in No Apparent Distress who is in the hospital to make sure she hasn't had a heart attack (rule out a Myocardial Infarction). And we think it's unlikely that she has had a heart attack (a *soft* rule-out).

If I learned nothing else during my first three months of working in the hospital as a medical student, I learned endless jargon and abbreviations. I started out in a state of primeval innocence, in which I didn't even know that "s̄ CP, SOB, N/V" meant "without chest pain, shortness of breath, or nausea and vomiting." By the end I took the abbreviations so much for granted that I would complain to my mother the English professor, "And can you believe I had to put down *three* NG tubes last night?"

"You'll have to tell me what an NG tube is if you want me to sympathize properly," my mother said. NG, nasogastric—isn't it obvious?

I picked up not only the specific expressions but also the ₄ patterns of speech and the grammatical conventions; for example, you never say that a patient's blood pressure fell or that his cardiac enzymes rose. Instead, the patient is always the subject of the verb: "He dropped his pressure." "He bumped his enzymes." This sort of construction probably reflects the profound irritation of the intern when the nurses come in the middle of the night to say that Mr. Dickinson has disturbingly low blood pressure. "Oh, he's gonna hurt me bad tonight," the intern might say, inevitably angry at Mr. Dickinson for dropping his pressure and creating a problem.

When chemotherapy fails to cure Mrs. Bacon's cancer, what ₅ we say is, "Mrs. Bacon failed chemotherapy."

"Well, we've already had one hit today, and we're up next, ₆ but at least we've got mostly stable players on our team." This means that our team (group of doctors and medical students) has already gotten one new admission today, and it is our turn again, so we'll get whoever is admitted next in emergency, but at least most of the patients we already have are fairly stable, that is, unlikely to drop their pressures or in any other way get suddenly sicker and hurt us bad. Baseball metaphor is pervasive. A no-hitter is a night without any new admissions. A player is always a patient—a nitrate player is a patient on nitrates, a unit player is a patient in the intensive care unit, and so on, until you reach the terminal player.

It is interesting to consider what it means to be winning, or ₇ doing well, in this perennial baseball game. When the intern hangs up the phone and announces, "I got a hit," that is not cause for congratulations. The team is not scoring points; rather, it is getting hit, being bombarded with new patients. The object of the game from the point of view of the doctors, considering the players for whom they are already responsible, is to get as few new hits as possible.

This special language contributes to a sense of closeness ₈ and professional spirit among people who are under a great deal of stress. As a medical student, I found it exciting to

discover that I'd finally cracked the code, that I could understand what doctors said and wrote, and could use the same
formulations myself. Some people seem to become enamored
of the jargon for its own sake, perhaps because they are so
deeply thrilled with the idea of medicine, with the idea of
themselves as doctors.

I knew a medical student who was referred to by the in- 9
terns on the team as Mr. Eponym because he was so infatu-
ated with eponymous terminology, the more obscure the
better. He never said "capillary pulsations" if he could say
"Quincke's pulses." He would lovingly tell over the multi-
named syndromes—Wolff-Parkinson-White, Lown-Ganong-
Levine, Schönlein-Henoch—until the temptation to suggest
Schleswig-Holstein or Stevenson-Kefauver or Baskin-Robbins
became irresistible to his less reverent colleagues.

And there is the jargon that you don't ever want to hear 10
yourself using. You know that your training is changing you,
but there are certain changes you think would be going a little
too far.

The resident was describing a man with devastating termi- 11
nal pancreatic cancer. "Basically he's CTD," the resident concluded. I reminded myself that I had resolved not to be shy
about asking when I didn't understand things. "CTD?" I asked
timidly.

The resident smirked at me. "Circling The Drain." 12

The images are vivid and terrible. "What happened to Mrs. 13
Melville?"

"Oh, she boxed last night." To box is to die, of course. 14

Then there are the more pompous locutions that can make 15
the beginning medical student nervous about the effects of
medical training. A friend of mine was told by his resident, "A
pregnant woman with sickle-cell represents a failure of genetic
counseling."

Mr. Eponym, who tried hard to talk like the doctors, once 16
explained to me, "An infant is basically a brainstem preparation." The term "brainstem preparation," as used in neuro-
logical research, refers to an animal whose higher brain

functions have been destroyed so that only the most primitive reflexes remain, like the sucking reflex, the startle reflex, and the rooting reflex.

And yet at other times the harshness dissipates into a strangely elusive euphemism. "As you know, this is a not entirely benign procedure," some doctor will say, and that will be understood to imply agony, risk of complications, and maybe even a significant mortality rate. 17

The more extreme forms aside, one most important function of medical jargon is to help doctors maintain some distance from their patients. By reformulating a patient's pain and problems into a language that the patient doesn't even speak, I suppose we are in some sense taking those pains and problems under our jurisdiction and also reducing their emotional impact. This linguistic separation between doctors and patients allows conversations to go on at the bedside that are unintelligible to the patient. "Naturally, we're worried about adeno-CA," the intern can say to the medical student, and lung cancer need never be mentioned. 18

I learned a new language this past summer. At times it thrills me to hear myself using it. It enables me to understand my colleagues, to communicate effectively in the hospital. Yet I am uncomfortably aware that I will never again notice the peculiarities and even atrocities of medical language as keenly as I did this summer. There may be specific expressions I manage to avoid, but even as I remark them, promising myself I will never use them, I find that this language is becoming my professional speech. It no longer sounds strange in my ears—or coming from my mouth. And I am afraid that as with any new language, to use it properly you must absorb not only the vocabulary but also the structure, the logic, the attitudes. At first you may notice these new and alien assumptions every time you put together a sentence, but with time and increased fluency you stop being aware of them at all. And as you lose that awareness, for better or for worse, you move closer and closer to being a doctor instead of just talking like one. 19

VOCABULARY

paragraph 1: intern
paragraph 2: primeval
paragraph 4: cardiac enzymes
paragraph 6: nitrates
paragraph 8: enamored
paragraph 9: eponym(ous), capillary, syndrome
paragraph 15: locution, sickle-cell (anemia)
paragraph 16: brainstem
paragraph 17: euphemism, dissipates
paragraph 19: atrocities, assumptions, fluency

QUESTIONS

1. In what ways is the special language or medical jargon Klass describes useful to doctors and medical students?

2. In what way did the pregnant woman with sickle-cell anemia represent "a failure of genetic counseling" to the resident (paragraph 15)? What point is Klass making in citing this statement?

3. What uses of medical jargon does Klass criticize? What uses if any does she praise? Is she critical of the doctor who refers to "a not entirely benign procedure" (paragraph 17)? Is she critical of doctors who seek to distance themselves from patients? Is she saying that all doctors do?

4. Is Klass critical of herself in mastering the language and putting it to use?

SUGGESTIONS FOR WRITING

1. Like Klass, you have probably had to learn a special language in beginning a course of study or training for a job. Describe how you learned the language and what uses you made of it. Then discuss gains or losses in having learned it.

2. Analyze the special language or jargon in several paragraphs from a textbook in one of your courses. Discuss what uses this language serves, pointing out any terms for which simpler words can be substituted without loss of meaning.

3. Rewrite a paragraph of a business contract using simpler words and sentences. Then discuss what is gained or lost in clarity and precision in rewriting the paragraph.

4. Analyze a published speech of a major political figure (in *Vital Speeches, Congressional Record,* the *New York Times* or another newspaper of record). Comment on the uses of euphemism, political jargon, and other language that you consider unfair or dishonest. Give your reasons, showing how the issue could be discussed in fair, honest language.

Russell Baker

RUSSELL BAKER *began his career in journalism as a reporter for the* Baltimore Sun, *and in 1954 began his long association with the* New York Times. *His column for the* Times *began in 1962. Baker is a keen observer of life in America and, as the essay reprinted here shows, a satirist of the pretentious language we often speak and write. His essays are collected in a number of books, including* All Things Considered *(1965),* So This Is Depravity *(1980), and* There's a Country in My Cellar *(1990). Baker has written about his life in* Growing Up *(1983) and* The Good Times *(1989). In 1979 he was awarded the Pulitzer Prize for Journalism.*

LITTLE RED RIDING HOOD REVISITED

In an effort to make the classics accessible to contemporary   1
readers, I am translating them into the modern American language. Here is the translation of "Little Red Riding Hood":

Once upon a point in time, a small person named Little Red   2
Riding Hood initiated plans for the preparation, delivery and transportation of foodstuffs to her grandmother, a senior citizen residing at a place of residence in a forest of indeterminate dimension.

In the process of implementing this program, her incursion   3
into the forest was in mid-transportation process when it attained interface with an alleged perpetrator. This individual, a wolf, made inquiry as to the whereabouts of Little Red Riding Hood's goal as well as inferring that he was desirous of

ascertaining the contents of Little Red Riding Hood's food-stuffs basket, and all that.

"It would be inappropriate to lie to me," the wolf said, dis- 4
playing his huge jaw capability. Sensing that he was a mass of repressed hostility intertwined with acute alienation, she indicated.

"I see you indicating," the wolf said, "but what I don't see is 5
whatever it is you're indicating at, you dig?"

Little Red Riding Hood indicated more fully, making one 6
thing perfectly clear—to wit, that it was to her grandmother's residence and with a consignment of foodstuffs that her mission consisted of taking her to and with.

At this point in time the wolf moderated his rhetoric and 7
proceeded to grandmother's residence. The elderly person was then subjected to the disadvantages of total consumption and transferred to residence in the perpetrator's stomach.

"That will raise the old woman's consciousness," the wolf 8
said to himself. He was not a bad wolf, but only a victim of an oppressive society, a society that not only denied wolves' rights, but actually boasted of its capacity for keeping the wolf from the door. An interior malaise made itself manifest inside the wolf.

"Is that the national malaise I sense within my digestive 9
tract?" wondered the wolf. "Or is it the old person seeking to retaliate for her consumption by telling wolf jokes to my duo-denum?" It was time to make a judgment. The time was now, the hour had struck, the body lupine cried out for decision. The wolf was up to the challenge. He took two stomach powders right away and got into bed.

The wolf had adopted the abdominal-distress recovery pos- 10
ture when Little Red Riding Hood achieved his presence.

"Grandmother," she said, "your ocular implements are of an 11
extraordinary order of magnitude."

"The purpose of this enlarged viewing capability," said the 12
wolf, "is to enable your image to register a more precise impression upon my sight systems."

"In reference to your ears," said Little Red Riding Hood, "it 13
is noted with the deepest respect that far from being under-
privileged, their elongation and enlargement appear to qualify
you for unparalleled distinction."

"I hear you loud and clear, kid," said the wolf, "but what 14
about these new choppers?"

"If it is not inappropriate," said Little Red Riding Hood, "it 15
might be observed that with your new miracle masticating
products you may even be able to chew taffy again."

This observation was followed by the adoption of an aggres- 16
sive posture on the part of the wolf and the assertion that it
was also possible for him, due to the high efficiency ratio of his
jaw, to consume little persons, plus, as he stated, his firm determination to do so at once without delay and with all due
process and propriety, notwithstanding the fact that the ingestion of one entire grandmother had already provided twice his
daily recommended cholesterol intake.

There ensued flight by Little Red Riding Hood accompanied 17
by pursuit in respect to the wolf and a subsequent intervention
on the part of a third party, heretofore unnoted in the record.

Due to the firmness of the intervention, the wolf's stomach 18
underwent ax-assisted aperture with the result that Red Riding
Hood's grandmother was enabled to be removed with only
minor discomfort.

The wolf's indigestion was immediately alleviated with such 19
effectiveness that he signed a contract with the intervening
third party to perform with grandmother in a television commercial demonstrating the swiftness of this dramatic relief for
stomach discontent.

"I'm going to be on television," cried grandmother. 20

And they all joined her happily in crying, "What a 21
phenomena!"

VOCABULARY

paragraph 2: initiated, indeterminate, dimension
paragraph 3: implementing, incursion, interface, alleged,
perpetrator, ascertaining

paragraph 4: intertwined, alienation
paragraph 6: consignment
paragraph 7: rhetoric
paragraph 8: interior, malaise, manifest
paragraph 9: lupine
paragraph 11: ocular, implements
paragraph 13: elongation
paragraph 15: masticating
paragraph 16: posture, propriety, ingestion, cholesterol
paragraph 18: aperture
paragraph 19: alleviated
paragraph 21: phenomena

QUESTIONS

1. The faddish language Baker parodies reflects faddish ideas. Here is one example: "An interior malaise made itself manifest inside the wolf." What current attitude toward human predators is Baker satirizing? How does the language help him to satirize the idea?

2. Red Riding Hood prefers the farfetched to the simple, as in the expression "ocular implements." What other examples can you find of euphemism, circumlocution, and other faults of diction (see pp. 520–521)?

3. What examples of repetitious phrasing and sentence padding do you find?

4. What kind of advertising language is Baker satirizing toward the end of his version?

5. What is the difference between the wolf's language and Red Riding Hood's? What does the wolf's language tell you about his personality and view of the world?

6. What other ideas is Baker satirizing in his telling of the story?

SUGGESTION FOR WRITING

Rewrite another fairy tale in the modish language of advertising or other contemporary jargons and styles. Let your choice of jargon and style make a point—or several points—as Baker's telling of "Little Red Riding Hood" does.

More on Faulty Diction

The following suggestions reflect some of the faults in diction that Russell Baker is satirizing in the essay on pages 516–518.

1. Using the same word more than once in a sentence can be confusing if the senses are different:

   > We were present for the presentation of the award.

   However, we need not avoid repeating a word if the senses are the same. Indeed, substitution can also be confusing:

   > The person who entered was not the individual I was expecting.

   Though *individual* is a popular synonym for *person*, it has other meanings. The substitution may confuse the reader.

2. Needless repetition can make sentences hard to understand:

   > There are necessary skills that writers need to make their ideas easy to understand and comprehensible.

3. Words that overlap in meaning can have the same effect:

   > The result of the survey should produce a change in policy.

   The words *result* and *produce* mean the same thing here. Better:

   > The survey should produce a change in policy.

4. Euphemism—providing a mild or pleasant substitute for a blunt term—can be a source of ambiguity. The euphemism *delinquent* to describe a juvenile criminal or the words *slow* and *retarded* to describe children who have trouble learning or are crippled mentally help us avoid giving pain. What words should we use in speaking about children who have trouble learning or have broken the law? We know the price of speaking bluntly, but also the price of hiding facts.

5. Circumlocution means taking the long way around—in other words, saying something in inflated language: saying "he has difficulty distinguishing the real from the imagined" when we mean "he lies." Euphemisms often depend on inflation of this kind.

6. Equivocal terms are also a source of ambiguity because they have double meanings. The word *exceptional* is widely used to describe bright children as well as crippled ones or children who have broken the law. We need to know what children we are talking about.

7. A cliché is a phrase or saying that has become trite through overuse: *sweet as sugar, conspicuous by his absence, outwore his welcome.* Clichés rob prose of conviction and vigor.

8. Mixed metaphors cause confusion and can be unintentionally funny:

   > Blows to one's pride stick in the craw.

9. Technical words or jargon can also have the same effect. The words *interface* (to describe the boundary between two independent machines) and *software* (to describe accessory equipment) are useful words in computer language. To quote H. W. Fowler, they become jargon in the sense of "talk that is considered both ugly-sounding and hard to understand"—when borrowed to describe other things. A conference is not an "interface," and referring to a book as "software" suggests something mechanical or perhaps dispensable.

Part 5

MATTERS OF STYLE:
THE SENTENCE

Introduction

This part of the book will show you how to make your sentences more effective as you draft and revise your paragraphs and essays. Unity and proper emphasis are just as important in sentences as they are in paragraphs. In fact, sentences can be loosely viewed as miniature paragraphs. For example, in the same way that the topic sentence of a paragraph states the core idea that the remainder of the paragraph develops, the main clause of a simple or complex sentence states the core idea that the rest of the sentence develops through its modifiers:

> I *heard* instead the shriek of brakes, the heavy throbbing of the once-a-day Braniff airliner into Minot, the shattering sirens born of war, the honk of a diesel locomotive which surely cannot call to faraway places the heart of a wakeful boy like the old steam whistle in the night. (Eric Sevareid, "Velva, North Dakota" [italics added])

The core subject and verb of this complex sentence (I *heard*) is completed by a series of modified objects—the final object further modified by a lengthy subordinate clause beginning with *which*.

Just as a series of main ideas combine in a single paragraph, so can simple and compound sentences form single sentences:

> You can walk down the streets of my town now and hear from open windows the intimate voices of the Washington commentators in casual converse on the great affairs of state [*simple sentence: main clause with compound predicate*]; but you cannot hear on Sunday morning the singing in Norwegian of the Lutheran hymns [*simple sentence: main clause with simple predicate*]; the old country seems now part of a world left long behind and the old-country accents grow fainter in the speech of my Velva neighbors [*compound sentence: two main clauses with simple predicates*]. (Sevareid)

And so can main and subordinate ideas, expressed in main and subordinate clauses and their modifiers:

> Attic and screen porch are slowly vanishing [*main clause*] and lovely shades of pastel are painted upon new houses [*main clause*], tints that once would have embarrassed farmer and merchant alike [*subordinate clause modifying the appositive "tints"*]. (Sevareid)

Though the parallel between paragraphs and sentences suggested here is not exact (main clauses do not always contain the most important idea of a sentence), it does suggest that, like

525

paragraphs, sentences build from cores to which subordinate ideas and details relate. And sentences, like paragraphs, also can contain two or more core ideas.

We write as we speak—stressing the core idea of a simple sentence and joining several core ideas into compound ones. We also place modifying words, phrases, and clauses in different positions in writing, as in speech, to gain different kinds of emphasis. In addition, we frequently make special use of the beginning and ending of the simple sentence for emphasis. We can, however, achieve emphasis in other ways. The following sections illustrate these possibilities.

26

Addition and Modification

As a paragraph usually begins with a topic sentence that states the subject or central idea, so the sentence may begin with a main clause that performs a similar job. Here is a sentence from Jane Jacobs' description of a New York street scene:

> Character dancers come on,
>> a strange old man with strings of old shoes over his shoulders,
>> motor-scooter riders with big beards and girl friends who bounce on the back of the scooters and wear their hair long in front of their face as well as behind,
>> drunks who follow the advice of the Hat Council and are always turned out in hats,
>>> but not hats the Council would approve.

The three additions—*strange old man*, *motor-scooter riders*, and *drunks*—make the main clause specific: they name the character dancers. Notice that these *appositives* (adjacent words or phrases that explain or identify another word) are considerably longer than the main clause. Notice, too, that the third appositive is itself modified. English sentences can be modified endlessly. They are not, however, because the reader would soon lose sight of the central idea. How long a sentence is often depends on how many ideas and details a reader can grasp.

Jane Jacobs

JANE JACOBS *has influenced current ideas on city architecture through her many articles and books. She has long been critical of city planning that breaks up close-knit neighborhoods like Hudson*

Street with housing projects and "cultural centers" that disperse people. "These thin dispersions lack any reasonable degree of innate
vitality, staying power, or inherent usefulness as settlements," she
writes in her book, The Death and Life of Great American
Cities (1961), which contains the following description of Hudson
Street in lower Manhattan. Jacobs is an effective stylist; her sentences, as this description shows, let us hear a personal voice—as if
she were talking to us informally about the everyday world.

HUDSON STREET

Under the seeming disorder of the old city, wherever the old   1
city is working successfully, is a marvelous order for maintaining the safety of the streets and the freedom of the city. It is a
complex order. Its essence is intricacy of sidewalk use, bringing with it a constant succession of eyes. This order is all composed of movement and change, and although it is life, not
art, we may fancifully call it the art form of the city and liken it
to the dance—not to a simple-minded precision dance with
everyone kicking up at the same time, twirling in unison and
bowing off en masse, but to an intricate ballet in which the
individual dancers and ensembles all have distinctive parts
which miraculously reinforce each other and compose an orderly whole. The ballet of the good city sidewalk never repeats
itself from place to place, and in any one place is always
replete with new improvisations.

The stretch of Hudson Street where I live is each day the   2
scene of an intricate sidewalk ballet. I make my own first entrance into it a little after eight when I put out the garbage can,
surely a prosaic occupation, but I enjoy my part, my little clang,
as the droves of junior high school students walk by the center
of the stage dropping candy wrappers. (How do they eat so
much candy so early in the morning?)

While I sweep up the wrappers I watch the other rituals of   3
morning: Mr. Halpert unlocking the laundry's handcart from its
mooring to a cellar door, Joe Cornacchia's son-in-law stacking
out the empty crates from the delicatessen, the barber bringing out his sidewalk folding chair, Mr. Goldstein arranging the

coils of wire which proclaim the hardware store is open, the wife of the tenement's superintendent depositing her chunky three-year-old with a toy mandolin on the stoop, the vantage point from which he is learning the English his mother cannot speak. Now the primary children, heading for St. Luke's, dribble through to the south; the children for St. Veronica's Cross, heading to the west, and the children for P.S. 41, heading toward the east. Two new entrances are being made from the wings: well-dressed and even elegant women and men with briefcases emerge from doorways and side streets. Most of these are heading for the bus and subways, but some hover on the curbs, stopping taxis which have miraculously appeared at the right moment, for the taxis are part of a wider morning ritual: having dropped passengers from midtown in the downtown financial district, they are now bringing downtowners up to midtown. Simultaneously, numbers of women in housedresses have emerged and as they crisscross with one another they pause for quick conversations that sound with either laughter or joint indignation, never, it seems, anything between. It is time for me to hurry to work too, and I exchange my ritual farewell with Mr. Lofaro, the short, thick-bodied, white-aproned fruit man who stands outside his doorway a little up the street, his arms folded, his feet planted, looking solid as earth itself. We nod; we each glance quickly up and down the street, then look back to each other and smile. We have done this many a morning for more than ten years, and we both know what it means: All is well.

The heart-of-the-day ballet I seldom see, because part of 4 the nature of it is that working people who live there, like me, are mostly gone, filling the roles of strangers on other sidewalks. But from days off, I know enough of it to know that it becomes more and more intricate. Longshoremen who are not working that day gather at the White Horse or the Ideal or the International for beer and conversation. The executives and business lunchers from the industries just to the west throng the Dorgene restaurant and the Lion's Head coffee house; meat-market workers and communications scientists fill the bakery lunchroom. Character dancers come on, a strange old man with strings of old shoes over his shoulders, motor-scooter riders with big beards and girl friends who bounce on the back of the scooters and wear their hair long in front of their faces as well as behind, drunks who follow the advice of the Hat Council and are always turned out in hats, but not hats the Council would approve. Mr. Lacey, the locksmith, shuts up his shop for a while and goes to exchange the time of day with Mr. Slube at the cigar store. Mr. Koochagian, the tailor, waters the luxuriant jungle of plants in his window, gives them a critical look from the outside, accepts a compliment on them from two passers-by, fingers the leaves on the plane tree in front of our house with a thoughtful gardener's appraisal, and crosses the street for a bite at the Ideal where he can keep an eye on customers and wigwag across the message that he is coming. The baby carriages come out, and clusters of everyone from toddlers with dolls to teenagers with homework gather at the stoops.

When I get home after work, the ballet is reaching its crescendo. This is the time of roller skates and stilts and tricycles, and games in the lee of the stoop with bottletops and plastic cowboys; this is the time of bundles and packages, zigzagging from the drug store to the fruit stand and back over to the butcher's; this is the time when teenagers, all dressed up, are pausing to ask if their slips show or their collars look right; this is the time when beautiful girls get out of MG's; this is the time when the fire engines go through; this is the time when anybody you know around Hudson Street will go by. 5

As darkness thickens and Mr. Halpert moors the laundry cart to the cellar door again, the ballet goes on under lights, eddying back and forth but intensifying at the bright spotlight pools of Joe's sidewalk pizza dispensary, the bars, the delicatessen, the restaurant and the drug store. The night workers stop now at the delicatessen, to pick up salami and a container of milk. Things have settled down for the evening but the street and its ballet have not come to a stop. 6

I know the deep night ballet and its season best from wak- 7
ing long after midnight to tend a baby and, sitting in the dark,
seeing the shadows and hearing the sounds of the sidewalk.
Mostly it is a sound like infinitely pattering snatches of party
conversation and, about three in the morning, singing, very
good singing. Sometimes there is sharpness and anger or sad,
sad weeping, or a flurry of search for a string of beads broken.
One night a young man came roaring along, bellowing terrible
language at two girls whom he had apparently picked up and
who were disappointing him. Doors opened, a wary semicircle
formed around him, not too close, until the police came. Out
came the heads, too, along Hudson Street, offering opinion,
"Drunk . . . Crazy . . . A wild kid from the suburbs."*

Deep in the night, I am almost unaware how many people 8
are on the street unless something calls them together, like the
bagpipe. Who the piper was and why he favored our street I
have no idea. The bagpipe just skirled out in the February
night, and as if it were a signal the random, dwindled movements of the sidewalk took on direction. Swiftly, quietly, almost magically a little crowd was there, a crowd that evolved
into a circle with a Highland fling inside it. The crowd could be
seen on the shadowy sidewalk, the dancers could be seen, but
the bagpiper himself was almost invisible because his bravura
was all in his music. He was a very little man in a plain brown
overcoat. When he finished and vanished, the dancers and
watchers applauded, and applause came from the galleries
too, half a dozen of the hundred windows on Hudson Street.
Then the windows closed, and the little crowd dissolved into
the random movements of the night street.

The strangers on Hudson Street, the allies whose eyes help 9
us natives keep the peace of the street, are so many that they
always seem to be different people from one day to the next.
That does not matter. Whether they are so many always-
different people as they seem to be, I do not know. Likely they

---

* He turned out to be a wild kid from the suburbs. Sometimes, on Hudson Street, we are
tempted to believe the suburbs must be a difficult place to bring up children.

are. When Jimmy Rogan fell through a plate-glass window (he was separating some scuffling friends) and almost lost his arm, a stranger in an old T shirt emerged from the Ideal bar, swiftly applied an expert tourniquet and, according to the hospital's emergency staff, saved Jimmy's life. Nobody remembered seeing the man before and no one has seen him since. The hospital was called in this way: a woman sitting on the steps next to the accident ran over to the bus stop, wordlessly snatched a dime from the hand of a stranger who was waiting with his fifteen-cent fare ready, and raced into the Ideal's phone booth. The stranger raced after her to offer the nickel too. Nobody remembered seeing him before, and no one has seen him since. When you see the same stranger three or four times on Hudson Street, you begin to nod. This is almost getting to be an acquaintance, a public acquaintance, of course.

I have made the daily ballet of Hudson Street sound more   10 frenetic than it is, because writing it telescopes it. In real life, it is not that way. In real life, to be sure, something is always going on, the ballet is never at a halt, but the general effect is peaceful and the general tenor even leisurely. People who know well such animated city streets will know how it is. I am afraid people who do not will always have it a little wrong in their heads—like the old prints of rhinoceroses made from travelers' descriptions of rhinoceroses.

On Hudson Street, the same as in the North End of Boston   11 or in any other animated neighborhoods of great cities, we are not innately more competent at keeping the sidewalks safe than are the people who try to live off the hostile truce of Turf in a blind-eyed city. We are the lucky possessors of a city order that makes it relatively simple to keep the peace because there are plenty of eyes on the street. But there is nothing simple about that order itself, or the bewildering number of components that go into it. Most of those components are specialized in one way or another. They unite in their joint effect upon the sidewalk, which is not specialized in the least. That is its strength.

QUESTIONS

1. The main clause in the first sentence of paragraph 3 is followed by a series of appositives explaining the *rituals of morning*. How many appositives do you find? Which of them is modified?

2. The colon in the following sentence introduces an addition that explains the main clause:

   > Two new entrances are being made from the wings: well-dressed and even elegant women and men with briefcases emerge from doorways and side streets.

   Does the colon in the succeeding sentence, in paragraph 3, serve the same purpose? What about the colon in the concluding sentence of the paragraph?

3. The second sentence of paragraph 5 might have been divided into four separate sentences. What does Jacobs gain by joining the main clauses through semicolons? Are the semicolons in paragraph 3 used in the same way?

4. Notice that the main clause of the first sentence of paragraph 6 is modified by the opening subordinate clause and by the phrases that follow, beginning with *eddying*. Try rewriting the sentence, beginning with *eddying*. What problems do you face in revising the sentence? Does your revision improve the sentence?

5. What point is Jacobs making about the "daily ballet" of Hudson Street? How do the various details illustrate her point?

6. Jacobs is defining what makes a New York street a neighborhood. How different is this neighborhood from yours?

SUGGESTIONS FOR WRITING

1. Explain why the specialization in each of the "bewildering number of components" that make up the street is the source of its strength. Show how Jacobs illustrates this strength.

2. Develop the following main clauses through addition of your own details. Use colons and semicolons if you wish:

   a. "Deep in the night, I am almost unaware how many people are on the street . . . ."

   b. "The crowd could be seen on the shadowy sidewalk . . . ."

   c. "People who know well such animated streets will know how it is . . . ."

27

Emphasis

The speaker of the following sentence, a witness before a congressional committee, repeats certain phrases and qualifies his ideas in a typical way:

> My experience is that we hold people sometimes in jail, young people in jail, for days at a time with a complete lack of concern of the parents, if they do live in homes where parents live together, a complete lack of concern in many instances on the part of the community or other agencies as to where these young people are or what they are doing.

Sentences as complex and disjointed as this one seems when transcribed are understood easily when spoken. In speaking, we often interrupt the flow of ideas to emphasize a word or phrase or to repeat an idea. Written punctuation sometimes clarifies the points of emphasis, but in a limited way. We cannot depend directly on vocal inflection for clarity and emphasis in writing; we can suggest these inflections by shaping the sentence in accord with ordinary speech patterns. Clearly written sentences stay close to these patterns.

The core of English sentences, we saw, can be expanded, and at length, if each modifier is clearly connected to what precedes it. To achieve special emphasis the writer may vary the sentence even more, perhaps by making special use of the end of the sentence—the position that in English tends to be the most emphatic:

> The cold passed reluctantly from the earth, and the retiring fogs revealed an army stretched out on the hills, *resting*. (Stephen Crane, *The Red Badge of Courage* [italics added])

Or the writer may break up the sentence so that individual ideas and experiences receive separate emphasis:

> The youth stopped. He was transfixed by this terrific medley of all noises. It was as if worlds were being rended. There was the ripping sound of musketry and the breaking crash of the artillery. (Crane)

534

English word order largely controls how we connect subordinate clauses to other elements in a sentence. The position of subordinate clauses that serve as nouns or adjectives (sometimes called noun clauses and adjective clauses) is rather fixed; the position of subordinate clauses that serve as adverbs (sometimes called adverb clauses) is not. The position of the adverb clause depends on its importance as an idea as well as on its length:

> I majored in zoology *because I like working with animals.*
>
> *Because I like working with animals,* I majored in zoology.

The position of the subordinate clause determines what information is stressed. In the first sentence, the subordinate clause seems to express the more important idea because it follows the main clause. In the second sentence, the main clause receives the emphasis. But the end of the sentence will not take the thrust of meaning if ideas appearing toward the beginning are given special emphasis.

Our informal spoken sentences show the least variation and depend heavily on coordination. The *stringy sentence* in writing—a series of ideas joined loosely with *and* and other conjunctions—is a heavily coordinated sentence without the usual vocal markers. The sentence *fragment*—a detached phrase or clause, or a sentence missing either a subject or a verb—sometimes derives from the clipped sentences and phrases common in speech.

Mark Twain

MARK TWAIN (*p.* 8) *worked as a river pilot from 1857 to 1861, and wrote about these experiences in* Life on the Mississippi, *published in 1883. Like the boy described in the passage reprinted here, Twain ran away to go on the river, but without immediate success: "Months afterward the hope within me struggled to a reluctant death, and I found myself without an ambition. But I was ashamed to go home." Eventually he did become a cub pilot on a river boat.*

THE STEAMBOATMAN

¹When I was a boy, there was but one permanent ambition among my comrades in our village on the west bank of the

Mississippi River. ²That was, to be a steamboatman. ³We had transient ambitions of other sorts, but they were only transient. ⁴When a circus came and went, it left us all burning to become clowns; the first negro minstrel show that ever came to our section left us all suffering to try that kind of life; now and then we had a hope that, if we lived and were good, God would permit us to be pirates. ⁵These ambitions faded out, each in its turn; but the ambition to be a steamboatman always remained.

⁶Once a day a cheap, gaudy packet arrived upward from St. Louis, and another downward from Keokuk. ⁷Before these events, the day was glorious with expectancy; after them, the day was a dead and empty thing. ⁸Not only the boys, but the whole village, felt this. ⁹After all these years I can picture that old time to myself now, just as it was then: the white town drowsing in the sunshine of a summer's morning; the streets empty, or pretty nearly so; one or two clerks sitting in front of the Water Street stores, with their splint-bottomed chairs tilted back against the walls, chins on breasts, hats slouched over their faces, asleep—with shingle-shavings enough around to show what broke them down; a sow and a litter of pigs loafing along the sidewalk, doing a good business in watermelon rinds and seeds; two or three lonely little freight piles scattered about the "levee"; a pile of "skids" on the slope of the stone-paved wharf, and the fragrant town drunkard asleep in the shadow of them; two or three wood flats at the head of the wharf, but nobody to listen to the peaceful lapping of the wavelets against them; the great Mississippi, the majestic, the magnificent Mississippi, rolling its mile-wide tide along, shining in the sun; the dense forest away on the other side; the "point" above the town, and the "point" below, bounding the river-glimpse and turning it into a sort of sea, and withal a very still and brilliant and lonely one. ¹⁰Presently a film of dark smoke appears above one of those remote "points"; instantly a negro drayman, famous for his quick eye and prodigious voice, lifts up the cry, "S-t-e-a-m-boat a-comin'!" and the scene changes! ¹¹The town drunkard stirs, the

clerks wake up, a furious clatter of drays follows, every house and store pours out a human contribution, and all in a twinkling the dead town is alive and moving. [12]Drays, carts, men, boys, all go hurrying from many quarters to a common center, the wharf. [13]Assembled there, the people fasten their eyes upon the coming boat as upon a wonder they are seeing for the first time. [14]And the boat *is* rather a handsome sight, too. [15]She is long and sharp and trim and pretty; she has two tall, fancy-topped chimneys, with a gilded device of some kind swung between them; a fanciful pilot-house, all glass and "gingerbread," perched on top of the "texas" deck* behind them; the paddleboxes are gorgeous with a picture or with gilded rays above the boat's name; the boiler-deck, the hurricane-deck, and the texas deck are fenced and ornamented with clean white railings; there is a flag gallantly flying from the jack-staff; the furnace doors are open and the fires glaring bravely; the upper decks are black with passengers; the captain stands by the big bell, calm, imposing, the envy of all; great volumes of the blackest smoke are rolling and tumbling out of the chimneys—a husbanded grandeur created with a bit of pitch-pine just before arriving at a town; the crew are grouped on the forecastle; the broad stage is run far out over the port bow, and an envied deck-hand stands picturesquely on the end of it with a coil of rope in his hand; the pent steam is screaming through the gaugecocks; the captain lifts his hand, a bell rings, the wheels stop; then they turn back, churning the water to foam, and the steamer is at rest. [16]Then such a scramble as there is to get aboard, and to get ashore, and to take in freight and to discharge freight, all at one and the same time; and such a yelling and cursing as the mates facilitate it all with! [17]Ten minutes later the steamer is under way again, with no flag on the jack-staff and no black smoke issuing from the chimneys. [18]After ten more minutes the town is dead again, and the town drunkard asleep by the skids once more.

---

* *"texas" deck*: The deck above the officers' quarters.

[19]My father was a justice of the peace, and I supposed he possessed the power of life and death over all men, and could hang anybody that offended him. [20]This was distinction enough for me as a general thing; but the desire to be a steamboatman kept intruding, nevertheless. [21]I first wanted to be a cabin-boy, so that I could come out with a white apron on and shake a tablecloth over the side, where all my old comrades could see me; later I thought I would rather be the deck-hand who stood on the end of the stage-plank with the coil of rope in his hand, because he was particularly conspicuous. [22]But these were only daydreams—they were too heavenly to be contemplated as real possibilities. [23]By and by one of our boys went away. [24]He was not heard of for a long time. [25]At last he turned up as apprentice engineer or "striker" on a steamboat. [26]This thing shook the bottom out of all my Sunday-school teachings. [27]That boy had been notoriously worldly, and I just the reverse; yet he was exalted to this eminence, and I left in obscurity and misery. [28]There was nothing generous about this fellow in his greatness. [29]He would always manage to have a rusty bolt to scrub while his boat tarried at our town, and he would sit on the inside guard and scrub it where we all could see him and envy him and loathe him. [30]And whenever his boat was laid up he would come home and swell around the town in his blackest and greasiest clothes, so that nobody could help remembering that he was a steamboatman; and he used all sorts of steamboat technicalities in his talk, as if he were so used to them that he forgot common people could not understand them. [31]He would speak of the "labboard" side of a horse in an easy, natural way that would make one wish he was dead. [32]And he was always talking about "St. Looy" like an old citizen; he would refer casually to occasions when he was "coming down Fourth Street," or when he was "passing by the Planter's House," or when there was a fire and he took a turn on the brakes of "the old Big Missouri"; and then he would go on and lie about how many towns the size of ours were burned down there that day. [33]Two or three of the boys had long been persons of consideration among us because they had been to St.

Louis once and had a vague general knowledge of its wonders, but the day of their glory was over now. [34]They lapsed into a humble silence, and learned to disappear when the ruthless "cub"-engineer approached. [35]This fellow had money, too, and hair-oil. [36]Also an ignorant silver watch and a showy brass watch-chain. [37]He wore a leather belt and used no suspenders. [38]If ever a youth was cordially admired and hated by his comrades, this one was. [39]No girl could withstand his charms. [40]He "cut out" every boy in the village. [41]When his boat blew up at last, it diffused a tranquil contentment among us such as we had not known for months. [42]But when he came home the next week, alive, renowned, and appeared in church all battered up and bandaged, a shining hero, stared at and wondered over by everybody, it seemed to us that the partiality of Providence for an undeserving reptile had reached a point where it was open to criticism.

[43]This creature's career could produce but one result, and it speedily followed. [44]Boy after boy managed to get on the river. [45]The minister's son became an engineer. [46]The doctor's and the postmaster's sons became "mud clerks"*; the wholesale liquor dealer's son became a barkeeper on a boat; four sons of the chief merchant, and two sons of the county judge, became pilots. [47]Pilot was the grandest position of all. [48]The pilot, even in those days of trivial wages, had a princely salary—from a hundred and fifty to two hundred and fifty dollars a month, and no board to pay. [49]Two months of his wages would pay a preacher's salary for a year. [50]Now some of us were left disconsolate. [51]We could not get on the river—at least our parents would not let us.

[52]So, by and by, I ran away. [53]I said I would never come home again till I was a pilot and could come in glory. [54]But somehow I could not manage it. [55]I went meekly aboard a few of the boats that lay packed together like sardines at the long St. Louis wharf, and humbly inquired for the pilots, but got only a cold shoulder and short words from mates and clerks. [56]I had to

---

* *mud clerk*: The second clerk on river steamers who went ashore to take account of freight.

make the best of this sort of treatment for the time being, but I had comforting day-dreams of a future when I should be a great and honored pilot, with plenty of money, and could kill some of these mates and clerks and pay for them.

QUESTIONS

1. How does Twain give equal emphasis to the many sights described in sentence 9? How do sentences 15 and 46 resemble sentence 9 in structure and emphasis?
2. How does sentence 11 build in emphasis? Sentence 16?
3. Rewrite sentence 19, subordinating one of the clauses. How does your revision affect the emphasis of ideas in the original sentence?
4. Combine sentences 35, 36, and 37 into a single sentence. What does your revision gain or lose in emphasis?
5. How does Twain build sentences 41 and 42 to give the end of the sentences the greatest emphasis?
6. Where does Twain mix short and long sentences to emphasize certain perceptions and feelings?
7. What emotions does Twain convey, and what examples can you cite of how sentence construction conveys these emotions and creates a mood?
8. How well does Twain convey the sense of childhood aspiration and frustration?

SUGGESTIONS FOR WRITING

1. Rewrite several of Twain's sentences, giving different emphasis to his ideas through a different coordination and subordination of sentence elements.
2. Twain says in his autobiography: "The truth is, a person's memory has no more sense than his conscience and no appreciation whatever of values and proportions." Discuss how his picture of the Missouri town and the coming of the steamboat illustrates this statement. Then develop the same idea from your own personal experience and observation.

28

Loose and Periodic Sentences

Sentences are sometimes classified as loose or periodic to distinguish two important kinds of emphasis: the use made of the beginning or the end of the sentence. The loose sentence begins with the core idea, explanatory and qualifying phrases and clauses trailing behind:

> It was not a screeching noise, only an intermittent hump-hump as if the bird had to recall his grievance each time before he repeated it. (Flannery O'Connor, *The Violent Bear It Away*)

If the ideas that follow the core are afterthoughts, or inessential details, the sentence will seem "loose"—easy and relaxed in its movement, perhaps even plodding if the content of the sentence permits:

> His eyes glittered like open pits of light as he moved across the sand, dragging his crushed shadow behind him. (Flannery O'Connor)

A subordinate element will not seem unemphatic or plodding, however, if it expresses a strong action or idea and the details cumulate:

> He beat louder and louder, bamming at the same time with his free fist until he felt he was shaking the house. (Flannery O'Connor)

Opening with modifiers or with a series of appositives, the periodic sentence ends with the core:

> Living this way by the creek, where the light appears and vanishes on the water, where muskrats surface and dive, and redwings scatter, I have come to know a special side of nature. (Annie Dillard, *Pilgrim at Tinker Creek*)

The strongly periodic sentence is usually reserved for moderate or unusually strong emphasis:

Partway down the long, very steep slope of Loma Vista Drive, descending through Beverly Hills, with the city of Los Angeles spread out far below the houses of sparkling opulence on either side, there is a sign warning "Use Lowest Gear" and, shortly after that, a sign that says "Runaway Vehicle Escape Lane 600 Feet Ahead." (James Stevenson, "Loma Vista Drive")

Watching the animals come and go, and feeling the land swell up to meet them and then feeling it grow still at their departure, I came to think of the migrations as breath, as the land breathing. (Barry Lopez, *Arctic Dreams*)

Most contemporary English sentences fall between the extremely loose and the extremely periodic. Compound sentences seem loose when succeeding clauses serve as afterthoughts or qualifications rather than as ideas equal in importance to the opening idea:

I was very conscious of the crowds at first, almost despairing to have to perform in front of them, and I never got used to it. (George Plimpton, *Paper Lion*)

Periodic sentences are used sparingly, with emphasis distributed more often throughout the whole sentence, as in Dillard's sentence above. Sometimes two moderately periodic sentences will be coordinated, with a corresponding distribution of emphasis:

Though reliable narration is by no means the only way of conveying to the audience the facts on which dramatic irony is based, it is a useful way, and in some works, works in which no one but the author can conceivably know what needs to be known, it may be indispensable. (Wayne C. Booth, *The Rhetoric of Fiction*)

John Steinbeck

JOHN STEINBECK (1902–1968) *was born in the Salinas Valley of California, the setting of many of his stories and novels. In 1962 he received the Nobel Prize for Literature—a testimony to the great reputation of his fiction throughout the world. His greatest work is undoubtedly* The Grapes of Wrath—*an account of the Joads, a family who, dispossessed of their Oklahoma farm during the Great Depression, make an arduous journey to California. Steinbeck's account of Depression poverty and the exploitation of migrant work-ers—awarded the Pulitzer Prize in 1939—remains a powerful one. Toward the beginning of the novel, Steinbeck describes a turtle mak-ing its own difficult journey—a hint of what is to follow. Steinbeck's sentences are notable for the various ways they convey the movement of the turtle up the embankment.*

THE TURTLE

[1]The sun lay on the grass and warmed it, and in the shade under the grass the insects moved, ants and ant lions to set traps for them, grasshoppers to jump into the air and flick their yellow wings for a second, sow bugs like little armadillos, plod-ding restlessly on many tender feet. [2]And over the grass at the roadside a land turtle crawled, turning aside for nothing, drag-ging his high-domed shell over the grass. [3]His hard legs and yellow-nailed feet threshed slowly through the grass, not really walking, but boosting and dragging his shell along. [4]The barley beards slid off his shell, and the clover burrs fell on him and rolled to the ground. [5]His horny beak was partly open, and his fierce, humorous eyes, under brows like fingernails, stared straight ahead. [6]He came over the grass leaving a beaten trail behind him, and the hill, which was the highway embankment, reared up ahead of him. [7]For a moment he stopped, his head held high. [8]He blinked and looked up and down. [9]At last he started to climb the embankment. [10]Front clawed feet reached forward but did not touch. [11]The hind feet kicked his shell along, and it scraped on the grass, and on the gravel. [12]As the embankment grew steeper and steeper, the more frantic were the efforts of the land turtle. [13]Pushing hind legs strained and slipped, boosting the shell along, and the horny head pro-truded as far as the neck could stretch. [14]Little by little the shell slid up the embankment until at last a parapet cut straight across its line of march, the shoulder of the road, a concrete wall four inches high. [15]As though they worked independently the hind legs pushed the shell against the wall. [16]The head upraised and peered over the wall to the broad smooth plain of cement. [17]Now the hands, braced on top of the wall, strained

and lifted, and the shell came slowly up and rested its front end on the wall. [18]For a moment the turtle rested. [19]A red ant ran into the shell, into the soft skin inside the shell, and suddenly head and legs snapped in, and the armored tail clamped in sideways. [20]The red ant was crushed between body and legs. [21]And one head of wild oats was clamped into the shell by a front leg. [22]For a long moment the turtle lay still, and then the neck crept out and the old humorous frowning eyes looked about and the legs and tail came out. [23]The back legs went to work, straining like elephant legs, and the shell tipped to an angle so that the front legs could not reach the level cement plain. [24]But higher and higher the hind legs boosted it, until at last the center of balance was reached, the front tipped down, the front legs scratched at the pavement, and it was up. [25]But the head of wild oats was held by its stem around the front legs.

QUESTIONS

1. The base idea in sentence 2 is *a land turtle crawled*. If this clause were moved to the end of the sentence, what change would occur in focus or meaning?

2. How does the structure of sentence 3 help us visualize the movement of the turtle? Is the sentence loose or periodic?

3. Consider this revision of sentence 7:

   His head held high, he stopped for a moment.

   Is the meaning of the original sentence changed?

4. Combine sentences 7, 8, and 9 into one sentence. What change in meaning, focus, or emphasis occurs?

5. Consider this revision of sentence 11:

   The hind feet kicking his shell along, it scraped on the grass and on the gravel.

   What is gained or lost in meaning or effect by the revision?

6. Sentences 11 and 12 both describe the action of the turtle—moving on the grass at the edge of the embankment, then moving up the steep part. What difference do you see in the structure of these sentences? How does each structure convey the action in a different way?

7. How does the coordinate structure of sentence 23 show that the movement of the legs and the tipping of the shell are not happening at the same time? How could Steinbeck change the structure of the sentence to show the two actions occurring at the same time?

8. How does the structure of sentence 24 help us to visualize the action here?

SUGGESTION FOR WRITING

Steinbeck's turtle seems to many readers symbolic of the Joad family in *The Grapes of Wrath*, the novel in which this description of the turtle appears. Dispossessed of their Oklahoma farm during the Great Depression of the 1930s, they make an arduous journey to California. Discuss the qualities or attitudes that Steinbeck might be symbolizing in the turtle.

ANNIE DILLARD *writes about her life in the Roanoke Valley of Virginia in* Pilgrim at Tinker Creek (1974)—*awarded the Pulitzer Prize in 1975. Dillard later lived in the Pacific Northwest and wrote about Puget Sound in a collection of essays,* Teaching a Stone to Talk (1982). *In* An American Childhood (1987) *she describes her early life in Pittsburgh. Her novel* The Living *was published in 1992. "It's all a matter of keeping my eyes open," Dillard tells us in* Pilgrim at Tinker Creek, *from which the following section is taken. "Nature is like one of those line drawings of a tree that are puzzles for children. Can you find hidden in the leaves a duck, a house, a boy, a bucket, a zebra, and a boot? Specialists can find the most incredibly well-hidden things."*

AT TINKER CREEK

¹Where Tinker Creek flows under the sycamore log bridge to the tear-shaped island, it is slow and shallow, fringed thinly in cattail marsh. ²At this spot an astonishing bloom of life supports vast breeding populations of insects, fish, reptiles, birds, and

mammals. ³On windless summer evenings I stalk along the creek bank or straddle the sycamore log in absolute stillness, watching for muskrats. ⁴The night I stayed too late I was hunched on the log staring spellbound at spreading, reflected stains of lilac on the water. ⁵A cloud in the sky suddenly lighted as if turned on by a switch; its reflection just as suddenly materialized on the water upstream, flat and floating, so that I couldn't see the creek bottom, or life in the water under the cloud. ⁶Downstream, away from the cloud on the water, water turtles smooth as beans were gliding down with the current in a series of easy, weightless push-offs, as men bound on the moon. ⁷I didn't know whether to trace the progress of one turtle I was sure of, risking sticking my face in one of the bridge's spider webs made invisible by the gathering dark, or take a chance on seeing the carp, or scan the mudbank in hope of seeing a muskrat, or follow the last of the swallows who caught at my heart and trailed it after them like streamers as they appeared from directly below, under the log, flying upstream with their tails forked, so fast.

⁸But shadows spread, and deepened, and stayed. ⁹After thousands of years we're still strangers to darkness, fearful aliens in an enemy camp with our arms crossed over our chests. ¹⁰I stirred. ¹¹A land turtle on the bank, startled, hissed the air from its lungs and withdrew into its shell. ¹²An uneasy pink here, an unfathomable blue there, gave great suggestion of lurking beings. ¹³Things were going on. ¹⁴I couldn't see whether that sere rustle I heard was a distant rattlesnake, slit-eyed, or a nearby sparrow kicking in the dry flood debris slung at the foot of a willow. ¹⁵Tremendous action roiled the water everywhere I looked, big action, inexplicable. ¹⁶A tremor welled up beside a gaping muskrat burrow in the bank and I caught my breath, but no muskrat appeared. ¹⁷The ripples continued to fan upstream with a steady, powerful thrust. ¹⁸Night was knitting over my face an eyeless mask, and I still sat transfixed. ¹⁹A distant airplane, a delta wing out of nightmare, made a gliding shadow on the creek's bottom that looked like a stingray cruising upstream. ²⁰At once a black fin slit the pink cloud on the water, shearing it

in two. [21]The two halves merged together and seemed to dissolve before my eyes. [22]Darkness pooled in the cleft of the creek and rose, as water collects in a well. [23]Untamed, dreaming lights flickered over the sky. [24]I saw hints of hulking underwater shadows, two pale splashes out of the water, and round ripples rolling close together from a blackened center.

[25]At last I stared upstream where only the deepest violet remained of the cloud, a cloud so high its underbelly still glowed feeble color reflected from a hidden sky lighted in turn by a sun halfway to China. [26]And out of that violet, a sudden enormous black body arced over the water. [27]I saw only a cylindrical sleekness. [28]Head and tail, if there was a head and tail, were both submerged in cloud. [29]I saw only one ebony fling, a headlong dive to darkness; then the waters closed, and the lights went out.

[30]I walked home in a shivering daze, up hill and down. [31]Later I lay open-mouthed in bed, my arms flung wide at my sides to steady the whirling darkness. [32]At this latitude I'm spinning 836 miles an hour round the earth's axis; I often fancy I feel my sweeping fall as a breakneck arc like the dive of dolphins, and the hollow rushing of wind raises hair on my neck and the side of my face. [33]In orbit around the sun I'm moving 64,800 miles an hour. [34]The solar system as a whole, like a merry-go-round unhinged, spins, bobs, and blinks at the speed of 43,200 miles an hour along a course set east of Hercules. [35]Someone has piped, and we are dancing a tarantella until the sweat pours. [36]I open my eyes and I see dark, muscled forms curl out of water, with flapping gills and flattened eyes. [37]I close my eyes and I see stars, deep stars giving way to deeper stars, deeper stars bowing to deepest stars at the crown of an infinite cone.

QUESTIONS

1. To make sentences 9 and 20 periodic, open them with the modifying phrases that conclude them. Do these revisions change the meaning of the sentences or merely change the emphasis?

2. Revise sentences 23 and 33 to put the opening modifiers at the end. What is gained or lost in emphasis?

3. Break sentence 7 into its component parts and combine them into shorter sentences. Then discuss the differences in effect or meaning from the original sentence.

4. How do the following revisions of sentence 11 change the emphasis and effect:

   a. Startled, a land turtle on the bank hissed the air from its lungs and withdrew into its shell.

   b. Hissing the air from its lungs, a startled land turtle on the bank withdrew into its shell.

   c. A land turtle, hissing the air from its lungs, withdrew into its shell, startled.

   Do the words *startled* and *hissing* refer clearly to the turtle in these revisions?

   How does the following revision change the effect of sentence 15?

   > Tremendous action—big action, inexplicable—roiled the water everywhere I looked.

5. How does sentence 37 build in emphasis?

6. What in the experience at Tinker Creek prompts the feelings Dillard describes in the final paragraph? What is the relationship between water and sky?

7. What implied thesis or idea is Dillard developing in the four paragraphs? What sentence comes closest to stating a thesis?

SUGGESTION FOR WRITING

Develop an implied thesis of your own through the details of an outdoor experience. You might build your description to the insight that you reached into the world of nature, as Dillard does.

29

Climax

Periodic sentences achieve climax by delaying the main idea or its completion until the end of the sentence. Even in loose or coordinated sentences, modifying or qualifying phrases and clauses following the main idea can be arranged in the order of rising importance—as in *I came, I saw, I conquered*. Here are sentences of Annie Dillard that do the same:

> But shadows spread, and deepened, and stayed.

> I close my eyes and I see stars, deep stars giving way to deeper stars, deeper stars bowing to deepest stars at the crown of an infinite cone. (*Pilgrim at Tinker Creek*)

A sense of anticipation, promoted through the ideas themselves, is necessary to climax. Anticlimax will result if the culminating idea is less significant than what has gone before. The resulting letdown may be deliberately comic:

> If once a man indulges himself in murder, very soon he comes to think little of robbery; and from robbing he next comes to drinking and Sabbath-breaking, and from that to incivility and procrastination. (Thomas De Quincey, *Supplementary Papers*)

John Updike

Born in Shillington, Pennsylvania, in 1932, JOHN UPDIKE began his long association with The New Yorker *early in his career and has published many of his poems, stories, and essays in that magazine. His collection of stories* The Music School *won the O. Henry Award in 1966. He received the National Book Award in 1963 for his novel* The Centaur *and the Pulitzer Prize and the American Book Award in 1981 for* Rabbit Is Rich. *His novel*

Rabbit at Rest *was awarded the Pulitzer Prize in 1991. The speaker in one of Updike's stories is describing his grandmother as he remembers her from his youth: "At the time I was married, she was in her late seventies, crippled and enfeebled. She had fought a long battle with Parkinson's disease; in my earliest memories of her she is touched with it. Her fingers and back are bent; there is a tremble about her as she moved about through the dark, odd-shaped rooms of our house in the town where I was born." His thoughts turn in this passage to happier days.*

MY GRANDMOTHER

[1]When we were all still alive, the five of us in that kerosene-lit house, on Friday and Saturday nights, at an hour when in the spring and summer there was still abundant light in the air, I would set out in my father's car for town, where my friends lived. [2]I had, by moving ten miles away, at last acquired friends: an illustration of that strange law whereby, like Orpheus leading Eurydice, we achieve our desire by turning our back on it. [3]I had even gained a girl, so that the vibrations were as sexual as social that made me jangle with anticipation as I clowned in front of the mirror in our kitchen, shaving from a basin of stove-heated water, combing my hair with a dripping comb, adjusting my reflection in the mirror until I had achieved just that electric angle from which my face seemed beautiful and everlastingly, by the very volumes of air and sky and grass that lay mutely banked about our home, beloved. [4]My grandmother would hover near me, watching fearfully, as she had when I was a child, afraid that I would fall from a tree. [5]Delirious, humming, I would swoop and lift her, lift her like a child, crooking one arm under her knees and cupping the other behind her back. [6]Exultant in my height, my strength, I would lift that frail brittle body weighing perhaps a hundred pounds and twirl with it in my arms while the rest of the family watched with startled smiles of alarm. [7]Had I stumbled, or dropped her, I might have broken her back, but my joy always proved a secure cradle. [8]And whatever irony was in the impulse, whatever implicit contrast between this ancient husk, scarcely female, and the pliant,

warm girl I would embrace before the evening was done, direct delight flooded away: I was carrying her who had carried me, I was giving my past a dance, I had lifted the anxious caretaker of my childhood from the floor, I was bringing her with my boldness to the edge of danger, from which she had always sought to guard me.

QUESTIONS

1. How does Updike construct sentence 3 to take advantage of the strong terminal position? Does the context justify the double emphasis given to *beloved*?

2. Sentence 3 develops through an accumulation of detail. Does the sentence develop a single idea? Could Updike break it up without interrupting the meaning or disturbing the effect?

3. What technique aids in achieving the climax in sentences 5 and 8? Does the same kind of sentence construction achieve it?

SUGGESTIONS FOR WRITING

1. Describe an episode involving a close relative or friend that reveals a special relationship. Let your details reveal the relationship; do not state it directly.

2. Compare Updike's depiction of his grandmother with N. Scott Momaday's depiction of his (p. 111), focusing on the chief similarity or difference in attitude or personal relationship.

30

Parallelism

The italicized words in the following sentence are parallel in structure; that is, they perform the same grammatical function in the sentence and, as infinitives, are the same in form:

> So long as I remain alive and well I shall continue *to feel* strongly about prose style, *to love* the surface of the earth, and *to take* a pleasure in solid objects and scraps of useless information. (George Orwell, *Why I Write* [italics added])

In speaking and writing, we make elements such as these infinitives parallel naturally. No matter how many words separate them, we continue the pattern we start. Indeed, our "sentence sense" tells us when a pattern has been interrupted. We know something is wrong when we read

> I shall continue to feel strongly about prose style, to love the surface of the earth, and taking pleasure in solid objects and scraps of useless information.

Parallelism is an important means to concision and focus in sentences. It also allows us to make additions to the sentence without loss of clarity.

A special use of parallelism is the balancing of similar ideas in a sentence for special emphasis:

> Violence ends by defeating itself. It creates bitterness in the survivors and brutality in the destroyers. (Martin Luther King, Jr., *Nonviolent Resistance*)

Notice that the parallel phrases here are of the same weight and length. Writers can balance clauses and occasionally whole sentences in the same way:

> Every landscape in the world is full of these exact and beautiful adaptations, by which an animal fits into its environment like one cog-wheel into another. The sleeping hedgehog waits for the spring to burst its metabolism into life. The humming-bird beats the air and

552

dips its needle-fine beak into hanging blossoms. Butterflies mimic leaves and even noxious creatures to deceive their predators. The mole plods through the ground as if he had been designed as a mechanical shuttle. (J. Bronowski, *The Ascent of Man*)

The marked rhythm of these sentences creates a highly formal effect by slowing the tempo. Such exact balance interrupts the natural flow of the sentence, giving emphasis to most or all of its parts. For this reason it is exceptional to find sentences as studied and formal as these in modern writing. But we do find a moderate balance used to give a greater emphasis to similar ideas than ordinary parallelism provides.

Ernesto Galarza

ERNESTO GALARZA (1905–1984), *the American labor leader, teacher, and writer, was born in Jalcocotán, Nayarit, Mexico, and came to the United States when he was six. He went to school in Sacramento, and later studied at Occidental College and at Stanford and Columbia universities, receiving his Ph.D. in history and political science in 1947. Galarza's youthful experience as a farm and cannery worker prepared him for his life's work organizing agricultural workers. He taught at various universities and as Regents Professor at the University of California, San Diego. His books include the autobiography* Barrio Boy *(1971), which describes his childhood in Mexico and California. The* Ajax *to which Galarza refers was his mother's sewing machine;* Coronel *was the family rooster in Jalcocotán.*

BOYHOOD IN A SACRAMENTO BARRIO

Our family conversations always occurred on our own kitchen porch, away from the gringos. One or the other of the adults would begin: *Se han fijado?* Had we noticed—that the Americans do not ask permission to leave the room; that they had no respectful way of addressing an elderly person; that they spit brown over the railing of the porch into the yard; that when they laughed they roared; that they never brought *saludos* to everyone in your family from everyone in their family when they visited; that *General Delibree* was only a clerk; that *zopilotes* were not allowed on the streets to collect garbage; that the policemen did not carry lanterns at night; that Americans didn't keep their feet on the floor when they were sitting; that there was a special automobile for going to jail; that a rancho was not a rancho at all but a very small hacienda; that the saloons served their customers free eggs, pickles, and sandwiches; that instead of bullfighting, the gringos for sport tried to kill each other with gloves?

I did not have nearly the strong feelings on these matters   2
that Doña Henriqueta expressed. I felt a vague admiration for the way Mr. Brien could spit brown. Wayne, my classmate, laughed much better than the Mexicans, because he opened his big mouth wide and brayed like a donkey so he could be heard a block away. But it was the kind of laughter that made my mother tremble, and it was not permitted in our house.

Rules were laid down to keep me, as far as possible, *un*   3
muchacho bien educado. If I had to spit I was to do it privately, or if in public, by the curb, with my head down and my back to people. I was never to wear my cap in the house and I was to take it off even on the porch if ladies or elderly gentlemen were sitting. If I wanted to scratch, under no circumstances was I to do it right then and there, in company, like the Americans, but I was to excuse myself. If Catfish or Russell yelled to me from across the street I was not to shout back. I was never to ask for tips for my errands or other services to the tenants of 418 L, for these were *atenciones* expected of me.

Above all I was never to fail in *respeto* to grownups, no mat-   4
ter who they were. It was an inflexible rule; I addressed myself to *Señor* Big Singh, *Señor* Big Ernie, *Señora* Dodson, *Señor* Cho-ree Lopez.

My standing in the family, but especially with my mother,   5
depended on my keeping these rules. I was not punished for breaking them. She simply reminded me that it gave her acute *vergüenza* to see me act thus, and that I would never grow up to be a correct *jefe de familia* if I did not know how to be a correct boy. I knew what *vergüenza* was from feeling it time and again;

and the notion of growing up to keep a tight rein over a family of my own was somehow satisfying.

In our musty apartment in the basement of 418 L, ours 6 remained a Mexican family. I never lost the sense that we were the same, from Jalco to Sacramento. There was the polished cedar box, taken out now and then from the closet to display our heirlooms. I had lost the rifle shells of the revolution, and Tio Tonche, too, was gone. But there was the butterfly sarape, the one I had worn through the Battle of Puebla; a black lace mantilla Doña Henriqueta modeled for us; bits of embroidery and lace she had made; the tin pictures of my grandparents; my report card signed by Señorita Bustamante and Don Salvador; letters from Aunt Esther; and the card with the address of the lady who had kept the Ajax for us. When our mementos were laid out on the bed I plunged my head into the empty box and took deep breaths of the aroma of *puro cedro*, pure Jalco-cotán mixed with camphor.

We could have hung on the door of our apartment a sign like 7 those we read in some store windows—*Aquí se habla español*. We not only spoke Spanish, we read it. From the *Librería Española*, two blocks up the street, Gustavo and I bought novels for my mother, like *Genoveva de Brabante*, a paperback with the poems of Amado Nervo and a handbook of the history of Mexico. The novels were never read aloud, the poems and the handbook were. Nervo was the famous poet from Tepic, close enough to Jalcocotán to make him our own. And in the history book I learned to read for myself, after many repetitions by my mother, about the deeds of the great Mexicans Don Salvador had recited so vividly to the class in Mazatlán. She refused to decide for me whether Abraham Lincoln was as great as Benito Juarez, or George Washington braver than the priest Don Miguel Hidalgo. At school there was no opportunity to settle these questions because nobody seemed to know about Juarez or Hidalgo; at least they were never mentioned and there were no pictures of them on the walls.

The family talk I listened to with the greatest interest was 8 about Jalco. Wherever the conversation began it always turned to the pueblo, our neighbors, anecdotes that were funny or sad, the folk tales and the witchcraft, and our kinfolk, who were still there. I usually lay on the floor those winter evenings, with my feet toward the kerosene heater, watching on the ceiling the flickering patterns of the light filtered through the scroll-work of the chimney. As I listened once again I chased the *zopilote* away from Coronel, or watched José take Nerón into the forest in a sack. Certain things became clear about the *rurales* and why the young men were taken away to kill Yaqui Indians, and about the Germans, the Englishmen, the Frenchmen, the Spaniards, and the Americans who owned the haciendas, the railroads, the ships, the big stores, the breweries. They owned Mexico because President Porfirio Diaz had let them steal it, José explained as I listened. Now Don Francisco Madero had been assassinated for trying to get it back. On such threads of family talk I followed my own recollection of the years from Jalco—the attack on Mazatlán, the captain of Acaponeta, the camp at El Nanchi and the arrival at Nogales on the flatcar.

Only when we ventured uptown did we feel like aliens in a   9
foreign land. Within the *barrio* we heard Spanish on the streets and in the alleys. On the railroad tracks, in the canneries, and along the riverfront there were more Mexicans than any other nationality. And except for the foremen, the work talk was in our language. In the secondhand shops, where the *barrio* people sold and bought furniture and clothing, there were Mexican clerks who knew the Mexican ways of making a sale. Families doubled up in decaying houses, cramping themselves so they could rent an extra room to *chicano* boarders, who accented the brown quality of our Mexican *colonia*.

VOCABULARY

barrio: neighborhood
Se han fijado?: Did you notice?
saludos: greetings
zopilotes: vultures, buzzards
un muchacho bien educado: a well-bred boy
atenciones: duties

respeto: respect
vergüenza: shame, embarrassment
jefe de familia: head of the family
puro cedro: pure cedar
Aquí se habla español: Spanish spoken here
Librería Española: Spanish Bookstore
rurales: rural mounted police
chicano: American of Mexican descent
colonia: colony

QUESTIONS

1. How does the author use parallelism in the third sentence of paragraph 1 to give equal emphasis to the various ideas?
2. How is the same use made of parallelism in paragraph 6?
3. Whole sentences can be parallel to one another. How much parallelism of this kind do you find in paragraph 3?
4. In general, how loose or how strict do you find the parallelism of Galarza's sentences? How formal an effect do his sentences create?
5. How do you believe children are best taught to respect people who are different from them culturally? How different from Galarza's was your training in manners?

SUGGESTIONS FOR WRITING

1. Galarza uses his account to say something about Mexican and American folkways and the changes brought about in moving from one world to another. Discuss what Galarza is saying, and comment on his attitude toward the changes he experiences.
2. Discuss the increased importance customs have when you find yourself in a new environment, perhaps in a new school or neighborhood. You might want to discuss changes in speech habits as well as changes in behavior.

31

Antithesis

When contrasting ideas are balanced in sentences and paragraphs, they are said to be in antithesis:

> History proves that dictatorships do not grow out of strong and successful governments, but out of weak and helpless ones. (Franklin D. Roosevelt)

> Shallow understanding from people of good will is more frustrating than absolute misunderstanding from people of ill will. (Martin Luther King, Jr., *Letter from Birmingham Jail*)

> We can no longer afford to take that which was good in the past and simply call it our heritage, to discard the bad and simply think of it as a dead load which by itself time will bury in oblivion. (Hannah Arendt, *The Origins of Totalitarianism*)

This moderate balancing to heighten the contrast of ideas is found often in modern writing, though usually in formal discussions. Like the exact balance of similar ideas, the balancing of sentences containing antithetical phrases is exceptional today. The following passage is the climax of a long book on the history of Roman society:

> Rome did not invent education, but she developed it on a scale unknown before, gave it state support, and formed the curriculum that persisted till our harassed youth. She did not invent the arch, the vault, or the dome, but she used them with such audacity and magnificence that in some fields her architecture has remained unequaled. (Will Durant, *Caesar and Christ*)

Martin Luther King, Jr.

Born in 1929, MARTIN LUTHER KING, JR., *was ordained in 1947 in the Atlanta church where his father was the minister. He*

558

graduated from Morehouse College the following year and received his Ph.D. from Boston University in 1953. In 1955 he rose to prominence in America and throughout the world as leader of the Montgomery, Alabama, bus boycott, and he continued as one of the leaders of the Civil Rights Movement until his assassination in Memphis on April 4, 1968. "From my Christian background I gained my ideals, and from Gandhi my technique," King said. It is the technique of passive resistance that he describes here. King's style of writing reflects the cadences of his speeches—influenced strongly by the style of the Old Testament prophetic books, to name just one of many sources.

NONVIOLENT RESISTANCE

Oppressed people deal with their oppression in three charac- 1
teristic ways. One way is acquiescence: the oppressed resign themselves to their doom. They tacitly adjust themselves to oppression, and thereby become conditioned to it. In every movement toward freedom some of the oppressed prefer to remain oppressed. Almost 2800 years ago Moses set out to lead the children of Israel from the slavery of Egypt to the freedom of the promised land. He soon discovered that slaves do not always welcome their deliverers. They become accustomed to being slaves. They would rather bear those ills they have, as Shakespeare pointed out, than flee to others that they know not of. They prefer the "fleshpots of Egypt" to the ordeals of emancipation.

There is such a thing as the freedom of exhaustion. Some 2
people are so worn down by the yoke of oppression that they give up. A few years ago in the slum areas of Atlanta, a Negro guitarist used to sing almost daily: "Ben down so long that down don't bother me." This is the type of negative freedom and resignation that often engulfs the life of the oppressed.

But this is not the way out. To accept passively an unjust 3
system is to cooperate with that system; thereby the oppressed become as evil as the oppressor. Noncooperation with evil is as much a moral obligation as is cooperation with good. The oppressed must never allow the conscience of the

oppressor to slumber. Religion reminds every man that he is his brother's keeper. To accept injustice or segregation passively is to say to the oppressor that his actions are morally right. It is a way of allowing his conscience to fall asleep. At this moment the oppressed fails to be his brother's keeper. So acquiescence—while often the easier way—is not the moral way. It is the way of the coward. The Negro cannot win the respect of his oppressor by acquiescing; he merely increases the oppressor's arrogance and contempt. Acquiescence is interpreted as proof of the Negro's inferiority. The Negro cannot win the respect of the white people of the South or the peoples of the world if he is willing to sell the future of his children for his personal and immediate comfort and safety.

A second way that oppressed people sometimes deal with 4 oppression is to resort to physical violence and corroding hatred. Violence often brings about momentary results. Nations have frequently won their independence in battle. But in spite of temporary victories, violence never brings permanent peace. It solves no social problem; it merely creates new and more complicated ones.

Violence as a way of achieving racial justice is both imprac- 5 tical and immoral. It is impractical because it is a descending spiral ending in destruction for all. The old law of an eye for an eye leaves everybody blind. It is immoral because it seeks to humiliate the opponent rather than win his understanding; it seeks to annihilate rather than to convert. Violence is immoral because it thrives on hatred rather than love. It destroys community and makes brotherhood impossible. It leaves society in monologue rather than dialogue. Violence ends by defeating itself. It creates bitterness in the survivors and brutality in the destroyers. A voice echoes through time saying to every potential Peter, "Put up your sword." History is cluttered with the wreckage of nations that failed to follow this command.

If the American Negro and other victims of oppression suc- 6 cumb to the temptation of using violence in the struggle for freedom, future generations will be the recipients of a desolate

night of bitterness, and our chief legacy to them will be an endless reign of meaningless chaos. Violence is not the way.

The third way open to oppressed people in their quest for 7
freedom is the way of nonviolent resistance. Like the synthesis
in Hegelian philosophy, the principle of nonviolent resistance
seeks to reconcile the truths of two opposites—acquiescence
and violence—while avoiding the extremes and immoralities
of both. The nonviolent resister agrees with the person who
acquiesces that one should not be physically aggressive
toward his opponent; but he balances the equation by agreeing with the person of violence that evil must be resisted. He
avoids the nonresistance of the former and the violent resistance of the latter. With nonviolent resistance, no individual or
group need submit to any wrong, nor need anyone resort to
violence in order to right a wrong.

It seems to me that this is the method that must guide the 8
actions of the Negro in the present crisis in race relations.
Through nonviolent resistance the Negro will be able to rise to
the noble height of opposing the unjust system while loving
the perpetrators of the system. The Negro must work passion-
ately and unrelentingly for full stature as a citizen, but he must
not use inferior methods to gain it. He must never come to
terms with falsehood, malice, hate, or destruction.

Nonviolent resistance makes it possible for the Negro to 9
remain in the South and struggle for his rights. The Negro's
problem will not be solved by running away. He cannot listen
to the glib suggestions of those who would urge him to
migrate en masse to other sections of the country. By grasping
his great opportunity in the South he can make a lasting contribution to the moral strength of the nation and set a sublime
example of courage for generations yet unborn.

By nonviolent resistance, the Negro can also enlist all men 10
of good will in his struggle for equality. The problem is not a
purely racial one, with Negroes set against whites. In the end,
it is not a struggle between people at all, but a tension
between justice and injustice. Nonviolent resistance is not

aimed against oppressors but against oppression. Under its banner consciences, not racial groups, are enlisted.

If the Negro is to achieve the goal of integration, he must 11
organize himself into a militant and nonviolent mass movement. All three elements are indispensable. The movement for equality and justice can only be a success if it has both a mass and militant character; the barriers to be overcome require both. Nonviolence is an imperative in order to bring about ultimate community.

A mass movement of a militant quality that is not at the 12
same time committed to nonviolence tends to generate conflict, which in turn breeds anarchy. The support of the participants and the sympathy of the uncommitted are both inhibited by the threat that bloodshed will engulf the community. This reaction in turn encourages the opposition to threaten and resort to force. When, however, the mass movement repudiates violence while moving resolutely toward its goal, its opponents are revealed as the instigators and practitioners of violence if it occurs. Then public support is magnetically attracted to the advocates of nonviolence, while those who employ violence are literally disarmed by overwhelming sentiment against their stand.

QUESTIONS

1. Note the sentences that conclude paragraph 1:

   > They would rather *bear those ills they have*, as Shakespeare pointed out,
   >> than *flee to others that they know not of.*

   > They prefer the *"fleshpots of Egypt"*
   >> to the ordeals of emancipation.

   What sentences in paragraph 5 contain antithetical elements? How exact is the antithesis? How many of these sentences are balanced to emphasize similar ideas?

2. How exact is the antithesis of ideas in paragraphs 8 and 10?

3. One way to moderate the tension of a passage containing considerable balance and antithesis is to vary the length of clauses

or sentences. To what extent are the sentences of paragraphs 5, 8, and 10 varied in their length?

4. What do balance and antithesis contribute to the tone of the passage? What kind of voice do you hear?

SUGGESTIONS FOR WRITING

1. Compare King's sentence style with that of another of his writings, for example, "Letter from Birmingham Jail." Discuss how the relative exactness of sentence balance and antithesis is used to moderate or increase the tension of the writing.

2. Compare a passage in the King James Version of the Bible with the rendering of the same passage in the Revised Standard Version. Comment on the differences you notice in the use of balance or antithesis.

32

Length

There is nothing inherently effective or ineffective, superior or inferior about long or short sentences, just as there is nothing inherently
effective or ineffective in a single note of the scale. How effective a
sentence is depends on what it does in a paragraph or essay. The very
short, disconnected sentences in a story by Ernest Hemingway effectively express the boredom a young war veteran feels on his return
home, but would probably also create a feeling of monotony in a
piece of writing on another subject:

> He did not want any consequences. He did not want any conse-
> quences ever again. He wanted to live alone without consequences.
> Besides he did not really need a girl. The army had taught him that.
> It was all right to pose as though you had to have a girl. Nearly every-
> body did that. But it wasn't true. You did not need a girl. That was
> the funny thing. ("Soldier's Home")

A sentence, as we have seen, often starts with the main idea and
then develops it:

> She was a spirited-looking young woman, with dark curly hair cropped
> and parted on the side, a short oval face with straight eyebrows, and a
> large curved mouth. (Katherine Anne Porter, "Old Mortality")

How much detail a writer can provide depends on how prominent the
main ideas are—whether in a sentence consisting of a single core
idea followed by a series of modifiers, as in Porter, or in one consisting of a series of connected core ideas or main clauses, modified as
in this sentence:

> Morrall would duck his head in the huddle and if it was feasible he
> would call a play which took the ball laterally across the field—a
> pitchout, perhaps, and the play would eat up ground toward the
> girls, the ball carrier sprinting for the sidelines, with his running
> guards in front of him, running low, and behind them the linemen
> coming too, so that twenty-two men were converging on them at a
> fair clip. (George Plimpton, *Paper Lion*)

564

Lewis Thomas

LEWIS THOMAS (*pp. 80–82*) *begins his essay on "matters of doubt" with a discussion of an important controversy of the 1960s. The English scientist and novelist C. P. Snow argued in* The Two Cultures and the Scientific Revolution (1961) *that scientists possess a culture little understood by "literary intellectuals," who have little knowledge of scientific ideas and are hostile to its achievements. "The scientific edifice of the physical world," Snow claimed, is "in its intellectual depth, complexity and articulation, the most beautiful and wonderful collective work of the mind of man." The English literary critic F. R. Leavis attacked these ideas, arguing that the achievements of modern science are not superior to those of the traditional culture, which created the human world and made science possible. Traditional literary culture, Leavis argued, provides a particular kind of "intelligence, a power—rooted, strong in experience, and supremely human," needed to respond to the rapid advances of science and technology. Thomas summarizes their views and, finding the controversy muddled, Thomas asks what the sciences and the humanities have in common and what attitude we should take in trying to understand the world.*

ON MATTERS OF DOUBT

The "two-cultures" controversy of several decades back has 1 quieted down some, but it is still with us, still unsettled because of the polarized views set out by C. P. Snow at one polemical extreme and by F. R. Leavis at the other; these remain as the two sides of the argument. At one edge, the humanists are set up as knowing, and wanting to know, very little about science and even less about the human meaning of contemporary science; they are, so it goes, antiscientific in their prejudice. On the other side, the scientists are served up as a bright but illiterate lot, well-read in nothing except science, even, as Leavis said of Snow, incapable of writing good novels. The humanities are presented in the dispute as though made up of imagined unverifiable notions about human behavior, unsubstantiated stories cooked up by poets and novelists, while the sciences deal parsimoniously with lean facts, hard data, incontrovertible theories, truths established beyond doubt, the unambiguous facts of life.

The argument is shot through with bogus assertions and false images, and I have no intention of becoming entrapped in it here, on one side or the other. Instead, I intend to take a stand in the middle of what seems to me a muddle, hoping to confuse the argument by showing that there isn't really any argument in the first place. To do this, I must try to show that there is in fact a solid middle ground to stand on, a shared common earth beneath the feet of all the humanists and all the scientists, a single underlying view of the world that drives all scholars, whatever their discipline—whether history or structuralist criticism or linguistics or quantum chromodynamics or astrophysics or molecular genetics.

There is, I think, such a shared view of the world. It is called *bewilderment*. Everyone knows this, but it is not much talked about; bewilderment is kept hidden in the darkest closets of all our institutions of higher learning, repressed whenever it seems to be emerging into public view, sometimes glimpsed staring from attic windows like a mad cousin of learning. It is the family secret of twentieth-century science, and of twentieth-century arts and letters as well. Human knowledge doesn't stay put. What we have been learning in our time is that we really do not understand this place or how it works, and we comprehend our own selves least of all. And the more we learn, the more we are—or ought to be—dumbfounded.

It is the greatest fun to be bewildered, but only when there lies ahead the sure certainty of having things straightened out, and soon. It is like a marvelous game, provided you have some way of keeping score, and this is what seems to be lacking in our time. It is confusing, and too many of us are choosing not to play, settling back with whatever straws of fixed knowledge we can lay hands on, denying bewilderment, pretending one conviction or another, nodding our heads briskly at whatever we prefer to believe, staying away from the ambiguity of being.

We would be better off if we had never invented the terms 5
"science" and "humanities" and then set them up as if they represented two different kinds of intellectual enterprise. I cannot
see why we ever did this, but we did. Now, to make matters
worse, we have these two encampments not only at odds but
trying to swipe problems from each other. The historians,
some of them anyway, want to be known as social scientists
and solve the ambiguities of history by installing computers in
all their offices; the deconstructionists want to become the
ultimate scientists of poetry, looking at every word in a line
with essentially the reductionist attitude of particle physicists
in the presence of atoms, but still unaware of the uncertainty
principle that governs any good poem: not only can the observer change the thing observed, he can even destroy it. The
biologists have invaded all aspects of human behavior with
equations to explain away altruism and usefulness by totting
up the needs of genes; the sociobiologists are becoming
humanists manqué, swept off their feet by ants. The physicists,
needing new terms for their astonishments, borrow "quarks"
from Joyce and label precisely quantitative aspects of matter
almost dismissively with poetically allusive words like
"strangeness," "color," and "flavor"; soon some parts of the universe will begin to "itch."

We have, to be sure, learned enough to know better than to 6
say some things, about letters and about science, but we are
still too reticent about our ignorance. Most things in the world
are unsettling and bewildering, and it is a mistake to try to
explain them away; they are there for marveling at and wondering at, and we should be doing more of this.

I do not mean to suggest that we are surrounded by un- 7
knowable things. Indeed, I cannot imagine any sorts of questions to be asked about ourselves or about nature that cannot
sooner or later be answered, given enough time. I do admit to
worrying, late at night, about that matter of time: obviously we
will have to get rid of modern warfare and quickly, or else we
will end up, with luck, throwing spears and stones at each
other. We could, without luck, run out of time in what is left of

this century and then, by mistake, finish the whole game off by upheaving the table, ending life for everything except the bacteria, maybe—with enough radiation, even them. If you are given to fretting about what is going on in the minds of the young people in our schools, or on the streets of Zurich or Paris or Sydney or Tokyo or wherever, give a thought to the idea of impermanence for a whole species—*ours*—and the risk of earthly incandescence; it is a brand-new idea, never before confronted as a reality by any rising generation of human beings.

I have an idea, as an aside. Why not agree with the Russians   8
about just one technological uniformity to be installed, at small cost, in all the missiles, theirs and ours: two small but comfortable chambers added to every vehicle before firing, one for a prominent diplomat selected by the other side, one for a lawyer selected at random? It might be a beginning.

Here's a list of things, taken more or less at random, that we   9
do not understand:

I am entitled to say, if I like, that awareness exists in all the   10
individual creatures on the planet—worms, sea urchins, gnats, whales, subhuman primates, superprimate humans, the lot. I can say this because we do not know what we are talking about; consciousness is so much a total mystery for our own species that we cannot begin to guess about its existence in others. I can say that bird song is the music made by songbirds for their own pleasure, pure fun, also for ours, and it is only a piece of good fortune that the music turns out to be handy for finding mates for breeding or setting territorial markers. I can say, if I like, that social insects behave like the working parts of an immense central nervous system: the termite colony is an enormous brain on millions of legs; the individual termite is a mobile neurone. This would mean that there is such a phenomenon as collective thinking, which goes on whenever sufficient numbers of creatures are sufficiently connected to one another, and it would also mean that we humans could do the same trick if we tried, and perhaps we've already done it, over and over again, in the making of language and the meditative

making (for which the old Greek word *poesis* is best) of metaphors. I can even assert out loud that we are, as a species, held
together by something like affection (what the physicists might
be calling a "weak force") and by something like love (a "strong
force"), and nobody can prove that I'm wrong. I can dismiss all
the evidence piling up against such an idea, all our destructiveness and cantankerousness, as error, error-proneness, built
into our species to allow more flexibility of choice, and nobody
can argue me out of this unless I choose to wander off to
another point of view.

I am inclined to assert, unconditionally, that there is one 11
central, universal aspect of human behavior, genetically set by
our very nature, biologically governed, driving each of us
along. Depending on how one looks at it, it can be defined as
the urge to be useful. This urge drives society along, sets our
behavior as individuals and in groups, invents all our myths,
writes our poetry, composes our music.

It is not easy to be a social species and, at the same time, 12
such a juvenile, almost brand-new species, milling around in
groups, trying to construct a civilization that will last. Being
useful is easy for an ant: you just wait for the right chemical
signal, at the right stage of the construction of the hill, and
then you go looking for a twig of exactly the right size for that
stage and carry it back, up the flank of the hill, and put it in
place, and then you go and do that thing again. An ant can
dine out on his usefulness, all his life, and never get it wrong.

It is a different problem for us, carrying such risks of doing 13
it wrong, getting the wrong twig, losing the hill, not even rec-
ognizing, yet, the outline of the hill. We are beset by strings
of DNA, immense arrays of genes, instructing each of us to be
helpful, impelling us to try our whole lives to be useful, but
never telling us how. The instructions are not coded out in
anything like an operator's manual; we have to make guesses
all the time. The difficulty is increased when groups of us are
set to work together; I have seen, and sat on, numberless
committees, not one of which intended anything other than
great merit, feckless all. Larger collections of us—cities, for

instance—hardly ever get anything right. And, of course, there is the modern nation, probably the most stupefying example of biological error since the age of the great reptiles, wrong at every turn, but always felicitating itself loudly on its great value. It is a biological problem, as much so as a coral reef or a rain forest, but such things as happen to human nations could never happen in a school of fish. It is, when you think about it, a humiliation, but then "humble" and "human" are cognate words. We are smarter than the fish, but their instructions come along in their eggs; ours we are obliged to figure out, and we are, in this respect, slow learners.

The sciences and the humanities are all of a piece, one and the same kind of work for the human brain, done by launching guesses and finding evidence to back up the guesses. The methods and standards are somewhat different, to be sure. It is easier to prove that something is so in science than it is to make an assertion about Homer or Cézanne or Wallace Stevens and have it stand up to criticism from all sides, harder still to *be* Homer or Cézanne or Stevens, but the game is the same game. The hardest task for the scientists, hardly yet begun, is to find out what their findings may mean, deep inside, and how one piece of solid information, firmly established by experimentation and confirmation, fits with that unlike piece over there. The natural world is all of a piece, we all know this in our bones, but we have a long, long way to go before we will see how the connections are made. 14

If you are looking about for really profound mysteries, essential aspects of our existence for which neither the sciences nor the humanities can provide any sort of explanation, I suggest starting with music. The professional musicologists, tremendous scholars all, for whom I have the greatest respect, haven't the ghost of an idea about what music is, or why we make it and cannot be human without it, or even—and this is the telling point—how the human mind makes music on its own, before it is written down and played. The biologists are no help here, nor the psychologists, nor the physicists, nor the philosophers, wherever they are these days. Nobody can explain it. It is a 15 mystery, and thank goodness for that. The Brandenburgs and the late quartets are not there to give us assurances that we have arrived; they carry the news that there are deep centers in our minds that we know nothing about except that they are there.

The thing to do, to get us through the short run, the years 16 just ahead, is to celebrate our ignorance. Instead of presenting the body of human knowledge as a mountainous structure of coherent information capable of explaining everything about everything if we could only master all the details, we should be acknowledging that it is, in real life, still a very modest mound of puzzlements that do not fit together at all. As a species, the thing we are biologically good at is learning new things, thanks to our individual large brains and thanks above all to the gift of speech that connects them, one to another. We can take some gratification at having come a certain distance in just the few thousand years of our existence as language users, but it should be a deeper satisfaction, even an exhilaration, to recognize that we have such a distance still to go. Get us through the next few years, I say, just get us safely out of this century and into the next, and then watch what we can do.

VOCABULARY

paragraph 1: polarized, polemical, parsimoniously, incontrovertible
paragraph 2: bogus
paragraph 5: encampments, reductionist, sociobiologists, manqué
paragraph 6: reticent
paragraph 7: incandescence
paragraph 10: mobile, neurone, cantankerousness
paragraph 13: stupefying, felicitating
paragraph 15: musicologists

QUESTIONS

1. In sentences containing semicolons in paragraphs 3, 5, 6, 13, and 15, the two parts of each might stand as separate sentences. What does Thomas gain by joining the two parts in each sentence? Could a colon substitute for the semicolon in each?

2. What purposes does the colon serve in paragraphs 5, 7, 9, 10, and 12?

3. Why does Thomas set off phrases with dashes rather than parentheses in paragraphs 3, 13, and 15, and the fifth sentence of paragraph 7? Could dashes substitute for the parentheses in paragraph 10?

4. What is the function of the single dash in paragraphs 2 and 10, and the fourth sentence of paragraph 7?

5. Combine the following sentences into longer ones. What is gained or lost by your revision?

> There is, I think, such a shared view of the world. It is called *bewilderment*. (paragraph 3)
>
> It is the family secret of twentieth-century science, and of twentieth-century arts and letters as well. Human science doesn't stay put. (paragraph 3)
>
> The biologists are no help here, nor the psychologists, nor the physicists, nor the philosophers, wherever they are these days. Nobody can explain it. (paragraph 15)

6. Thomas might have broken the fifth sentence ("This would mean") and the final sentence ("I can dismiss") of paragraph 10 into a series of shorter ones. What does he gain by not doing so?

7. What does Thomas mean by *bewilderment*, and how does he illustrate the idea?

8. What are the *humanities*, and how does Thomas explain the term in the course of the essay?

9. How does Thomas explain the statement that "the natural world is all of a piece"? How does the statement relate to his general thesis? Where does Thomas state it? Does he restate it in the course of the essay?

SUGGESTIONS FOR WRITING

1. Paragraph 4 contains a series of compound and compound-complex sentences (that is, sentences containing all main or independent clauses or a mix of independent and subordinate or dependent clauses). Rewrite the paragraph, breaking it into shorter sentences, or subordinating independent clauses where

possible. Then discuss how your revision changes the emphasis and tone of the original paragraph.

2. Provide a list of things you would like to understand most about yourself and the world, and suggest ways a college education may help you to reach an understanding. You may wish to discuss why a college education cannot provide full or partial answers.

3. Thomas states that "human knowledge doesn't stay put." Illustrate this statement from your own experience.

Part 6

ESSAYS ON WRITING

Introduction

In the first essay that follows, Mark Twain stresses the unconscious powers of mind that come into play in the act of composition. Twain refers to "an automatically-working taste . . . which selects and rejects without asking you for any help, and patiently and steadily improves itself without troubling you to approve or applaud." But that taste has been shaped by what the writer has read; Twain takes note of the "model-chamber" in which writers store those effective sentences they find as they read. Though writers shape their sentences unconsciously, drawing upon these model sentences, the act of writing becomes conscious when they reject sentences that don't make sense and experiment with sentences that are different from the ones they usually write.

John Ciardi agrees with Twain that reading is essential to the writer: "No writer can produce good writing without a sure sense of what has been accomplished in the past within his form." But, Ciardi adds, the writer does not adhere to the past but rather innovates: "it is impossible to venture meaningful innovation unless one knows what he is *innovating from*." But more so than Twain, Ciardi stresses the conscious side of creativity, which he defines as "the imaginatively gifted recombination of known elements into something new." Practiced writers possess a power of mind akin to that described by Twain—in Ciardi's words, "a second attention lurking in the mind at the very moment [writers] have felt the need to be most indivisibly absorbed in what they are doing." The competent writer, like the competent reader, must possess "fluency," which Ciardi defines as "the ability to receive more than one impression at the same time."

Walker Gibson deals with a different kind of decision—that of the style the author chooses, sometimes unconsciously, sometimes deliberately. He states in his book on prose styles, *Tough, Sweet, and Stuffy*, that each choice "is significant in dramatizing a personality or voice, with a particular center of concern and a particular relation to the person he is addressing." The author may have reason to question the style of a piece of writing under review, sensing that the piece does not "sound right," though the content seems satisfactory. We have all had this experience in beginning a letter, then starting again, sensing we are writing in a style—or voice—that conveys a false impression or image of ourselves. We continue experimenting

577

until our sentences establish the desirable relation to the person addressed. The main job of revision, we sometimes discover, is to find the appropriate style or voice.

In his essay on revision, William Zinsser focuses on what happens in the course of writing and afterwards, as we rethink and revise initial drafts. Zinsser gives the same advice that George Orwell does in his classic essay "Politics and the English Language." In his discussion of how to avoid ready-made words and phrases, Orwell suggests how these words and phrases find their way into a piece of writing: "When you think of something abstract you are more inclined to use words from the start, and unless you make a conscious effort to prevent it, the existing dialect will come rushing in and do the job for you, at the expense of blurring or even changing your meaning." Zinsser shows how to deal with this problem of ready-made words and ideas. "The secret of good writing is to strip every sentence to its cleanest components," he states, and he illustrates how to do so.

These four essayists by no means suggest all the ways writers proceed or engage in revision. They agree, however, that the act of writing is not aimless or undirected. Zinsser and Gibson in particular show that writers give attention to what they have written—to its clarity and effectiveness—at some stage in the process and sometimes at all stages.

Mark Twain

MARK TWAIN's *description of life in the* Missouri *river town where he grew up and his experience as a cub pilot on a* Mississippi *steamboat appear earlier in this book. His numerous stories, novels, sketches, and essays seem the work of a writer who lets a tale or comment develop leisurely, in the manner of the relaxed yarn spinner. This impression is deceptive, for Twain was attentive to the craft, as all good storytellers and writers must be. Yet, he tells us in this short statement on writing, he allowed his imagination to shape the work, without constant awareness of means and effects. Rather, he depended on the "model-chamber" he describes and on "an automatically-working taste" that came to him through wide reading. Twain suggests one way that writers develop their craft.*

THE ART OF COMPOSITION

Your inquiry has set me thinking, but, so far, my thought fails 1
to materialize. I mean that, upon consideration, I am not sure
that I have methods in composition. I do suppose I have—I
suppose I must have—but they somehow refuse to take shape
in my mind; their details refuse to separate and submit to classification and description; they remain a jumble—visible, like
the fragments of glass when you look in at the wrong end of a
kaleidoscope, but still a jumble. If I could turn the whole thing
around and look in at the other end, why then the figures
would flash into form out of the chaos, and I shouldn't have
any more trouble. But my head isn't right for that today, apparently. It might have been, maybe, if I had slept last night.

However, let us try guessing. Let us guess that whenever we 2
read a sentence and like it, we unconsciously store it away in
our model-chamber; and it goes with the myriad of its fellows
to the building, brick by brick, of the eventful edifice which we
call our style. And let us guess that whenever we run across
other forms—bricks—whose color, or some other defect,
offends us, we unconsciously reject these, and so one never
finds them in our edifice. If I have subjected myself to any
training processes, and no doubt I have, it must have been in

this unconscious or half-conscious fashion. I think it unlikely that deliberate and consciously methodical training is usual with the craft. I think it likely that the training most in use is of this unconscious sort, and is guided and governed and made by-and-by unconsciously systematic, by an automatically-working taste—a taste which selects and rejects without asking you for any help, and patiently and steadily improves itself without troubling you to approve or applaud. Yes, and likely enough when the structure is at last pretty well up, and attracts attention, *you* feel complimented, whereas you didn't build it, and didn't even consciously superintend. Yes; one notices, for instance, that long, involved sentences confuse him, and that he is obliged to re-read them to get the sense. Unconsciously, then, he rejects that brick. Unconsciously he accustoms himself to writing short sentences as a rule. At times he may indulge himself with a long one, but he will make sure that there are no folds in it, no vaguenesses, no parenthetical interruptions of its view as a whole; when he is done with it, it won't be a sea-serpent, with half of its arches under the water, it will be a torchlight procession.

Well, also he will notice in the course of time, as his reading $\quad$ 3 goes on, that the difference between the *almost right* word and the *right* word is really a large matter—'tis the difference between the lightningbug and the lightning. After that, of course, that exceedingly important brick, the *exact* word—however, this is running into an essay, and I beg pardon. So I seem to have arrived at this: doubtless I have methods, but they begot themselves, in which case I am only their proprietor, not their father.

John Ciardi

Poet, editor, and translator JOHN CIARDI (1916–1986) *was the author of forty books of poetry and criticism. He was poetry editor for* Saturday Review *from 1956 to 1972, writing a column "Manner of Speaking" for that magazine. These columns and other essays are collected in* Dialogue with an Audience (1963) *and*

Manner of Speaking (1972). His *distinguished translation of* Dante's Divine Comedy *was published in its full edition in* 1977. *Ciardi was director of the Bread Loaf Writers' Conference at Middlebury College from* 1955 *to* 1972. *The essay that follows was presented to the conference in its inaugural year.*

WHAT EVERY WRITER MUST LEARN

The teaching of writing has become practically a profession by now. There is hardly a college in the land that does not offer at least one course in "creative writing" (whatever that is) by some "teacher of writing" (whoever he is). There are, moreover, at least fifty annual writers' conferences now functioning among us with something like fifty degrees of competence. And there seems to be no way of counting the number of literary counselors, good and bad, who are prepared to promise that they can teach a writer what he needs to know. 1

I am myself a "teacher of writing," but though it be taken as a confession of fraud I must insist, in the face of all this "teaching" apparatus, that writing cannot in fact be taught. What a writer must have above all else is inventiveness. Dedication, commitment, passion—whatever one chooses to call the writer's human motivation—must be there, to be sure. But to require human motivation is only to assume that the writer is a human being—certainly not a very hard assumption to make. Art, however, is not humanity but the *expression* of humanity, and for enduring expression the one gift above all is inventiveness. 2

But where, in what curriculum ever, has there been, or can there be, a course in inventiveness—which is to say, in creativity? The truly creative—whether in art, in science, or in philosophy—is always, and precisely, that which cannot be taught. And yet, though it seems paradoxical, creativity cannot spring from the untaught. Creativity is the imaginatively gifted recombination of known elements into something new. 3

And so, it may seem, there is no real paradox. The elements of an invention or of a creation can be taught, but the creativity must be self-discovered and self-disciplined. A good 4 teacher—whether in a college classroom, a Parisian café, or a Greek market place—can marvelously assist the learning. But in writing, as in all creativity, it is the gift that must learn itself.

The good teacher will be able to itemize a tremendous amount of essential lore. He can tell a would-be novelist that if an incidental character is given a name that character had best reappear in the later action, and that if he is not going to reappear he should be identified simply as "the supply sergeant," "the big blond," "the man in the red waistcoat," or whatever. He can point out that good dialogue avoids "he averred," "he bellowed," "he boomed," "he interpolated," and that it is wise to write simply "he said," indicating any important direction for the tone of voice in a separate sentence. He can demonstrate that in all fiction the action must be perceived by someone, and he can defend in theory and support by endless instances that in effective fiction one does not allow more than one means of perception within a single scene. He can point out to would-be poets that traditional rhyme and traditional metrics are not indispensable, but that once a pattern has been established the writer must respect it. And he can then point out that within the pattern established at the start of the student's poem certain lines are metrically deficient and certain rhymes forced.

He may "teach" (or preach) any number of such particulars. And if he is a good man for the job he will never forget that these particulars are simply rules of thumb, any one of which may be violated by a master, but none of which may be safely ignored by a writer who has not yet learned they exist.

Belaboring such particulars is a useful device to the would-be writer, who under a competent teacher may save himself years of floundering trial-and-error. Writers are forever being produced by literary groups of one sort or another, and one of the most important things a writer acquires in the give-and-take of a good literary group is a headful of precisely such particulars. The most important thing a teacher of writing can do is to create a literary group in which he teaches minimums while the most talented of his students learn maximums—

very largely from fighting with one another (rarely, if ever, from mutual admiration).

But if writing requires a starting talent that a man either 8 has or has not and which he cannot learn, and if the teachable elements are not enough to make a writer of him, what is it he must learn? What are the measures by which his gift comes to know itself?

The answers to that question must be given separately, and 9 if they are so given they must be put down one after the other with some sort of natural implication that the order in which they are given is keyed to their importance. Such mechanical necessity (and it is one of the most constant seductions of the classroom) must not be allowed to obscure the far greater likelihood that the answers all exist at the same time in the behavior of a good writer, and that all are equally important. That, too, is part of what must be learned. As is the fact that no one set of generalizations will ever suffice. But one must begin somewhere. I offer the following six points as the most meaningful and the most central I have been able to locate.

1. *Something to Write About*

"You have to give them something to write about," Robert 10 Frost once said in discussing his classroom principles. His own poems are full of stunning examples of the central truth that good writers deal in information, and that even the lofty (if they are lofty) acreages of poetry are sown to fact. Consider the opening lines of "Mending Wall":

> Something there is that doesn't love a wall,
> That sends the frozen-groundswell under it,
> And spills the upper boulders in the sun;
> And makes gaps even two can pass abreast.
> The work of hunters is another thing:
> I have come after them and made repair
> Where they have left not one stone on a stone,
> But they would have the rabbit out of hiding,

> To please the yelping dogs. The gaps I mean,
> No one has seen them made or heard them made,
> But at spring mending-time we find them there . . .

I intend no elaborate critique of this passage. I want simply to make the point that it contains as much specific information about stone walls as one could hope to find in a Department of Agriculture pamphlet.

Frost states his passion for the *things* of the world both in 11 example and in precept. "The fact is the sweetest dream the labor knows," he writes in "The Mowing." One has only to compare that line with R. P. T. Coffin's "Nothing so crude as fact could enter here" to understand an important part of the difference between a poet and something less than a poet.

Even so mystical a poet as Gerard Manley Hopkins (I misuse 12 the word "mystical" in order to save three paragraphs, but let me at least file an apology) is gorgeously given to the fact of the thing. Consider: "And blue bleak embers, ah my dear,/ Fall, gall themselves, and gash gold-vermilion." (I.e., "Coal embers in a grate, their outside surfaces burned out and blue-bleak, sift down, fall through the grate, strike the surface below, and are gashed open to reveal the gold-vermilion fire still glowing at their core.")

The writer of fiction deals his facts in a different way, but it 13 will not do to say that he is more bound to fact than is the poet: he simply is not required to keep his facts under poetic compression; keep hard to them he still must. Consider Melville's passion for the details of whaling; or Defoe's for the details of criminality, of ransoming an English merchant captured by a French ship, or of Robinson Crusoe's carpentry. The passion for fact was powerful enough in these masters to lure them into shattering the pace of their own best fiction, and to do so time and time again. And who is to say that a man reading for more than amusement, a man passionate to touch the writer's mind in his writing, has any real objection to having the pace so shattered? All those self-blooming, lovingly managed, chunky, touchable facts!

For a writer is a man who must know something better 14
than anyone else does, be it so little as his own goldfish or
so much as himself. True, he is not required to know any one
specific thing. Not at least until he begins to write about it.
But once he has chosen to write about X then he is responsible for knowing everything the writing needs to know about
X. I know of no writer of any consequence whatever who did
not treasure the world enough to gather to himself a strange
and wonderful headful and soulful of facts about its going
and coming.

2. An Outside Eye

Nothing is more difficult than for the writer to ride his passion 15
while still managing to observe it critically. The memoirs of
good writers of every sort are studded with long thoughts on
this essential duplicity, this sense of aesthetic detachment, of
a second attention lurking in the mind at the very moment
they have felt the need to be most indivisibly absorbed in what
they are doing.

The writer absolutely must learn to develop that eye outside 16
himself, for the last action every writer must perform for his
writing is to become its reader. It is not easy to approach one's
own output as if he were coming on it fresh. Yet unless the
writer turns that trick any communication that happens will
either be by accident or by such genius as transcends the possibility of discussion.

For the writer's relation to his writing is a developing rela- 17
tion. The writing starts as a conceptual buzz. Approaching the
writing thus with the buzz loud in the head, one may easily
believe that anything he sets down is actually full of that starting buzz. But one must remember that the buzz is there before
the writing, and that should some accident interfere with the
actual writing the buzz would still be there. A writer in a really
heightened state could jot down telephone numbers and actually believe that he has set down a piece of writing that accurately conveys his original impulse.

The reader, however, is in a very different situation. He [18] comes to writing committed to no prior emotion. There is no starting buzz in his head, except by irrelevant accident. It is the writer's job to make that reader buzz. Not, to be sure, to make every reader buzz—the world is full of the practically unbuzzable—but to make the competent reader buzz. Simply to say, "I buzz," is not enough. To make the reader experience the original buzz with nothing but the writing to create the buzz within him—that is the function of every sort of literature, the communication of experience in experienceable terms. The disciplines of any art form are among other things ways of estimating the amount of buzz the form is transmitting.

3. Fluency

As noted, one does not hope to reach all readers, but only the [19] competent. In one way the qualifications of a good reader are the same as those of a competent writer. Both must achieve fluency. By fluency I mean the ability to receive more than one impression at the same time. To create or to experience art one must be both technically and emotionally fluent.

A pun is a simple example of the necessity for technical flu- [20] ency. The two or more faces of a pun must be received at the same instant or all is lost. The news comes over the radio that the Communist leader of Pisa has been chastised by Moscow for making overtures to the left-center parties for a unified front, and the happy punster says, "Aha, a Lenin tower of a-Pisa-ment!" then settles back in his moment of personal splendor. This golden instant from my autobiography—but what good is even glory if it has to be explained? "I don't get it," says the guest who will never be invited again, and the evening is ruined.

The pun, of course, is only the simplest example of the need [21] for technical fluency. Unless the writer and the reader have in common the necessary language of simultaneity in its millions of shadings, the best will die en route.

The need for emotional fluency is analogous. Good writing 22 constantly requires the writer to perceive and the reader to receive different sets of feelings at the same instant. Both the writer and the reader must be equal to the emotion of the subject dealt with. Shakespeare can put a world into *Hamlet*, but where is that world when a five-year-old child or an emotionally-five-year-old adult attempts to read or to see the play? Whatever he may see, it is certainly not Shakespeare. A reader who is emotionally immature, or who is too psychically rigid (the same thing really) to enter into the simultaneity of the human experiences commonly portrayed in literature, is simply not capable of any sort of writing with the possible exception of the technical report, the statistical summary, or that semi-literate combination, the Ph.D. thesis.

4. A *Sense of the* Past

No painter can produce a good canvas without a broad knowl- 23 edge of what has been painted before him, no architect can plan a meaningful building except as he has pondered the architecture of the past, and no writer can produce good writing without a sure sense of what has been accomplished in the past within his form.

There are legions of poets today who are trying belatedly to 24 be Wordsworth, and legions of fictioneers who are trying to be Louisa May Alcott. I imply no attack here on either Wordsworth or Alcott. I simply make the point that it is too late to be either of them again. Both of them, moreover, did a better job of being themselves than any of their imitators can aspire to. As the Kitty-cat bird in Theodore Roethke's poem said: "Whoever you are, be sure it's you."

Nor does one learn the past of his form only to adhere to it. 25 Such an adherence, if overdedicated, would be a death in itself. I mean, rather, that it is impossible to venture meaningful innovation unless one knows what he is *innovating from*. With no exception I am able to think of, the best innovators in our literature have been those who best knew their past tradition.

I am saying simply that a writer must learn to read. He 26
must read widely and thoughtfully, and he must learn to read
not as an amateur spectator but as an engaged professional.
Just as the football coach sees more of the play than do the
coeds, so the writer must learn to see more of what is happening under the surface of the illusion than does the reader
who simply yields to the illusion. William Dean Howells, then
editor of *The Atlantic*, paid what he intended as a supreme
compliment to one of Mark Twain's books when he reported
that he had begun the book and for the first time in many
years had found himself reading as a reader rather than as an
editor. A happy indulgence and a gracious compliment, but
once the writer has allowed himself that much it becomes his
duty to reread the book with his glasses on—not only to enter
into the illusion of the writing, but to identify the devices (*i.e.*,
the inventions) by which the illusion was created and made to
work upon him. And here, too, he must experience his essential duplicity, for the best reading is exactly that reading in
which the passion of the illusion and the awareness of its
technical management arrive at the same time.

5. A *Sense of the Age*

The true writer, that is to say the writer who is something more 27
than a competent technician, has a yet more difficult thing to
learn. He must not only know his human and artistic past; he
must learn to read the mood of his world under its own names
for itself. He must become an instrument, tuned by devices he
can never wholly understand, to the reception of a sense of his
age, its mood, its climate of ideas, its human position, and its
potential of action. And he must not let himself be deceived
into thinking that the world answers to the names it gives
itself. Hitler's agencies once gave a great deal of attention to
what they called "Strength-through-Joy." It was the product of
this Strength-through-Joy that Lord Beaverbrook called at the
time "the stalwart young Nazis of Germany." The names were
"strength," "joy," and "stalwarts." Yet any man today can see

that those who answered to these shining names contained within themselves possibilities for action that must answer to much darker names. Any man can see it—now. I think it is very much to the point that all of the best writers sensed it then, and that the better the German writers were, the earlier they left Germany. Good writing must be of its times and must contain within itself—God knows how but the writer must learn for himself—a sense of what Hippolyte Taine called "the moral temperature of the times," what the Germans call "der Zeitgeist," and what English and American writers have come to call "the climate."

6. Art Is Artifice

And along with all else, as an essential part of his duplicity, his commitment, his fluency, and his sense of past and present, the writer must learn beyond any flicker of doubt within himself that art is not life itself but a made representation of life. He must learn that it is no defense of a piece of fiction, for example, to argue, "But that's the way it happened." The fact that it happened that way in the world of the *Daily News* does not make it happen to the reader within the world of the writing. 28

The writer's subject is reality but his medium is illusion. Only by illusory means can the sense of reality be transmitted in an art form. That complex of pigment-on-canvas is not four maidens dancing, but it is the managed illusion whereby Botticelli transmits his real vision of the four seasons. Those words on paper are not Emma Bovary, but they are the elements of the illusion whereby we experience her as a living creation. The writer, like every artist, deals in what I have come to call the AS-IF. As-if is the mode of all poetry and of all imaginative writing Is is the mode of what passes for reality and of all information-prose. Is is more real than as-if? One must ask: "More real for what purposes?" I have no argument with, for example, the research chemists. I mean rather to hold them in considerable admiration. But though many of them think of themselves as 29 the IS-iest men in the world, which of them has ever determined a piece of truth except by setting up and pursuing a starting hypothesis (let me leave accident out of consideration)? And what is a starting hypothesis but an AS-IF? "Let us act AS-IF this hypothesis were true," says the researcher, "and then see how it checks out." At the end of ten, or a hundred, or ten thousand starting AS-IF's lurks the nailed-down IS of valence, or quanta, or transmutation of elements. Maybe. And then only until the next revolution in IS outdates the researcher's results.

At the far end of all the AS-IF's a man, and particularly a   30
writer, can summon from himself, there lurks that final IS (maybe) that will be a truth for him. But not all of the truth will be told at one time. Part of the truth, I think the most truth, a writer must learn is that writing is not a decorative act, but a specific, disciplined, and infinitely viable means of knowledge. Poetry and fiction, like all the arts, are ways of perceiving and of understanding the world. Good writing is as positive a search for truth as is any part of science, and it deals with kinds of truth that must forever be beyond science. The writer must learn, necessarily of himself and within himself, that his subject is the nature of reality, that good writing always increases the amount of human knowledge available, and that the one key to that knowledge of reality is AS-IF. His breadth and depth as a human being are measured by the number of AS-IF's he has managed to experience; his stature as a writer, by the number he has managed to bring to life in his work.

For no man in any one lifetime can hope to learn by physi-   31
cal experience (IS) all that he must know and all that he must have experienced in order to be an adequate human being. No writer can hope to engage physically enough worlds of IS to make his imagination and his humanity pertinent. Only by his vicarious assumptions of AS-IF can the writer learn his real human dimension, and only as he dedicates his writing to the creation of a meaningful and experiencable new AS-IF can he hope to write well—to write as no school can teach him to write, but he must learn for himself if he cares enough, and if he has gift enough.

William Zinsser

WILLIAM ZINSSER, *whose essay "The Right to Fail" appears earlier in this book, has had a long and varied career as a journalist, critic, columnist, and teacher of writing. His numerous essays are collected in* The Lunacy Boom (1970) *and other books. In this essay from his book* On Writing Well (5th ed., 1994), *Zinsser discusses the clutter that infects so much American writing today, and he emphasizes the importance of revision and editing in the act of writing. In the sample extract included in the essay, Zinsser gives an example of his own revising and editing.*

SIMPLICITY

Clutter is the disease of American writing. We are a society strangling in unnecessary words, circular constructions, pompous frills and meaningless jargon. 1

Who can understand the viscous language of everyday American commerce: the memo, the corporation report, the business letter, the notice from the bank explaining its latest "simplified" statement? What member of an insurance or medical plan can decipher the brochure explaining his costs and benefits? What father or mother can put together a child's toy from the instructions on the box? Our national tendency is to inflate and thereby sound important. The airline pilot who announces that he is presently anticipating experiencing considerable precipitation wouldn't think of saying it may rain. The sentence is too simple—there must be something wrong with it. 2

But the secret of good writing is to strip every sentence to its cleanest components. Every word that serves no function, every long word that could be a short word, every adverb that carries the same meaning that's already in the verb, every passive construction that leaves the reader unsure of who is doing what—these are the thousand and one adulterants that weaken the strength of a sentence. And they usually occur in proportion to education and rank. 3

During the 1960s the president of my university wrote a let-   4
ter to mollify the alumni after a spell of campus unrest. "You
are probably aware," he began, "that we have been experiencing very considerable potentially explosive expressions of dissatisfaction on issues only partially related." He meant the
students had been hassling them about different things. I was
far more upset by the president's English than by the students'
potentially explosive expressions of dissatisfaction. I would
have preferred the presidential approach taken by Franklin D.
Roosevelt when he tried to convert into English his own government's memos, such as this blackout order of 1942:

> Such preparations shall be made as will completely   5
> obscure all Federal buildings and non-Federal buildings
> occupied by the Federal government during an air raid for any
> period of time from visibility by reason of internal or external
> illumination.

"Tell them," Roosevelt said, "that in buildings where they   6
have to keep the work going to put something across the windows."

Simplify, simplify. Thoreau said it, as we are so often re-   7
minded, and no American writer more consistently practiced
what he preached. Open *Walden* to any page and you will find a
man saying in a plain and orderly way what is on his mind:

> I went to the woods because I wished to live deliberately,   8
> to front only the essential facts of life, and see if I could not
> learn what it had to teach, and not, when I came to die, dis-
> cover that I had not lived.

How can the rest of us achieve such enviable freedom from   9
clutter? The answer is to clear our heads of clutter. Clear thinking becomes clear writing; one can't exist without the other. It's
impossible for a muddy thinker to write good English. You may
get away with it for a paragraph or two, but soon the reader will
be lost, and there's no sin so grave, for the reader will not easily be lured back.

Who is this elusive creature, the reader? The reader is some- 10
one with an attention span of about 30 seconds—a person
assailed by other forces competing for attention. At one time
these forces weren't so numerous: newspapers, radio, spouse,
home, children. Today they also include a "home entertainment center" (TV, VCR, tapes, CDs), pets, a fitness program, a
yard and all the gadgets that have been bought to keep it
spruce, and that most potent of competitors, sleep. The person snoozing in a chair with a magazine or a book is a person
who was being given too much unnecessary trouble by the
writer.

It won't do to say that the reader is too dumb or too lazy to 11
keep pace with the train of thought. If the reader is lost, it's
usually because the writer hasn't been careful enough. The
carelessness can take any number of forms. Perhaps a sentence is so excessively cluttered that the reader, hacking
through the verbiage, simply doesn't know what it means. Perhaps a sentence has been so shoddily constructed that the
reader could read it in several ways. Perhaps the writer has
switched pronouns in midsentence, or has switched tenses, so
the reader loses track of who is talking or when the action took
place. Perhaps Sentence B is not a logical sequel to Sentence
A—the writer, in whose head the connection is clear, hasn't
bothered to provide the missing link. Perhaps the writer has
used an important word incorrectly by not taking the trouble to
look it up. The writer may think "sanguine" and "sanguinary"
mean the same thing, but the difference is a bloody big one.
The reader can only infer (speaking of big differences) what the
writer is trying to imply.

Faced with such obstacles, readers are at first tenacious.
They blame themselves—they obviously missed something,
and they go back over the mystifying sentence, or over the
whole paragraph, piecing it out like an ancient rune, making
guesses and moving on. But they won't do this for long. The
writer is making them work too hard, and they will look for one
who is better at the craft.

5 --

is too dumb or too lazy to keep pace with the ~~writer's~~ train
of thought. My sympathics are ~~entirely~~ with him. ~~He's not
so dumb.~~ (If the reader is lost, it is generally because the
writer ~~of the article~~ has not been careful enough to keep
him on the ~~proper~~ path.

This carelessness can take any number of ~~different~~ forms.
Perhaps a sentence is so excessively ~~long and~~ cluttered that
the reader, hacking his way through ~~all~~ the verbiage, simply
doesn't know what *it* ~~the writer~~ means. Perhaps a sentence has
been so shoddily constructed that the reader could read it in
any of *several* ~~two or three different~~ ways. ~~He thinks he knows what
the writer is trying to say, but he's not sure.~~ Perhaps the
writer has switched pronouns in mid-sentence, or ~~perhaps he~~
has switched tenses, so the reader loses track of who is
talking ~~to whom,~~ or ~~exactly~~ when the action took place. Perhaps Sentence B is not a logical sequel to Sentence A -- the
writer, in whose head the connection is ~~perfectly~~ clear, has
not *bothered to provide* ~~given enough thought to providing~~ the missing link. Perhaps the writer has used an important word incorrectly by not
taking the trouble to look it up ~~and make sure.~~ He may think
that "sanguine" and "sanguinary" mean the same thing, but)
~~I can assure you that~~ (the difference is a bloody big one ~~to the
reader.~~ *The reader* ~~He~~ can only ~~try to~~ infer ~~what~~ (speaking of big differences) what the writer is trying to imply.

Faced with *these* ~~such a variety of~~ obstacles, the reader
is at first a remarkably tenacious bird. He ~~tends to~~ blame*s*
himself. ~~He~~ He obviously missed something, ~~he thinks,~~ and he goes
back over the mystifying sentence, or over the whole paragraph,

6 --

piecing it out like an ancient rune, making guesses and moving
on. But he won't do this for long. ~~He will soon run out of
patience.~~ (The writer is making him work too hard ~~→ harder
than he should have to work~~ — (and the reader will look for
~~a writer~~ one who is better at his craft.

The writer must therefore constantly ask himself: What am
I trying to say? ~~in this sentence?~~ (Surprisingly often, he
doesn't know.) ~~And~~ Then he must look at what he has ~~just~~
written and ask: Have I said it? Is it clear to someone
encountering ~~who is coming upon~~ the subject for the first time? If it's
not, ~~clear,~~ it is because some fuzz has worked its way into the
machinery. The clear writer is a person ~~who is~~ clear-headed
enough to see this stuff for what it is: fuzz.

I don't mean ~~to suggest~~ that some people are born
clear-headed and are therefore natural writers, whereas
others ~~other people~~ are naturally fuzzy and will ~~therefore~~ never write
well. Thinking clearly is ~~an entirely~~ conscious act that the
writer must force ~~keep forcing~~ upon himself, just as if he were
embarking ~~starting out~~ on any other ~~kind of~~ project that requires ~~calls for~~ logic:
adding up a laundry list or doing an algebra problem ~~or playing
chess.~~ Good writing doesn't ~~just~~ come naturally, though most
people obviously think it does. ~~it's as easy as walking.~~ The professional

Two pages of the final manuscript of this chapter from the First Edition of On Writing Well. Although they look like a first draft, they had
already been rewritten and retyped—like almost every other page—
four or five times. With each rewrite I try to make what I have written
tighter, stronger and more precise, eliminating every element that is
not doing useful work. Then I go over it once more, reading it aloud,
and am always amazed at how much clutter can still be cut.

Writers must therefore constantly ask: What am I trying to say? Surprisingly often they don't know. Then they must look at what they have written and ask: Have I said it? Is it clear to someone encountering the subject for the first time? If it's not, some fuzz has worked its way into the machinery. The clear writer is someone clearheaded enough to see this stuff for what it is: fuzz.

I don't mean that some people are born clearheaded and are therefore natural writers, whereas others are naturally fuzzy and will never write well. Thinking clearly is a conscious act that writers must force upon themselves, as if they were working on any other project that requires logic: adding up a laundry list or doing an algebra problem. Good writing doesn't come naturally, though most people obviously think it does. Professional writers are constantly being bearded by strangers who say they'd like to "try a little writing sometime"—meaning when they retire from their real profession, which is difficult, like insurance or real estate. Or they say, "I could write a book about that." I doubt it.

Writing is hard work. A clear sentence is no accident. Very few sentences come out right the first time, or even the third time. Remember this in moments of despair. If you find that writing is hard, it's because it *is* hard. It's one of the hardest things people do.

Walker Gibson

> In Tough, Sweet, and Stuffy (1966), WALKER GIBSON *describes three kinds of talker—the Tough Talker, a person who is "centrally concerned with himself" whose style is "I-talk"; the Sweet Talker, who makes a special effort to be nice to us and whose style is "you-talk"; and the Stuffy Talker, who "expresses no concern either for himself or his reader." Gibson states that "these are three extreme possibilities: the way we write at any given moment can be seen as an adjustment or compromise among these three styles of identifying ourselves and defining our relation with others." In the following*

chapter, Gibson describes the Stuffy Talker and analyzes typical stuffy writing.

STUFFY TALK:
The Rhetoric of Hollow Men

Leaning together,
Headpiece filled with straw. Alas!

The voice we hear in an ad is not the official voice of the cor- 1
poration that pays the bill. The voice in the ad is a highly fictitious created person, speaking as an individual in a
particular situation. In a bathtub, for instance. No corporation
could ever say, officially, "I never, never bathe without Sardo."
The official voice of a corporation appears, I suppose, in its
periodic reports to its stockholders, or in its communications
with government agencies.

I define official prose, accordingly, as language whose voice 2
speaks for an organization rather than for an individual. And
nobody says a good word for it, not even its authors. The composing of officialese suffers from circumstances, however, that
make the job especially difficult, and possibly some small sympathy is in order. For just as such prose speaks for a group of
people rather than for a single writer, so in its actual composition a number of people are likely to be lending a hand. And in
writing, two hands are usually worse than one.[1]

Anyone who has worked on a committee preparing a docu- 3
ment to be signed by all fellowwriters knows some of the difficulties. Disagreements of opinion and emphasis can produce
a voice that is hardly a voice at all. Constant qualification
makes for weakness. The various writers, all too aware of their
audience as real people, may try to anticipate hopelessly conflicting prejudices and objections. Everybody has a point he

---

[1] Actually, in various works on the subject, there has been precious little sympathy for the writers of officialese, who are an easy mark for critical abuse. Among numerous discussions of official style, all fairly bloodthirsty, I recommend: George Orwell's famous essay, "Politics and the
English Language," in *Shooting an Elephant and Other Essays* (1950), Robert Graves and Alan
Hodge, *The Reader over your Shoulder* (1946), and Robert Waddell, *Grammar and Style* (1951), which
contains an entertaining "grammar of Basic Jargon." See also, for an earlier attack, Sir Arthur
Quiller-Couch, *On the Art of Writing* (1916).

wants included, but what is worse, no one feels any personal responsibility for the tone of the whole. Nobody cares, really. Contrast the situation of the single writer alone at his desk, who can establish a single speaking voice and an ideal assumed reader to listen to it. Yet a great deal of modern prose is written, or at any rate rewritten, not at a lonely desk but around a table where everybody talks at once. The loss of personality almost inevitable under such circumstances should cause us anguish whenever, as so often happens, we have to read or write the prose of organization life. When we speak of official prose as *stuffy*, we are referring, I think, directly to this loss of personality. (Not that you need a committee to produce stuffiness.) Stuffiness may imply, by way of the stuffed shirt, that the speaker has no insides, no humanity. It is scarecrow prose. Other familiar metaphors also seem to recognize an emptiness within; thus we speak of the "inflated" language of officialese, the speaker in that case being filled with gas, or hot air.

What is the rhetoric of such hollow men, and how can it be 4
improved, if it can?

Take a handy example, the federal government's much- 5
publicized report, "Smoking and Health," issued early in 1964. The text quoted in the newspapers ("Summary and Conclusions") begins this way:

> In previous studies the use of tobacco, especially cigarette 6
> smoking, has been causally linked to several diseases. Such
> use has been associated with increased deaths from lung can-
> cer and other diseases, notably coronary artery disease, chron-
> ic bronchitis, and emphysema. These widely reported findings,
> which have been the cause of much public concern over the
> past decade, have been accepted in many countries by official
> health agencies, medical associations, and voluntary health
> organizations.

> The potential hazard is great because these diseases are 7
> major causes of death and disability. In 1962, over 500,000 peo-
> ple in the United States died of arteriosclerotic heart disease
> (principally coronary artery disease), 41,000 died of lung cancer,
> and 15,000 died of bronchitis and emphysema.

Another cause of concern is that deaths from some of 8
these diseases have been increasing with great rapidity over
the past few decades.

Lung cancer deaths, less than 3,000 in 1930, increased to 9
18,000 in 1950. In the short period since 1955, deaths from
lung cancer rose from less than 27,000 to the 1962 total of
41,000. This extraordinary rise has not been recorded for cancer of any other site. While part of this rising trend for lung
cancers is attributable to improvements in diagnosis and the
changing age-composition and size of the population, the evidence leaves little doubt that a true increase in the lung cancer has taken place.

This is by no means an extreme example of stuffiness, and 10
I quote it to give the official voice its due. And I reaffirm my
modest sympathy with the authors, who must have had to
compose this document under difficult circumstances. There
were ten of them on the committee, professional experts
chosen by the Surgeon General, presumably strong-minded
men of varying opinions. A separate committee staff was also
involved. There must have been considerable debate about
phrasing as well as more "substantial" matters, and no doubt
uneasy compromises had to be made. A consciousness of
audience must have been high in the writers' minds. On one
hand the document had to be acceptable to the scientific
community, particularly to those scientists who had participated in various earlier projects on which this report was
based. On another hand, the document was surely addressed
to legislators and officials with the expectation of their taking
the "remedial action" called for. On still a third hand, these
multidextrous writers must have wished to reach the smoking
public directly, and they surely anticipated the reprinting of
key passages like this one in the daily press. We may, as I say,
sympathize with the practical difficulties of multiple author-
ship and multiple readership, but it does not follow that we
have to like the results. For this is a Stuffy voice.

For a harder look at the created personality, I take a shorter 11
passage from the page in the committee's report where one

might suppose both writer and reader to be especially attentive. It is a point where, if anywhere, the committee might be
expected to speak directly and plainly, with a minimum of hot
air.[2] Here is the much-quoted conclusion under the heading
"Lung Cancer":

> Cigarette smoking is causally related to lung cancer in men; 12
> the magnitude of the effect of cigarette smoking far outweighs
> all other factors. The data for women, though less extensive,
> point in the same direction.
>
> The risk of developing lung cancer increases with duration 13
> of smoking and the number of cigarettes smoked per day, and
> is diminished by discontinuing smoking.
>
> The risk of developing cancer of the lung for the combined 14
> group of pipe smokers, cigar smokers, and pipe and cigar
> smokers is greater than for nonsmokers, but much less than
> for cigarette smokers.
>
> The data are insufficient to warrant a conclusion for each 15
> group individually.

"Cigarette smoking is causally related to lung cancer in 16
men. . . ." Causally related? Probably there is some good reason why the committee could not say simply "Cigarette smoking causes lung cancer in men." What good reason could there
be? Perhaps the latter phrasing suggests that smoking is the
only cause of lung cancer? Perhaps it suggests that all smoking
necessarily causes lung cancer? But our faint understanding of
the committee's anxiety for caution and clarity, in the light of
its complex audience, should not prevent us from deploring
the alternative. For by using the passive verb (*is related to*) and
its odd modifier (*causally*), the writers deprive their language
not only of strength but of responsibility. Note that in this
sentence the committee's voice isn't doing any relating itself;
all it's saying is that something is or has been related to something—by someone else. Very scientific, very "objective." Then

---

[2] In the version published in book form, the following prefatory remark describes the intention
in this section of the report: "Realizing that for the convenience of all types of serious readers
it would be desirable to simplify language, condense chapters, and bring opinions to the forefront, the Committee offers Part I as such a presentation." *Smoking and Health*, Public Health
Service Publication No. 1103, U. S. Government Printing Office, p. 5.

we read on (to finish the first sentence): "the magnitude of the effect far outweighs all other factors." The magnitude is doing the outweighing, not the austere members of this committee. The choice of language in the following sentence ("data . . . point in the same direction") is of course similar. An abstraction (data) is pointing, not a human finger. Explained in these terms, we can understand why the voice in this first paragraph sounds so disembodied and the wording sounds so awkward.[3]

A key characteristic of Stuffy rhetoric is just this refusal to 17 assume personal responsibility. It is accomplished by at least two stylistic techniques, both of which we have just witnessed. One is the use of the passive verb. (Military prose, among others, is full of this gambit: *it is ordered that . . . it is desired that. . . .* Who ordered, who desired? With such rhetoric, buck-passing becomes child's play.) The other technique is a preference for abstract nouns as the subjects of active verbs. The doer of the action is not a human somebody, certainly not the speaker himself. It is Magnitude, or Data, buzzing along while the speaker merely notes the unarguable results.

It is as if the speaker, in this first paragraph, had made a 18 determined effort to keep *people* out of the discussion, including himself. Whether this was done to promote a kind of official tone for the sake of legislators, or to sound mathematical and cautious for the sake of scientists, or simply out of stuffy habit, I cannot tell. But the effort partly breaks down in the second paragraph. "The risk of developing lung cancer increases with duration of smoking." This is still clothed in pretty abstract dress, but there has been a significant change, for now we are suddenly seeing the situation almost from an individual smoker's point of view. The statement seems far less rigorously mathematical when the subject of the sentence is a word

---

[3] The pussyfooting language seems at odds with the conviction about *cause* that the Committee evidently did feel. The book version of the report contains a statement about this conviction, after some cautious warning about the Committee's use of the word "cause." "No member was so naive as to insist upon monoetiology in pathological processes or in vital phenomena." Nevertheless, "granted these complexities were recognized, it is to be noted clearly that the Committee's considered decision to use the words 'a cause,' or 'a major cause,' or 'a significant cause,' or 'a causal association' in certain conclusions about smoking and health affirms their conviction." (*Smoking and Health*, p. 21.) What interests me here is that this conviction is affirmed in language that almost removes the affirmers from the scene.

like *risk*, though of course the riskiness is based on numbers. And the writers' own risk seems abruptly much greater, for now they do seem to be taking responsibility for a more ambitious assertion: "the risk increases." It is hard to understand why they had to be so awkwardly impersonal and cautious in their first paragraph, if they were going to come out so flatly in their second.

In the third paragraph the voice continues, rather woodenly, 19 with "risk," and then moves into a terrible tangle as the writers, trying to deal with three groups of smokers, produce an almost unreadable mess. "Pipe smokers, cigar smokers, and pipe and cigar smokers." This sort of thing is easily perpetrated by a voice that cares as little about its reader as this one does. Then in the final sentence of the passage the voice backs away again into its posture of impersonal no-responsibility. "The data are sufficient to warrant a conclusion. . . ." Data are insufficient only if somebody says so. Once again, the subject of the verb is the data, not the interpreters of the data.

No doubt the data are insufficient to warrant a conclusion, 20 but I find insurmountable the temptation to rewrite the committee's prose into plainer English, and politer.

> Cigarette smoking is the major cause of lung cancer in 21 men, and probably in women too.
>
> The longer one smokes, and the more cigarettes one 22 smokes per day, the greater the chance of developing lung cancer. This risk is reduced when one stops smoking.
>
> People who smoke pipes or cigars, or both, also risk can- 23 cer, but to a lesser degree than cigarette smokers. We cannot say exactly what the risk is for each of these groups.

For any number of reasons, possibly even good reasons, this 24 version might be unacceptable to the advisory committee. But at least we can examine some of the ways in which the revision was accomplished, and so focus on some rhetorical characteristics of Stuffiness. In the first place, of course, human responsibility has been introduced, in the opening sentence, by the simple tactic of removing the passive verb and making a more positive statement. (The statement *seems* to be justified by the original.) The original's willingness to speak of "the risk" in its second paragraph is retained in the revision, and the smoker's own involvement in the situation is further encouraged by the introduction of "people" in the revised third paragraph. Finally, the committee's responsibility is made explicit in the revised last sentence, by changing "The data are insufficient to warrant . . ." into "We cannot say exactly what. . . ."

These changes suggest that I have tried to make a scarecrow 25 into a human being. By what other means can one humanize the quality of a Stuffy voice? One way is to reduce sharply the sheer number of words, in this case by something over one-quarter. Stuffy voices talk too much, although for sheer gratuitous verbosity a Sweet voice does pretty well too. The Stuffy voice characteristically uses longer words, and the revision shows a clear rise in proportion of monosyllables, and an even clearer drop in proportion of words of more than two syllables. Stuffy voices modify nouns almost as generously as adwriters, and they are exceedingly fond of the noun adjunct construction. Whereas the original contained nine adjectives and nine noun adjuncts (like *cigarette smoking*), the revision contains three of each. Finally, repetition in the original is very high (the "wooden" effect alluded to), and this repetition, while still present in the revision, has been reduced. A list of this information may be of interest:

	Original	Revision
Total number of words	106	76
Average sentence length	21	15
Proportion of monosyllables	57%	69%
Proportion of words over two syllables	18%	5%
Adjectives and noun adjuncts	18	6

Such "rules" as these figures suggest are familiar enough, 26 and many a popular treatise on writing has been based on the simpleminded proposition that simple words and sentences are always better than complex ones.[4] But that is not the point at all. It depends! In true Stuffy Talk, we feel a disparity between the simplicity of the situation, as we feel it ought to be defined, and the pretentiousness of the lingo. As so often in literary matters, we have to appeal finally to extraliterary considerations—our sense of a "proper" definition of the circumstances. Thus we resent a voice haranguing us from a high horse, not just because his horse is high, but because the situation seems to us to be worthy of a more modest perch. If you are composing a preamble to a new nation's constitution, you have a perfect right to climb up on a high horse. On the other hand, if you're trying to get people to stop smoking. . . .

But this is not to say at all that the problem of cancer and smoking is frivolous: the tone of my revision remains serious, even though I have brought the voice down from on high and into closer contact with the listener. I did not go so far as to invoke the intimacy of the Sweet Talker, or even the Tough Talker. The occasion remains, as it must, official and formal. Nevertheless it is true that in revising I have imposed upon the committee's style some of the Tough Talker's manners. A little Tough Talk goes a long way, sometimes, as an antidote to Stuffy Talk, and I have no doubt that most committee reports would be more palatable if the language could be brought somewhat into line with Tough Talk's rhetoric. But easy does it. Whereas a little Toughness can be wholesome, a little Sweetness can be sickening. How facile it would be to reduce an official voice to mere cuteness, in a flurry of public-relations informality. For instance take this sentence from the original committee report: 27

---

[4] Extraordinary efforts, over the past quarter century and more, have been devoted by psychologists and others to devising formulas for measuring "readability." The best-known of these formulas are those constructed by Rudolph Flesch (*The Art of Plain Talk*, etc.). Readability, or Reading Ease (Flesch's term), refers entirely to the comfort and efficiency of the reader in "understanding" the words in front of him. Most of the formulas proposed to measure this quality depend heavily on simple computations of sentence length and word length. These formulas, as their inventors usually concede, are not concerned with *style* in my sense, as the expression of a personality on paper. No doubt such formulas may be helpful to some writers in improving style—especially the style of Stuffy Talk—but the experts in readability are not worried about what happens to the voice when their formulas are applied. See George R. Klare, *The Measurement of Readability* (Ames, Iowa, 1963).

The risk of developing lung cancer increases with duration of smoking and the number of cigarettes smoked per day, and is diminished by discontinuing smoking.

My revision offered this alternative:

The longer one smokes, and the more cigarettes one smokes per day, the greater the chance of developing lung cancer. This risk is reduced when one stops smoking.

A reviser interested in promoting informality could easily become too interested. He could, for instance, bring the voice still closer to the reader by the simple introduction of the second-person pronoun:

The longer you smoke, and the more cigarettes you smoke per day, the greater your chance of developing lung cancer. This risk is reduced when you stop smoking.

This begins now to look like the clubbiness of Sweet Talk—a degree of admonitory intimacy that the members of the committee would no doubt, and rightly, consider beneath their dignity. And from here it is only a step to the full saccharine flavor of Sweet Talk itself:

No doubt about it—when you smoke cigarettes you're running a scientifically-proved risk of lung cancer. That is, if you're a man. And if you're a woman, you're probably running a risk that's almost as certain. | 28

Fact is, the longer you've smoked, and the more cigarettes you smoke every day, the likelier you are to develop cancer. But scientific data demonstrate that you can lower that risk any time you care to—just stop smoking. | 29

If you smoke cigars or a pipe (or both), you're still risking cancer. But a good deal less than you are if you stick to those cigarettes. | 30

So why not cut out expensive, evil-smelling, disease-laden cigarette smoking for good? Like the Surgeon General says you should. | 31

Examples of Stuffy Talk abound. Of our three styles, it is the   32
easiest to recognize and define; perhaps it is easy to compose
too. Consider another example, from another branch of government. Not long ago the pay envelopes of academicians
included a document stating a new ruling by the Internal Revenue Service. This ruling, a welcome one to its recipients, concerned certain deductible expenses on the part of professors.
It began this way; and it needs no comment:

REVENUE

Advice has been requested concerning the deductibility for   33
Federal income tax purposes of research expenses, including
traveling expenses, incurred by college and university professors in their capacity as educators.

The facts presented are that the duties of a professor   34
encompass not only the usual lecture and teaching duties but
also the communication and advancement of knowledge
through research and publication. Appointments are commonly made to college and university faculties with the expectation that the individuals involved will carry on independent
research in their fields of competence and will put that
research to use in advancing the body of learning in that area
by teaching, lecturing, and writing. It is customary, therefore,
for professors to engage in research for the above purposes.
Where the research is undertaken with a view to scholarly publication, the expenses for such purposes cannot usually be
considered to have been incurred for the purpose of producing
a specific income-producing asset. . . .

Based on the facts presented, it is held that research ex-   35
penses, including traveling expenses properly allottable
thereto, incurred by a professor for the purposes of teaching,
lecturing, or writing and publishing in this area of competence, as a means of carrying out the duties expected of him in
his capacity as a professor and without expectation of profit
apart from his salary, represent ordinary and necessary business expenses incurred in that capacity and are therefore
deductible under section 162(e) of the Code.

I take a final example of Stuffy Talk from another end of aca- 36
demic life. Here is the voice of the academic institution itself,
a passage from the catalogue of a liberal arts college setting
forth its policy on admissions.

ADMISSIONS

Admission to X College is a selective process, since each 37
year many more qualified candidates apply for admission
than can possibly be accommodated. In considering the
factors involved in the selections, academic ability, and
achievement, community citizenship and leadership, character, and personality are considered most important. Special
emphasis is placed on the candidate's record of achievement
throughout his secondary school years. Specifically, selection
of candidates is based on information obtained from the following sources: (1) the secondary school record, including
rank in class; (2) the College Entrance Examination Board's
Scholastic Aptitude and Achievement Tests; (3) a personal
interview with a member of the Admissions staff, or with a
designated representative; (4) the recommendation of the
school.

X College admits undergraduates for the Bachelor of Arts 38
degree only. For practical reasons of adjustment to college
life and the proper arrangements of a program of study, X
admits freshman students only in September, at the beginning of the fall semester. The freshman class is limited by the
capacity of the dormitories. An early application is advised. It
is expected that candidates who live within a reasonable distance of the College will visit X sometime before January of
their senior year of secondary school.

The Admissions office is open for appointments through- 39
out the year except on Saturday afternoons and Sundays.
(During the months of July and August appointments and
interviews are not scheduled on Saturdays.) An appointment
with the Admissions Officer may be arranged by writing or
phoning the Admissions Office at least two weeks in advance
of the intended visit.

As every parent, teacher, and teenager knows, admission to ⁴⁰ college these days is a desperate business. But the assumed author here could hardly care less. Certainly he admits no difficulties on his part, and his passive verbs do their efficient work of evading responsibility. "Special emphasis *is placed* . . . , selection of candidates *is based*. . . ." Note that it is quite possible to be Stuffy within a very short sentence: "An early application *is advised*." In the face of all these passives, the poor applicant has nobody to argue with. The machine grinds on. There is no hint here about what actually happens in the "admissions process"—who pores over the documents, how he or they do make decisions, what the relative importance may be of the four sources of information. Furthermore an interview with an Officer whose very title rates a capital O is already a formidable undertaking. Surely teenagers have enough troubles, without having to face the blank face of prose like this.

Glossary

allusion An indirect reference to a presumably well-known literary work or an historical event or figure. The phrase "the Waterloo of his political career" is a reference to Napoleon's disastrous defeat at the Battle of Waterloo in 1815. The allusion implies that the career of the politician under discussion has come to a disastrous end.

analogy A point-by-point comparison between two unlike things or activities (for example, comparing writing an essay to building a house) for the purpose of illustration or argument. Unlike a comparison (or contrast), in which the things compared are of equal importance, analogy exists for the purpose of illustrating or arguing the nature of one of the compared things, not both.

antithesis The arrangement of contrasting ideas in grammatically similar phrases and clauses (*The world will little note, nor long remember, what we say here, but it can never forget what they did here*—Lincoln, *Gettysburg* Address). See *parallelism*.

argument Proving the truth or falseness of a statement. Arguments are traditionally classified as *inductive* or *deductive*. See *deductive argument* and *inductive argument*. Argument can be used for different purposes in writing. See *purpose*.

autobiography Writing about one's own experiences, often those of growing up and making one's way in the world. The autobiographical writings of Mary E. Mebane and Eudora Welty describe their childhood in the South.

balanced sentence A sentence containing parallel phrases and clauses of approximately the same length and wording (*You can fool all the people some of the time, and some of the people all the time, but you cannot fool all the people all of the time.*—Lincoln).

cause and effect Analysis of the conditions that must be present for an event to occur (*cause*) and of the results or consequences of the event (*effect*). An essay may deal with causes or with effects only.

classification and division *Classification* arranges individual objects into groups or classes (GM cars, Chrysler cars, Ford cars). *Division* arranges a broad class into subclasses according to various principles (the broad class GM *cars* can be divided on the basis of their transmission or manufacturing unit).

cliché A once-colorful expression made stale through overuse (*putting on the dog, mad as a wet hen*).

coherence The sense, as we read, that the details and ideas of a work connect clearly. A paragraph or essay that does not hold together seems incoherent. Transitions are a means of coherence.

colloquialism An everyday expression in speech and informal writing. Colloquialisms are not substandard or "illiterate" English. They are common in informal English and occur sometimes in formal English.

comparison and contrast The analysis of similarities and differences between two or more persons, objects, or events (A and B) for the purpose of a relative estimate. The word *comparison* sometimes refers to the analysis of similarities and differences in both A and B. *Block comparison* presents each thing being compared as a whole (that is, if the comparison is between A and B, then features a, b, c of A are discussed as a block of information, then features a, b, c of B are compared to A in their own block of information). *Alternating comparison* presents the comparable features one by one (a, a, b, b, c, c).

complex sentence A sentence consisting of one main or independent clause and one or more subordinate or dependent clauses (*The rain began when she stepped outside*).

compound sentence A sentence consisting of coordinated independent clauses (*She stepped outside and then the rain began*).

compound-complex sentence A sentence consisting of two or more main or independent clauses and at least one subordinate or dependent clause (*She stepped outside as the rain began, but she did not return to the house*).

concrete and abstract words Concrete words refer to particular objects, people, and events (Valley Forge, Franklin Delano Roosevelt, the Rocky Mountains); abstract words refer to general shared qualities (heroism, courage, beauty). Concrete writing makes abstract ideas perceptible to the senses through details and images.

concreteness Making an idea exist through the senses. Writing can be concrete at all three levels—informal, general, and formal. See *concrete and abstract words.*

connotation Feelings, images, and ideas associated with a word. Connotations change from reader to reader, though some words probably have the same associations for everybody.

context The surrounding words or sentences that suggest the meaning of a word or phrase. Writers may dispense with formal definition if the context clarifies the meaning of a word.

coordinate sentence A sentence that joins clauses of the same weight and importance through the conjunctions *and, but, for, or, nor,* or *yet,* or through conjunctive adverbs and adverbial phrases (*however, therefore, nevertheless, in fact*) following a semicolon.

deductive argument Reasoning from statements assumed to be true or well-established factually. These statements of assumptions are thought sufficient to guarantee the truth of the inferences or conclusions. In formal arguments they are called *premises*. A valid argument reasons correctly from the premises to the conclusion. A sound argument is true in its premises and valid in its reasoning. See *enthymeme, syllogism*.

definition Explaining the current meaning of a word through its etymology or derivation, its denotation, or its connotations. Denotative or "real" definitions single out a word from all other words (or things) like it by giving *genus* and *specific difference*. Connotative definitions give the associations people make to a word. See *connotation*.

description A picture in words of people, objects, and events. Description often combines with narration and it may serve exposition and persuasion.

division See *classification and division*.

enthymeme A deductive argument that does not state the conclusion or one of the premises directly. The following statement is an enthymeme: *Citizens in a democracy, who refuse to register for the draft, are not acting responsibly*. The implied premise is that the responsible citizen obeys all laws, even repugnant ones.

essay A carefully organized composition that develops a single idea or impression or several related ideas or impressions. The word sometimes describes a beginning or trial attempt that explores the central idea or impression instead of developing it completely.

example A picture or illustration of an idea, or one of many instances or occurrences that is typical of the rest.

exposition An explanation or unfolding or setting forth of an idea, usually for the purpose of giving information. Exposition is usually an important part of persuasive writing. Example, process analysis, causal analysis, definition, classification and division, and comparison and contrast are forms of exposition.

expressive writing Essays, diaries, journals, letters, and other kinds of writing that present personal feelings and beliefs for their own sake. The expressive writer is not primarily concerned with informing or persuading readers.

figure of speech A word or phrase that departs from its usual meaning. Figures of speech make statements vivid and capture the attention of readers. The most common figures are based on similarity between things. See *metaphor, personification, simile*. Other figures are based on relationship. See *allusion*. Metonymy refers to a thing by one of its qualities (*the Hill* as a reference to the United States Congress). Synecdoche refers to a thing by one of its parts (*wheels* as a reference to racing cars). Other figures are based on contrast between statements and realities. See *irony*. Related to irony is *understatement*, or saying less than is appropriate (*Napoleon's career ended unhappily at Waterloo*). Hyperbole means deliberate exaggeration (*crazy about ice cream*). Paradox states an apparent contradiction (*All great truths begin as blasphemies*—G. B. Shaw). *Oxymoron,* a kind of paradox, joins opposite qualities into a single image (*lake of fire*).

focus The limitation of subject in an essay. The focus may be broad, as in a panoramic view of the mountains, or may be narrow, as in a view of a particular peak. For example, a writer may focus broadly on the contribution to scientific thought of scientists from various fields, or focus narrowly on the achievements of astronomers or chemists or medical researchers, or focus even more narrowly on the achievements of Albert Einstein as representative of twentieth-century science.

formal English Spoken or written English, often abstract in content, with sentences tighter than colloquial ones and an abstract and sometimes technical vocabulary. See *general English* and *informal English*.

general English A written standard that has features of informal and formal English. See *formal English* and *informal English*.

image A picture in words of an object, a scene, or a person. Though visual images are common in writing, they are not the only kind. Images can also be auditory, tactile, gustatory, and olfactory. John Keats's line *With beaded bubbles winking at the brim* appeals to our hearing and taste as well as to our sight. His phrase *coming musk-rose* appeals to our sense of smell. Images help to make feelings concrete.

implied thesis The central idea of the essay, suggested by the details and discussion rather than stated directly. See *thesis*.

inductive argument Inductive arguments reason from particulars of experience to general ideas—from observation, personal experience, and experimental testing to probable conclusions. Inductive arguments make predictions on the basis of past and present experience. An argumentative analogy is a form of inductive argument because it is based on limited observation and experience and therefore can claim probability only. Analysis of causes and effects is inductive when used in argument.

"inductive leap" Making the decision that sufficient inductive evidence (personal experience, observation, experimental testing) exists to draw a conclusion. Sometimes the writer of the argument makes the leap too quickly and bases conclusions on insufficient evidence.

informal English Written English, usually concrete in content, tighter than the loose sentences of spoken English. The word *informal* refers to the occasion of its use. A letter to a friend is usually informal; a letter of application is usually formal. See *formal English* and *general English*.

irony A term generally descriptive of statements and events. An ironic statement says the opposite of what the speaker or writer means, or implies that something more is meant than is stated, or says the unexpected (*He has a great future behind him*). An ironic event is unexpected or is so coincidental that it seems highly improbable (*The fireboat burned and sank*).

jargon The technical words of a trade or profession (in computer jargon, the terms *input* and *word processor*). Unclear, clumsy, or repetitive words or phrasing, sometimes the result of misplaced technical words (*He gave his input into the decision process*).

loose sentence A sentence that introduces the main idea close to the beginning and concludes with a series of modifiers (*The car left the expressway, slowing on the ramp and coming to a stop at the crossroad*). See *periodic sentence*.

metaphor An implied comparison that attributes the qualities of one thing to another (the word *mainstream* to describe the opinions or activities of most people).

mixed metaphor The incongruous use of two metaphors in the same context (*the roar of protest was stopped in its tracks*).

narration The chronological presentation of events. Narration often combines with description and it may serve exposition or persuasion.

order of ideas The presentation of ideas in a paragraph or an essay according to a plan. The order may be *spatial*, perhaps moving from background to foreground, or from top to bottom, or from side to side; or the order may be *temporal* or chronological (in the order of time). The presentation may be in the order of *importance*, or if the details build intensively, in the order of *climax*. The paragraph or essay may move from *problem* to *solution* or from the *specific* to the *general*. Some of these orders occur together—for example, a chronological presentation of details that builds to a climax.

parallelism Grammatically similar words, phrases, and clauses arranged to highlight similar ideas (*There are streets where, on January nights, fires burn on every floor of every house, sending fragrant smoke through the cold black trees. There are meadows and fields, long rows of old oaks, bridges that sparkle from afar, ships about to leave for Asia, lakes, horses and islands in the marsh.*—Mark Helprin). See *antithesis*.

paraphrase A rendering of a passage in different words that retain the sense, the tone, and the order of ideas.

periodic sentence A sentence that builds to the main idea (*Building speed as it curved down the ramp, the car raced into the crowded expressway*). See *loose sentence*.

personification Giving animate or human qualities to something inanimate or inhuman (The sun *smiled* at the earth).

persuasion The use of argument or satire or some other means to change an audience's thinking and feeling about an issue.

point of view The place or vantage point from which an event is seen and described. The term sometimes refers to the mental attitude of the viewer in narration. Mark Twain's *Huckleberry Finn* narrates the adventures of a boy in slave-owning Missouri from the point of view of the boy, not an adult.

premise See *syllogism*.

process An activity or operation containing steps usually performed in the same order. The process may be mechanical (changing a tire), natural (the circulation of the blood), or historical (the rise and spread of a specific epidemic disease, such as bubonic plague, at various times in history).

purpose The aim of the essay as distinguished from the means used to develop it. The purposes or aims of writing are many; they include expressing personal feelings and ideas, giving information, persuading readers to change their thinking about an issue, inspiring readers to take action, giving pleasure. These purposes may be achieved through description, narration, exposition, or argument. These means may be used alone or in combination, and an essay may contain more than one purpose.

reflection An essay that explores ideas without necessarily bringing the exploration to completion. The reflective essay can take the form of a loosely organized series of musings or a tightly organized argument.

satire Ridicule of foolish or vicious behavior or ideas for the purpose of correcting them. *Social satire* concerns foolish but not dangerous behavior and ideas—for example, coarse table manners, pretentious talk, harmless gossip. George Bernard Shaw's *Arms and the Man* is a social satire. *Ethical satire* attacks vicious or dangerous behavior or ideas—religious or racial bigotry, greed, political corruption. Mark Twain's *Huckleberry Finn* is an ethical satire.

simile A direct comparison between two things (A *growing child is like a young tree*). See *figure of speech, metaphor*.

simple sentence A sentence consisting of a single main or independent clause and no subordinate or dependent clauses (*The rain started at nightfall*).

slang Colorful and sometimes short-lived expressions peculiar to a group of people, usually informal in usage and almost always unacceptable in formal usage (*nerd, goof off*).

style A distinctive manner of speaking and writing. A writing style may be plain in its lack of metaphor and other figures of speech. Another writing style may be highly colorful or ornate.

subordinate clause A clause that completes a main clause or attaches to it as a modifier (She saw *that the rain had begun*. *When it rains*, it pours).

syllogism The formal arrangement of premises and conclusion of a deductive argument. The premises are the general assumptions or truths (*All reptiles are cold-blooded vertebrates. All snakes are reptiles*) from which particular conclusions are drawn (*All snakes are cold-blooded vertebrates*). This formal arrangement helps to test the validity or correctness of the reasoning from premises to conclusion. See *deductive argument*.

symbol An object that represents an abstract idea. The features of the symbol (the fifty stars and thirteen horizontal stripes of the American flag) suggest characteristics of the object symbolized (the fifty states of the Union, the original confederation of thirteen states). A *sign* need not have this representative quality: a green light signals "go" and a red light "stop" by conventional agreement.

thesis The central idea that organizes the many smaller ideas and details of the essay.

tone The phrasing or words that express the attitude or feeling of the speaker or writer. The tone of a statement ranges from the angry, exasperated, and sarcastic to the wondering or approving. An ironic tone suggests that the speaker or writer means more than the words actually state.

topic sentence Usually the main or central idea of the paragraph that organizes details and subordinate ideas. Though it often opens the paragraph, the topic sentence can appear later—in the middle or at the end of the paragraph.

transition A word or phrase (*however, thus, in fact*) that connects clauses and sentences. Parallel structure is an important means of transition.

unity The connections of ideas and details to a central controlling idea of the essay. A unified essay deals with one idea at a time.

Index

Copyrights and Acknowledgments

621